FINANCIAL SERVICES TECHNOLOGY

PROCESSES, ARCHITECTURE AND SOLUTIONS
SECOND EDITION

Randall E. Duran

CENGAGE

Australia • Brazil • Mexico • Singapore • United Kingdom • United States

Financial Services Technology: Processes, Architecture, and Solutions, Second Edition
Randall E. Duran

Senior Regional Director:
Janet Lim

Senior Product Manager:
Charles Ho

Senior Editorial Manager:
Lian Siew Han

Senior Development Editor:
Tanmayee Bhatwadekar

Development Editors:
Kenneth Chow
Ng Wei Yi
Elaine Chew
Willie Ong

Senior Regional Manager,
Production and Rights:
Pauline Lim

Production Executive:
Rachael Tan

Copy Editor:
Irene Yeow

Cover Designer:
Lee Meng Hui

Compositor:
diacriTech

© 2018 Cengage Learning Asia Pte Ltd

For product information and technology assistance, contact us at
Cengage Learning Asia Customer Support, 65-6410-1200

For permission to use material from this text or product,
submit all requests online at **cengageasia.com/permissions**
Further permissions questions can be emailed to
asia.permissionrequest@cengage.com

ISBN: 978-981-4780-86-5

Cengage Learning Asia Pte Ltd
151 Lorong Chuan #02-08
New Tech Park (Lobby H)
Singapore 556741

Cengage Learning is a leading provider of customized learning solutions with office locations around the globe, including Singapore, the United Kingdom, Australia, Mexico, Brazil, and Japan. Locate your local office at **www.cengage.com**

Cengage Learning products are represented in Canada by Nelson Education, Ltd.

To learn more about Cengage Learning Solutions, visit **cengageasia.com**

Every effort has been made to trace all sources and copyright holders of news articles, figures and information in this book before publication, but if any have been inadvertently overlooked, the publisher will ensure that full credit is given at the earliest opportunity.

Printed in Singapore
Print Number: 01   Print Year: 2017

To
my family

BRIEF CONTENTS

CONTENTS

ABOUT THE AUTHOR

Randall E. Duran is the Chief Information Officer of 1st Financial Bank USA and Chairman of Catena Technologies Pte Ltd, a Singapore-based Fintech firm that he founded and served as the Chief Executive Officer for over ten years. He is also an Adjunct Faculty at Singapore Management University (SMU). Randall received his bachelors and masters degrees in computer science from the Massachusetts Institute of Technology (MIT).

Randall began his career in Silicon Valley in the early 1990s, pioneering the development of digital market data distribution systems, working with investment banks in New York to implement those solutions. He then went on to work with banks in London and Europe, designing and implementing enterprise application integration platforms. In 1998, Randall moved to Singapore and was involved in the implementation of the first generation of automated dealing systems foreign exchange. He spent over 15 years in the Asia-Pacific region. During that time, he implemented technology solutions for dozens of financial institutions across the Asia-Pacific region and in North America, and has been involved with banking projects focused on cybersecurity, architecture design, business process management, customer relationship management, and high-performance computing.

Randall began his involvement with SMU in 2002 teaching a prototype course on financial markets technology. Later, he helped the university design and develop its Master of IT in Business–Financial Technology (MITB Fintech) program and taught courses on corporate and institutional banking technology and financial markets technology. He has researched and published in the areas of managing technology, prototyping for innovation, enterprise integration architecture, mobile banking, business process management, and high-performance computing.

Randall is on the American Bankers Association (ABA) Payments Systems Committee, part of the ABA Cyber and Information Security Working Group, and is also a member of the Financial Services Information Sharing and Analysis Center (FS-ISAC) Data Analytics Working Group.

PREFACE

For those in the financial services industry, learning by doing is the primary mode of gaining knowledge. While it can be effective, it is a trial-and-error process where mistakes are often repeated. Depending on individuals' learning aptitude, the responsibilities that they are given, and whom they work with, they may learn very much or very little. To acquire a broad range of knowledge, people must work in many different roles, departments, geographies, and institutions. This process does not make it easy to advance during the early stages of their careers. Likewise, it is not a reliable or scalable way for financial institutions to develop talent.

I have experienced the learning-by-doing process first-hand. I had the great fortune to work with people in many different financial institutions and technology vendors over the years, who have greatly contributed to my understanding of the industry. In spite of that, I believe that the learning-by-doing system has many limitations: the knowledge transfer process is inefficient and slow, it is not repeatable, and students' success largely depends on their luck and ability to find good mentors.

Moreover, the real world is not the ideal environment for introducing or explaining core concepts. Classroom learning provides a better forum for understanding industry principles and practices, but it is limited by the level of substance and depth that can be delivered during class sessions. Reading-based learning can help provide a solid foundation for practice-based learning both in the classroom and in industry. Hence, this book has been written to help both people currently working in the financial services industry and those entering it to build their knowledge of financial services technology quickly and efficiently.

Target Audience

This book was originally designed for the Singapore Management University's Master of IT in Business–Financial Technology program. It addresses topics that are covered in the Retail Banking Technology, Corporate and Institutional Banking Technology, and Financial Markets Technology courses. The book has been written both to support these courses as well as to serve as a standalone source of information for those who are not able to participate in the MITB Fintech program.

Even though it is oriented as a technology book, many business topics related to financial services are covered as well. I believe that effective use of technology requires a solid understanding of the business context that it will be used within. The transition between business strategy and business processes, and between business processes and their technology implementations is fluid. Thus, learning about the details of how to define the best data structures for banking systems, the most efficient C++ trading algorithms, or the best Java object models seems less critical than learning about how banking operations work and can best leverage technology.

This book has been written to serve different audiences. Technologists should find it useful to understand more about financial services and how technology solutions support their business functions. Likewise, the book can provide people with a business background a better understanding of the different technology platforms available to them, and how they can best be applied for different purposes. For those new to the financial industry, this book can serve as a primer that can accelerate their career development. Alternatively, for those who are already in the industry, it can help fill in knowledge gaps that cover different areas that they may have heard about, but have no direct experience in.

Case Studies

Throughout the book, I have included case studies to highlight practical aspects of various considerations that are discussed. For the most part, I have included relatively recent events as case studies, but have also reached further back in time when issues encountered years back are still applicable today. Also, many of the case studies are focused on failings; however, the intention is not to convey a negative tone about the industry. In contrast, many case studies that are provided by vendors, markets research groups and the like, tend to only focus on the positive aspects of the solutions they discuss. My view is that by identifying, studying, and understanding problems with technology and business environments, hopefully we can better avoid making the same mistakes in the future. Likewise, some financial institutions are discussed more often than others. This does not imply that those mentioned are better or worse than others. It is more the case that there happened to be relevant information that could be easily acquired to illustrate a point, which happened to relate to that institution. In general, larger financial institutions tend to have more news coverage, so they will show up more frequently.

Organization of the Chapters

Readers may want to approach this book as follows. Chapter 1 should be useful for those new to the industry or with limited experience to better understand the environment that financial service firms operate in and the challenges they face when implementing technology solutions. Chapters 2–5 will be useful for those who want to become more familiar with business process, technology architecture, solution implementation, and technology infrastructure considerations, as they pertain to financial services. Chapters 6–12 will be of interest to those readers involved with retail and commercial banking. Chapters 13–15 are most applicable to those who are or would like to develop solutions for financial markets. Finally, Chapters 16–20 will benefit readers across different business areas who are interested in better understanding some of the cross-functional technical and business concerns that relate to financial services.

Note that American English is used throughout the book, except when referring to cheques, where the British spelling variant is used. This helps avoid any confusion with the other meanings of "check," for example, it is always good to check your cheque. Also, the entity names –such as Wool World, Kiwi National Bank, Coats R Us, and Dragon Bank– used in examples within this book are purely fictitious; any similarities to actual companies with similar names are coincidental and unintended. I welcome any feedback or suggestions regarding this book and its contents. Communications are best sent via email to red@financialservicestechbook.com. Also, all instructors' and students' resources related to the book are available at http://www.cengageasia.com/duran.

NOTES ON THE SECOND EDITION

Time passes quickly, and many things change. I had intended to update this book several years after the first edition's publication to fill in gaps in content that I did not have time to address initially and discuss new trends. However, I had not anticipated how quickly the industry would continue to evolve and change. Accordingly, much of the new material in this edition relate to innovation and major changes that have occurred in the financial services industry over the past few years.

Since the publication of the first edition, I have changed my career role, moving from the Fintech world directly into the banking world. You might say that before, working as a software solution vendor and technology consultant, I was on the outside looking in on the world of banking. More recently, I have found myself on the inside looking out. This change has provided me with new perspectives and a better appreciation for the importance of IT infrastructure and operations, regulation and compliance, and the challenges that cybersecurity present to financial institutions. Likewise, I have also come to better understand the many aspects of the payments industry. As a result, this second edition has additional content that examines these areas.

ACKNOWLEDGEMENTS

I would like to thank Steve Miller and Enoch Ch'ng for their ongoing support in the Singapore Management University Master of IT in Business–Financial Technology (FinTech). Also, thanks to Ramona J. Duran, Lawrence J. Duran, and Anne Sam for their editing and proofreading assistance. I also greatly appreciate Tom Hayhurst's and Chris Dalton's detailed reviews and suggestions regarding content and focus on several of the chapters. Furthermore, I would like to thank my other MITB FS teaching colleagues as well as my many current and former work associates. Many of the ideas contained herein are not entirely my own and are based on insights gained from working with and studying the research of other industry professionals. The Endnotes section in each chapter contains general bibliographical references that were used to develop the chapter content, as well as specific cited references.

A number of industry practitioners and academics have reviewed sections of the book, providing corrections and useful suggestions. In particular, I owe thanks to the following people (in alphabetical order by family name): Alyce Campbell, Ivan Choong, Andrew Clarke, Gayathri Dwaraknath, David Fleet, Paul Griffin, Venkateswaran Govindarajan, Aaron Hallmark, Pieter Hamman, Jeremy Hebblethwaite, Susan Hwee, V. Kannan, Pervez Kazmi, Low Teng Yong, Keith MacDonald, Simon McNamara, Alan Megargel, Ng Yet Kuan, Ong Whee Teck, George Papp, Ian Rae, Abdy Salimin, Nancy Selph, Venky Shankararaman, Surindar Singh, Grace Soh Hooi Gim, Kevin Steppe, Mark Sutheran, Teng Soon Lang, Roderick Theseira, and Zhang Li. Special thanks goes to Paul Cobban and DBS bank for making available the information used in Case Study 17-1.

I also greatly appreciate the assistance I received from my editors, Kenneth Chow and Han Lian Siew, in bringing this project to fruition, as well as Cengage Learning Asia for seeing the value in the book's continued publication.

Thanks to DBS Bank, NYSE Technologies, and Standard Chartered Bank for providing permission to reprint their photographs and graphics to help illustrate key points throughout the book. *Automated Trader* magazine was also very kind in allowing me to use some of its survey statistics.

1 Introduction

Chapter Overview

1.1 BUSINESS DRIVERS

1.2 TECHNOLOGY DRIVERS

1.3 BUSINESS OPPORTUNITIES

1.4 BUSINESS CHALLENGES

1.5 STAKEHOLDER ALIGNMENT

1.6 SUMMARY

FURTHER READING

ENDNOTES

Information technology (IT) can add great value to the financial services sector by addressing the needs of key stakeholders: the institution's customers, business functions, operations functions, risk management functions, IT functions, and regulatory bodies. However, creating business solutions that fulfill the needs of diverse groups is a challenging task. It is a complex process that involves balancing conflicting business requirements, managing technology limitations, and navigating through organizational and external politics. Despite the challenges, IT solutions can provide many benefits to financial institutions, supporting their growth and enabling them to develop new lines of business. New customer-focused solutions can make financial institutions more competitive and enable them to dominate market segments. Customers also benefit from improved convenience and access to diverse financial products. On the other hand, ineffective use of technology and the inability to deliver IT solutions can lead to customer dissatisfaction, employee frustration, and business stagnation.

The business environment has become less hospitable for financial institutions in recent years. The tougher regulatory environment established in the aftermath of the **Global Financial Crisis** of 2008 has made the consolidation and growth of financial institutions more difficult (Figure 1-1). At the same time, financial institutions have already reaped the benefits from many of the productivity gains that could be achieved easily through the use of technology; greater effort will be required to realize further improvements. In many cases, the inefficiencies caused by past growth provide resistance to new growth and profitability. Hence, the time is ripe for making critical structural changes to financial institutions' business processes, IT infrastructure, and operations.

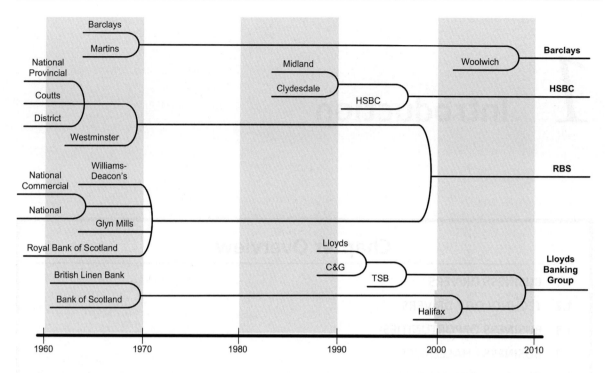

Figure 1-1 Consolidation of banks in the United Kingdom

This book examines considerations related to creating business solutions for the financial services industry, which includes banks and other types of firms that operate in the financial markets. It presents a framework for discussing how technology is used to support operational processes, IT architecture, and business solutions. It reviews these concepts in the contexts of banking and financial markets, and examines real-world examples of the challenges facing financial institutions. Many topics that are touched upon in this introduction will be revisited and discussed in-depth in subsequent chapters.

This chapter begins by providing a historical review of the evolution of banking businesses and technology. Next, it presents the current business opportunities and challenges facing financial institutions. And finally, it discusses the importance of aligning and balancing the needs of different stakeholders when implementing solutions. The goal is to call attention to general concerns of financial institutions so as to provide the context for the following chapters, which focus more on specific technology and business concerns. This introductory chapter and the chapters that follow begin with a case study that highlights a common problem that banks and other financial institutions face and, in some cases, how they solve them. Additional case studies are interspersed within each chapter.

Case Study 1-1

Reducing Costs by Reengineering Technology and Processes at HSBC

Banking IT solutions come in many forms. They may enable new products or services; alternatively, solutions may support consolidation and efficiency improvements. Growth, along with mergers and acquisitions, often lead to duplicated systems across multiple locations, increased complexity, and reduced productivity. To remain competitive and enable the development of new solutions, it is often necessary to streamline IT systems and business operations.

As Hong Kong Shanghai Banking Corporation (HSBC) grew to serve over 14 emerging market countries as well as many developed markets, it found itself needing to strengthen its operating model by streamlining processes and technology across its geographic centers. The bank had reached a stage where, as of 2007, it had 55 core banking systems, 24 credit card systems, 41 Internet banking platforms, and 130 data centers supporting over 10,000 branches worldwide.

To tackle the overall state of complexity that had evolved over time, HSBC embarked on its "One HSBC" program, a massive process and IT reengineering effort that aimed to improve customer experience and reduce the bank's production costs. A major goal of the effort was to manage and view information at the customer level, rather than the system-driven account level. When complete, this strategy, in conjunction with consolidated technology platforms, would enable the bank to provide a single customer view across multiple banking channels, including call centers, Internet banking, and physical branches.

Furthermore, standardizing systems platforms across all its operation centers helped to reduce development and operational costs. As part of the consolidation, many manual processes were automated so as to reduce execution time and overall delivery cost. For example, these changes helped reduce the call center process for handling lost debit cards from 13 steps to five steps. The bank's goal, with respect to its systems environment, was to pare down to just one core banking system, reduce its banking platform to a third of its original size, and consolidate to only four primary data centers.

Despite all the obvious benefits that can be achieved, it is rare for financial institutions of this size to take on change initiatives of this scale. One of the main impediments to such an overhaul is convincing management that the potential benefits justify the costs and risks. One HSBC program was a multiyear project with an implementation cost of over US$1 billion per annum. The program's progress was made public as part of the bank's 2008 annual report, and the initiative had the backing of the chief executive.

As part of this ongoing initiative, in 2011, HSBC set out to save US$3.5 billion over three years. The bank sought to cut costs by reengineering business processes and streamlining IT systems. A key goal was to reduce complexity. Relocating software development operations to lower-cost locations and buying more off-the-shelf software packages were also targeted as ways of achieving cost savings. By 2014, HSBC had had achieved cost savings of $5.7 billion. While improved IT and operational efficiencies greatly contributed to this cost reduction, HSBC had also reduced its headcount by 13% and stopped operating in 15 countries.

The drive to lower expenses continued into 2015, when the bank announced it was aiming, within two years, to reduce spending by up to $5 billion annually. Some of the cost reduction would come from job cuts, of nearly 10% of the bank's staff, and withdrawing from Brazil and Turkey. However, a large part of the savings would be achieved through an investment of $1 billion on accelerating digital and automation programs. New core investment initiatives included improving online channels and productivity; automating and reengineering operations; and optimizing its software development processes and technology infrastructure. A key goal of the plan was to further simplify infrastructure platforms and eliminate 750 software applications.

While HSBC, being one of the largest banks in the world, is relatively unique in its scale and geographic coverage, its business and technology challenges are not unusual. Small- and medium-sized banks also have an overabundance of business processes and systems and are under pressure to reduce expenses. Thus, leveraging new technologies, consolidation, integration, and resource optimization are necessities for most financial institutions. As illustrated by HSBC's saga, cost savings and efficiency improvement initiatives are not a one-time event. Changes in the banking environment, such as new regulatory demands, and competitive pressures, require that banks continually improve their technology and operations to manage costs.

Sources: HSBC Holdings plc 2008 Interim Report; "The IBS Interview: Ken Harvey, HSBC," *International Banking Systems Journal*, IBS Publishing, Issue 18.4, December/January 2009, http://www.ibsintelligence.com/index.php?option=com_content&view=article&id=12685: ken-harvey-hsbc&catid=176:2008&Itemid=33; King, Leo, "HSBC Streamlining IT in £2bn Cost-saving Drive," *Computerworld UK*, May 11, 2011, http://www.computerworlduk.com/news/it-business/3279194/hsbc-streamlining-it-in-2bn-cost-saving-drive; HSBC, "HSBC—Actions to Capture Value from Our Global Presence in a Changed World: Investor Update 2015," June 9, 2015, http://

(Continued)

Questions

1. How might these change initiatives affect customers' experiences with the bank's services?
2. How could management overcome resistance within an organization to the rationalization of business processes and the consolidation of IT systems?
3. Why would redundant processes and systems remain after banks merge or are acquired?
4. What are the disadvantages of allowing overlapping business processes and systems to persist?

1.1   BUSINESS DRIVERS

Understanding the evolution of a financial institution's businesses can enable better development of IT solutions and addressing of IT-related concerns. Managers and solution implementers can make better decisions on how to create new business solutions when they understand how different contributing factors have led to decisions that shaped solutions that were developed previously. This section examines how financial services have evolved, and identifies the changes that have shaped and transformed the industry over the past several decades. The following industry-wide changes will be reviewed in this section: increased competition, increased scale, new revenue sources, new delivery channels, regulatory changes, and increased complexity. In most cases, these factors have been interdependent, as illustrated in Figure 1-2.

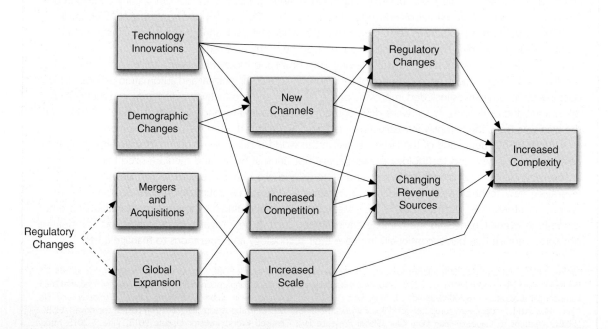

Figure 1-2 Factors influencing banking evolution

1.1.1 Increased Competition

The greatest change affecting the banking industry has been the shift from financial services being a protected market to a more competitive market. This transformation has occurred at different rates in different geographies and was initially spawned by regulatory changes. Competition has caused a domino effect, with the more competitive banks taking the lead, setting higher standards, and attaining a position of strength for subsequent industry consolidation. Increased competition reduced profit **margins** for many traditional products and services that became commoditized over time. However, it has also presented opportunities for creating new products and services that commanded higher premiums. A more competitive banking environment benefits industry leaders; however, it in turn creates an ongoing struggle to maintain a dominant position. The gap between the leading and lagging institutions gradually diminishes over time, and new products and services eventually become old and commonplace.

For many years the competitive threat to financial institutions was from other financial institutions that were able to enter new geographic markets. More recently competition has come from startup financial technology, or "Fintech," companies that aim to disrupt incumbent financial institutions. Fintech companies seek to leverage technology more effectively and provide innovative financial products and services that are more attractive to customers than those provided by traditional institutions. By nature of being technology oriented, rather than having a financial services charter, Fintech firms are often not subject to the same regulatory requirements as financial institutions, providing them with greater flexibility and agility with regard to their business strategy. Likewise, as startups, Fintech companies are not encumbered by pre-existing business lines and legacy IT systems. The impact of Fintech on financial institutions will be covered in more depth in Chapter 20 and is also highlighted in some of the chapters in Parts Two and Three.

1.1.2 Increased Scale

Increased competition led to consolidation across the industry, enabling banks to take advantage of economies of scale. The largest banks engaged in what is referred to as **universal banking**—providing a comprehensive set of products and services including deposit taking and lending, derivatives trading, securities trading and underwriting, fund management, and insurance. Increased scale helped reduce unit costs, lower risk by increasing **diversification**, and improve return on investment for large IT infrastructure expenditures. International expansion provided the opportunity to extend existing products to new markets. However, introducing existing products to new markets is complicated; regulatory requirements, customer preferences, and business practices vary across different countries and have to be addressed.

Increased scale, particularly where it came about through the consolidation of multiple entities, had a major impact on the IT and operations of financial institutions, as highlighted in Case Study 1-1. Larger business operations, along with increased competition, often necessitated the integration of what were previously separate siloed* business functions. One goal of integration was to eliminate duplicated functions and systems to achieve greater efficiency. Another goal was to find synergies across business lines that, when combined, could create greater business value and provide new opportunities. For instance, the integration of systems and services across business units has enabled banks to bundle together multiple products and services, such as deposits, credit cards, and payment facilities, into what appear to the customers as consolidated offerings. Integrating business capabilities also supported cross-selling, that is, expanding the usage of existing products across different customer segments.

---

* Silos are a metaphor for business functions or IT systems that are vertically integrated but are not linked with one another. The original reference comes from farming where grain is stored in tall cylindrical structures, referred to as silos, often placed in rows next to one another. The term "smokestacks" is also used interchangeably with silos and has the same meaning.

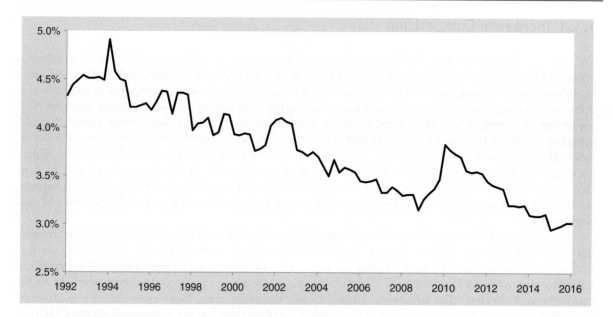

Figure 1-3 Changes in US banks' net interest margin over time

1.1.3 Changing Revenue Sources

Over time, banks have increased their focus on fee-based revenue and relied less on income derived from the net interest margin, which is the difference between the interest income that the bank receives and pays out. An extended period of low interest rates and shrinking net interest margins, as shown in Figure 1-3, has put pressure on the bottom lines of banks and other financial institutions, particularly money market funds [1]. As compared with revenue derived from net interest, fees provide an income source that is less sensitive to interest rates and business cycles. Shifts in interest rates and customers' credit quality usually do not directly impact fees. Furthermore, growth in fee-based income does not require financial institutions to increase the size of their balance sheets, as is the case with lending. Balance sheet growth is generally undesirable because it often requires institutions to raise additional capital; hence, promoting fee-based products and services has been a common goal for financial firms over the past several decades. As a case in point, as of 2009, more than 60% of earnings of banks in the United Kingdom were from fee-based income [2].

1.1.4 New Delivery Channels

New customer delivery channels, such as phone and Internet banking, have supported the growth and profitability of banks, enabling an increase in volume and a reduction in transaction costs, as illustrated by Case Study 1-2. Whereas the cost of processing a transaction initiated at a bank branch might cost just over a dollar, the cost of processing the same transaction through the call center would be just over 50 cents, through an automated teller machine (ATM) at around 30 cents, and through the Internet or mobile banking at less than 5 cents [3]. The exact values of channel costs will vary by country and institution but their proportions will be similar. In addition to benefiting banks, new channels have increased customer convenience, enabling transactions to be initiated from home, work, and while shopping or in transit. Likewise, being able to reach out to customers through their mobile phones has made it easier for banks to communicate with customers on a continuous basis.

New delivery channels have provided many benefits, but have more tightly intertwined IT with the business processes of banks. Accordingly, banks' business staff have had to become more IT literate

---

Case Study 1-2
Leveraging Digital Channels to Reduce Costs and Improve Service

As discussed in Case Study 1-1, one of the core initiatives that HSBC was pursuing as part of its 2015–2017 cost savings plan was to invest in and better leverage digital channels and capabilities, with the overall goal being to enable growth at lower cost. Shifting customer interactions and transactions to self-service channels can reduce the need for front-office staff and enable a greater number of customers to be serviced at a lower marginal cost. For example, making use of email and text messages to provide information about account balances could reduce the number of inbound requests to a bank's call centers, so that fewer customer service representatives are required to handle customer inquiries.

Digital channels can also provide better tools for front-office staff, such as tellers and relationship managers, to increase their productivity. Providing banking IT system capabilities on mobile devices, such as tablet computers, can enable branch staff to get out from behind their counters or desks to engage with customers more dynamically in the branch environment or visit customers at locations outside of the branch. This flexibility can improve front-office staff productivity and increase the number of meetings that a relationship manager has per week. Likewise, making all the information about the customer—i.e., all their different accounts, transactions, and interaction history—available to relationship managers through online channels can help ensure the customer's needs are fully addressed during a single engagement.

Along with other initiatives to reduce the amount of back-office and administration work required, making better use of digital channels was a critical part of achieving HSBC's goal of lowering expenses. By making these changes, the bank planned to reduce the overall number of its branches by 12%.

Source: HSBC, "HSBC—Actions to Capture Value from Our Global Presence in a Changed World: Investor Update 2015," June 9, 2015, http://www.hsbc.com/~/media/HSBC-com/InvestorRelationsAssets/investor-update-2015/group.

---

so that they can understand how technology can be leveraged to support business goals, and also to understand its risks and limitations. Likewise, banks' IT staff have had to learn more about customers and the banks' business requirements to develop effective IT solutions. Furthermore, the introduction of new channels and channel-related processes has also brought on new business risks. Identifying and mitigating these risks are only possible by having business users and IT solution implementers understand each other's domains and work closely together.

1.1.5 Regulatory Changes

For many years, many of the regulatory changes were favorable to financial institutions in that new laws broke down the barriers that limited growth and expansion.* The changes in financial service regulation in the United Kingdom are a case in point. In 1971, Competition and Credit Control that was introduced by the Bank of England allowed retail banks to operate in the commercial market and reduced the amount of liquid assets clearing banks were required to hold by more than half. Subsequently, in 1979, the United Kingdom lifted foreign exchange (FX) controls that previously limited FX dealing for an authorized subset of banks. In 1986, securities regulation reforms were enacted, which enabled brokers to trade on their own accounts and **market makers** to act on customers' behalf.

---

* For more details on the effects of regulatory changes on banks, see the chapter on Government Policies and Regulation in *Bank Management: A Decision-making Perspective* (ISBN: 978-981-4416-13-9).

Similar types of changes occurred in North America. Deregulation ultimately led to consolidation within the industry, the formation of universal banks, and the creation of financial institutions that were so large that their failure could imperil the entire global financial system.

Over the past decade however, the tide has changed. The Global Financial Crisis brought into question the economic and societal benefits of having large and relatively unrestricted financial institutions. Accordingly, a host of new regulations was introduced. In the United States, the Dodd-Frank Wall Street Reform and Consumer Protection Act came into effect in 2010, bringing about sweeping reforms. In Europe, the final form of the Markets in Financial Instruments Directive II (MiFID II) was issued in 2011, which includes a host of new rules related to securities and derivatives markets. Furthermore, new risk management guidelines defined by the Basel III Accord in 2010 are poised to affect financial institutions worldwide. Coping with ongoing regulatory changes is one of the major challenges that banks will continue to face in the years to come. Note that Dodd-Frank, MiFID II, and Basel III will be discussed in more detail in the chapters that follow on Banking Contexts (Chapter 6), Capital Markets Contexts (Chapter 13), and Market Risk Management (Chapter 18).

1.1.6 Demographic Changes

More recently, the rise of the Millennial generation has become a driving factor for banks' businesses. The term **Millennials** refers to the generation of people born between 1980 and 1994, and in the United States, they are the largest age group within the population. Compared with other generational groups, Millennials are more open to using alternatives to banking services, such as nontraditional payment services and peer-to-peer lending. They prefer communications through digital channels such as email, text messages, Internet banking, and mobile applications. As shown in Figure 1-4, use of mobile banking and mobile payment services has been found to increase significantly as age decreases [4]. Younger consumers also are more averse to using credit cards, preferring debit and prepaid cards as alternatives. Catering to Millennials' needs and preferences is of great importance for financial institutions, not only because of the large size of that demographic, but also because younger customers represent greater long-term revenue generation potential for banks.

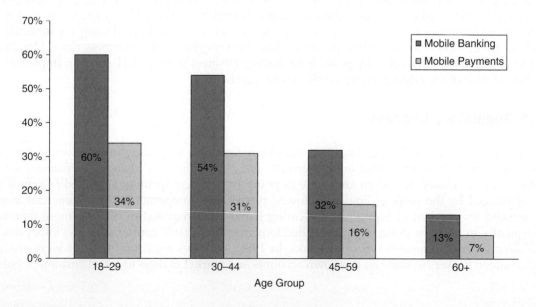

Figure 1-4 Use of mobile services in the past 12 months by age

1.2 TECHNOLOGY DRIVERS

IT has developed at a rapid pace and has supported the evolution and transformation of financial institutions. Today, the financial services industry is highly dependent on technology, and IT is an integral part of most business processes and solutions. Yet, for all the benefits afforded by new technology, the ongoing technological change has also introduced complications. One of the greatest IT challenges facing financial institutions is dealing with **legacy systems**—IT systems and applications that have become outdated. This section reviews how technology has changed over time and the implications of those changes for financial institutions. The topics discussed include advances in technology infrastructure, adoption of distributed computing, improvements in data processing and management, the emergence of solution building blocks, the use of middleware platforms that facilitate IT system integration, and the shift toward software that is designed to more flexibly support business process.

1.2.1 Technology Infrastructure

The capabilities of IT infrastructure in terms of hardware, software, and networks have improved markedly over the past several decades. The hardware processing speed and memory of mobile phones today exceed what was available to run core banking systems two decades ago. Likewise, user interfaces are much more flexible, powerful, and intuitive as compared with the punch cards and terminal screens that once dominated software applications. In the 1980s and 1990s, banking systems had to be designed to work around the limitations of low-bandwidth voice-only phone lines; today, high-bandwidth Internet and fourth-generation mobile data connections can easily reach a large number of end customers.

Technology has greatly influenced banking products and services and has become the foundation of banking solutions. For many years, the primary challenge was to find ways to circumvent technological limitations such as memory available and CPU speeds; however, many of them are no longer relevant.

While many of the old concerns have fallen away, new solution development and management challenges have emerged. Having more implementation options creates the challenge of choosing the best platform for the given solution purpose. Cost, performance, stability, and skills availability must all be considered. Furthermore, as the rate at which new technology offerings are introduced increases, so does the rate at which existing technology becomes obsolete. Over time and without intention, a hodgepodge of IT systems can easily emerge. Hence, "refreshing" and consolidating technology platforms have become major concerns for financial institutions.

1.2.2 Distributed Processing

Increases in computer-processing power combined with reduction in the cost of hardware and network bandwidth have led to the wide-scale use of IT within banks. Furthermore, the migration from centrally located **mainframe computers** to servers and desktop workstations has enabled financial institutions to easily relocate computing resources. In many cases, the capture and processing of information are decentralized, and extend to branches and customers' homes and offices via the Internet. Financial services firms have a high degree of flexibility with respect to where processing work is performed, because few, if any, physical elements are involved in the execution of financial transactions.

As banks grew more geographically diverse, distributed computing capabilities became essential. They allow customers to access banking services from many different locations, and also enable banks to electronically route manual processing work to lower-cost locations. However, distributed computing also led to a number of challenges related to the management, monitoring, and efficient usage of decentralized applications. Ironically, these concerns have led to initiatives aimed at centralizing computer resources—as was once the case when all computing was carried out on mainframe computers. Examples of this trend can be seen in the adoption of **thin client**, remote desktop, and **virtualization** technologies by financial institutions. Now, many financial institutions must grapple with the challenge of determining which parts of their IT infrastructure should be centralized and standardized, and which parts should be left to local and regional business units to source, manage, and customize.

1.2.3 Data Processing and Management

Banking-related data processing and management practices have advanced in the past several decades. One major change has been the shift from overnight batch processing to real-time processing. Advances in networking and **distributed systems** technology made it more practical to deliver information in real time for immediate processing. Real-time posting of financial transactions has enabled banks and customers to view current information, as opposed to potentially stale information from the end of the previous day. Real-time price delivery also fundamentally changed securities and FX trading practices. It enables traders to view and make decisions based on continuously updated price information rather than having to periodically check with potential counterparties to determine the current price. Moreover, the availability of real- time **market data** that can be processed by software applications has enabled many of the functions once performed by traders to be automated.

The increased use of distributed systems had the side effect of creating new stores of standalone data, often creating duplicate copies of customer and transaction information. At first, having the power to access data more freely and bypassing the restrictions and delays of centralized database administration was liberating. However, this ability ultimately created problems with data management, aggregation, synchronization, and reconciliation. Disparate data sources made it difficult to obtain a consolidated view of customer and transaction information that was dispersed across multiple systems. Similarly, the need to aggregate information related to market exposures created a major challenge for risk managers of financial institutions. Accordingly, consolidating data across IT systems has become a major area of concern for financial institutions.

1.2.4 Solution Building Blocks

The evolution of technology also led to a fundamental shift in how IT solutions can be developed, as shown in Figure 1-5. Initially, in-house software development teams developed IT solutions for financial institutions. As technology platforms matured and commonality between different solutions across organizations was identified, software vendors began producing more generic business IT solutions that could address the needs of many customers. More recently, flexible enterprise technology platforms have emerged that enable financial institutions to assemble solutions by combining pertinent components and incorporating application-specific business logic. Using enterprise platforms as a base for building IT solutions is in some ways similar to using prefabricated concrete slabs to build buildings: it speeds up the construction process, helps ensure structural integrity, and allows for various building shapes and structures to be built. Table 1-1 shows common enterprise platforms that support solution development.

Besides enterprise platforms, other application frameworks and standards, such as Spring and XML, also helped make it more practical to assemble solutions rather than exclusively buying or building them. Layered architecture models (discussed in greater detail in Chapter 3) have also provided a model for decomposing IT solutions into components, many of which could be implemented using enterprise platforms. As the assembly-based solution implementation gained momentum, more vendors began supporting this approach, making application easier. More recently, the trend has been to provide customers and other third parties with direct access to banks' internal technology solutions by providing application programming interfaces (API) that are accessible externally (discussed in more detail in Chapter 20).

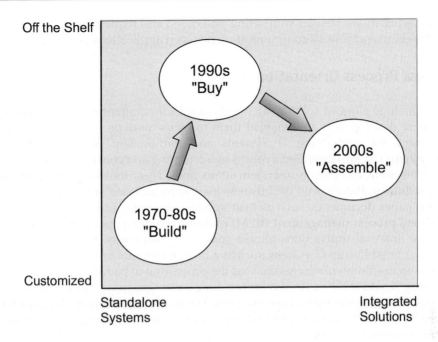

Figure 1-5 Solution implementation approaches

Table 1-1 Technologies and enterprise platforms that support solution development

Function	Tools
Data capture	Scanning/imaging, bar codes, optical character recognition technologies
Data entry	Web browser and development tools (e.g., HTML5)
Data management	Enterprise data management (EDM) platforms and common operational data stores
Business logic management	Rules engines and complex event processing (CEP for short)
Access to system functions	Remote procedure calls (RPC for short), web services technologies, and representational state transfer (ReST for short) technologies
System-oriented workflow	Business process management (BPM) platforms
Human-oriented workflow	BPM platforms
Management reporting	Data warehousing, business intelligence, and real-time dashboard display technologies

1.2.5 Enterprise Application Integration

The shift from monolithic solutions to more flexible solutions that were assembled from multiple enterprise systems and business applications brought the use of enterprise application integration (EAI) technology to the forefront. EAI and its cousins, middleware-oriented messaging and **enterprise service buses (ESBes)**, provided a common "glue" that linked systems and platforms together. EAI interface standards provided a standard way for IT systems to present their application functions for use by other applications. Besides supporting pull-based and request/reply interactions, EAI also enabled push-based, asynchronous communication between applications.

1.2.6 Business Process Orientation

Advances in technology allowed solution architects to shift their attention away from basic concerns related to software development and enabled them to focus more on how business processes were implemented using the underlying IT systems and middleware platforms. **Business process management systems (BPMS)** provided a means of integrating and consistently managing person-to-person, system-to-system, and person-to-system interactions. These tools provided a robust framework for composing solutions, and allowed the business logic to be accessed and inspected more readily.

By scanning paper documents, such as loan application forms, at the point they were received and using **business process management (BPM)** platforms to route the images for processing, it was possible to make financial transactions almost completely paperless. Similarly, where transaction information was entered into an IT system, such as a branch terminal or Internet banking application, business process orchestration platforms enabled the processing to be fully automated in many cases. Manual processing would still be required for handling exception cases, but a large proportion of the process steps would not require human involvement. The resulting **straight-through processing (STP)** helped financial institutions achieve significant gains in efficiency, reductions in transaction processing time, and improvements in accuracy.

1.3 BUSINESS OPPORTUNITIES

The business opportunities available to different financial institutions and groups within institutions vary significantly. The geographical markets that financial institutions operate within, along with their current business and technology capabilities, determine which opportunities are available to them. For example, in some countries, the majority of small and medium enterprises may still be managed on a cash basis, creating opportunities related to the frequent cash deposits at bank branches. In other countries, almost all of the corporate banking may be done electronically, providing a different set of opportunities. Thus, financial institutions must search for ways to innovate within the context of their environment.

The rate of innovation within the financial service industry has increased substantially in recent years. Ongoing improvements in business practices and technological capabilities have provided an abundant source of possibilities for new offerings. Increased competition and the commoditization of existing products have also driven banks to become more innovative. This section will discuss how financial institutions can take advantage of business opportunities by introducing new products, new services, new channels, and new business models, and by improving service levels.

1.3.1 New Products

Rather than introducing completely new products, financial institutions will typically enhance or extend existing products, reformulate them to address the needs of different customer segments, or combine them to form new products. For example, exotic foreign exchange (FX) options (discussed in more detail in Chapter 12) are based on simpler option products that were enhanced to meet additional customer needs. Alternatively, the creation of financial products that are compliant with Islamic Sharia law is an example of how pre-existing products, such as deposits and loans, can be adapted to fit new demographic market requirements. **Dual currency investments (DCI)** also demonstrate how banks can combine existing products, such as time deposits and FX options, to address specific customer risk-return needs.

Typically, new product offerings provide banks with a short-term competitive advantage. The pricing of new and complex financial products is often less transparent and there are fewer competitors, providing higher profit margins. Over time, however, competitors will come up with their own copies of new products that are successful, reducing their profitability. In turn, other new products will need to be created to take their place. However, it is not easy to develop new products. Technical, regulatory, and operational hurdles must often be overcome, and hidden risks of new products can offset their expected benefits.

1.3.2 New Services

Developing new services provides financial institutions with both direct and indirect benefits. Services can help generate fee revenue, directly contributing to the bottom line. Nonetheless, free services can also produce financial benefit by increasing customer loyalty or improving the operational efficiency within banks, which helps lower expenses. For example, consider a bank that provides a service that automatically notifies customers regarding the status of their loan applications. Proactive notification could improve customer perception of the bank's responsiveness and, at the same time, reduce the need for customers to call the bank to make status inquires. In turn, the volume of inbound calls that the bank's call center must process would be reduced, lowering operating costs and, thus, improving profitability.

New services can also help customers manage their finances and improve their financial security. Like new products, new services are often extensions or add-ons to existing services. For example, for many years, banks have provided bank-to-bank payment services to customers. These have been relatively cumbersome for customers to use, requiring knowledge of the other party's bank account information, creating privacy concerns. These transactions would often settle the next day. More recently, some banks have begun offering new payment services that more easily allow their customers to make payment to other banks' customers electronically by only knowing their mobile phone number or email address. Likewise, these services typically provide near real-time settlement of the funds transfer. In many cases, competition from Fintech firms have driven banks to offer new and innovative services. Both long-standing and new payment technologies are discussed in Chapter 9.

1.3.3 New Channels

As discussed in Section 1.1.4, the delivery of financial services to customers has changed significantly due to the introduction of new technology and channels. This trend looks likely to continue into the future, with further adaptation of existing channels and introduction of new channels. For instance, Internet banking applications leverage basic web browser technology, but financial institutions have yet to take full advantage of Internet-based social networking, video content delivery, and mobile access. Likewise, smartphones and tablet computers are becoming more ubiquitous, powerful, and multifunctional, bringing about a wide range of possibilities for extending and creating new mobile banking solutions (see Case Study 1–3). As of 2014, 87% of the adult US population had mobile phones and 71% of mobile phones were smartphones. Furthermore, smartphone users were also more likely to take advantage of mobile banking and mobile payment services than users of other types of mobile phones.

New channels mostly provide indirect benefits for banks, and are not usually a source of revenue by themselves, although at least one study of US consumers showed that customers who used online banking were more likely to use other services that were revenue-generating. Additional channel capabilities can help increase the sales volumes of products by providing easier access to services and information. For example, enabling customers to check, using their mobile phones, that their account balances are not near their credit limit while they are shopping could lead them to make additional credit card purchases. Supporting new delivery channel services can extend the reach of financial institutions to new customer segments, particularly younger customers. New low-cost channels, such as text messages sent to mobile applications over the mobile Internet, can also be used to replace existing higher cost channels, such as text messages sent via mobile operator networks. Additionally, online channels have gotten high marks for customer satisfaction [5].

Case Study 1-3
Mobile Phones Change the Banking World

The emergence of the mobile Internet in combination with new mobile handset capabilities has enabled new services to be developed. The cameras, Bluetooth, near-field communication (NFC) capabilities, and fingerprint scanners in smartphones have all spurred innovation in the financial services arena.

The cameras in mobile phones have been used to facilitate transactions, simplify account opening, and provide enhanced security. One of the earliest uses of the mobile phone's camera within banking was to provide **remote deposit capture** services, so that customers could deposit cheques by taking photos of them and uploading the images to their bank (discussed in more detail in Chapter 7). Another way that the camera has been used is to capture barcode or quick response (QR) code information to facilitate mobile payments. The camera, in conjunction with optical character recognition, has also been used to capture driver license information to populate the fields in online account applications more quickly and provide better "know your customer" information for customers who open accounts online. Banks have also used the camera as a biometric security tool that provides another way to authenticate users, capturing and comparing the pattern of veins in the eye to identify users.

While Bluetooth connectivity has been available in mobile phones for many years, only more recently has it started to become more relevant for banking applications. The introduction of smart watches connected to mobile phones via Bluetooth, provides another platform for banks to quickly and easily provide information to customers. Also, some banks have begun testing beacons, Bluetooth devices that connect to customers' mobile phones when they are nearby, in branches. Beacon technology can be used to send messages to customers when they walk by, or are inside, a branch.

The introduction of NFC capabilities in mobile phones enabled major mobile contactless payment initiatives to move forward. Android Pay, Apple Pay, and other mobile wallet services enable customers to make contactless transactions at retail merchants using their mobile phones. In some cases, the provider of the phone operating system (OS) limits access to the NFC chip so that only the phone provider's mobile wallet can be used. Thus, control over the mobile payment infrastructure has begun to shift away from banks and more toward the phone OS providers. Some banks are also working on rolling out NFC-enabled ATMs, so that a mobile phone can be used in place of a debit card to withdraw cash.

Mobile phones' fingerprint scanners provide another means of identifying the user of mobile banking applications. Fingerprint authentication can be used in conjunction with traditional username/password login credentials to provide an extra layer of security. Alternatively, fingerprint authentication can be used instead of username and password credentials to speed up the application login process, providing greater convenience for customers. Also, some mobile wallets use fingerprint scanning to authorize payment transactions.

Many mobile technologies and their potential applications are still in their early stages of development and understanding. Mobile devices' ability to support biometric identification holds great promise for supplementing or supplanting passwords as a means of authenticating users. On the other hand, it has been predicted that the global positioning systems in mobile phones could provide banks with a means for banks to offer customers real-time, personalized offers based on their location. Yet there has been little visible progress in this area. While some mobile features may not turn out to be smashing successes, others will likely have far-reaching effects on how banks interact with their customers.

Sources: Nash, Kim, "Wells Fargo to Verify Customers through Eye Prints," *Wall Street Journal*, April 26, 2016, http://blogs.wsj.com/cio/2016/04/26/wells-fargo-to-verify-customers-through-eye-prints/; Barret, Brian, "Your Phone Will Replace Your Wallet at the ATM, Too," *Wired*, January 28, 2016, http://www.wired.com/2016/01/cardless-atms/; Macheel, Tanaya, "Mobile's Future Is Here—Too Bad So Many Banks Are Stuck in the Past," *American Banker*, July 6, 2016, http://www.americanbanker.com/news/bank-technology/mobiles-future-is-here-too-bad-so-many-banks-are-stuck-in-the-past-1090073-1.html.

1.3.4 New Business Models

Financial institutions can go beyond introducing new products and services, and find new business models to harness. New business models may involve innovative pricing schemes, reaching new customer segments, and linking financial services together with products and services provided by other industries. Leveraging new business approaches can provide a means of growth when an existing market has become saturated, or it can be a guerrilla tactic used to counteract the incumbent strength of larger rivals.

The introduction of self-serve discount brokerages in the 1990s is one example of how relatively small brokers used a new business model to create a formidable challenge for larger rivals. Over time, this model came to dominate retail equities trading in many countries. Another example of a new business model that emerged was digital-only banking, where transactions were only supported over the Internet and phone, and by mail. While this business model has not become pervasive like discount brokerages did, it created a new niche that may further evolve into something more significant (digital-only banking is discussed further in Chapter 16).

More recently, Fintech companies have introduced business models that leverage mobile payment, peer-to-peer payment, and nontraditional lending services. For the most part, Fintech companies' business models have avoided the requirement to become chartered financial institutions and the regulatory burdens that go along with such charters. Likewise, some banks have been moving toward digital-only business models that abandon support for higher-cost physical channels, such as branches, and rely on lower-cost electronic channels.

1.3.5 Improving Service Levels

Many opportunities that financial institutions can take advantage of do not require innovation; rather, they involve improving the existent business processes and IT solutions. Digitizing paper and voice-based transactions can reduce costs and transaction processing time, thereby improving profitability, customer satisfaction, and overall competitiveness. Likewise, by analyzing how business processes are executed, in some cases it is possible to achieve major gains without automation. Streamlining manual activities so that there are fewer delays and removing bottlenecks can also produce major benefits (see Chapter 2 for more discussion on process improvement).

For example, by improving existing processes and automating manual activities, it may be possible to reduce mortgage loan approval time from days to hours. Similarly, by optimizing how customer service representatives in branches perform tasks, it is possible to reduce customer queuing time and help ensure relationship managers sell appropriate financial products to customers. Improving existing processes and IT systems provides great potential for financial institutions to enhance their business.

1.4 BUSINESS CHALLENGES

Besides having many opportunities, financial institutions face many challenges. Just as competition in other industries led to better and cheaper products over time, similar pressure exists in the financial services industry. Technology enables automation of manual activities, such as taking customer orders, enabling banks to charge less and offer better services. Innovators that gain competitive advantages put pressure on the rest of the industry. In turn, the profit margins associated with disrupted business areas can diminish greatly over time. The challenges discussed in this section include competition, complexity, risk, regulation, and cost pressures.

1.4.1 Competition

For much of the twentieth century, regulatory restrictions curtailed competition in the financial services industry. As a result, for many years, banks' services were performed during limited "bankers' hours," the hours banks would be open for business, typically from 10:00 am to 3:00 pm on weekdays. Over the course of time regulations became less restrictive, opening up competition. New market entrants were able to compete by providing better pricing and services. Hence, today bankers' hours no longer exist as a concept. Some banks provide extended branch hours up to 7:00 pm, and many provide 24-hour service through call centers and via the Internet. Regulatory changes, technological advancement, new channel development, and international expansion have created a new environment where financial institutions must constantly work to fend off new competition.

One example of how technology has driven competition is in the equity and derivatives exchange market. After regulatory changes made it easier to set up new exchanges, new entrants found a lucrative market catering to the needs of high-frequency traders that used automated trading strategies. These new challengers became a major threat to the long-established exchanges, often requiring the incumbents to acquire their new rivals to maintain a market share (consolidation of exchanges is discussed in more detail in Chapter 14). Other industries are also adding to the competition. For example, in the United States, there has been an ongoing battle between banks, their Fintech competitors, and mobile phone operating system makers for ownership of the mobile wallet application that supports contactless retail payments (covered in Chapter 9). Likewise, new technologies, such as Bitcoin have also broadened the field of competitors that financial institutions must contend with.

1.4.2 Complexity

Over time, the business processes and IT systems environment of financial institutions have increased in complexity. Mergers and acquisitions, ongoing regulatory changes, use of new technologies, and adoption of additional service delivery channels have all increased the complexity level. Global expansion and the addition of service sourcing options by banks have also increased the complexity by dispersing IT systems and the execution of business processes across many different locations. Consequently, increased complexity has led to greater **operational risk**. For example, the likelihood of an IT system failure is higher in a complex systems environment than in a simple one. Similarly, internal controls may be more easily circumvented when business processes are complex than when they are simple. Root causes of problems are also more difficult to identify in complex environments.

Complexity can also lead to inefficiency and create diseconomies of scale. Normally, as an organization grows in size, its profitability benefits from economies of scale. However, such benefits may only apply up to a certain size, and in some cases, organizational, process, and IT system complexity may cause profitability to decrease as size increases. Limits on economies of scale and some evidence of diseconomies of scale have been observed by a number of studies examining the banking industry [6].

It is not uncommon for financial institutions to reach a point where tackling complexity becomes a strategic concern, as highlighted in Case Study 1-1. **Technical debt**—choosing a suboptimal technical design or implementation that is easiest to deliver in the short term, but creates more work in the long term in terms of maintenance—often accrues through a series of decisions to try to achieve immediate business goals (Case Study 1-4). Accordingly, at some point it is necessary to streamline the integration between systems to improve transaction processing speed, decrease manual effort required, and reduce operational risk. In many cases, business applications were originally designed to be standalone applications for use within a single business function, such as trade finance. Over time, though, it became necessary for financial institutions to integrate their systems to improve the accessibility of information. An integrated view of customer holdings across different business lines is required to support risk management and reporting. System integration is also necessary to support high transaction volumes via straight-through processing—that is, ensuring transactions require no manual processing to complete.

Implementing customized system-to-system links for a few business applications is manageable, but not for a large number of them. As the number of applications increases, there is a combinatorial explosion* of the number of linkages required. As illustrated in Figure 1-6, implementing full point-to-point connectivity between four applications requires six linkages, eight applications require 28 linkages, and 12 applications require 66 linkages. Since financial institutions often have dozens, if not hundreds, of systems to integrate, it is easy to end up with integration "spaghetti." Changing one IT system requires many interfaces to be re-implemented and may impact many other systems, thereby severely limiting an organization's ability to change rapidly.

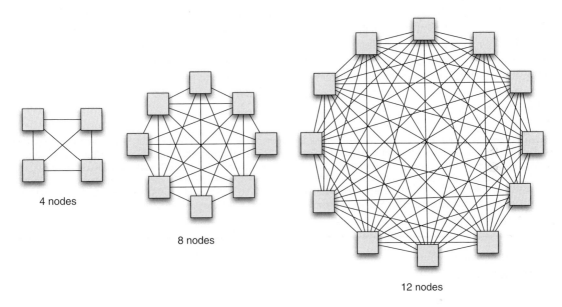

Figure 1-6 Increasing interconnection complexity for four, eight, and 12 nodes

---

Case Study 1-4
Deutsche Bank Battles Complexity by Streamlining IT Systems

As one of the first industries to leverage computer technology, financial institutions have had to bear the burden of dealing with outdated technology, which has continued to grow over time. Since the 1960s, banks have added many IT systems and business processes; however, old ones have not been retired at the same rate. As a case in point, Deutsche Bank's IT systems environment became overly complex because of its aim to, as quickly as possible, take advantage of profit opportunities. Over a number of years, it allowed individual business units within the bank to use disparate and incompatible IT systems to help grow their business—around 80% of the bank's 7,000 applications came from different vendors. Integration between systems was an afterthought, and as a result, the processing and reconciliation of trades became onerous and time consuming.

(Continued)

---

* The number of linkages required increases by $n(n-1)/2$, where n is the number of systems being connected.

(Continued)

Over the course of many years, overall process complexity and technical debt grew to the point where it was weighing heavily on Deutsche Bank's business operations. Over three years, the bank had been hit with over $10 billion of regulatory fines, some of which were related to weak controls in its trading operations. Likewise, during the 2015 bank stress tests in the United States, which Deutsche Bank failed, the bank was unable to extract some information that was requested by regulators. Moreover, human error in one of the bank's manual trade settlement processes led to a mistaken $6 billion transfer of funds to a hedge fund customer, which fortunately, was retrieved the next day.

In 2015, the bank's new co-chief executive declared that Deutsche Bank had "lousy systems, very slow processes" and launched a major initiative to remove and replace its legacy systems and reengineer its operations. Key goals would include retiring outdated IT systems, automating manual processes, strengthening internal controls, standardizing procedures and IT systems, and improving reporting. Such predicaments— where too much focus was put on short-term objectives leading to reduced productivity and increased risk in the long term—and the subsequent change initiatives that are required to remediate them are not uncommon in banks.

Sources: Arnold, Martin and James Shotter, "Deutsche Bank Streamlines IT Systems in Effort to Cut Costs," *Financial Times*, March 28, 2016, http://www.ft.com/cms/s/0/eb90b750-f4c2-11e5-9afe-dd2472ea263d.html; Boulton, Clint, "Deutsche Bank Digging out of Technical Debt, While Moving to the Cloud," *CIO*, Nov 11, 2015, http://www.cio.com/article/3004538/cio-role/deutsche-bank-digging-out-of-technical-debt-while-moving-to-cloud.html; Arnold, Martin, "Deutsche Bank to Rip out IT Systems Blamed for Problems," *Financial Times*, October 26, 2015, http://www.ft.com/intl/cms/s/0/29e44356-7bf0-11e5-98fb-5a6d4728f74e.html; Arnold, Martin and Katie Martin, "Deutsche Bank in $6bn 'Fat Finger' Slip-up," *Financial Times*, October 19, 2015, http://www.ft.com/cms/s/0/0546944a-7682-11e5-a95a-27d368e1ddf7.html.

1.4.3 Risk

Achieving effective risk-adjusted returns is a fundamental challenge for financial institutions. Market, counterparty credit, and operational risk must be managed effectively to achieve long-run profitability. Unlike many othe industries, by design, financial institutions have dedicated risk management units that help ensure that risks are identified, measured, and controlled; however, risk managers cannot be at all places at all times. Risk must be considered on an ongoing basis by business, technology, and operations functions. The risk management function has a similar function as the fire department. Firemen try to control fires that are starting or have started and work to help prevent them in the first place; nevertheless, they cannot stop carelessness or negligence. If everyone does not do his or her part, buildings will burn down. Thus, it is important for bank management and employees to think through the near- and long-term risk implications of their decisions. They must consider where potential risks may emerge, their significance, how they can be mitigated, and at what cost. Likewise, management must be aware of and manage the institution's dependence on the knowledge or capabilities of specific individuals. If only a few key people understand an institution's core business processes, internal controls, or IT systems, their departure can greatly increase its operational risk.

Operational risk—the risk that an institution may incur losses due to operational failures, such as breakdown of controls that leads to internal or external fraud, downtime of critical systems, and mistakes in the implementation of pricing or valuation models—relates directly to how business processes and IT systems are designed and managed and is a major concern for financial institutions. Whereas an automobile manufacturer is unlikely to go out of business because of the failures of one machine or machine operator, the potential losses that financial institutions can face due to failures of operational controls can be enormous. A prime example of the importance of operational risk management is the 200-year old financial institution, Barings Bank, which collapsed due to the manipulation of data, failure of control processes, and the impropriety of one man (discussed in more depth in a case study in Chapter 19). Almost two decades later in 2011, multinational broker MF Global went bankrupt due to poor implementation of market risk management (discussed in more depth in a case study in Chapter 18). Managing losses due to poor risk management practices has been an ongoing problem that will likely continue into the future.

In recent years, cybersecurity has become a critical risk area for financial institutions. Some banks have to defend against upwards of 30,000 cyberattacks per week. Such defenses are not perfect and occasionally breaches will occur, causing major reputational damage. In 2014, JPMorgan's computer systems were breached by a criminal gang, which was able to steal the names, phone numbers, and email addresses of more than 80 million people. This information was subsequently used in a scheme to illicitly manipulate stock prices [7].

1.4.4 Regulatory Change

Regulatory changes have been a key concern for banks in recent years and will continue to be a major challenge in the years to come. The number of regulatory changes per year steadily increased from around 8,000 in 2008 to over 14,000 in 2011, amounting to over 60 per working day [8]. The largest source was the United States, which accounted for 57% of regulatory changes issued. Europe followed second with 22% and Asia took third place with 15%. Generally, regulatory requirements are not optional and will have hard deadlines by which financial institutions must be compliant. Unfortunately, effort focused on implementing regulatory changes draws resources away from other revenue-generating and cost-saving initiatives. Given the scale of regulatory changes that are engulfing financial institutions, focus on regulator changes can easily dominate their agenda.

One approach to coping with regulatory change is to find a way to combine them with other initiatives so that some forward business momentum is produced. Investment in changes that implement regulatory requirements can be leveraged to develop other capabilities as well. For example, the Foreign Account Tax Compliance Act (FATCA) enacted by the US government in 2010 requires financial institutions globally to provide it with detailed tax information on American persons and entities as well as their holdings starting in 2013. This requirement is quite onerous both from the perspectives of businesses and IT systems. Aggregating, validating, and filing the necessary information is a major undertaking. One approach might be to implement a solution that only addressed FATCA-specific requirements. Alternatively, the solution could be built in a way so that some of its underlying components could be reused to implement other types of solutions in the future. For example, if the FATCA solution was built on top of an enterprise data management platform, the same platform could also be used to implement other types of solutions, such as customer relationship management.

While some regulatory changes, such as FATCA and Basel III, will affect financial firms globally, most regulations are country-specific. Multinational financial institutions face the greatest regulatory challenge, having to comply with multiple regulatory regimes. Accordingly, multinational banks may choose to provide limited or no services in countries that have relatively small markets, to avoid the additional regulatory overhead. In some cases, financial institutions will choose to locate their business operations in countries where the regulatory environment is most favorable. When the majority of regulations is being generated in North America and the minority is produced in Asia, an additional consideration is where financial firms should locate their business entities, operation centers, and IT systems to minimize the amount of regulation-related disruption that they must endure.

1.4.5 Cost Pressures

In recent years, several factors have led to increasing expenses for banks and other financial institutions, squeezing their profitability. As a result, they have had to make tough choices regarding investment priorities, balancing what they want with what they need. A key contributor to additional expenses has been regulatory requirements. Preparation and participation in stress tests, tighter anti-money laundering controls, and better oversight of traders have been given priority to avoid large regulatory fines and the negative press that often accompanies compliance failures. To provide some perspective on the scale of investment in regulatory compliance, consider Citibank, which as of 2015, was estimated to have 26,000 employees focused on compliance activities [9].

Another major contributor to rising expenses has been spending on cybersecurity. Financial institutions' information security costs have swelled as a result of the increase in cyberattacks and data breaches that have occurred in recent years. As banks and other financial institutions have much to lose in terms of financial, regulatory, and reputational damage, they have a strong incentive to maintain adequate security despite the high and rising costs. Taking JPMorgan Chase as an example, as of 2016, the bank was planning to spend $500 million to strengthen its cybersecurity capabilities. The impact of the costs of cybersecurity is more extreme for smaller banks, because they do not have the scale or resources to support large expenditures on information security, yet are subject to similar types of risks as larger banks.

1.5   STAKEHOLDER ALIGNMENT

While IT solutions can help financial institutions take advantage of opportunities available and overcome challenges, they will only be successful if they are aligned with the needs of all of the key stakeholders. For financial services solutions, key stakeholders usually include the firm's management, customers, operations, technology, and regulatory compliance groups, as shown in Figure 1-7. Stakeholders will typically be concerned about how solutions address their objectives and affect their **key performance indicators (KPIs)**—the metrics by which they are formally evaluated. They will also all be wary of new risks that the solutions may introduce. Their focus may include short-term and long-term considerations.

For example, consider the hypothetical case of a bank that is creating a technology-based solution to provide online banking services through a mobile application that runs on smartphones. Stakeholders will have different concerns that are related to their specific needs and points of view. Management will want to make sure that the solution achieves targets for return on investment and that the application is delivered quickly to market. The banks' customers will want the application to be easy to use, constantly available, and free of defects. The bank's operations function will want to ensure that questions or problems that customers have with the application does not result in increased call volume to the bank's call centers. IT will want the application to be scalable, free of defects, and easily maintainable. Regulators will want to make certain that the application is in line with the bank's overall strategy and that risks associated with the solution have been considered and mitigated by the bank's management.

The relative importance of stakeholders' needs will depend on the organization and the type of solution being implemented. Nevertheless, it is important to ensure that all the stakeholders are

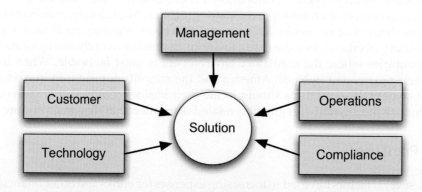

Figure 1-7 Stakeholders involved in financial service IT solutions

considered from the outset. For instance, if regulatory, audit, and IT security compliance concerns are not considered as part of a solution's requirements, functionality that is not compatible with those objectives may inadvertently be implemented. Compliance issues can become showstoppers that will potentially require solutions to be redesigned, causing major delays and cost overruns. Similarly, if operational concerns are not considered upfront, complications discovered during the deployment may be difficult to remediate, increasing operational and support costs. This section reviews the needs and objectives of the five key stakeholders.

1.5.1 Management Concerns

Since management decides which solution initiatives will be pursued, along with their scope and scale, its needs and views are often given the highest priority. One important management goal will be to ensure that the IT solutions developed are aligned with the company's overall strategy and future plans. Financial institutions' management must weigh the merits of different solutions and prioritize them accordingly. Cost, return on investment, how benefits will be measured, when benefits will be realized, and potential risks are typical management considerations for solutions. Furthermore, solutions may be categorized as strategic, tactical, and maintenance-related. Initiatives should be balanced across all three categories. Case Study 1-4 highlights the outcome when there is too much focus on tactical initiatives, while ignoring maintenance-related and strategic needs.

Management must also make sure that IT solutions are flexible. Given the pace of change in the financial services industry, solutions need to be able to be changed quickly to adapt to new market and regulatory requirements. Likewise, flexibility is necessary to innovate and rapidly take advantage of new technology. In contrast, many financial institutions are saddled with legacy IT systems that are difficult to change and integrate, which hamper new solution initiatives. While little can be done about poor technology decisions made in the past, management can learn from previous mistakes and help ensure that the future IT environment can be more easily adapted to new requirements.

Moreover, risk management is a major concern for banks' board of directors and senior executives. Poor quality, late delivery, instability, and inadequate controls within technology solutions can damage

---

Case Study 1-5

Reputational Risk

Besides market, credit, and operational risk, financial institutions must also be concerned about their reputations. A financial institution's reputation can be quickly tarnished by one incident or a series of incidents, prompting customers to move their business to competitors or decreasing the firm's market value. One danger is that minor issues can be blown out of proportion by the media or through social media. For example, in 2012, Goldman Sachs faced public criticism after it became known that its employees had referred to its customers as "muppets" in internal emails. While the actual financial damage incurred might not have been that severe, the effects of embarrassment to the banks' management and employees should not be underestimated.

As a case in point, UK bank Lloyds TSB faced a number of challenges when a bank employee autonomously changed a customer's phone banking password from "Lloyds is pants"* to "no it's not." Subsequently, when the customer tried to change it back, he met resistance from a call center agent who

(Continued)

---

* "Pants" is British slang for "rubbish" or "bad."

(Continued)

went on to disallow various other passwords that were disapproving of the bank or suggested that a competitor was better, as well as the word "censorship." While making for amusing news reading, this was not the kind of customer service that the bank's management wanted to project and, therefore, it issued a public apology for the incident.

When solutions and business processes are designed, it is difficult to predict how they will be used or misused. Often, concerns will be focused on preventing fraud, rather than reckless usage. Without having full knowledge of the business environment, it is hard to determine exactly how situations like this can be avoided completely. Training staff might help, but it does not guarantee prevention. One possibility might be to route sensitive requests, such as changing of a password, to specific agents who have special system access rights, are trained to deal with a wide range of customer situations, and are trusted to act responsibly. Financial institutions must continuously work to avoid being cast into the public spotlight due to a mishap or error in judgment.

Sources: "A Noisy Exit," *Economist*, March 14, 2012, http://www.economist.com/blogs/schumpeter/2012/03/goldman-sachs; "Man's 'Pants' Password Is Changed," *BBC News*, August 27, 2008, http://news.bbc.co.uk/2/hi/uk_news/england/shropshire/7585098.stm.

---

a financial institution's' reputation (Case Study 1-5). Accordingly, management must ensure that the technology solution delivery process that is used is robust and executed effectively, discussed in depth in Chapter 4.

1.5.2 Customer Concerns

From an IT solutions perspective, there are two types of customers: internal and external (Figure 1–8). Internal customers are the financial firm's employees that are responsible for front-office sales and operations. External customers are the consumers and companies to whom the financial institution provides products and services. In some cases, internal customers may be the only users of an IT solution, as is the case with a bank's customer relationship management platform. On the other hand, both internal and external customers may be users, as is the case with an Internet banking platform. Internal customers will administer and manage the system, while external customers will be the ones performing transactions on the Internet-banking website.

Common customer concerns include cost, convenience, ease of use, quality of service, and security. They will want a solution that is low cost, convenient, easy to use, always available, and highly secure. Unfortunately, some of these requirements are in conflict. For example, highly secure solutions are often difficult to use. How trade-offs should be made between these considerations will depend largely on the type of customers. For instance, cost may be less of a concern for a solution that is provided to internal customers who are fixed income traders in a large investment bank, compared with one that is provided to branch tellers in a small retail bank. External corporate customers may be more concerned about how banks' solutions integrate with their own processes and systems rather than ease of use, which is of greater importance to retail customers. A major challenge for financial firms is to match their products and services to customer needs, as opposed to designing technology solutions to fit their own organizational structures and objectives.

Some financial institutions have adopted a more customer-centric approach. The idea behind this strategy is to design processes and IT solutions around customers' preferences, rather than the institution's organizational structure. For instance, customer-centric call-center support would enable the service representative to handle customer inquiries without having to transfer them to different departments to handle different requests. Sometimes, however, IT solutions may not directly provide

Figure 1-8 External and internal customers (© Standard Chartered Bank. Reprinted with permission.)

benefit to external customers. In these cases, it is important to consider the indirect effects that may occur. The effects of IT solutions, both positive and negative, on operations staff will also impact external customers whose transactions they process.

1.5.3 Operational Concerns

Business operations groups are usually governed by KPI and **service-level agreements (SLA)**. SLA defines the acceptable ranges for service provision, often described in terms of the average and maximum allowable processing time and **throughput**. Alternatively, SLA may be defined in terms of absolute cutoff times; for example, all payment forms received by 3:00 pm will be settled on the same day. A primary concern for operations is how IT solutions will affect their KPI and SLA both in the short and long term. Solutions that do not contribute to the improvement of operations groups' performance measurement are unlikely to be embraced. Moreover, even when IT solutions provide long-term benefits, their adoption may face resistance because short-term performance may suffer due to the additional effort and risk required to change existing operational processes and working practices.

Operational concerns* associated with IT solutions are usually focused on the maintenance of internal controls, efficiency, flexibility, and exception management. Particularly during the automation of manual processes, it is critical to ensure that the controls that are incorporated into operational processes are not lost. For example, if a paper form-based payment process involves two different people to approve transactions to achieve **separation of duties**, the IT solution should follow a similar structure. Likewise, while IT solutions generally improve operational efficiency, poorly designed user interfaces can, in some cases, reduce efficiency. Flexibility can be greatly enhanced by making solutions' runtime behavior configurable, as opposed to being hardcoded. Exceptions, by definition, will not be handled by IT solutions so manual operational processes must deal with these special cases. If there are many exceptions or if the cost of processing exceptions is high, operational costs will balloon as well.

Consistency and continuity, that is, stability, are also operational concerns. One way of increasing the stability of operational processes is to minimize the number of changes made to them. The

---

* For more discussion on banks' operational concerns, see the chapter on Managing Technology and Operations in *Bank Management: A Decision-making Perspective* (ISBN: 978-981-4416-13-9).

greater the number of changes, the higher the likelihood that defects may be introduced, causing the degradation of operational KPI and SLA. Hence, operational managers are often averse to change. The challenge is to find the optimal balance between implementing technology-related changes to improve efficiency and limiting the frequency of changes to maintain stability.

1.5.4 Information Technology Concerns

Standardization, technology risk, cost of development and maintenance, and geographical distribution are all concerns regarding the IT functions of financial institutions. Standardizing hardware, software, and networking equipment helps to simplify the IT environment and lower costs. Technology risks can come in many forms. Defects in software applications, IT security vulnerabilities, and poorly designed IT solutions are common concerns that increase a financial firm's operational risk. Given the significant amount that financial institutions spend on technology, around 8% of their revenue, it is not surprising that the cost of IT solutions is a major concern [10]. Total cost of ownership is a good measure of cost because IT solutions often last between five and ten years, if not more, and support and maintenance costs can be significant, easily exceeding the development cost over time.

Geographical distribution becomes a concern when financial institutions have business activities performed or IT systems deployed at more than one location, which is usually the case. Distributed business operations will require that sufficient network capacity is available to link them together. Likewise, it will be necessary to decide where to locate IT equipment and staff. Data centers may be situated in the same locations as business operations or in remote locations. Availability and cost of physical space, power, and cooling capacity are relevant factors in deciding where to locate IT equipment. Firms may also decide to locate IT systems and staff in low-cost offshore locations or outsource them to a third party, further complicating logistical management and requiring coordination across multiple time zones. As discussed in Case Study 1-1, HSBC's 2015–2017 cost-management strategy included the movement of operations to low-cost locations so that more than 60% were based offshore to achieve between $175 and $200 million in savings.

In some cases, financial institutions manage IT and business operations functions together as a single unit, referred to as technology and operations. This arrangement is beneficial because many business processes are executed by a combination of IT systems and operations staff. There are also cost benefits to reducing the number of operational units and interfaces between them. So, it may be the case that in practice, IT and operational concerns are combined or intertwined. Within this book, IT and business operations functions will be discussed separately to better emphasize each function's specific considerations and concerns.

1.5.5 Regulatory and Compliance Concerns

When delivering financial service IT solutions, failing to adequately address regulatory and compliance requirements can be disastrous. Hence, it is critical that IT solutions comply with regulatory directives, are reviewed for legal potential concerns, do not have control or security vulnerabilities, and are adequately monitored. Compliance functions are predominantly focused on controlling business risks. Accordingly, people who are in compliance functions generally do not have engineering backgrounds; instead, they may be trained as lawyers or accountants. The same holds true for senior management (Case Study 1-6). It follows that in many cases, the first step toward achieving a positive stakeholder relationship is education. It helps if compliance staff understand technology capabilities and limitations, and that IT staff understand the business risks that must be avoided. Through mutual understanding and with appreciation of each other's point of view, IT and compliance functions can work together effectively and find common ground.

A key success factor for developing banking solutions is to consider, address, and obtain buy-in from key stakeholders. Failing to achieve this can result in delays, cost overruns, and project failures.

Case Study 1-6

Technology Knowledge Gap in the Boardroom

One of the major challenges that banks face is lack of technology knowledge in the boardroom. A 2016 study of 109 large banks across the world found that of their non-executive directors, overall only 6% had professional technology experience. Many banks' boards had none. In this regard, banks compared poorly to other industries, such as consumer goods and healthcare.

Having depth of technology expertise within a bank's board of directors is important for several reasons. First, a good understanding of IT is important for shaping and driving business strategy, which in the current day, is heavily reliant on rapidly evolving digital channels. Second, without sufficient technical knowledge, it is difficult for a bank's board to assess the merits, risks, and effectiveness of multiyear technology initiatives, such as the core system replacement and technology rationalization initiatives, as discussed in Case Study 1-1. Third, technology knowledge is essential to fend off competition from Fintech companies, to determine which threats are material and how best to address them. Lastly, younger, technology-savvy directors can help boards better understand and manage the threat of cybercrime, which is a major concern for banks and other financial institutions.

While having technology expertise in the boardroom may be optional today, in the future it may be less so. Government officials in the United States have called for publicly traded companies to disclose whether their boards have cybersecurity experience. Likewise, regulators have become increasingly concerned about financial institutions' reliance on technology and their ability to manage it effectively. There have also been recommendations to form board-level technology committees to provide the necessary level of attention to information technology and the risks that it presents.

Sources: Arnold, Martin, "Bank Directors Have Lack of Technology Know-how, Study Finds," *Financial Times*, October 26, 2015, http://www.ft.com/intl/cms/s/0/352210c4-7b17-11e5-a1fe-567b37f80b64.html; Wack, Kevin, "Get Tech Expertise in Your Bank's Boardroom," *American Banker*, January 4, 2016; Jenkins, Patrick, "Boards Urged to Appoint Younger Directors to Tackle Cyber Threat," *Financial Times*, December 14, 2015, http://www.ft.com/intl/cms/s/0/66e4c356-a27a-11e5-bc70-7ff6d4fd203a.html; Bravard, Jean-Louis, "All Boards Need a Technology Expert," *Harvard Business Review*, September 23, 2015, https://hbr.org/2015/09/all-boards-need-a-technology-expert.

Balancing conflicting stakeholder objectives is often a major challenge: management wants a low-cost solution, whereas the compliance function wants a high level of control and security; business users want regular improvements to service, whereas operations want stability; and customers want the latest technology to be supported, whereas IT wants standardization, to minimize the number of platforms that must be supported. It is important to begin working with the stakeholders as early as possible when creating technology solutions so that optimal compromises can be achieved.

1.6 SUMMARY

This chapter covered:

- the evolution of financial services and technology;

- current opportunities that could benefit financial institutions;

- ongoing challenges that financial institutions must address; and

- the key stakeholders relevant to financial institutions' IT solutions.

The chapters that follow provide an overview of how technology-based solutions can be used to support, manage, and automate business processes in financial institutions. They present techniques and technologies that support IT solutions development and explain how they are applied in real-world contexts. Throughout the book, case studies are used to help illustrate the topics discussed.

The book is divided into four parts. Part One (Chapters 2, 3, 4, and 5) provides a primer on foundational areas that support solution development and delivery. Part Two (Chapters 6, 7, 8, 9, 10, 11, and 12) provides an overview of bank business functions and discusses how technology-based solutions support them. Part Three (Chapters 13, 14, and 15) reviews how financial institutions operate in capital markets and examines how they use technology. Part Four (Chapters 16, 17, 18, and 19) discusses the functional and technology considerations that span across multiple business lines within financial institutions. The final chapter (Chapter 20) looks at emerging technology and discusses how innovation can help improve financial services.

FURTHER READING

A "Further Reading" section can be found following the summary at the end of each chapter. This section provides reference to supplemental background information and materials that provide more in-depth coverage of concepts found within the chapter. Besides the sources listed for each of the case studies, materials that were relied upon to develop each chapter's content are referenced in its Endnotes section.

This book focuses primarily on financial services technology, architecture, processes, and solutions. Due to scope constraints, it does not try to provide detailed explanations of financial products or business-related management concerns. For more detailed coverage of business-related topics, readers may refer to *Bank Management: A Decision-making Perspective* by Koch, MacDonald, and Duran (Singapore: Cengage Learning Asia, 2013) (ISBN: 978-981-4416-13-9).

ENDNOTES

1. Federal Financial Institutions Examination Council (US), Net Interest Margin for all U.S. Banks [USNIM], retrieved from FRED, Federal Reserve Bank of St. Louis, https://fred.stlouisfed.org/series/USNIM, July 9, 2016.

2. Davies, R., P. Richardson, V. Katinaite, and M. Manning, "Evolution of the UK Banking System," *Bank of England Quarterly Bulletin* 50, issue 4 (2010): 321–332.

3. Claessens, S., T. Glaessner, and D. Klingebiel, "Electronic Finance: Reshaping the Financial Landscape around the World," *Financial Sector Discussion Paper* no. 4, The World Bank, 2000.

4. Board Of Governors of the Federal Reserve System, "Consumers and Mobile Financial Services 2015," March 2015.

5. Fiserv, "Insights From the 13th Annual Consumer Trends Survey," August 2015, https://www.fiserv.com/resources/2014-fiserv-consumer-trends-survey.aspx

6. Davies, R., P. Richardson, V. Katinaite, and M. Manning, "Evolution of the UK Banking System," *Bank of England Quarterly Bulletin* 50, issue 4 (2010): 321–332.

7. Fernandes, D., "Small Banks Face the Greatest Risk from Hackers," *Boston Globe*, March 24, 2016, https://www.bostonglobe.com/business/2016/03/24/small-banks-face-greatest-risk-from-cyber-hackers/ptIWIWZh9ldFIbBxyQfx1K/story.html.

8. Brooke, M., "Financial Groups Hit by Flood of New Rules," *Financial Times*, December 8, 2011, http://www.ft.com/cms/s/0/158171f6-218e-11e1-a19f-00144feabdc0.html.

9. Noonan, L., "Banks Face Pushback over Surging Compliance and Regulatory Costs," *Financial Times*, May 28, 2015, https://next.ft.com/content/e1323e18-0478-11e5-95ad-00144feabdc0.

10. "From Clipboards to Keyboards," *Economist*, May 7, 2007, http://www.economist.com/node/9196289?story_id=9196289.

— — —

11. "Deutsche Bank Executing Strategy 2020," October 29, 2015, https://www.db.com/ir/en/download/Deutsche_Bank_Strategy_2020_29_October_2015.pdf.

12. Millennial Banking Insights and Opportunities, Fair Issac Corporation, 2014.

13. Carrns, A., "More Young People Ditching Credit Cards," *New York Times*, June 29, 2013, http://bucks.blogs.nytimes.com/2013/06/20/more-young-people-ditching-credit-cards/?nl=your-money&emc=edit_my_20130624&_r=0.

PART ONE
FOUNDATIONS

2 Business Process Management

The strategies and objectives of banks are realized primarily through the implementation of business processes. Business processes, which include sales, operational, and management processes, define people's functional roles, determine the activities they will perform, and specify how tasks will be carried out. Banks depend heavily on the robustness of their business processes because they are used for implementing internal controls that help prevent fraud, ensure regulatory compliance, and avoid risk-related losses. Business processes also serve as an institutional memory that provides a record of how past mistakes could have been avoided and should be prevented in the future.

Over the years, the execution of business processes has transitioned from activities that were performed manually using paper-based instructions to partially and fully automated information technology (IT) systems. Today, the majority of banks' information is stored electronically, and many business activities, such as calculations, checks, and communication, are executed by software applications. In business areas such as payments and foreign exchange (FX) trading, almost all transaction processing is implemented using **straight-through processing (STP)**. With STP, IT systems are used to initiate and process transaction fulfillment, from the time an order is placed to the time its **settlement** is completed. The processing is fully automated, requiring no manual intervention except in rare cases when there are processing exceptions. Financial products and services that involve high transaction volumes, that is, hundreds of thousands or millions of transactions per day, require STP to be cost effective, but also to keep error rates manageable. When manual processes are used, human error is inevitable. Accordingly, process execution error rates are higher when manual processing is involved than when full automation is achieved.

In business areas such as **investment banking** and specialized types of lending, a large proportion of processing is performed manually. In many cases, these transactions are not practical to automate for a number of reasons. If the transaction type occurs infrequently, the cost of automating it may not be justifiable. Alternatively, transactions that involve extensive negotiation or subjective judgment are usually not candidates for automation because of the complexity of the rules involved that would need to be encoded into software logic. Likewise, as new financial products evolve, they are often changed rapidly, making it difficult for IT systems to keep up with the current state of business practices. Initially, manual procedures may be preferred since they can be adapted more easily and quickly than IT systems.

Many of the business processes in banks involve a combination of people and IT systems, and much of the business process logic is embedded in and executed by IT systems. As a result, banks often fall into the trap of being IT centric, with IT systems determining how business activities are performed, instead of being the other way around. If the implementation of the IT systems perfectly matches business requirements, IT centricity is not a concern. However, IT systems are often purchased from vendors and implement generic business processes that, therefore, cannot exactly match each and every bank's business requirements. Even custom-developed systems may not perfectly match current business requirements due to budget constraints, requirement misunderstandings, and new requirements that arise over time. Hence, banks commonly face the challenge of shifting from IT-centric business processes to more flexible process-centric models where business processes can be managed and modified independently of core business IT systems.

Business process management (BPM) describes a set of tools and techniques that help companies systematically control and improve their business processes. As organizations grow, entropy increases and processes become more complex and inefficient. BPM helps address these concerns and enables the automation of manual processes. More importantly, BPM can help support agile development practices and reduce the time required to implement business processes that support new products and services. It can also make it easier to change and improve existing business processes, which is often necessary to adapt to changing market conditions and to new regulatory requirements. However, as highlighted in Case Study 2-1, in some cases process improvement efforts will precede or be performed in parallel with implementation of BPM.

It is not uncommon for core banking systems, helpdesk, and case management systems to have workflow capabilities embedded within them. In some cases, these facilities can be helpful for providing small-scale or application-specific process management outside of a more heavyweight BPM platform. However, those implementations will not realize all the benefits that BPM provides and will need to be managed and maintained independently from the BPM platform.

Case Study 2-1

Delivering Better Customer Experience by Improving Operational Processes

In 2010, the head of technology and operations at Singapore-based DBS Bank launched a process-improvement initiative that focused on improving service quality. The primary objectives of the program were to increase customer focus and the overall maturity level of the bank's operational processes. Soon thereafter, a new CEO came on board and expanded the program to include business as well as operational processes, with the broader goal of improving customer experience throughout the bank.

Unlike many other improvement programs, which often take months or years to show results, DBS's initiative was designed to show substantial benefits within a few weeks of implementation. To realize this goal, information technology (IT)-related changes were avoided and only manual processes were changed. The rationale behind this approach was that there were abundant inefficiencies in their manual processes that could be immediately addressed to achieve substantial gains. Making changes to IT systems would require significantly more time to implement and, thus, delay the realization of the initiative's benefits.

DBS's process improvement approach was largely based on **Lean** manufacturing techniques that had been pioneered decades earlier by the Toyota Motor Corporation in Japan. One of the key principles of Lean is the identification and elimination of waste in processes. Waste in banking processes can take many forms. For example, the time taken to transport documents from one building to another does not improve customer experience so it can be considered as waste. Rekeying information into different computer systems and fixing processing errors are also common forms of "waste" found in banking processes.

To focus efforts, DBS organized week-long workshops that involved the process improvement team as well as people involved in different parts of the particular business process that was targeted. During the workshop, the current process state was mapped, and then handoffs, delays, and inefficiencies were identified. Next, a new "future state" version of the process was designed that addressed these concerns and, in turn, reduced the customer's waiting time and the bank's processing effort. To ensure that the future state was implemented quickly and that delays in obtaining management approval did not slow down progress, the new approach was presented to managers midway through the workshop. Before leaving the workshop, these managers had to either approve or reject the suggested improvements. Approved changes could then be tested and refined during the remaining part of the workshop.

Often, a series of relatively small changes can compound over time to make processes less efficient. For instance, outsourcing scanning and data entry appeared to be advantageous from a cost and resourcing perspective, but ended up adding days to the process cycle time. Likewise, seating bank staff according to job role made sense from a human resources and staff management perspective, but made processing customer transactions less efficient. Simple changes, such as having all the people required to complete a transaction work in the same physical space, greatly improved processing efficiency and the speed at which business processes could be completed. While technology, such as **business process management systems (BPMS)**, can help manage workflow between physically separated workers, it can be faster to ask a colleague a quick question across desk partitions than to route a case back for rework.

Nevertheless, convincing managers to change existing processes is not easy. Resistance can be encountered when changes to employees' responsibilities, physical locations, or working methods are proposed; this is especially true when the proposals come from those seen as outsiders who are not directly involved with the business function. The process improvement team used two approaches to help avoid and get past such resistance. The first approach was to run experiments to test the proposed processing changes with a small group so that the benefits could be demonstrated and doubts eliminated. The second approach was to involve the people executing the business processes in the process improvement effort. Their involvement helped build support for the changes, as well as made sure that the changes proposed could be readily implemented.

By running an ongoing series of process improvement workshops that were targeted at high-impact business processes, DBS was able to achieve substantial gains. In its first year, the bank's process improvement initiative saved 90 million customer hours, which is defined as the number of hours customers wait to have their transactions completed. This achievement surpassed the expected target of saving 10 million customer hours. Besides improving customer service, the efficiency improvements also saved the bank over 82,000 working hours. This time saving led to reduced cost, enabled business volumes to be increased, and supported business expansion in new areas.

With operations in 15 countries and over five million customers in Singapore and Hong Kong, there is ample room for improvement in the processes at DBS. Accordingly, to help accelerate the rate that gains

(Continued)

(Continued)

were realized across the bank, DBS increased the size of its process improvement team from two to ten people. Moreover, even though substantial gains were realized by only making changes to manual processing steps, at some point going forward, it will also become necessary to incorporate technological changes into the bank's process improvements. Including changes in IT systems will slow the rate at which process changes can be implemented, but they will also help achieve substantial and wide-reaching business benefits.

Even in large organizations, benefits can be quickly realized when process-oriented improvements are given the appropriate level of focus and attention. In the years prior to implementation of its process improvement and customer experience initiatives, DBS had consistently trailed behind its peers in annual customer satisfaction surveys and come in last in the 2010 rankings. However, it saw a major turnaround in the 2011 survey results: DBS achieved the number one ranking, beating both local and foreign bank competitors.

Sources: Interviews with Paul Cobban, Managing Director of Customer Experience and Operational Excellence at DBS, 2011; Ng, Magdalen, "What a Difference a Year Makes for DBS," *Straits Times*, March 24, 2012, http://www.straitstimes.com/BreakingNews/ Singapore/Story/ STIStory_781186.html.

Questions

1. To be successfully applied at other financial institutions, how might DBS's process improvement strategy need to be adjusted?
2. What challenges might the process improvement initiative have faced without direct backing from the bank's top management?
3. What would the advantages and disadvantages of relying solely on experts in the process improvement team to redesign the bank's processes be?
4. What strategies could be used to overcome resistance to process changes?
5. What are the benefits of making the improvement efforts short and intensive?

This chapter provides a brief overview of what constitutes BPM and how it can be applied to financial services. It then discusses specific benefits that financial institutions can gain from using BPM. Next, approaches to applying BPM in financial institutions are explored along with suggestions for overcoming common challenges that may be encountered. An example of how BPM can be applied in the context of syndicated lending is then reviewed. The chapter ends with the presentation of a model for evaluating the maturity of BPM capabilities of banks.

2.1 OVERVIEW OF BUSINESS PROCESS MANAGEMENT

BPM involves many concepts, techniques, and technologies. Since it is beyond the scope of this chapter to provide a comprehensive explanation of BPM, only the main BPM concepts that are relevant to financial services will be reviewed. The Further Reading section at the end of this chapter refers readers to additional sources that provide more detail on the topics introduced here. Likewise, subsequent chapters in this book will further illustrate the concepts introduced here.

BPM functions are implemented using **business process management systems** (BPMS) that orchestrate process activities performed by both people and IT systems and integrate the content of information contained in documents and data stored in IT systems. Whereas workflow systems have traditionally been oriented toward people-to-people interactions and document-based activity management, BPMS support person-to-person, system-to-system, and person-to-system interactions. Depending on the BPMS that are used, functions such as process modeling, process execution simulation, business rules management, real-time activity monitoring, and post-execution analysis may be integrated into the same software package. Alternatively, they may be divided across multiple vendor products or components.

The following subsections will discuss process modeling, process analysis and solution design, process execution, process monitoring, and process automation. Business process modeling will be covered in greater depth because it is the foundation for process execution and monitoring. Likewise, whereas process execution and process monitoring support business operations, process modeling also provides another key benefit—knowledge management. Consistent, well-documented, and easily accessible business process information provides great value to almost every banking function.

2.1.1 Business Process Modeling

At many a bank, asking three people who are involved with a business process how it is executed will often produce three similar, but different, answers. Front-line staff understand the fine details of the processes that they execute, but those activities may only be a small part of the entire business process. Conversely, managers will usually understand the big picture of how processes work and fit together, but not be aware of the details. When processes are implemented in software, often only the people who wrote the program understand what it is supposed to do, and only those who have tested the software will understand what it really does. To help address these limitations, process modeling provides a better way of describing and understanding how banks implement their business processes.

Modeling business processes provides several benefits. One is that processes that can be easily visualized are easier to change. Another is that conflicting views and misunderstandings related to process behavior can be identified. Most importantly, though, is that the processes become more portable. When process models are documented in a complete, consistent, and well-structured manner, the execution of the processes can be more readily transferred between people and places.

Providing support for formal process modeling is probably one of the most important contributions that BPM has provided to financial services and other industries. Traditionally, flowcharts have been the preferred tool for business users who tend to be graphically oriented. Unfortunately though, there tends to be little education in and discipline around flowcharting techniques. Hence, the quality and consistency of flow charts are largely dependent on the individuals who construct them.

Another challenge with using flowcharts to document business processes is that the computer-based drawing and diagramming tools used to create them are little better for managing information than manual tools such as paper and pencil. That is to say, they do not provide a way of managing, organizing, and analyzing the information contained in the flowchart diagrams. To illustrate the concerns related to flowcharts, consider the business processes described using the flowchart shown in Figure 2-1.

In this case, no layout guidelines or abstraction principles have been applied. As a result, too much information is presented in a haphazard manner, making it difficult for anyone other than the person who created it to implement, review, or validate the process. Likewise, multiple views are mixed together, making it difficult to fully conceptualize the process from a workflow, personnel, or systems perspective. Mixing together, on a single diagram, information related to all of these viewpoints will, in many cases, lead to more confusion than insight. Often, these problems occur because the staff at banks have not received any formal training on how to document business processes. As a result, they may focus on users' interactions with the IT system, rather than on the form and function of the activities performed in the business process. Process models are not meant to be procedure manuals and, thus, should generally avoid implementation-specific details, which will usually change at some point in the future.

The aim of using formal process modeling techniques is to avoid these types of problems. Specific techniques and tools have been developed to support the description of business processes. One of the cornerstones of this business process modeling is the use of rich process modeling standards, both notations and languages. The Business Process Modeling Notation (BPMN) and Business Process Execution Language (BPEL) are two such common standards. Unlike flow charts, these tools have been designed specifically to cater to the definition of complex business process requirements and to aid the automated execution of business processes.

As an alternative to the flowchart shown in Figure 2-1, a process-modeling tool could be used to create the BPMN diagram shown in Figure 2-2. Note here that with BPMN's use of swim lanes, the groups and roles are obvious, and it also separates this information from the task descriptions. A standard left-to-right, top-to-bottom orientation makes it easier to interpret diagrams produced by different people. Furthermore, overly detailed information is removed and can be captured in subprocesses as necessary, simplifying the high-level view. Often, process models that are designed to be executable are not well suited for communicating how a process works. Fine details that are necessary for execution are not required to understand the general function or behavior of a process. Hence, many of the business process models presented in this book are not complete or accurate from a process-execution standpoint. They have been abbreviated, truncated, and summarized to help readers focus on and understand specific process considerations.

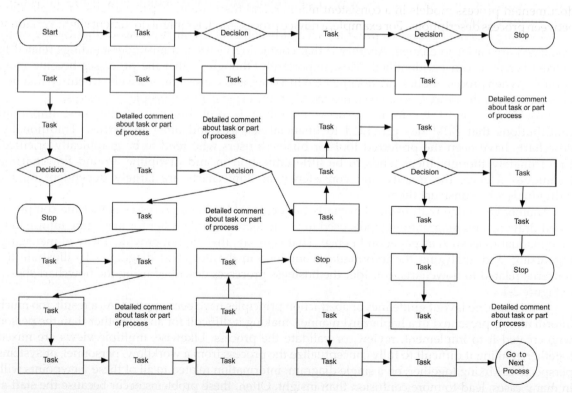

Figure 2-1 Example of a convoluted process description

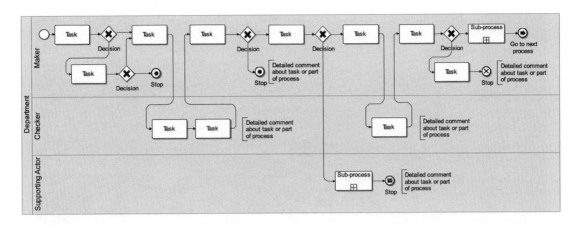

Figure 2-2 Example of a well-structured process model

While diagrams with similar qualities could potentially be created using simple diagramming tools, they are usually not. Process modeling tools and methodologies are usually required to help enforce discipline and to ensure that good practices are followed. One of the key benefits of using a structured process-modeling language is that process-modeling tools can be used to validate process model diagrams, verifying that they are consistent and complete.

Ideally, when process modeling tools and techniques are applied, some level of standards will be enforced. Process models should be manually validated to ensure that different people have documented process models in a consistent manner, and there are no gaps, overlaps, or duplication between process descriptions. For example, a novice process modeler might document slight variations in the same process by making multiple copies of the process model and small changes to each copy, rather than creating multiple flow branches within a single process model. While both approaches are valid, the latter approach makes it clear that differences are variations of the same process as opposed to constituting completely separate processes.

Depending on the process modeling tools that are used, they may also support capabilities such as capturing and managing business rules that are more complex than simple if-then logic in a tabular form, similar to spreadsheets. Advanced tools may support the capture of various types of attributes associated with tasks, such as the IT systems involved, the data accessed, and related risks and constraints on the task's execution, such as cutoff time requirements. With these attributes defined, process-modeling tools can enable filtering and reporting based on attribute values. For example, if an IT system is going to be upgraded, a report could be generated that lists all of the business process tasks that make use of that system and would be potentially affected.

Moreover, the technology used to document and communicate business process details is of less importance than the analysis method used to capture and express the information. As a case in point, practitioners of **Lean*** process improvement techniques often use whiteboards, paper, and sticky notes to interactively model processes in group workshops, rather than software-based process modeling applications (Figure 2-3). Note, however, low-technology modeling approaches cannot be easily translated into business processes that are automated and executed using BPMS.

---

* As discussed in Case Study 2-1, the "Lean" methodology seeks to improve processes by identifying and eliminating process waste.

Figure 2-3 Another type of process modeling technology (© DBS Bank. Reprinted with permission.)

2.1.2 Process Analysis and Solution Design

Once business processes have been modeled, it is then necessary to analyze how they can best be implemented using automated and manual processing. Automatable tasks must be identified and system integration dependencies evaluated. Cost-benefit analysis will then be required to determine the activities for which automation is practical. In some cases, the locations where manual work is to be performed may be chosen from multiple different physical sites, both within a country and overseas. User interfaces will also need to be designed to support manual processing steps. Moreover, regulatory considerations must be taken into account. There may be restrictions by national governments as to where customers' data may reside and where it can be processed. Such restrictions can have a significant impact on process execution and solution design.

2.1.3 Business Process Execution

Business process execution manages the information flows and activities that have been defined in process models. Process execution typically fits into two categories: orchestration of short-lived system-driven processes (henceforth referred to as **stateless process orchestration**) and long-lived processes that require people's involvement (henceforth referred to here as **stateful process orchestration**). While not all cases will necessarily cleanly fit into one category or the other, they are useful for examining how different types of processes are structured, and what technology is required to support them.

2.1.3.1 Stateless process orchestration

A large number of processes are involved in the coordination of data flows between systems. For example, when customers view a summary page of their account balances on an Internet-banking website, several different systems will be involved with verifying their identity, checking what information and transactions they are entitled to access, and retrieving the different account balances and other information from multiple back-end IT systems. Other than the user who initiates the request, there is no human interaction that is required to fulfill the transaction. While system-to-system integration is the most critical requirement for implementing these types of services, it is also necessary to orchestrate the flow of data and functions provided by different IT systems to form a single logical workflow.

The short-lived nature of these interactions, where a transaction is completed in seconds or less, allows for, and in some ways requires, the processing state to be maintained only temporarily in memory and not be kept in longer-term storage, such as files on disk or in a database. Perhaps referring to this type of process orchestration as "stateless" is somewhat of a misnomer, since state is maintained, albeit for very short periods of time. However, processing state is usually not robustly maintained. If the hardware that is running the process orchestration software were to fail, there would be no persistent record of what point the processes that were in progress had reached, because their processing state was only maintained in memory. Accordingly, upon recovery, when the processes were reinitiated, they would have to be run from the beginning again. Stateless process orchestration is faster and can support greater volumes because it does not require the overhead of writing information to disk, which is typically orders of magnitude slower than writing information to random access memory (RAM).

Stateless process orchestration can be achieved through different approaches. One approach is to distribute the workflow logic in the individual components that are responsible for interacting with each of the systems providing data. In this case, there is no centralized location where the workflow is executed. An information bus architecture, as shown in Figure 2-4, uses multiple adapters to integrate different systems. Adapter components can implement simple workflows individually that, when combined, execute more extensive business processes. For example, the adapter for source system

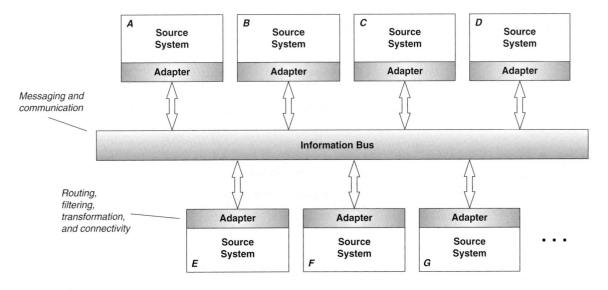

Figure 2-4 Integration using an information bus architecture

A could have logic encoded in it to send information on a specific channel* of the information bus that source system B is listening to. The adapter for system B receives the information and performs calculations which are added to the information received from system A, and sends the enriched information on another channel of the information bus that both systems C and D are listening to, and so on. The adapters implement a loosely coupled workflow by coordinating on which channels they are sending and receiving information. A single source system's adapters may send and receive information on multiple different channels, depending on the complexity of the workflow.

There are several problems with this approach. First, the workflow logic is difficult to visualize and manage because it is distributed across multiple components. Second, determining the status of a workflow depends on tracking its state across multiple components by checking the status of each one. Third, changes made in one component may have unintended workflow-related effects on other components.

An alternative approach is to centralize process orchestration, as shown in Figure 2-5. In this case, the process orchestration workflows are managed and executed by a common component. As a result, the adapters linking source systems are less aware of the context in which they interact. This approach makes it possible to manage the entire workflow as well as monitor its execution status in one place. Stateless process orchestration architectures that are more complex tend to make use of centralized coordination.

For example, using the process orchestration architecture, source system adapters would communicate with the process orchestration layer, not with one another. The process orchestration layer would receive information from system A, and the workflow logic coded in the process orchestration layer would forward the information to system B. After performing calculations, system B would send the enriched information back to the process orchestration layer, which would then send it to systems C and D. Furthermore, the process orchestration layer could implement calculations that are not source system-specific, avoiding having to embed that logic into the adapters. This approach helps simplify the adapters and make their function more specific to the source system for which they provide connectivity.

---

* The idea of a channel on the information bus is a logical concept and is also referred to as topics and subjects, depending on the implementation platform used for the information bus.

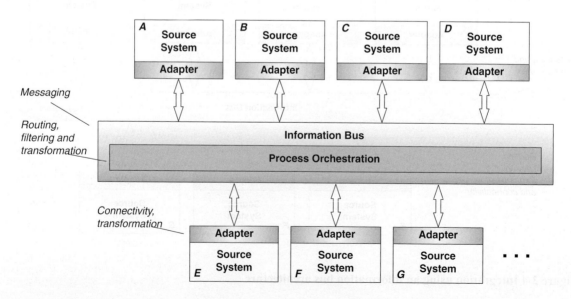

Figure 2-5 An information bus architecture with integrated stateless process orchestration

2.1.3.2 Stateful process orchestration

Stateful process orchestration, i.e., business process management, involves tracking and monitoring of process activity that requires persistent storage, usually in the form of a database. Redundant disk-based storage facilities are used so that if the server that hosts the primary instance of the process orchestration platform fails, an instance running on another server can be relied upon to continue providing service. People-oriented processes also typically require user interfaces and user and role management facilities. Hence, IT platforms that support stateful process orchestration tend to be much larger and more complex than stateless process orchestration platforms. To provide further context, Table 2-1 compares the various attributes associated with stateless and stateful process orchestration.

While business processes that only involve IT systems can be frequently managed using stateless process orchestration techniques, processes that involve people generally take more time and require stateful management. For instance, the process that underlies retrieving a customer's account balance and presenting it for online access could be performed without maintaining anything more than a transient state. On the other hand, a new account-opening process, which requires several stages of review and approval, would require the processing state to be maintained throughout the execution of the process. The speed advantage provided by stateless process orchestration is critical for ensuring that the account balance is retrieved in a timely manner. The customer would expect it to take a few seconds or less to complete such a transaction, and tens of thousands of those transactions may occur per day, or per hour, depending on the number of customers that are serviced. Alternatively, customer expectations for the time required to open a new account will be minutes, if not hours, and far fewer of those transactions will be performed per day.

Processing of paper-based credit card applications is one example of where process management is applicable. Multiple people-oriented activities are required, such as collection of application forms, data entry, documentation verification, credit scoring, as well as card fulfillment processes. Different people will perform these tasks over a period of time that spans hours, if not days. A BPMS supports the execution of this type of process by providing data entry and management capabilities for each business activity as well as controlling the flow of activities between individuals, based on predefined business rules. Process management can help govern how activities are performed and validate that tasks are performed as intended, particularly where manual procedures have a high degree of variability as to how they are executed by different individuals.

Automating business processes using process management tools can significantly improve operational efficiency and reduce operational errors. Paper-based processes can easily go awry, such as when documents fall behind desks, get stuck to one another, or are inadvertently damaged

Table 2-1 Comparison of stateless and stateful process orchestration

Attribute	Stateless Process Orchestration	Stateful Process Orchestration
State management	Must be handled by workflows, e.g., process tasks must explicitly write state information to database or file	Built-in persistence
Development of user interface	Oriented toward workflow and data transformation	Oriented toward workflow and form building
End user interface	N/A	Data display, data entry, and activity management interfaces
Work processing	Real-time events or batch-triggered processing	Work allocated to queues, roles, or individuals

(for example, when coffee is spilled on them). These types of problems are easily avoidable and preventable when business processes are managed using electronic records instead of paper ones. Automated business processes also facilitate more effective process monitoring, which can also help reduce **operational risk**.

Furthermore, business process modeling can help identify how manual tasks can be parallelized and support improved workflow design. In turn, stateful process orchestration can efficiently distribute those tasks to be worked on in parallel to multiple people in the same room or across continents. For example, manual processing is often managed by splitting up paper forms into batches that are distributed to individual processing staff members who are expected to complete those forms within a fixed time period, such as by the end of the day. However, this work allocation method is inherently inefficient since some people will work faster than others and some cases may take more time than others to process. Thus, some people will be done with their work early, while others have extra work items left over at the end of a given processing period. Batch processing also makes it difficult to prioritize work items because it requires finding specific documents within the different batches and manually sorting paper records. Alternatively, BPMS typically manage work in centralized electronic queues that can be easily searched and sorted. People will either pull work from the queue when they are ready or have it pushed to them automatically. Central management is more efficient for distributing work, ensuring that no one is left without work to do while others are clearing a backlog.

Electronic management of information and tasks also enables new methods of parallel execution and work specialization that are not practical for paper-processing methods. For example, besides dividing the task of entering manual data from forms by assigning individual forms to different people, data entry of scanned images can also be subdivided into physical sections on the forms. Specific field areas on each form can be electronically "clipped" and routed to the specific people for data entry. This approach potentially enables greater efficiency and quality since the type of work that individuals are focused on is consistent from one activity to the next. It also provides another security- and control-related benefit by limiting access of processors to customer data. The chance of customers' personal information being compromised by the individuals processing the information is lower if those working with the data records only have access to a small subset of fields. That is to say, knowing only an account number is not particularly useful for a would-be fraudster, if he or she does not also know the name of the customer associated with that account number.

2.1.4 Business Process Monitoring

A common maxim is that it is hard to improve what you do not measure. Hence, the ability to monitor and measure processes is fundamental to being able to improve them. For manual processes, monitoring and measurement are troublesome because the people doing the processing work naturally generate little status information. Tracking might be possible, but it will potentially slow down the process itself, and the management of the tracking information itself is not a trivial task.

Time and motion studies are a well-known approach to measuring business process activities to help improve efficiency. Time and motion studies require a third party that is not involved with processing to measure the time taken to execute workflow tasks at a detailed level. One challenge is that the mere presence of a monitor may cause the people performing the process to behave differently, resulting in a skewed measurement. Furthermore, the measurements performed are only a snapshot of one or perhaps a few instances of the processes, by one of possibly many people who perform the tasks. All of the possible variations and exceptions in the process flow are not measured, and the effects of changes over time to both the process and the means of processing are not captured.

Automating the execution of business processes using BPMS largely addresses these problems. The fact that process status information is constantly recorded makes it possible to easily determine the current status of a process as well as its state history over a period of time. This can make it easier to analyze the time that was required to complete individual tasks and of how often specific branches within a process flow were executed. These capabilities support real-time monitoring for exception and service-level management, as well as efficiency and performance monitoring (Case Study 2-2). Monitoring facilities are often provided in the form of dashboards or reporting facilities that are built into BPM execution infrastructure.

Process monitoring supports a number of different management initiatives. First and foremost, it can help drive resource optimization. By determining in real time that a process bottleneck is occurring at one stage of a process, resources can potentially be reallocated to reinforce that position. Detailed process execution statistics can also provide the foundation for process improvement initiatives such

---

Case Study 2-2

Business Activity Monitoring of Payments Processing

Business activity monitoring (BAM) is a term used to describe the monitoring of business processes that may be managed by BPM platforms or be implemented independently by IT systems. Like other types of monitoring, BAM provides business-level dashboards that can be used to monitor the real-time health of business operations and trigger alerts and actions when processing exceptions occur. Banks' payment processes are often split across multiple business units and IT systems, and high transaction volumes make it impractical to manually monitor payment transaction flows. Accordingly, payments processing is one of the areas that can benefit significantly from BAM.

A cheque-processing project by Bank of America (BoA) illustrates how BAM can be applied and the benefits that it can yield. In 2004, BoA began to migrate from processing paper-based cheques to processing digitized images of the cheques. Processing scanned images rather than handling paper copies saved BoA billions of dollars per year in operational costs, and also made real-time monitoring of cheque processing more practical. When processing cheques, BoA encountered over half a million processing exceptions per day because of cheques missing critical information or signatures. Bank staff that handled the exception cases would handle on average 2,500 cases per day. Hence, it was important to ensure that there were no breaks in the flow of information and that no processing bottlenecks occurred. Processing delays could cause settlement cutoff times to be missed and interest penalties to accrue.

To provide real-time business monitoring, BoA implemented a BAM solution and also created a monitoring service group that was responsible for providing business process monitoring services to the bank's business units. The monitoring group tracked cheque-processing statistics, watching for deviations that might indicate processing problems were emerging. It also monitored IT system-level information to determine if there were any failures with scanning equipment, intersystem communication, or software applications. The group's goal was to proactively take actions that would help maintain service levels. The monitoring group was also tasked with analyzing how processes could be improved based on the process information that it captured.

When implementing business process and activity monitoring and solutions, it is important to determine which information should be displayed and tracked, and which information can be disregarded. Typically, the more information that is presented, the less attention each piece of information will receive. A good way of determining what information should be actively monitored is to identify who will use the information and what actions they will potentially take depending on its information status.

Sources: Cheetham, Jonny, "Business Activity Monitoring: A New Way to Control the Payments Process?" *Gtnews*, August 8, 2005, http://www.gtnews.com/webforms/article_detail.aspx?id=10737461758; Gassman, Bill, "Business Activity Monitoring and Electronic Check Clearing," Gartner Research, ID Number: G00205313, September 15, 2010.

as Lean and **Six Sigma**.* Moreover, capturing the exact frequency of different process variations can also help improve the accuracy of accounting initiatives such as activity-based costing.

2.1.5 Business Process Automation

For banks, most business processes involve some level of automation so as to reduce error rates and operational costs. It is not uncommon for employee costs to account for over half of a financial institutions' ongoing operational expenses. Thus, the benefits of being able to reduce manual processing costs are significant. Automation also minimizes the need to have trained and capable staff ready to handle increases in transaction volumes and spikes in processing demand.

While STP is the ideal end goal, it is not always possible. Certain activities, such as signature verification and data entry of handwritten information, are still done more accurately and efficiently by people rather than computers. Likewise, freeform document content analysis, which is required for processing payment instruction letters and trade finance **letters of credit (L/Cs)**, are almost entirely dependent on human analytical skills. Certain functions may also not be cost effective to automate. An activity that occurs once a month and takes a few minutes to manually execute is probably not worth spending man-days or man-months to automate. Hence, it is critical that automation initiatives

---

Case Study 2-3

Business Process Management Solutions at Credit Suisse

Credit Suisse is a multinational bank based in Switzerland with a worldwide presence and has a strong focus on providing investment banking and wealth management services. Like many banks, Credit Suisse dealt with issues stemming from slow transaction processing times and a lack of integration between business processes. Credit Suisse also suffered from a lack of structure for defining the steps that employees should follow to ensure that processes were fulfilled correctly. Furthermore, in some cases, it was difficult to determine the current status of a transaction's processing at any given time.

To address these problems, the bank's approach was to apply BPM tools and techniques to implement solutions. BPM provided a solution platform that supported process modeling, prototyping, execution, monitoring, and business-rule maintenance. Specifically, BPM was used to create solutions that addressed needs in the areas of trade finance, securities settlement, closing of accounts, and special-order handling.

The BPM solution for trade finance focused on automating manual processes and eliminating paper-based communication with customers. The approach taken to improve these areas was to build a solution that combined the strengths of a BPM system with the capabilities of other existing IT systems. The solution enabled the bank to simplify tracking of customer transactions, increase overall process productivity, and improve service availability, for example, by enabling service to be provided on weekends.

On the other hand, the primary purpose of the BPM-based account-closing solution was to streamline a disorganized process that involved many people and communications mechanisms. The solution approach was to redesign the process and build the new implementation on top of a BPM system. The streamlined implementation used the BPM system to manage and track the communications. This new solution controlled and monitored the tasks that needed to be completed by different users to help ensure that all the steps were carried out in the right order. The reduction of error rates was an important benefit gained from implementing this solution.

---

* Six Sigma aims to improve the quality of the outputs that processes produce by minimizing process defects and variability.

The BPM solution that supported the securities settlement was focused on replacing an old mainframe-based application that was difficult to maintain and enhance to meet new business requirements. In this case, the bank chose to build its own process-execution environment and to structure the system using a more modular, service-based approach. Business-process modeling software was used to support the process-analysis effort. The solution enabled the bank to process over 30,000 cases daily, with only 0.01% of the cases requiring manual intervention. These improvements reduced operating costs and process cycle times significantly.

The bank's special-orders solution addressed the problem of slow processing times for out-of-the-ordinary customer requests. In particular, the objective was to improve coordination between the parties involved with fulfilling special requests, who often spanned multiple departments, so as to minimize delays. To address this problem, Credit Suisse implemented person-to-person workflow management on top of a BPM system. As a result of implementing the solution, the cycle time for special orders was reduced, as was the amount of administrative work involved. These gains, in turn, helped increase worker productivity and customer satisfaction.

The problems that these solutions address are quite typical of those encountered in banks. Likewise, the benefits that were realized are also representative of the types of gains that are commonly achieved using BPM. In this case, Credit Suisse applied different BPM tools and techniques to optimize information, system, and human interactions as part of its business processes.

Source: Küng, Peter and Claus Hagen, "The Fruits of Business Process Management: An Experience Report from a Swiss Bank," *Business Process Management Journal* 13, issue 4 (2007): 477–487.

not target automating every process and activity. Cost-benefit analysis is required to prioritize and define cutoffs for automation activities. Moreover, before automation efforts even begin, it is beneficial to review whether process activities are really required, or if there is a way to optimize the business process so that they are no longer necessary.*

2.2 BUSINESS PROCESS MANAGEMENT BENEFITS

BPM can provide strategic benefits and greatly improve the return on investment in IT achieved by financial service firms. It supports efficiency improvements and process changes by reducing non–value-adding complexity, enabling scalability and growth, encouraging standardization of processes, and providing control and audit-tracking capabilities that help fulfill regulatory requirements. Using BPM to automate "business as usual" processes enables operations staff to apply their skills to handling more complex cases. Thus, back-office workers can be shifted from performing simple tasks, such as document verification and process flow tracking, to performing more challenging work, such as the development and delivery of new financial products and services. This section examines how BPM helps financial institutions achieve strategic benefits, and Case Study 2-3 provides examples of how BPM can provide benefits in various different business contexts.

2.2.1 Supporting Agile Development of Products and Services

Developing new products and services is part of the core strategy of most financial institutions, and the effectiveness by which new business ideas are mapped into working solutions determines how well an organization will be able to innovate. There are many challenges to be addressed when transitioning from ideas to solution implementations.

---

* Elimination of non-value-adding process activities is one of the primary goals of Lean.

Commonly, the delivery team, who are responsible for the detailed implementation, may not be fully aware of the objectives or intentions of the business person who came up with the original idea and only expressed it in high-level terms. Also, there are many uncertainties that cannot be fully understood in advance; therefore, upfront assumptions must be made with the expectation that they will probably be changed at a later stage of the development process. Furthermore, the implementation of supporting systems, for example, software applications and software integration, may become dependencies, thus, creating obstacles for moving a new solution idea forward.

Use-case descriptions, storyboards, and business narratives provide a means of describing and defining new business ideas, but they fall far short of demonstrating the idea. Business innovation requires additional effort to conceptualize the ideas so that they can be effectively communicated to and evaluated by others. It is difficult for solution designers to foresee all the potential uses for a solution and problems that may be encountered in implementing a new concept. Prototyping helps validate assumptions and provides an opportunity to explore alternative uses.

BPM can provide a platform for implementing and testing new financial products and services. BPM supports the capture and refinement of requirements and enables rapid prototyping as well as solution implementation. Using a BPM platform, it is possible to apply agile development techniques as opposed to relying on traditional long-cycle waterfall methods of implementation. Additionally, BPM's process execution capability provides a means of expanding the scale of process implementations. Thus, rather than just serving as a model that has a limited lifetime, a BPM-based prototype can be easily extended and further developed into a pilot system or full-scale solution implementation. On the other hand, ideas that are determined to have less potential or are overly difficult to implement can then be abandoned so that they do not draw resources away from other more practical opportunities.

2.2.2 Change Impact Analysis and Management

In many cases, the adaptation of existing business processes is of equal or greater importance than supporting the development of new products and services. Changes in the market environment and new regulatory requirements have become an ongoing concern for financial institutions, and significant time, cost, and risk are involved with changing existing business processes. BPM tools and techniques can help business users understand the full impact of potential changes and manage their implementation.

Process modeling digitally captures process information that relates specific business activities with IT systems, operational risks, documents, fees, internal controls, and financial products. This information can then be utilized to analyze the scope and impact of process changes. For example, if an IT system is to be replaced, the processes and activities that will be affected can be more easily determined. Likewise, if new regulations change the rules regarding how and when customer fees may be charged, the impact on existing processes, from front-office call-center operations to back-office statement generation, can be more easily determined.

Moreover, managing changes to ongoing business processes is not straightforward. For long-lived transactions, such as mortgage loans, multiple different versions of a process may need to be supported simultaneously. Older transactions may need to follow an older business process, whereas new transactions must be implemented using an updated process. Keeping track of which version of a particular process should be applied to each transaction instance can be complicated and contribute to operational risk. BPMS generally support process versioning, so the system will guide users as to which process steps will be followed for particular transactions, rather than relying on people to always determine and take the correct course of action themselves.

2.2.3 Process Improvement

Given that often competitors can easily copy financial products and services, the execution quality of business processes is one of the few remaining sustainable competitive advantages. It takes significant time and effort to implement effective and efficient business processes. Accordingly, banks that can take and maintain a lead in process improvement can differentiate themselves from their competitors.

Process improvement methodologies typically involve either applying incremental changes to or completely reengineering existing processes. As depicted in Figure 2-6, the scale of process changes undertaken with process improvement efforts affects both risk and return. Small, incremental changes will produce few returns but will also involve relatively little risk. On the other hand, major changes, such as those that involve organizational restructuring, can produce major gains, but can also lead to significant problems if they do not go as planned or have unintended side effects.

BPM facilitates process improvement by providing a means of documenting and verifying existing "as is" processes and describing future "to be" optimized processes. Additionally, some process modeling tools support simulation, allowing the effects of process changes to be evaluated prior to implementation. For example, process simulation can help estimate the effect of eliminating a processing step, increasing the resources allocated to it, or moving it to another stage of processing.

BPMS can enable process changes to be easily prototyped so that business and operations users can better understand what the new process will look like in practice. Executing business processes using a BPM platform also helps generate and capture "telemetry" data related to the execution of business processes. Statistics related to the processing time taken for each activity can easily be measured, and the number of flows through certain branches, such as exception cases, can also be determined. A process that captures the same volume and depth of information as manual processes would not be practical to implement without BPM due to the measurement and data collection overheads that would be involved.

2.2.4 Process Standardization

The ability of financial institutions to grow in size and scope has been a critical factor in their overall success. Effective growth requires that proven processes are reused when expanding and extending the organization. Likewise, as discussed in Case Study 2-4, sometimes it is necessary to rationalize multiple similar processes to a smaller set of common best-practice processes to improve efficiency. Most banks have developed a standard set of procedures that incorporate the collective experience that has been gained over time, thus, forming a set of organizational best practices. Common examples include concepts such as **separation of duties**,* use of audit trails, and reconciliation procedures. However, best practices are often only verified through checks by banks' audit and compliance functions late in the implementation cycle, rather than being formally integrated into the design of business processes.

The development and reuse of process templates that can be utilized as organizational blueprints is critical for supporting growth. Process templates provide abstractions of common process patterns that can be further customized and extended for specific purposes, while ensuring that best practices and streamlined structures are utilized. Incorporating best-practice guidelines into templates can also

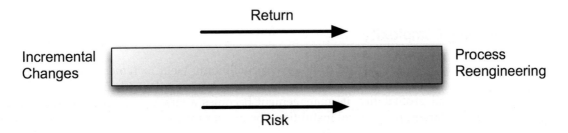

Figure 2-6 The spectrum of process change

---

* Defining separate "maker" and "checker" roles in banking business processes is a common means of implementing internal controls to prevent fraud and operational errors.

help ensure that they are consistently applied across all applicable processes. For example, process templates could be structured in a way so that when exceptions, i.e., unexpected situations in process flows, are corrected, they are processed again from the beginning of the process rather than having a separate reentry point somewhere in the middle of the process. Implementing this flow structure is important because sometimes the actions taken to correct an exception case can undo work or invalidate verification tasks performed at an earlier stage of the process.

Processes based on well-defined standards are easier to implement and manage because they lead to commonality and consistency between processes. Commonality and consistency, in turn, make processes easier to learn and support. Standardized processes also enable managers to examine variations between processes to better assess the basis and justifications for differences between them. A multinational bank, for example, might have an enterprise-wide process that is the baseline for unsecured lending that includes a standard set of credit verification, credit monitoring, and limit management procedures. Variants could be created from this template to cater for different types of unsecured lending products related to cash lines, credit cards, and trade finance.

A repository or library of best-practice process blueprints can facilitate growth of new business areas, integration required by mergers and acquisitions, and expansion into new geographic markets. Standardized processes can also be customized to fit country-specific considerations. For example, in some countries, consumer credit limits may be determined by applying algorithms to customer consumer credit histories in conjunction with results from credit reporting services, whereas in other countries, government regulations may limit a customer's credit to be a multiplier of his or her monthly salary. While local process implementations might vary significantly, as a general principle, the process implementations should be as close as possible to the blueprint and, therefore, to one another. That is to say, one would not expect to see structurally different process designs or implementations for different product adaptations or geographic regions. The same core business principles should be reflected in functionally similar processes.

Process modeling, a key component of BPM, facilitates the development of process templates and organization blueprints by providing tools for creating abstractions and providing a means of logically separating what processes do from how they do it. Abstraction is critical to help process planners focus at the right level at the right time. Given the complexity of banking processes, it is easy to get lost in detail, especially for operations staff, who are often used to focusing at a very detailed hands-on level. Abstraction through process modeling also helps draw attention to the alternative paths that may occur within workflows to help ensure that business processes implementations are well thought-out and are as complete as possible.

Process standardization can improve the speed at which new banking operations are set up. BPM also supports business growth by helping to manage complexity. Controlling complexity will often determine whether a financial institution continues to be effective as it grows, or gradually becomes dysfunctional as the burden of maintaining of processes and IT systems increases.

2.2.5 Managing Complexity

Because efforts to simplify and reduce complexity usually only yield incremental benefits, they are often thought of as "house cleaning" activities. However, when complexity becomes an impediment to growth and overall profitability, its management becomes a strategic concern, as illustrated by Case Study 1-1. The larger the financial institution, the greater the number of different business units and the geographical diversity. Ideally, the benefits arising from economies of scale should be linear; however, the costs and overhead of interactions between additional organizational units can increase exponentially. This increased overhead can easily offset benefits generated by economies of scale.

The negative effects of process complexity are observed across many different types of financial firms and can be addressed to some extent through **enterprise application integration (EAI)**. However, the benefits achieved by consolidating information and automating manual steps are limited. To wholly address the problem of multisystem complexity, it is important to recognize that, fundamentally, most IT systems are partial implementations of business processes. Thus, focusing on improving end-to-end business-process workflows also helps overall IT efficiency so that financial institutions can achieve higher returns on their IT investments. Moreover, the less time financial institutions' staff need to focus on the mechanics of executing processes, the more time they have to focus on value-adding activities, such as addressing customer needs and innovation.

With the expansion of business operations, new processes and activities within processes are often added without considering the removal of processes and steps that are no longer necessary. Often business processes grow organically, adapting to changes in the environment over time. In some cases, people may be unclear on the purpose of "legacy" processes that were put in place many years previously. Particularly, in complex environments, there may be consternation over removing or changing legacy processes because of the uncertainty over what new problems might occur as a result. Consequently, new processes may be built upon poorly designed, pre-existing processes, rather than redesigning or cleaning up the legacy processes.* Also, as expansion requires more people and IT systems, additional effort must be spent on managing ongoing business operations. Increased organizational overhead also reduces the time available to spend on identifying and managing critical exceptions.

While complexity cannot be eliminated, it can be controlled. BPM is a powerful tool for combating complexity because it can help deal with complexity on multiple levels. Process modeling provides a means of making complexity more visible and providing a medium for shared understanding. It is difficult to counteract something that is not understood. Process modeling also enables inefficiencies to be examined more easily and potential failure points within organizational processes to be identified. Process management allows processes to be adapted and changed in a controlled manner over time, thereby supporting ongoing change and expansion. Furthermore, by automatically generating an electronic audit trail, process monitoring helps business users understand how growth in transaction volume, the number of resources applied, and organizational interactions affect the efficiency and profitability of business processes.

Case Study 2-4

Achieving Cost Savings through Business Process Automation and Reengineering

HSBC began as a trade bank based in Hong Kong in 1865 and grew to become Europe's largest bank with offices in over 85 countries. For many years, it was organized as a conglomeration of separate banks that were governed by a common set of polices and maintained a congruous culture, but where each region was managed separately. This federated structure led to duplication of business processes and a proliferation of IT systems. For instance, the bank had over 40 different processes for opening accounts for retail banking products across its various locations. The lack of standardized business processes and IT systems was problematic for both HSBC and its customers. The bank suffered from inefficiency and high expenses due to the effort involved in maintaining so many processes and IT systems. Multinational customers were forced to do business with the bank in different ways in different countries, potentially complicating customers' efforts to standardize their processes.

(Continued)

---

* In some ways this is comparable to human DNA, where many of the genes are thought to be nonfunctional "junk" that was carried over from our ancestors.

(Continued)

To address these challenges, HSBC set out to develop more consistency across its different businesses. Ideally, HSBC would have a relatively small set of processes and IT systems that implemented and supported all of its business processes. Unfortunately, this goal is usually impractical because banks' products are tailored to specific jurisdictions, customers, and individual transactions. Hence, developing internally or sourcing externally a standard set of IT banking systems that can accommodate the level of variation required across all of HSBC's locations would be extremely difficult, time consuming, and costly.

In 2005, HSBC procured a BPMS to provide a global platform for rules-driven workflow automation. To help spur use of the platform, the bank set up BPM centers of excellence in India and Chicago. Centers of excellence are typically groups within an organization that have a high level of knowledge of and expertise with a particular software application or business area and are used to support implementation projects across the organization. Initially, the BPMS was targeted to automate projects in the areas of global payments and cash management, Asia-Pacific retail lending, and securities processing. Also, reengineering operational processes was one of the key initiatives to reduce headcount and costs, with specific goals of reducing complexity and operational risk, and enabling the bank to become more agile and dynamic.

Through these initiatives, by 2012 HSBC had realized cost savings of over $400 million and had reduced paper consumption by 14%. It also aimed to save another $80 million by reengineering and automating processes in its contact centers. In its 2015–2017 cost savings plan, the automation and reengineering of its operations remained a core initiative, with the simplification of business processes, process improvement, and automation remaining key objectives. The workflow capabilities that BPM provides underpinned this initiative, in particular, where it could help automate and eliminate manual verification activities. It is not uncommon for banks' business processes to involve manual checking of data values or calculations, which can be done much more efficiently by computers. HSBC's goal, through these and other changes, was to save over $100 million. Given the thousands of different processes that banks like HSBC perform every day and the many new ones that they create every year, leveraging BPM and applying process improvement techniques is a never-ending campaign.

Source: HSBC, "Simplifying HSBC," May 2012; "HSBC: Re-engineer, Redesign and Reap the Rewards," *Finance Director Europe*, May 17, 2012; HSBC Selects Pegasystems Software As Global Standard; Pegasystems' SmartBPM to Be Enterprise BPM Toolset," October 4, 2005, https://www.pega.com/about/news/press-releases/hsbc-selects-pegasystems-software-global-standard-pegasystems-smartbpm-be; HSBC, "HSBC—Actions to Capture Value from Our Global Presence in a Changed World: Investor Update 2015," June 9, 2015, http://www.hsbc.com/~/media/HSBC-com/InvestorRelationsAssets/investor-update-2015/group.

2.2.6 Reducing Operational Risk

Complexity is just one of many factors that contribute to the operational risk of financial institutions. Fraud, customer confidentiality breaches, and regulatory noncompliance are other common operational risk concerns. From a process perspective, operational risk can derive from weak process design, weak process execution, or both. Weak process design may have insufficient risk controls or it may have loopholes that can be exploited to circumvent controls. Alternatively, weak process execution may invalidate robust process design by failing to implement the design as intended. As a case in point, in 2010, Deutsche Bank was required by the Singapore courts to pay an unspecified amount of damages to one of its private banking customers after the bank's employees allegedly panicked and prematurely closed out the customer's FX positions without the proper authorization [1]. Given the limited information available about the case, it is unclear whether processes governing the timing and authorizations required to close out a customer's positions were absent or if they were present but were disregarded. Nevertheless, process failures in this example led to the bank realizing losses due to operational risk.

Business process modeling supports robust process design by enabling clear and concise documentation of process structure, the interactions between different functional roles, and how risk controls are instituted. Process models can also be extended to include fictitious roles that are malicious to help identify and analyze how potential process weakness could be exploited. Furthermore, process models help highlight how changes may potentially create new weakness or neutralize the effects of existing safeguards.

BPMS control process execution and help ensure that business processes are implemented as designed. They help prevent unplanned deviations from standard operating procedure, thereby strengthening process execution practices. BPM can also be used to help implement and enforce internal controls. Restricting employees' access or requiring secondary approval to perform certain functions can avoid operational mishaps caused by judgmental errors or sloppy execution of processes. Business process monitoring can also be used to identify suspicious or nonstandard process execution patterns.

Section 6.6 provides a more in-depth example of how BPM can be used to implement robust process design and process execution in the context of financial planning services provided by banks to customers.

2.2.7 Supporting Flexible Sourcing and Location Operating Models

In recent decades, financial institutions have sought to take advantage of flexible sourcing and location models to optimize their cost structures and take advantage of larger resource pools to support growth. A key trend has been for financial institutions to engage in business process outsourcing (BPO), where they transition some operational responsibilities to third-party companies. Financial institutions have also shifted work activities to in-house operations in locations such as India and China, where labor and operation costs are lower. Accomplishing either of these approaches requires that existing business processes are well understood and can be effectively communicated and transferred across and within organizations.

The success of BPO and relocating where processes are executed is highly dependent on process modeling because it is the starting point for capturing and communicating how tasks should be performed. BPMN and other internal guidelines for documenting business processes help provide a common vocabulary for communicating process information across languages and cultures. On the contrary, poor or incomplete process documentation can greatly increase the business risk involved with migrating business processes and increasing the time and effort required to implement the transition.

Using BPMS can also enable and support the transition of work between parties and locations. When the process logic is encoded in a BPMS, it is less vital for people performing the processes to understand the details of how the processes are structured. Accordingly, less training is necessary for new people, in different locations or organizations, to perform the business processes. Likewise, there is reduced risk that a transition will lead to misunderstanding by the new implementers as to how processes should be performed. The BPMS is the definitive source of truth for that information, rather than the previous implementers.

2.3 APPLYING BUSINESS PROCESS MANAGEMENT

Having reviewed the strategic benefits that BPM can provide to banking and other financial institutions, it is also important to consider the practical issues encountered when applying BPM. To realize wide-scale benefits with BPM, significant challenges must be overcome and numerous pitfalls avoided. This section discusses approaches for implementing BPM and identifies common problems that are encountered.

2.3.1 Tactical and Strategic Implementations

Financial institutions often have business objectives that are not fully aligned across the organization, and which, at times, may even be in conflict with one another. Typically, the performance of front-office business units is measured by revenue growth and profit margins. For these groups, ongoing innovation is critical to remaining competitive and meeting performance targets. On the other hand, back-office operational units are commonly gauged by the **throughput**, timeliness, stability, correctness, and consistency of the services that they provide. Hence, their inclination is to have as few and as small changes as possible so as to not disrupt working processes and systems or introduce new problems. This difference in objectives usually leads to the front office being fast-paced and IT-driven, and the back office being slow to change and, accordingly, more paper-based.

To realize strategic benefits with BPM, management of business processes must go beyond groups or departments and address the needs of processes that stretch across the entire organization. Both business and technology requirements must be considered so that interactions between people and systems are efficient and contribute positively toward the business goals. Interactions should be viewed as closely connected parts of a single business process rather than as a loose integration of disparate systems and operations. Yet, budgeting models, differing internal objectives, and limitations of IT systems can hinder the implementation of enterprise-wide BPM.

To get around these challenges, BPM can be applied incrementally in stages and built up from tactical, cross-department implementations, to more value-adding enterprise-wide strategic deployments. Using this approach, BPM is implemented in multiple stages. Four possible stages are identified as follows:

- **Stage 1: Allocation and tracking**. BPM is applied in the least invasive way, not directly affecting the processing, but rather providing a wrapper around it just to help track and monitor activity. By directing people to perform tasks based on the process definition and the current workload, resource utilization can be managed more dynamically. Likewise, by having workers record their current task status, it is possible to more easily track the location of specific cases and identify when **service-level agreements (SLAs)** are falling short or being exceeded.

- **Stage 2: Routing of scanned images**. Where Stage 1 helps manage the processing of paper-based workflows, Stage 2 works to minimize the use of paper by scanning documents at their entry point within the business process. . BPMS electronically route the scanned images to the people who are responsible for processing them. Thus, a waste of time and logistics related to moving paper copies is eliminated, and the chance of loss or damage of documents is minimized. The benefits in terms of reduced effort and **cycle time** can be very significant, particularly where different geographic sites are involved.

- **Stage 3: Routing based on elementized information**. An important limitation encountered with Stage 2 BPM implementations is that activities cannot be managed within the BPMS based on the data contained in the scanned documents. This pixilated form of information does not adequately convey the meaning of the words and numbers that it represents. Manually capturing the information into electronic, elementized records either during or after scanning addresses this limitation and makes it possible for the BPMS to route workflow based on information extracted from the scanned documents. Hence, validation and exception checking can be performed automatically within the system, rather than requiring manual checks to be performed on the scanned images. Note that information that is captured electronically, such as through forms on a website, at the source will be available as elementized form fields from the start and will not require extra effort to have routing rules applied to it.

  It is also possible for the BPMS to present the data in an optimized form to the people performing the process tasks. That is to say, instead of having to search the entire scanned image to find a particular piece of relevant information, the BPMS can present that one piece of data directly to the user as part of a customized application screen. For instance, a form for opening an account may have 20 different pieces of information on it. If at one stage of processing only the address is to be verified, rather than displaying all 20 data fields to the user, just the customer address can be displayed.

- **Stage 4: Rule consolidation and management**. Beyond Stage 3, the more advanced capabilities of BPM can be applied. In extensive and complex workflows, business rules can become more difficult to manage. Hence, a **rules engine** may be used as part of the BPM architecture to consolidate and rationalize the processes' business rules. Likewise, real-time monitoring of the business process execution can be used to track SLAs and help identify problems as they occur, so that preemptive action can be taken.

These stages are only representative, and will be actualized in different ways within organizations. Some organizations may skip Stage 1 entirely and choose to go directly to Stage 2 or 3. Others may choose to implement Stage 1 for certain processes, and Stages 2 and 3 for other processes. Some of the advanced capabilities in Stage 4 may be applied in limited forms in conjunction with the implementation of other stages. How these different stages will be implemented largely depends on the level of expected benefits or return on investment that is required from the changes. In some cases, major regulatory changes can be used as a springboard for improving BPM capabilities of banks and improving existing business processes.

2.3.2 Business Process Management and Enterprise Platforms

In the context of industry changes, traditional application-driven IT architectures presented a number of challenges. Functional systems, such as front-office trading and back-office securities-processing systems, were often designed for specific purposes and were segmented by business lines. These systems would have overlapping functionality, but there would also be gaps in their capabilities when they were combined to address beginning-to-end business requirements. Additionally, business IT systems utilized different hardware platforms and did not provide open interfaces, making their integration, customization, and extension difficult to implement. Financial service applications have been generally focused on departmental functions rather than beginning-to-end business processes, so many different people and systems were required to execute a single customer-focused banking process to completion.

Over the past few decades, a number of technologies have evolved that enable banks to address many different challenges. **Service-oriented architecture (SOA)** and EAI technology provided both the framework and tools for financial institutions and systems vendors to better link IT systems together. Imaging and enterprise content management (ECM) systems facilitated the transition from paper-based processing to network-based distribution and management of information. Web browsers and thin-client interfaces enabled a larger number of process participants to access data capture and dissemination facilities more easily.

BPM has evolved to provide a framework that supports process modeling, management, and monitoring. It can incorporate an SOA foundation that provides access to process-specific data from a number of different sources. But more importantly, BPM can circumscribe a large part, if not all, of the manual user activities involved in executing business processes.

Imaging, SOA, web, and content management technology have been available for some time and have generated significant benefits for financial institutions. However, many of these benefits have only been realized at a tactical level, being applied to address solution-level requirements, and have not produced broad-based benefits that span across the organization. Business process orchestration provides a way to coordinate an enterprise's processes, whether they involve systems or people, and to address both short- and long-lived business processes. Hence, process orchestration is the keystone that enables strategic BPM benefits to be realized.

2.3.3 Linking Business Process Management with Service-oriented Architecture

Even where BPM is used as a framework for managing business and data services, in many cases the alignment of business processes and services is not an integral part of the solution-delivery process. This gap may be due to organizational factors; often business analysts work separately from software architects and there is little, if any, interaction between the two groups. Business analysts may not have sufficient technical depth to be able to say whether an SOA design is sufficient to meet the needs of the business process. Conversely, software architects may not have sufficient business domain knowledge to determine whether the SOA design is fit for the purpose.

The BPM-SOA implementation may follow a top-down or bottom-up approach. A top-down approach will drive the service definitions based on the business-process definitions. Typically, the mapping between the data services that are required by the business processes with existing systems will be implemented at a lower level of the data services layer, as presented in the channel-services architecture discussed in Chapter 3. The benefit of using a top-down approach is that the structure of the data and business service interfaces are determined by the business processes, not the reverse. Alternatively, a bottom-up approach often leads to service definitions that closely resemble the structure of the systems that they provide access to. The mapping of how they are utilized by business processes will be performed at the top level of the data-services layer, or possibly in the business-services layer.

Using either approach, defining mappings between business processes and software services during the design process is essential. If the business processes and the software services are designed and implemented independently, there will likely come a point during integration testing when incongruence is discovered. For example, a business or data service utilized by a business process may require an identifier that is not available at that step of the process. For example, the business process uses the customer identifier (ID), but the service requires the account ID. Mapping out in advance the services that will be called in order by individual tasks within business processes can help prevent this type of problem.

2.4   A BUSINESS PROCESS MANAGEMENT EXAMPLE

To help illustrate how process modeling and BPM can be applied in practice, this section reviews BPM in the context of **syndicated lending**, where multiple banks will join together to form a syndicate to provide funding to a single borrower. Banks engage in syndicated lending primarily at two levels: as an arranger or as a participant. Arranging banks help to manage the syndication process and entice participants to join the syndicate. Arranging banks are typically oriented toward providing investment-banking services and seek to generate fee income from the transaction. Alternatively, participant banks benefit by increasing their lending capacity and reaching customers and markets that they might not normally have access to directly. By fulfilling only a portion of the total loan amount, participant banks can avoid overexposing themselves to a single counterparty or industry sector as they may if they are the sole creditor, covering the entire loan amount. For instance, in 2000, Hong Kong International Theme Parks Limited used syndicated lending to raise US$425 million in capital to finance its Hong Kong Disneyland theme park and resort complex. Chase Manhattan Bank led the financing and a total of 32 banks participated in the syndicate.

Figure 2-7 shows a simplified process model view of the parties and activities involved with originating and fulfilling a syndicated loan. The process model clearly shows the main parties involved, i.e., the borrower, Bank A, and Bank B, in separate pools. The roles that Bank A and Bank B serve are

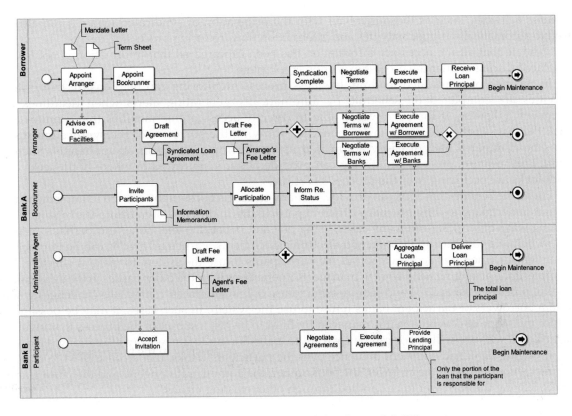

Figure 2-7 A process model view of syndicated loan origination and fulfillment

identified as swim lane designations. Bank A acts as the mandated arranger, the bookrunner, and the administrative agent, whereas Bank B only acts as a participant. In an alternative scenario, the roles that Bank A plays may have been performed by other banks instead. For ease of reading, Figure 2-7 only shows one pool associated with a single participant bank; however, in practice, many participant banks would be involved. Likewise, many of the activities shown would constitute subprocesses, of which the details are not shown.

The process model also shows the documents involved with the process, such as the mandate letter, term sheet, and information memorandum. Flow lines connect activities to one another. Gateways, shown as diamonds, indicate where flows branch based on conditional logic, execute in parallel, and converge. Start and end shapes, denoted by circles, identify whether flows begin or end independently, or link to other processes. Text annotations help highlight key points that help clarify the model description.

In contrast to process models, textual descriptions of processes often vary dramatically in their structure and level of detail. They may be documented in terms of functional roles, activities, supporting documents, or a combination of some or all of these. Textual descriptions of complex interactions can be confusing, however, because of ambiguities related to the sequence of events and exactly which parties are involved at each stage. Business-process models help address these concerns by providing a consistent graphical framework that clearly identifies relationships between process participants and individual activities.

Besides using process modeling to document the syndicated lending process, a BPMS could be used to manage it as well. A BPMS can help control and track manual, multiparty, paper-based business activities, such as those involved with the origination of syndicated loans. It can also be used to automatically trigger activities and information flow, reducing processing delays. The system can validate that all the necessary information has been captured so that information is not lost or misplaced during or after the process execution is complete.

In the case of syndicated lending, business-process monitoring can help ensure that critical activities are completed on schedule by automatically generating alerts when deadlines are imminent. Likewise, if the borrower is able to directly access online facilities that monitor and track the state of the processes, tasks related to notifying the borrower of the syndication status could be eliminated and/or easily automated using electronic communication channels such as email. Furthermore, process monitoring can provide better visibility as to where bottlenecks and roadblocks are occurring over the process's lifetime.

For all the benefits that BPM can provide, in many cases it is not straightforward to implement. It is a major undertaking to convince many different participants in different organizations to change their existing ways of working—in many cases, using pen and paper, the telephone, and perhaps email—and switch to a software application and electronic documents. Particularly, BPM can be impractical to implement when it is necessary for all the participants to use the system to make it effective. For example, if the arranging bank were to manage its interactions with the other parties in the syndicated-lending processes using BPM and require them to use online interfaces, it may face challenges where certain borrowers or participant banks refuse to use the system. In such cases, it may be possible to reduce the scope of coverage that is managed by BPM to be just a subset of the process that involves participants who are willing, or can be coerced, to transitioning to a new way of working. Hence, if the arranging bank had sufficient influence over the participant banks, it could use BPM to manage the interactions between the arranger, the bookrunner, the administrative agent, and the participating banks, leaving the borrower to be handled through other existing means.

2.5 TARGETING AND MEASURING BUSINESS PROCESS MANAGEMENT MATURITY

Whether or not they explicitly recognize it, all financial institutions are at some level of BPM maturity. It is important for organizations to have a framework that is used to gauge and target BPM maturity levels. Without one, it will be less clear where improvement is needed and how much effort is required to achieve desired competency levels. Maturity targets will also vary between institutions. Large financial institutions may target higher maturity in areas such as process execution and governance to ensure consistency of service and manage risk. On the other hand, smaller financial firms may target higher maturity in process modeling and monitoring to help improve their agility and efficiency. Based on the current and target BPM maturity levels identified, companies can develop a roadmap for developing additional BPM capabilities.

Figure 2-8 shows a BPM maturity model for financial services that is partially based on concepts and structures used by the Capability Maturity Model Integration (CMMI) for Services [2] and the Open Group Service Integration Maturity Model (OSIMM) [3]. Unlike the CMMI and OSIMM models, which are designed to be pan-industry and focus specifically on services and software integration, this framework is oriented more specifically toward the financial institutions' BPM capabilities. While the model shows distinct boundaries separating all of the measurement dimensions across each of the levels, in practice, the BPM capabilities of companies in different areas will vary across different levels of maturity. For example, their capabilities for process execution may be at level 3, their process modeling at level 2, and their process monitoring at level 1. The following subsections will discuss the characteristics of financial services firms at each of the different maturity levels.

	Level 1 Chaotic	Level 2 Managed	Level 3 Standardized	Level 4 Optimized	Level 5 Innovative
Process Governance	No Governance	Variable Localized Governance	Common Centralized Governance	Continuous Improvement Practices	Scenario Planning and Analysis
Process Modeling	In People's Heads	Inconsistent Procedure Documentation	Standardized Process Models	Rationalized Process Models	Process Change Impact Analysis
Process Execution	Inconsistent	Repeatable but Inconsistent	Repeatable and Consistent	Variance Control	Dynamic Resource Allocation
Process Monitoring	Inconsistent Aggregated Reporting Metrics	Inconsistent Detailed Reporting Metrics	Standardized Detailed Reporting Metrics	Reactive Real-time Process Monitoring	Future Process State Prediction

Figure 2-8 A BPM maturity model for financial services

2.5.1 Level 1: Chaotic

Level 1 maturity is characterized by inconsistency, and is largely unstructured and unmanaged. There will be little, if any, process governance and different people may execute the same processes in different ways. There will be no formal documentation of how things should be done, or if it does exist, processes are described at such a high level that it is difficult to repeat by anyone other than the person who regularly performs the activity. Typically, no BPMS facilities will be available within the organization. While there will be some level of management reporting, statistics are likely to be high-level aggregate values, such as total transactions processed per day, and may be quantified differently across various business processes.

It is rare to see financial institutions operating in a chaotic state for two reasons. First, regulatory requirements generally preclude such poor operational practices. Second, poorly managed financial institutions will generally succumb to competitive pressures. Competitors who have higher levels of maturity will provide better levels of service and operate more cost efficiently and with fewer defects. However, it may be the case that pockets within organizations may be effectively operating at this level. Likewise, exception cases that occur infrequently may be managed at this low level of process management competency.

2.5.2 Level 2: Managed

Level 2 maturity provides a stable basis for operation. Basic process governance ensures that common patterns and best practice controls are implemented as part of process design and enforced during process execution. Processes are documented at a sufficient level of detail, but may be documented in different ways by different people and groups. Some combination of flowcharts, textual use-case descriptions, and process models may be used. More detailed process documentation enables process execution to be more repeatable, but different groups may implement the same business processes using different approaches. More detailed process reporting metrics will be available, but their structure and presentation will vary. In some cases, detailed information will be provided in periodic reports; in other cases, more frequently updated dashboards may be utilized.

Many financial institutions, particularly small- and medium-sized ones, operate at the second level of maturity. It enables them to be functional, but stifles their growth and causes variable levels of service delivery. BPMS may be used tactically in some departments, but their use may be limited to stateless or stateful process orchestration. While they operate more efficiently than organizations at level 1 maturity, they are unable to take advantage of process and platform reuse. Some processes will be automated or implemented by prepackaged systems, but automation is likely to be implemented as point solutions rather than as an integrated platform design.

2.5.3 Level 3: Standardized

When financial institutions reach level 3 maturity, they typically have centralized functions that are responsible for managing process governance and modeling at an enterprise or divisional level, for example, across **retail banking**. Comprehensive, start-to-finish business process models will be available and be directly associated with executable versions of the process. Focus will be on standardization and consolidation to achieve better consistency and economies of scale. Besides being repeatable, the level of service provided by process execution will be consistent. A consistent monitoring and service-level management framework will be used to track process execution and react to exceptions and variances. More automation will be used to reduce processing times and exceptions that are due to manual processing errors.

Larger financial institutions tend to be the ones that have process maturity at the third level. The size of their operations requires standardization to maintain efficiency. Some institutions have engaged in large-scale process modeling efforts, in some cases driven by outsourcing and offshoring initiatives. Likewise, they have more capital capacity to invest to achieve standardization, and their scale can justify dedicated process governance and management functions that serve as a central resource that supports solution delivery efforts across the organization. BPMS will be implemented at divisional or enterprise levels, and will be able to support both stateless and stateful process orchestration. Somewhat ironically, standardization and centralization are more easily implemented in smaller organizations than in larger ones even though they tend to receive less attention in smaller firms. Standardization and centralization are very much a change-management exercise. The more parties and locations that are affected by the change, the greater the effort required to effect it.

Case Study 2-5

Improving Customer Onboarding with Process Reengineering and Automation

Few, if any, processes in banking are more important than account opening. It is often customers' first impression of a bank's processes and may lead to customers doing more business, or discourage them from doing so, in the future. If there are problems or delays with the account-opening processes, customers may abandon the banking relationship altogether. Hence, many banks have shifted their focus toward streamlining the account-opening and customer-onboarding process. As a case in point, Singapore-based OCBC bank invested more than $14 million in automation technology that eliminated paper forms and records and streamlined the account-opening process.

As of 2011, OCBC had used its account opening processes to service over 200,000 new accounts each year, with the vast majority opened at the bank's branches. The process was primarily paper-driven and required customers to sign multiple forms and present their personal identification documentation when setting up new accounts and purchasing new financial products. It also required the bank's front-office staff to navigate between 36 different screens that were presented by six different IT systems.

To improve the customer experience and improve efficiency, OCBC set the goal of reengineering the account-opening process to be so simple and intuitive that new employees could open new accounts without receiving any training. One major change to the process was to capture customers' signatures on an electronic pad once rather than requiring customers to sign multiple physical forms. Also, customers' personal identification documents, such as passports and government identity cards, were scanned and loaded directly into the banking IT system at the branch. This change eliminated the need to make copies of the customers' documents and then transport those copies to a central processing location, increasing efficiency and reducing processing time.

Additionally, OCBC installed screen displays that could swivel so that the customer could see and verify the information captured during the account-opening process. Verifying the information at the start of the process helped to reduce the likelihood of manual input mistakes or miscommunication, reducing the likelihood of errors and avoiding the higher cost of correcting these later in the process.

The new account-opening process and the IT system that supported it took 16 months to implement and was rolled out in all of OCBC's 56 branches. The benefits achieved were decreasing the time to open accounts by half and reducing the back-office costs associated with the transportation, storage, and management of physical documents. Taking better advantage of technology at branch locations, where many transactions are initiated, is one of the many ways that banks can streamline processes, eliminate manual steps, and improve customer service.

Source: Siow Li Sen, "OCBC Makes Account Opening a Breeze," *Business Times,* November 17, 2011.

2.5.4 Level 4: Optimized

Whereas maturity level 3 provides a solid delivery-capability competency that sustains business operations, levels 4 and 5 provide advanced capabilities that can offer broader competitive advantages. For example, at lower maturity levels process governance is typically focused on controlling how processes were defined, executed, and managed. At maturity level four, the focus shifts to continuous improvement of existing processes. Likewise, process modeling goals shift from developing consistent and well-documented process models to optimizing and rationalizing existing process models (Case Study 2-5). In turn, process execution focuses on controlling the frequency of exceptions and keeping variance within statistical limits, that is, within some number of standard deviations, rather than absolute limits. Process monitoring is able to identify resource bottlenecks in real time so that situations that would lead to excessive process variance can quickly addressed so that service levels are maintained.

A limited number of financial institutions have achieved level 4 maturity. Continuous process improvement has probably received the most attention in recent years. There is still a vast amount of inefficiency and process waste that can be found and eliminated across the financial services industry. There has also been a shift to combine real-time monitoring with **complex event processing (CEP)** platforms (discussed more in Chapter 15) so that real-time actions can be taken within processes automatically based on a set of predefined rules. For example, real-time monitoring and reaction can be used to help prevent fraud when a series of business process activities are detected that match a particular fraud pattern.

2.5.5 Level 5: Innovative

The fifth level of maturity concentrates on prediction and adaptation of future states. In the context of process governance, scenario analysis is used to assess the effects of potential process changes, using static analysis of process models as well as simulation. Process monitoring will be oriented toward assessing what is likely to happen rather than what has already happened so that process execution resources can be dynamically allocated to effectively address upcoming needs.

Because these capabilities are dependent on having already achieved lower-layer maturity capabilities, only a small number of banks have developed capabilities at this level. One area that has received more attention is the ability to predict and take special action when process-monitoring facilities predict that service levels are likely to be breached.

Compared with other industries, such as telecommunications, manufacturing, and logistics, the financial services industry is behind from a business process perspective. Historically, high profit margins in combination with growth by merger and acquisition has allowed financial institutions, for the most part, to ignore maturity concerns. However, as the business environment has become less hospitable, it is likely that financial institutions will have to improve their maturity to remain competitive and support future growth.

2.6 SUMMARY

This chapter covered:

- key BPM tools and techniques;

- the benefits that BPM provides to financial institutions;

- approaches used by financial institutions to implement BPM; and

- a method for assessing the BPM maturity of financial institutions.

The next chapter will focus on solution architecture and how SOA platforms can be constructed to support BPM and the development of IT solutions.

FURTHER READING

Books

Dumas, M., M. La Rosa, J. Mendling, and H. A. Reijers, *Fundamentals of Business Process Management* (New York: Springer, 2013).

Gitlow, H. S. and D. M. Levine, *Six Sigma for Green Belts and Champions: Foundations, DMAIC, Tools, Cases, and Certification* (New Jersey: FT Press, 2004).

Havey, Michael, *Essential Business Process Modeling* (California: O'Reilly Media, 2005).

Hayler, R. and M. Nichols, *Six Sigma for Financial Services: How Leading Companies Are Driving Results Using Lean, Six Sigma, and Process Management* (New York: McGraw-Hill, 2006).

Shankararaman, V., J. L. Zhao, and J. K. Lee, *Business Enterprise, Process, and Technology Management: Models and Applications* (Pennsylvania: IGI Global, 2012).

Weske, Mathias, *Business Process Management: Concepts, Languages, Architectures* (Berlin: Springer, 2007).

Papers

Chan, V. C. T., D. K. W. Chiu, M. Watson, P. C. K. Hung, H. Y. Hu, H. Hu, and Y. Zhuang, "Designing a Credit Approval System Using Web Services, BPEL, and AJAX," *IEEE International Conference on e-Business Engineering* (2009): 287–294.

Hammer, M., "Reengineering Work: Don't Automate, Obliterate," *Harvard Business Review*, July–August 1990, https://hbr.org/1990/07/reengineering-work-dont-automate-obliterate.

Hammer, M., "Process Management and the Future of Six Sigma," *MIT Sloan Management Review* 43, issue 2 (2002): 26–32.

Rabhi, F. A., H. Yu, F. T. Dabous, and S. Y. Wu, "A Service-oriented Architecture for Financial Business Processes: A Case Study in Trading Strategy Simulation," *IEEE International Conference on Services Computing, SCC '06*, Springer-Verlag, September 18–22, 2006.

Scheer, A. W. and M. Nüttgens, "ARIS Architecture and Reference Models for Business Process Management," in *Business Process Management, LNCS 1806*, eds. W. van der Aalst et al., pp. 376–389 (London: Springer-Verlag, 2000).

Shankararaman, V. and P. Kazmi, "Unifying EA, BPM and SOA through a Synergistic Framework," *CEC '11 Proceedings of the 2011 IEEE 13th Conference on Commerce and Enterprise Computing* (2011): 286–293.

Shankararaman, V., Gottipati, S. and Duran, R., "A Retail Bank's BPM Experience", Journal of Information Technology Case and Application Research, 2012, 14:3; pp 33-51, http://www.tandfonline.com/doi/abs/10.1080/15228053.2012.10845705#.VPB2nYdDaZY

Shostack, G. L., "Designing Services That Deliver," *Harvard Business Review*, January 1984, https://hbr.org/1984/01/designing-services-that-deliver.

Periodicals

Business Process Management Journal, published by Emerald Insight.

Web

ARIS Express, http://www.ariscommunity.com/aris-express.

Intalio BPM, http://www.intalio.com/bpm.

OMG/Business Process Management Initiative, http://www.bpmn.org.

Oryx, http://bpt.hpi.uni-potsdam.de/Oryx/WebHome.

ENDNOTES

1. Leong, G., "Court Rules Deutsche Bank Closed Client's Positions Prematurely," *Business Times*, December 3, 2010.

2. Carnegie Mellon Software Engineering Institute, *CMMI for Services, Version 1.3* (Pensylvania: Carnegie Mellon University, 2010).

3. The Open Group, *The Open Group Service Integration Maturity Model (OSIMM), Version 2*, 2011, http://www.opengroup.org/soa/source-book/osimmv2/model.htm.

— — —

4. Gadanecz, B., "The Syndicated Loan Market: Structure, Development and Implications," *BIS Quarterly Review* (2004): 75–89.

5. Loan Market Association, "Guide to Syndicated Loans," http://www.lma.eu.com/uploads/files/Guide_to_Par_Syndicated_Loans.pdf.

6. Esty, B. C., "Structuring Loan Syndicates: A Case Study of the Hong Kong Disneyland Project Loan," *Journal of Applied Corporate Finance* 14 (2001): 80–95.

3 Solution Architecture

Chapter Overview

The architecture of a solution will often determine its success or failure. A well-designed solution should be easy to modify, be able to accomodate system and component failures, and support future growth. On the other hand, a poorly designed solution may have to be modified many times during development, leading to delivery delays. Likewise, poorly designed solutions may fail critical tests during user acceptance testing or not meet customer expectations in production use. Yet, for all its importance, solution architecture often receives relatively little attention and is not well understood by many business and information technology (IT) staff in financial institutions.

To understand solution architecture in the banking context, it is useful to first take a step back and examine IT architecture in a broader context. The Institute of Electrical and Electronics Engineers (IEEE) standard 1471–2000 identifies the following basic considerations that characterize IT architecture:

- the organization of a system and its components;

- the relationships between components and the environment; and

- the principles guiding the design and evolution of a system.

Beyond these basic considerations, architecture addresses important nonfunctional concerns, such as integration and resilience requirements.

IT architecture focuses on many different areas. Some categories of architecture are enterprise, software, hardware, network, and security. Enterprise architecture, for example, focuses at a high level on how IT systems are structured and linked across an organization's divisions, groups, and geographies. Hardware architecture, on the other hand, focuses more closely on the physical implementation of an IT system.

It is also useful to differentiate architecture and design. Typically, architecture focuses on macro considerations, ensuring that the high-level design, that is, the architecture, addresses the underlying stakeholders' needs. Alternatively, design can be thought of as making the more detailed choices that are possible within the context of the overall architecture, in order to make localized optimizations as appropriate.

This chapter reviews the architectural considerations that are most relevant to solutions implemented for the financial services industry. As IT architecture is a pervasive subject, this chapter aims only to highlight and provide a brief explanation of key architecture principles. Rigorous examinations of architecture principles and practice can be found in other texts, some of which are referenced in the Further Reading section at the end of this chapter. The following sections of this chapter discuss abstraction, architecture patterns, architectural considerations for banking solutions, data management, application programming interfaces, cloud computing, architectural considerations related to using cloud services (Case Study 3-1), and the role of the solution architect. Note that for the sake of brevity, the term "banking solution" will be used subsequently to refer to IT solutions used by a broad range of financial institutions, not just banks.

Case Study 3-1

The Growth of Cloud Computing in Financial Services

With the introduction of cloud computing in the mid-2000s, the financial services industry seemed like a market that was well suited to use cloud services. Banks' risk management and derivative pricing calculations periodically required intensive central processing unit (CPU) resource usage. A common approach was to deploy high-powered and expensive computer hardware on desktops and in data centers that was underutilized much of the time. Hence, the cloud computing business model, where third parties provide computing services on demand much like power utilities, appeared to be a good fit for financial institutions. However, as of 2017, the utilization of cloud computing in financial services was still developing and not fully established.

To gain traction in the banking world, the service delivery models used by cloud computing providers had to overcome a number of barriers. One major concern was security. For financial institutions, it was critical to restrict access to IT systems and sensitive information to maintain customer trust and avoid running afoul of regulators. Previously, some banks were badly affected when third-party outsourcing partners experienced security breaches that led to the banks' customer information being compromised (see Case Study 4-3). Another major concern was reliability. IT system outages can bring financial markets trading and customer transaction processing to a standstill, causing direct monetary losses and regulatory ire. Furthermore, customer confidence could be easily eroded by IT system failures, causing reputational damage. Cloud services were, for the most part, reliable; however, in 2011, one of the largest and best-known public cloud services, Amazon's EC2 service, suffered a major outage, reinforcing doubts regarding the practicality of using cloud services for mission-critical functions. Moreover, the communication links that companies use to access cloud services must also be highly resilient.

The slow rate of adoption of Internet-based shared cloud computing by financial institutions led to the emergence of another cloud computing model: the private cloud. Private clouds differed from public clouds in a number of ways. First, as the name implies, private cloud services were not open to the general public—

their access and usage were limited to financial institutions. Second, private cloud services went beyond basic hardware and operating system provisioning. Software and data services commonly used by banks were included in private cloud offerings, increasing the benefits that financial firms could obtain by using cloud services. Private cloud software-as-a-service (SaaS) offerings were better matched to the interests of financial institutions. Being able to shift software management responsibilities, such as the implementation of periodic software operating system and software application updates, as well as hosting and operation, to a third party provided many benefits. Smaller institutions will especially gain from not having to allocate capital for large upfront investments in hardware and software licenses.

The hybrid cloud model, which combines use of both private and public clouds, also grew to meet financial services firms' needs. With a hybrid cloud, the bank will manage some computing services in-house and third parties will provide other services. ING, a bank based in the Netherlands, took this approach to consolidate its data centers. Third parties would own and operate the data centers, which would also be used by other companies, and ING would manage its applications within that environment. This model provided ING with a dynamic cost structure, where it would only pay for capacity when it was required. Another example is where Bank of New York Mellon created a hybrid cloud to enable software developers to set up new environments quickly and easily, avoiding the administrative overheads associated with procuring and configuring new hardware.

NASDAQ was one of the first financial institutions to make full use of the public cloud, leveraging Amazon's public cloud facilities for storing data for a market data replay service. By using cloud storage, NASDAQ was able to incrementally increase its storage capacity as the volume of data that it provided grew, without requiring investment in additional hardware. US-based bank Capital One has also embraced Amazon's cloud services with the goal of reducing the number of data centers from eight to three and avoiding having to invest in complex and costly technology infrastructure. Other big banks have included using cloud platforms as part of their strategic plans to reduce costs. HSBC planned to use cloud platforms for some of its systems that were not business-critical, such as those used by its human resources department, as part of its plan to save more than $300 million between 2015 and 2017. Likewise, Deutsche Bank was aiming to ramp up its use of private cloud services to 80% by 2020 to help reduce its IT operations costs by more than $700 million.

While public cloud computing offerings are gaining ground, they still have a ways to go before achieving widespread adoption across the financial services industry. Some institutions may be experimenting, but relatively few have made substantial use of them. Bankers still have reservations about allowing data, which are an asset that underlies banks' competitiveness, to be stored within third-party cloud services. A major concern is that cloud service providers may not provide the same level of stewardship and protection for sensitive data as banks do. If a bank's customer data were breached through its cloud service provider, regulators would hold the bank accountable and take it to task, not the service provider. Nonetheless, cloud providers are starting to incorporate features such as encryption and monitoring, and regulators are beginning to become less apprehensive about the technology, which makes it more practical for banks to leverage cloud services. As a case in point, by establishing additional controls and technology standards, and using data encryption, Singapore-based DBS bank was able to create a hybrid cloud platform that leverages Amazon's public cloud infrastructure.

Sources: "Keys to the Cloud Castle," *Economist*, May 18, 2011, http://www.economist.com/blogs/babbage/2011/05/internet_security; "Amazon Failure Takes Down Sites across Internet," *Associated Press*, April 21, 2011, http://www.cnbc.com/id/42706104/Amazon_Failure_Takes_Down_Sites_Across_Internet; Crosman, Penny," Cloud Computing Begins to Gain Traction on Wall Street," *Wall Street and Technology*, January 6, 2009, http://www.wallstreetandtech.com/it-infrastructure/212700913; Crosman, Penny, "ING Taps HP and Colt to Build Cloud-ready Data Centers," *American Banker*, June 6, 2012, http://www.americanbanker.com/issues/177_109/ING-HP-Colt-build-cloud-data-centers-1049907-1.html; Boulton, Clint, "Deutsche Bank Digging Out of Technical Debt, While Moving to the Cloud," *CIO*, November 11, 2015, http://www.cio.com/article/3004538/cio-role/deutsche-bank-digging-out-of-technical-debt-while-moving-to-

(Continued)

(Continued)

cloud.html; HSBC, "HSBC—Actions to Capture Value from Our Global Presence in a Changed World: Investor Update 2015," June 9, 2015, http://www.hsbc.com/~/media/HSBC-com/InvestorRelationsAssets/investor-update-2015/group; Rexrode, Christina and Emily Glazer, "Amazon Web Services Takes Aim at Big Banks," *Wall Street Journal*, February 23, 2016, http://www.wsj.com/articles/amazon-web-services-takes-aim-at-big-banks-1456227994?mg=id-wsj; DBS, "DBS to Leverage Amazon Web Services Cloud," https://www.dbs.com/newsroom/DBS_to_leverage_Amazon_Web_Services_Cloud.

Questions

1. What specific cost advantages can cloud computing offer to financial institutions?
2. Which types of financial services use cases would be well suited for leveraging cloud platforms?
3. What steps can service providers take to help make the cloud model be more attractive to financial institutions?
4. How can the availability of public and private cloud services be incorporated into solution architecture planning?
5. What trade-offs should be considered when deciding to implement all or parts of solutions in the cloud?

3.1 ABSTRACTION

Before delving into specific considerations related to solution architecture, it is first helpful to understand abstraction and its importance in architecture. Abstraction refers to the process of reducing a description to its most basic features so as to provide a generalized representation. Table 3-1 gives an example of how a textual technical description can be abstracted. Irrelevant details have been omitted to enable the essence of the function to be understood. In Chapter 4, abstractions are discussed in a business context; they can help explain how solutions are connected with business goals and how tasks interrelate to fulfill a business function.

An important benefit of using abstractions is that they enable architects to focus on high-level structures and objectives. Abstracting and clearly communicating the core features of a business process or solution architecture help ensure that the detailed implementation will follow that structure. Thus, abstraction is integral to solution design and is essential for developing large or complex systems. The following sections discuss how abstraction supports different architecture-related functions. Relevant examples from both banking solutions and analogous situations in the physical world are presented to help provide context.

Table 3-1 Abstraction examples

Specific Description	Abstraction
The FET process matches the TRANS_ID field in each swap transaction record to the 31a field in the SWIFT confirmation message.	There is a reconciliation process between the front office (trading) and back office (clearing).
The CMPL system, which operates on a Sun Ultra 20 platform running Solaris 10, receives SOAP messages over 10 GB Ethernet through a CISCO 2503 and converts the SOAP messages to FIX messages that are transmitted using IBM MQ. The following messages are transferred via SOAP: order request, order confirmation, order accepted, execution matches, and order expiry value.	There is an order routing system that runs on a UNIX platform and makes use of various middleware.

3.1.1 Enabling Top-down Planning

During the planning stages of solutions, definition and use of high-level abstractions are essential to ensure that the technical approach fits with primary solution goals, stakeholders' needs, and organizational environment. Whereas detailed descriptions make it difficult for planners and reviewers to concentrate on the most important considerations, abstractions can focus more selectively on form and function so as to support top-down planning and design. Top-down analysis starts with the most essential requirements, mapping onto the simplest design, and then gradually adds more detail, as needed, to meet the full set of requirements and provide a comprehensive level of design information. As part of the top-down design, abstraction helps support decomposition of solutions into system components and decomposition of system components into modules that serve specific functions.

Consider the following as an example related to civil engineering that helps illustrate how abstraction supports top-down planning. When designing transportation connectivity across two sections of a city, a planner might first consider the current and future traffic needs. Then, taking into account the existing transportation infrastructure and land-use restrictions, the planner could determine whether it is most appropriate to convert existing roads to an expressway, build an elevated highway, or dig a tunnel. Low-resolution maps or sketches are typical abstractions that would be used to support this next depth of planning. If a tunnel is determined to be the best option, then the tunnel's depth, path, and circumference can be considered; high-level blueprints best serve this level of planning.

Architectural abstraction enables things that are relevant at each stage of top–down planning to receive the appropriate level of focus. If every concern and consideration were presented all at once, it would be difficult to identify and concentrate on the most important ones.

3.1.2 Controlling Focus

Abstraction helps hide details so that the most important qualities can be easily observed, enabling the identification of relevant patterns and structures. Sometimes it is important to view the forest as a whole, and at other times to see the trees within it. Information that is removed from one view can be shifted into another view to which it is most relevant. Reducing the complexity shown in a view makes it easier to analyze the information that is presented. For example, consider technical descriptions of both an abacus and a personal computer. Few similarities would be found when comparing descriptive views of each technology that included all of the detailed physical, functional, and operational characteristics. However, by hiding most of the detail, such as the construction materials, shape, size, power source, and user interface characteristics, and examining only the functional considerations, their similarities become immediately apparent.

Often, implementers have difficulty letting go of details when they move into architecture or business-planning roles. For software development, technology support, and operations, paying attention to details is important. However, architects must suppress the urge to immediately delve into the details. For instance, when designing an airport, the architect may choose to focus on different levels of detail such as:

- the surface materials used for the landing strip;

- the length and width of the landing strip and distance from the terminal;

- the number of landing strips and their orientation;

- the location of the airport and its immediate surroundings; and

- the function of the airport in its broader surroundings (for example, is it the only airport, one of many, commercial or military, and so on).

There is no definite rule as to how much time should be spent focusing on each of these levels. The architect or planner would probably spend more time on high-level considerations, leaving details such as the length and width of the landing strip to be addressed by other designers who have specific knowledge of the landing requirements of various planes. Nevertheless, there may be benefits to examining specific details at an early stage of planning to validate the overall approach. It would be important to confirm that the ground where the landing strips are planned can support the weight of an Airbus A380 aircraft, for example. Certain small but critical details must be verified before completing the architecture planning because they can potentially invalidate the overall design.

In the context of banking solutions, abstraction helps separate different levels and types of concerns so that they can be addressed independently. High-level software architecture need not include details about low-level system interfaces. Similarly, high-level integration architecture should focus on system communication interfaces and connectivity, but not on hardware configuration details.

Where attention should be focused will vary on a case-by-case basis, and is best guided by practical experience. When a project is concluded, architects should perform a post-mortem analysis. For instance, such analysis might identify that more time should have been spent early on evaluating performance-related design considerations. By identifying the mistakes that were made, architects can learn and achieve better results on future projects. Accordingly, architects should be engaged for the full duration of solution delivery projects: at the start of the project, to develop the design; in the middle, to ensure implementation adheres to the design; and at the end, to assess the impact of the choices made.

3.1.3 Facilitating Communication

By distilling concepts, abstractions help communicate information. Usually, people who are not familiar with a solution will better understand its design if they are first presented with core, high-level information. As illustrated in Table 3-1, many details are irrelevant when explaining what a system does or how it works. For communication purposes, less is more. Removing detail and providing a more concise description help facilitate understanding.

Textual descriptions are useful for providing detail, but graphical representations are often better tools for conveying structural information. Size, spatial relationship, shape, shading, and color can all be used to quickly and distinctly convey information diagrammatically. However, graphical representations often become overloaded when they contain too much information. Likewise, they can be confusing when they include information without a clear purpose or provide inconsistent information. The best way to present abstractions in graphical form is usually not obvious; it may take several iterations of refinement to develop a good representation.

Although it may seem somewhat counterintuitive, using a drawing software package to create architecture diagrams can do more harm than good. The availability of fancy graphics and clip art often leads to their overuse and misuse; instead, basic shapes can sometimes be best used to represent simple concepts. Pictorial and graphical representations may be used inappropriately by the diagram creator or misinterpreted by the diagram reader. Figure 3-1 shows an example of a bad architecture diagram. While this example is fictitious, it is not unlike many of those that are found both in industry and academia. The diagram highlights the following poor practices:

- too much information presented, for example, there are too many boxes (30) and lines;

- inconsistent level of detail, for example, some flow lines are labeled while others are not;

- graphics inconsistently used, for example, pictures are used for some representations and boxes are used for others, and different images are used for the same type of entity (CCA network versus TEF network);

- differences denoted by colors cannot be differentiated when printed in black and white;

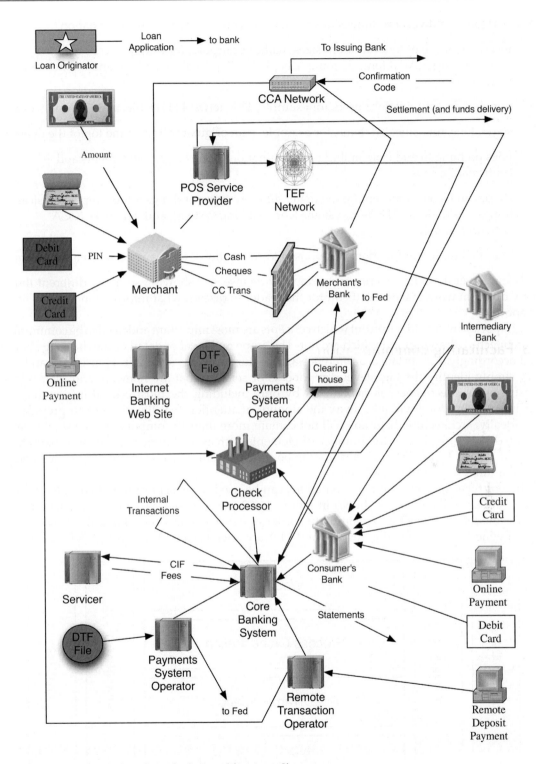

Figure 3-1 An overloaded and confusing architecture diagram

- horizontal and vertical dimensions not used to convey any specific information;

- inconsistent use of fonts and font sizes, without purpose, for example, core banking system in larger Arial font, customer's bank detail in small Arial font, and online payment in Times font;

- nonobvious abbreviations used, for example, TEF network, DTF file, and CCA network;

- standalone, unconnected items, for example, loan originator flow at the top of the diagram;

- lines pointing to and from ambiguous destinations, for example, statements and confirmation code;

- shapes and icons representing too many different types of things, for example, physical things (cash), data (DTF file), systems (core banking system), and networks (CCA network); and

- lines that represent functions as opposed to connections, for example, internal transactions.

While none of these issues are very serious by themselves, showing so many different things in so many different ways makes it difficult for the reader to discern what information is really relevant and important.

It is important to consider upfront which concepts are most important and need to be communicated in an architecture drawing, and which are not. The scope and level of detail of the drawing should be limited accordingly. For instance, a reference architecture view, as shown in Figure 3-2, can be used to very simply identify the high-level components or services that are relevant, and their relations. An abstraction's effectiveness is maximized by only including the most critical information. Each box or line that is added will take away the amount of attention that the viewer can provide to the others. Ideally, architecture diagrams will not contain more than 15 components in a single view. As highlighted by Figure 1-6, as the number of elements increases, the more difficult a diagram is to follow and absorb. If significant details need to be shown, multiple views should be created and used at different times with different audiences.

Different types of graphical representations can be used to present different considerations. For instance, sequence diagrams, as shown in Figure 11-12, can be used as a more succinct alternative to process model diagrams for explaining the order in which events occur. Logical functional views, several of which are shown in Figures 11-8 and 14-9, are often used to describe high-level connectivity

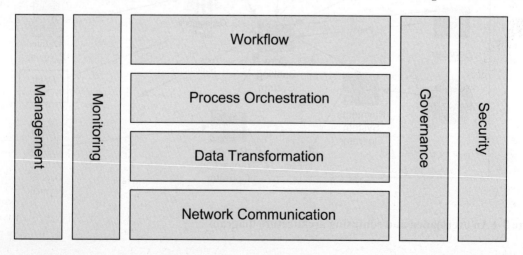

Figure 3-2 A reference architecture view

and interactions between components. Venn diagrams, as shown in Figure 17-2, can also be used to logically partition problems and help narrow down the areas of focus; that is, the area where the circles intersect.

3.1.4 Making Use of Multiple Views

Architecture considerations can be abstracted and communicated in different ways, providing multiple views of a solution. Figure 3-1 shows why multiple views should be used. The figure includes information about physical locations of hardware, network addresses, information flows, and subsystem functions; these make it cluttered and difficult to follow for someone who is not familiar with the immediate context. An alternative approach would be to design several different diagrams, each of which contains information about a single aspect. For instance, one diagram could show only information related to the hardware configuration and physical deployment, whereas another diagram could show the information types and flows.

When presenting a visual representation of architecture information, it is more important to ensure that the information is presented clearly and consistently rather than conforming closely to standards such as the unified modeling language (UML) or business process modeling notation (BPMN). Sometimes, closely adhering to standards can be counterproductive for communication purposes because they require additional detail to be included that is unnecessary for communication purposes and may be distracting to the viewer.

The audience and specifics of the solution play a major role in determining which views to present. In most cases, three views are primarily used to describe a solution:

- a business process model that shows the overall logic and behavior of the system
- a logical diagram that shows the main functional modules and information flows
- a physical diagram that shows the server and network hardware configuration

However, other types of diagrams may be constructed to provide supplemental information, or to more readily communicate certain types of information. For example, if a solution spans multiple locations, geographical diagrams could also be useful for describing the architecture.

Moreover, having a small number of well-constructed architecture diagrams greatly contributes to a solution's success as they will enable different people to quickly understand the solution's function and structure. Many projects struggle due to the absence of good architecture diagrams; poorly constructed diagrams and missing diagrams may cause confusion and lead to misunderstandings.

3.1.5 An Abstraction Example: A Three-tier Architecture

To help explain how abstractions are used in solution architecture, this section examines tiered architecture abstractions, specifically the channel-services architectural model that works well in conjunction with **service-oriented architecture (SOA)**. SOA aims to create functionally oriented abstract interfaces to applications using common interface standards. The channel-services model helps map application functions into specific types of service categories. This model helps logically separate the type of functionality that services provide. For example, it helps avoid embedding channel-specific logic, such as only allowing Internet banking transactions from 5:00 am to 11:00 pm, in business-specific components, like a credit card payment service. The channel-services model also helps business users and system implementers view systems in terms of the types of business services they can provide, rather than just as standalone business applications. In contrast to an SOA-based channel-services view of a system's capabilities, a monolithic standalone system view of a trade finance application is depicted in Figure 10-11.

3.1.5.1 Evolution of tiered architectures

To understand how tiered architectures are used, it is helpful to understand their evolution. To begin with, solution architectures were single tiered. Application-process instances managed all data in memory and persisted data using the local file system. As applications grew in number and had multiple users, it became necessary to centralize data storage. This led to two-tier architectures that comprised application and database layers. The proliferation of presentation technologies, for example, **thick client** and web browser user interfaces, drove the separation of business logic and application functions from data presentation functions. Hence, the three-tier model came into existence, separating data presentation, business logic, and data management. This model further evolved as applications were implemented over multiple delivery channels, including internal networks, the Internet, and mobile phones. This final evolutionary stage is referred to in this text as the "channel-services" architecture. The channel-services architecture is commonly found in financial services, and is presented in a business context in Figure 16-6.

Tiered architecture models are abstractions that can be applied to functional, physical, and component-level views. For example, physical hardware can be logically separated into groups of database, application, and web server hosts. Likewise, in the software-component context, tiered architectures are implemented as relational database management systems, application server and business logic containers, and web server containers. Not every solution will strictly follow the three-tier separation model; nonetheless, it is a useful tool for logically decomposing solutions. Note that Chapter 5 discusses the hardware and software components that underlie the channel-services architecture abstraction.

3.1.5.2 Channel-services architecture

The channel-services architecture is a three-tier architecture abstraction that is useful for showing how a single solution can be decomposed functionally and how different solutions share similar functions. As shown in Figure 3-3, the model consists of three layers: channel, business, and data services. The

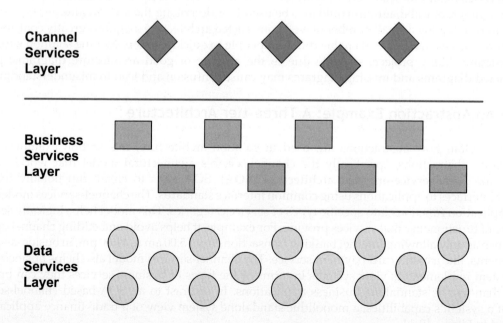

Figure 3-3 Channel-services architecture

diamonds, rectangles, and circles represent services provided in each layer. The white space between the shapes shown in the channel-services diagram, that is, the "glue" that connects all the systems and components, will usually be implemented using middleware technology. Sometimes, middleware will be shown as a separate layer. **Messaging middleware**, web services, **enterprise service bus (ESB)**, and process orchestration technologies are all commonly used to link components.

Channels provide connectivity to internal and external customers or partners. Automatic teller machines, internal thick client applications, web-based Internet applications, and phone services are all examples of delivery channels. Channel services provide common interfaces to each channel that can be reused by different systems and different lines of business, for example, retail and **commercial banking**. As part of the logical separation from the business and data layer, components that reside in the channel layer should not include any business logic (for example, fee calculation formulas) or assumptions about data representation or structures (for example, the "Z" code in field 37 of the CUST_DETAILS table means that the customer is over his or her credit limit).

Business services encapsulate specific business functions such as pricing or fee-calculation services, business-process workflow logic, and data aggregation and manipulation functions such as reporting. Business services will typically access information via the data layer, manipulate it, and then provide it to the channel layer. As part of the logical separation from the channel and data layer, components that reside in the business layer should not include logic related to channels (for example, only send alerts via short message service between 8:00 am and 9:00 pm) or assumptions about where and how data will be accessed (for example, connect to the database at network address 10.0.2.33 and do an SQL join operation on the CUST_DETAILS and the TRANS_DETAILS tables).

Data services provide logical abstractions that access various data stores such as databases and information gateways, and data stores contained within specific banking applications. Data services may provide access to a centralized **operational data store** or to individual databases that are scattered across the organization. In many cases, data services, which are defined at a logical level, will orchestrate data retrieval and aggregation from multiple databases or systems and present it through the service interface in a consolidated form. As part of the logical separation from the business and data layers, components that reside in the data layer should not implement any channel-specific logic (for example, that only account balances can be accessed via the mobile channel) or business logic (for example, workflow state transition logic).

The channel-services model is useful for understanding the scope and boundaries of the solution. It shows how their functionality and data potentially overlap and where gaps exist. This abstraction is useful for designing SOAs. It helps to identify how separate services should be defined, encapsulated, and reused in each of the layers. It is important to note that the services defined in each layer correspond to business concerns, not system concerns. One of the primary goals of abstraction is to hide system-specific interfaces and present them as more generic functions. For example, instead of having applications subscribe to foreign exchange prices using a vendor's application programming interface (API), data would be accessed through a generic rates service that resides in the data services layer. The rates service would hide the vendor's API, and may integrate price data from other vendors as well.

The channel-services model can also be used to map system boundaries. In some cases, a core system may occupy most of the diagram space, and only a few satellite systems may show up on the periphery. Alternatively, in other environments, more systems may provide a range of diverse services, sharing the space more equally. Figure 3-4 shows an example of how existing banking systems could potentially be mapped onto a channel-services model. In practice, the mapping would vary by financial institution and the particular systems that it uses.

The logical separation provided by channel-services architecture provides a useful model for how to construct services and decompose systems. However, in some cases, it will not be clear which layer specific solution functions should be fit into, and in other cases, there may be justifications for deviating from the model structure. For example, there may be situations where incorporating business calculation logic into channel frontends or into databases greatly improves performance or significantly simplifies the design. Hence, deviations may be warranted from time to time.

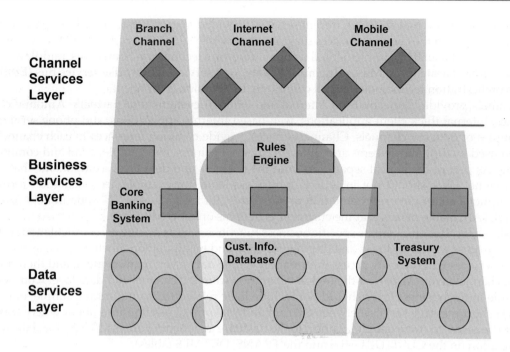

Figure 3-4 Mapping of banking systems onto a channel-services architecture

3.1.5.3 Other tiered architecture models

Besides the simple channel-services abstraction described above, there are other more elaborate ways to represent architectures. For instance, the Solution Architecture for N-Tier Applications (SANTA) model is one of many alternative architecture reference models [1]. The SANTA model is composed of six horizontal layers and six vertical pillars. The horizontal layers relate to:

- access and interaction
- business processes
- composite services
- services and components
- integration and communication
- enterprise resources

The six vertical pillars, on the other hand, relate to runtime infrastructure and development processes, specifically:

- operational management
- security
- hosting environment
- application and service frameworks

- cross-cutting aspects and patterns

- modeling and development tools

Whether it is appropriate to use a simple three-tier view or a more complex and detailed model will depend on the purpose and audience of the analysis. When communicating information to a team of trained architects, more complex models like SANTA provide a rich and precise framework for decomposing and describing solution design. When communicating design information to broader audiences, using a simpler and more straightforward three-tier model is usually the more practical approach.

Tiered architecture models can also be used to represent architecture concepts that are not related to software services. For instance, a three-tier abstraction composed of a compute layer, a network layer, and a storage layer can be used when a more hardware-oriented representation is required. Alternatively, a multilayer view could be used to explain the different functions performed by network communication protocols, such as the case with the seven-layer ISO OSI Reference Model [2].

3.2 ARCHITECTURE CONCEPTS

It is important that IT solutions developed fit into the financial institution's architecture roadmap and make use of common architecture principles, patterns, and standards. The following subsections explain each of these considerations.

3.2.1 Roadmap

An architecture roadmap describes the intended architecture end state and the plan to get there based on the current state of the architecture. Architectures are not created simultaneously—they are built up in stages. A roadmap defines those stages so that priorities can be set and the delivery scope can be limited. For example, an architecture roadmap defined to implement the reference architecture shown in Figure 3-2 may assume the following form:

Stage 1: Implement workflow layer and related governance processes

Stage 2: Add the network communications layer and monitoring

Stage 3: Add process orchestration and related governance processes

Stage 4: Add management and security facilities

Stage 5: …

Based on this roadmap, near-term solution delivery projects should be targeted to implement Stage 1 architecture components. Follow-on projects can then leverage those components, for example, workflow, and implement Stage 2 components, and so on. In this fictitious example, presumably the organization had a driving business need to implement workflow; roadmaps of other organizations might place the implementation of process orchestration or network connectivity first.

If no roadmap is in place, individual projects will likely implement technologies inconsistently, with limited capabilities, and without a clear objective. If the roadmap does not clearly show that workflow is a strategic architecture component for the organization, a near-term solution delivery project may choose a low-cost tactical workflow platform that cannot be easily leveraged by other projects in the future. Hence, later projects may need to use different workflow platforms to fulfill their needs, leading to duplicated workflow systems and increasing cost and complexity.

The concept of an architecture roadmap is further illustrated in Section 3.4.

3.2.2 Guiding Principles

Guiding principles are defined to help resolve ambiguity and simplify decision making. They also help provide consistency across the architecture's implementation. Some examples of architectural guiding principles are as follows:

- Data validation logic should be centralized and not distributed across components.

- Calculations should only be performed in the business layer, not the data or presentation layers.

- By default, all back-end components should be written in Java and run on Linux.

By making core decisions clear in advance, confusion and debate can be avoided in the future. While guiding principles that will cater to each and every possible consideration cannot be defined, a set of well-thought-out principles can address a wide range of concerns.

3.2.3 Patterns

Whereas principles provide guidelines to follow, architecture patterns provide common building blocks that can be reused to construct solutions. Revisiting the airport example, if an architect had to design a new airport terminal, it would be impractical to start from scratch. Rather, it would be beneficial to examine the existing designs of other airports to look for common structures that have already been proven to work. For instance, a common pattern in the design of modern international airport terminals is to have arrivals on one level and departures on another. While there are other ways of constructing terminals, such as using partitions on a single level to achieve separation, certain patterns have been proven as being the most effective and are, therefore, regularly reused.

An example of an architecture pattern relevant to financial services is the structure of adapters—the components that communicate data from one system to another. Simply, adapters can be viewed as a pattern of interconnecting pipeline components that perform different functions and are supported by modules that perform more generic functions. Figure 3-5 shows a common pattern structure for designing adapters.

Using a proven design, such as that in Figure 3-5, would help prevent mistakes like performing data validation before data normalization. Changing the order will prevent validation rules from being easily reused across different adapters. Similarly, combining data validation and data transformation functions could make maintenance more difficult.

Identification and definition of patterns have grown into a cottage industry, with many books and websites dedicated to this approach. Patterns are very useful; however, care must be taken not to become overly dependent or fixated on them. In many cases, generic patterns may not be suitable for the design of specialized components, for example, the ones that require very high performance. Likewise,

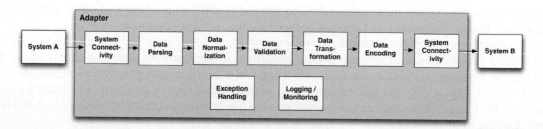

Figure 3-5 A common design pattern for adapters

referencing patterns in designs usually requires ever-present familiarity with the pattern nomenclature and their meanings. For example, talking about a design in terms of a façade pattern (that is, a layer that provides a simplified interface) will not be helpful unless everyone is clear about what that pattern represents.

The antithesis of using known good design patterns is to start from scratch. The folly of many inexperienced designers and architects is to think that they can come up with something better than the collective experience of hundreds or thousands of past projects. Alternatively, they may be lazy about researching what has been done previously, or not know where to look for the information. Beginning anew is appropriate in a few situations; however, it is generally more desirable to avoid discovering and repeating mistakes that already have been encountered before. Design is evolutionary; good designs will survive and be publicized, whereas bad designs will only persist if they are reintroduced due to technical ignorance.

3.2.4 Standards

Whereas architecture principles provide high-level guidelines and architecture patterns provide high-level reusable design abstractions, architecture standards specify the details of how solutions should be implemented. Architecture standards often cover considerations such as the versions of the software development platform used (for example, HTML5), the means by which database tables should be accessed (for example, via stored procedures), and how systems should communicate with one another (for example, SOAP over HTTP). Standardization helps minimize the complexity that arises from using disparate technologies and implementation techniques. Defined standards can help narrow employee skill requirements and make it easier for enterprise-wide support functions to be developed.

3.3 SOLUTION ARCHITECTURE CONSIDERATIONS

When architecting banking solutions, a number of nonfunctional requirements must be considered. These include resilience, scalability, performance, security, auditability, maintainability, geographic distribution, and cost. The specific solution and the business context will determine the level of attention received by each of these concerns. The following subsections summarize these concerns. Additionally, these topics will be revisited in later chapters and discussed in context of specific financial services business needs.

Case Study 3-2

The US$60 Million Instability Problem

In June 2007, the London Stock Exchange (LSE) launched a new version of its TradElect electronic trading system. With the goal of remaining at the cutting edge of technology, the exchange engaged a large consultancy and spent £40 million (approximately US$60 million) to upgrade its core trading system. The new solution platform used off-the-shelf server hardware and software architecture based on Microsoft Windows technologies. The upgrade was considered to be the chief executive officer's (CEO's) flagship project.

Five months after the system launch, the LSE had to extend its closing auction due to a system fault that stopped the distribution of live prices for 40 minutes. What is more, in September 2008, another system failure halted trading for seven hours, almost the entire trading day. The outage occurred on the day that

(Continued)

(Continued)

European shares saw the greatest gains in five months. Many traders were incensed that, due to the outage, they were unable to take advantage of the market's upswing. This problem also occurred as a number of new competitors, whose trading capabilities were not affected by the LSE outage, were rapidly gaining market share at the expense of the LSE.

At that time, technology accounted for 47% of LSE's total expenses, and the TradElect system upgrade contributed to a sizable portion of that cost. As part of the TradElect deal, over 100 employees from the consultancy that implemented the upgrade were transferred to become LSE headcount. Hence, when a new CEO took over in May 2009, cutting costs and replacing the TradElect system became a top priority. Rather than build a new system or purchase an existing system, the LSE decided to spend US$30 million to purchase a small Sri Lankan company, MillenniumIT, that built and deployed exchange systems for smaller exchanges, mostly in developing nations.

The MillenniumIT system was based on a Linux and UNIX-based software environment that ran on off-the-shelf server hardware. At that time, the company claimed to achieve transaction times of 0.13 milliseconds, faster than the 2.7 milliseconds taken by TradElect and 0.4 milliseconds for the LSE's fastest direct competitor. Moreover, besides gaining a new trading platform, the purchase also provided LSE with its own low-cost specialized offshore development center.

However, the acquisition of MillenniumIT was not a cure-all for the LSE. A two-hour outage occurred during the first stage of the migration, when the LSE migrated its Turquoise trading venue to the new platform. This glitch further weakened confidence in the LSE's ability to deploy resilient systems and delayed the migration of the LSE's main **market order** book to the new system by months.

Resilience is of paramount importance to exchanges. Whereas a system failure at a bank will usually only affect that bank's customers, system failures at exchanges affect the entire market and market participants around the world. Surely, a number of factors—human, technological, and organizational—contributed to the outages that the LSE faced. However, it can also be argued that the architectural decision to implement the TradElect system upgrade using a software platform that at the time was not commonly associated with mission critical systems was extremely bold, if not misguided. By choosing technology that had not already been proven for resilient trading systems, the LSE squandered its time, money, and credibility.

Sources: Jones, Sarah and Ambereen Choudhury, "LSE Breaks Down in Biggest Failure in Eight Years," *Bloomberg*, September 8, 2008, http:// www.bloomberg.com/apps/news?pid=newsarchive&sid=a9bRidj83NBQ; Grant, Jeremy, "Rolet Speeds In to Push Change at LSE," *Financial Times*, July 18, 2009, http://www.ft.com/cms/s/0/ab39993c-7301-11de-ad98-00144feabdc0.html; King, Leo, "London Stock Exchange to Replace TradElect," *CIO UK*, September 7, 2009, http://www.cio.co.uk/news/3201214/london-stock-exchange-to-replace-tradeelect; King, Leo, "London Stock Exchange Completes First Live Linux Test," *Computerworld*, October 13, 2010, http://www.computerworlduk.com/ news/it-business/3243905/london-stock-exchange-completes-first-live-linux-test; Grant, Jeremy, "Sabotage Fears As LSE Platform Crashes," *Financial Times*, November 2, 2010, http://www.ft.com/cms/s/0/939dc20c-e6b0-11df-99b3-00144feab49a.html.

3.3.1 Resilience

Resilience is a critical concern for banking solutions (Case Study 3-2). System failures can lead to both direct and indirect monetary losses. Direct losses can occur when a financial institution is unable to process its own transactions in a timely manner due to a system failure. Similar losses may occur when processing customer transactions—the bank may need to reimburse the customer for forgone profits or losses incurred due to processing delays. Regulatory penalties resulting from outages may also be imposed. Potential sources of indirect loss include reputational damage and loss of customer confidence. There is also a potential loss of business if customers choose to transact through competitors while the bank's system is down.

Resilience is usually measured by required total uptime, represented as a percentage value expressed in nines. For instance, four nines uptime (99.99%) equates to approximately 52 minutes of downtime per year. This requirement can be further qualified as to whether or not it includes planned downtime, that is, scheduled maintenance periods. Resilience is achieved at a system level using active-active or **active-passive configurations**. An **active-active configuration** shares the load continuously between two or more nodes. Alternatively, an active-passive configuration only has one active node. If the active node fails, another passive node will become active and take over processing. These two design patterns are commonly used to implement fault-tolerant hardware, software, and network configurations.

Besides system-level resilience, most financial institutions must cater for site-level disaster recovery (DR) as well. DR usually requires that operational capability be brought online at a separate physical location within a given time period (for example, 24 hours). Often, the hardware at **DR sites** will be regularly used for other purposes, such as testing, when not required for DR. In cases of primary site failure, development or test software processes or virtual machines will be shut down, and new production software instances will be started to replace the failed primary site's functions. It is also possible to have an active-active DR configuration where each production site can take over the load and act as the DR site for the other site(s).

Resilience can be achieved by a number of means; sometimes it may be accomplished entirely through hardware or software. Often, the optimal resilience configuration is achieved by taking advantage of both hardware and software fault-tolerance mechanisms. Cloud computing technologies also can enable new approaches for achieving resilience. For instance, in some cases DR environments may be implemented more cost effectively in cloud environments, where the full cost of their operation is only realized in the case of an actual DR event.

It is important to clearly define resilience requirements early on so that they can be fully incorporated into the solution architecture. Trying to implement resilience after solution construction has begun may require fundamental design changes and significant rework, leading to increased cost. Furthermore, end-to-end processing must be considered, including linkages to systems outside of the immediate solution scope. Weak links must be identified and compensated for across the entire processing chain.

Resilience considerations related to technology infrastructure are covered in Chapter 5 and with respect to payment systems is discussed in greater detail in Chapter 9.

3.3.2 Scalability

Scalability describes the ability to increase a solution's capacity to meet greater usage demands. The type of capacity that must be increased will depend on the particular solution and the business environment in which it is used. Scaling to support increased transaction volume is a common requirement; in some cases, transaction volumes may increase exponentially over time. Scaling to support a greater number of users, connections, and locations are also common scalability needs.

As shown in Figure 3-6, solution scaling can be achieved either "vertically" by increasing the size of the server, or "horizontally" by adding more servers. It is also possible to combine horizontal and **vertical scaling**. When faster processors are used for vertical scaling, no special design requirements are imposed on the software. If vertical scaling is achieved by adding more processing cores within the same server, the software will most likely need to be designed to support multithreading so that it can take advantage of the multiprocessor environment. Vertical scaling can be very expensive when there is a nonlinear increase in cost for hardware performance. There may also come a point where the current computing capability has been reached so adding more powerful hardware is not possible or practical economically. Hence, relying on vertical scaling can potentially lead to absolute capacity limitations.

Horizontal scaling requires that multiple instances of the software can be run in parallel across different machines in a networked environment. The processing is either dynamically load-balanced

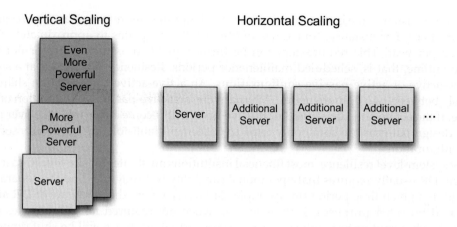

Figure 3-6 Scaling using vertical and horizontal approaches

or statically partitioned across the different instances. Grid and cloud computing are examples of how horizontal scaling can be used in the extreme. Generally, from a design perspective, horizontal scaling is the preferred approach as it provides better flexibility and is not dependent on the availability of a more powerful server. Scalability and horizontal scaling patterns are discussed in more detail in Chapter 11, in context of market data delivery, and in Chapter 12, in context of performance considerations.

As is the case with resilience, it is crucial that scalability requirements are evaluated and kept in mind from the beginning. Fundamental design limitations that may ultimately limit the capacity of the solution must be analyzed and carefully considered. Redesigning a single-threaded solution to become multithreaded can be costly; redesigning a single instance solution to support multiple instances that are distributed across the network will be even more costly. In the context of designing an airport, supporting increased air traffic may require building an additional landing strip. If this option is not planned for in advance, the land adjacent to the airport that is required for expansion may be difficult to obtain; this in fact, has been a problem for London's Heathrow airport, among others.

3.3.3 Performance

System performance is important for many different reasons. Often it is a matter of convenience for users and service levels for customers. Alternatively, certain transactions may require high performance because they are time sensitive. For example, foreign exchange transactions are based on real-time market prices that fluctuate continuously. Thus, delays in the delivery of price quotations could lead to trades that are initiated based on stale information, resulting in unprofitable transactions. Other types of banking services, such as payments, require consistent performance to ensure that processing can be completed before a predefined cutoff time.

Defining requirements for solution performance and measuring conformance to those requirements are not always straightforward. For instance, performance could be measured as the absolute maximum end-to-end processing time or average time, or make use of additional statistical measures such as the standard deviation of a sample. It is not uncommon for financial transaction volumes to occur in bursts, for example, at market opening, at lunchtime, and at the end of the month, so usually, performance under both peak and average volumes must be considered. At the requirements and design stage, it is necessary to agree with business users what needs to be measured and how it should be measured. Only when these metrics have been clearly defined is it possible to design the solution to meet those needs and verify that the solution provides the performance specified.

It is not uncommon for business users to avoid defining exact performance numbers, provide fuzzy numbers that are hard to quantify, or provide overly demanding requirements. This is often due to the fact that the business users themselves are unsure about what level of performance will actually be required. It is the architect's duty to work with business users to develop sensible performance requirements and to identify approaches for validating those requirements as soon as possible to allow for adjustments, if necessary. Alternatively, if poorly defined performance requirements are accepted, there is a substantial risk that the solution delivered will be inadequate. Having to rearchitect a system that fails to meet performance expectations when it is discovered late in the implementation cycle can lead to long delays and significant additional costs.

Performance considerations are discussed further in context of exchange trading systems in Chapter 14.

3.3.4 Security

For many financial services solutions, it is necessary to ensure that they are secure and have adequate risk controls. Security is relevant for systems where improprieties can cause direct or indirect monetary losses. Fraud is a major concern where monetary transactions are involved. Customer data privacy has also become a major security concern. Both internal and external security breaches must be prevented, with the damage done by internal bad actors often being the greater threat. The level of time and effort—in other words, cost—applied to prevent security breaches should be based on the severity of the loss that would be incurred and the likelihood of occurrence. Implementing security measures comes at a cost and must be fit within limited budgets. Hence, it is necessary to allocate security resources based on cost and benefit to ensure that the best practical level of security is achieved.

Major security considerations for financial institutions are authentication, authorization, confidentiality, nonrepudiation, and accountability. Authentication verifies identification of the people involved in business interactions. Nonrepudiation ensures that after completing a transaction, an involved party cannot deny its legitimacy. Privacy ensures that unauthorized parties cannot access sensitive information. Access control, that is, authorization, ensures that authenticated users can only access the data and services required as per their role. Detection ensures that any security or control breaches will be identified quickly.

The importance and impact of the complexity that is created by information security in solution architecture cannot be underestimated. The management and administration of security information is a complex problem within itself. Accordingly, most financial institutions have dedicated functions or groups that have the requisite skills to assess and manage security. This function defines security standards, verifies that solution designs comply with standards, and tests solutions to ensure that the final implementation is also conformant. In some cases, the security function is managed outside of the technology and operations divisions within financial institutions as part of the accounting or audit functions. Banks will also engage third parties to run security penetration tests to validate the robustness of solutions' security implementations.

It is important that solution architects consult with the security group in the early stages of design, and get their ratification of the architecture before beginning implementation. Otherwise, there is a risk that security issues that require redesign may be raised later, during user acceptance testing or just prior to production rollout, causing time delays and increased cost.

While weak security is an obvious concern, so is uncompromisingly strict security. Overbearing security measures can impair usability, impede operational processes, and sometimes be counterproductive. For instance, many financial institutions have security policies such that developers cannot access production systems. While this rule provides a number of security benefits, it makes debugging and fixing problems that occur in production environments or that involve production data much more difficult. Hence, business users, architects, and security managers must work together to find the most effective and practical way to implement security measures. CyberSecurity is covered in greater depth in Chapter 17.

3.3.5 Auditability

Auditability is related the security considerations of nonrepudiation and accountability; it ensures that a nonalterable record is kept to track important events or interactions after they have occurred. Usually, auditability is more of a business-level application concern rather than a technology-related concern. However, technology can be used to help support auditability requirements. Common approaches to ensure auditability include:

- marking data records as deleted or specifying in the record the date at which they are no longer valid, rather than deleting them entirely;

- recording data modifications as a reversal of the original record and creation of the new modified record, rather than changing the data fields directly;

- identifying a "**system of record**" that is designated as the master source for specific types of information; and

- reconciling data records between the system of record and other systems that share the same information to ensure intersystem consistency and integrity.

The need for auditability as part of control systems is also discussed in Chapter 17.

3.3.6 Adaptability and Maintainability

Once developed, solutions are dynamic and their architectures often have a limited lifetime. Solutions typically follow the lifecycle shown in Figure 3-7. Business and technological evolution necessitates change, and will eventually make most solution architectures obsolete over time as new product features are required, new channels are introduced, and the cost of technology changes (Case Study 3-3). For example, the introduction of the Internet and mobile phone channels has had a significant impact on banking solutions and the architectures used to implement them. Globalization has also brought about considerable changes to solution architecture. Keeping in mind adaptability and maintainability when designing solutions can significantly improve their longevity.

Adaptability and maintainability describe the ability of solutions to be changed and supported. The longer a solution is expected to operate, the more important these aspects become. The key goal is to ensure that the solution is flexible so that it can easily accommodate future change requests without requiring major rework. For instance, designing a solution so that it is open, modular, and portable will make it more adaptable than a closed design, which is often the case with monolithic applications. Likewise, incorporating flexible logging and monitoring facilities in a solution makes solutions easier to support and maintain. Exposing parameters as settings that can be configured at runtime rather than hardcoding them into the solution will also help provide flexibility.

Planning for change is essential. Changes should be expected during the use stage of the solution lifecycle, and sometimes may also occur during development. The architecture design should consider

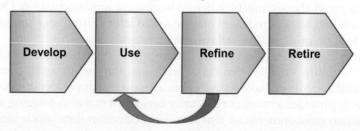

Figure 3-7 Solution lifecycle

lifecycle factors such as the planned longevity of the solution, the areas that are most likely to change, how redeployment will be managed, and whether the solution is ultimately likely to be replaced in its entirety or piecemeal. Ignoring these considerations is a shortsighted approach that can increase **technical debt** and often leads to greater levels of effort to be required in the future. That said, software solutions have limited timelines and budgets, so a compromise between short- and long-term goals must be achieved.

The architecture challenges related to managing the long lifecycles of core banking systems are discussed in Chapter 7.

Case Study 3-3

The Architecture of a Fixed-income Analytics Solution

Salomon Brothers developed the Yield Book fixed income (that is, bond) analytics solution in the late 1980s. The Yield Book application was originally named and modeled after physical books that were used to compute the prices of bonds. The solution was driven by the introduction and growth in popularity of more complex fixed-income securities such as collateralized mortgage obligations and asset-backed securities. Whereas earlier, simpler fixed-income products could be priced by manual computations, the only effective way to evaluate the performance and risk characteristics of these securities was to use sophisticated software that ran on high-end computer hardware.

In the beginning, the Yield Book solution was built using a distributed, client-server architecture. This was in contrast to many financial services applications of that time that were hosted on mainframes and accessed via dumb terminals. The solution provided analytical computation services directly to Salomon's customers, communicating from the bank's data center over leased phone lines to workstations at their customers' offices. Changes to the business requirements and rapid advances in technology led the solution architecture to evolve through three different forms.

The initial architecture made use of a local server deployed at the customer site to perform analytical computations and provide the user interface. Data needed to support the computations was transferred to each of the local servers on a nightly basis from Salomon's central servers. The architectural approach performed well initially, but ran into problems when new, more complex financial instruments were introduced—they put a heavy load on the local server's CPU and, thus, took significantly longer to compute.

The second-generation architecture addressed this problem by moving the CPU-intensive calculations off the customers' local servers and onto more powerful servers in Salomon's data center. This architectural change addressed the immediate performance issues, but still encountered scalability limitations related to the support of the local servers. As the number of customers using the solution increased, a substantially greater support effort was required to manage, maintain, and update the customers' local servers.

The third-generation architecture was significantly different in that there was no server deployed to end-customer sites. Instead, the database, analytical, and user interface components were housed at Salomon's data center, and only a remote display environment was installed on customers' workstations. Using a centralized approach simplified the management and maintenance of the solution, and enabled more efficient use of hardware resources by load-balancing calculations across a centralized pool of servers.

At the outset, it is difficult to envision how a solution will need to evolve. For financial services solutions, it is not uncommon to refactor the architecture on a periodic basis to take advantage of recent advances in hardware, software, networking, and channel technologies, or to address changing requirements. The challenge is to determine the best direction to take in the near term that will also support change in the future.

Source: Battifarano, Ernest, "Lessons from Developing the Yield Book," in *Creating Value in Financial Services: Strategies, Operations, and Technologies,*, eds. Edward L. Melnick, Praveen R. Nayyar, Michael L. Pinedo, and Sridhar Seshadri, pp. 219–252 (Massachusetts: Springer, 1999).

3.3.7 Geographic Distribution

Geographic distribution is an architectural concern for financial institutions that span multiple geographies. Deployment of solutions in different locations provides options as to where processing and data storage can be deployed. Also, when solution implementations span national boundaries, local regulations may affect how functionality is implemented and restrict where data can reside. Table 3-2 lists three common approaches for managing solution resources geographically.

In practice, there can be many subvariations for each approach. For example, a centralized solution implementation that supports multiple countries could be single-instance multi-tenant —where only only one copy of the software is run and it designed to handle multiple users— or multi-instance single-tenant —where the software is designed to cater to only one user and thus multiple copies of the software is run to support multiple users. For the single-instance multi-tenant implementation, the solution would be designed to concurrently support the different sets of rules and data required by different countries. A single instance would run and support all locations. For the multi-instance single-tenant case, the solution could be designed to support the business rules and data for just a single country. Separate instances of the solution would be run, and each instance would be configured to meet the requirements of the country it supports.

Centralization and distribution of processing operations in the context of trade finance are discussed further in Chapter 10.

3.3.8 Cost

Ideally, the sequence of activities for delivering solutions would be to define the requirements, design the architecture, and then determine the budget required. However, this is rarely the case. Usually, the budget is determined in advance, and the requirements and design have to fit it. Large budgets will provide for many implementation options, whereas small budgets will allow for few. Accordingly, when developing the solution architecture, the goal is to maximize the near- and long-term value that the solution will provide, given the limited resources available.

Balancing benefits with costs requires trade-offs. Determining which architectural trade-offs are best is especially complex because there are many different dimensions, for example, delivery time, effort, performance, resilience, security, flexibility, and cost, and their relationship may not be linear. For instance, consider the cost of increasing performance, measured as **throughput**. A 10% increase in throughput may be achievable by tuning existing components, a 20% increase

Table 3-2 Common approaches for managing solution resources geographically

Approach	Description	Benefits	Drawbacks
Centralized	Processing of data that is managed and maintained at a central location	Economies of scale High level of reuse Simplified management	Can become bottleneck Central authority may not be responsive to local needs
Federated	Some functions managed centrally while others delegated to regional or local implementation	Increased flexibility Common functions can be standardized and reused	More complicated to manage
Distributed	Localities have full autonomy	Greatest flexibility	Duplication of functions No standardization or reuse Difficult to manage

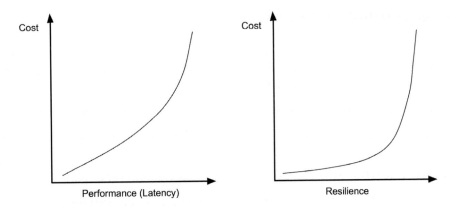

Figure 3-8 Examples of nonlinear cost relationships

may require replacing hardware components, and a 30% increase could require redesign and redevelopment. Whereas the increase in throughput in this example is linear (10%, 20%, 30%), the related increases in implementation time, effort, and cost will likely increase much more quickly, rising by 10%, 50%, and 100%, respectively.

Figure 3-8 shows a hypothetical example of two nonlinear relationships between the performance and cost and resilience and cost. Due to the relative shapes of the two curves, investing low to moderate amounts would produce more benefit in resilience than in performance. However, whether the investment should favor resilience over performance is further determined by the relative importance that the business requirements assign to each factor. Furthermore, there may be interdependencies between some factors. For example, solution performance is often inversely proportional to scalability— as volume or number of users increases, performance often decreases.

In practice, such trade-offs need to be assessed across many different factors. Using a consistent framework or method for analyzing trade-off decisions helps ensure consistency and substantiate why decisions were made. For example, a decision framework could try to quantify the benefits provided by different options in monetary terms so that the relative merits and costs can be more easily compared. This method can be combined with other methods, such as an explicit prioritization scheme; for example, agreeing that security is most important, followed by resilience, and then performance. Alternatively, explicit weightings could be used as guidelines; for example, no more than 8% of the budget should be spent on solution security.

In Chapter 13, cost will be discussed in greater detail as an architectural concern in relation to trading platforms used by fund managers and buy-side traders and where they source components for those systems.

3.4 ENTERPRISE ARCHITECTURE

Some architectural approaches, such as modular design, can be implemented exclusively at the solution level. Other architectural concerns, such as data management, integration, and SOA, are better managed across multiple solution deliveries. If they are addressed at the individual solution level, they end up being limited, tactical implementations. Alternatively, if these architectural concerns are addressed at the enterprise level, across multiple solutions, they can become strategic assets. All new solutions will become much easier to deliver if there is a reusable library of off-the-shelf business, data, channel, and integration services that they can leverage. This section will discuss the relevance of enterprise-level data and integration architecture, how they can support solution development, and how they can be developed over time through multiple solution implementations.

3.4.1 Reference Data Architecture

Much of the nontransactional data managed within financial institutions are shared between systems and are duplicated copies of the "master" data from a system of record. This data is commonly referred to as **static data** or **reference data**, and often includes:

- customer information (for example, names, addresses, account numbers, and relationships);

- securities information (for example, symbol name, instrument type, dividend structure, and maturity date);

- end-of-day prices (for example, used for portfolio revaluation and mark-to-market);

- limits (for example, counterparty credit limits and daily **settlement** limits); and

- holiday schedules for determining settlement dates (discussed further in Chapter 6).

The system of record is the designated source (sometimes referred to as the "golden" source) from which other downstream IT systems obtain validated and unadulterated reference data. For example, customer information may come directly from a core banking system in the form of a **customer information file (CIF)**. On the other hand, customer information may be aggregated from multiple different systems and maintained in a customer information system that provides access to information via service interfaces.

Many financial institutions have only rudimentary **enterprise data management (EDM)** technology implementations. Each solution implementation may be responsible for retrieving, importing, and merging end-of-day batch files that contain the current reference data images. This decentralized approach is inefficient and can be prone to errors. However, EDM has gained more attention in recent years. Providing centralized processes and technology that support master data cleansing, validation, distribution, and integration helps minimize the effort that solutions must undertake to access and contribute to master data.

3.4.2 Integration Architecture

Integration is vital for providing a **"single view of the customer,"** that is, having all relevant data readily available for use during interactions with customers, and for achieving **straight-through processing (STP)**. Few solutions are completely standalone, and most require integration with other systems. Generally, the greater the number of systems that must be integrated as part of technology solution implementation, the lower the probability is of successful delivery within the defined timeframe. When extensive system integration is required, it is almost assured that some variables, unknowns, and dependencies will surface to cause problems. For example, core banking systems have a large number of external interfaces; accordingly, core system replacement projects generally encounter significant cost and delivery risk related to integration.

System integration is usually not simple or straightforward. In some cases, the interfaces that the different systems provide will conform to open technical standards, and in other cases, they will not. Even when standard data formats are used, multiple different standards may need to be accommodated. Hence, the data mapping and translation between systems still present a formidable challenge. Furthermore, integration often requires external support. Owners of systems in other departments will need to provide, at a minimum, details on the available interfaces that can be used by the solution for integration and support for testing. Time or resources may not always be readily available from system owners to support system integration needs, creating critical dependencies.

Many of the challenges related to system integration can be partially addressed when financial institutions have an enterprise-level integration architecture in place. Figure 3-2 provides a view of the high-level components that can be combined to create an integration architecture. SOA and ESB technologies are readily available and can be used to help provide all solutions with basic network transport, data transformation, and process orchestration facilities. The analogy of an "information bus" is often used to refer to a technology platform that enables applications to easily share information with one another in a standard way, just as various types of cards inside computers share information via a hardware bus. Integration platform concepts are discussed in more depth in Chapter 2.

3.4.3 Solution-driven Enterprise Architecture

Getting started and gaining momentum are major challenges for creating enterprise-level architectures for both data management and integration. Architecting an SOA is relatively easy compared with the logistics of implementing it. Resources are rarely available to migrate existing systems and services to a new SOA platform, or even purchase the infrastructure required to support common services across the enterprise. Solution implementations, and their architectures, provide a means of building enterprise architectures piecemeal. While this is not the most expeditious way of implementing a new architecture, it is a practical one and requires significantly less direct funding and organizational change than a total strategic platform overhaul.

Figure 3-9 shows how an SOA can be built up over time. Common services can be introduced through prototypes and expanded in full solution deliveries. By delivering a series of solutions that leverage the same architecture, increased benefit from existing services can be achieved and the portfolio of services available can be continually expanded.

By understanding the enterprise's architecture objectives and coordinating with the enterprise architecture team (or possibly the chief information officer), the solution architect can ensure that the architectural approach produces the maximum results. Solution implementations can provide a vehicle for prototyping, piloting, testing, validating, and extending new technology platforms. The key to this strategy is to intertwine technology goals with business targets and link project-specific aims with enterprise-level objectives, rather than trying to address them independently.

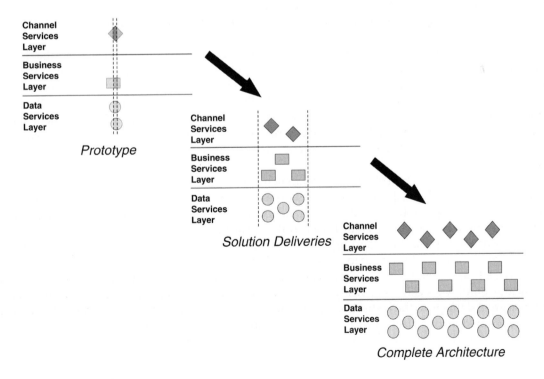

Figure 3-9 Using solutions to migrate to enterprise architecture

3.5 DATA MANAGEMENT

Besides the considerations related to reference data, as discussed in Section 3.4.1, there are many other data management considerations that must be addressed, and it is one of the most critical architecture challenges. Data management considerations need to be addressed at both the solution and enterprise levels. Specific data management considerations include logistical management, quality management, classification and control, segregation, and protection. This section will briefly examine these factors in the context of financial services solutions.

Logistical management ensures that data can easily get to where it needs to be used and can be combined with other data to produce the required information. Messaging middleware and/or other integration techniques may be used to extract and transfer information from their source to the required destinations, at the appropriate times. For example, it may require that over-the-counter (OTC) derivative trading information be fed from a number of different source systems at a certain time of the day to a system that aggregates the information and submits it for regulatory reporting purposes.

Data quality management ensures that the data is accurate, complete, and consistent. It starts with the data capture or input processes which may involve manual entry of information. Where manual entry is used, data values can be mistyped or the electronic input forms may be flawed. For example, an electronic form could accept a 12-character field value and insert it into an eight-character database field, truncating it in the process. Data can also be corrupted when it is shared between systems and converted from one format to another. The format transformation logic that is implemented may not account for certain data exception cases, and when they occur may lead to blank fields or faulty data. Furthermore, the same data provided by multiple different sources may be inconsistent, requiring reconciliation processes to determine which value is correct. Duplicate data records are another source of data quality problems. For example, two records in the same system may exist for a single customer, one under the customer's full name and the other under a nickname or alias. Stale data can also create data quality problems. If a linkage between systems becomes broken, updates may not occur as expected, leading to the downstream system having outdated information that, if used, could produce erroneous results.

Data classification underlies data access control and segregation. Determining the level of sensitivity of information (e.g., secret, confidential, public) and designating and identifying the information as such enable access to it to be restricted and tracked, as appropriate for the type of data. For example, personally identifiable information (PII) that includes passport number or, in the United States, social security number can be used to impersonate customers and support fraudulent **account takeover** attempts. Accordingly, this information needs to be identified and carefully managed to help avoid any unintentional leakage or data breaches, which can violate privacy laws and lead to major legal ramifications.

Segregation and protection of sensitive data, such as PII, within the physical and logical architecture support its protection. Sensitive data, especially databases holding large quantities of sensitive data, should be stored on specially restricted and managed servers and networks that have limited logical, physical, and network access. **Second-factor authentication** should be used to provide user access to applications, and applications and tight network firewall controls should be implemented to limit network access to servers. Entire databases or, at a minimum, the sensitive fields within them should be encrypted. Data access and removal should be tracked and audited. Without such protections, hackers or malicious employees can more easily walk away with vast amounts of sensitive information that can cause great damage to the institution and its customers. Some of the largest data breaches in recent years have been due to the lack of such controls and more specifically, allowing sensitive data stores to reside on the main corporate network.

3.6 INTERFACES

The availability and design of internal and external APIs largely determine the effort required to integrate systems and replace them over time. One architecture consideration is the communication technology used to provide the API. Common communication methods used to implement APIs include:

- REpresentational State Transfer (REST)

- Simple Object Access Protocol (SOAP)

- Executable application code—JAR files, static or shared libraries

- Database stored procedures with ODBC/JDBC connectivity

- XML messages sent via message queuing (MQ)

It is often the case that several of these protocols, if not all of them, will be used within a financial institution.

Besides the communication protocol that is used, equally, if not more important, is how the API structures the data that it provides access to, as well as the methods support to access that data. An analogy is to think of data as the nouns and the methods as the verbs. For example, a core banking system could provide a SOAP interface that provides a number of methods—e.g., *GetAccountDetails()*, *CreateAccount()*, etc.—for accessing account information and a standard structure for the data fields that describe the account record, e.g., AccountNumber, AccountBalance, etc.

One important consideration with API design is which methods to expose. In one sense, it would be ideal if all applications and data were exposed through APIs. This would provide the ultimate flexibility for designing and constructing other applications that make use of those APIs. However, more practically, there may be dangers exposing certain functions, such as administrative capabilities, because they could present security concerns or create risks that activities external to the application might negatively affect the integrity of the application. Likewise, the effort to design and implement APIs for all an application's functions is a major undertaking, and hence, is often not practical. Accordingly, often only a subset of an application's functions is exposed through APIs, creating the challenge of deciding which interfaces should be provided. If the wrong set of interfaces, or too few interfaces, are implemented, design limitations may be encountered that require extra work in the future for projects that use the APIs.

Another key consideration with API design is determining what level of granularity information should be provided. For example, a core banking system could expose API methods, such as GetAccountInfo(), that provide access to account information with a course level of granularity, possibly returning dozens of fields. Alternatively, it could provide API methods that have a fine level of granularity like GetAccountBalance(), which only returns one field. Course granularity is useful when many data fields are required, but may lead to slow performance when only one field is necessary, since all the data field information provided by the API must be transferred over the network and parsed by both the sender and the receiver. On the other hand, fine granularity is convenient for accessing individual fields, but becomes burdensome for accessing larger sets of data. In this case, multiple API calls would be required, which also can lead to slow performance and excessive communication overhead. Providing both APIs that provide both course and fine granularity might seem the best approach, except that it may significantly increase the amount of implementation and maintenance work required.

Beyond API design considerations, financial institutions also must consider how to work with APIs that are presented by third-party applications. One approach is to not give them any special consideration and use them as-is. When a third-party API uses an uncommon interface protocol, this can create significant work for each integration project that needs to make use of the API. Another approach is to build API wrappers that sit on top of third-party APIs to provide access through commonly used communication protocols and possibly to present the data in a more standard format. The wrapper API is used for integration and serves as a buffer to the underlying third-party API. In theory, this approach also helps minimize the changes required if the underlying third-party system is replaced with a new one. Only the wrapper layer internals would require re-implementation. The wrapper's exposed interface would not change, so other systems connecting to it would not be affected by the change. In practice, however, it is usually not that simple, since the characteristics of the wrapper API are often derived from the characteristics of the underlying system. Furthermore, building and maintaining wrapper APIs require a nontrivial amount of effort.

Recently, banks and other financial institutions' focus for APIs has shifted more toward providing public APIs that can be used externally. Opportunities related to providing payment capabilities to third-party websites and mobile applications have helped to drive this trend. But more generally, providing public APIs also enables innovation by allowing other companies to build upon the online services that banks provide. This topic is explored further in Chapter 20.

Case Study 3-4

HSBC Reduces Costs by Simplifying and Streamlining IT Architecture

One of the cornerstones of HSBC's 2015 cost reduction initiative, which was discussed in Case Study 1-1, was to simplify and streamline its IT architecture. A large part of this effort was focused on simplifying its software application architecture. The bank targeted to eliminate approximately 11% of its applications, which numbered around 6,700 in total. Two IT system rationalization projects that HSBC had planned were to consolidate its 41 consumer Internet banking applications to just 14 and eliminate eight of its 11 business Internet banking applications.

The bank also sought to reduce costs by improving its data management. One focus area was to invest in and leverage global standards for data. Another was to improve customer data so that it could be more easily managed digitally and leveraged to help automate business processes. Often legacy business processes maintain information on paper forms, requiring manual processing and leading to higher costs. Likewise, legacy IT systems that have poor integration capabilities can lock up data within them, limiting its usefulness. These problems do not usually solve themselves, and thus, concerted effort is required to improve data access and management.

Another area HSBC was aiming to simplify was to reduce the number of independent data warehouses that were managed and maintained within different countries' operations. Ideally, banks would have a single data warehouse for the entire organization, but often this is impractical for very large organizations because of the scale of their data and also the need to collect and synchronize the information across multiple time zones. On the other hand, it is not uncommon for decentralized IT management to lead to different countries or business units building local data warehouses that serve their own immediate purposes, but which results in excessive costs for redundant hardware, software licenses, management, and administration.

Source: HSBC, "HSBC—Actions to Capture Value from Our Global Presence in a Changed World: Investor Update 2015," June 9, 2015, http://www.hsbc.com/~/media/HSBC-com/InvestorRelationsAssets/investor-update-2015/group.

3.7   ARCHITECTURAL CONSIDERATIONS RELATED TO USING CLOUD SERVICES

When architecting a solution, it is important to consider which aspects are suitable for cloud computing. Factors that largely affect cloud suitability include:

- enterprise cloud computing strategy;

- purpose and users of the solution;

- dependencies on other internal systems;

- off-the-shelf resources and capabilities that can be leveraged either internally or from a cloud environment; and

- type of information stored in the cloud, i.e., account and/or personally identifiable information.

These factors will vary significantly depending on the type and the size of the institution and the specific solution. For example, a standalone application that is designed to be used by consumers and is developed by a Fintech startup whose strategy is to leverage open source technology would be well suited for cloud implementation. On the other hand, a solution developed by a medium-sized bank for its internal users that has extensive integration with in-house systems and requires several commercially licensed components would be less suitable for deploying in a cloud environment.

For Fintech companies, making use of cloud-based resources is a logical starting point because it helps avoid the expenditure of upfront capital, which is often very limited, on hardware and software licenses. Likewise, using cloud services makes it easier to take advantage of the declining cost of technology over time and leveraging the economies of scale that cloud service providers can achieve. The availability of readily available, off-the-shelf components and services within the cloud environment–such as databases, development platforms, and network firewalls–can reduce time to market so that new business opportunities can be taken advantage of more quickly. The vast menu of services offered by cloud service providers enables customized environments to be rapidly created and easily changed in the future. Infrastructure capacity can be adjusted both up and down to optimize cost and fulfill variable demand levels over time.

Established financial institutions face more hurdles to overcome when implementing technology solutions in cloud environments. Arduous procurement and vendor management processes may need to be completed, and review and approval of the vendor's information security may be required. Where internal standards dictate that solutions are built using commercial infrastructure components, such as vendor-supplied databases and web servers, additional licenses may need to be purchased to support a cloud implementation. However, while cloud services may be impractical for production deployment of some technology solutions, it may be suitable to provide an environment for their development and testing, so that the cost of these environments is incurred only when they are in use. Additionally, new and relatively standalone technology solutions can provide the opportunity for banks to experiment with cloud services. The lessons learned from these pioneering efforts can benefit future projects and potentially lead the way for migrating systems that are hosted on premise to cloud platforms.

Migration of existing applications to cloud environments may only make business sense in certain situations. For example, modern, web-based applications are more practical to migrate, whereas applications that run on mainframe or minicomputers would involve substantially greater effort. Immediate drivers can help lead the way for cloud migration. For example, if the capacity limits of an on-premise data center are being reached, migrating some applications to a cloud environment could provide additional headroom to the data center. Likewise, migration to cloud services may make sense when planning technology "refreshes", where outdated hardware would normally be scrapped and replaced by newer systems.

While cybersecurity, resilience, and regulatory concerns are major factors when considering the use of cloud services, these concerns are not completely new to outsourcing. Cloud services can be viewed as part of the spectrum of outsourcing that also includes the use of third-party data centers and software as a service (SaSS) application platforms, both of which are common within financial services. Likewise, as cloud service providers have turned their focus more towards financial services, their capabilities in these areas have evolved to better address these concerns. Ironically, in some cases, the cybersecurity and resilience capabilities of cloud service providers may exceed those of some financial institutions. In particular, small- and medium-sized banks, which have relatively small IT budgets, may be better off using cloud-based services rather than hosting systems in their own local data centers.

Integration is another important architecture consideration. For instance, consider a cloud-based application that is "chatty", i.e., has frequent communication interactions, with other on-premise applications. To function effectively, this type of application may require increased communication bandwidth from on-premise data centers to the cloud environment. The application performance may also suffer because of the latency in communication between the two sites which is amplified by the need for many back-and-forth interactions to complete a single transaction. Furthermore, larger organizations may make use of multiple cloud service providers, leading to increased complexity. For instance, different cloud service vendors may use different and incompatible standards. System resilience and failover recovery behavior can also become more complicated when interdependent components are spread across multiple cloud and on-premise environments.

Moreover, having an enterprise-level cloud strategy is important for providing guidance for how cloud services can and should be applied within various solution contexts. Such a strategy should outline the criteria and potential use cases for using cloud services, the process for sourcing cloud services, and preferred vendors. Without such guidelines, individual projects and departments may lack a mandate to move forward with cloud services or, alternatively, may move forward with services that are not in line with the company's overall objectives. There is also the potential to end up with a hodgepodge of cloud capabilities that arise as different solutions independently choose different cloud services to meet their immediate needs. This can lead to a proliferation of cloud vendor relationships, redundant or overlapping services, and added complexity that increases ongoing support and maintenance costs.

3.8   THE SOLUTION ARCHITECT'S ROLE AND RESPONSIBILITIES

The role of the solution architect is multifaceted. In some cases, the role of the architect overlaps with those of the project manager and the business solution manager. Together they are the team responsible for the solution's delivery. In other cases, their goals may conflict. For example, adequate architecture planning and execution may require more time than the project plan and budget have allocated. In this case, the architect will have to work with the other managers to make them understand the importance of architecture planning so that they will increase the resources allocated for this purpose. In some cases, it may be unwise to implement a solution if sufficient effort cannot be spent planning and overseeing the architecture. The long-term costs and risks introduced by delivering a poorly architected solution can outweigh the benefits that the solution generates. Likewise, allowing individual solutions to implement their own disparate architectures can, over time, lead to high support and maintenance costs at the enterprise level (Case Study 3-4).

As illustrated in Figure 3-10, solution architecture should be driven by business and IT strategy. This implies that the architect should have a clear understanding of the institution's business objectives and the solution's motivation. Solution requirements are not always clear and explicit. Accordingly, the solution architect must help elucidate and analyze both business and technical requirements, focusing principally on the nonfunctional requirements discussed in Section 3.3. The solution architect must also work with stakeholders to understand their objectives and develop concrete architecture requirements from them.

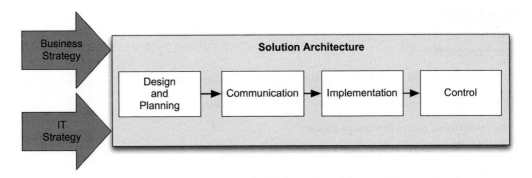

Figure 3-10 Drivers and functions of solution architecture

Besides translating business and IT strategy concerns into architecture requirements, the following are some of the important aspects of the solution architect's role:

- **Design and Planning**. The solution architect has the primary responsibility for defining technical-scope boundaries, identifying and selecting technical alternatives, and managing trade-offs. The solution architect must also ensure that the solution architecture is aligned with broader enterprise architecture objectives. Framework and component reuse are paramount.

- **Communication**. The value of a good plan or design can be greatly diminished if it is not clearly understood. Hence, the solution architect must champion key architecture principles and potential technology risks to key stakeholders. Communicating the rationale behind key design choices also helps to build support for the architecture.

- **Implementation**. Even with good communication, there is no guarantee that solution architecture will be implemented as planned. Therefore, the solution architect must review the solution implementation as it progresses to ensure that it matches the target solution architecture as closely as possible.

- **Control**. The solution architect must identify key architectural risks and develop strategies to mitigate them. Over time, risks must be monitored and managed if they reach significant levels. Solution architecture must also be controlled over the extended lifetime of a solution. Refinements and adaptations of a solution should track the target architecture. Likewise, the solution architecture may need to be revised over time to accommodate new requirements and technology advances, as discussed in Case Study 3-3.

Across these various stages of delivery, the solution architect should assess the effectiveness of the design decisions that were made. The objective should be to draw out lessons learned and incorporate them into the organization's knowledge base of architectural design patterns and best practices so that they can be applied to future solutions.

It is important that the solution architect has the requisite background and experience for the job, and has sufficient time dedicated to the project. Many a project has suffered from having a part-time architect who has too many other commitments and does not spend enough time developing, documenting, and communicating the architecture design. Problems can also occur when architects with very narrow experience are used in place of more broadly focused solution architects. Likewise, architects who are oriented toward one particular software platform, such as Java or Microsoft .NET, may see the software platform as the architecture, rather than just being one type of implementation. Good solution architects avoid technology biases, knowing that today's hot technology will be tomorrow's legacy platform.

3.9   SUMMARY

This chapter covered:

- how abstraction is used to communicate solution architecture;

- how different views can be used to describe a solution;

- the benefits of using design patterns;

- major architectural concerns for banking solutions;

- how enterprise architecture fits together with solution architecture,

- the importance of data management and system interfaces to solution architecture;

- architectural considerations related to using cloud services; and

- the role and responsibilities of a solution architect.

This chapter focused on the high-level considerations related to IT solution architecture in the context of financial services. The next chapter will cover the IT solution requirement analysis techniques and delivery processes.

FURTHER READING

Books

Brooks, F. P., *The Mythical Man-month: Essays on Software Engineering* (New Jersey: Addison-Wesley Professional, 2005).

Clements, P., R. Kazman, and M. Klein, *Evaluating Software Architectures: Methods and Case Studies* (New Jersey: Addison-Wesley Professional, 2001).

Fowler M., K. Beck, J. Brant, and W. Opdyke, *Refactoring: Improving the Design of Existing Code* (New Jersey: Addison-Wesley Professional, 1999).

Gamma, E., R. Helm, R. Johnson, and J. M. Vlissides, *Design Patterns: Elements of Reusable Object-oriented Software* (New Jersey: Addison-Wesley Professional, 1994).

Hohpe, G. and B. Woolf, *Enterprise Integration Patterns: Designing, Building, and Deploying Messaging Solutions* (New Jersey: Addison-Wesley Professional, 2003).

Lim, E., Taksande, N., Seaman, C., "A Balancing Act: What Software Practitioners Have to Say about Technical Debt," *IEEE Software* (November/December 2012): 22–27.

Krafzig, D., K. Banke, and D. Slama, *Enterprise SOA: Service-oriented Architecture Best Practices* (New Jersey: Prentice Hall, 2004).

Rozanski, N. and E. Woods, *Software Systems Architecture: Working with Stakeholders Using Viewpoints and Perspectives* (New Jersey: Addison-Wesley Professional, 2005).

Papers

Armbrust M., A. Fox, R. Griffith, A. D. Joseph, R. Katz, A. Konwinski, G. Lee, D. Patterson, A. Rabkin, I. Stoica, and M. Zaharia, "A View of Cloud Computing," *Communications of the ACM* 53 (2010): 50–58.

Booch G., "Draw Me a Picture," *IEEE Software* (January/February 2011): 6–7.

Duran, R. E., "Case Study: Enterprise Integration and Process Improvement," in *Enterprise Architecture and Integration: Methods, Implementation and Technologies*, eds. Wing Lam and V. Shankararaman, pp. 240–254 (Pennsylvania: IGI Global, 2007).

Emmerich, W., E. Ellmer, and H. Fieglein, "TIGRA—An Architectural Style for Enterprise Application," *Proceedings of the 23rd International Conference on Software Engineering*, 2001.

Hammond, J. S., R. L. Keeney, and H. Raiffa, "Even Swaps: A Rational Method for Making Trade-offs," *Harvard Business Review* (March 1998): 137–149.

Natis, Y. V. and M. Pezzini, "Twelve Common SOA Mistakes and How to Avoid Them," *Gartner Research Report G00152446*, 2007.

Paoli, H., C. Holtmann, S. Stathel, O. Zeitnitz, and M. Jakobi, "SOA in the Financial Industry—Technology Impact in Companies' Practice," in *Handbook on Information Technology in Finance*, eds. D. Seese, C. Weinhardt, and F. Schlottmann, pp. 9–28 (Berlin: Springer, 2008).

Rivera, Roberto, "Am I Doing Architecture or Design Work?" *IT Professional* (November/December 2007): 46–48.

Periodicals

Both of these journals cover current software architecture issues, providing practice summaries and case studies. They are written more for professionals than for academics.

- *IEEE IT Professional*
- *Communications of the ACM*

Web

"Banking Industry Architecture Network," http://www.bian.org.

"Wikipedia Overview on Design Patterns," http://en.wikipedia.org/wiki/Design_pattern_(computer_science).

ENDNOTES

1. Shan, T. C. and W. W. Hua, "Solution Architecture for N-Tier Applications," *IEEE International Conference on Services Computing* 2006 (SCC '06): 349–356.

2. Zimmermann, H., "OSI Reference Model—The ISO Model of Architecture for Open Systems Interconnection," *IEEE Transactions on Communications* 28 (1980): 425–432.

— — —

3. Enfield, R., "Reviewing Your Organization's Approach to Data Management," *Journal of Securities Operations & Custody* 3, issue 2.

4 Technology Solution Delivery

Chapter Overview

4.1 DEFINING FINANCIAL SERVICE INFORMATION TECHNOLOGY SOLUTIONS

4.2 FULFILLING BUSINESS OBJECTIVES

4.3 SOLUTION DELIVERY STRATEGIES

4.4 SOLUTION DELIVERY PROCESSES

4.5 DELIVERY PROCESS EXECUTION

4.6 SUMMARY

FURTHER READING

ENDNOTES

There are varied opinions on the usefulness of technology and how it is best applied. In 2003, a contentious paper in the Harvard Business Review (HBR) titled "IT Doesn't Matter" [1] argued that when information technology (IT) becomes more widely available and commoditized, as is the case now, its strategic importance decreases. Some research [2] supports this view, particularly in the financial services industry, by showing that in the United States and Europe, increased IT spending has not shown a positive correlation to profitability. However, it is important to note that the HBR article also suggests that the commoditization effect is less relevant to firms that utilize specialized IT solutions since they are less prone to replication.

A more recent view, also from HBR, is that IT affords a competitive edge [3] in winner-take-all industries where high IT spending is the norm. This research holds that new technologies enable improvements in the operating models of firms. Also, it suggests that widespread dissemination of successful operating models and innovations throughout the organization can yield a strategic advantage. It concludes that these advantages can be achieved by embedding business processes in IT systems and using IT as the means of service distribution.

It is in the context of these views that the overall importance of technology to the financial services industry should be considered. On the one hand, it can be argued that a significant portion of the business of financial institutions, for example, loans, deposits, and **remittances**, has been commoditized. On the other hand, specialized applications can provide banks with a competitive advantage in markets, in areas such as mobile banking, complex derivatives, and risk management. Furthermore, given its historical development, financial services could be viewed as a winner-takes-all industry; in many cases, larger and more aggressive firms have grown, whereas less competitive firms have often been forced to merge or be acquired.

Over the past decade, competition from companies in other industries and Fintech upstarts have raised the ante for how traditional financial institutions approach the delivery of technology solutions. Google and Uber have shown how firms that leverage technology most effectively can dominate entire industries and marginalize established companies in those markets. Likewise, Amazon is able to roll out changes to their production software environment several times a minute, every day, using continuous delivery techniques. Accordingly, banks have had to rethink the approaches they use and the frequency with which new services are delivered to customers.

Rather than considering the value of IT to the entire financial services industry, it is more meaningful to consider it in a narrower context. The importance of technology to individual institutions will largely depend on the markets in which they compete and from where they derive their competitive advantage. Ultimately, these factors will be the drivers determining which solutions a bank implements and how the solutions are delivered. The Yield Book platform that Salomon Brothers initially created in the 1980s, discussed in Case Study 3-3, is an example of how investing in a technology solution provided the investment bank with a competitive advantage in the fixed income trading markets. This solution evolved and continued to serve customers over several decades. Ultimately, Yield Book was sold to the London Stock Exchange, along with fixed income indexes, in 2017 for $675 million [4].

This chapter will examine what constitutes an IT solution in that context and in terms of what is important from the perspective of sales and management, also referred to as the "Business." First, the objectives of IT solutions for financial services are reviewed along with the strategies for delivering the solutions (Case Study 4-1). Then, these concepts are presented in the context of a broader framework that describes the process of how solutions are typically delivered. Going forward, for brevity, the term "IT solution" will be used to refer to technology solutions used by financial services firms, including banks, brokers, and institutional customers.

Case Study 4-1

Banks Embrace Agile Software Development

For decades the "waterfall" software development model has dominated financial services. This traditional approach of plan-driven project management begins with a lengthy process of gathering and documenting requirements for a new software solution. Typically, software development work will not begin in earnest until documentation of requirements is completed and has been signed off by key stakeholders. With this model, business analysts are a buffer between the business users and the software developers, and the requirements documentation serves as the means of communication between the two groups. After the requirements analysis effort is complete, a sequential process of software design, development, testing, and deployment ensues. When the waterfall delivery approach is used, often business users will not see any part of a solution working until close to the end of the project. As a result, flaws in requirements, wrong assumptions, and misunderstandings are only identified late in the project cycle, leading to significant rework and major delays in delivery.

In the early 2000s, the "agile" software delivery model was established to provide an alternative to the waterfall model, and address many of the problems that the waterfall model presented. A key principle that underpins the agile methodology is to minimize the lag between project inception and software delivery. Short development cycles, referred to as sprints, are typically a month or less in duration and are used to deliver partial functionality. These intermediate releases can be evaluated, learned from, built upon, and improved. Also, agile relies upon collaboration between software developers and customers. Communication through informal conversations and dialogs is preferred over using formal written documentation. These qualities help projects progress more quickly and better adapt and cope with changes, often in the business requirement or related to technology. Unlike the waterfall methodology, project stakeholders and end-users are involved throughout the project and can see progress sooner. By providing feedback early in the development process, they are able to help ensure that what they receive at the end of the project meets their needs. In recent years, banks have increased their use of agile methods and realized significant gains as a result.

In South Africa, Standard Bank adopted agile as a response to counter competition from banks that had a strong digital presence. Standard Bank's goal was to speed up software delivery cycles while reducing cost and improving performance. Key changes that were made in applying agile, was to shift to short delivery cycles, use an iterative learning approach, and take advantage of increased team collaboration and colocation. Instead of spending a large proportion of project time producing volumes of requirements documentation that had to be read and interpreted by software developers and testers, Standard Bank assembled a multidisciplinary team that worked together to define a smaller set of requirements. The effort saved on managing documentation was instead focused on implementing new features and incorporating customer feedback to improve subsequent releases. By using agile, Standard Bank realized cost reductions of up to 70% and productivity increases of up to 50%.

In the United States, Capital One has been a big adopter of agile, with 85% of its software development projects using that delivery approach. Using agile, the bank was able to shorten software project delivery time from six months to three and significantly reduce costs. Likewise, it deploys around 400 product releases a month with 95% of those meeting business expectations. Greater involvement of business users in software development projects has been a key factor in the success of agile at Capital One. Also in the United States, BBA Compass uses agile for about 50% of its software development projects, including its mobile payment application. JP Morgan Chase has been using agile to re-implement its website and chose to break down the effort into three-week sprints so that improvements could be demonstrated and reviewed quickly and on an ongoing basis.

For all its benefits, there are a number of challenges that banks can encounter when introducing agile. One common challenge is getting the people who begin working in an agile team to change their mindsets. When using the agile methodology, peoples' roles and activities are not as clear-cut as they are with other development methodologies. The agile working environment is more fluid and less predictable. While some people may find this kind of working environment exciting, others may be less comfortable and may struggle with uncertain timelines and rapid changes to the scope of work. In particular, using an agile approach makes it difficult to come up with definitive schedules for completion and effort estimates for overall budgeting purposes. Furthermore, agile does not mesh well with a top-down, hierarchical management structure because agile depends on team members to regularly make key decisions that affect the delivery process. These hurdles can be overcome, but may cause setbacks. For example, Standard Bank had to put a stop to one of its first agile pilot projects because of lack of management support in certain business areas.

Banks and other financial institutions will likely continue further adoption of agile techniques and find ways to integrate them into their product development strategies. Many Fintech competitors have been taking advantage of the speedier time-to-market, rapid adaptation, and productivity benefits that agile provides. Banks that fail to gain these same strengths by using agile will find themselves disadvantaged in a quickly moving and highly competitive marketplace.

Source: Pollack, Lisa, "How Project Management Turned into a Scrum," *Financial Times*, August 12, 2015, http://www.ft.com/cms/s/0/144bda3a-39ac-11e5-bbd1-b37bc06f590c.html; Crosman, Penny, "Agile Development Is Reshaping Tech at Banks Like Chase and BBVA," April 5, 2016, American Banker, http://www.americanbanker.com/news/bank-technology/agile-development-is-reshaping-tech-at-banks-like-chase-and-bbva-1080281-1.html; Blumberg, Sven and Stüer, Christian, "Becoming a Digital Bank," McKinsey, April 2016, http://www.mckinsey.com/business-functions/business-technology/our-insights/becoming-a-digital-bank; MacSweeney, Greg, "Capital One Delivers 85% of Software through Agile," *Bank Systems & Technology*, March 31, 2014.

Questions

1. What types of banking applications would be best suited for agile development? Which applications would find it more difficult to make use of agile?
2. What are some benefits provided by having short development cycles, i.e., sprints?
3. How might shifting to agile affect the different stakeholders, as identified in Chapter 1?
4. Compared with the waterfall model, how can using agile better support innovation?

4.1 DEFINING FINANCIAL SERVICE INFORMATION TECHNOLOGY SOLUTIONS

By definition, a solution involves the resolution of a problem or difficult situation. In the context of financial services, IT solutions aim to address business and operational problems, and to improve efficiencies or enable new business opportunities. The upshot of this fairly broad definition is that any number of things can be considered to be an IT solution. For example, a simple spreadsheet that calculates loan interest payments could potentially be an IT solution. Since the imperative challenge for banks is to be able to deliver large-scale solutions, this book will focus on solutions that require many personnel and long timeframes to implement.

Besides defining the boundaries of what a solution is, it is also important to consider the different forms assumed by IT solutions. Solutions may be reengineered implementations of existing processes. They can also initiate entirely new business processes as may be required to support a new financial product or service. On the other hand, IT solutions may not correspond to specific products or services; instead, they may relate to ancillary functions such as risk management, accounting procedures, or service-delivery channels. For example, data warehousing and business intelligence solutions are often not related to any one financial product or service.

IT is generally viewed as a force for positive change, serving as a principal tool for improving process efficiency; however, there are negative aspects of IT as well. For example, badly managed IT can become an inhibiting force that ends up reducing efficiency. There is also the danger that technology can become the focus, rather than the means, of delivering business value. Also, it is quite easy to implement technology that delivers little or no value to the business. In degenerative cases, technology ends up dictating how the bank's business processes are defined and executed.

Whereas solutions are sometimes driven by a systems-oriented technology-focused viewpoint, this book considers solutions from a process-oriented business perspective. Solution designers should focus on understanding the underlying business processes and ensuring that the IT systems used to construct technology solutions are subordinate to the needs of those processes. From a practical standpoint, this may not always be possible, but it should nonetheless be the goal.

4.2 FULFILLING BUSINESS OBJECTIVES

Fundamentally, solutions represent an implementation of a bank's corporate strategy. While defining a clear and well-directed strategy is important to overall business success, doing so becomes inconsequential if the strategy cannot be executed effectively. Unfortunately, sometimes when solutions are developed, the strategic considerations are quickly forgotten and the focus is placed primarily on tactical considerations. Hence, it is necessary to design the solution delivery plan such that both strategy and tactics are adequately addressed as part of the solution-delivery effort.

Effective strategy implementation depends on management, and is a top-down effort. If the bank's senior management does not effectively define and communicate its key goals and objectives, it is unlikely that solution-delivery efforts will be able to address them. Furthermore, strategic concerns must be mapped to initiatives and then integrated into the solutions' requirements and design. The following subsections discuss how business strategy can be integrated into IT solutions viewed from different levels of detail.

4.2.1 The 30,000-foot View: Why and What

From an airplane flying at 30,000 feet, only large geographic features are visible. The focus is on which direction you are headed and the best route to get there, and instrumentation is required for guidance. Similarly, in the solution context, from the highest viewpoint, the strategic goals of the bank must be

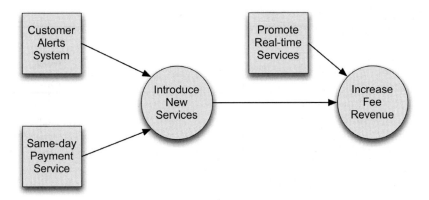

Figure 4-1 A results chain

taken into consideration. The solution must be viewed in terms of how it contributes to the bank's overall strategy and how it relates to other strategic initiatives. Tools, such as a strategy map and results chain analyses, can be used to relate strategic goals with initiatives, which in turn correspond to solutions. Mapping out these relationships is critical so that:

- the alignment between goals, initiatives, and solutions is clear;

- the business value of solutions can be easily communicated; and

- the relationship between solutions and initiatives can be understood.

Figure 4-1 shows how a "results chain" can be used to graphically identify goals and initiatives upon which a strategic objective is dependent. The circles represent business goals and the squares represent initiatives required to achieve those goals. A results chain is useful, in this example, for explaining how initiatives such as the "Customer Alerts System" are necessary to achieve the end objective of increasing fee revenue. Initiatives will often correspond one-for-one with solution implementations.

It is important that solution designers and delivery managers are able to conceptualize solutions at a high level. Senior management and peers will usually need to understand *what* the solution is and *why* it is important to give their support. Because the primary audience is senior management, who are often pressed for time to review details, the presentation of solutions at a 30,000-foot level must be very succinct, and is often achieved by using graphics and presentation slides.

4.2.2 The 10,000-foot View: What and How

When flying an airplane at 10,000 feet, the outlines of more detailed features, such as farms, cities, and roads, are visible, and navigation by visual identification becomes more practical. Beyond the high-level view presented to senior management, solution descriptions must also be presented in more depth, that is, at a level relevant to middle managers. Middle managers will want to know *what* the solution is in more detail and *how* it will affect them. Business process abstractions and high-level requirement specifications are commonly used to present solutions at this intermediate level. Additionally, at this level, it becomes relevant to sketch out a high-level solution architecture, which has been discussed in detail in Chapter 3.

Figure 4-2 shows an abstracted process model for a hypothetical fee-management solution. At this level of analysis and presentation, the activities have minimal detail and the focus is on understanding the most likely flow, also referred to as the "golden path" or "main flow." Much of the focus may be

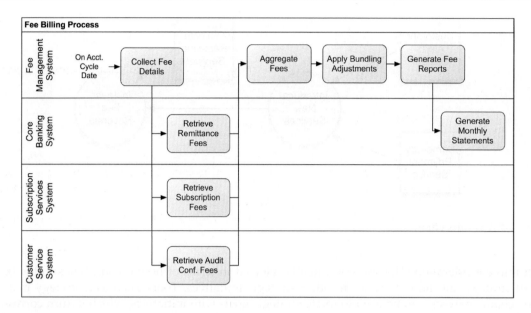

Figure 4-2 A high-level process model

on understanding how interactions will cross boundaries, such as systems, organizational groups, or geographical locations. This information can be effectively presented by layering process-flow diagrams on top of "pools" and "swim lanes."

It is at this level that the overall shape and form of the solution is agreed upon. There is enough detail for key stakeholders to feel comfortable with what will be delivered, but not so much detail that they are overwhelmed by irrelevant information. At this intermediate level, it is important that the focus does not become too detailed, as the low-level view is where more detail is appropriate.

4.2.3 The 2,000-foot View: Who and How

Flying at 2,000 feet, it is possible to see major details of buildings, cars, and landing strips. Visual cues are used to guide the plane in for landing and to watch for other aircrafts in the vicinity. In the case of IT solutions, after the high-level design has been finalized, there is a large amount of work necessary to specify requirement and design considerations in sufficient depth so that the end product will be robust and complete. Unlike management, for whom detail is distracting and abstractions are best served, the implementers of the solutions will need detailed information to help remove ambiguity and avoid misunderstandings regarding function and design.

Detailed business process models, **use case** descriptions or **user stories**, and design specifications produced by the business analysts and designers all serve to enable solution developers and testers to understand exactly what should be built, *how* it should work, and *who* will be involved. Figure 4-3

> Alternate flows:
> 2a. Customer has over $500,000 in current account assets
> 2a1. Monthly account service fees are waived
>
> 2b. Customer was converted from a Ready Account to a current account
> 2b1. Apply Ready Account service fees as per business rule #43
> . . .

Figure 4-3 A detailed use-case specification

- As a customer, I want monthly account service fees waived
  - current account assets over $500,000

- As a customer, I want to retain the same fee structure when changing account types
  - Ready Account converted to current account

Figure 4-4 A user story specification

shows an example of the detailed use-case specification describing the behavior of different alternate flow cases. In larger solutions, it would not be uncommon to have hundreds of alternate flows and business rules defined in the detailed use-case specifications. Alternatively, user stories may be used to capture detailed requirements, as shown in Figure 4-4.

It is important that the high-, medium-, and low-level solution views be presented clearly. A good high-level design will help ensure that the purpose and function are clear; however, if the detailed specifications are neglected, the end product may diverge far from its intended form. On the other hand, detailed specifications are usually not a good tool for communicating the value and function of a solution to senior and middle management.

4.3   SOLUTION DELIVERY STRATEGIES

Having considered how solutions should be defined at various levels for different purposes, the next major consideration is how to most effectively perform solution delivery activities. Before getting into the detailed mechanics of solution delivery, it is first important to ensure that a clear delivery strategy is in place. Developing the delivery strategy will typically involve creating a high-level delivery plan, identifying risks, and pinpointing the building blocks that will serve as core components of the solution and evaluating trade-offs between different approaches.

4.3.1   High-level Delivery Planning

Continuing with the airplane analogy, even the most talented pilots flying the most modern aircraft prepare a flight plan before takeoff as standard practice. The flight plan will identify the takeoff and landing points, expected flight time, and alternate landing locations in case of bad weather. Similarly, for solutions, one cannot understate the importance of having a high-level plan that covers how long it will take to be implemented, who will need to be involved, potential issues and risks, and alternative delivery strategies that can be adopted if problems occur.

Defining solution scope and priorities is the cornerstone of solution delivery. Without a clear scope, the delivery has no clear endpoint or success criteria. Many people will have different ideas as to what the scope comprises; hence, it is critical to find a consensus on the scope and communicate that clearly. Likewise, even within the in-scope items, there will be differing levels of relative importance. When trade-offs need to be made, it is important to understand in advance what is critical as opposed to what is in the "nice-to-have" category. In many cases, defining what is not in scope and what is less important is as critical as defining what is in scope.

Besides establishing the core requirements, the solution delivery strategy must determine which solution building blocks will be the most beneficial to use. Answering the following basic questions will help identify the best underlying components to use:

- Is the expectation to build or buy the system?

- What existing enterprise platforms can be leveraged to reduce cost and effort and improve quality?

- Which **legacy system** components should be avoided, if possible?

- What enterprise platforms are not currently in place that could be partially implemented as part of the solution delivery effort?

- What level of involvement does the bank intend to have in the solution delivery and what aspects will third-party vendors be responsible for?

- How can the solution's development and operation leverage cloud infrastructure?

The expected lifetime and total cost of ownership of the solution must also be factored into the delivery strategy. While it may seem counterproductive to consider the end of something before even beginning it, this exercise helps clarify the underlying principles behind the solution's purpose and facilitates decision making during the solution-delivery process. For example, the cost of incurring a six-month delay to incorporate additional functionality may not be acceptable for a solution that has a planned lifetime of three years, but could be for a solution that has an expected lifetime of ten years. Similarly, the trade-off between high startup costs and low maintenance costs, and vice versa, will be impacted by the expected lifetime of the solution.

Furthermore, it is necessary to validate that the high-level delivery plan is actually feasible (Case Study 4-2). It is quite possible to specify requirements and constraints for something such that it becomes economically impossible to build. If the delivery team is not confident that the implementation is viable at a high level, the solution scope should be redefined or the initiative may need to be reconsidered altogether. For example, if a request for proposal may lead to no solution proposals that are suitable, there may be a problem with the underlying requirements or the communication of the requirements.

4.3.2 Assessing and Managing Risks

Risk management is critical to successfully delivering solutions. As discussed in the previous section, one of the most important risks that must be controlled is solution scope. Other risks that often need to be addressed are technology, vendor, project delivery, and cost risks, which are discussed below.

Technology risks usually arise when solutions make use of new technology. New technologies may not work as expected because either the technology is not fit for purpose or the expectations of how the technology will be used are unrealistic. For example, early mobile phone web-browsing solutions that used the Wireless Application Protocol (WAP) communications did not do well because the interface turned out to be slower and less user-friendly than expected. While problems with new technologies are common, another concern is the possibility of old technology not being able to keep up with new

Case Study 4-2
Ensuring that the Solution Scope Is Deliverable

It is not uncommon for stakeholders to try to fit too many things into a solution. Even when the delivery scope is not overloaded, implementation can be more difficult than expected. Close examination will often reveal complications with even the simplest of tasks. If a solution is too complex or difficult to begin with, it is likely to become unmanageable and even undeliverable at some point in the future. The more "moving parts" there are, the greater the likelihood that something will break or fail to work as expected.

An example of a solution failure that was caused by overloading the solution scope was Bank of America's MasterNet trust accounting system. The development effort spanned over six years and resulted in a loss of US$78 million. A number of factors contributed to the project's failure, including starting with a high level of functional complexity, significant technical challenges, and underestimation of the project's scope and difficulty.

Source: Szilagyi, J. G., "Bank of America's Masternet System: A Case Study in Risk Assessment," http://csse.usc.edu/classes/cs510_2001/notes/masternet.pdf.

business requirements. Not updating technology and trying to continue using dated and rickety systems is a risk in itself.

Vendor risks are often caused by problems with the vendor's technology or its inability to meet schedule deadlines. The vendor's financial health or its poor service levels can also translate into risks. Using vendors to implement technology solutions can be beneficial because they can provide flexibility leverage for resourcing and technology provision. However, because vendors are separate companies, banks do not have the same level of control over vendors as they do with their own internal resources. Also, vendors may not provide sufficient visibility into resource or delivery problems, providing less time for the bank to manage such problems when they eventuate.

Project delivery and cost risks tend to go hand in hand with scope management, technology risks, vendor risks, and personnel risks. An inexperienced project manager or delivery team has a higher chance of encountering problems with a solution delivery. If the project schedule is tightly constrained and has a large number of dependencies, the effects of a few unexpected problems can become compounded and cause significant delays and cost overruns. Recognizing that a solution-delivery project is too complex and, subsequently, reducing the scope and dependencies is an important way in which project delivery risk can be reduced. Contingency plans also help to reduce the impact of risks when they do occur. For example, an alternative vendor might be kept in reserve to take over the delivery responsibilities if the primary vendor fails.

4.3.3 Evaluating Trade-offs

When delivering any type of solution, making trade-offs is inevitable. From the very beginning, the delivery strategy must decide how to balance the number of features, time-to-market, quality, and cost. Limited budgets dictate that only a finite number of resources can be allocated in various proportions to try to address a broad range of requirements. It is necessary to decide and define which aspects of a solution are the most and the least important; it is unrealistic to believe that all concerns are of equally high value. Moreover, if management does not define the relative importance of criteria related to trade-off decisions, their importance may be determined more randomly based on the opinions and preferences of the implementers.

A major point in time where trade-offs must be considered is when making the decision whether to buy, build, assemble, or outsource solution construction and delivery. Table 4-1 presents common approaches for implementing IT solutions and generalizations of the trade-offs encountered.

The buy and build approaches for creating IT solutions have been in place for many years and are fairly well understood. Alternatively, a hybrid approach may involve the assembly of components

Table 4-1 Trade-offs between different solution delivery approaches

Approach	Benefits	Drawbacks
Buy	Effectiveness of existing products can be better understood Short time-to-market	Lack of differentiation from other banks that use the product Must live with the product's limitations
Build/develop	Flexibility and uniqueness Can be designed and customized to match the bank's processes and environment	Longer time-to-market Higher maintenance cost Sufficient skills and resources must be available
Assemble "best of breed"	Flexibility Broad range of capabilities	Multiple vendor systems or components must be integrated and supported Risk that a single component mismatch compromises the solution
White-labeled/hosted solution	Minimal effort involved to implement and launch Faster time-to-market May have cost advantages for some business models	Minimal differentiation from other banks that use the solution High level of vendor dependency Cost structure may not be efficient for some business models

from different vendors and their integration to form a single solution; this is also known as the "best of breed" approach. For example, with the hybrid approach, the reference data underpinning a solution may be managed and maintained by an **enterprise data management (EDM)** system provided by one vendor, and that data may, in turn, be accessed by components that implement the business logic related to financial services transactions that is provided by another vendor. **White labeling**, on the other hand, utilizes a third-party provider to manage the solution as a service to the bank instead of providing a system (Case Study 4-3).

If the choice is made to build a solution in-house, the different options for sourcing development and testing resources must be considered. Local in-house resources, offshore in-house resources, local contracted resources, and offshore contracted resources may all be options. Each has its benefits and drawbacks related to cost, risk, and delivery capabilities that must be considered. Another approach for building solutions is for a financial institution to only define requirements and hand over implementation responsibilities to a vendor that specializes in custom software development.

Solution implementation choices will sometimes be driven by the misunderstanding of cost structures and by organizational bias. For example, a financial institution that has a large in-house software development capability may view building as being more cost effective than buying. Avoiding the 15–20% maintenance fees that solution vendors often charge for off-the-shelf products may seem particularly attractive. In reality though, maintenance costs are usually higher for custom-built solutions. This is because solution vendors are able to divide the cost of maintenance across multiple customers, whereas the costs of maintaining a custom-built solution will only be borne by the institution for or by which it was built. Maintenance services provided by software vendors also typically include bug fixes and improvements that other customers may have requested, as well as other product enhancements.

Case Study 4-3
A White-label Bill-pay Solution

One example of a white-label solution is CheckFree provided by the company Fiserv. Online electronic bill payment services were relatively slow to take off in the United States as compared with Europe and Asia. However, as it gained popularity, banks in the United States were faced with the decision of how to provide the service to their customers. As an alternative to building or purchasing bill-payment systems, CheckFree provides a hosted service that is integrated into the banks' existing Internet banking websites. When customers select the bill-payment option, they are routed to CheckFree's website to perform the transaction. CheckFree also provides back-end payment processing. CheckFree provides electronic bill-payment services to Wachovia, Bank of America, and many other institutions.

Using a white-label system like CheckFree can be inviting for smaller banks that do not have the economies of scale to justify buying or building a dedicated system. Per-transaction pricing is well suited for cases where the transaction volumes are expected to be low. Likewise, time-to-market is usually low with a white-label solution because the platform is already in place and has been designed to integrate with external systems.

The downsides of using a white-label solution are that there is a high level of dependence on the vendor. Whereas banks have a high degree of control over their own internal processes and environments, they will not have the liberty with an externally hosted solution. Resiliency of white-label solutions is one major concern; security is another. As a case in point, early in 2009, a security breech at an Internet domain registrar caused some 160,000 customers that used CheckFree's service to be redirected to a malicious server in the Ukraine. Consequently, banks that used the CheckFree's white-label service to provide bill-payment services to their customers may have inadvertently exposed them to an additional security risk.

Sources: CheckFree Corporation website, http://www.checkfree.com; McMillan, Robert, "CheckFree Warns 5 Million Customers after Hack," *Computerworld,* January 6, 2009, http://www.computerworld.com/s/article/9125078/CheckFree_warns_5_million_customers_after_hack.

Another common problem that is encountered when making solution trade-offs is that too much emphasis may be placed on upfront cost. This orientation is detrimental because often, solutions that have the lowest upfront costs may have higher long-term costs. They may be more difficult to support or maintain, or may have limited flexibility that limits future business agility. There is also the risk that being excessively frugal will lead to a proliferation of small tactical solution implementations. Instead of tackling several problems simultaneously by spending more and implementing a broader strategic solution, business sponsors end up spending more overall, but in small, incremental quantities.

4.3.4 Solution Delivery Logistics

The location and identity of the developers and testers of a solution may, at first, seem to be low-level implementation details. However, these considerations are of strategic interest because the logistics of the delivery effort can make or break it. In the current world of global sourcing, many resourcing options— internal and external, local or remote—are available. In theory, mixing and matching these options can provide the optimal cost structure and talent pools. Practically, however, there are interfacing costs to separating activities across organizations, geographies, and time zones. For example, having dual development teams in Hong Kong and Texas may seem like a good idea because it provides round-the-clock implementation. Even so, this approach may be counterproductive when questions arise in one location and the other location is not available to respond because of the time zones invovled. Moreover, in such cases, the timings of conference calls are typically inconvenient for at least one of the parties, if not both.

A solution-delivery strategy must balance gains that can be achieved from multisourcing, with the resulting additional complexity and risks. It may be practical to spread a delivery effort that requires 20 labor-years' worth of work across three locations and two vendors. On the other hand, it may be more cost effective to execute a project that only requires one labor-year of effort at one location using a single organization (the bank or a vendor). There is no exact formula that can be used to determine the best logistical arrangement, but strategic guidelines should be identified early so that the solution-delivery managers can identify the parameters within which to work.

4.4 SOLUTION DELIVERY PROCESSES

Finding an opportunity and making sure that it is aligned with key stakeholders' needs do not always translate into an effective business solution. A lot of work must be done between the time a business idea is formulated and the time the end solution is rolled out to users. One way to understand the processes between the beginning and the end of solution delivery is to split the process into two major phases: solution conception and solution instantiation. Each bank has its own specific process that it follows to deliver solutions. Rather than focusing on any single bank's processes, the following subsections look at the common, high-level tasks involved in both solution conception and instantiation.

4.4.1 Solution Conception

The solution conception phase serves as a filtering mechanism for business ideas to ensure that capital is applied to only the best ideas and those that are aligned with the bank's overall strategy. That is to say, due to resource limitations, only a small fraction of potential solutions will be implemented. The solution conception phase is critical for refining initial ideas, verifying feasibility, evaluating the return on investment, and gaining consensus support within the organization. Figure 4-5 shows a high-level view of the solution conception process. Some organizations refer to the conception phase, or similar types of activities, as the "discovery" phase.

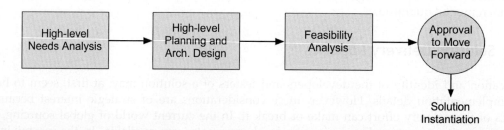

Figure 4-5 Solution conception process

4.4.1.1　High-level needs analysis

Translating a business idea to a solution requires that the business needs (requirements) are well understood early on. The considerations of what the solution will be and why it is valuable must be articulated in the context of the organization's business strategy. If a solution's purpose is ambiguous or the scope is too diffused, it is unlikely to move forward or be successful. Hence, the initial needs analysis is key to a solution's overall success. Regulatory considerations and the potential compliance impact of the solution also need to be assessed at an early stage, as they may present major hurdles or even roadblocks. The considerations and techniques discussed in Section 4.2.1 are typically applied at this stage of the process.

4.4.1.2　High-level planning and design

Once the general scope of the solution is understood, a high-level sketch of how it can be constructed can be drafted. High-level planning and design should combine an internally focused, top-down analysis of the bank's current environment and capabilities with an externally focused review of what solution building blocks and systems are available in the market. The overall solution-delivery timeline and budget are also defined at this stage; these factors will determine the overall size and shape of the solution. The considerations and practices discussed in Section 4.3 are typically applied at this stage of the process.

　　One of the more critical considerations that the high-level design will address is the amount of integration that will be undertaken as part of the solution. It is not uncommon for system integration to represent 30–45% of a major solution implementation effort. System integration is the bane of solution delivery because it is usually complicated and increases the number of dependencies on other systems. While system integration is good because it helps streamline processes and achieve **straight-through processing (STP)**, too much integration can make a solution expensive and unfeasible. For instance, integrating with one system as part of a solution effort might take a couple of months and cost tens of thousands of dollars. Integrating with seven systems could take a year and cost several hundred thousand dollars. Integrating with 30 systems could easily take years and cost millions of dollars. Hence, identifying the scope of integration is necessary at an early stage of solution planning.

4.4.1.3　Feasibility analysis

Feasibility analysis focuses on identifying and validating assumptions that were made during the high-level planning and design stage. The considerations reviewed by the feasibility analysis will be dependent on the solution. It is good practice to perform a bottom–up review of the existing environment to determine if there are any potential limitations or stumbling blocks that will interfere with the solution delivery as planned. Looked at another way, feasibility analysis can be compared to the due diligence that would be involved prior to building a skyscraper. The composition of the underlying soil, the types and costs of building materials available, and regulatory restrictions on building height all need to be confirmed in advance of commissioning the project. If one site or design is found to be impractical, other alternatives can be identified.

　　It is often said that the devil is in the details; this is especially true of delivering solutions. While things may look fine from the 30,000-foot level in terms of how a solution can be implemented, it is necessary to investigate and identify potential roadblocks. Particularly in cases where system integration is required, it is not uncommon to find cases where:

- interfaces are not available to access systems;
- interfaces may be available, but extremely expensive to utilize;

- access to a system is dependent on it being upgraded first; or

- cooperation of a another party is required, for example, a vendor or separate division.

While these challenges can often be worked through, they need to be understood upfront so that they can be incorporated into the solution delivery plan. If major integration concerns are discovered after the project has begun, timelines and budgets will need to be revised, leading to additional scrutiny by management and potentially killing the entire initiative.

Feasibility analysis requires the solution plan to be communicated to front-line business, operational, and technical staff to identify and understand any issues and concerns. It is sometimes helpful to undertake a small proof-of-concept exercise to demonstrate the feasibility of implementing new technologies or processes. Showing a working prototype can help dispel myths and concerns that might otherwise linger, and thereby improve overall confidence in the delivery plan. Proof-of-concepts can be as simple as demonstrating connectivity between two systems, showing a mock-up of a user interface, or testing process changes to show their viability and effectiveness.

4.4.1.4 Approval to move forward

The mechanics of evaluating which potential solutions should move forward to be instantiated varies with the organization. In many cases, a consensus will be reached by a group of key stakeholders, often representing different divisions within the bank. Approval by such a committee or council may be through a formal meeting, informal discussions, or possibly both. Detailed cost-benefit analysis may be required so that the return on investment can be compared with an internal hurdle rate or with the returns of other solutions that are competing for funding. However, in some cases, a solution may be able to move forward solely with the support of one or two senior executives, for example, the chief information officer and chief executive officer.

After the solution has been approved, formal contract negotiations may begin with external vendors such as service providers or systems suppliers. It is possible that final agreement on the commercial terms may delay the solution instantiation phase; however, in many cases, project planning and design can get started in parallel, while the commercial agreement is being finalized. To help get things going and avoid delays, a letter of intent that guarantees certain starting payments and documents mutual agreement as to a high-level pricing structure may be provided by the bank to the vendor(s) prior to contract signing.

4.4.2 Delivery Approach

Before examining the steps involved in solution instantiation, it is useful to consider the different ways in which they can be executed. Table 4-2 describes common project delivery approaches used for delivering IT solutions.

The most effective approach in any particular case will be determined by the following factors: the size of the project, its perceived risk, the experience levels of the project manager and project team, and the quality of the requirements. For example, the code-and-fix approach might be adequate for a very small project but could be disastrous for a large one. Similarly, in cases where the project team only has experience using the waterfall approach, it may not be practical to use an iterative approach. Fuzzy requirements, or requirements that are expected to change, can pose significant challenges to the waterfall approach. In such cases, an iterative approach is often more practical. Moreover, in some organizations, different delivery approaches may coexist or be fused into hybrid models.

In general, there has been a trend for financial institutions to move from large, waterfall-based solution deliveries to smaller, iterative deliveries (Case Study 4-4). Shorter delivery cycles are generally preferable because they require less upfront planning and financial commitment, and business value

Table 4-2 Common project delivery approaches used for solutions

Approach	Description	Benefits	Drawbacks
Waterfall	Each phase of development follows the other in one continuous flow to produce the end deliverable.	Well-understood methodology that is sequential and easily tracked.	Slow to deliver visible results. Misunderstandings show up late in the delivery process.
Iterative	Multiple minicycles are executed, usually with an interim deliverable at the end of each cycle. The end deliverable is built up and refined over the course of multiple iterations.	Progress is visible early. Ideas can be adapted and refined during the delivery process. Facilitates stakeholder involvement through ongoing delivery reviews.	Management and project teams may be less familiar with the process. More difficult to estimate total project duration given that requirements are not complete upfront.
Code and fix	Minimal structure around the implementation process. Functionality is implemented in an indiscriminate manner.	Does not incur delays for planning and requirements gathering.	Lack of planning can lead to major structural flaws that make the solution unworkable in the long run.

can be more quickly. Earlier delivery and use also help identify misunderstandings in requirements and design flaws sooner so that they can be corrected in subsequent iterations. Breaking the delivery up into pieces is also more manageable from a project resource standpoint, providing teams with nearer-term goals to focus on and allowing for successes to be celebrated much sooner and more often. Moreover, as the financial services landscape has become more competitive over the last decade with emergent Fintech companies competing in the same space as banks and other financial institutions, time-to-market has become an increasingly important concern for new offerings. Whereas ten or 20 years ago, an 18–36-month project delivery schedule would have been the norm for a major solution implementation, today, business value is often expected to be produced within a 3–6-month timeframe, with subsequent releases to be provided at similar intervals.

Constraints related to time and cost may also be factors in the chosen delivery approach. Where strict time or cost limitations must be adhered to, it is often necessary to treat the requirement scope as a variable consideration. To this point, iterative delivery approaches often involve "time-boxing" techniques. Requirements will be implemented in priority order within the time or funding available, and some lower priority requirements will be expected to remain outstanding when time or funding limits are reached.

Besides deciding the project delivery approach, it is also necessary to decide whether the delivery process should be lightweight or heavyweight. A lightweight process minimizes required formal documentation and project tracking. It tends to work best for smaller projects with highly skilled, experienced staff that are accustomed to working together as a a team and operate in a more casual, i.e. less regulated, environment. A heavyweight process tracks, measures, and documents project activities and deliverables more carefully. A heavyweight delivery process is usually required for larger projects, or when less skilled or inexperienced workers make up a large proportion of the delivery team or is required by regulators or auditors. Carnegie Mellon University's Capability Maturity Model Integration (CMMI) is an example of a heavyweight process that is commonly used by service providers to ensure repeatable delivery and consistent quality. Unfortunately, the overhead costs of implementing and maintaining CMMI levels 4 and 5 delivery capabilities are usually impractical for most organizations.

Case Study 4-4

Revamping Solution Delivery to Achieve Cost Savings

Simplifying its software development was a key initiative of HSBC's 2015 cost reduction strategy, which was introduced in Case Study 1-1. The bank's goal was to gain over $775 million in savings by 2017. Of that, more than $475 million of the savings was to be realized by consolidating software development by reducing the number of vendors used for software development and relocating more software development work offshore. The rest of the savings, more than $300 million, was to be gained by buying more off-the-shelf software solutions and to building better software using agile development techniques.

With regard to vendor consolidation, reducing the number of vendors used provides greater volume of work for the vendors that remain, enabling them to achieve greater economies of scale and, thus, at least in theory, provide lower cost services. Likewise, having fewer vendors reduces the amount of administrative overhead, e.g., contract and invoice processing, and vendor management work, e.g., service level agreement monitoring and due diligence checking that banks are commonly required to perform. However, when banks limit the number of vendors they use, they risk vendor lock-in situations, where incumbent vendors are less competitive because they know that, by the policy of limiting the number of vendors used, it is difficult for the bank to bring in new, alternative vendors to provide comparable products or services.

HSBC planned to achieve its goal of relocating more software development offshore by increasing the amount of software development performed in India and China from 50% to 75%. Software engineers' and related professionals' salaries in emerging markets are usually less than half of those in the United Kingdom, Western Europe, and the United States. While using offshore resources provides savings on a per-resource basis, it can create additional coordination work, and it also does not fit well with agile development methods, which aim to have teams colocated.

With regard to using more off-the-shelf software, HSBC's target was to implement around 40% of new applications using market-standard, third-party offerings. This approach would reduce time to market and also reduce development and maintenance costs. Like custom-tailored clothing, customized software applications are expensive to make and also often unnecessary. In most cases, an off-the-shelf alternative is good enough. That said, prepackaged applications rarely provide an exact match to business requirements, so trade-offs are required.

HSBC's target of increasing the use of agile software development methodologies is in line with industry trends. While the definition and implementation of "agile" methods vary from one organization to the next, typical features include colocation—ideally in the same room—of all resources involved with the software development project; a collaborative environment that is centered around frequent, informal communication; incremental and iterative software deliveries; work units broken down into smaller-sized chunks; and more closely knit project teams. Much of the goal of using agile is to better support fluid business models and cope with unpredictable business requirement and technology changes. Yet, as pointed out in Case Study 4-1, shifting to use agile methods has its own challenges.

While HSBC's cost savings initiatives are well oriented for producing cost savings, none of them is a silver bullet that will magically solve the problem. Their implementation will be the real challenge and determine their overall success. It is often the case that a fix for one problem, such as high costs, can lead to several new problems, such as reduced quality or flexibility.

Sources: HSBC, "HSBC—Actions to Capture Value from Our Global Presence in a Changed World: Investor Update 2015," June 9, 2015, //www.hsbc.com/~/media/HSBC-com/InvestorRelationsAssets/investor-update-2015/group; Cao, Lan and Balasubramaniam Ramesh, "Agile Software Development: Ad Hoc Practices or Sound Principles?" *IEEE IT Professional*, March/April 2007.

4.4.3 Solution Instantiation

Solution instantiation is the post-approval process of delivering the project. Figure 4-6 shows the main activities required for solution instantiation. The following subsections will discuss these activities.

4.4.3.1 Project planning

With respect to project planning and management, relatively little is unique to financial services, and it is a topic that has been studied extensively. Please refer to the Further Reading section at the end of this chapter for more resources on this topic.

4.4.3.2 Requirements analysis

After the scope and key objectives have been set out in the solution conception and project-planning stages, it is critical that a complete and understandable set of requirement specifications be produced. The importance of this stage cannot be overemphasized. After lack of stakeholder support, inadequate

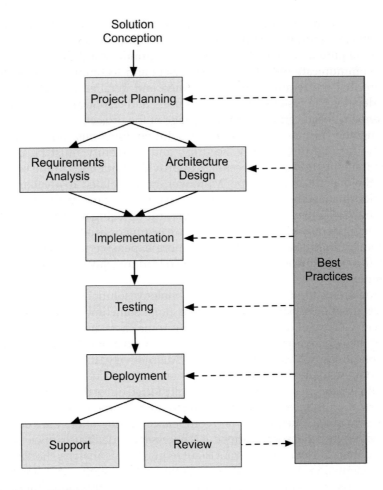

Figure 4-6 Solution instantiation process

requirements are the second most significant contributing factor to project failure [5]. Often, the underlying cause of midstream project changes is inadequate upfront requirements. While having well defined software requirements may seem obvious, it remains a concern for even some of the largest and most experienced organizations.

To help illustrate how the requirement development analysis process can go awry, consider the following situation. Business users identify a problem or opportunity and a manager is assigned to move a solution initiative forward. The manager is then tasked with documenting the requirements, possibly with the help of a business analyst. Because the organization does not have a standard methodology for analyzing and documenting requirements, the requirements are documented as a list of bullet points or a spreadsheet with a list of features. Requirement lists, sometimes viewed as "wish lists," often have mixed levels of detail that leave room for a wide range of interpretations; hence, they can cause problems and delays due to misunderstandings later in the implementation process.

In this example, the first critical failure is not having a well-defined methodology for performing requirements analysis. Applying a methodology provides structure to the requirements-gathering effort and helps ensure that it is consistent and complete. Formal methodologies can also impel the requirements-analysis effort to go into greater depth so that the details of ambiguous requirements are better understood. Process-oriented methodologies, as discussed in Section 4.2.2, are useful because they examine needs in the context of end-to-end business processes rather than focusing on system features.

It is also critical to have a skilled business analyst assist in developing the requirements; business users rarely have sufficient training or time to perform this function well. The business analyst should be familiar with the requirements-analysis methodology, understand the business concepts, and be able to effectively communicate with the business users and technical implementers. The business analyst must ensure that the requirements are defined and detailed to sufficient depth so that the implementers can develop the system. The business users and technical team should then review and validate the requirement specifications at an early stage of the project.

Besides defining the business processes and solution functions, nonfunctional requirements such as availability, **throughput, latency**, security, and scalability must be considered. Defining nonfunctional requirements upfront is necessary to provide guidelines to the solution architect and help to determine the overall project scope. Moreover, needs related to ancillary functions, such as reporting, application management, and administrative monitoring, must also be captured during the requirements analysis. Often these considerations end up being afterthoughts that are identified when a solution is being deployed into user acceptance testing or production. Trying to address them late in the development lifecycle is usually much more expensive to implement than if they were incorporated from the start. Late identification can also lead to delays to production deployment and overall project completion.

The business requirements documented for technology solutions often include regulatory and other compliance requirements. Banking IT solutions must sometimes cater to customer information privacy and data secrecy laws of different countries. In some cases, it may be possible to address such concerns outside of the solution implementation context by obtaining prior customer consent as part of the terms and conditions defined for the service. Alternatively, it may be necessary to design the solution so that certain activities, such as the initiation of transactions, are performed in the home country and that only certain types of information are transferred out of the country for remote processing. That is to say, information that can be used to directly identify the customer, such as their name or address, may not be sent abroad. Regulatory and compliance considerations are examined in Chapter 19.

To develop good requirement specifications, it is necessary to dedicate sufficient time to the analysis effort. Unfortunately, there is a tendency to want to cut requirements analysis short and get on to the "real work," that is, implementation. This usually comes at the cost of greatly extending the implementation time because the end target was ambiguous or unclear, and as a result, significant rework was required to address changes late in the development process. Even after the requirements analysis has been completed, clarification and refinement will be necessary. Hence, it is useful to put in place a formal process for tracking requirements-related questions and ensuring their timely clarification.

4.4.3.3 Architecture design

Nonexistent and weak solution architecture designs are a common cause of IT project failure. Given the importance of this topic, solution architecture is covered in depth in Chapter 3.

4.4.3.4 Implementation

Where the implementation of a solution involves significant software development, often it will extend or enhance an existing software application. In this case, it is common that a separate branch of the source code will be created to accommodate changes related to the new solution being implemented, while the main branch is used for bug fixes and other minor enhancements. Alternatively, solution development may occur on the main branch and bug fixes and other major features will be implemented in separate branches. Ultimately, the branches will need to be merged so that there is a single common code base that includes all of the application functionality. The coordination of creating and merging source code branches can involve substantial effort in complex environments. Furthermore, retesting is usually required after the code merge is complete to ensure that flaws in the merging process did not introduce new defects.

Traditional development approaches perform code merges infrequently, usually when new functionality has been completed and fully tested. A more contemporary approach is to use continuous integration (CI), where source code changes are more regularly merged into the main source code branch and immediately validated using automated tests. This approach is beneficial in that it finds bugs earlier in the development lifecycle and makes it easier to identify which changes introduced them. It also avoids the need for major code merge and testing exercises. CI platforms will typically trigger a build of the application whenever new source code is committed to a shared source code repository. When the build is completed, the CI platform will then initiate automated tests that verify the new code has not compromised the integrity of the application. If the changes create build problems or cause tests to fail, the CI platform will send out notifications so that the problems can be quickly addressed.

4.4.3.5 Testing

Compared with solutions for many other industries, testing and quality assurance (QA) of IT solutions differ in several ways. First, due to the high-value nature of financial service applications, the cost of post-implementation failures can be very high. Whereas the cost of a word-processing application crashing in an ordinary business operation may be a few hours of lost work, the cost to a bank of a payment system failure can be millions of dollars. Second, besides functional completeness, critical nonfunctional concerns such as operational security and resilience must also be verified as part of the quality assurance process. Moreover, the close interrelationship between manual and automated activities in financial services requires that IT solutions be validated in the context of end-to-end business processes. A solution may appear to be fully functional in an isolated test environment, but may be unfit for use in a wider context.

Extensive work has gone into developing tools and techniques for system testing and QA. Having said that, the maturity level that different financial institutions have reached with respect to testing and quality varies greatly. In some organizations, QA is a centralized function that is responsible for developing a competency in that area and provides resources to solution-delivery efforts as and when needed. Other organizations may leave it up to the development group or solution-delivery effort to determine how QA is implemented. Centralization has many benefits and is generally preferable, but requires greater organizational coordination.

Automating software tests is critical for reducing the effort required to perform quality assurance, reducing the time required to deliver solutions, and improving the consistency of the testing that is performed. There is, however, substantial upfront investment involved with creating automated tests, perhaps equal to or greater than the effort of creating the application source code that is being tested. Hence, it is necessary to evaluate which test cases make sense to automate, considering factors such as the effort required to automate the test cases, the effort required to manually execute the test cases, and how often the test cases are likely to be executed. Also note that automated unit- and application-level tests may be necessary to support continuous integration software development processes.

4.4.3.6 Deployment and support

Unfortunately, deployment and support considerations are often not sufficiently considered when planning solution delivery. The success of a solution will ultimately be judged by its effectiveness in a production environment, and not by its performance during acceptance testing. The smoothness by which a solution is deployed and supported will largely contribute to how successful its launch is perceived. Hence, it is beneficial to incorporate deployment and support concerns into the design and acceptance testing phases of the solution delivery. Particularly where the end users are bank customers, post-delivery deployment and support issues will be of critical importance.

Immediately after production deployment, support needs will usually require the solution development and testing team to be ready to investigate problems or questions that arise. The quick release of "hot fixes" or "patches" may be required to address production issues that were not or could not be identified during user acceptance testing. For example, solutions deployed on the bank's customers' workstations may encounter conflicts with other software that is also installed on the workstation. Alternatively, the security configuration of the production network environment may be different from the test network environment. Identifying such situations in advance is difficult due to the wide range of target environments that could be encountered. Additionally, functional gaps or flawed assumptions in the requirements may become apparent during deployment. These discoveries may lead to change requests that must be quickly retrofitted into the software and be redeployed to ensure the solution's success.

4.4.3.7 Identifying and applying best practices

It is critical to perform a post-delivery review upon completing a solution delivery, irrespective of the overall success of the effort. This review should be accomplished through analysis of project artifacts and group discussions. The group review should include members of each of the main groups involved in the project, including the project management, the business, the architect, the implementers, the QA testers, as well as deployment and support staff (Figure 4-7). The review and summary report should include quantitative information that is available, such as how the project effort tracked to plan. Quality factors, such as number of defects found at different stages of the delivery process, and attributable factors should also be examined.

The main objectives of review should be to identify:

- what worked well and should be repeated in future delivery efforts;

- what did not work well and should be avoided or done differently in future delivery efforts; and

- what should have been done but was not, and should be incorporated into the process for future delivery efforts.

Figure 4-7 Successful solutions begin by having everyone understand the big picture (© DBS Bank. Reprinted with permission.)

By identifying lessons learned, the delivery process can be refined and improved, and a set of best practices can be codified and used to achieve continuous improvement.

Let us look for a moment at the same concept in the context of a different industry—the airline industry. In the United States, the US Federal Aviation Administration (FAA) is responsible for ensuring the safety and effective operation of the airline industry. The "black boxes" on planes, recordings of air traffic control communications, equipment reviews, and interviews with the people are all used to identify potential problems related to technology, process, and people. Based on its findings, the FAA will issue best practice guidelines, recommendations, and restrictions for all airlines to follow to ensure the highest level of safety for future flights. Besides investigating crashes, which occur infrequently, the FAA also investigates near misses (that is, when two aircraft fly too close to each other) and other reported problems in order to gather a larger set of data for analysis. Minor issues that occur in one situation may be magnified in other situations, leading to more severe consequences. Hence, regular detailed review and analysis are necessary.

In the context of IT solutions, the idea behind identifying and applying best practices is to avoid making the same mistake twice and to learn from others' mistakes and successes. Issues that cause minor problems for one project may be encountered again as major concerns for other projects. Over time, collected lessons learned and best practices can become a corporate asset and a form of knowledge capital.

There is a wide disparity as to how banks formally capture, maintain, and apply best practice information. Often, information exists, but is embedded in the collective experience of individuals rather than being documented in a more persistent form that can be easily accessed and extended. When knowledge resides only among employees, it can be easily lost when they leave the organization. However, even when employees with the relevant knowledge and experience are present in an organization, they may not always be accessible to provide the needed advice. Hence, a key challenge for banks is to determine how best to capture this information and ensure that it is disseminated and applied as part of the ongoing solution delivery process.

4.5 DELIVERY PROCESS EXECUTION

While having a well-defined solution delivery process will help avoid common problems and failures, people's execution of that process will ultimately determine the overall level of success. Usually, there must be a champion for the solution whose primary concern is to ensure that the solution is planned, delivered, and deployed successfully. This person can be thought of as the "solution-delivery manager," and is one who has overarching business responsibility and whose career options will be heavily dependent on the solution's success.

Depending on the organization and project, it may be the case that the roles of the solution-delivery manager and project manager are combined in the same person. Irrespective of whether the roles are combined in one individual or split between multiple people, it is important to differentiate them. Whereas the role of the project manager is to ensure effective planning and execution of the project, the role of the solution manager is to have and realize a vision of what the solution can achieve for the organization and ensure that that vision is achieved.

Before any solution can be implemented, the inertia must be overcome. First, key stakeholders must be convinced that it is a good idea (Case Study 4-5). Even when the stakeholders are on board, a lot of work is still needed to get all the relevant parties to commit to support the delivery effort. Once commitments are secured, getting the follow-through on those commitments may still be a challenge. Great effort is required to convince those who do not support the solution, and to overcome other hurdles. It is the responsibility of the solution manager to navigate through these different challenges and sustain the overall momentum of the project.

Case Study 4-5
Stakeholder Involvement

Issues related to stakeholder involvement were identified as contributing to project failure over 20 years ago. Two decades later, it remains a major concern for solution delivery. Often, the focus of solution delivery goes into the mechanics of the project management or the technology itself, while neglecting stakeholders' issues and social processes. For example, in the context of delivering enterprise resource planning solutions, it is estimated that human factors constitute 57% of difficulties, whereas process and technology factors account for only 27%. The statistics for delivering financial services solutions are probably quite similar.

Having the end users involved with the design of solutions is critical to gaining their support and acceptance. Particularly where new processes are involved, end users should be involved in testing and validating them. In this vein, implementing a **change management** plan is important for involving stakeholders to help smooth their transition to the new system. Having a close linkage between solution developers and end users, ideally where developers sit with the users for a "test drive" of the system at early stages, helps keep key stakeholders involved and gives them a sense of ownership. This approach also helps highlight pitfalls or misassumptions early in the implementation process, when they can more easily be corrected.

Integrating the end users and developers is not as easy as it sounds; both parties have to come to the table. End users may not be willing to invest their time or the IT group may not be open to integrating feedback into the development process. Hopefully, with better education about the effects on quality and costs, less isolated development will occur in the future and there will be more focus on stakeholder involvement.

Source: Legris, P. and P. Collerette, "A Roadmap for IT Project Implementation: Integrating Stakeholders and Change Management Issues," *Project Management Journal* (December 2006): 64–75.

An important function of the solution-delivery manager is to keep up the delivery team's motivation and the stakeholders' interest through the course of the project. Creating an IT solution is often an uphill battle for those involved in the delivery process. The solution manager must ensure that a sufficient level of energy is maintained so that the delivery effort does not stall. Motivation may be achieved through incentives, disincentives, personal commitments, or a combination of all of these factors.

Toward the end of the project, the solution-delivery manager's challenge is to drive it to closure. This may involve convincing people to make trade-offs between functionality and delivery timeframes, and may require compromising on end goals or restructuring. The solution-delivery manager must have the perseverance to battle on when things become difficult. Often, a successful solution-delivery manager's track record as well as his or her interactions with peers and the management will serve as the basis for his or her promotion to more senior management positions.

4.6 SUMMARY

This chapter reviewed financial services IT solutions from the point of view of the business and project delivery functions, and covered the following topics:

- how IT solutions derive from corporate strategy and objectives;

- techniques for defining business requirements at various levels of abstraction depth;

- the process for deciding whether IT solutions are feasible and should be implemented;

- the high-level process for delivering IT solutions; and

- how the ultimate success of an IT solution depends on the stakeholders and the people involved in its delivery.

This chapter focused on how technology solutions are delivered in the context of financial services. The next chapter will examine IT infrastructure and operational considerations.

FURTHER READING

Books

Cockburn, A., *Writing Effective Use Cases* (Massachusetts: Addison-Wesley Professional, 2000).

————, *Agile Software Development: The Cooperative Game*, 2nd ed. (Massachusetts: Addison-Wesley Professional, 2006).

Flinn, J. A., *The Success Healthcheck for IT Projects: An Insider's Guide to Managing IT Investment and Business Change* (Singapore: John Wiley & Sons, 2010).

Humble, J. and Farley, D., *Continuous Delivery: Reliable Software Releases through Build, Test, and Deployment Automation* (Addison-Wesley Professional, 2010).

Kaner, C., J. Bach, and B. Pettichord, *Lessons Learned in Software Testing* (New York: John Wiley & Sons, 2001).

Kaplan, R., *The Strategy-focused Organization: How Balanced Scorecard Companies Thrive in the New Business Environment* (Massachusetts: Harvard Business School Press, 2001).

Kulak, D. and E. Guiney, *Use Cases: Requirements in Context*, 2nd ed. (Massachusetts: Addison-Wesley Professional, 2003).

McConnell, S. *Rapid Development: Taming Wild Software Schedules* (Washington: Microsoft Press, 1996), Chapter 3.

———, *Software Estimation: Demystifying the Black Art* (Washington: Microsoft Press, 2006).

Thorp, J., *The Information Paradox* (Toronto: McGraw-Hill Higher Education, 2003). This book is out of print, but is available online at http://www.fujitsu.com/us/news/publications/books/ ip.html.

Web

Capability Maturity Model Integration, http://www.sei.cmu.edu/cmmi.

Project Management Resources, University at Buffalo, http://www.tks.buffalo.edu/pm.

Tree Swing Analogy Cartoon, http://www.projectcartoon.com.

ENDNOTES

1. Carr, N., "IT Doesn't Matter," *Harvard Business Review* (May 2003): 41–49.

2. Beccalli, E., "Does IT Investment Improve Bank Performance? Evidence from Europe," *Journal of Banking & Finance* 31 (2007): 2205–2230.

3. McAfee, A. and E. Brynjolfsson, "Investing in the IT That Makes a Competitive Difference," *Harvard Business Review*, July 2008.

4. Hussain, N. B., "LSE to buy Citi's bond data and indexes business for $685 million," Reuters, May 30, 2017, https://www.reuters.com/article/us-citigroup-m-a-lse-idUSKBN18Q0FZ.

5. Kappelman, L. A., R. McKeeman, and L. Zhang, "Early Warning Signs of IT Project Failure: The Dominant Dozen," *Information Systems Management* 23, issue 4 (2006): 31–36.

5 Technology Infrastructure and Operations

Chapter Overview

5.1 TECHNOLOGY INFRASTRUCTURE

5.2 MANAGING TECHNOLOGY OPERATIONS AND INFRASTRUCTURE

5.3 SUMMARY

FURTHER READING

ENDNOTES

There are many layers and dimensions to the technology infrastructure that financial institutions use to run their business. Software applications that customers and staff use on a daily basis to retrieve information and transact, often get the most attention. However, there are a multitude of components and services that software applications are dependent on to provide service. Should any of these components become unavailable, the software application could suffer a service outage that would potentially cause financial and reputational damage to the institution (Case Study 5-1).

As of 2015, banks collectively spent over $180 billion on information technology, with more than two-thirds of that expenditure going toward maintenance of existing systems [1]. While investment in new technologies often gets the limelight, the reality is that existing infrastructure and systems dominate the IT landscape of banks. Today's exciting new technology platform becomes tomorrow's legacy system that has to be managed with all the rest. Like it or not, "keeping the lights on" takes priority over implementation of new systems.

The hardware and software environments that banks use to operate their IT systems are large and complex. Computer hardware, operating systems (OS), databases, software applications, middleware, and networking equipment must be regularly patched for flaws and security vulnerabilities, and eventually reach a point where the vendor no longer supports the component, so that it must be upgraded or replaced. The cost of implementing and testing these ongoing changes is substantial, and an estimate is that the cost of maintaining IT systems consumes three-quarters of banks' IT spending. It is no wonder that from a cost perspective, cloud-based and managed service provider solutions have become attractive.

The design and management of technology infrastructure are critical to the businesses of financial institutions. Availability, capacity, and security must be maintained across all components and continuously over time. Breakages can occur due to changes, such as those caused by patching and upgrades. Underlying components can become overloaded due to changes in usage patterns or the addition of new software applications. Components that were thought to be secure can become unsecure overnight when new vulnerabilities are discovered. The effort involved to sustain even moderately complex infrastructure environments is never-ending.

It is important to be familiar with the types of components used by financial institutions to implement their technology infrastructure and to understand the issues related to their management. This chapter will provide an overview of the most relevant components, discussing their function and role in the overall IT architecture ecosystem. Specifically, the hardware and software components that support end-user software applications will be examined along with other communication-related components and physical infrastructure required to support technology solutions. Infrastructure operation and management considerations are also presented.

Case 5-1

System Operation Woes at Royal Bank of Scotland

In June of 2012, Royal Bank of Scotland (RBS), one of the largest banks in the United Kingdom, had a critical IT systems outage that affected more than 17 million of the bank's customers. The outage was the result of a routine upgrade of a vendor system that prevented the overnight batch from being processed on schedule. It took three days to resolve the problem, which caused a backlog of 100 million unprocessed payments to accumulate. The bank's customers were unable to make transactions or access their accounts for several days. Payment delays affected paycheck deposits and bill payments leading to public concern as to whether the customers' credit histories would be tainted in cases where they were unable to make loan payments as a result of the outage.

To help deal with the service interruption, RBS extended the opening hours of over 1,000 branches, doubled the number of call center staff, and stayed open on Sunday. The bank also offered to waive fees incurred by its customers. Resolving the problem cost RBS £175 million. On top of that, the bank committed to spend an extra £750 million over a three-year period to improve the resilience and security of its IT systems. Additionally, the Financial Conduct Authority (FCA), a financial regulator in the United Kingdom, performed an investigation into the incident that resulted in RBS incurring a fine of £56 million for technology failures. As a consequence of the system upgrade problem, RBS's chief executive did not receive a bonus that year.

Three years later, in June of 2015, an IT system failure caused RBS to delay the processing of over 600,000 customer payments. While not of the same scale as the 2012 problem, this case highlights that these types of problems are often chronic, not acute. IT system operation and maintenance are an ongoing challenge to banks and other financial institutions. RBS's troubles were far from unique. In August of 2015, HSBC ran into a payments software failure that delayed the processing of 275,000 payments.

Banks employ vast and complex IT infrastructure environments with many interdependencies. Interconnections can amplify small problems and turn them into major disruptions. Changes to the environment are continually required, such as patching, upgrades, and replacement of components. Unfortunately, changes introduce risks: patches may contain bugs or incompatibilities, upgrades may introduce new system behaviors, and implementation mistakes can corrupt the systems that they are meant to fix. Likewise, while banks' IT systems are designed to be resilient, "hidden" dependencies or environmental changes can undercut the protection against failures that the design was supposed to provide.

Operating and managing IT systems remain a critical concern for financial institutions. Failures can lead to financial and reputational damage and increased regulatory scrutiny. Likewise, time spent remediating problems and doing damage control is time lost on technology improvement and innovation. Yet the

(Continued)

(Continued)

challenge appears to be growing over time, as the pace of technology innovation accelerates. The size and age of financial institutions also play into the likelihood of problems and their severity. The larger the IT environment and the more legacy systems involved, the greater the complexity and the increased likelihood of major IT systems problems unfolding.

Questions

1. Other than implementing IT system resiliency, what steps can banks take to minimize the likelihood of system failures from occurring?
2. What steps can banks take to minimize the impact when system failures occur?
3. Why might the £750 million investment that RBS made to improve its IT systems not have prevented the 2015 incident?
4. Is minimizing IT environment changes a practical strategy for limiting the risks associated with system operation and maintenance?
5. Besides the financial and reputational costs banks pay for service failures related to IT systems, what are some of the other internal costs that can result from these problems?

Sources: Moore, Elaine, "Customers Face Fallout from RBS Failure," *Financial Times*, June 29, 2012, http://www.ft.com/cms/s/0/13ea4bc2-c136-11e1-8eca-00144feabdc0.html; "RBS CEO Hester to Waive Bonus After IT Debacle," Reuters, June 29, 2012, http://www.reuters.com/article/2012/06/29/rbs-hester-bonus-idUSL6E8HTD2J20120629; Dunkley, Emma, "RBS's Tech Wake-up Call to Banks," *Financial Times*, June 17, 2015, http://www.ft.com/intl/cms/s/0/0efa0e4a-1502-11e5-9509-00144feabdc0.html; Dunkley, Emma, "RBS under Pressure over New IT Failure," *Financial Times*, June 17, 2015, http://www.ft.com/intl/cms/s/0/41c4579c-14d8-11e5-a51f-00144feabdc0.html; Dunkley, Emma, Clear Barrett, and John Aglionby, "Royal Bank of Scotland Fined £56m for IT Meltdown," *Financial Times*, November 20, 2014, http://www.ft.com/intl/cms/s/0/3e8d7d5e-7084-11e4-9129-00144feabdc0.html; Dunkley, Emma, "Royal Bank of Scotland Braces for Fines over IT Meltdown," *Financial Times*, November 17, 2014, http://www.ft.com/intl/cms/s/0/7c5458ec-6e45-11e4-bffb-00144feabdc0.html; Masters, Brooke, Elaine Moore, and Jim Pickard, "The Upgrade that Downed Royal Bank of Scotland," *Financial Times*, June 25, 2012, http://www.ft.com/cms/s/0/4ecdb67c-beb9-11e1-b24b-00144feabdc0.html; Arnold, Martin, "HSBC Systems Failure Delays 275,000 Payments," *Financial Times*, August 28, 2015, http://www.ft.com/intl/cms/s/0/9657d306-4d7c-11e5-b558-8a9722977189.html.

5.1 TECHNOLOGY INFRASTRUCTURE

5.1.1 Overview

The following subsections provide descriptions of core technology infrastructure components and their functions. In many cases, simplified explanations are provided that omit technical details, that while relevant, could easily diminish the readability of this chapter. As shown in later figures, infrastructure components can be very simply represented as boxes and lines. Boxes represent physical or logical components and lines represent the connectivity between them and the outside world.

Another way to think about components is by the category of service that they provide and their interdependencies. Figure 5-1 shows a way of representing this as "stacks" of logical components where each stack represents a category; the positioning of the components denote their place in the hierarchy or dependencies on other related components. Some types of components, such as hardware and operating system, networking communications, and software applications, are well suited for this type of representation. However, telecommunication, physical infrastructure, and monitoring and administration components are not easy to categorize this way. Likewise, there can be some overlap. For instance, often storage components, such as network attached storage devices, include CPUs and memory as part of their design so could be categorized as hardware as well as storage.

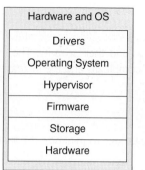
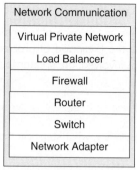
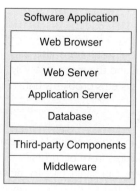

Figure 5-1 Stacks of logical components

It should be kept in mind that while these representations can be useful for high-level conceptualization, they are imprecise. For example, in the Network Communication stack shown in Figure 5-1, it could be argued that network adapters and switches should be at the same level in the stack. In the Software Application stack it is unclear whether third-party components, such as software libraries, and middleware should go above, below, or next to the application server, so they are shown near but separate from the main stack. Nevertheless, in many cases, imperfect but simple representations are often better than overly complicated precise ones.

It is also important to understand that much of the scale and complexity of the infrastructure components and their environments has been omitted. For example, where a single Database box is shown in Figure 5-1, multiple databases from different vendors may be used in practice, and for each vendor, multiple instances and versions may be running. Likewise, the diagrams later in this chapter do not convey that for each hardware component shown, multiple components may actually be running to provide resilience and provide sufficient capacity.

Whole component environments may also be duplicated across different physical locations, such as branches, call centers, regional operational centers, and disaster recovery locations. As well, multiple environments may be replicated within a single location. It is common practice to have separate software development, testing, and production environments, all of which have an implementation of software application stack components. Note, however, that in nonproduction environments, certain stack components differ from the production environment due to cost and connectivity constraints.* For example, SAN storage may be available in the production environment, but not in the development environment, so that local disk storage is used there instead.

5.1.2 Hardware and Operating System Infrastructure

This section reviews the components shown in the Hardware and OS stack shown in Figure 5-1. The components will be discussed in order from bottom to top, to help show how each layer functionally builds upon the others.

5.1.2.1 Hardware

Over the past 20 years, the relative low cost, broad compatibility, and flexibility of operating systems used have made commodity hardware the workhorse of the financial services industry. Generally

---

* This discrepancy sometimes causes software runtime problems to be encountered in production that were not seen in nonproduction environments, and vice versa.

defined as using an IBM-PC compatible central processing unit (CPU), commodity hardware can be sourced from many different vendors and delivered in many different configurations. For the most part, hardware that is tied to just one operating system—such was the case with Sun Microsystems in the 1990s—have fallen by the wayside, with Apple Macintosh being the exception. Similarly, mini- or midrange computers, such as the IBM AS/400 and its descendants, have gained only limited traction in banking.

At the other end of the spectrum from commodity hardware, mainframe computers have maintained their dominance in certain areas of financial services, mainly core banking and payments. The strength of mainframes is in their ability to process extremely high volumes of transactions and in their overall reliability. Their weakness lies in the orientation toward batch processing and its relative difficulty integrating with non-mainframe systems. Mainframes are also very expensive to purchase, operate, and maintain. Yet the cost and risk of migrating critical applications from mainframes to commodity hardware are more than most financial institutions can handle.

5.1.2.2 Storage

Persistent data storage is the foundation of IT systems. It is where information is managed and maintained. Many people think of the hard drives in their personal computers or external USB drives as the primary means of data storage. In the enterprise context, they are less relevant, and in some ways problematic. From a security standpoint, it is paramount that sensitive data be tracked and protected. That goal is much more easily achieved when sensitive data is stored in a centralized location rather than distributed across the local storage on hundreds, or possibly thousands, of individual workstations. Likewise, ensuring that the integrity of data is maintained through backups is much simpler if data storage is centralized rather than distributed.

In place of local disk drives, smaller operations may use network attached storage (NAS) devices. NAS provides a collection of disk drives that appear to be a single logical shared file system. NAS disk arrays are generally configured as redundant arrays of independent disks (RAID), to ensure that if a single disk fails, the information stored on it can be recovered from redundant information that is stored on the other disks.

Larger institutions generally use storage area networks (SANs) as their primary storage of application and enterprise data. Whereas a NAS is a single hardware device that houses and manages multiple disks, a SAN is a coordinated group of devices that manage multiple disks that are typically linked together over a dedicated private network. SANs are commonly connected to computer servers with fiber-optic cables over which the high-performance Fiber Channel network protocol is used. Like NAS, SAN provides RAID resiliency and may include different types of disk storage, i.e., both fast and slow hard disk drives. More expensive, fast disks within a SAN are usually allocated to performance-sensitive applications such as databases that software applications rely upon. On the other hand, slow disks within a SAN are allocated to less critical functions, such as on-disk backup or archival storage.

One of the principle benefits of using a SAN, is that it implements storage virtualization, where many different storage devices are made to appear as a single storage service. Centralization improves the efficiency of management and provision of storage resources. A single logical storage service can support a wide range of applications, at the same time hiding the details underlying storage implementation. This enables storage devices to be added to increase overall capacity in a way that does not impact the hosts and applications that are making use of the SAN.

Tape backup systems, another type of storage, are used typically for two purposes: to back up data that is stored on hard disk and to archive information so that it no longer needs to be stored on hard disk drives. Tape backup serves as a means of recovery in case of storage device failures or catastrophic disk failures or data corruption. If the tapes are stored offsite, which is generally advisable, they can also enable recovery in disaster scenarios, such as if an entire site were rendered inoperable by fire or flood.

5.1.2.3 Firmware

Firmware refers to the low-level instructions that are "baked into" computer hardware and used to load the operating system when the computer is turned on or rebooted. Firmware is usually written to persistent programmable memory chips on the computer circuit boards. Firmware may need to be updated periodically and, thus, require patching the hardware itself as well as the operating system running on the hardware. Upgrading firmware is typically more involved and risky than patching operating systems. If something goes wrong during the upgrade process, the entire hardware device can be rendered inoperative.

5.1.2.4 Hypervisors

Many financial institutions make use of host virtualization, where multiple "virtual" servers are run together on the same hardware. Each virtual server, also referred to as a virtual machine, is instantiated as an operating system that shares the physical server's resources—microprocessors, memory, disk, network connectivity, and hardware peripherals—with other operating system instances running on the same physical server. The hypervisor is the operating system that manages and coordinates the different virtual servers' interaction with the hardware. A simplified analogy would be to think of virtual servers as clouds in the sky and the hypervisor as the sky itself.

The hypervisor loads and runs different virtual machines, which are stored on disk as bootable operating systems and their file systems. They may also be stored as runtime images that reflect the state of the operating system and running applications at the time the image is snapshotted and saved. For each virtual machine the hypervisor controls:

- the number of microprocessor cores on the physical server that are accessible or dedicated to a virtual machine;

- network access to other systems that the physical server is connected to;

- network access to other virtual machines running within the hypervisor;

- the amount of physical memory that is available; and

- the amount of physical disk space that is available.

Virtualization enables many different software applications to run in their own dedicated operating system environment on the same physical hardware. This avoids the problems encountered when running multiple applications on the same physical server with a single operating system. Applications running in the same operating system may encounter incompatibilities within that environment and may have runtime behaviors that interfere with one another. Virtualization also enabled better economies of scale for commodity hardware systems. Fewer, more powerful servers could be used, saving space, power, and cooling resources, and providing fewer physical servers to manage and maintain. Virtualized servers can also make more efficient use of CPU computing power and available memory. Hence, many institutions are moving away from using standalone servers toward virtualized ones.

Figure 5-2 shows how virtualized and standalone servers compare from a logical architecture standpoint. Whereas standalone physical servers run a single operating system, multiple virtualized operating systems (virtual machines) are run within a single physical server (the host system). The hypervisor hosts multiple virtual machines, each of which will, in turn, have software applications that run within its virtualized operating system environment. For the most part, applications running within virtual machines will not be aware that they are not running on a standalone server. Furthermore, the multiple different types and versions of operating systems can be run side by side within a virtual

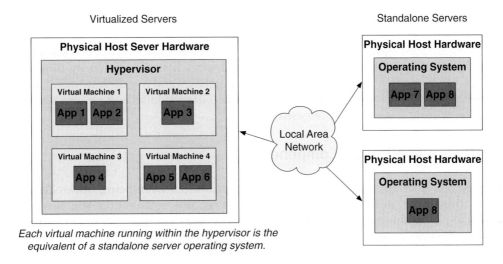

Figure 5-2 A comparison of virtualized and standalone servers

server host. For example, the hypervisor running within a virtual server host could run both Windows 8, Windows 10, and Linux virtual machines.

For all the benefits that virtualization provides, there are a few downsides. One is that hardware failures or downtime required, possibly for operating system upgrades or patching, on the physical host system will affect multiple virtual servers and the applications that are running on them. In comparison, the impact on standalone servers is limited to a single operating system and one set of applications. Another downside is that it is easy for virtual machines to proliferate, because usually adding a new virtual machine does not immediately require purchase of new hardware. However, over time, uncontrolled growth of new virtual machines can greatly increase capacity requirements for storage, memory, and CPU. Growth in the number of virtual machines leads to increased system management and patching effort, and capacity monitoring in a virtualized environment can be more complicated than it is in an environment purely made up of physical servers.

5.1.2.5 Operating systems

The operating system is the framework that enables applications to access the microprocessor to execute program instructions and memory, and provides access, in conjunction with drivers, to other hardware devices such as disk drives, displays, and network interfaces. Typically, operating systems provide high-level interfaces to these resources. For example, operating systems present disk drives as file systems rather than specific sectors on physical disks. Common operating systems used in financial services are Linux and Microsoft Windows used on commodity server and workstation hardware, and z/OS used on mainframe hardware. Linux is also run on mainframe computers, but it is much more commonly run on commodity hardware. Microsoft Windows dominates the desktop environment, although there are pockets of desktop users running Mac OSX on Macintosh hardware. Linux and Microsoft Windows are the predominant operating systems running on commodity hardware servers.

Operating system patches are released quite frequently, on a weekly or monthly basis, and occasionally on an ad hoc basis to address newly discovered, critical flaws. They typically address bugs and security vulnerabilities. Major operating system upgrades occur anywhere from an annual basis to occurring every few years. Upgrades provide new features and functions, and may significantly change the behavior of the underlying platforms that software applications run on, in some cases requiring applications to also be upgraded so that they can run on a new version of the operating system.

5.1.2.6 Drivers

Various drivers are used by the operating system to provide a common way of accessing the network, peripherals, databases, printers, scanners, and other devices that are offered by different vendors. Alternatively, other types of drivers, such as those for databases and middleware components, may be loaded directly by software applications. Drivers can become outdated and require upgrades as new versions of the operating systems are released.

5.1.3 Software Application Components

Over the past few decades, software applications have shifted from being thick-client standalone systems to thin-client multi-tiered applications. It is not uncommon for modern banking applications to rely upon more than four different technology components to perform its function. This section will review some of the more common components used to run software applications. The components described here underlie the channel-services architecture described in Chapter 3.

5.1.3.1 Databases

Relational databases (RDBs) are the primary means by which software applications store and manipulate information. Both commercial and open-source RDBs are available and used extensively within homegrown applications as well as packaged third-party applications. Storage of application data in an RDB provides centralized persistent storage that can be readily used for information management and reporting purposes. Applications usually interact with RDBs dynamically using a query language, such as structured query language (SQL), or using stored procedures, which is query language code that is compiled and stored as runtime procedures within the RDB. Using stored procedures is preferable.

Besides managing application data, RDBs are often used for storing parameters that applications use to determine how they will operate during runtime. By changing the parameter values in the database, system operators can change an application's behavior without having to make changes to the source code and then building and deploying a new application. For example, the foreign currencies supported by a banking application would likely be defined as a parameter in an RDB rather than as a static list that is included in the source code. This design allows new currencies to be added and existing currencies removed with minimal effort, i.e. by executing a SQL command.

Typically, software applications will access one or more databases. One database is the primary one used to store its information, whereas the others may provide supplemental information or transactional capabilities. Most databases are run in the same physical location as other application components. While it is possible to access databases over wide area network (WAN) connections, communication delays can significantly impair the overall application performance.

Beyond relational databases, other types of databases are also used for specific purposes. Column-oriented databases are commonly used for storing large volumes of market data pricing information, often in memory instead of on disk, to provide super-fast processing and retrieval, which are important for algorithmic trading applications. NoSQL databases are another type of nonrelational databases that are popular for big data applications. NoSQL databases manage data across a multitude of commodity servers, enabling high scalability and resilience.

5.1.3.2 Application servers

Application servers typically are where the business logic is implemented in tiered software applications. Application servers are usually runtime engines that execute programming language instructions. However, they may also work with higher-level, graphical languages that are converted to Java or other machine-level language instructions. For example, the component that "runs" the instructions defined in process orchestration or business process management languages, as discussed in Chapter 2, is effectively serving as an application server.

The goal of storing the business logic in the application server, rather than in the database or the application display logic, is to centralize where it is kept. This approach reduces maintenance effort. For example, imagine if there was a requirement to change the interest rate calculation in a banking application. Ideally, the calculation would be contained in a single function in the source code that application server executes. That said, in practice it would not be uncommon for the calculation to be in multiple functions in the application server. However, it would be more problematic, from a maintenance standpoint, for the calculation logic to also be implemented in the database in the form of a stored procedure and/or the frontend application code that is managed and executed by the web servers.

Finding and changing the business logic becomes more complicated and involved if the logic is outside of the application server. Usually one type of software developer will write programming code for the application server, whereas other types of developers write code for the database and web servers. Hence, a one-person job can turn into a two- or three-person job. Also, instead of having to just deploy one component, an application server module to make the change, database and web server modules may also need to be deployed.

That said, in practice, there are times when it does make sense to implement business logic in other components, usually for performance or efficiency reasons. In some cases, business logic will be implemented in stored procedures where calculations need to be applied across large sets of data. It is less efficient to try to extract large volumes of data and manipulate it externally, than have the database apply the calculations to the data directly. Likewise, often business logic validation will be applied in the frontend code that the web server executes, to speed up the user interface. It is much faster for the user interface code to do some simple checks—for example, using the Luhn algorithm* to determine if a credit card number is well formed—than to make a call to the application server over the network to do the same validation.

5.1.3.3 Web servers

Unlike an application server, which can provide service over a number of different interfaces and communication protocols, web servers provide service for HTTP requests, receiving and return HTML content, which is typically displayed by the requestor in a web browser. Web servers can deliver static, predefined web page content or can deliver dynamic, programmatically generated content. Typically, scripts—such as Java Server Pages (JSP), Active Server Pages (ASP), and Common Gateway Interface (CGI) scripts—running on the web server will support and provide functions for generating dynamic HTML based on parameters they receive as part of the request. In many cases these scripts will make requests to an application server to retrieve information or perform calculations.

5.1.3.4 Middleware

Middleware is a somewhat open-ended term, but in this context it will be considered as the communication components that "glue" all the other components together. Communication protocols, such as web services or representational state transfer (ReST) interfaces are a very simple form of message-oriented middleware (MOM), providing the capability for higher-level communication —i.e. transferring records and fields, rather than encoded bytestreams— between application components. For instance, implementations of the Java Message Service (JMS) provides features such as message queuing and supports both point-to-point and publish-subscribe delivery paradigms. Message brokers, beyond providing connectivity between applications, also provide basic message transformation capabilities.

---

* The Luhn algorithm is a checksum formula that is used to validate credit card and other identification numbers.

5.1.3.5 Web browsers

Web browsers have evolved to become the primary user interface for thin-client applications. The introduction of HTML version five provided capabilities that enabled more complex and user-friendly applications to be developed with greater ease using HTML and run in web browsers. Yet, for all the benefits that web browsers provide application developers, they come with their own set of complecations as well. Code compatibility between different browsers and different versions of the same browser can vary. An application that works in the Chrome browser may not display well or certain functions may not work in the Internet Explorer browser, or vise versa.

Where financial institutions provide browser-based applications to the public, there is no control over what browser and browser version customers will use. This requires extensive compatibility testing for each new major release or laying down very limiting requirements, such as only one particular browser is supported and only specific versions of that browser. Where thin-client applications are used internally within an institution, the browser type and version can be more easily controlled, helping to reduce the amount of testing that is required. However, the challenge arises when the version of the browser used reaches its end of support and it is necessary to upgrade to a newer version of the browser. This necessitates testing and making compatibility changes to potentially hundreds of internal web-based applications, which is no small undertaking and may take many months to complete. Generally, banks do not have the option of continuing to use unsupported browsers in the long term, because they no longer receive security updates.

The other challenge that thin-client applications face using browsers is accommodating multiple screen sizes. Historically, browser-based applications were designed for desktop-sized screens. As web browsers on mobile phones and tablets became popular, in many cases, companies designed separate websites and applications for smaller-screen, mobile devices. This led to two challenges. First, two separate sets of source code had to be maintained, one for desktop-sized screens and another for mobile phones. Second, mobile devices came in many sizes so a single version of a mobile website might fit well on a small mobile phone, but be less effective on a notepad- or tablet-sized device. Development frameworks that support responsive web design have addressed this problem by allowing a single version of the source code that allows the framework to automatically adapt the content and display structure to the size of the user's display.

5.1.3.6 External interfaces and APIs

It should be said that no application is an island, or at least relatively few are. Applications often need to interface with other internal applications, third-party service providers, and cloud-based services. This creates another layer of complexity and introduces additional change-related risk. The behavior of third-party interfaces may change, causing software applications to break or behave differently. A vendor or third party may also stop supporting an interface version that is currently in use by an application, requiring it to upgrade to a newer version, which in turn necessitates regression testing of, potential changes to, and redeployment of applications that access the interface.

5.1.4 Communication Infrastructure

5.1.4.1 Network communications

Network communications is the backbone of IT systems. It enables interconnectivity between applications, client-to-server communications, and the development of distributed applications. A number of different components support network communications.

5.1.4.1.1 Ethernet connectivity

To provide local area network (LAN) communication, network switches, hubs, and network interface cards (NIC) facilitate communication over physical cables or radio waves. Typically financial institutions eschew using wireless LANs and prefer physical connectivity because physical connectivity is more secure. Physical access control measures, such as door locks, are an added layer of security limiting access to wired networks. While in theory, encryption can be used to protect wireless LANs, in practice, wireless LAN encryption has been found to have vulnerabilities.

Network switches and hubs serve as a central point for connecting multiple devices that have NICs that support the Ethernet communication protocol. Hubs allow all the network traffic to flow between all the devices they are connected to. Switches limit the network traffic such that each device sees to that which is destined for it, and filters out traffic destined for other devices. Hence, switches provide a more efficient form of distribution and have superseded hubs for providing Ethernet connectivity. A hypervisor may also implement a virtual switch to manage network traffic between virtual machines that run within the hypervisor.

5.1.4.1.2 Routers

Network routers link together disparate LANs (also known as network segments), and route network traffic between them. They also provide connectivity to WANs, such as the Internet. Routers determine where to deliver messages on LANs based on Internet protocol (IP) addresses, which are assigned to each device on the network. Routers may be very simple, such as those that are used for home networks, which usually include switch functionality in the same hardware device. Alternatively, they may be more sophisticated, such as those used by enterprises. More advanced routers and network switches provide virtual LAN (VLAN) capabilities. VLANs are individual network segments that are configured within the router or managed switch. The Ethernet ports connected to the router can be arbitrarily configured to be part of a particular VLAN. VLANs provide tremendous flexibility without having to physically change the cabling on devices or add additional network hardware.

5.1.4.1.3 Load balancers

Network load balancers are used to distribute network traffic, such as inbound requests to a web server, across multiple servers that can respond to those requests. The load balancer makes it look to the requestors that there is only one server to connect to, while behind the scenes it forwards the requests to an available resource to fulfill the request. The load balancer also forwards the responses from the server back to the requestor. Usually the load balancing will be limited to specific types of services, such as web server traffic, and from specific sources, i.e., the Internet.

5.1.4.1.4 Firewalls

Firewalls are used to restrict the flow of network traffic between devices connected to the network. Firewalls are most commonly implemented as network devices that forward or block network traffic, but also can be implemented as software on servers or workstations that protect only that computer. A hypervisors may also implement a virtualized firewall to protect the virtual machines that are running within the hypervisor. Firewalls can be configured to allow or deny network message traffic:

- between networks;
- between networks and specific network devices; and
- between specific network devices.

While firewalls are effective tools for controlling access to networks and IT systems, they can also become impediments to implementing new systems. Newly installed or deployed software applications may require network connectivity that is blocked by default by firewalls. Accordingly, their testing and operation may be delayed until the required access is configured in the firewalls, which often may require additional administrative procedures and approvals, as discussed later in Section 5.2.1.2.

Firewalls can also allow or restrict traffic on specific network ports. A network port is a logical "channel" that network devices use for specific purposes, similar to how there are numeric television channels. While some ports can be used for any purpose, other ports have defined services associated with them. For example, web clients send HTTP requests to web servers' port 80. Secure shell, which is used for remote logins, uses port 22. By restricting network traffic access to specific ports on specific servers, firewalls help prevent illicit use of services on the computers they protect. For example, a web server might have a known security vulnerability associated with its secure shell implementation. By having a firewall block all network access to port 22 and allowing access to port 80 on the web server would effectively mitigate the risk of the security vulnerability while still allowing the server to perform its primary function.

5.1.4.1.5 Virtual private network

A virtual private network (VPN) is commonly used for providing secure external access for employees and connectivity to third parties. A VPN creates an encrypted session between computers or networks over public or unsecured networks. For employees connecting remotely, usually VPN client software is installed on laptops that connect to VPN gateways that reside at the financial institution. Often second-factor authentication mechanisms, such as hardware tokens that generate unique one-time passcodes, will be used in conjunction with the VPN client software to provide additional security. Alternatively, a VPN connection may be set up between VPN hardware gateways at two locations. For example, instead of utilizing dedicated connectivity to a vendor or customer via leased phone lines, less critical connections may use VPN connections to securely communicate over the public Internet.

5.1.4.2 Telecommunications

While Internet connectivity often comes to mind when thinking about communication technology in financial services, telephone communication is still prevalent. Telephones are used for internal communications and communication with customers. Customer phone communications may be routed to individual staff members, routed to call centers, or handled by automated response units.

5.1.4.2.1 Telephone exchange

The telephone exchange, also referred to as a private branch exchange (PBX) or phone switch, is the primary component that links phone headsets and automated response units with the external public switched telephone network. The exchange will connect to one or more trunk lines from telecommunication companies and allow line connections to be shared by many telephone stations. It will also link to other systems such as automated response units and dialers. The telephone exchange system is the heart of an organization's phone communications and is a critical system component.

5.1.4.2.2 Automated response unit

Automated response units (ARUs), also referred to as interactive voice response (IVR) and voice response units (VRUs), commonly are used handle customers' service requests in place of or prior to interactions with customer service agents. ARUs enable customers to enter and retrieve information about their account using the keypad of a touchtone phone or by saying voice commands which the ARU will respond to with prerecorded or computer-generated speech. ARUs have programmable menu options and are integrated with the phone exchange system and other information systems, such as the core banking system.

ARUs enable customers to perform common transactions without having to talk with an agent. In turn, ARUs reduce the number of calls that agents in a call center need to process, so that fewer agents are required. ARU can also provide round-the-clock service cost effectively. Even if customers ultimately need to talk with agents, ARUs help by capturing customer information, such as account numbers, before the agent answers the call, saving the agents time that would otherwise be spent during the call to get this information. If the ARU is integrated with the software that the agent is using, the information collected can be used to automatically retrieve the customer account information for the agent so that he or she is ready to provide service when the call is connected.

5.1.4.2.3 Dialer

Financial institutions that have extensive outbound calling requirements, such as those that perform debt collection, may choose to invest in a predictive dialer. The dialer is fed a list of telephone numbers that it automatically dials and, if a connection is made, will route the call to an agent. Predictive dialers maximize the likelihood that an agent will be available to answer a connected call by analyzing the the time taken to complete call activities and the frequency of call connections, and adjusting the outbound call rate accordingly. Eliminating the need for agents to manually dial numbers and ensuring that time spent between calls is minimized greatly increases call center efficiency, enabling more calls to be made with fewer people.

5.1.4.3 External connectivity

All financial institutions require external connectivity to communicate with customers, service providers, other financial institutions, and regulators. Leased lines are commonly used to provide dedicated links between different locations and can be used to provide telephone or network connectivity. Unlike regular phone lines, leased lines only provide continuous connectivity between two locations and do not have a phone number associated with them. T-1 communication lines that provide a data transmission rate of 1.544 Mbit per second, supporting up to 24 voice channels, are commonly used to provide leased line services. The capacity of a leased line can be split between voice and data connections. In all but small institutions, leased lines are typically used to connect to Internet service providers (ISPs) and for call center connectivity.

As an alternative to supplementing leased lines, financial institutions may contract with telecommunication providers to use their packet-switched networks, such as multiprotocol label switching (MPLS), to provide connectivity between multiple sites. In this case, there are not dedicated fixed-bandwidth connections between sites. Instead, the telecommunication provider is responsible for routing information, voice or data, through nodes through its internal network while meeting agreed service levels related to capacity and latency.

Figure 5-3 shows a simplified example of how network connectivity could be configured between multiple sites and with a mission-critical third-party services provider, such as a vendor that is hosting the core banking system. Multiple communication links to and from multiple data centers are used to prevent the failure of any one communication link or data from disrupting service. Note that the satellite office does not have its own ISP connection. Instead, requests for Internet access from the satellite office would be routed over the MPLS network to one of the other locations, to use the other office's Internet connection.

It is not uncommon to use a combination of leased line and packet-switched communications to provide redundancy. Likewise, redundant leased lines may be provisioned from multiple carriers to avoid the risk that the failure of a single carrier would cause a break in service. Failures involving external connectivity have the potential to render call centers and Internet banking websites unreachable by customers. Redundancy provided by using different telecommunication providers must also consider the physical location of their cables and switching centers. If two different providers share the same fiber optic cable and it is cut by accident during construction work, resilience will not be achieved.

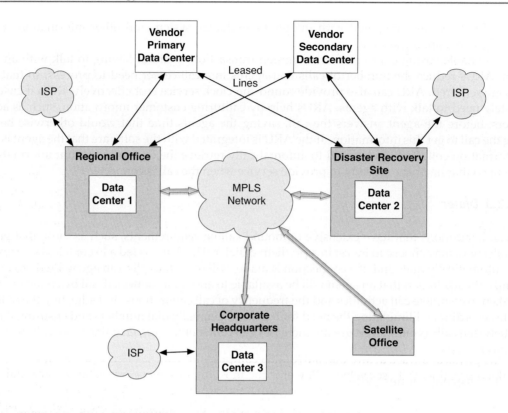

Figure 5-3 External network connectivity

Likewise, similar problems will occur if the providers' switching centers are in the same geographic area, which is impacted by a widespread power outage.

5.1.5 Core and Peripheral Components

In addition to the infrastructure components discussed in the previous sections, there are a plethora of other components that are vital for normal business operations. Some of these systems include:

- core banking
- customer relationship management
- accounting
- imaging and image storage
- statistical analysis/risk analysis
- internal email, instant messaging and calendar management
- external email gateways
- customer email distribution
- master data management
- content management

- system monitoring and management

- domain name service (DNS)

- directory services—e.g., Lightweight Directory Access Protocol (LDAP)

- system availability/performance monitoring

- cybersecurity monitoring and management (discussed further in Chapter 17)

- time synchronization service

Beyond the infrastructure within financial institutions, the infrastructure utilized by third-party service providers is also a critical dependency. Examples of important third-party providers include core banking system providers, payment processors, email distributors, and mobile short message service (SMS) aggregators and distributors. As a case in point, in January of 2013, customers at a number of Canadian banks—including Royal Bank of Canada, TD Canada Trust and CIBC—were unable to process Visa credit card transactions because of a power disruption in the data center of a third-party service provider. The provider, Total System Services, was used by Visa to process authorizations for credit card transactions in Canada [2].

5.1.6 Physical Infrastructure

Often the physical infrastructure that surrounds computer systems is often taken for granted, yet it is critical to operation of those systems. Power is the most important concern. The power requirements for a financial institution's data centers can be enormous, and in some cases can reach levels beyond what is available in a particular geographic area, especially if other data centers nearby have high or growing power consumption requirements. Power outages must be catered for, usually by using a combination of uninterruptible power supplies (UPS), which provide short-term power continuity, usually measured in minutes. UPS may be implemented through multiple units that serve individual server racks, or as centralized units that supply large portions of the entire data center. UPS are usually further backed up by diesel power generators that can provide power for days, assuming the availability of fuel.

Heating, ventilation, and air conditioning (HVAC) is a close second to power in terms of importance to the systems operating in a data center. Computer and communications hardware generate a large amount of heat that needs to be dissipated. Overheating in a single machine rack or across a data center can cause equipment to malfunction or possibly become damaged on a small or widespread scale. Centralized cooling and heating units are typically used to maintain the temperature of a data center within acceptable levels. Machine racks and the hardware within the racks may be oriented so that heat output from hardware flows toward specific "hot" and away from "cold" aisles. Air conditioning units will feed cool air in to the cold aisles and draw warm air from the hot aisles. Cooling capacity should be in excess of current requirements to accommodate the addition of new hardware or replacement of existing hardware with units that generate higher levels of heat. Likewise, the outside temperature may increase, placing additional stress on air conditioning units.

Fire detection and suppression capabilities are also important. Detection can be achieved through the use of smoke and heat monitoring as well as more advanced very early smoke detection alert (VESDA) systems. VESDA systems suck in air from the data center and sample the quality continuously using a laser-based sensor that can detect fires before combustion occurs, such as when wires are smoldering. Fire suppression is commonly achieved using sprinkler or clean agent systems. Sprinklers have heat-sensitive valves that will release water when the temperature exceeds a specific threshold. The release of water on computer systems will usually damage them, resulting in extended downtime for the hardware affected, so clean agent systems flood the affected area with gas that can reduce the temperature and the availability of oxygen that the fire feeds on. While clean agent systems are more expensive to install and maintain than sprinklers, in case of fire, they cause less damage and downtime.

Data centers also may have environmental and video surveillance monitoring. Environmental monitoring may include heat, moisture, humidity, and airflow. Video cameras are commonly placed at the entrance and exits of data centers and sometimes within a data center in the isles between hardware racks for security purposes. Individual racks may also have cameras monitoring access to hardware within them.

Many or all of the systems mentioned have network interfaces that provide status information. Accordingly, an abundance of real-time data is available for monitoring the health of physical systems. Furthermore, individual hardware components may also have temperature sensors that can generate alerts if heat thresholds are exceeded.

5.2 MANAGING TECHNOLOGY OPERATIONS AND INFRASTRUCTURE

Managing IT infrastructure can be likened to having to continually clean and replace mechanical parts on a commercial jet while it is flying with passengers onboard. Customer expectations to have 24/7 access to online services have raised the bar that financial institutions must meet in managing their infrastructure and IT operations. Likewise, the complexity of the underlying technology that supports online services and the rate it is changing have been steadily increasing. This combination presents a major challenge for financial institutions.

The management of IT operations and infrastructure will to a large extent determine the quality and reliability of the services it offers to customers. Having an operational framework that addresses considerations such as competence, control, consistency, capacity, cost, agility, and customer focus is important to help align the capabilities and services provided by IT with the institution's overall business strategy.* Competence and capacity concerns relate to technical skills and resources being able to meet current and future business needs. Operational controls address regulatory requirements and help mitigate other types of operational risk, helping to ensure consistency, i.e., service levels will be maintained at specified levels. For example, banks usually restrict system administration access to the servers in their production Internet banking environment to a very small subset of IT staff. This operational control helps reduce the chance that someone who is unqualified or unfamiliar with that environment from inadvertently making a change that disrupts online banking services.

Policies, procedures, and standards, as discussed in Chapters 2 and 3, also support management of IT operating environments. Policies provide guidelines for what and how things should be done, helping to avoid confusion and prevent conflicting actions. Procedures provide detailed instructions for performing specific activities, so that they are performed consistently and as intended. Standards reduce variability. Generally, heterogeneity of IT infrastructure is undesirable because it increases the breadth of skills that are required to maintain and support the environment. For example, it is common for banks to set standards as to which vendor's database product should be used, when a choice is available. This approach better allows a knowledge competency to be developed and leveraged for that technology. It also reduces the number of different products that need to be updated and patched and the number of vendor relationships that must be maintained. However, having fewer vendors can limit the choices available and potentially lead to vendor lock-in.

Risk management is an important part of technology management. The list of potential technology-related problems that could occur is never-ending. On the other hand, financial and human resources are limited. Thus, as discussed in Chapter 18, it is necessary to evaluate both internal and external risks in terms of their likelihood and impact, and prioritize them accordingly. Ideally, controls would be put in place to mitigate the risks that have the highest priority. Unfortunately, the practicality and cost of risk mitigation are also considerations that come into play. Hence, mitigating controls will only be implemented for the

* For more discussion on these considerations, see the chapter on Managing Technology and Operations in *Bank Management: A Decision-making Perspective* by Koch, MacDonald, and Duran (Singapore: Cengage Learning Asia, 2013) (ISBN: 978-981-4416-13-9).

set of risks that are of sufficiently high severity and which can be practicably addressed. In the context of IT infrastructure, many of the risks are related to failures that cause service downtime.

A cross-industry estimate of the average total cost of unplanned data center outages in 2016 was $8,851 per minute and the average duration of partial and total outages was 95 minutes [3]. Figure 5-4 shows the root causes of unplanned outages from a 2016 study, with infrastructure-related problems—IT equipment, UPS, HVAC, and generator failures—accounting for over half of the downtime cost. Besides cybercrime-related downtime, which is also discussed in Chapter 17, human error and

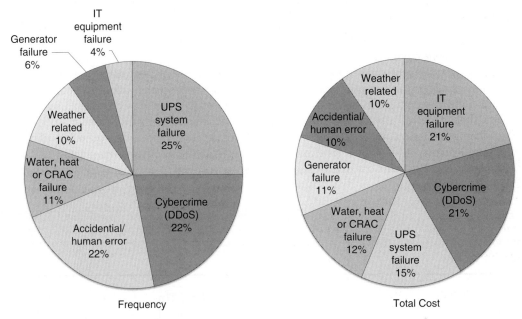

CRAC: Computer room air conditioner
DDoS: Distributed denial of service (see Chapter 17 for more information).

Figure 5-4 Underlying causes of unplanned outages

Case 5-2

The Causes and Costs of Data Center Outages

A cross-industry study of the cost of unplanned data center outages of organizations in the United States found that their cost averaged around $740,000 per incident. The maximum sum reported totaled over $2,400,000 and a downtime of over two hours. Overall, the cost of outages had increased by 38% between the first study in 2010 and the third one in 2016. Business disruption and lost revenue were the main factors behind the costs, representing 63% of the outage cost, followed by reductions in end-user productivity and IT productivity, which represented 27%.

While in all of the studies UPS system failure was the most common cause of unplanned data center outages, it was not the greatest contributor to outage costs. On the contrary, IT equipment failure had the greatest cost impact, even though it had, in 2016, the lowest rate of occurrence (see Figure 5-4). This implies that although IT equipment failure is less common, when it does occur the duration of the outage caused

(Continued)

(Continued)

by it is longer than other types of outages. This is not too surprising since IT equipment failures could be caused by problems in any one of many different layers, such as the CPU hardware, network connectivity, operating system, or software application components. Often identifying the root cause of IT equipment failure can be a long and arduous process, and rarely can fixes be put in place until the underlying problem is sufficiently understood. Also, after the initial problem has been fixed, there may be follow-on issues that must be addressed. For instance, in 2016, the Singapore Exchange suffered a disk failure that caused trading to be halted for the good part of a day. The failover from the primary to the secondary system was performed within an hour of when the problem occurred. However, application-level issues caused by the failover, where clearing confirmation messages were not sent or were sent multiple times, required trading to be halted so that clearing members could reconcile their orders.

Interestingly, cybercrime showed the greatest increase in the cause of data center outages. Distributed denial of service (DDoS) attacks can flood the external network connections with data centers as well as overwhelm software components, such as web and DNS servers, so that they are unable to service other requests. Cyber attacks represented only 2% of outages in 2010, whereas they grew to 18% in 2013, and 22% in 2016. Throughout the studies, human error remained relatively constant, causing around 23% of outages.

Of the 15 industry segments, the total cost of unplanned data center outages was greatest for financial services. Hence, financial institutions have plenty of incentive to take steps to ensure that their IT infrastructure is resilient.

Source: Ponemon Institute, "Cost of Data Center Outages," January 2016, http://www.emersonnetworkpower.com/en-US/Resources/Market/Data-Center/Latest-Thinking/Ponemon/Pages/2016-Cost-of-Data-Center-Outages-Report.aspx; Hui, C. "SGX trading outage caused by disk failure", *Channel News Asia*, July 19, 2016, http://www.channelnewsasia.com/news/singapore/sgx-trading-outage-caused/2967760.html.

weather-related failures accounted for the rest of the downtime. This information sets the stage for the discussion in Case Study 5-2 and the subsections that follow. Infrastructure maintenance and support will be considered in the context of how infrastructure failures can be prevented or curtailed. IT environment management strategies that help prevent human error will be reviewed. IT system resilience will be discussed in the context of how it can help prevent downtime from IT system failures and weather-related problems. The managing of the human element of IT operations is examined. Finally, considerations related to using to outsourced and cloud platforms are reviewed.

5.2.1 Infrastructure Maintenance and Support

The Center for Internet Security's Cyber Hygiene campaign sums up security best practices in five words: count, configure, control, patch, and repeat [4]. These topics will be discussed more in the security context in Chapter 17, but in this section these practices, except for configuration, will be examined in terms of their impact on IT operations. *Counting* equates to IT asset management, *control* to change management, and *patching* to system updates and upgrades. The *repeat* imperative somewhat conflicts with the operational objective of minimizing changes to help ensure stability. Unfortunately, stasis is not an option. Financial institutions' risks from cybercrime require that security-related maintenance be given high priority, but also be balanced with other operational management considerations.

5.2.1.1 IT Asset management

IT asset management sounds simple and straightforward, but in practice can become quite onerous. Knowing what hardware is connected to the network and what software is running on that hardware is an ongoing battle when users can easily plug or unplug a laptop to or from a LAN or install new software on a workstation or server. From a security standpoint, IT asset management is important for identifying unauthorized devices that may present a threat or serve as a vector for attack. All IT systems have vulnerabilities and regular patching helps address that risk. However, hardware and software components that are not accounted for may not be patched, causing them to be greater risks.

The components discussed in Section 5.1—hardware, network, telecommunications equipment, as well as software application components and the applications themselves are a multitude of things that need to be cataloged and tracked. Besides IT equipment directly owned by the institution, components and systems managed or maintained by third parties that reside on the institution's network must also be considered. In some cases, IT asset management is achieved through manual tracking. Spreadsheets can serve as the registry and may be manually updated periodically. Alternatively, automated asset management solutions provide a more robust solution, whereby software is used to catalog active IT systems and inventory their contents, storing the information in a database that supports reporting and analysis.

5.2.1.2 IT environment change management

Change management, also referred to as change control, in financial institutions' technology environments is critical for maintaining stability and security. Properly evaluating changes' potential effects and controlling their implementation reduce the risk of accidents that might disrupt service or compromise security. The greater the importance of the system environment, the greater the need for change management. For example, in a bank's development environment, developers may make changes to development servers with little consideration. If they inadvertently impair the server by making a change, the impact is limited to the developers using that server. On the other hand, a system administrator making changes on the production network will have more demanding change management requirements, since error made there could potentially cripple key business systems.

The main activities in an IT change control process are notification of the change through a change request, oversight and governance to approve the change, and controlling the implementation of the change. The information that may be contained in a request is:

- what the change is;
- if the change has been already tested in other environments;
- why the change is required;
- who will make the change;
- when the change will be made;
- how the change will be verified once applied;
- the steps that are performed to implement the change;
- what the recovery steps are in case something goes wrong with, or because of, the change;
- what risks are associated with the change; and
- if any business service will be disrupted or impacted during the implementation of the change.

This documentation serves both as a procedure for executing the change that can be easily reviewed and also serves as a record of what changes were made for audit purposes. It also provides accountability if something goes wrong as to what process was followed in evaluating and approving the change. The request notifications and their approvals may be managed on paper, electronically through email and spreadsheets, or using a software system.

Typically, a change advisory board, composed of IT and business representatives, will be notified of the change request and will be responsible for evaluating the rationale for making the change and risk associated with the change request. The review process may elicit additional information about the change and ultimately the request will be approved, if appropriate. Periodic change review meetings are often used to review batches of change requests, rather than deal with each request one by one.

Control over the implementation of changes is in many cases achieved using manual procedures whereby the person who will be making the change is trained to not perform any changes to a particular environment or system without receiving prior approval for the change request. This is less than ideal, since it is still possible—if steps of the change management process are intentionally or unintentionally bypassed—for production environment changes to be made without completing the change management process. For example, under the pressure of trying to fix a problem that has taken the Internet banking system offline, a system administrator may make a change on one of the production servers, forgetting that he should have gotten proper approval to do so first. Completely preventing such situations is difficult; however, tools such as file and configuration integrity monitoring systems can help detect when changes have been made unexpectedly, potentially indicating that the change management process may not have been followed.

5.2.1.3 System updates and upgrades

From an operations standpoint, because changes can break working system environments, it is best to make changes as infrequently as possible. From a system update and upgrade perspective, changes would only be made if they provided material benefit that offset the risk of making the changes. For example, if a software update, also referred to as a patch, was issued by a software vendor, the patch would only be applied if it was a known problem that was affecting users or addressed a imminent security risk. Likewise, if a new version of the software became available, the software would only be upgraded if the new features were of significant value to users. Unfortunately, this model does not hold in most financial services IT environments.

As highlighted by the Center for Internet Security's Cyber Hygiene initiative, patching is a critical part of ensuring information security. Hence, regular patching of systems is required to minimize vulnerabilities that are available for bad actors to try to exploit. Upgrading hardware and software components is also usually inevitable, because at some point vendors stop supporting—i.e., providing patches for—old versions of their systems, which compels financial institutions to upgrade so that they can ensure that their systems do not have untreatable security weakness. Regulators frown on financial institutions running unsupported software or hardware.

To put the scale of effort involved with updates in perspective, consider all the components discussed in Section 5.1 and imagine that each component may be provided by multiple vendors, and that there are multiple instances of those vendors' components in multiple business locations. Some vendors may only release updates a few times a year, whereas others may release updates monthly or weekly. The volume of systems and patches that need to be applied to them creates an ongoing need for IT operations staff, and possibly other IT and business groups, to be engaged in the patching process.

A key challenge with patching, from an IT operations perspective, is the potential unintended impact of patches that are applied to production systems. System updates that address one problem, may introduce another. For example, an operating system patch may inadvertently cause an application running on the operating system to break. Hence, the model of allowing the application to "pull" its own updates from the vendor on its own is not practical for many mission-critical systems. For example, an operating system could automatically download and install a patch and inadvertently break an application running on top of the operating system because the application is incompatible with the patch. Hence, patches and updates updates are usually "pushed" by administrators to systems.

Patches will be pushed in other test environments first and monitored to determine if any ill effects are observed. After a validation period, they will be pushed to other, more critical environments.

The logistics of applying patches to all systems is another difficulty that must be managed. Patching of systems may cause temporary service unavailability, the timing of which must be coordination with users. Additionally, some systems may be off the network when the system patching effort is underway, and it may be the case that the updating process may not be successful on all systems. Thus, tracking and verification of patching is required, and remedial activities may be required after the initial updating exercise. Automated asset management solutions can help track the application of updates across the network, and automated patching solutions are valuable for saving staff time and making the process more efficient.

Component upgrades, often triggered by end of support for installed versions, often involve more significant risk than patching. Major version upgrades of operating systems and software application components usually contain many new features and may change the underlying implementation of the software. Such major changes are more likely to create incompatibilities or demonstrate new behavior that may not be desirable or acceptable. Hence, more in-depth testing is required for system upgrades, often requiring testing by quality assurance and business users as part of the validation process. One type of upgrade that has major implications is web browser upgrade. Because many internal software applications in financial institutions rely on web browsers to provide the frontend, the number of applications, both homegrown and vendor-provided, that are affected can be very large. Just the testing effort to validate if any application functions are broken by the new browser version can require man-years of effort.

5.2.2 Resilience

Beyond information security concerns, most financial institutions are required, by regulators and for their own risk management purposes, to have resilient hardware, software and network infrastructure. Resilience may be implemented locally within a site by having redundant systems, also referred to as high availability (HA), as well as between sites to provide disaster recovery (DR) capabilities that support business continuity plans (BCP). There are standard architecture models for implementing high availability and disaster recovery, which are discussed in Chapters 3 and 7. However, application-specific complications sometimes arise, particularly related to the ongoing synchronization of data between servers or sites. Usually, only one "master" copy of a data can and will exist.

Offsite backups are also important for ensuring that critical information is preserved in cases where online data may be corrupted pervasively or where a bad actor destroys or renders data unusable. As a case in point, ransomware has become a major concern for institutions. Ransomware is a type of malware that encrypts data files, making them unusable unless a sum of money, a form of ransom, is paid. In worst-case scenarios, ransomware could reach online backups, rendering them unusable. The "air gap" provided by offline and offsite backups helps mitigate these kinds of risks.

System resilience capabilities will often be verified during routine maintenance activities such as patching or the deployment of new software components. While one system is taken offline to be updated, its resilient backup will continue to provide service.* While this demonstrates a certain level of resilience, full DR testing should be performed periodically to ensure that the resilience mechanism works as intended on a broader scale. Full-scale DR testing can also help find hidden dependencies between systems. For example, a pair of application servers may be resilient across two sites, but its operation may be dependent on a DNS configuration that is only available at the primary site.

---

* This is not the case where the resilience design readily caters for failover from the primary instance to the secondary, but not from secondary back to the primary. This is sometimes the case for databases where the primary instance is the master copy, and the secondary instance is only designed to be used to in a disaster recovery situations.

While the application server may appear to be resilient, if the primary site was rendered inoperable, the DNS dependency would impair the operation of the application server at the DR site. DR testing that severs the connectivity between sites will help identify these types of dependencies so that they can be addressed before a real site outage occurs.

For all its merits, full DR testing is a major undertaking and can be highly disruptive to IT and business operations. It requires significant time to plan and execute the testing and must be done in a way that avoids or minimizes impact to ongoing operations. In some cases, it may not be practical to simulate a complete disaster recovery failover. For example, it is not unusual for IT system services to be designed to be transferred to a backup site in case of disaster, but there may be no easy way to return those services back to the original primary site. This limitation can make it difficult to test a full failover of the system during a DR test exercise.

There are many steps financial institutions can take to ensure that their IT capabilities ensure business continuity. However, they have little direct control over external dependencies, such as the operations of service providers that they depend on as highlighted by Case 5-3. The more service providers that are relied upon, the greater the likelihood that external factors will cause downtime or service disruption. Hence, vetting the capabilities and operational practices of critical service providers is paramount. Vendor management practices are discussed in Chapter 19.

Case 5-3

Resilience Lessons Learned from Past Catastrophes

Catastrophes are inevitable, and the best outcomes from them are the lessons learned that can be applied to lessen the impact of future disasters. Likewise, not all the problems related to catastrophes that financial institutions encounter will be technology-related. Personnel and logistical consideration are also key dependencies for IT operations. Lessons learned from the extensive flooding in New Orleans, Louisiana caused by Hurricane Katrina in 2005 highlighted some of these considerations.

One problem area was related to disruption of communications. Failures of landline and cellular phone services made it difficult to locate and provide instructions to stranded personnel. Likewise, in some areas postal mail delivery was delayed for months, disrupting the processing of paper cheque deposits and payments.

Another concern was staff's ability to get to recovery locations. Damaged or inaccessible roads, evacuation orders, and health hazards can all prevent staff from being able to execute their roles to support business continuity activities. Furthermore, if employees' families or homes are at risk, they cannot be relied on to be able to fulfill their BCP responsibilities.

The unavailability of electrical power for extended periods caused IT system downtime. The fuel stock for generators was insufficient and in many cases it was not possible to source additional fuel to keep them running. Moreover, a number of business operation centers suffered major damage or were entirely destroyed.

In general, the BCP of financial institutions affected by Hurricane Katrina was able to quickly restore operations. That said, the extended duration of and access limitations imposed by the flooding went beyond the BCP considerations of some institutions. Hence, it is important that financial institutions be ready to improvise and face unexpected challenges in every DR situation. DR plans and planning help institutions prepare for bad situations, but cannot be expected to address every possible consideration or outcome.

Sources: Federal Financial Institutions Examination Council, "Lessons Learned from Hurricane Katrina: Preparing Your Institution for a Catastrophic Event," June 15, 2006, https://www.federalreserve.gov/newsevents/press/other/20060615a.htm.

5.2.3 IT Operations Personnel

The activities discussed in Section 5.2 depend heavily on people for their successful implementation. The effectiveness of having advanced technology and well-defined processes will be limited by the ability and motivation of staff supporting them. IT operations staff need to have a combination of diverse capabilities. They require in-depth knowledge of infrastructure technology and how the business uses that technology to develop effective architecture designs and make good decisions about changes to the environment. IT operations staff need be disciplined and have meticulous execution skills to ensure that no implementation steps are skipped, either intentionally or unintentionally. They also require resourcefulness and strong problem-solving skills, to be able to quickly and effectively address unexpected troubles that arise.

The wide range of skills and knowledge required to run IT operations is never available in a single person or in all staff; it is distributed across multiple people. This creates the need for managers to understand and keep track of every individual's capabilities so that they can be combined and applied effectively to complete projects or solve technical problems. Furthermore, it is important to ensure that technical knowledge and capabilities are shared by multiple people, so that the unavailability of a single individual does not create significant risk because that person is the only one who understands a particular process or component. Good documentation of the IT environment and operational procedures is also vital for supporting cross-training and providing a backstop for being able to deliver services when the normal resources that perform those functions are unavailable.

Operations management and troubleshooting will span across multiple groups within IT. Production problems with applications that have been developed internally will often require the involvement of software development and quality assurance groups. Production problems with third-party systems may require the involvement of the application support team that supports that application or business function and possibly the vendor as well. Problems with data file uploads or downloads between IT systems may require database administrators to implement corrective action. Business units may also be involved with problem resolution activities to help identify the best course of corrective action or determine if workarounds are possible to address specific concerns.

Tools that help organize and track operational activities can boost productivity and reduce implementation time by helping to tasks are not forgotten or disregarded, causing delays. It is not uncommon for a given individual who is part of the IT operations staff to be working on IT project requests for other IT groups, IT operations-related projects, as well as production problems, all in the same day. Hence, it is important to capture, prioritize, and track tasks and IT operations activities that need to be completed. Helpdesk software is commonly used for capturing service requests, assigning those requests to individuals, and tracking their completion. Helpdesk software may be a standalone package or be integrated with or be a part of other issue and project-tracking software applications that are used to manage other IT activities such as the software development lifecycle, i.e., software development, testing, and deployment activities. Use of task management software also helps provide management with reporting around service levels, resource loading, and productivity.

5.2.4 Outsourced and Cloud Platforms

The infrastructure and management processes described in this chapter correspond to what medium- and large-sized financial institutions would typically have in place. Smaller banks and Fintech companies may not have the financial resources and skills available to implement and support extensive technology infrastructure and, thus, would be more likely to leverage outsourced and cloud-based platforms. That said, as financial institutions come under greater pressure to reduce costs, as discussed in Chapter 1, larger institutions are seeking to take advantage of outsourced and cloud-based infrastructure services. This is consistent with an overall management strategy of focusing resources on what provides competitive advantage, and, in most cases, operating data centers and managing software application environments does do not provide a competitive advantage to most banks.

One approach that has been used by larger banks over the past several decades to try to reduce IT operations costs has been to outsource operational support services. Typically Usually with this approach, a third-party service provider is engaged on a long-term basis, typically between five and ten years, to operate and manage some combination of hardware, storage, network, and software application infrastructure. In many cases, some or most of the bank's IT operations staff are transitioned to become employees of the vendor. This approach has had mixed success. One of the key limitations that it has faced is that while the operating approach may change, the underlying systems remain the same. Support effort and operational cost are directly related to the complexity of the underlying environment that is being maintained. Hence, adjusting the IT operations approach is, in many ways, treating the symptom rather than the cause of the problem. Simplifying IT infrastructure and migrating IT systems to platforms that are easier to maintain would likely result in more substantial savings.

The complexity and interdependencies within banks' existing environments are also a key challenge for moving existing systems from internal data centers to external environments that are operated by third parties. That is to say, to move one component externally, might require moving or recreating several other components that it is dependent on, and those components have further dependencies that must be relocated, and so on. This type of complexity is also the reason why often IT-related expenses increase over time, even as the cost for the same level of computing power continues to drop over time. Layers of hardware and software components that have been built up over time are difficult to disentangle, consolidate, and relocate, and in turn, limit the advantages that using new technology can provide.

As highlighted in Case 5-4, it is imperative that banks tackle this type of complexity to achieve cost-cutting objectives. By mandating that some proportion of IT systems be migrated to outsourced and cloud environments, management can encourage IT staff to think beyond the bounds of existing operating models and to reconsider assumed limitations and restrictions. During this process, trade-offs will need to be made. Cost savings and flexibility can be gained, but often only by incurring new risks. In some cases, the trade-off will be worthwhile; in other cases, it will not. Accordingly, banks

---

Case 5-4

Reducing Infrastructure Complexity and Moving to the Cloud to Reduce Costs

It is not uncommon for revenue-generating business initiatives to take priority over more mundane maintenance activities. Replacing and upgrading hardware platforms is often one of those necessary but tiresome maintenance activities that ties up resources, requires extensive coordination, and takes significant time to complete. The complexity that arises from the plethora of hardware, operating systems, and other technology infrastructure that banks use makes ongoing maintenance difficult and time consuming. It can take years to fully migrate off of - and decommission hardware and operating systems that are approaching their end of support. The more platforms that are used, the greater the number of platforms that will be in the process of being retired. With this in mind, it is not surprising that Deutsche Bank estimated that, as of 2015, 35% of the hardware that its systems used was close to the end of its support lifecycle or had past it.

(Continued)

(Continued)

To address this challenge, as part of the bank's Executing Strategy that was communicated by its CEO and CFO in 2015, Deutsche Bank set out as a major goal to reduce the complexity of its IT infrastructure by 2020. The overall objective is to reduce operating costs by around €800 million. Key elements of this initiative included reducing the number of end-of-support hardware and software platforms from 166 to none, shrinking the number of operating systems that it used from 45 to four, and increasing the use of private cloud services from 20% to 80%. Since the complexity of the existing environment often holds back the adoption of cloud services, it made sense to link these initiatives together.

To make real headway in addressing the problems related to the complexity of technology infrastructure, it is necessary to tackle the problem at an executive level, so that as a priority, it is put on par with other business initiatives. The goals that Deutsche Bank set are very aggressive, and will be challenging to complete within five years. Nevertheless, even achieving partial success should provide significant cost savings and, more importantly, provide greater flexibility for new IT-driven business initiatives.

Sources: Boulton, "Deutsche Bank digging Digging out Out of technical Technical debtDebt, while While moving Moving to the cloudCloud", ," CIO, Nov 11, 2015, http://www.cio.com/article/3004538/cio-role/deutsche-bank-digging-out-of-technical-debt-while-moving-to-cloud.html; Cryan, J. and Schenck M. "Executing Strategy 2020", ," *Deutsche Bank*, 29 October 29, 2015, https://www.db.com/newsroom_news/Strategy_2020_-_Press_Presentation_engl._29.10.2015.pdf.

must assess where the greatest benefits can be achieved while incurring the least additional risk, and which IT systems can be migrated with the fewest complications.

5.3 SUMMARY

This chapter covered:

- important hardware and communication components;
- key software application components;
- the complexity of managing IT infrastructure and operations; and
- challenges encountered with managing and supporting IT infrastructure.

This is the last chapter in Part One that covers the foundation topics. The following chapter begins the next part, which is focused on banking-related business functions, and begins by examining the context in which banks operate and the characteristics of their customers.

FURTHER READING

Books

1. Behr, K., G. Kim, and G. Spafford, *The Visible Ops Handbook: Implementing ITIL in 4 Practical and Auditable Steps*, (Information Technology Process Institute, June 15, 2005).

2. Limoncelli, T.A., C.J. Hogan, and S.R. Chalup, *The Practice of System and Network Administration, Second Edition* (Addison-Wesley Professional, July 15, 2007).

Web

Financial Institutions Examination Council (FFIEC) IT Handbook: Operations, http://ithandbook.ffiec. gov/it-booklets/operations.aspx.

Financial Institutions Examination Council (FFIEC) IT Handbook: Business Continuity Planning, http:// ithandbook.ffiec.gov/it-booklets/business-continuity-planning.aspx.

ENDNOTES

1. Arnold, M. and T. Braithwaite, "Banks' Ageing IT Systems Buckle under Strain," *Financial Times,* June 18, 2015, http://www.ft.com/intl/cms/s/0/90360dbe-15cb-11e5-a58d-00144feabdc0.html.

2. Luxen, M. and R. Piffer, "Visa Credit Card System Back Up and Running Nationwide after Temporary Disruption," *Toronto Star,* January 28, 2013, https://www.thestar.com/news/ gta/2013/01/28/visa_credit_card_system_down_across_canada.html.

3. Ponemon Institute, Cost of Data Center Outages, January 2016, http://www.emersonnetworkpower. com/en-US/Resources/Market/Data-Center/Latest-Thinking/Ponemon/Pages/2016-Cost-of-Data-Center-Outages-Report.aspx.

— — —

4. Center for Internet Security, Cyber Hygiene Toolkit, https://www.cisecurity.org/cyber-pledge/ tools/index.cfm.Case 5-3

PART TWO
BANKING TECHNOLOGY

6 Banking Contexts

Banks provide valuable services to customers and play an important role in society. They act as intermediaries, providing an important source of capital by pooling depositors' funds and making those funds available to companies and individuals. Banks also provide transactional capabilities that enable customers to make payments and settle the purchase and sale of securities. Furthermore, they enable customers to transfer risk, such as foreign exchange (FX) risk, to the financial markets and help facilitate trade by providing guarantees and insurance.

The types of customers served and business provided depend partially on the size of the banking institution. Small banks may focus on only a single line of business such as deposit taking and lending or credit card issuance, and may primarily serve only one subgroup of customers, for example, nonaffluent retail customers. Medium-sized banks typically have multiple lines of business and serve a broader range of customers, for example, consumers and corporations. Large banks provide almost all categories of banking services, including FX dealing and **investment banking**, and cater to almost all customer segments.

Banks' locations also determine the type of business they engage in and the category of customers they serve. In mature financial markets, such as the United States and the United Kingdom, banks provide a wide range of services and, in some cases, provide customers with access to capital markets for investment purposes, along with traditional banking services. In other markets, such as Asia, trade facilitation and FX risk management provide profitable lines of business. In large developing markets, such as China and India, the growth of consumer credit services provide a major opportunity for banks.

Besides influencing customers' needs, location also determines the regulations that banking institutions must abide by. Regulatory requirements underlie macrolevel considerations, such as which lines of business a bank can engage in and how much capital it must maintain. Regulation also governs microlevel concerns, such as individual customer lending limits and lending qualification standards. Thus, the success of banks is dependent not only on developing business lines that address specific needs of their customers, but also on providing products and services that are within regulatory limits. While this strategy may sound simple, many complications arise because customer needs and regulatory requirements change over time and vary by location.

Moreover, over the past decade, competition from Fintech companies have had a major impact on banks' business models, particularly in the United States and Europe. They encroached upon core business areas are such as lending, payments, and providing financial advice (Case Study 6-1). In many cases, the relationships between banks and Fintech companies is that of being frenemies; they may compete with one another, but in some market circumstances, it makes sense to be partners. The challenges that Fintech companies present to banks will be discussed in more detail in the chapters that follow.

Case Study 6-1

Rise of the Robo-advisers

Providing financial advice to customers is one of the core services that bankers provide to their customers, and this area has become one of the latest technology battlegrounds. Technology startups began by offering the service of robo-advisers, online applications that use automated algorithms to provide customers with guidance about investment decisions without any interaction with bank staff. Customers provide information about their financial circumstances and goals through an online robo-adviser application and receive suggestions on the amount of money that should be invested in different asset classes and specific investment vehicles, such as mutual funds. The robo-advisory service could also make, for a fee, the recommended transactions on behalf of the customer.

The robo-advisory innovation is a way of providing wealth and investment advisory services to a broader audience and at a lower cost. In the United States and United Kingdom, new regulations increased the cost for investment advisers to operate, making it less attractive for them to provide services to customers with relatively small, but not insubstantial, amounts to save. In particular, the mass affluent customer market is a prime target for robo-advisory services. Also, younger customers were more familiar with digital channels, so online robo-advisory tools appealed to young professionals between the ages of 25 and 45.

Fintech firms were the first to enter into and capitalize upon the robo-advisory market. As of 2016, robo-advisers were estimated to manage around $45 billion worth of assets. One of the largest independent robo-advisory firms claims to have $5 billion in assets under management and 175,000 customers. Furthermore, in 2015 the world's largest fund manager, Blackrock, purchased FutureAdvisor, a robo-advisory firm that was founded in 2010. Instead of providing robo-advisory services to its customers, Blackrock instead sold the services of FutureAdvisor's platform to banks and brokers, which in turn offered the robo-advisory services to their customers.

Royal Bank of Scotland (RBS) was one such bank that partnered with Blackrock to use its FutureAdvisor service. The move came as RBS scaled back its face-to-face investment advice offering, eliminating 220 adviser positions. To access an investment adviser, it increased the minimum amount that it required customers to have for investment purposes from £100,000 to £250,000. By providing robo-advisory services, RBS was able to continue offering investment advice to existing customers who no longer qualified for face-to-face service, as well as additional customers who had at least £500 to invest. Other large UK banks, such as Barclays, Lloyds, and Santander UK, were also expected to begin providing robo-advisory services to their customers as well.

Robo-advisory services are of interest to both large and small banks. On the large side, UBS partnered with Fintech startup SigFig Wealth Management to provide robo-advisory services to UBS's investment advisers, rather than providing them directly to customers. The goal was to reduce the time advisers need to spend constructing investment portfolios and enable them to spend more time helping customers make the best choices. On the small side, Cambridge Savings chose SigFig as a way of offering high-tech wealth management features to its customers without making a large investment in software applications. Prior to engaging in the partnership with SigFig, Cambridge Savings did not provide any wealth management services to its retail customers. The partnership enabled it to offer its robo-advisory service to customers with $2,000 or more on deposit and charges a 0.5% annual management fee. Like many other banks that leverage technology partners' platforms, Cambridge Savings offers SigFig's service under its own brand, ConnectInvest.

While robo-advisers provide numerous benefits to financial institutions and their customers, they also have shortfalls. One limitation of robo-advisers is that the online questionnaires that they provide to customers may not elicit all the information that is necessary to provide the most accurate investment advice. Likewise, when explaining recommendations, robo-advisers cannot provide customers with the same level of interaction as professional advisers can. High-quality interaction is most important for customers who have complicated financial situations. Another concern is that, in formal business terms, typically robo-advisory services provide investment "guidance" rather than "advice." The key to this distinction is that customers who receive investment advice can demand restitution or claim compensation if they are provided with unsuitable advice. Customers who receive financial guidance do not have this right and must determine themselves whether recommendations are suitable for their needs. Accordingly, the terms and conditions for using robo-advisory services usually make customers responsible for ensuring the recommendations provided are in their best interest.

Robo-advisers have gained significant traction in recent years, but still capture only a very small part of the investment advisory market. It is yet to be seen how much they will displace, rather than just supplement, services provided by professional investment advisers. With robo-advisory fees costing typically 65–85% less than face-to-face professional services, the economics make them attractive to customers. Moreover, even before robo-advisers came on the scene, banks' record for providing investment advice was less than stellar. A 2015 regulatory review of wealth management and private banking services in the United Kingdom found that around 60% of customers were receiving unsuitable advice. The coming years will determine just how big the opportunity is for automated, self-service investment advice and how banks will take advantage of new technologies to remain competitive in the investment advisory space.

Sources: Rovnick, Naomi, "Wealth Managers Giving Unsuitable Advice, Warns City Watchdog," *Financial Times*, December 9, 2015, http://www.ft.com/cms/s/0/431236d4-9e88-11e5-b45d-4812f209f861.html; Dunkley, Emma, "RBS Cuts Face-to-face Service and Brings in 'Robo-advisers'," *Financial Times*, March 13, 2016, http://www.ft.com/intl/cms/s/0/10df9f22-e90f-11e5-bb79-2303682345c8.html; Dunkley, Emma and Martin Arnold, "UK Banks Set to Launch 'Robo-advisers'," *Financial Times*, January 22, 2016, http://www.ft.com/intl/cms/s/0/afb03182-c107-11e5-9fdb-87b8d15baec2.html; Welsch, Andrew, "Wells Fargo to Test Robo-adviser Next Year," *American Banker*, July 19, 2016, http://www.americanbanker.com/news/bank-technology/wells-fargo-to-test-robo-adviser-next-year-1090262-1.html; Broughton, Kristin, "How Banks Are Co-opting the Robo-advisory Revolution," *American Banker*, July 25, 2016, http://www.americanbanker.com/news/bank-technology/how-banks-are-co-opting-the-robo-advisory-revolution-1090281-1.html; Fein, Melanie, "Robo-advisers Aren't All They're Cracked Up to Be," *American Banker*, October 7, 2015, http://www.americanbanker.com/bankthink/robo-advisers-arent-all-theyre-cracked-up-to-be-1077106-1.html.

Questions

1. What considerations would lead a bank to partner with a Fintech company to provide robo-advisory services to its customers rather than building the technology solution itself? Conversely, what factors would lead a bank to building the solution?
2. How could banks use hybrid approaches that combine both human- and robo-advisory services?
3. What are some new risks that banks which offer robo-advisory services face? On the other hand, what risks do banks that do not offer these services face?
4. Why would this technology emerge from and be made popular by Fintech firms rather than by banks?

This chapter reviews the different types of bank customers and the banking business environment. Bank customers—such as consumer, corporate, and institutional—are described, and their varied banking needs are delineated by subsegment. Common opportunities and challenges that banks face are also presented. This chapter also introduces a transaction lifecycle model, and the design and setup stage of the lifecycle is examined in detail. Finally, an example of a solution that addresses both retail customer needs and regulatory requirements is presented.

6.1   CUSTOMER SEGMENTATION

To understand banking solutions that are applied in different environments, it is necessary to first know how banks categorize their customers and how customer segment needs differ. To begin with, consider how corporate customers differ from retail customers. Key differences include:

- **Number of customers**. There is a significantly larger number of retail customers than corporate customers.

- **Assets per customer**. On average, corporate customers have significantly more assets than retail customers.

- **Customer information availability**. More information is available about corporations' finances, particularly publicly listed ones that must periodically perform financial reporting for regulatory purposes.

- **Customer revenue diversification**. Individuals' revenue streams are usually dominated by one source of income—their employment, whereas corporations may have multiple customers and conduct business across multiple business and geographical markets.

- **Number and types of products and services required**. Consumer banking services are focused on investments, lending, and financial advisory services. Corporations have more complex needs, such as supporting import/export trade activities, hedging, and cash management.

- **Concentration of risk**. Due to the relatively small size of transactions with a large number of customers, the exposure of retail banks to the **credit risk** of any one customer is minimal. Transactions with corporate customers can be much larger, and transactions can occur with multiple risk-dependent entities, such as parent corporations and their subsidiaries.

- **Regulatory requirements**. Consumer banking often has regulatory restrictions that are designed to protect customers against unfair practices and inappropriate products. These concerns are less pertinent to corporate banking customers.

While these considerations can be used to differentiate consumer and corporate customers, they can also be applied within those groups to create subsegments. This section will review how banks' lines of business are typically organized and divided into lines of business focused on consumer banking, commercial banking, institutional banking, and investment banking. It will also examine the characteristics used to segment retail and corporate customers.

6.1.1   Consumer Banking Customers

Consumer banking, commonly referred to as **retail banking**, constitutes a large percentage of the overall banking business, and is generally an integral part of capitalist societies. Banks have been providing basic needs, such as securing deposits from and lending to individuals, for hundreds

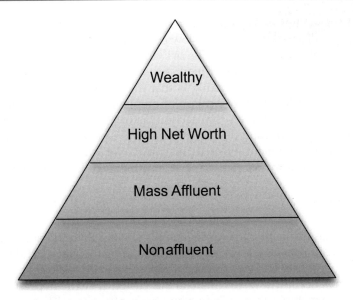

Figure 6-1 Four core retail customer segments

of years. All the same, only in the last century has consumer banking become ubiquitous. Retail banking services have flourished, moving from simple loans and deposits to include revolving credit, payment services, and distribution of related products, such as insurance.

To understand consumer banking, it is helpful to study the characteristics of retail customers, their needs, and how they are viewed from a banking perspective. Figure 6-1 shows the four core retail customer segments. At a very high level, retail customers can be categorized as either wealthy or nonwealthy. Private banking divisions within banks usually focus on wealthy customers. Alternatively, specialized private banks may address their needs. Nonwealthy retail customers can be further divided into three core categories: high net worth, mass affluent, and nonaffluent. The following subsections will examine the characteristics and banking needs of each of these latter three categories in more detail.

6.1.1.1 Nonaffluent

Nonaffluent customers account for the largest potential number of banking customers worldwide. While, by definition, they have limited monetary deposits, they often have recurrent borrowing needs. Typical products used by nonaffluent customers include payment/chequing accounts, mortgages, and possibly third-party products, such as life insurance policies. In some markets, they may also have access to credit cards and automobile loans. It is not uncommon for this customer segment to have relatively few choices with regard to banking alternatives. As a result, banks that service this segment will often impose high fees and interest rates on credit facilities. This income is necessary to offset the cost of providing services and the higher credit default rate that they incur compared with affluent customers.

For banks, the nonaffluent segment comprises a large customer base and, thus, requires banking services to be provided efficiently. The products and services offered must be oriented toward cost-effective distribution and scalable delivery. Likewise, banks must structure bundled offerings so that profitability is achieved across the set of products and services provided. For example, it is practical for banks to provide free chequing services when customers' minimum account balances are over a certain threshold so that the bank's net interest **margin** earned exceeds the cost of processing customers' payments. Additionally, the credit risk for nonaffluent customers will be more tightly coupled with economic cycles and the value of their collateral. When job losses or other hardships occur, nonaffluent customers have little or no financial safety net.

While nonaffluent customers, as a group, may be sensitive to economic conditions, individual credit risk exposures will be small and have relatively low correlation. This risk feature is beneficial to banks when they serve large numbers of customers. The risk exposure of the group as a whole is characterized by a normal distribution, and no single nonaffluent customer can cause a large loss for the bank.

An interesting aspect of consumer banking is that there is relatively little information available to banks to evaluate their customers. Verification of employment history, salary information, credit bureau reports, and analysis of customers' transaction history provide relevant, but often incomplete, information about customers' profit and risk potential. This is especially true for nonaffluent customers, who may have little, if any, employment and credit history available. Hence, banks can face a predicament as to how to best offer products and services to such customers while sufficiently controlling risk.

6.1.1.2 Mass affluent

In many countries the mass-affluent banking segment is smaller than the nonaffluent one, and mass-affluent customers' deposits provide a low-cost source of funding for banks. While the definition of mass affluent varies between countries and financial institutions, it usually includes customers with between $250,000 and $3 million in net assets. Loans made to this customer segment present relatively little risk, and mass-affluent customers typically consume many types of services. These customers have a larger pool of funds available that can be applied to a broader range of savings and investment products. Likewise, their higher disposable income makes lending for large-ticket consumer goods less risky.

Since mass-affluent customers have more diverse banking needs, more banks will find them attractive as customers and will compete for their business. Beyond the acquisition of customers, there is also the opportunity to persuade customers to consolidate funds and concentrate their business with one bank. The financial supermarket concept, which has gained significant ground in the United States, has been an effective tool for providing customers with consolidated access to a wide range of financial services including savings, payments, mortgage, credit cards, **mutual funds**, and equities.

In the context of the investment products that banks offer, banks' fiduciary duty to their customers is an important concern. As part of this obligation, banks are assumed to have the trust and confidence of their customers, and must ensure that they are acting in good faith to serve the customers' best interests. This can present an interesting ethical challenge, since banks have a similar obligation to shareholders to maximize profits. Hence, the role of regulators is to ensure that these two objectives are adequately balanced. Furthermore, banks' fiduciary obligations will vary by the types of customers that they serve. Banks' responsibilities toward nonaffluent and mass-affluent customers differ from those toward private banking and institutional customers. For example, due to their perceived risk, banks generally do not offer alternative investment products, such as hedge funds, to retail and corporate customers. However, in many cases, they do offer these products to the top end of these segments, that is, private banking and institutional customers (Case Study 6-2).

Case Study 6-2

Banks' Responsibilities to Customers

Banco Santander, a bank based in Spain that has a large presence in Latin America, took the unusual step in January 2009 of offering its private banking customers €1.38 billion in compensation. This action was driven by the bank's role in offering investment funds to customers who had invested in fraudulent investment schemes linked with Bernard L. Madoff. The Ponzi scheme perpetrated by Madoff caused Santander's customers to lose €2.33 billion. Providing compensation to customers was viewed by some as the bank's acknowledgement of its own responsibility for the losses and was an attempt to repair its reputation.

Interestingly, institutional customers were not included in this repayment offering. The bank considered the institutional customers to have sufficient investment knowledge so as to be responsible for their own investment decisions. Institutional customers were, apparently, viewed as being capable of performing their own due diligence, whereas private banking customers were not and had to rely on the bank's expertise.

This is a case of banks taking on risk by nature of being distributors of third-party products. Santander was not the only bank facing this issue as a result of Madoff's fraud. Likewise, it was not the first time that Santander had to offer compensation related to failures of third parties. Previously, the bank provided compensation to clients who bought products backed by Lehman Brothers' guarantees. Lehman Brothers declared bankruptcy in September 2008.

Source: Werdigier, Julia and Victoria Burnett, "Santander Offer Pressures Rivals to Match It," *New York Times*, January 27, 2009, http://www.nytimes.com/2009/01/29/business/worldbusiness/29santander.html?_r=1&dbk.

6.1.1.3 High net worth

High-net-worth customers are generally considered as individuals with a minimum of between one and ten million dollars of funds, excluding the asset value of their primary residence. The cutoff depends on the market and bank. Typically, this segment is better suited for developing a more intimate customer relationship with a designated **relationship manager (RM)**. Likewise, the fee structure may vary from the normal retail structures. For instance, fees may be based on an annual percentage of funds deposited rather than per transaction or, alternatively, they may be waived altogether.

Products and services offered to the high-net-worth segment are often oriented toward wealth preservation and the most efficient growth of funds. Taxes, estate planning, and privacy become more significant considerations, and some banks provide advisory services in these areas. Beyond individual accounts, there may also be trust accounts that are managed by the banks. Likewise, where customers are owners of family businesses, more complex financial transactions that involve business assets and aggregated family wealth are common.

Given the spectrum of retail customers, an important decision for banks is which type of customers to target. Obviously, they want to target the most profitable ones; however, this objective is complicated by the fact that profitability in retail banking is determined by a combination of customer preferences, products and services offered, balances maintained by customers, the amount of market competition, and the fee structures implemented by banks. Moreover, as highlighted in Case Study 6-2, external factors can also affect the profitability of the products and services that banks offer.

Demographic factors such as age and income are not necessarily good predictors of customer profitability. Generally, profitable customers can be found in any segment and, in theory, banks can make unprofitable ones profitable by adjusting their fees and interest rates. Moreover, while segmentation can be a useful tool for organizing business activities, it does not necessarily lend itself to viewing customers from the standpoint of lifetime value and risk. For instance, a nonaffluent customer with low profitability today may be on the path to becoming a more profitable mass-affluent customer.

6.1.2 Private Banking and Wealth Management

Discussion of high-net-worth individuals provides a logical stepping-stone to a brief review of private banking and wealth management. High-net-worth and wealthy customers have unique needs that banks have a strong interest in satisfying. In many cases, private banking and wealth management customers may be experts in their primary business, but may be too busy or simply lack the requisite skills to actively manage their money. Hence, there is an opportunity for banks to fill this gap by providing financial tools and management services.

Owing to the relatively small number of customers served by private banking and the potential for large profits, it is more practical to customize products to address specific needs of wealthy customers. Customization may come in the form of providing specialized products, such as alternative investment funds, that are oriented toward specific investment objectives, or may instead be structured products that match customers' unique needs. Services can also be customized to address general needs, such as providing money management educational seminars for heirs of wealthy families. Alternatively, they can be customized to cater to idiosyncratic customer relationship needs, such as having a dedicated RM who is available by phone 24 hours a day, seven days a week.

A critical challenge for private banking and wealth management is having processes and systems that can address diverse and complex requirements. Core banking systems often do not support the broad range of financial products that are offered to private banking customers; additional systems may be required. Consolidating customer balances and holdings across all products and systems for statement reporting purposes is also not easy. In cases where IT systems have not been fully integrated to address this requirement, manual processes will be necessary. Likewise, many of the products offered to private banking customers may be sourced from other financial firms. Therefore, product-distribution management processes may be as important as services that come from within the bank.

As discussed in Case Study 2-3, private bank customers' special requests may require business processes to be designed and implemented on demand. Providing such dynamic services can be very costly and involve significant operational risk. It is common for certain banks to specialize in wealth management and serve only the wealthy and, possibly, the high-net-worth segments. By limiting their focus, these banks are able to orient their technology and operations in ways that other banks, which serve larger markets, would find difficult.

6.1.3 Corporate and Institutional Banking Customers

As with retail customers, banks typically segment their corporate customers, also referred to as "wholesale" banking customers, into different categories to help establish segment-specific business strategies. Common corporate customer segments include small- and medium-sized enterprises (SMEs), large national corporations, and large multinational corporations (MNCs). Institutional customers can be another form of corporate customer, but are often grouped separately for business purposes. In some cases, banks may choose to structure the segmentation differently, potentially with finer granularity or by ignoring some segments altogether. However, these four categories, as shown in Figure 6-2, are useful for examining how different types of corporate customers determine product, service, and solution strategies.

Banks commonly use annual revenue, or turnover, to categorize corporate customers. Measures such as turnover can be viewed as proxies for the potential volume of business that a customer may conduct with the bank. This volume of business, in turn, would be proportional to the expected earnings, or profit, that the bank could potentially derive from the customer. For example, a customer that has a turnover of only $500,000 is not likely to generate the same level of net interest margin or transaction fees as a customer whose annual turnover is $500 million. Hence, the products, services, and cost structures offered to different types of customers must take into account the quantity of and types of transactions they are likely to conduct.

Although turnover is commonly used for segmentation purposes, corporate customer segmentation criteria will vary across banks and markets. Annual revenue that is comparably large in one market or currency may be considered small in another. Likewise, banks' orientations may largely determine how customers are segmented. Smaller, local banks may focus on a limited range of corporate customers and, thus, may choose to focus only on the lower half of the pyramid shown in Figure 6-2 and create additional categories within those subgroups. Alternatively, universal banks may choose to target only the top half of the pyramid in many foreign markets and ignore the larger, bottom half altogether.

The characteristics, needs of, and opportunities provided by SMEs, large national corporations, and large MNCs are examined in the following subsections. Institutional customers will be examined in Section 6.1.3.5.

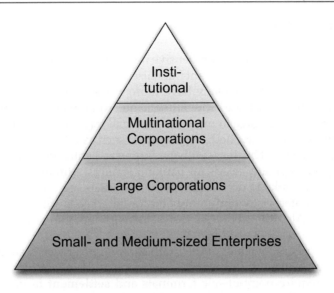

Figure 6-2 Four core wholesale customer segments

6.1.3.1 Small businesses

Small businesses* have unique characteristics and needs. For the purposes of illustration, small businesses might include a retail bakery, a construction contractor, or a Fintech startup. Depending on the country and type of business they operate in, they may work on a cash-only basis, have few employees, and use insurance to protect themselves against losses that could cripple the business. Small businesses may be growing rapidly, or they can be long-time established businesses that are not oriented toward growth at all.

Generally, small businesses have fewer banking options than other segments. Large banks and multinational banks may choose to ignore this segment of the market because it may be impractical to support a large number of relationships and offer market-specific products. Also, small businesses are less likely to be directly involved in international trade and, therefore, may not require FX-related services or may only use very basic products such as FX spot conversions (FX products are covered in Chapters 11 and 12).

Banking products commonly provided to small businesses include savings and current accounts, fixed deposits, overdraft facilities, secured lending, bill payment, and revolving credit. However, the specific services actually offered will vary by country, and special services provided to customers will depend on market-specific factors. For example, in a market where many small businesses operate in a cash-only environment, banks may offer cash collection services so as to provide greater convenience to customers and also reduce transaction volumes at bank branches. Similarly, where customers are physically distant or face inconveniences in reaching bank branches, remote document collection services can help simplify the process of opening accounts. Such services could verify documentation completeness at the customer's premises, thereby streamlining the account opening process.

The products, services, and solutions offered to small businesses must be structured such that they can support large numbers of customers who perform relatively few transactions. Hence, "self-serve" channels, such as Internet banking, are a preferred strategy for servicing small-business customers. Product customization is also generally not practical for small-value transactions and, as a result, banks will generally only offer standardized products to small-business customers.

---

* For the purpose of this analysis, only incorporated businesses are considered as small businesses. Other forms, such as sole proprietorships, are considered to be in the realm of consumer banking.

6.1.3.2 Medium-sized enterprises

Medium-sized enterprises have more comprehensive needs. For the purposes of illustration, medium-sized enterprises may include a small restaurant franchise, a textile factory, or an automobile dealership. Compared to small businesses, they usually have more employees and higher levels of trade with suppliers and customers, and may have growth financing requirements. Given their greater breadth, medium-sized enterprises may engage in more international trade and, in turn, require trade finance, foreign currency accounts, and use FX hedging products, such as FX forwards.

Often, banks prefer to conduct business with medium-sized enterprises than with small-sized ones due to the former segment's greater needs for banking services. Minimum balances and transaction levels required by various banks to do business with customers are more easily met by these firms. Typically, medium-sized enterprises' **remittance** and funding needs are on a much greater scale than those of small businesses. Also, the credit risk associated with medium-sized companies can be lower than that of smaller companies (Case Study 6-3).

Medium-sized enterprises use some of the same banking products as small businesses, but also require additional products to support the increased scope of their activities. Merchants who accept credit and debit cards require point-of-sale terminals and **settlement** facilities. More sophisticated payment facilities may be offered in conjunction with trade and treasury-related products. Given the wider range of products available to customers, it is logical for banks to also provide more extensive advisory services. Banks can help corporate customers match their specific needs to the banks' financial products. There is also the opportunity for banks to provide outsourced services, such as payroll processing, where the lack of efficiencies of scale make it less practical for medium-size companies to perform those services in-house.

Wider product usage also provides an opportunity for providing bundled offerings. Combining products and services that have different profit margin levels enables banks to form aggregated offerings that are both profitable and attractive to customers. It also makes it harder for customers to directly compare fee structures with those of competitors. For example, a bank might package a no-fee chequing account, but require a higher aggregate balance and levy higher-than-average overdraft charges. Trade finance products may be offered at a competitive rate, but FX spreads (that is, the difference between the buy and sell prices for the currency) charged for related transactions may be wide.

Case Study 6-3

Risk Characteristics of Different Customer Segments

SMEs play a major role in the economies of many countries and provide an important market for many banks. For example, in France, more than 440,000 SMEs contribute to about 60% of the countries' total employment figure. Although SMEs provide a large base for deposits and fees, subsegments of SMEs exhibit different risk characteristics. A study published in 2004 assessed the probability of default of a large population of French and German SMEs. This group was segmented into three subgroups with annual turnovers in ranges of €150,000 to €1 million, €1 million to €5 million, and €5 million to €40 million.

This analysis showed that overall the sensitivity of SMEs to macroeconomic factors was relatively low and that on average, the correlation of firms' credit risk with these factors decreased as their turnover increased. However, the credit-risk characteristics of the different SME subgroups varied. In terms of default probabilities, the smallest segment of SMEs was less risky than the mid-sized segment; however, both these segments were more risky than the SME segment that had the highest annual turnover.

These results could be interpreted as indicating that it is less risky to lend to SMEs that have larger revenues than those with smaller revenues. However, it was also found that, as a whole, the SMEs with the lowest revenues provided the greatest diversification across economic sectors, which improved the credit risk characteristics of holding their debt when aggregated in a loan portfolio. Conversely, larger SMEs exhibit low correlations between credit risk and turnover but on average, they have an increased risk of correlation when combined as a group of loans in a portfolio. The analysis also showed that the credit characteristics of the small SME subgroup was found to resemble retail loans and suggested that they could be treated as such.

Source: Dietsch, Michel and Joel Petey, "Should SME Exposures Be Treated As Retail or Corporate Exposures? A Comparative Analysis of Default Probabilities and Asset Correlations in French and German SMEs," *Journal of Banking & Finance* 28 (2004): 773–778.

6.1.3.3 Large corporations

Large corporations are much more complex than SMEs and, accordingly, require more sophisticated treatment as customers. Commercial airlines, privatized postal services, and utility companies are examples of large corporations. Compared to SMEs, they typically have a much larger number of employees and more developed internal processes and systems, such as enterprise resource planning systems, to support business operations. While operating primarily in one market, they may have foreign subsidiaries and a substantial number of customers in other countries.

Many banks prefer to conduct business with large corporations because they are easier to assess and offer lower risks. However, a single bank may not be able to serve all their needs; therefore, large corporations are likely to have multiple banking relationships due to the counterparty credit limits imposed by individual banks. Moreover, large corporations are not limited to using banks as they also have the option to obtain financing in the capital markets by issuing equity or bonds.

In addition to the products offered to SMEs, banks also offer large corporations syndicated loans, investment banking services, and more complex risk-management and investment products, such as FX options. Given the more complex requirements of large corporate customers, there is an opportunity for banks to customize the products and services provided so as to address very specific needs. New products can be created on an as-needed basis to capture market opportunities.

Although large corporations can offer profit opportunities for banks, there are some potential risk trade-offs. For example, risk management across more complex corporate structures is a challenge presented by larger businesses. When a large corporation does business through multiple local subsidiaries, overall counterparty credit risk and profitability may need to be tracked aggregately across all these entities.

6.1.3.4 MNCs

MNCs share many characteristics with large national companies, with the addition of more complex capital structures and many foreign entities. Some examples of MNCs are Starbucks, DHL, and Levi Strauss & Co. MNCs' business considerations are generally more complicated than those of large corporations. For example, they may choose to borrow in one currency or country to fund business activities involving other currencies or countries, thus, requiring more complex risk hedging products such as cross-currency interest rate swaps (discussed in Chapter 12). Likewise, profit and loss may be managed between subsidiaries to optimize tax efficiencies across various countries. Depending on the firm's orientation, the finance function may be highly centralized and tightly controlled or, alternatively, considerable autonomy may be provided to regional or national operations.

Some MNCs will have effectively created a bank within the corporation, raising capital that provides a source of funding for various internal needs. For example, an MNC's bond issuances in the United States could fund business activities in China. Likewise, FX exposures may be managed, to a large extent, internally. For example, at a corporate parent level, a purchase by one subsidiary requiring conversion of ¥200 million to US dollars (USD) in Japan may be offset, for currency hedging purposes, by a transaction by another subsidiary in the United States that requires the conversion of USD and yields ¥180 million. Taken in aggregate, the net exposure would only be ¥20 million (netting concepts are covered in Chapter 9). Instead of having each of the two subsidiaries independently perform large foreign currency transactions with banks in Japan and the United States, an MNC can instead perform a single hedging transaction for the smaller net amount on behalf of both subsidiaries. This transaction could occur in yet a third country, where the MNC's corporate treasury is based.

Due to their sophistication and large scale, MNCs are managed, in some cases, as institutional customers rather than corporate customers. Their finance and treasury departments may have trading and **market data** systems that are as sophisticated as banks' data systems. MNCs' transaction volumes also allow them to negotiate lower fees on banking services. Integration and efficiency of **straight-through processing (STP)** between the customer's IT systems and the bank's become more important. Moreover, banks also provide value to MNCs by providing investment banking services and by customizing banking products to meet MNCs' specific needs.

Banks doing business with MNCs must manage global counterparty credit and settlement limits effectively. For example, a simple approach to credit-limit management would be to divide the total loan exposure or FX exposure allowable to an MNC (and all its subsidiaries) by country. However, this approach is disadvantageous in that limits in one country may be fully utilized, while other countries still have available limits. This situation prevents the MNC from conducting more business in the country where the limit has already been fully utilized, whereas they may not want nor need to transact in the other countries where the limit has not been reached. Tracking and managing limits globally can help MNCs utilize limits more effectively, thereby increasing banks' global revenues and profits. Management of counterparty credit limits is discussed in more depth in Chapter 8.

6.1.3.5 Institutional banking customers

Institutional customers are typically financial firms or large MNCs that operate on a scale similar to financial firms. In both cases, the size of individual transactions or the total volume of transactions would be expected to be much greater than that for other corporate customers. Financial institutions that are treated as institutional customers may include various types of funds such as **pension funds**, mutual funds/unit trusts, or hedge funds. Banks may also deal with insurers, brokers, and other banks, both smaller and similar sized, that are considered as institutional customers. In the case of MNCs, a very large company like ExxonMobil or Royal Dutch Shell may be treated as an institutional customer because its annual revenue is over a trillion dollars.

Regulatory and industry treatment of institutional customers will often differ from that of retail and corporate customers. Institutional customers will expect lower costs for products and services and higher levels of service. They are also expected to have greater market knowledge and savvy; hence, protections, both regulatory and legal, that are provided to other types of customers may not apply to institutional customers.

As highlighted in Case Study 6-4, there are no hard and fast rules as to how banks segment their customers, and segmentation strategies may change over time. The approach to segmentation will vary by country, by market segment, and by financial institution. Most importantly, creating predefined groups of customers makes it easier to design products and services that match each group's unique characteristics and needs.

Case Study 6-4
Varying Approaches to Customer Segmentation

The means by which banks categorize customers for marketing and servicing purposes will vary between regions, countries, and individual institutions. Even within a single country market, the parameters that banks use to determine which businesses qualify as corporate customers can differ. For example, a 2005 study of the Italian banking sector found the average range of turnover (that is, annual revenues) required by Italian banks to be between €1.5 and €250 million. However, this range varied significantly, with at least one bank having a minimum turnover requirement of €15 million, which was much higher than the average minimum. Another had a maximum of €100 million, which was much less than the average maximum.

The turnover range that each bank chose to define the boundaries for its corporate customer segment determined the number of potential target customers. A bank that chose to define corporate customers as those with turnovers between €2.5 million and €300 million had a potential target customer base of 255,000. Then again, another bank that chose to define a minimum of €15 million and had no maximum had a potential customer base of only 7,000 customers. Clearly, within Italy, the proportion of small- and mid-sized customers is relatively large.

One fundamental question is whether enterprise turnover is the best top-level segmentation criterion. Alternative measures include the size of the lines of credit, total business volume, and the growth rate of enterprises' turnover. Overall, enterprise turnover is used in Italy, as well as many other parts of the world, because it is objective and simple to use. Nevertheless, these and other measures can be useful for providing second-level segmentation. Breaking down the macro or strategic segments into second-level categories can help focus on the needs and revenue potential of specific customers, as well as support product positioning.

The predominance of SMEs in Italy and many other countries provides opportunities for local banks to better understand and cater to their specific needs. However, small banks need to find ways to provide more comprehensive banking services, beyond the basic ones that they offer, to meet the broader needs of their customers. One possibility is to form alliances with Fintech companies and other financial institutions to leverage their capabilities. For example, whereas many SMEs are family owned, they could benefit from combining corporate and private banking activities. Therefore, finding ways to integrate corporate and private banking services is also a means for these banks to provide value to their customers.

Source: Caselli, Stefano, "Corporate Banking Strategies: Products, Markets and Channels," in *Strategy and Organization of Corporate Banking*, ed. Giacomo De Laurentis, pp. 37–62 (New York: Springer-Verlag, 2005).

6.1.4 Investment Banking Customers

It is important not to confuse corporate and institutional banking with investment banking, although there is some overlap. Investment banking focuses on providing security underwriting, brokerage, and merger and acquisition activities. Corporate and institutional banking, on the other hand, focuses on providing general banking needs—such as investment, financing, remittances, risk management, and support for cross-border transactions. There are, however, clear intersections and synergies between the two business areas. For example, a bond issuance in a foreign currency may necessitate FX transactions. Likewise, raising funds in the debt and equity markets can be seen as an extension and alternative to raising funds through bank loans. However, the two business areas are usually managed separately within banks, and many banks do not engage in investment banking activities at all.

6.2 OPPORTUNITIES

In many banks, there is an opportunity to transform business and interactive models from being bank-centric to being customer-centric. Traditionally, business processes have been designed to fit and are organized around the structure and constraints of banks' business units. As a result, customer interactions were often disjointed and segmented along business lines or support functions. For example, a bank may provide one phone number for general corporate banking inquiries and another for corporate Internet banking technical support. The customer-centric business model has been gaining some traction, but still has significant room for growth. Limited IT system integration and siloed business operations are still common and create barriers for implementing customer-centric business services. Hence, by defining business metrics in terms of customer needs and experiences and redesigning processes and IT systems to meet those targets, banks can greatly improve the quality of services they deliver. Case Study 2-1 provides an example of how a customer-centric focus can be applied in practice.

The design of channels and implementation of customer relationship management (CRM), covered in Chapter 16, is a common area where banks can improve their customer focus. Historically, it was not uncommon for channel implementations to be tied to specific IT systems, for example, the core banking system or particular types of products such as FX. Likewise, in many cases, CRM was viewed as an IT system rather than as a set of service delivery processes supported by an IT system that contributed to the customer experience. Over time, some banks have migrated to more system-agnostic channel implementations and focused on streamlining their CRM processes. By doing so, they have been able to provide more consistent and seamless service experiences to customers, regardless of the channels used. Nonetheless, there are still many opportunities for banks to improve their internal processes and technology to improve customer experience. Channels and CRM are discussed in depth in Chapter 16.

Banks also have the opportunity to grow by expanding into new markets. In some cases, new markets may be found in different geographies, enabling banks to move out of saturated or stagnant markets into more demographically favorable ones. For instance, Japan and parts of Europe are facing

Figure 6-3 Emerging markets offer high growth potential (© Standard Chartered Bank. Reprinted with permission.)

negative population growth and have mature banking markets, but in places such as China, India, Africa, and South America the populations are still growing and the banking markets are relatively underdeveloped (Figure 6-3). It is estimated that by 2020, Asia-Pacific trade flows will grow on average by 7% per year, and Asia will account for 60% of global trade volumes [1]. Furthermore, as of 2014, two billion unbanked people were estimated to be living in developing countries, with over a half of them in Asia-Pacific and South Asia regions [2].

There are also opportunities to service underserved market segments, particularly the unbanked. In both developed and emerging markets, there is a segment of the population that does not have ready access to banking services and has to make use of licensed and unlicensed moneylenders, cheque-cashing services, pawnshops, and money transfer agents. In developed countries, many of the unbanked are immigrants. For example, in the United States, it is estimated that there are more than 17 million adults who do not have bank accounts.

On the other hand, in developing nations, banks are not designed or incentivized to provide services to large segments of the population, thus creating a gap in the market. In many cases, banks have an opportunity to expand their services to this untapped market by leveraging IT, such as using mobile phones, and redesigning banking products and processes to provide more cost-effective service offerings. Mobile phone usage also greatly exceeds Internet usage in most developing countries. Hence, it is not surprising that developing markets have shown the greatest affinity for mobile payments. Figure 6-4 shows the percentage of respondents of a poll of 30,000 people in 63 countries as to the likelihood of their making a mobile payment directly to another person in the next six months. In markets where banks have not stepped up to address these needs, companies in other industries have done so. For instance, in Kenya, Pakistan, and the Philippines, telecom operators have begun providing payment services in conjunction with mobile phone In China, online marketplace company Alibaba and social media company WeChat dominate the mobile payments market.

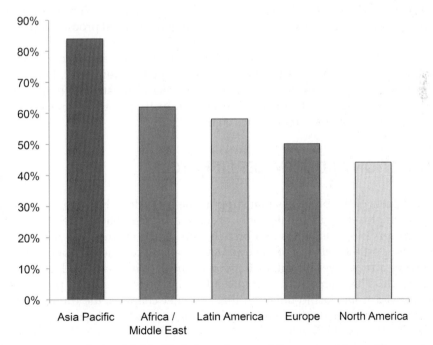

Figure 6-4 Consumers somewhat or highly likely to make a mobile payment to another person in the next six months (2016)

Source: Nielsen, "Mobile Money", October 2016, http://www.nielsen.com/content/dam/nielsenglobal/kr/docs/global-report/2016/nielsen_global_mobile_money_report_final.pdf.

6.3 CHALLENGES

As will be discussed in Chapter 19, dealing with regulatory changes is one of the greatest challenges that the banking industry currently faces. The Dodd-Frank Act has curtailed the universal banking business model (discussed in Chapter 1). Increased capital requirements and tighter risk controls required by regulation has reduced banks' profitability and made it more difficult for them to achieve the high profit margins that they have historically enjoyed. Furthermore, financial product innovations, which in part contributed to the Global Financial Crisis, now face increased regulatory oversight. As a case in point, in 2012, the Financial Services Authority issued guidelines on how products should be developed and marketed to customers in the United Kingdom [3].

Many banks reined in their lending activities during the Global Financial Crisis due to the weak economy and higher capital requirements. This funding shortage put further stress on customers and also provided an opportunity for new competitors to enter the market. In many markets, SMEs faced considerable difficulty in obtaining bank loans in the wake of the financial crisis and, thus, were attracted to alternative forms of nonbank financing. For example, an independent exchange was set up to enable firms to sell their accounts receivable invoices to institutional investors to get faster access to working capital. Likewise, large retailers, such as Walmart, were able to help provide **liquidity** to smaller suppliers by offering invoice discounting programs, where invoice payments would be expedited if the supplier provided additional discounts. Money managers also raised capital to create investment funds that were designed to provide loans to medium-sized firms. Fintech companies have created marketplace lending platforms that enable investors to easily provide financing to SMEs. While none of these offerings are likely to replace traditional lending in the foreseeable future, they have created new competitive niches in the financial services landscape that banks must now address.

Moreover, customers' trust in banks has suffered in recent years, partly due to common perception that banks engaged in excessive risk taking in search of profits, and were the cause of the Global Financial Crisis. Also, numerous cases of banks' mis-selling of financial products raised the question of whether they favored profits over customer relationships. Banks' unwillingness or inability to provide credit to firms and individuals when they required liquidity the most also soured customers' views on banking relationships. The Occupy Wall Street protests staged in New York, London, and Frankfurt highlighted the general discontent with the financial services industry. Although as time has past, much of the angst has dissipated, the financial services industry must continue to work to restore the level of customer trust and support that it once enjoyed.*

6.4 TRANSACTION AND SERVICES LIFECYCLE

Often, only small parts of the processes that support the lifecycle of banking transactions or services are visible. Bank employees will usually only observe activities that are related to their particular functions, such as servicing customers at a branch, and not be aware of all the other functions that are necessary to support the delivery of the transaction or service. The six-stage framework shown in Figure 6-5 provides a high-level logical abstraction of the activities involved in financial transaction and services lifecycle. This framework provides a holistic view of banking processes that identifies the activities involved from start to finish. In this and later chapters, the framework will be used to examine the activities associated with delivering banking products and services.

---

* The 'phantom account' scandal that was publicized in 2016, where Wells Fargo's employees opened millions of new accounts on behalf of customers without their permission, discussed in Case Study 19-4, did not help make a case for looser regulatory oversight.

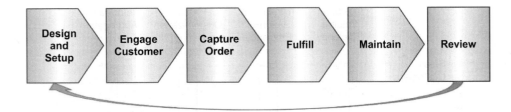

Figure 6-5 Transaction and services lifecycle model

A high-level summary of the lifecycle is as follows:

1. **Design and setup**—activities related to the creation and validation of banking products and processes, and the setup and configuration of supporting IT systems.

2. **Engage customer**—processes and supporting technologies that are used to market and sell products and services to customers.

3. **Capture order**—activities related to the acquisition of customer order details and obtaining an agreement that legally executes the transaction.

4. **Fulfill transaction**—processes and technologies that follow order capture and support fulfillment activities, such as transaction confirmation, accounting, disbursement, and remittance.

5. **Maintain transaction**—activities that are required over time to support long-lived products and services.

6. **Review**—processes that evaluate the effectiveness and profitability of products and services and feed back to the design and setup stage of the lifecycle, initiating changes to support improvement.

6.5 LIFECYCLE FOCUS: DESIGN AND SETUP

This section examines the design and setup stage of the lifecycle. First, it will discuss how customer segmentation considerations are factored into the design and setup of financial products and processes. Then, the setup of reference data, which is required by many different financial services IT systems, is discussed.

6.5.1 Segmentation-related Design Considerations

A number of segment-related considerations affect how IT solutions are designed, constructed, and deployed. Figure 6-6 shows the relationship between corporate customer segment size and the importance of customer volume efficiency, transaction volume efficiency, product customization, and information aggregation as solution considerations.

Banks must be able to efficiently handle large numbers of customers when catering to SMEs. Products, services, and solutions must be optimized to support large numbers of customers with minimal overhead cost. Streamlining per-customer operational processes, such as account openings, deposits, and payments is paramount. Consequently, banks have used channels such as thin branches, Internet banking, and mobile banking and related solution technologies to provide services more efficiently and cost-effectively to smaller customers. For instance, thin branches may be small branch setups that have only one or two employees and may be located in the premises of another business, such as a supermarket or department store.

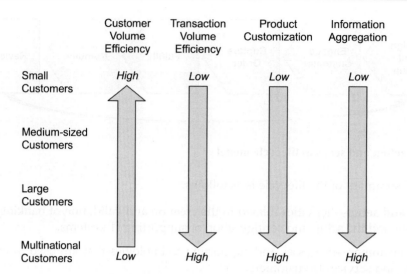

Figure 6-6 Solution considerations for different corporate segments

Efficiently handling large transaction volumes becomes more crucial when supporting large corporate customers and MNCs. While the total number of customers is smaller, the number of transactions, such as payments and FX, may increase dramatically. Hence, supporting electronic data interchange channels, aggregation, STP, and exception handling become more important.

As noted earlier, customizing products for small corporate customers is usually impractical from a profitability standpoint. The cost of the time required for bank staff to sufficiently understand customers' needs and tailor a customized product that matches their requirements could easily overrun the expected profit on the transaction. Even if the profit is commensurate, providing customization for a large number of customers is usually challenging with regard to staff training and availability, solution support, and operational processing efficiencies. Alternatively, it is more practical to customize products, services, and solutions for a small number of large corporate customers and MNCs. As these customers regularly transact in multimillion dollar units, the profit margins associated with customization of those transactions can more easily justify the effort and risk involved for banks.

Finally, requirements related to customer information aggregation and management increase dramatically in relation to company size. Typically, small companies will generate relatively little financial information and may only be obligated to report their financial condition on an annual basis. On the other hand, MNCs often have dozens of subsidiaries spread around the world, with each reporting on a quarterly basis. Rating agencies and other third parties may also provide information about larger corporations that may also be relevant to the bank's decisions regarding customer transactions. Effective and timely capture of customer information, along with its management, is crucial when monitoring the risk associated with large corporations and MNCs.

6.5.2 Reference Data Setup

One example of a nonobvious concern that must be addressed in the design and setup of banking and trading systems is the initial configuration and administration of reference data. Calendar reference data is one example of information that business processes and IT systems require to determine valid trading dates and settlement dates. The fact that business days and holiday schedules vary by country complicates calendar implementations. For example, business days run from Monday through Friday in many countries, whereas in the United Arab Emirates (for instance, Dubai) business days range from Sunday through Thursday. Likewise, as shown in Table 6-1, national holidays will vary from

Table 6-1 An example of settlement holidays for major currencies

	USD	EUR	JPY	GBP	CHF	CAD	AUD	HKD	KRW	SEK
June 23, 2017										X
June 26, 2017										
July 1, 2017								X		
July 3, 2017					X					
July 4, 2017	X									
July 5, 2017										
July 6, 2017										
July 17, 2017			X							
August 1, 2017					X					
August 7, 2017						X	X			
August 9, 2017										
August 11, 2017			X							
August 15, 2017									X	
August 20, 2017										
August 28, 2017				X						
September 1, 2017										
September 4, 2017	X					X				
September 16, 2017										
September 18, 2017			X							

country to country and must be taken into consideration when making cross-border payments or settling FX transactions.

Constructing and maintaining holiday calendars are not trivial tasks. In some cases, holidays follow simple rules and repeat on an annual basis, for example, Thanksgiving in the United States falls on the fourth Thursday in November. In other cases, the holidays may move in accordance with the lunar calendar, for example, Hari Raya and the Lunar (Chinese) New Year, requiring more complicated algorithms. Furthermore, there is the possibility of new holidays being added by governments on an ad hoc basis, such as when a parliamentary election date is scheduled. Hence, providing a user-friendly way of configuring and managing trading calendar information can be an entire IT solution by itself.

Calendar information is embedded within many different IT systems, causing logistical challenges when updates are required. Ideally, calendar information will be stored in a bank's **enterprise data management (EDM)** system, which maintains the master copy of reference data, such as currencies and securities details. The EDM system will be integrated with other downstream systems so that it can feed calendar changes to those systems without requiring human intervention. If an EDM system is not used, bank operations staff will need to manually update the calendar configurations in each system.

Calendar information is utilized at several different stages of the transaction lifecycle, specifically when engaging customers, capturing orders, fulfilling transactions, and maintaining transactions. For example, banks should only quote FX **forward rates** (explained in Chapter 11) for settlement dates that are valid for both the currencies exchanged, and the rates provided will depend on the number of days until settlement. IT systems responsible for capturing the FX forward trade details and settling the trade amounts, as well as other systems, will also need calendar information to verify that the specified transaction dates are valid. When calendar details are set up incorrectly, significant problems can arise. Incorrect prices could be quoted, payments could be settled on the wrong dates, and IT systems could disallow a valid order entry.

6.6   SOLUTION CONSIDERATIONS: FINANCIAL PRODUCT ADVICE

While as highlighted in Case Study 6-1, some investment advisory services are being automated, the vast majority of the services provided are provided through interactions with bank staff. To help put some of the considerations related to customer segmentation into context, this section looks at how banks' investment advisers provide financial advice to customers from a solutions perspective. For brevity, the problem has been simplified and abstracted to its core considerations. In practice, however, there are many more complications that must be considered.

6.6.1   Business Context

As discussed previously, providing financial advice to both retail and corporate customers provides a major opportunity for banks to establish long-lasting relationships with customers. However, it also creates additional responsibilities; to provide appropriate advice to customers, banks must understand the customers' needs, capabilities, and risk preferences. Obtaining information can help banks make better choices about how much and what types of credit to offer customers, thus improving banks' risk management. Providing sound financial advice can also help improve the loyalty of customers. Instead of seeing the bank as a provider of commodity services, an institution can develop a relationship that has more depth and reduces the likelihood that customers will shift their business to a competitor because of monetary incentives.

Customers also benefit from receiving objective advice that helps them select products for their short- and long-term financial goals. Customers may not be able to evaluate their own financial needs objectively; furthermore, their knowledge of the available financial products available may be limited. Hence, banks are well positioned to provide independent assessment and guidance.

While providing many benefits, taking on an advisory role requires that banks have processes and controls in place to ensure that prudent and unbiased advice is provided. A fundamental risk is that banks' staff could either intentionally or unintentionally give unsuitable advice to customers. For example, badly designed financial incentives for bank personnel, that is, commissions, could lead to intentional biases, such as selling specific products that yield the highest commissions rather than the products that best serve the customers' needs. On the other hand, unintentional biases could arise in cases where the bank staff are not sufficiently knowledgeable about the financial products available or do not adequately assess customers' financial needs and conditions.

6.6.2   Stakeholder Needs

Based on the business context described above, four primary stakeholder needs can be identified:

- **Customer**—wants to receive objective and accurate advice so that he/she can purchase the most appropriate products.

- **Financial consultant**—wants to provide good advice so as to establish a long-term relationship. Depending on compensation structure, he/she may also want to promote specific or large quantities of products to meet sales targets.

- **Bank management**—wants to sell financial products, avoid risks associated with providing inaccurate advice, and also make use of information related to customers' financial needs, condition, and preferences as best as possible.

- **Regulator**—wants to ensure that customers are treated fairly and are not taken advantage of by financial institutions.

While a detailed analysis might identify additional requirements or constituencies within these groups, for a high-level discussion, these primary stakeholders and the concerns identified are sufficient.

6.6.3 Business Processes

It is useful to consider the financial planning advisory business processes in two forms. The first form is a simple service delivery process that addresses the most basic needs of the customer and the financial consultant. The activities shown in Figure 6-7 represent a process that might be used by less advanced financial institutions. This approach reflects an elementary method that lends itself to improvement. For the purposes of this example, the solution will be focused on nonaffluent and mass-affluent retail banking customers.

In the elementary process, the financial consultant initially retrieves two types of information about the customer: his or her profile and financial holding details. This information, along with the risk-profile information obtained through discussions with the customer, will be used by the financial consultant as the basis for deciding which products to recommend to the customer. The recommendation is based on the financial consultant's knowledge, training, experience, and opinion. No record is kept of the customer's and financial consultant's interactions.

As an alternative, Figure 6-8 shows an "improved" version of the process that addresses all of the stakeholders' needs. The first major improvement is that the customer's risk-profile information that is obtained during the advice session is stored or updated in the customer's profile data. Another improvement is the addition of an explicit step of analyzing the fit of the financial products offered with the customer's risk profile. This analysis utilizes a documented set of rules for making the decisions. Furthermore, the product recommendations are recorded for future reference.

The improved version also shows the related, but separate, compliance-related business process. Information stored by the financial consultant about the customer's risk preferences and the products recommended can be cross-checked against the product compatibility rules defined at that time to determine if appropriate recommendations were made. Discrepancies can be investigated and remedial action taken, if necessary. Other compliance-related processes, not shown, could also periodically

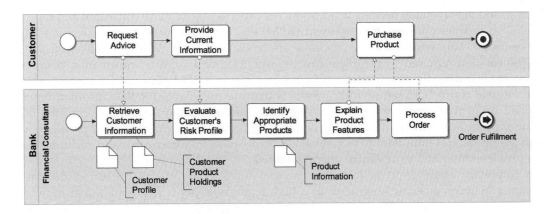

Figure 6-7 An elementary process for providing financial advice to customers

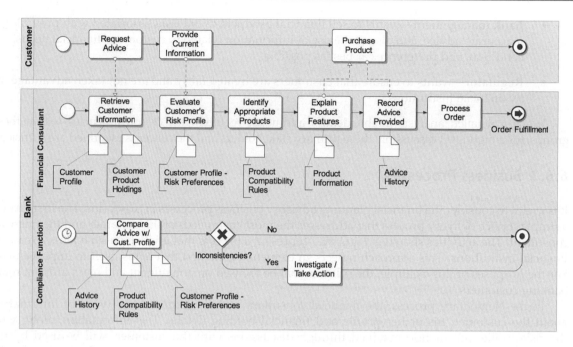

Figure 6-8 The improved process for providing financial advice to retail customers

prompt RMs to check with customers to see if the customers' risk profiles had changed, and, if so, suggest changes to their investment holdings. Similarly, there would also be marketing-oriented business processes that support management reporting and analysis needs. These could compare risk profiles and investment objectives with available products, compare product recommendations with product purchases, and examine changes in customers' risk profiles over time. Note, however, that for brevity, the marketing workflows are not shown in Figure 6-8.

The improved version offers significant benefits. Specifically, the use of a predefined and explicit set of rules for analyzing product compatibility with customer needs reduces the chances of the financial consultant making inappropriate recommendations. Having an explicit set of rules helps prevent individual biases from unduly influencing customers' financial choices, hence avoiding "product pushing" by financial consultants. These rules can be updated periodically as new products are added or when new regulations come into effect. Recording the customers' risk preferences and the financial consultants' recommendations also provides an audit trail that helps support compliance, marketing, and management review. In addition, the process will be more consistent and repeatable.

Ideally, a **business process management (BPM)** execution platform, as discussed in Chapter 2, would be used to help ensure that the processes are carried out as intended, provide electronic access to the information required to complete process activities, and capture information obtained and decisions made during the financial planning process. Using a BPM platform for execution can help enforce internal controls. It can identify products that are unsuitable for the customer, based on a predefined set of rules, and prevent them from being offered to the customer during the financial planning process, rather than solely relying on the compliance check process to find problems at some point in the future. It is important to stop mistakes before or as they occur to avoid additional work to correct problems later and to minimize operational risk.

An important observation is that the financial advisory processes presented do not differ significantly between customer segments at a high level. Whether it is a nonaffluent individual or a medium-sized corporation, the high-level activities described in a best-practice reference model should be almost the same. However, as the process details are further identified, the differences will become more apparent. The information gathering activities will vary based on the type of customer, as will the rules associated with recommendations. For mass-market customers, these rules would be standardized and adhered to strictly. Alternatively, within the processes catering to high-value customers, both retail and corporate, many of the rules could be replaced by guidelines or suggestions, placing greater reliance on the judgment of highly trained bank staff.

6.6.4 Solution Implementation

There are a few different ways by which these business processes could be implemented as solutions. One possibility is that the process could be entirely manual and paper based. Financial consultants can be trained to retrieve paper files of customer records and manually update the documentation when necessary. While an entirely manual implementation of the elementary version is feasible for small numbers of customers, this approach is not practical for the improved process because of the likely complexity that would be involved with evaluating the applicability of the product compatibility rules. Furthermore, manual management and storage of information becomes even less practical when it is being updated and accessed by multiple parties. Likewise, the scalability problems of an entirely manual process would make it unsuitable for serving the larger retail and wholesale customer segments.

An improved version of the solution would be where all the information resources were centralized so that all parties could access them more easily. Ideally, access to information would be provided electronically to simplify logistical concerns, and so that access could also be more easily controlled and monitored. A simple solution could be implemented by providing a basic customer information application that allows financial consultants to view and update a customer information database.

A further improvement to the solution would be to semiautomate and manage the process execution. This automation would be in the form of a software application that manages and tracks the flow of activities that the financial consultants perform and also captures information relevant to that process. The advantage of this approach is that the system would control the process steps, thus reducing the risk of the financial consultants inadvertently, or intentionally, skipping steps or taking incorrect actions. Some of the required data could be collected automatically and other entered data could be validated within the application workflow. Such a solution could be implemented either as standalone software or as a workflow application within a **business process management system (BPMS)**.

In the context of the last two solution approaches described, it is useful to assess the business benefits of automating the process, as opposed to simply managing the information. In the case where enabling data-access is the main focus of the solution, the "recommend products" step of the process would require the consultant to record in a database which products were recommended. However, there is the possibility that the financial consultant could err by doing any of the following:

- forgetting to record the recommendations;

- recording the recommendations incorrectly; or

- correctly recording inappropriate recommendations.

Trying to determine which of these occurred, after the fact, could be problematic.

Alternatively, a solution that controls the process workflow would automatically record the information and the process steps that led to the final set of recommendations, as well as the recommendations themselves. This solution approach would decrease the number of mistakes that would occur with manual noting of this information, reduce the the number of tasks that the financial consultant must perform, and also reduce the chance of making incorrect recommendations. Furthermore, it would not be necessary to retrain the financial consultant when changes occur to the rules governing which products should be offered to customers under different circumstances. Instead, the rules embedded in the solution implementation would simply be changed, thereby causing new application workflow behavior. As a result, the solution would lead the financial consultant and the customer down different decision tree paths.

Of course, the benefits provided by the workflow-based solution come at a cost. First off, a new workflow behavior would need to be designed, implemented, and supported. If there is an existing BPM or workflow infrastructure in place, the effort could be reduced, but substantial efforts related to requirements analysis and testing would still be required. Second, integration with banks' information systems would be required. Also, a new database might need to be created to store the product recommendation history information.

Ideally, even better automation could be achieved by linking this process to downstream product-fulfillment processes. For example, recommendation of a loan product could automatically trigger and pass relevant customer details to the banks' loan origination system. Similarly, recommendation of an insurance product could lead to an additional set of workflows that capture additional policy application information and electronically route it to an external system that initiates the fulfillment by an **insurance company** (Case Study 6-5).

Banking solutions are achieved by assessing the broader needs of the stakeholders, developing processes to address those needs, and then creating efficient and cost-effective implementations of the processes. The approach and scope of implementation will depend largely on the make-up of an institution's customers, goals, and budgets. A very small bank may find that the costs of automation are too high to realize sufficient return on investment. Mid-sized institutions may determine that partial automation yields the greatest benefits, or may choose to invest more to achieve full automation with the objective of achieving other strategic benefits as a result. Large institutions may decide that the return on investment can easily be achieved, but complications related to budgeting and system integration may limit the scope of automation efforts.

Case Study 6-5

Bancassurance

While banking products address a large portion of customers' financial service needs, insurance companies also provide products that address savings and risk-management needs. In many markets, particularly in Europe and Asia, banks have formed partnerships with insurance companies to sell insurance products to their customers. This arrangement is commonly referred to as bancassurance. Bancassurance typically utilizes branch staff and tellers to sell insurance products. Certain bank staff may be trained as specialists by the insurer and deployed to bank branches. In Italy, for example, bancassurance accounts for more than €3 billion in life insurance sales.

Banks offer a wide range of insurance products to different customer segments. Within the consumer-banking segment, products such as renters' insurance, which covers personal home belongings, are marketed to nonaffluent customers. Automobile and homeowners' insurance is targeted at the mass affluent, and insurance covering luxury items, such as jewelry, and collectables, such as fine art, is marketed to wealthy customers. Likewise, services, such as those designed to help prevent and detect identity theft, can be marketed to all consumer segments. A number of different types of insurance offerings can be provided to commercial banking customers, including protection against damage to or loss of commercial vehicles, professional liability claims, lawsuits related to employment practices, and workers' compensation claims.

The distribution capabilities of banks' branches provide an efficient channel for selling life insurance products, serving as an alternative to offerings provided by commissioned agents and over the Internet. This distribution arrangement also provides banks with the opportunity to generate fee income on third-party products that may appeal to customers different from those whom the banks serve with their standard products. Furthermore, selling third-party insurance products does not increase banks' capital requirements. Due to this mutually beneficial arrangement, life insurance sales through bancassurance are expected to continue growing in the coming years, particularly in the Asia-Pacific region due to the size of the markets there. As of 2016, it was estimated that the bancassurance market sizes in China, South Korea, and Taiwan were $82 billion, $51 billion, and $42 billion, respectively.

Sources: Tutt, Nigel, "Bancassurance Model Seen Key to Life Product Sales," *Reuters*, July 27, 2009, http://uk.reuters.com/article/2009/07/27/bancassurance-idUKLNE56Q05720090727; "DBS, Aviva Extend Bancassurance Partnership in Singapore and HK," *Channel NewsAsia*, July 30, 2009, http://www.channelnewsasia.com/stories/singaporelocalnews/view/445712/1/.html.
Takeuchi, Y., "Bancassurance Operations in the Asia-Pacific Region - FALIA Bancassurance Survey 2016," *Foundation for the Advancement of Life & Insurance Around the World*, http://www.falia.or.jp/assets/pdf/research/FALIA%20Bancassurance%20Survey%2020161201.pdf.

6.7 SUMMARY

This chapter provided background information on:

- approaches used by banks to segment customers;

- services provided to different customer segments;

- opportunities and challenges faced by banks;

- transaction and services lifecycle model;

- common considerations addressed in the design and setup stage of the transaction and services lifecycle; and

- approaches for providing solutions that support the financial planning advisory services of banks.

Having reviewed the basic concerns and considerations of banks and their customers, the next six chapters examine IT considerations related to common banking lines of business in more detail. The next chapter discusses deposits and cash management, and the subsequent chapters cover lending and debt collection, payments, trade services and finance, treasury and FX, and treasury derivatives.

FURTHER READING

Papers and Articles

Craig, V. V., "Merchant Banking: Past and Present," *FDIC Banking Review* (September 2001): 29–36.

"Global Banking Outlook 2017," *Ernst & Young*, http://www.ey.com/gl/en/industries/financial-services/banking—capital-markets/ey-global-banking-outlook-2017.

"2015 FDIC National Survey of Unbanked and Underbanked Households," *Federal Deposit Insurance Corporation*, https://www.fdic.gov/householdsurvey/.

"Small Business Credit Survey 2016," *Federal Reserve Bank of New York*, https://www.newyorkfed.org/smallbusiness/small-business-credit-survey-employer-firms-2016.

"Slings and Arrows: A Special Report on International Banking," *Economist*, May 9, 2015, http://www.economist.com/news/special-report/21650290-financial-technology-will-make-banks-more-vulnerable-and-less-profitable-it.

Koderisch, M., G. Wuebker, J. Baumgarten, and J. Baillie, "Bundling in Banking—A Powerful Strategy to Increase Profits," *Journal of Financial Services Marketing* 11 (2007): 268–276.

Periodicals

Journal of Banking & Finance

Journal of Corporate Treasury Management

International Journal of Bank Marketing

Web

Bank of England Quarterly Bulletin, http://www.bankofengland.co.uk/publications/quarterlybulletin.

FDIC Quarterly, http://www.fdic.gov/bank/analytical/quarterly/index.html.

Financial Times, http://www.ft.com.

ENDNOTES

1. Wong, J., "DBS Expands Asia-Pacific Factoring Network," *Finance Asia*, May 3, 2011, http://www.financeasia.com/News/256088,mandates-and-payments-roundup-may-3.aspx.

2. "Universal Financial Access 2020", *World Bank*, http://ufa.worldbank.org/global-progress.

3. Financial Services Authority, "Retail Product Development and Governance—Structured Product Review," March 2012, http://www.fsa.gov.uk/library/policy/final_guides/2012/fg1209.

— — —

4. "Markets for Minnows," *Economist*, April 15, 2010, http://www.economist.com/node/15908493.

5. Davies, R., P. Richardson, V. Katinaite, and M. Manning, "Evolution of the UK banking system," *Bank of England Quarterly Bulletin* 50 (2010): 321–332.

6. Campbell, D. and F. Frei, "The Persistence of Customer Profitability: Empirical Evidence and Implications from a Financial Services Firm," *Journal of Service Research* 7 (2004): 107–123.

7. "On the Side of the Angels," *Economist*, February 25, 2012, http://www.economist.com/node/21547994.

8. "Alienated: Tapping the Market for Financial Outsiders," *Economist*, March 10, 2011, http://www.economist.com/node/18335131.

7 Deposits and Cash Management

In ancient Greece, around 700 BC, affluent individuals would store their gold and silver at the temple of Apollo in Delphi, which acted as one of the first banks in Western history. Because of temples' sanctity and the fact that they were tied to the Greeks' common religion, rather than being associated with any specific Greek state, temples provided relative security for storing wealth. Likewise, the virtue of the temples' priests instilled trust in the temples being a safe place for depositors' money. Temples also had militias that protected them. Today, a similar structure still applies, but with fundamental changes in the mechanisms used. Individuals and corporations store their money—which is usually represented and stored in electronic, rather than physical form—at banks for safekeeping and to earn interest. Bankers' integrity is reinforced by governance by and accountability to regulatory and judicial bodies. Banks' physical security is maintained by the police, and banks invest substantial sums on technology to protect themselves from cybersecurity-related threats.

Deposits are the foundation of banks' products and services. Lending funds to receive interest—how most banks make a large part, if not most, of their income—is dependent on having funds to lend, the majority of which comes from customer deposits. Retail customers deposit cash to build up savings for large purchases, investments, and retirement. Corporations keep working capital in bank deposits. A key reason that customers deposit funds at banks is because of the safety that banks provide. In most developed markets, bank accounts come with some level of government backing or guarantee. Another reason that customers maintain their cash deposits at banks is for the convenience of being able to access them. Banks provide customers with cash management facilities for administering funds between accounts within a bank and payment services for transferring funds to accounts at other banks. Today, most of these services are provided electronically and do not require customers to have physical access to their bank.

Cash management facilitates the movement of funds between accounts and investment vehicles. It is most relevant in the context of helping corporate customers manage their **liquidity.** Companies' options for cash management remained relatively unchanged until the 1980s (Case Study 7-1). One of the major changes that led to innovations in cash management was the rise of global corporations. By taking advantage of banks' services, global corporations are able to operate using **federated** cash management models that pool and optimize their funding. They are also able to achieve cost savings and take better advantage of economies of scale with their financial transactions.

The advent of **digital currencies**, such as bitcoin, has also introduced a new store of value that individuals and corporations can potentially deposit and manage through financial institutions. However, the means by which digital currencies are stored and managed present new risks for financial institutions that provide products and services for them. Likewise, since digital currencies have been in existence for only a short period of time, it is quite possible that new risks will be discovered going forward. Hence, the legitimacy and longevity of digital currencies are still unclear, and banks' role in supporting them has yet to be established.

This chapter examines the role that banks and technology play in providing deposit and cash management services to customers. First, the reasons why customers need deposit and cash management services are explored. Second, the opportunities and challenges that banks face when providing these services are discussed. Third, technology solution considerations for **core banking systems** and architecture considerations related to resilience are examined. Finally, the future of cash notes and the evolution of digital currencies are considered.

Case Study 7-1

Implementing Global Cash Management

Motorola, one of the largest global producers of electronic devices, has a large number of subsidiaries and units in different countries that require ongoing cash-flow management to fund operations and purchases from suppliers. Whereas historically, the local entities would manage their payment and FX exposures, starting in the mid-1970s, Motorola began centralizing these functions in two phases.

The first phase of this global initiative was to implement **netting** of payments between autonomous Motorola companies that traded with one another. Whereas intracompany payments amounted to approximately US$5 billion, the main objective was to have a central treasury function manage foreign currency payments and exposures. The business goal was to reduce cash flows between entities while also reducing the number and size of FX transactions that were required. The information technology (IT) implementation of this objective was relatively straightforward, with each of the netting participants uploading a daily file of their transaction information to the netting system. Subsequently, email messages were used to notify the participants if they would need to pay funds to or receive funds from the corporate treasury.

The second phase focused on external netting and centralization of payments. In this regard, each of Motorola's subsidiaries would provide a file with details of payments due to suppliers on a weekly basis. The payments netting center would then make the external vendor payments via cheque or electronically, and advise each of the subsidiaries of their net position, that is, the total amount they needed to pay the netting center. Electronic data interchange (EDI) messaging was also used to communicate payment-status information to the vendor.

In the implementation of the second phase, Citibank played a central role in facilitating global payments. Motorola would send supplier payment information using EDI messages to Citibank in London. Citibank would then effect payments to the suppliers' banks using the SWIFT network or via the bank's cheque issuing centers in New York and London. At the time, Citibank was one of the few banks that could offer such services based on its existing global communications network and presence in many different countries.

These cash management changes yielded significant benefits. The first phase yielded savings of over US$6 million per annum. The second phase reduced the value of payments that had to be settled by over US$2 billion. The subsidiaries also enjoyed the benefits of reduced administrative overhead and operational errors. Yet, for the benefits that were gained, significant challenges, more organizational than technical, were faced in implementing the netting strategies. For example, despite the clear cost benefit that was possible, resistance was encountered in shifting from the subsidiaries' local payment operations to a centralized corporate model.

Motorola's pioneering initiative provides a representative example of the business drivers and implementation challenges involved with corporate cash management, and shows how financial institutions can support this function. Today, cash management services are offered to corporations of all sizes by numerous regional and global financial institutions, and many banks obtain a significant portion of their revenue and profit from the provision of cash management and transactional services.

Source: Holland, C., P. Christopher, G. Lockett, J. M. Richard, and I. Blackman, "The Evolution of a Global Cash Management System," *Sloan Management Review* 36, issue 1 (Fall 1994): 37–47.

Questions

1. What approaches could Fintech companies use to offer cash management solutions that could compete with banks' offerings?
2. What advantages do established banks have over new entrants for providing cash management services?
3. What financial benefits would Citibank have gained from providing cash management services to Motorola?
4. How could banks leverage modern technology to cost-effectively provide similar cash management services to small and medium-sized corporations?

7.1 DEPOSIT TAKING

Deposit taking is an unglamorous but critical banking activity. Customer savings deposits provide banks with an inexpensive and "sticky" funding for their lending activities. Typically, banks have access to several sources of funding: equity, long-term debt, short-term debt instruments and agreements, and customer deposits. While equity and long-term debt provide a steady and secure source of funding, their cost is relatively high. Alternatively, the cost of short-term borrowing is lower, but funding costs vary from month to month and year to year. The cost and availability of short-term funding depends both on prevailing interest rates and market **liquidity**, and counterparties willing to lend to banks on a short-term basis. For instance, during the **Global Financial Crisis** in 2008, few lenders were willing to provide short-term funding to banks. As a result, when banks' short-term debt obligations matured, they faced the problem of replacement funding being only available in the financial market at exorbitant costs. Hence, short-term debt is not sticky—there is no guarantee that it will be readily available when needed. In contrast, once customer deposits are acquired, they do not need to be regularly replaced as a source of funding. Even though customers can withdraw bank deposits, the likelihood that they withdraw funds en masse is low and typically new deposits from one set of customers will replace the funds lost through withdrawals from another set of customers.

While it might seem as though all banks would have access to customer deposits, some do not. Investment banks, for instance, by their nature are not in the business of taking customer deposits. Likewise, banks that specialize in specific types of lending, such as credit card issuance, may only have very limited current (chequing) and savings deposit facilities. Supporting current and savings accounts is not particularly complicated; rather, the bulk of the effort goes into providing multichannel access to these accounts. For example, most customers require access to their funds via automated teller machines, through debit cards, and over the Internet for bill payment. Significant time, effort, and cost are required to implement and maintain each of these channels.

Banks that accept customer deposits compete with other banks on the interest rates and the types of savings plans offered. Some banks provide business solutions that enable customers to set savings goals, calculate saving amounts, and track their saving progress over time. These solutions may also automatically transfer a portion of direct salary deposits to a special savings account. Besides helping customers save to reach specific monetary goals, saving solutions also provide banks with information about customers' expected future cash inflows and outflows.

Holding on to customers' deposits has become more difficult as competition has increased. In many cases, the younger generations are more concerned with service and convenience and are less risk averse with regard to products that they purchase. Accordingly, banks must provide customers with easy access to their accounts and flexible banking services (for example, mobile banking and Internet bill payment) as well as provide innovative types of savings products. For example, banks in many Asian countries offer foreign currency deposit products and enhanced yield products, such as **dual currency investments (DCI)**, as a way of providing depositors with the opportunity to achieve higher yields on their savings when domestic interest rates are low. DCIs are able to provide higher nominal interest rates by incorporating additional risk into the product, where under certain conditions loss of interest and possibly principal may occur.

Moreover, to accept deposits banks must first be able to receive the customer's funds. While this sounds elementary, in many cases it is more complicated than it would appear. In countries where Automated Clearing House (ACH) and General Interbank Recurring Order (GIRO) payments are prevalent, such as many countries in Europe, this is less of a concern because funds can be easily deposited electronically. However, in other markets where use of cash notes and paper cheques are common, banks face logistical challenges in collecting and processing these financial instruments in physical form. With regard to cash notes, in some markets banks have provided special services to support small, cash-only businesses that routinely amass large volumes of paper notes over the course of a business day. For instance, in Singapore some banks' automated teller machines (ATMs) are designated for and only support deposit of cash notes. With regard to paper cheques, which are still relatively common in the United States, many banks have leveraged technology to implement **remote deposit capture (RDC)** solutions.

Prior to 2004, the US Federal Reserve required cheques to be physically transferred from payees to their banks, and then from their banks to regional cheque processing centers for processing. However, in 2004, the Check Clearing for the 21st Century Act (also known as Check 21 Act) was passed, which allowed cheque recipients to process the cheques using the scanned image rather than the physical copy. This change greatly reduced logistical problems, for example, loss, destruction, and delays associated with cheque processing, and also opened up new opportunities for new business solutions.

This change in the law along with widespread use of cameras with mobile phones and scanners, led banks to offer RDC services. In the retail context, typically banks will provide customers an applicaiton that supports RDC to install on their mobile phones. Customers use the application to enter the details of the payment, capture images of the front and back of the cheque, and transmit this information over the mobile Internet to the banks' servers for processing. In the corporate context, the process is similar but a personal computer is used in place of a mobile phone and a scanner is issued instead of a camera.

RDC has been popular with bank customers because it improves funds availability, does not require trips to bank branches to make deposits, and provides a later cutoff time for deposits. Besides increasing the convenience for customers, RDC also reduces the volume of paper cheques that banks need to handle and scan and reduces the processing costs. Figure 7-1 shows how for a major US-based bank, customer use of self-service deposit channels, such as RDC and ATMs, has grown and the cost advantage they provide [1]. Although cheques are slowly becoming obsolete in the United States, solutions such as RDC that combine service, channel, and process innovation make the continued

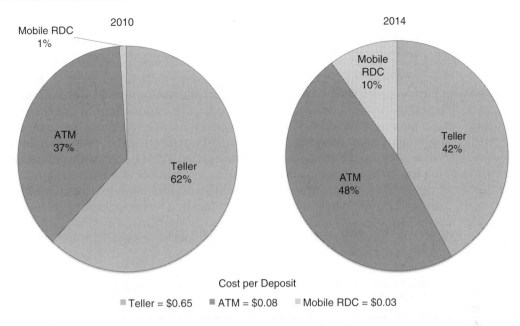

Figure 7-1 Shift in use of deposit channels by consumer households and relative costs

usage of cheques much more efficient. However, as simple and straightforward as RDC sounds, it creates new avenues for fraud. For example, using RDC, a fraudster could quite easily use RDC to deposit the same cheque twice at two different banks. The underlying processes and issues involved with RDC are more complicated than might appear on the surface, as highlighted in Case Study 7-2.

Case Study 7-2

Managing the Complexities of Remote Deposit Capture

Comerica Bank launched its RDC offering to its customers in 2006. Within two years, it managed to support cheque processing at 2,000 different customer locations, and reached the point where it was processing over 650,000 items and US$2.63 billion in deposits on a monthly basis. Comerica Bank used a third-party vendor to implement its remote capture technology, which helped reduce the amount of work the bank had to do to implement RDC. However, there were still many complications that the bank had to address.

Development, rollout, and support of the RDC service involved many different parts of the bank. Marketing and communications staff determined how to position and promote the product. Sales people, relationship managers, and customer service representatives were the front-line staff that worked with customers to ensure that the service met their needs. Risk management and credit administration staff were also involved in the design and were also users of the system. The bank's legal department was responsible for drafting and reviewing vendor and customer agreements so that they addressed relevant RDC considerations, such as liability, and also for ensuring that the solution was compliant with applicable laws and regulations. IT and operations staff, along with the vendor, were responsible for designing, implementing, testing, supporting and maintaining the RDC solution. From the IT standpoint, security, scalability, and image quality were key considerations. Optical character recognition (OCR) was also an important part of the technology. It enabled the courtesy amount, i.e., the dollar value written in numbers, and the legal amount, i.e., the dollar value written in words, to be captured without requiring human intervention.

(Continued)

(Continued)

One major compliance-related requirement that complicated Comerica's solution was to "know your customer" (KYC). There were several considerations associated with KYC that had to be addressed. One was ensuring that the nature of RDC customers' businesses were in line with the bank's strategy and target market. Another concern was that new RDC customers could involve substantial upfront effort in underwriting. Likewise, the transaction histories and behavior patterns of RDC customers had to be studied and understood as part of the risk underwriting process. Furthermore, Comerica needed to ensure that its RDC business operations could be adequately observed and examined. While this is often achieved through onsite visits to customers, this approach was not practical given that many of Comerica's customers were remote, spread across 41 states and three foreign countries. These considerations were crucial because during the early stages of customers' use of the RDC service, Comerica had to underwrite the customer's risks associated with the service. That is to say, if a customer were to incur financial loss related to the RDC solution, inadequate KYC due diligence could lead to claims that the service was unsuitable for the customer, shifting the liability to the bank.

Source: McCarty, Daniel J., "Best Practices in Product Development: A Case Study of Remote Deposit Capture," Journal of Payments Strategy & Systems 3, issue 2 (2009): 157–170.

7.2 CASH MANAGEMENT

7.2.1 Corporate Banking Context

Banks typically provide the following types of cash management services to customers: account management and access facilities, receivables management, liquidity management, international cash netting, and payment facilities. An overview the first four of these areas will be presented in the following subsections, and payment facilities will be covered in depth in Chapter 9.

7.2.1.1 Account management and access facilities

A fundamental need of a bank's customers is to determine their financial position, which in turn usually requires access to bank account balance information. Needs related to accessing account information include being able to see current (real-time) account balances, monitor cash movements, retrieve historical statement information, check the status of outstanding payments (such as cheques), and see mark-to-market valuation, that is, a reflection of current market prices of foreign currency holdings. With regard to currency valuation, when customers have accounts denominated in foreign currencies, in some cases, balances will be presented in both the accounts' underlying currencies and the customer's base currency so that aggregate account totals can be summed in the base currency.

Besides retrieving balance information, customers also need to be able to transfer funds between accounts. Transfers may be simple, such as moving funds from a current to a savings account, in which case they can be fulfilled through accounting entries within the bank's core banking system. On the other hand, they may be complicated, as is the case with transfers between different accounts of differing currencies. For example, a transfer between a Japanese yen (JPY) denominated account to an Australian dollar (AUD) denominated account would require currency conversion from JPY to AUD. This conversion, in turn, requires the use of an FX rate that may be determined in a number of ways. One possibility is that the rate is based on the bank's "counter" rate, defined at the beginning of the day; another is that the rate is derived from the real-time spot rate with an added **margin**; it is also possible that the rate is determined by a previous hedging transaction, such as a forward FX contract.

Corporate customers often have multiple bank accounts spread across different financial institutions or in the same financial institution across different countries. Similarly, conglomerates may have multiple individual accounts with a single bank for each of its subsidiaries. This disaggregation of funds presents corporate customers with a problem related to tracking and maintaining balances and, thus, provides banks with an opportunity to provide account information consolidation services. While for many reasons, corporate customers may need to have many distributed accounts, for other reasons, they may also require a consolidated view of those same accounts.

Corporate customers also have systems that require bank account information. For example, it will be necessary for corporate customers to reconcile their bank account balances in the **general ledger (GL)** with their bank account statements. This reconciliation process is used to determine which payables have been settled and which receivables are outstanding. Bank charges, account transfers, and currency exchanges will also be verified. Furthermore, large corporate customers may also have dedicated cash and treasury management systems that require integration of bank account transaction and balance information.

By delivering account statement information electronically, banks enable customers to aggregate balance information across multiple accounts and institutions more easily and integrate account information into their internal systems. Electronic statements provided via the Internet banking website may be delivered using display-oriented formats, such as HTML, or in application-oriented formats, such as a file with text values separated by commas. Alternatively, they may be provided through the bank's electronic channel interfaces via host-to-host communications (for example, secure file transfer protocol) using electronic data interchange formats, such as the SWIFT MT940 standard. The SWIFT MT940 electronic account statement is an international standard for the paperless transmission of account information. This standard is used to support integration with customers' cash management, treasury systems, and accounting applications. SWIFT will be discussed in more depth in Chapter 9.

7.2.1.2 Receivables management

Besides enabling payments, banks can help corporate customers collect and manage their receivables. Banks can automate collection from the customers of corporate customers through the domestic electronic payment network, for example, via GIRO or ACH transfers. In this case, the end customer would authorize the bank to withdraw from their account a fixed or variable amount on a periodic basis.

Utility companies commonly employ such collection facilities. Similarly, banks can help corporate customers debit their customers' credit card accounts to pay outstanding invoices. Lockbox services are a mail-processing outsourcing function provided by banks. As part of this service, banks provide post office boxes that are specified as the destinations for corporate customers' payments in the form of cheques. They maintain the post office boxes, open the mail that is received, and process any cheques that it contains. They then electronically capture relevant data in the mail contents, deposit cheques, and generate reports. Such services can be useful for mid-sized firms that cannot take advantage of economies of scale to internally process large numbers of paper-based payments. Besides improving processing efficiency, lockboxes can reduce "mail float" time, that is, the time that funds are unavailable because they are in transit, improving cash flow and increasing interest revenue.

Corporate customers may also work together with banks so that they are included as a payment destination in the bill-payment systems that banks provide to their customers. Alternatively, billers may need to coordinate with third-party nonbank electronic bill-payment services, as discussed in Case Study 4-3.

Moreover, many banks provide foreign cheque clearing and settlement services. Typically, cheques presented for deposit that are issued by a foreign bank will be repatriated to their country of origin, cleared locally, and then the funds will be transferred electronically from the bank that issued the cheque to the depositor's bank. Due to logistics and the number of parties involved, foreign cheque processing is often slow and involves substantial fees.

7.2.1.3 Liquidity management

An important function that corporate treasuries provide is to optimize liquidity, that is, the availability of a firm's cash resources. For many years, the primary aim of liquidity management was to maximize interest earned on surplus funds and minimize interest paid on fund shortfalls. However, during the **Global Financial Crisis** of 2008, companies' options for obtaining short-term funding from external sources dried up and, thus, it became more important for corporations to be able to manage their own internal liquidity effectively. This section will briefly review how banks help customers manage their liquidity by providing cash sweeping, pooling, and netting services.

7.2.1.3.1 Cash sweeping

Sweeping funds enables corporate customers to maximize returns on cash surpluses and minimize interest expense on cash shortfalls. Sweeping usually involves the movement of end-of-day balances from subaccounts to a single master account. The resulting state of the accounts is that the subaccounts have zero balances, and funds are concentrated in the master account. The master account may be interest bearing, or the concentrated funds may be invested on an overnight basis to achieve higher returns. Sweeping is an automated service provided by banks that reduces unnecessary administrative work for customers.

7.2.1.3.2 Cash pooling

Cash pooling is similar to cash sweeping, except that it involves notional consolidation of balances without the physical movement of funds between accounts. As with sweeping, the balances across multiple accounts—dispersed across separate, but linked corporate entities—are aggregated for interest compensation purposes. Pooling arrangements may be for accounts in the same currency and the same country. Alternatively, banks may support more complex arrangements of pooling balances across multiple countries, and possibly even multiple currency accounts. A key benefit of pooling is that it allows the corporation to minimize interest-related expenses and fees by notionally offsetting funding excesses and shortfalls across multiple individual accounts. Large fund amounts, attained by aggregating balances, may also be placed in money market instruments to yield higher returns on cash holdings.

As an example of pooling, consider a corporation with two subsidiaries, entities A and B. Entity A may have a surplus of funds, whereas Entity B may have short-term borrowing requirements to cover a liquidity shortfall caused by trade activities. Without pooling, Entity A may make a small amount of interest revenue on its excess funds, and Entity B may require the use of short-term lending facilities or trade financing that incurs interest charges and possibly bank fees. With pooling, the customer could notionally fund Entity B's shortfall with Entity A's excess, thereby saving the cost of the spread between the borrowing cost and the return on deposit, as well as any related transaction fees.

In the multi-entity corporate context, cash pooling is attractive because it preserves the autonomy of subsidiaries' accounts. It does not affect the control of funds and has minimal impact on the entities' record keeping. However, as with sweeping, it does require that all pooled accounts be maintained with the bank providing the pooling service.

7.2.1.3.3 Netting of cash settlements

As discussed in Case Study 7-1, netting offsets corporate intracompany payment obligations so that only the net difference needs to be settled. Third parties, such as suppliers, may also participate in netting arrangements. Netting eliminates the need for gross settlement, thereby reducing fund movements and the resulting funds-transfer costs. It also reduces the FX conversions required and consolidates FX positions so that larger, centralized positions can be traded at more favorable rates. The concept of netting is explained in more depth in Chapter 9 in the context of payments.

7.2.2 Retail Banking Context

Cash management services in the retail banking context are quite similar to that for corporate banking, but generally simpler. For example, individuals have fewer accounts to manage, which makes sweeping less relevant. Likewise, they do not deal in sufficient volumes to justify pooling or netting arrangements. In fact, many banks offer integrated retail accounts that provide cheque and electronic payment and overdraft facilities, and also bear interest. Online bill payment and cash withdrawal capabilities have greater relevance to retail customers. Also, as international travel and overseas work assignments have become more common, there has been an increasing need for retail customers to be able to make cross-border payments, money transfers, and cash withdrawals.

Over the past several decades, in many developed markets bank deposits have faced competition from other investment options, such as investment accounts that provide access to stocks and mutual funds (also known as unit trusts). Accordingly, some banks offer investment accounts as part of their cash management options. These may be provided in conjunction with the investment banking division of a larger bank, or in partnership with another bank or other firm that provides those services. By providing both cash and investment management services banks can provide "one stop shopping" for their customers. This benefits both the banks and their customers, by increasing banks' wallet share and improving customers' convenience in accessing these services.

Moreover, personal financial management (PFM), i.e., budgeting tools, have also become an important feature for retail cash management (Case Study 7-3). Offerings to customers range from simple end-of-year reports on the customer's credit card spending trends to more complex aggregated views of customer financial information and cash flows across multiple accounts at different financial institutions. Graphical data visualization may be used to help customers understand concepts such as budgets and net worth. Often PFM tools will enable customers to set goals, such as a saving or spending, and help track their progress toward those goals. Email, text message, or mobile application alerts may also be used to provide information about payments that are due, low balances, and milestone achievements toward saving or spending goals.

Case Study 7-3

The Growth and Evolution of Personal Financial Management Tools

Online personal financial management tools were popularized by Fintech companies in the early 2000s. Some of the biggest and most successful firms offering online PFM services also provided aggregation services that pulled users' financial information from accounts held in different financial institutions so that all bank account balances, credit card and mortgage debt, and retirement savings information could be viewed and analyzed in a consolidated form. Integrating this information required customers to provide their credentials, i.e., username and password, to the PFM service so that it could access their online banking accounts at other institutions.

Banks' responses to these PFM services were mixed. Some, such as Citibank, partnered with established Fintech companies to integrate their PFM services into the banks' websites to provide budget planning and account aggregation capabilities to customers. On the other hand, other banks rejected Fintech PFM providers and saw them as a threat or a nuisance. In their view, Fintech PFMs intermediated the online relationship banks had with their customers, and enabled rates and fees to be more easily compared with those of other financial institutions. PFM aggregators also generated much more traffic that hit banks' online banking websites than actual customers and accessed more pages, putting heavier loads on the bank's websites and back-end systems. Furthermore, the fact that PFMs held customers' login credentials created additional security risks for banks.

(Continued)

(Continued)

If hackers breached the PFM aggregator's systems and the login credentials were compromised, the banks and their customers could end up bearing the fallout from fraudulent use of those accounts.

Partially in response, some banks have created their own PFM solutions, with the aim of providing unique, defining features. USAA bank released a standalone mobile application called Savings Coach that responds to voice commands and integrates games into the saving process. HSBC has run pilot tests with a mobile application called Nudge that would spur customers to change their spending behavior based on their goals, comparing their current spending patterns with past behavior and with the spending of other similar types of consumers. Alerts are used to reinforce positive saving or spending behavior and warn against overspending. It is yet to be seen if banks can divert or wean their customers away from Fintech PFM services by developing their own capabilities in this area.

Sources: Crosman, Penny, "Online Banking Design Succeeds or Fails on Feedback, Details: Citi's Weber," *American Banker,* January 28, 2013, http://www.americanbanker.com/issues/178_19/citigroup-s-weber-on-the-keys-to-online-banking-design-1056204-1.html; Cumming, Chris, "PFM Sites Seek Thaw in Frosty Relationship with Banks," *American Banker,* December 31, 2015, http://www.americanbanker.com/news/national-regional/pfm-sites-seek-thaw-in-frosty-relationship-with-banks-1078583-1.html; Wisniewski, Mary, "USAA Launches New App to Help Millennials Save," *American Banker,* July 28, 2015, http://www.americanbanker.com/news/bank-technology/usaa-launches-new-app-to-help-millennials-save-1075714-1.html; Wallace, Tim, "HSBC Prods Customers to Spend Less and Save More," *The Telegraph,* January 19, 2016, http://www.telegraph.co.uk/finance/newsbysector/banksandfinance/12106290/HSBC-prods-customers-to-spend-less-and-save-more.html.

7.3   OPPORTUNITIES

For banks, an attractive feature of offering cash management services is that it generates both fee- and float-based revenue. Yet, unlike lending, these services do not have a material impact on the bank's balance sheet and, hence, do not require the bank to raise additional regulatory-mandated capital. Cash management services also produce little, if any, credit, market, and interest-rate risk. Fee-based revenue is invaluable when revenue from lending activities is under pressure. The year 2008 was particularly brutal for banks, during which many banks experienced massive losses related to loans and derivatives. One bright spot was corporate transactional services, which continued to contribute to the bottom line and helped offset losses in other areas. A case in point is Deutsche Bank, which in the fourth quarter of 2008 incurred over €3 billion in losses related to trading, a large portion of which was related to credit positions in the US automotive sector. At the same time, its transaction-oriented businesses, which included cash management and trade finance, generated over €750 million in net revenue and showed double-digit growth compared with the previous year.

There is also the opportunity for banks to help their customers save more. Studies show that, at least in the United States, millennials are particularly needful in this area. As of 2014, people 35 years old and under had a negative savings rate of minus 2% [2]. They also had fewer investment accounts and investments, including savings accounts and time deposits, than the previous generation had at the same age. Millennials' household wealth was also lower by comparison. Reasons cited for their lack of savings include the complexity of investments offerings combined with Millennials' limited understanding of the risks investments present and rewards that they can provide. Accordingly, banks can benefit by creating savings products that address these concerns. For example in the United Kingdom, Santander marketed a relatively simple '123' account that paid 1% interest on deposits above £1,000, 2% on deposits greater than £2,000, and 3% on funds deposited above £3,000 and up to £20,000.

Banks can also take advantage of bundling other products and services to encourage deposits from specific customer segments. For example, to lure affluent frequent travelers, a bank could offer higher interest rates, waive fees for overseas ATM withdrawals, and provide free travel insurance provided to customers who maintain a high deposit balance. Alternatively, banks often reduce or eliminate fees based on the amounts customers have on deposit, and also some offer special savings accounts that offer better rates but are only accessible through online channels. In some cases, banks provide preferred lending interest rates to customers that have pre-existing deposit accounts. Providing additional services to existing customers results in lower acquisition costs as well as makes it easier to examine customer behavior patterns.

7.4 CHALLENGES

While cash management services offer benefits to both the bank and its customers, factors such as price competition, processing efficiency, and operational risk are crucial concerns. Processing efficiency, which underlies price competitiveness, requires that only a minimal amount of manual processing be performed so that large transaction volumes can easily be supported. That is to say, STP is necessary to ensure low transaction costs and high levels of customer service.

Opening accounts so that customers are able to make deposits is not always simple or straightforward. Numerous know-your-customer checks are required to ensure that the bank is not creating a stepping-stone for money laundering. (Regulatory compliance concerns related to account opening are discussed in more depth in Chapter 19.) Likewise, business in some industries is off limits for banks to deal with. For example, legal marijuana distribution businesses in US states such as Colorado have encountered major challenges when trying to gain access to banking facilities. Where banking regulations have not kept up with changes in state laws, gray areas exist and financial institutions generally would err on the conservative side and not do business with unsanctioned customers.

Fraud is another concern when taking deposits. As a case in point, in 2014, 29 people were arrested in Chicago for perpetrating a scheme called "card cracking" that cost banks millions of dollars in losses [3]. As part of the scheme, fraudsters leveraged social media to recruit young banking customers, convincing them to provide the debit card and PIN for their accounts and accept a counterfeit cheque for deposit. Once the cheque was deposited in the account, the fraudster would withdraw the funds before the bank was able to determine the cheque was counterfeit. The customer would then claim that they lost their debit card and that it was used to withdraw the funds. The customer expected to receive a kickback for participating in the fraud. In this case, under US Regulation E, the customer was protected and the bank was liable for the losses. Hence, something as basic as opening an account and accepting a deposit can have significant risk implications.

In recent years, low, and in some cases negative, interest rates have created major changes for banks to attract customer deposits and maintain profitability of saving products. For instance, as of 2016, providing the '123' account mentioned in Section 7.3 was costing Santander UK over one billion dollars per year. Initially, this prompted Santander to more than double the monthly fee for the account, but ultimately required the bank to cut the interest rate on the account to an even 1.5%. What is more, some banks in Europe and the United Kingdom started, or warned they may start, to apply negative interest rates to customer deposits. This would effectively require customers to pay to keep their money at a bank. While this type of change would clearly create new challenges for banks' business models, it would also pose new technology challenges. It is unlikely that few, if any, core banking systems have been designed to support negative interest rates for savings and current accounts. Hence, significant changes to core platforms and other supporting systems would be required to accommodate this requirement and manual account adjustments could be required while the system changes required to handle negative interest rates are being implemented.*

---

* Increases in interest rates that began in 2016 and continued through 2017 alleviated the concern that banks may have to implement negative savings rates. Nonetheless, the potential impact of this unexpected situation is interesting to consider from an IT systems perspective.

7.5   SOLUTION CONSIDERATIONS: CORE BANKING SYSTEMS

In the broader context of deposit taking and lending, core banking systems are a good place to begin reviewing architecture considerations. The definitions of core banking systems vary but, at a minimum, they generally provide transaction processing and account management functions. They support current and savings accounts and loan products. Payments processing functionality is also usually implemented in core banking systems. Over time, core banking systems have evolved to include additional functionality and may include support for treasury products, multichannel connectivity, and customer relationship management (CRM) facilities. Typically, core banking systems primarily support the capture order and fulfillment stages of the transaction lifecycle and, to some extent, transaction maintenance. Additional IT systems are usually required to support activities related to engaging the customer for complex transactions and for some transaction maintenance activities.

The functions provided by a bank's core banking system will vary with the size and geographic location of the institution. For example, a small bank may rely predominantly on a single core banking system for the majority of its business activities. Alternatively, a large bank may have separate IT systems for its service delivery channels, CRM, credit card processing, treasury, trade finance, and risk management. Core banking product vendors generally design their products to be modular so that customers can license and use the parts of the system that best fit their needs. Figure 7-2 shows how the modules of the FLEXCUBE retail core banking system from Oracle are organized, and how it links with other banking IT systems.

While one might assume that each bank will have one "core" banking system, in fact, several such systems may coexist per bank. There may be one system that is used for deposits and loans and

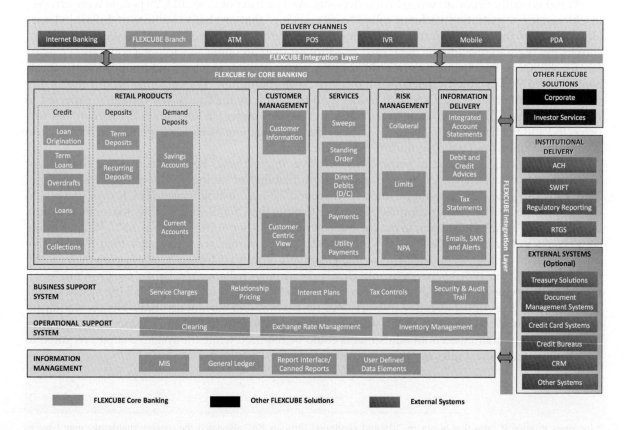

Figure 7-2 Reference architecture of a modern retail core banking platform (© Oracle Corporation 2012. Reprinted with permission. Oracle and Java are registered trademarks of Oracle and/or its affiliates.)

another that is used for credit cards. Alternatively, a legacy core banking system may be used at a bank's headquarters and different, newer technology may be deployed for overseas operations. It is also possible that multiple locations use the same core banking software, but run their own separate system instance that is configured or customized to support local requirements.

In the 1960s, core banking systems emerged as software systems custom-developed by banks that ran on mainframes. In the 1970s and 1980s, hardware and software vendors began to offer core banking solutions, and in the 1990s, core banking solutions offerings became available on minicomputers and commodity hardware that ran operating systems such as UNIX and Windows. These newer core banking platforms could be accessed more easily and had better support for integration than mainframe systems. In some cases, the operation and maintenance of core banking systems may be outsourced to third-party vendors. For example, some banks contract with service providers to provide, operate, and maintain the core banking system for their credit card operations. In conjunction with these services, other services, such as the printing and mailing of statements, manufacturing and distribution of credit cards, and fraud monitoring of account activity may be outsourced.

Since their inception, core banking platforms have presented innumerable challenges for banks. Core banking systems can be quite complex due to their growth over time and the wide range of functions that they provide. Also, a large proportion of core banking systems still run on mainframe hardware, for which there is limited expertise available. Moreover, there is a fundamental paradox that surrounds core banking. Because it is so crucial for day-to-day operations, it is risky and undesirable to make major changes to it. At the same time, because it is central to so many business functions, most business-related changes will involve the core banking system in some way. As the financial services market has become faster moving—largely due to competition from Fintech companies—being able to quickly make changes to the core banking environment has become a strategic concern for banks.

Maintenance and migration of core banking systems remain major concerns at many banks. Maintenance of 10-, 20-, or even 30-year-old systems can be costly and time consuming. Often, new technology solutions will be limited by the existing capabilities of the core banking system. While migrating to a newer and more functional core banking system might seem to be the obvious solution, it is difficult to achieve this in practice. The bank's processes will have been largely designed around the core banking system, and changing the system will require altering a substantial number of business processes as well. Likewise, because management and users are intimately familiar with what they already have, it can be difficult for them to predetermine if alternative implementations will meet their needs.

Legacy core banking systems present a formidable challenge for solution architects. Since they cannot be easily replaced, it is important to find ways to work around their functional and technical limitations. To address functional concerns, a common strategy is to minimize solutions' dependencies on the core system. New functionality is built or purchased as components that run external to the core banking system. Technically, core banking functions may be encapsulated using service-oriented wrappers that enable the system's functions to be more easily accessed by other components. This strategy can also help to decouple system integration from system-specific interfaces so that it is easier to replace the core system in the future.

More advanced architecture considerations include how to most effectively integrate the core banking functions into the overall transaction lifecycle. Besides booking and fulfilling transactions, the information contained in core banking systems is also critical for sales, marketing, and management reporting purposes (Case Study 7-4). Customization strategies are also important because business-process workflows are often implemented as part of the core banking system logic. Approaches for customizing or supplementing these workflows to meet bank-specific requirements can be achieved by paying the vendor to modify the software, making use of the software's configuration options, or using external workflow facilities, as discussed in Chapter 2, in conjunction with the core banking system.

Making a subset of the execution logic configurable at runtime is a common approach for making prepackaged software, such as core banking platforms, more adaptable and maintainable. Runtime configuration is generally implemented using parameters, scripting languages, and plug-in architectures. Parameters that specify simple binary or enumerated options can either be defined in

---

Case Study 7-4
Core Banking Success Factors

The successful deployment and use of core banking systems are dependent on a number of factors, of which technology is only one. A case study of a German bank's use of a core banking system for loan processing found that the system's perceived success varied significantly among the bank's business units, and the perception was partially attributable to the business users' background and level of interaction with the information group.

One measure of success was how efficiently the branches used the core banking system. Of the four branches described in the study, one branch chose to record customer transaction data initially in spreadsheets rather than in the core system. The data was rekeyed from the spreadsheets to the core system after the transaction had been completed. The same branch indicated that users found the core system to be slow, complicated, and uncomfortable to use. The screens of the core system were not customizable and required the user to enter three-letter codes to navigate between functions; it took up to an hour-and-a-half to enter a standard loan transaction.

Branch users were less satisfied with the system than back-office staff. While the core system catered to most back-office functions, it provided less benefit to the branches. Of the three main activities that the branches engaged in—consulting, sales, and processing—the core system only supported loan processing. Unfortunately, the core system was focused on serving a specific part of the transaction and services lifecycle, rather than supporting business activities from start to finish.

On the other hand, when it comes to replacing core banking systems, success is more dependent on having the ability manage large-scale projects and the perseverance to see the effort through to the end. To put this in perspective, consider Commonwealth Bank in Australia, which replaced its legacy, batch-based core banking system with a more modern one that was designed to provide realtime capabilities. The project began with a four-year schedule and AU\$580 budget. Ultimately, it took six years to complete and cost AU\$1.3 billion. The project had 1,500 people working on it on a full time basis, and the migration of data from the old to new system involved 53 million customer records, 1.2 million term deposit accounts, and 10 million retail deposit and transaction accounts.

Source: Beimborn, D., J. Franke, H. T. Wagner, and T. Weitzel, "The Influence of Alignment on the Postimplementation Success of a Core Banking Information System: An Embedded Case Study," *Proceedings of the 40th Hawaii International Conference on System Sciences—2007*, http://www.computer.org/portal/web/csdl/doi/10.1109/HICSS.2007.541; Fitzsimmons, C., "CBA takes \$1.3bn SAP punt on real-time banking", *Financial Review*, August 19, 2013, http://www.afr.com/technology/cba-takes-13bn-sappunt-on-realtime-banking-20130818-jyxen; Foo, F., "CSC questions CBA core banking upgrade", *Australian*, July 7, 2011, http://www.theaustralian.com.au/business/technology/csc-questions-cba-core-banking-upgrade/news-story/3641617bd3640a35a570928d65d65402; Lohman, T., "Commbank IT modernisation spending tips \$1.1b", *Computerworld*, February 9, 2011, https://www.computerworld.com.au/article/376024/commbank_it_modernisation_spending_tips_1_1b_/; Pearce, R., "More work needed on CBA's backend systems, says bank's digital chief", *Computerworld*, September 20, 2016, https://www.computerworld.com.au/article/607151/more-work-needed-cba-backend-systems-says-bank-digital-chief/.

---

configuration files or databases, often using graphical user interfaces. Interpreted scripting languages and workflow editors allow more complex data structures to be defined and conditional and control logic to be implemented in conjunction with core product functions. Plug-in facilities provide flexibility by enabling separate modules to be programmed independently and then linked into the core system. The configuration approach used will vary by the type of system and user requirements. Parameterization is the most common approach, but many systems also support plug-in capabilities, and a relatively small number have workflow facilities built in.

7.6 ARCHITECTURE CONSIDERATIONS: RESILIENCE

Given the potential problems that banks can face when holding and handling customers' money, it is critical that their IT systems and business processes are resilient. From a technology perspective, being fully resilient requires fault tolerance at all levels and in all stages in the processing chain, including application-level resilience, hardware resilience, network resilience, and telecommunication-link resilience. From a business process perspective, resilience requires development of a **business continuity plan (BCP)** and the readiness to execute it when technical or operational failures occur. Basic concepts related to resilience were introduced in Chapters 3 and 5, and this section will explore resilient architecture configurations in more detail.

Resilient architectures can be divided into two categories, active-active and active-passive. In **active-active configurations**, two or more active services are run in parallel, sharing the processing load. If one of the service instances fails, the remaining instances will take over its load so that processing continues with minimal interruption. With active-passive architectures, only one service will be actively doing processing and one or more services will be on standby, waiting to take over in case the active service fails.

Active-passive configurations come in several different flavors: hot standby, warm standby, and cold standby. With **hot standby configurations**, the passive service will be running in parallel with the active service and receiving the same input information. However, the hot standby service will not complete the actions that the active service performs, such as sending out messages or writing to a database, unless it takes over because the active service is unavailable. Hot standby fault tolerance takes the shortest time to recover in case of a failover, because the passive service is already in step and synchronized with the active service. Usually, hot standby failover logic is implemented at the application level.

On the other hand, with **warm standby configurations**, the passive service does not begin running until the active service fails. **Hardware clustering** is a common approach for implementing warm standby fault tolerance. In a hardware cluster, one or more hardware servers are kept idle so that they are ready to take over the function of another hardware server in case of failure of the active server. Commonly, when the warm standby server begins to take over, it will assume the network identity, that is, the Internet protocol address of the active server. Warm standby configurations are simpler than hot standby configurations because they do not require any special application-level logic to be implemented. However, longer failover delays will be incurred. Since all the necessary software applications are not already running, they will need to be launched on the standby server during the failover transition.

Cold standby configurations are generally associated with **disaster recovery (DR) sites**. Software solutions are installed on cold standby servers but not actively run, and may not necessarily be ready to run on short notice. Where hot standby failover may be measured in seconds and warm standby failover is measured in minutes, cold standby recovery often takes hours.

Even with all the protection that resilient architectures provide, they are not foolproof. Botched operational procedures and software upgrades can undermine almost any IT platform. Likewise, unlikely and/or unexpected events, such as the terrorist attacks on September 11, 2001 in the United States and the earthquake and tsunami in March of 2011 in Japan, can challenge and sometimes even overwhelm robust system designs. Thus, business continuity planning is essential. BCP considers potential failure points and conditions and then identifies steps and defines procedures for alleviating critical failures. In some cases, recovery strategies may involve backup or DR IT systems. In other cases, strategies may temporarily revert to completely manual processes that only require pen and paper (Case Study 7-5).

To be effective, BCPs must be regularly exercised. If DR failover tests are not performed periodically, fears that a DR strategy may not work as planned may inhibit its use in times of emergency. Likewise, it is important that clear guidelines be in place as to when DR failovers should be initiated so as to help avoid delays, confusion, and conflict when problems occur. It is better not to have to make critical decisions on the fly in times of distress. Key decisions are best thought through in advance so that clear instructions and guidelines can be prepared and relied upon when dealing with crisis situations.

Case Study 7-5

The Impact of Poor Core IT System Resilience

In 2002, three banks—Dai-ichi Kangyo Bank, Fuji Bank, and Industrial Bank of Japan—merged to form Mizuho Bank and Mizuho Corporate Bank. As part of the merger, the banks had to integrate their core banking systems, which were developed and supported by three different IT vendors. Unfortunately, this major undertaking did not go as planned, and Mizuho experienced major IT system failures immediately following the launch of the merged entities. During the incident, most of the bank's 7,000 ATMs malfunctioned, over 30,000 customers were double-billed, and over 2.5 million payments were delayed.

Both the Bank of Japan and the Financial Services Agency (FSA) conducted onsite examinations that resulted in the FSA issuing a business improvement order to Mizuho Financial Group. Mizuho submitted a report that promised to address the issues that led to the failure. The special advisers who had led the merger accepted responsibility for the debacle and resigned, and also the banks' senior executives were penalized with six-month pay cuts of between 15% and 50%.

Nine years later, Mizuho Bank had another major system failure following the magnitude 9.0 earthquake and tsunami that hit northeast Japan in March 2011. The earthquake itself was not the cause of the problem; rather, it was the large number of transfers to two bank accounts set up to receive charitable donations following the quake. The banks' 38,000 ATMs were out of service for three days, and at one point, the bank had more than one million payment transactions, including salary payments, waiting to be processed. It took a total of ten days to completely restore the bank's IT systems. The outage also resulted in a backlog of work for tellers who were inundated with over 200,000 customer requests for cash withdrawals while the ATMs were down. The bank branch's online transaction systems were down at the time as well, leading to the use of paper forms that had to be manually processed when the systems were back online.

It is difficult to attribute two major failures such as these at the same institution as coincidence or bad luck. The timing of the second outage was especially distressing for customers who were already suffering from the earthquake, the tsunami, and the many aftershocks that followed. In April 2011, it was announced that the President and CEO of Mizuho Bank would resign, accepting responsibility for the debacle. Mizuho Financial Group also announced that it would merge the retail and corporate banks to help improve management and decision-making processes to prevent similar problems from occurring in the future.

Senior management resignations and regulator sanctions will only have a limited effect if the institution does not change from within and address the underlying concerns. While simple, superficial changes can be made to address the problem symptoms, it takes considerable time and effort to institute the changes necessary to prevent recurrences. The larger the organization, the harder it is and the longer it takes to bring about meaningful changes.

Sources: Miyake, Kuriko, "Japan Urges Mizuho to Recover from System Errors," *ComputerWorld*, April 11, 2002, http://www. computerworld. com/s/article/70211/Japan_urges_Mizuho_to_recover_from_system_errors; "Ex-Mizuho Chiefs' Allowances Eyed," *Japan Times*, April 22, 2002, http://www.japantimes.co.jp/text/nb20020622a3.html#.T_agEJHwlg8; Belson, Ken, "Bank Group's Debut Adds to Japan's Woes," *New York Times*, April 10, 2002, http://www.nytimes.com/2002/04/10/business/bank-group-s-debut-adds-to-japan-s-woes.html; Bank of Japan, "The Bank's Closer Monitoring of Mizuho Financial Group," June 19, 2002, http:// www.boj.or.jp/en/announcements/release_2002/ fsk0206a.htm; "System Glitch Aftershocks Weigh On Mizuho Bank," *Nikkei*, April 1, 2011; Fujioka, Chisa, "Mizuho Bank Head to Resign over Computer Glitch," *Reuters*, April 23, 2011, http://www.reuters.com/ article/2011/04/23/us-mizuho-idUSTRE73M06I20110423; Ohinata, Hirobumi, "Mizuho President to Resign for Computer Failure," *Asahi Shimbun*, April 24, 2011, http://en.occa.mard.gov.vn/Crawl-Content/ Mizuho-president-to-resign-for-computer-failure-Asahi-Shimbun/2011/4/24/46971.news; Fukase, Atsuko, "Tech Crash Hits Japan Bank," *Wall Street Journal*, March 21, 2011, http://online.wsj. com/article/SB10001424052748704433904576212310659262754.html; Sato, Shigeru, "Mizuho to Merge Retail, Corporate Banking Units by 2013," *Bloomberg*, September 16, 2011, http://www.bloomberg.com/news/2011-09-16/mizuho-to-merge-retail-corporate-banking-units-by-2013-1-.html.

7.7 CASH AND DIGITAL CURRENCIES

Are digital currencies sounding a death knell for cash notes and government-issued currencies? This section examines some of the trends and considerations related to the future of cash notes and digital currencies.

7.7.1 Cash Notes

A 2016 survey of American adults showed that 62% of them thought it was likely or very likely that they would live in a cashless economy in their lifetime [4]. Trends point in this direction, with more than half of the survey participants under 30 saying that they were already comfortable without having cash. Likewise, from 2011 to 2016, the number of Americans that only pay for things using cash has dropped from 32% to 24%. Although the trend is clear, the elimination of cash notes and coins may still be a long time in coming.

While the use of cash may dwindle over time, to completely eliminate it would require a government edict. Governments have had some success in small reforms in cash usage, such as the phasing out of the one-cent coin in Australia and Singapore. However, larger-scale initiatives to phase out payment instruments have been mixed. For instance, in 2009 the UK Payments Council* set out a plan to eliminate the use of paper cheques by 2018. The rationale for this change was the decline in cheque usage and an estimated £200 million in savings that would be achieved from migrating the remaining usage to electronic payments. By 2011, the initiative was abandoned after a backlash by consumer groups and small businesses, which claimed a higher level of trust in the cheques over other payment methods. On the other hand, by government edict, India was able to demonetize its largest denomination cash notes, which accounted for 86 percent of the cash in circulation by value, within just a few months at the end of 2016. Key goals of this change included fighting corruption and countering tax evasion.

The experiences in the United Kingdom and India highlight how preferences towards cash and other paper payment instruments differ between countries. In parts of Europe, cash is still king. For instance, as of 2016, in Germany more than 75% of payments are made in cash and in Italy, the number is 83%. In contrast, in countries like Sweden, cash payments only represent between 5% and 7% of the value of payments made, and cash is typically used by tourists rather than Swedish nationals. Across northern Europe it is not uncommon for shops not to accept cash. In Japan, even though mobile and contactless-card payments enjoy widespread use for small purchases, many restaurants only accept cash and it is not uncommon for larger purchases and payments to be made using cash notes. Some of the dynamics affecting the use of cash include the maturity of electronic payment channels, consumer preferences, and fees associated with using electronic payments. The latter can be often substantial for merchants that accept credit card payments. Figure 7-3 shows the use of cash, by transaction volume, across several developed markets, as of 2014 [5].

Electronic payments provide three key advantages over cash payments: convenience, cost, and security. Electronic payments do not require the payer and the payee to physically handle funds, avoiding the need to hold and handle cash notes. For businesses, the cost of managing cash is significant. Cash notes and coins must be regularly checked for counterfeits, counted, stored, and transported. At each stage of handling, there is the risk of theft or fraud. For governments, cash transactions are problematic because they provide a means of transacting without record, facilitating tax evasion, and money laundering.

Yet, using cash also has a number of benefits that continue to make it attractive to use. The fact that it provides anonymity and cannot be easily tracked is appealing to people who are

---

* The Payments Council was a financial institution industry body that defined strategy for UK payment mechanisms up until 2015.

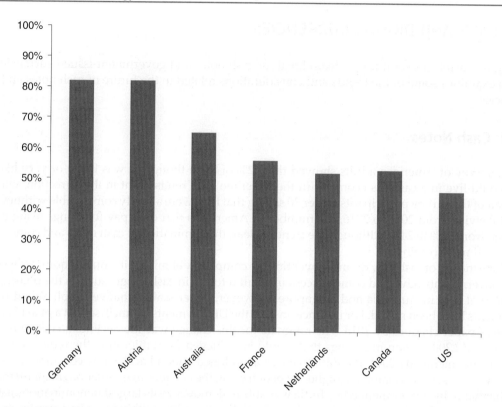

Figure 7-3 Cash payments as share of transaction volume

concerned about their privacy. On the other hand, merchants, banks, and other entities regularly use information generated from customers' electronic transactions for marketing and analysis purposes. This information can potentially fall into the wrong hands or made publically available if a data breach were to occur. Cash also provides a trusted backup when electronic payment systems are unavailable. Major catastrophes such as earthquakes and floods can knock out power or networks for large areas for extended periods of time, restricting the use of electronic payments. Furthermore, paying with cash has been shown by researchers to affect how much consumers are willing to spend on purchases and to make them focus more on the cost of items, which is helpful for people who are on a budget [6].

The rise of mobile and peer-to-peer payments, discussed in Chapter 9, may help lead consumers away from cash, encouraging them to replace their wallet with their phone. There is also a tipping point when the number of cash transactions becomes so small that the cost of supporting them stops making economic sense. Nonetheless, challenges arise in accommodating foreign visitors and unbanked nationals in a cashless market. It is hard to say whether the vision of a cashless economy will really come to pass in the next 50 years. Perhaps some countries will come close or even succeed, but given where things are today, it is difficult to imagine cash disappearing on a wide-scale basis.

7.7.2 Digital Currencies

Over the past decade digital currencies have grown from a novelty, of interest only to a small group of technologists, to a potentially disruptive force within the financial services industry. In hindsight, the emergence of digital currencies is not that surprising given that today most financial assets, including bank deposits, primarily exist as digital records. Likewise, some of the motivations behind digital currencies, such as avoiding centralized control of the currency or the payment system and privacy of transactions, are features that the existing financial system is not oriented toward.

This subsection will briefly examine digital currencies, focusing mostly on Bitcoin, since it was the prototype for modern digital currencies and still is the predominant digital currency. There is some variation in the terminology used for financial technologies such as Bitcoin; they are also referred to as virtual currencies and cryptocurrencies. This section will refer to them as digital currencies, and will sidestep any debate as to which is the best term to use. **Distributed ledgers**, such as blockchain, are the core technology that serves as the foundation for modern digital currencies. Many consider distributed ledger technology to be the real gem that has emerged from the invention of Bitcoin, and see great potential for its use in financial services outside of digital currencies. Blockchain and distributed ledgers will be examined separately in Chapter 20 and discussed both in the context of digital currencies as well as other applications.[*]

Since the inception of Bitcoin, arguably the starting point for modern digital currencies, digital currencies have had a bumpy ride. Figure 7-4 shows some of the major events that have occurred with digital currencies over the past decade. The following sections examine a number of different aspects of and considerations related to digital currencies, focusing primarily on those, such as Bitcoin, that are based on decentralized distributed ledgers.

7.7.2.1 Motivations

The digital currencies' reason for being revolves around three key considerations: ideological factors, improved transaction processing, and producing financial benefits for the inventors. Ideological considerations often get the most attention, largely because of a reference in the Bitcoin source code to the poor state of banks during the Global Financial Crisis of 2008. Digital currencies, such as Bitcoin, offer a way to eliminate dependencies on traditional financial institutions and circumvent centralized control and restrictions, such as those that national governments may impose, over the currency and the payment system that supports it. For example, digital currencies have been used to get around capital controls and restrictions on foreign currency purchases in China and Greece. In theory, users

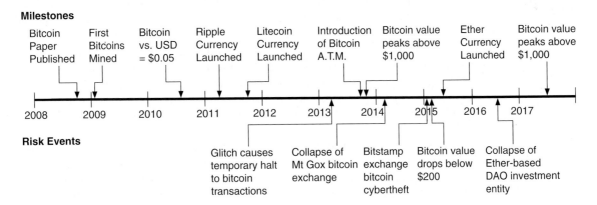

Figure 7-4 Digital currency timeline

---

[*] Since new payment systems are a large part of digital currencies' design and implementation, their discussion might be more appropriate in Chapter 9. However, given the great volume of material already contained in the chapter on payments, the author chose to include it in this chapter since storing funds in bitcoin accounts is an alternative that customers have to depositing money in bank accounts.

who wholly adopt digital currencies have the potential to operate outside of existing mainstream monetary and payment systems. The anonymity that digital currencies can provide is also attractive from an ideological perspective to those who place high value on their privacy.

Digital currencies have the potential to provide better transactional capabilities in several ways. First, by design, digital currencies have global reach and are not linked to the users' geographical location. For cross-border payments, digital currencies eliminate the need to make use of international payment systems,* such as SWIFT, and national automated clearing house (ACH) payment systems. Accordingly, users of digital currencies can avoid the fees that they charge and are not limited by the cutoff times that they impose. Use of a distributed payment system, where funds are transferred directly between users' account, also avoids credit and liquidity risks that the use of financial intermediaries can present, e.g., in the case when Lehman Brothers collapsed in 2008. There are no direct costs associated with maintaining digital currency accounts and transaction fees are low, compared with many other forms of money transfers and card payments. The overhead of accepting payments by digital currency are also low and primarily involve setting up a digital currency account and wallet.

Users can realize financial benefit directly from digital currencies in two different ways. One way is that they can participate as facilitators in the payment system, and in doing so, earn transaction fee revenue. Another way is that they can act as speculators on the value of the digital currency versus other, sovereign, currencies—i.e., currencies issued by national governments—that it can be converted into. In this context, digital currencies can be equated to a commodity or asset class. Speculating on digital currencies comes with significant risk in that digital currencies have no intrinsic value and their worth is largely determined by supply and demand. Digital currencies' value also depends on expectations of their future value and continued acceptance of them as a medium of exchange. The supply of digital currencies is usually predetermined by their technical design. Demand for digital currencies can have high variability depending on interest in the currency, acceptance level, and level of competition of other digital currencies. Events that highlight the risks of a digital currency, such as a major cybertheft of digital currency, can damage confidence and sharply reduce demand.

7.7.2.2 Characteristics

While the implementation specifics vary from one digital currency to another, for the most part they have a number of common characteristics. The use of new digital ledger technologies is probably the characteristic that stands out the most. Whereas traditional currency and payment systems have relied on the centralized ledgers that are operated and maintained by commercial and national central banks, digital currencies typically make use of distributed ledgers that are openly accessible to all participants in the payment system. This structure provides a high level of redundancy for information storage and transaction processing, compared with traditional, centralized payment systems. The distributed ledger serves as a means of recording holdings and transfers of assets, and serves as the authoritative record of ownership. Hence, the integrity and robustness of this mechanism is critical to the viability of digital currencies.

Most digital currencies use cryptography to validate transaction. Accordingly, they are referred to as cryptocurrencies. Public key encryption, also referred to as asymmetric encryption, is leveraged so that a cryptocurrency user digitally signs his or her transactions using a private key which can then be authenticated by others using the user's public key (see the Further Reading section at the end of this chapter for more information about asymmetric encryption). Cryptographic hash functions, such as SHA-256, are also generated and used as part of the process of validating and recording transactions in the digital ledger. Because cryptography underpins most digital currencies, it is critical that the cryptographic logic has been implemented correctly; otherwise flaws could lead to a fundamental compromise of the currency, making it worthless. Likewise, the protection of digital currency users'

---

* Covered in Chapter 9.

private keys is paramount. If a private key is lost, the digital currency account can no longer be accessed. Likewise, if the private key is compromised, the account could be accessed by someone other than the user and the funds held in the account stolen.

Some digital currencies, notably those most widely used, enable transactions to be made without disclosing the identity of the parties performing the transactions. The ability to make pseudonymous payments is ideal for those who highly value their privacy, but also can be used for illicit purposes as well. Digital currencies have become the payment method of choice for facilitating many illegal activities, ranging from selling illegal goods and services online to complying with ransom demands. Pseudonymity also enables users to circumvent tax reporting and regulatory restrictions. So far, this feature has precluded traditional financial institutions from providing services that support or involve digital currencies that are publicly available. It flies in the face of know-your-customer (KYC) requirements that underlie financial institutions' obligations to support laws related to anti-money laundering (AML) and combating the financing of terrorism (CFT).

Another important characteristic of many digital currencies is that their transactions are irrevocable. That is to say, once a transaction has been recorded and verified in the distributed ledger, it cannot be undone (without a fundamental change to the digital currency system, as discussed in Case Study 7-6). This feature is attractive to the receivers of digital currency payments, because there is little doubt regarding the permanence of the funds received, compared with other traditional payment mechanisms such as credit card and ACH payments, where payments can be reversed in the case of unauthorized transactions or disputes over a purchase. On the other hand, for the sender of digital currency payments, there is no means to recover funds in case of fraud or in case mistakes, such as using a wrong account number or transfer amount.

7.7.2.3 Participants

This subsection outlines the various participants, or actors, involved in digital currency transactions, based on a Bitcoin transaction as an example.

Users. A wide range of market participants including consumers, merchants, and criminals may choose to use digital currencies. They can obtain digital currency units by converting other sovereign currencies to a digital currency, selling goods or services in return for digital currency, receiving a payment from another digital currency user, or by acting as a digital currency miner. Users can dispose of digital currency units by converting digital currency to another sovereign currency, paying digital currency in return for goods or services, or making a payment to another digital currency user.

Wallet providers. Digital wallets provide a means for users to store the cryptographic keys, access the account balance, facilitate transactions, and maintain transaction history information. Digital wallets can reside on users' computers or mobile devices, or they may reside on the Internet as a cloud-based application.* Note that the user's digital currency is "stored" in the distributed ledger, not in the digital wallet. The dependability and security of the digital wallet are paramount. If the cryptographic keys are lost or corrupted, the user will no longer be able to access his or her digital wallet account. If the keys are stolen, they can be used as credentials to access the user's digital currency account and withdraw funds.

Exchanges. Given the limited acceptance of digital currencies in the broader commercial market, exchanges that provide trading services that enable users to convert digital currencies to sovereign currencies and vice versa are an important part of the digital currency ecosystem. Typically, exchanges will offer to buy and sell one or more digital currencies at advertised exchange rates against major sovereign currencies, such as the US dollar, euro, Japanese yen, and Chinese yuan, as well as against other digital currencies. They accept users' payments in sovereign currencies in different forms, such as electronic transfers from bank accounts or credit or debit card transactions, to fund the purchase of digital currencies.

---

* While use of a digital wallet provided by a third party is common, it is not a necessity. Users can create and maintain their own digital wallets.

Miners. Miners are individuals or groups of individuals that provide computational services to perform computationally intensive Proof of Work calculations to validate sets of transactions that are candidates to be added to a decentralized distributed ledger, such as Bitcoin's of blockchain.* In return for providing these services, miners receive units of the digital currency, either through issuance of new currency or by means of a transaction fee provided by the user initiating the transaction being validated. The validation performed by miners prevents counterfeit digital currency units from being used and stops the same digital currency units from being used simultaneously in multiple transactions. Some mining operations are formed by pools of miners or commercial businesses, which may provide mining services across multiple digital currencies. Professional miners may invest in specialized hardware that is optimized to perform cryptographic calculations at a much higher speed than standard commodity hardware.

Besides the key participants highlighted above, there are a host of other actors that make up the digital currency ecosystem. Inventors are necessary to create a digital currency in the first place, and maintainers act as the caretakers of the algorithms and mechanisms that underlie digital currencies. ATM providers enable users to exchange sovereign currency for digital currency and vice versa. Exchanges also act as market data providers for digital currencies, providing information related to prices, volumes, and volatility. Although some financial institutions have made investments in digital currency exchanges, banks have yet to become mainstream participants in the digital currency ecosystem.

7.7.2.4 Risks

A number of factors contribute to the risks associated with holding and using digital currencies. By nature of the newness of the technology that digital currencies use, it is likely that only a subset of the risks will be understood at any given point in time, with more waiting to be discovered. The evolutionary nature of digital currency technology also means that innovations will probably lead to new risks. This section discusses some of the fundamental risks that characterize the use of digital currencies, including technical, security, financial, and legal concerns. Consideration is primarily focused on digital currencies that use decentralized ledgers, such as Bitcoin.

Digital currencies involve a number of technical risks. First and foremost is the risk that a flaw in the design or implementation of the digital currency algorithm or other software that is associated with it, as highlighted in Case Study 7-6, could undermine users' trust in the currency. There is also the risk that the self-interested inventors of a currency would design it in a way, such as building in undisclosed features, that provides them a means of achieving financial gain at the expense of other users. Likewise, the mechanisms for validating digital currency transactions often rely on building consensus across a majority of miners in the network. If cybercriminals are able to obtain sufficient computing power to achieve a majority, they could potentially create fraudulent transactions.

Digital currencies, by nature, are highly dependent on the availability of access to computing devices and the Internet. Hence, digital currencies would provide little value to their users in catastrophic situations that involve widespread power outages or network failures, e.g., major floods. For the user, protecting their private keys and digital wallets is also a concern. If these data are not adequately backed up, loss or failure of the computing or memory storage holding the key could lead to loss of all digital funds associated with that key. Unlike the passwords associated with Internet banking accounts, there is no mechanism for resetting for cryptographic keys when they are lost.

Security risk is perhaps the most critical risk of all for digital currencies. Participants across the digital currency ecosystem are prime targets for hackers. For example, cybercriminals may target individual users' digital wallets and cloud-based wallet providers to steal cryptographic keys. Also,

---

* There are also Proof of Stake implementations that achieve validation consensus based on level of ownership rather than computational effort.

digital currency exchanges have been prime targets for cybercriminals because of the greater value that they hold. In 2014, Tokyo-based Mt. Gox, the largest Bitcoin exchange at the time, suspended withdrawals and later filed for bankruptcy after discovering that $480 million worth of Bitcoin had been stolen. About a year later, another major Bitcoin exchange, Bitstamp, froze user accounts and blocked transactions after hackers stole $5 million. Unlike regulated bank accounts, digital currencies have no underlying laws to resolve reimbursement disputes or governing bodies to provide oversight and help ensure that users' interests are protected.

Price volatility has been a major area of risk for users of digital currencies. For instance, in the days following the collapse of the Mt. Gox exchange, Bitcoin lost more than 35% versus the US dollar. For digital currency speculators, this risk may be more tolerable, but for individuals and merchants it is a material concern. High levels of volatility have curbed the broader adoption and use of digital currencies. One factor that contributes to their volatility is that digital currencies have no intrinsic value or government backing. That is to say, digital currencies only have monetary value if enough users believe that they have value.

The day-to-day price value of digital currencies, when exchanged with other sovereign currencies, is also greatly affected by the availability of liquidity—i.e., the number of available buyers and sellers of the digital currency. That is to say, if a digital currency has relatively little demand one day, sellers will find few buyers and, thus, buyers will push prices down. Conversely, if it is in high demand the next day, sellers will have the upper hand in setting the trading price, driving the value of the digital currency higher. However, as the adoption of a digital currency increases and there are more buyers and sellers actively participating in the market, liquidity has less effect on price volatility.

Digital currencies' limited legal status and regulations also present risks for users and other participants, casting doubt on their current and future obligations. Traditional legal contracts are the primary means of defining obligations between parties using digital currencies; however, it is possible that new laws could cause those contracts to be unenforceable. Changes in regulatory treatment could also negatively affect the use and value of digital currencies. As a case in point, the move in 2017 by China's central bank to more heavily regulate Bitcoin transactions in China, triggered a sharp drop in the volume of domestic Bitcoin trading. Likewise, new taxation requirements could introduce additional costs for users of digital currencies, reducing their attractiveness. While digital currency exchanges are registered in some countries, they are for the most part unregulated. Accordingly, users who experience losses due to fraud, theft, or failure of a counterparty to fulfill their obligations have very limited recourse for seeking compensation.

7.7.2.5 Banks' Positioning

For the most part, banks have steered clear of digital currencies. This is not surprising since handling new and unregulated financial instruments could create extensive and unknown risks for these heavily regulated institutions. Because of uncertainty over legal and compliance requirements as well as cybersecurity concerns, established financial institutions have not offered services related to digital currencies and, for the most part, do not support transactions with digital currency intermediaries, such as exchanges. Financial institutions have shown more interest in the distributed ledger technology that most digital currencies are based on (as discussed in Chapter 20), rather than the digital currencies themselves.

In many cases, banks have viewed digital currencies as a threat that has the potential to undermine their control over parts of the financial system. If widespread adoption of digital currencies were to occur, financial institutions could find themselves disintermediated, particularly in the areas of merchant and peer-to-peer payments. With the potential to become a disruptive force in their markets, banks have kept a wary eye on the progress and development of digital currencies.

By far, nations' central banks, which issue and control sovereign currencies, face the greatest threat by currencies that are outside of their remit. If a subset of the world's population were to exclusively use digital currencies, they would be outside the direct economic influence of the central banks.

Likewise, if the volume of digital currency usage were sufficiently high, a price crash could potentially disrupt the financial stability of other currencies and financial markets. While this scenario is still far from being a reality, it behooves central banks to monitor digital currencies and determine how and when these risks could eventually be realized.

Nevertheless, commercial and central banks have been testing the waters to better understand how they might fit into the digital currency market. In 2015, US-based USAA bank integrated its digital channels with a Bitcoin wallet provider so that the bank's customers could view their bitcoin wallet holdings alongside their bank account information. In 2016, digital bank WB21, which specializes in multicurrency accounts and cross-border payments, announced that it would accept Bitcoin transfers to deposit funds into customer accounts that were denominated in other currencies. Mitsubishi UFJ Financial Group has partnered with a digital currency exchange with the aim of improving international payments. Moreover, Canada's central bank has been leading an experiment along with other large Canadian banks to use distributed ledger technology to create a digital version of the Canadian dollar. While this currency was designed for interbank payments, rather than for public usage, it highlights how traditional financial institutions are working to understand how they can integrate with and benefit from technological changes.

7.7.2.6 Evolution

The fact that digital currencies are generally open-source projects makes it easy for new digital currencies to propagate. Since the advent of Bitcoin, hundreds of alternative cryptocurrencies, "alt-coins", have come into being. While the ability to create new digital currencies provides the opportunity for innovation and fast evolution, it also creates uncertainty about the longevity of both up-and-coming as well as established digital currencies. The success of new digital currencies is dependent on achieving a sufficient level of acceptance and use. The greater the number of digital currencies competing for use, the fewer that are likely to succeed. Likewise, established digital currencies continually face the risk that their dominance could be displaced by a new challenger that gains greater popularity.

The reasons why digital currencies are invented vary. In some cases, the motivation may be for inventors to profit by obtaining a large amount of the currency at its start. However, in many cases the primary goal has been to improve upon Bitcoin. Common adaptations have been to modify the algorithms used to validate transactions that are stored in the distributed ledger as well as other dynamics of the digital currency such as the speed at which it processes transactions and its total supply and rate of growth. Furthermore, some new digital currencies have been created more with the objective of supporting innovative payment solutions, rather than to stand by themselves as a store of monetary value.

To understand how digital currencies vary and are evolving, this subsection will briefly compare three of the most popular digital currencies—Litecoin, Ripple, and Ethereum—with Bitcoin. Litecoin, as the name suggests, is very similar to Bitcoin, but includes several changes designed as improvements. One of the main selling points of Litecoin is that the average time it takes to verify a block of transactions is a quarter of Bitcoin's time (2.5 minutes versus 10 minutes). This reduces the time users must wait for transactions to be confirmed, and supports higher volumes of transactions. Another key difference is that Litecoin miners use a different encryption algorithm for verifying user transactions. The algorithm, Scrypt, is more memory intensive, making it more difficult for miners to gain advantages over other miners by investing in customized hardware to speed up the transaction mining process. Also, the total supply of Litecoin is capped at 84 million, versus 21 million for Bitcoin.

Ripple's currency XRP is just part of the Ripple payment network. The Ripple network provides payment, real-time gross settlement, and currency exchange services. The network itself supports transactions in other cryptocurrencies as well as sovereign currencies, and use of XRP is not required when using the Ripple network. Like Bitcoin, XRP transactions are included in a publicly available distributed ledger, but it uses a consensus algorithm to verify transactions rather than a Proof of Work mechanism. Thus, XRP does not require miners or mining. Also, the total number of XRP is fixed at 100 billion. Additionally, Ripple provides real-time confirmation for transactions.

Ether, like Bitcoin, uses a blockchain to record its transactions and makes use of miners who are rewarded with Ether currency for validating transactions by performing Proof of Work calculations. Rather than using SHA256 as a Proof of Work algorithm, Ether uses the EtHash algorithm, which is memory intensive, and which hinders use of customized hardware that is often used by mining pools, and is oriented more toward the technology that is used by individual miners. New transaction blocks on Ether's blockchain are verified every 15 to 17 seconds. Besides serving as a digital currency, Ether forms the basis of a virtual computing platform called Ethereum that supports "smart contracts"— software-based binding financial agreements that does not involve human mediators or courts of law for enforcement. The idea behind smart contracts is that Ethereum blockchain transactions can include conditions for execution of transactions that can be independently verified by the Ethereum platform.

Whereas Litecoin varies in relatively minor ways from Bitcoin, Ripple and Ether are fundamentally different in that they go far beyond serving as just a digital currency, and provide platforms for implementing new types of payment services. In particular, Ripple's cross-currency settlement capabilities have garnered interest from financial institutions. For example, in 2016 a consortium of international banks performed a trial using Ripple to perform cross-border settlements, where its XRP currency could provide instant liquidity to the system in the case of shortages of the other currencies being settled.

Beyond these dominant digital currencies, new ones appear regularly with new features. For example, Zcash was developed in recent years to provide greater privacy for digital currency transactions. Zcash transactions can be confirmed by the blockchain network without having to record the payment addresses of the users. In contrast, Bitcoin records users' payment addresses on the blockchain. Through complex data analysis it is possible in many cases to link a bitcoin payment address to individuals using the payment network.

7.7.2.7 Potential

So far, the overall success of digital currencies has been limited. On one hand, there are thousands of businesses across the world that accept Bitcoin for payment. On the other hand, that number is a very small proportion of the number of businesses that accept traditional, sovereign currencies. Needless to say, in most places you cannot go to your local grocery store or favorite restaurant and pay with digital currency. For payments, the network effect is critical. If too few parties make use of a payment instrument or services, it will not be viable. The challenge is finding ways to accelerate usage soon after introduction so as to reach the point where a sufficient number of mainstream participants, such as consumers and merchants, use the digital currency to sustain it. So far, no digital currency has achieved widescale use.

Digital currencies' broader uptake hinges on their ability to fill an unmet market need. Sad to say, gap that Bitcoin was able to fill was facilitating payments for illicit activities. It is commonly used for cybercriminal ransom demands. Nonetheless, features such as faster transaction speeds, low costs, and transnational reach have the potential to make a compelling offering if a matching use case that is sufficiently common can be found. Cross-border, cross-currency payments seem to have a reasonably close fit. Moreover, use cases must have sufficient incentives for all participants, including users and intermediaries, such as miners. Likewise, competition for payment services from traditional financial institutions will also challenge digital currencies' growth. For example, the transaction cost advantages provided by digital currencies could be undercut by banks reducing their fees on payments.

For a digital currency to achieve widespread adoption may require institutional support from the likes of banks, regulators, and governments to help give them more legitimacy. However, the idea of centralized control or management of digital currencies is counter to the structural basis for many digital currencies, such as Bitcoin. This raises the question of how well a marriage between digital currencies and traditional currencies would work. Likewise, there is the question of how interested traditional financial institutions are in digital currencies. While some institutions are publicly touting their experimentation with them, privately, the broader view is that digital currencies like Bitcoin will be transient or only capture a negligible portion of the market.

Market fragmentation also threatens the overall success of digital currencies. While Bitcoin has maintained the lead in terms of usage, other digital currencies compete with it for usage and acceptance. Although it is not exactly a zero-sum game, the limited demand for digital currencies means that funds invested or transacted in one digital currency are funds that are not being applied to others. Incumbent digital currencies constantly bear the threat that a new challenger will displace them. The digital currency market as a whole would benefit more from having a just few contenders that that participants could work with, rather than having to try to choose one of many, hoping that it will be successful in the end. Market fragmentation makes it harder for any one digital currency to achieve a critical mass of support from participants, which if achieved, would help propel the entire market to a more prosperous and stable state.

Perhaps what could provide the greatest boost for digital currencies is the development of and support for the financial technologies that are available for most sovereign currencies. Interest-bearing deposits, lending, and price volatility hedging capabilities would help put digital currencies more on par with sovereign currencies and would help increase the attractiveness of holding and using digital currencies. While banks and other established financial institutions have the strongest capabilities in these areas, it is questionable whether they will take the lead in providing these services. Based on what has been seen so far, it seems more likely that, if anyone, Fintech companies will fill this gap. Digital currencies would also benefit greatly if governments were to encourage, or at least provide grounds for, their financial institutions to integrate and make use of digital currencies. While this seems less likely in large developed markets, smaller nation-states that aim to serve as financial services hubs could capitalize on this unfulfilled need.

Less than ten years since the launch of Bitcoin and with some of the most popular digital currencies only having launched in the past few years, it is still relatively early in their overall lifecycle. Many new digital currencies will undoubtedly be developed and many of the existing ones will be further tested. Given the relatively small number of users, digital currencies' efficiency, scalability and resilience—standard features for mainstream payment systems—have yet to be demonstrated for handling high volumes of transactions. Moreover, the jury is out on whether digital currencies and banks can find synergies that will support the growth of both industries. The answer to the question of whether digital currencies will have a place in history as a financial technology that fundamentally changed the world financial system or whether they will be remembered as an interesting innovation that attained

---

Case Study 7-6

Lost in the Ether

Many critics of digital currencies have pointed to the risks that are yet to be discovered with this new technology. There is also the potential for hackers to undermine the security of the payment system, intermediaries, or the digital currency itself. While previous cyberthefts of digital currency had involved exchanges such as Mt. Gox and Bitfinex, in June of 2016 a new type of hacking attack occurred against a flaw in the programming of a virtual entity that used the digital currency Ether, and posed new questions and challenges for digital currencies, as well as the platforms that support and make use of them.

Bitcoin experts launched Ether in 2014 with great fanfare as having the potential to dethrone Bitcoin as the leading digital currency. Development of Ether was partially driven by a discord within the Bitcoin community on how it should evolve. Beyond serving as a digital currency, Ethereum also provided a platform for creating automated virtual organizations and developing virtual markets that used Ether as their currency. However, due to its greater complexity, Ethereum was thought by some to likely face more security concerns, compared with simpler systems such as Bitcoin.

The decentralized autonomous organization (DAO) was one such virtual organization that was created using Ethereum. The DAO existed only on the Internet, and in May of 2016, through crowd funding, it raised over $150 million of Ether, which represented 14% of the total amount of Ether. The goal of the DAO was to invest in startup businesses, serving as a type of venture capital fund that was investor directed, as opposed to being run by managing partners. Investment candidates would provide proposals in the form of business plans and smart contracts. If the DAO's investors approved the project, the DAO would automatically release funds to the company per the terms of the smart contract.

In June of 2016, the DAO faced a calamity when a hacker attacked it and stole more than 3 million Ether, the equivalent of 60 million US dollars at the time. Ether lost 30% of its value on online exchanges shortly thereafter. It is thought that the hacker took advantage of a programming error related to DAO's smart contracts. Fortunately, though, for the DAO's investors, as a feature of the DAO's design, the DAO-like virtual entity that the hacker transferred the stolen Ether to could not transact using currency until several weeks after the heist. This provided Ethereum developers with an opportunity to try to rectify the situation.

The solution that was chosen was to add a new set of rules into Ethereum's computer code and create a "hard fork" of its blockchain. This type of software upgrade was not backward compatible, was risky, and was typically only used to implement critical bug fixes. The new rules that were implemented applied only to accounts related to the DAO and were designed to recover the funds that were invested in the DAO, so that they could be returned to investors, effectively dissolving the DAO. The alternative would be to do nothing and let the DAO investors shoulder the loss, potentially leading to legal action against the DAO and Ethereum.

This operation was the first time a protocol change had been implemented on a major digital currency to thwart a cybertheft. It spurred major debate as to whether it was the right course of action. Cryptocurrency purists believed the rules that are implemented for digital currencies should not include any special cases for specific transacting parties and that the blockchain should be inviolable. However, Ethereum's online polling showed that the majority of Ether's holders, by value, supported the fork, which made the change viable. However, the hard fork was only partially effective because a version of the original Ethereum code continued to be developed and supported by a group that was opposed to the idea of implementing a hard fork. In turn, this resulted in the formation of a new digital currency, "Ether classic," which continued to be used alongside the mainstream Ether currency.

This case highlights the potential risks of new technology that often is only fully tested when it is used, sometimes with potentially dire consequences. Likewise, it shows the unpredictable nature of digital currencies' evolution.

Sources: Popper, Nathaniel, "Ethereum, a Virtual Currency, Enables Transactions That Rival Bitcoin's," March 27, 2016, http://www.nytimes.com/2016/03/28/business/dealbook/ethereum-a-virtual-currency-enables-transactions-that-rival-bitcoins.html?_r=0; Waters, Richard, "Automated Company Raises Equivalent of $120m in Digital Currency," *Financial Times*, May 16, 2016, https://www.ft.com/content/600e137a-1ba6-11e6-b286-cddde55ca122; Peck, Morgen E., "'Hard Fork' Coming to Restore Ethereum Funds to Investors of Hacked DAO," *IEEE Spectrum*, July 19, 2016, http://spectrum.ieee.org/tech-talk/computing/networks/hacked-blockchain-fund-the-dao-chooses-a-hard-fork-to-redistribute-funds; "DAO May Be Dead After $60 Million Theft," *IEEE Spectrum,* 17 June 2016, http://spectrum.ieee.org/tech-talk/computing/networks/dao-may-be-dead-after-40million-theft; Finley, Klint, "A $50 Million Hack Just Showed That the DAO Was All Too Human," *Wired*, June 18, 2016, https://www.wired.com/2016/06/50-million-hack-just-showed-dao-human; Vigna, Paul, "Ethereum Gets Its Hard Fork, and the 'Truth' Gets Tested," *Wall Street Journal*, July 20, 2016, http://blogs.wsj.com/moneybeat/2016/07/20/ethereum-gets-its-hard-fork-and-the-truth-gets-tested/?cb=logged0.17972590150118084; del Castillo, Michael, "The DAO Hacker Is Getting Away," CoinDesk, August 8, 2016, http://www.coindesk.com/ethereum-dao-hacker-getting-away-classic.

only a small user base and peripheral usage is yet to be written. Progress and developments over the coming years will provide clues to what that answer will be.

7.8 SUMMARY

This chapter covered:

- the importance and complications involved with accepting customer deposits;
- how banks' cash management services benefit corporate and retail customers;
- core banking system technology;
- how IT system resilience is implemented; and
- factors affecting use of cash notes and the evolution of digital currencies;

The next chapter will examine how banks provide lending services to their customers.

FURTHER READING

Books

Allman-Ward, M. and J. Sagner, *Essentials of Managing Corporate Cash* (New Jersey: John Wiley & Sons, Inc., 2003).

Dolfe, M. and A. Koritz, *European Cash Management: A Guide to Best Practice* (New Jersey: John Wiley & Sons, Inc., 1999).

Papers and Articles

Badev, A. and M. Chen, "Bitcoin: Technical Background and Data Analysis", US Federal Reserve Board, October 7, 2014.

Beer, C., E. Gnan and U. W. Birchler (eds.), "Cash on Trial," *SUERF Conference Proceedings 2016/1.*

Epstein, E., "Two Faces to a Cashless Future," *ABA Banking Journal,* May/June 2017Nakamoto, S., "Bitcoin: A Peer-to-peer Electronic Cash System," bitcoin.org, October 31, 2008, https://bitcoin.org/bitcoin.pdf.

Fung, B. and H. Halaburda, "Understanding Platform-based Digital Currencies," *Bank of Canada Review,* Spring 2014.

Gandal, N. and H. Hałaburda, "Competition in the Cryptocurrency Market", Bank of Canada Working Paper/Document 2014-33.

Lam, W., "Ensuring Business Continuity," *IT Professional* 4, issue 3 (May/June 2002): 19–25.

Leising, M., "The Ether Thief", *Bloomberg,* Jun 13, 2017, https://www.bloomberg.com/features/2017-the-ether-thief/.

Mols, N., P. Niels, P. Bukh, D. Nikolaj, and P. Blenker, "European Corporate Customers' Choice of Domestic Cash Management Banks," *The International Journal of Bank Marketing* 15 (1997): 255.

Segendorf, B., "What is Bitcoin?" *Sveriges Riksbank Economic Review* (2014): 2.

"The Dangers Linked to the Emergence of Virtual Currencies: the Example of Bitcoins," *Banque de France Focus,* issue 10, December 5, 2013.

Web

Asymmetric Encryption Explained, http://etutorials.org/Programming/Programming+.net+ security/Part+III+.NET+Cryptography/Chapter+15.+Asymmetric+Encryption/15.1+Asymmetric+Encryption+Explained/.

Capgemini Core Banking Systems Survey, http://www.hr.capgemini.com/m/hr/tl/Core_Banking_ Systems_Survey_2008.pdf.

Crypto-currency Market Capitalizations, http://coinmarketcap.com/all.html.

ENDNOTES

1. Smith, G., "Consumer and Community Banking," JPMorgan, February 24, 2015.

2. Zumbrun, J., "Younger Generation Faces a Savings Deficit," *Wall Street Journal*, November 9, 2014, http://www.wsj.com/articles/savings-turn-negative-for-younger-generation-1415572405.

3. Guarino, M., "Chicago Police Arrest Rapper and 28 Others for 'Cracking Cards'," *The Guardian*, October 30, 2014, https://www.theguardian.com/world/2014/oct/31/chicago-police-arrest-rapper-and-28-others-for-cracking-cards.

4. "Gallup: Most Expect Cashless Economy in Lifetime," *ABA Journal*, July 15, 2016, http://bankingjournal.aba.com/2016/07/gallup-most-expect-cashless-economy-in-lifetime.

5. Bagnall, J., D. Bounie, K. P. Huynh, A. Kosse, T. Schmidt, S. Schuh, and H. Stix, "Consumer Cash Usage: A Cross-country Comparison with Payment Diary Survey Data," European Central Bank Working Paper, no. 1685, June 2014.

6. Chatterjee, P. and Rose, R., "Do Payment Mechanisms Change the Way Consumers Perceive Products?," *Journal of Consumer Research*, April 2012.

— — —

7. de Soto, J. H., "Money, Bank Credit, and Economic Cycles," Ludwig von Mises Institute, 2012.

8. Moore, E.,"Loyal Customers Receive Tailored Rates," *Financial Times*, June 10, 2011, http:// www.ft.com/cms/s/2/a33c9750-9386-11e0-922e-00144feab49a.html.

9. Dunkley, E., "Santander's Flagship 123 Accounts Costs It Almost £1bn," *Financial Times*, August 29, 2016, http://www.ft.com/cms/s/0/270d4b6a-6aaa-11e6-ae5b-a7cc5dd5a28c.html.

10. Deutsche Bank Investor Relations, "Deutsche Bank Reports Net Loss of EUR 3.9 Billion for the Year 2008,"February 5, 2009, https://www.db.com/ir/en/content/ir_releases_2009_7249.htm.

11. "Card Cracking," American Banker Association website, http://www.aba.com/tools/function/cyber/pages/card-cracking.aspx.

12. Wallace, T., "German Savers Hit by Negative Interest Rates," *The Telegraph*, August 12, 2016, http://www.telegraph.co.uk/business/2016/08/12/german-savers-hit-by-negative-interest-rates/.

13. Wallace, T. and K. Morley, "Savers Fear Negative Interest Rates As Natwest Warns Businesses Might Have To Pay to Hold Cash," *The Telegraph*, July 25, 2016, http://www.telegraph.co.uk/news/2016/07/25/savers-fear-negative-interest-rates-as-natwest-warns-businesses/.

14. Warwick-Ching, L. and D. Law, "Cheques to Disappear by 2018," *Financial Times*, December 16, 2009, https://www.ft.com/content/2408f13c-ea94-11de-a9f5-00144feab49a#axzz1RiIole8v.

15. Moore, E., "Decision to Abolish Cheques Reversed," *Financial Times*, July 12, 2011, https://www.ft.com/content/39c4ab04-ac96-11e0-a2f3-00144feabdc0.

16. "Europe's Disappearing Cash: Emptying the Tills," *Economist*, August 11, 2016, http://www.economist.com/news/finance-and-economics/21704807-some-europeans-are-more-attached-notes-and-coins-others-emptying-tills.

17. Stempel, J., "Bitcoin Is Money, US Judge Says in Case Tied to JPMorgan Hack," *Reuters*, September 20, 2016, http://www.reuters.com/article/us-jpmorgan-cyber-bitcoin-idUSKCN11P2DE.

18. "An Abridged History of Bitcoin," *New York Times*, November 19, 2013, http://www.nytimes.com/interactive/technology/bitcoin-timeline.html?_r=1&#/#time284_8155.

19. Lee, T. B., "Major Glitch In Bitcoin Network Sparks Sell-off; Price Temporarily Falls 23%," *Ars Technica*, March 12, 2013, http://arstechnica.com/business/2013/03/major-glitch-in-bitcoin-network-sparks-sell-off-price-temporarily-falls-23.

20. "Bitcoins and Banks: Problematic Currency, Interesting Payment System," UBS Global Research, March 28, 2014.

21. Dougherty, C. and G. Huang, "Mt. Gox Seeks Bankruptcy After $480 Million Bitcoin Loss," *Bloomberg*, February 28, 2014, https://www.bloomberg.com/news/articles/2014-02-28/mt-gox-exchange-files-for-bankruptcy.

22. "Hackers Steal $5 Million from Major Bitcoin Exchange," *Fortune*, January 5, 2015, http://fortune.com/2015/01/05/bitstamp-bitcoin-freeze-hack.

23. Macheel, T., "Bitcoin Inches Closer to Mainstream with USAA Partnership," *American Banker*, November 4, 2015, http://www.americanbanker.com/news/bank-technology/bitcoin-inches-closer-to-mainstream-with-usaa-partnership-1077686-1.html?zkPrintable=true.

24. "WB21 Is the First Digital Bank Accepting Bitcoin Deposits," WB21 press release, June 14, 2016, https://www.wb21.com/WBPressRelease14.06.16.

25. "What Is the Difference between Litecoin and Bitcoin?" CoinDesk, April 2, 2014, http://www.coindesk.com/information/comparing-litecoin-bitcoin.

26. https://ripple.com.

27. https://www.ethereum.org/ether.

28. Popper, N., "Ethereum, a Virtual Currency, Enables Transactions That Rival Bitcoin's," *New York Times*, March 27, 2016, http://www.nytimes.com/2016/03/28/business/dealbook/ethereum-a-virtual-currency-enables-transactions-that-rival-bitcoins.html.

29. "Ripple and R3 Achieve Breakthrough in Cross-Border Bank Payments," *Fortune*, October 20, 2016, http://fortune.com/2016/10/20/ripple-r3.

30. Bank for International Settlement, "Digital Currencies," November 2015.

31. European Central Bank, "Virtual Currency Schemes: A Further Analysis," February 2015.

32. Popper, N., "Zcash, a Harder-to-trace Virtual Currency, Generates Price Frenzy," *New York Times*, October 31, 2016, http://www.nytimes.com/2016/11/01/business/dealbook/zcash-a-harder-to-trace-virtual-currency-generates-price-frenzy.html.

33. Wolf, M., "India's bold experiment with cash", *Financial Times*, February 21, 2017, https://www.ft.com/content/e3f2aaa8-f77d-11e6-bd4e-68d53499ed71?mhq5j=e1.

34. Kelly, J., "Fearing return to drachma, some Greeks use bitcoin to dodge capital controls", *Reuters*, July 3, 2015, http://www.reuters.com/article/us-eurozone-greece-bitcoin-idUSKCN0PD1B420150703.

35. Deng, C., "China Bitcoin Rules Would Require Exchanges to Verify Clients' Identity", *Wall Street Journal*, March 17, 2017, https://www.wsj.com/articles/china-bitcoin-rules-would-require-exchanges-to-verify-clients-identity-1489721593.

36. Eha, B., "MUFG Aims to Use Bitcoin to Improve Cross-Border Payments", *American Banker*, October 27, 2016, https://www.americanbanker.com/news/mufg-aims-to-use-bitcoin-to-improve-cross-border-payments.

8 Lending and Debt Collection

Lending has been an activity practiced since ancient times and plays an important role in business and government. In the 1800s, banks financed the shipping of goods between Britain, Europe, and the Americas. Likewise, the purchase of the Louisiana territory by the United States was partially financed by British banks. Today, bank lending is a key underpinning of the theory of corporate finance, and the proceeds derived from lending underlie the business models of most banks.

However, for all the benefits that loan financing has provided, governments have had to protect consumers from predatory lending practices. As far back as 1750 BC, the Code of Hammurabi set out to regulate the interest charged on the lending of money. Since then, governments have enacted **usury laws** that limit the interest rate that may be levied on customers. These laws have had both positive and negative effects. For example, in 1978, the US state of South Dakota eliminated interest rate caps. This move enabled banks to relocate their credit card issuance business there and operate nationally without regard to other states' usury laws.

The dangers associated with lending practices are not limited to customers. While the one million bank foreclosure filings in the third quarter of 2009 were a painful memory to many customers who purchased homes, banks also suffered significant losses. Declines in property values and illiquidity in the housing market left banks facing a worst-case scenario. In some instances, the losses on property loans were so great that the banks making the mortgage loans became insolvent. In the year 2009 alone, over 130 banks failed in the United States.

Banks clearly bear risks when lending and look for interest rates and fees to offset those risks. The competitive advantage and profitability of banks are determined by the combination of which customers they lend to, the amount lent, and the return produced on the capital utilized. Some banks choose to focus on making high-value loans in one particular segment or geography, leveraging expertise in that area. Other banks opt to take advantage of the law of large numbers, making loans to a large and diversified base of customers, in the hope that unrelated individual losses will be averaged out over a large number of loans.

In recent years, banks have faced new sources of competition for their loan products. Fintech companies provided marketplace-lending services that introduced new approaches to lending, disrupting banks' traditional business models (Case Study 8-1). Technology companies have also began providing credit services. For instance, as of 2017, Amazon had originated over \$3 billion

---

Case Study 8-1

Increasing Competition from Fintech Companies in Lending Markets

For centuries, banks have dominated the lending markets, for the most part competing with one another, thanks to restrictions by national governments that made it difficult for nonbanks to enter the market. However, over the past decade, banks have begun to face more significant competition from new contenders—Fintech companies providing unsecured credit to consumers. By taking advantage of business models that incur lower expenses than banks' business models and leveraging technology to approve loans more quickly than most banks, marketplace lenders have gained a small but important foothold in the financial services markets.

Fintech companies, such as Lending Club and Prosper, that facilitate marketplace (also referred to as peer-to-peer) lending rely on a different source of funds than banks use. Bank lending generally relies on customer deposits to provide the underlying capital that is used to make loans. In contrast, marketplace lenders use money provided by debt investors to directly fund loans to consumers and businesses. Additionally, marketplace lenders often exclusively use low-cost online channels to originate and service loans. Banks, on the other hand, rely much more on face-to-face or phone-based communication for these activities. Moreover, whereas banks are middlemen between depositors and borrowers, marketplace lenders are middlemen between investors and borrowers. Marketplace lenders typically make money by charging transaction fees, rather than earning interest. Instead, the interest from loans goes to the investors in the loans. Also, they are not subject to the credit risk of the borrowers; losses resulting from defaults in loan repayments are borne by the investors.

Borrowers who wish to receive loans through marketplace lenders set up profiles for themselves on the lender's website. Borrower profiles typically include information about the borrower's credit history and credit score, the amount of the loan, the purpose of the loan, and information about the borrower's income and existing debt level. Loan amounts can range from a thousand to tens of thousands of dollars. Marketplace lenders use proprietary algorithms to assess the borrower's likelihood of default and, if the borrower is sufficiently creditworthy, to determine the interest rate and fees to be charged on the loan. What makes marketplace lending attractive to consumers is that the interest rates marketplace lenders charge borrowers are often lower than they would pay for similar credit if it were provided by a bank.

Investors can search through marketplace lenders' information about prospective borrowers' loans and determine which ones they want to invest in. By funding as little as \$25 per loan, investors can selectively spread their risk across many different borrowers, reducing the amount of loss from any single loan default. Investors are also able to sell the debt they are owed to other investors on a secondary market, which provides them with liquidity so that they do not have to necessarily keep funds locked up in the loan for its entire tenure. Investors in marketplace loans may be individuals or institutions. Furthermore, to help attract investors, some marketplace lenders publicly provide information about the performance history of their loan portfolio, including net return and charge-off rates. Marketplace lenders' funding models are continuing to evolve. In 2017, several marketplace lenders began securitizing some of their loans so that they could be sold as bond offerings. As part of this arrangement, the lenders kept a small percentage of loans on their balance sheet, so that they would share some financial risk with investors, in case of loan defaults.

While the financial products that marketplace lenders provide generally compete with banks, in some cases, there are synergies. Some smaller banks have partnered with marketplace lenders to offer unsecured consumer loans to their customers. They jointly market loans via digital channels to the bank's customers and the bank takes a cut of the revenue generated by the loan, which is originated by the marketplace lender. As an example, a US-based community bank, BankNewport, which had a total of 15 branches, decided to partner with Lending Club to offer unsecured consumer loans to its customers. The bank had previously given up that business because it could not compete with larger banks which had greater economies of scale.

While marketplace lenders have achieved significant growth in recent years, they have had to overcome challenges as well. Around 2008, both Lending Club and Prosper were compelled to register with the US Security Exchange Commission and change the structure of their business model. Instead of investors having debt obligations tied directly to the borrower, the structure was changed so that investors received notes issued by the marketplace lenders that were secured by debt repayments made by of the borrower. This new model subjected investors to credit risk of both the marketplace lender as well as the borrower. Additionally, in 2016, marketplace lenders faced increased difficulty in attracting investors—particularly institutional investors, such as pension funds, hedge funds, and insurance companies—causing the interest rate the lenders charged to borrowers to rise. Moreover, one of the gunmen in the attack in San Bernardino in 2015 had borrowed $28,500 from a marketplace lender weeks before the attack, possibly using the funds to purchase weapons, raising the question of the legitimacy of the borrowers using marketplace lending and the true purpose for their seeking of funding.

Clearly marketplace lenders provide a valuable service to customers who might otherwise not be able to obtain credit or might have to pay a higher price if they used a bank. Yet, there are also concerns about their place in the ecosystem, operating methods, and stability. One concern is that with the growth of marketplace lending, more money is shifting into the "shadow" banking system, which regulators have less influence over, and that could potentially contribute to new financial crises. Also, the automated algorithms that marketplace lenders use to assess credit may inadvertently discriminate against particular groups within the population, potentially leading to unfair lending practices. Marketplace lending, at its current size and incarnation, also has yet to face the effects of a major recession. Shifts in economic cycles and regulatory changes in the coming years will likely determine whether marketplace lenders can further establish their businesses and continue to grow or whether they will be choked by new market conditions and tighter regulatory restrictions.

Questions

1. What credit products at banks are most vulnerable to competition from marketplace lenders?
2. What risks might banks face when partnering with marketplace lenders?
3. What other financial products might marketplace lenders expand into as a natural extension to unsecured credit lending?
4. What types of regulatory changes could have a major effect on marketplace lenders and how might those changes impact them?

Sources: www.prosper.com; www.lendingclub.com; Kim, Jane, "Peer-to-Peer Lender Relaunched," *Wall Street Journal*, April 28, 2009, http://www.wsj.com/articles/SB124088142201761953; Sterngold, James, "Lending Club and Smaller Banks in Unlikely Partnership," Wall Street Journal, June 23, 2015, http://www.wsj.com/articles/lending-club-and-smaller-banks-in-unlikely-partnership-1435015121; Corkery, Michael, "As Lending Club Stumbles, Its Entire Industry Faces Skepticism," *New York Times*, May 9, 2016, http://www.nytimes.com/2016/05/10/business/dealbook/as-lending-club-stumbles-its-entire-industry-faces-skepticism.html; Koren, James and Jim Puzzanghera, "Loan to San Bernardino Shooter Draws Scrutiny to Online Lending Industry," *Los Angeles Times*, December 11, 2015, http://www.latimes.com/business/la-fi-prosper-regulation-20151210-story.html; Bisbey, A., "Pay Attention: LendingClub's First Securitization is a Big Deal," *American Banker*, June 26, 2017, https://asreport.americanbanker.com/news/pay-attention-lending-clubs-first-securitization-is-a-big-deal.

worth of loans to small businesses that sell goods on Amazon's website [1]. Amazon funds the loans from its balance sheet and uses sellers' merchandise that is in its warehouses as collateral. The extensive information that Amazon has about the sellers' product sales and customer service levels provide it with unique insights that can be used to make more astute credit decisions. Clearly, while lending was a relatively staid business in the past, it has been shaken up by new players in the market that are using technology to gain a competitive edge.

Business processes and technology are fundamental to lending. This chapter examines considerations related to lending to both retail and corporate customers and to debt collection. Opportunities and challenges related to lending are discussed, including how Fintech companies are supplementing as well as encroaching on banks' lending businesses. Next, an overview of counterparty risk is provided. The transaction lifecycle for secured lending is reviewed, and credit evaluation processes are examined in depth. Then, the architectural considerations related to banks' debt collection functions are studied. Finally, specific solution considerations related to lending applications are discussed.

8.1 LENDING

Banks engage in many types of lending activities. Lending is commonly provided in the form of fixed-term loans or revolving credit facilities. Credit lines may be either committed or uncommitted facilities. When banks provide a **committed line of credit** to a customer, as long as the customer does not break the covenants of the lending agreement, the bank is legally obliged to lend the funds up to the credit limit specified in the lending agreement. On the other hand, when a bank provides an **uncommitted line of credit**, it has the option to cancel or suspend the credit line. This section will further review the lending activities of banks in the context of corporate and **retail banking**.

8.1.1 Corporate Banking Context

In contrast to standardized products, like overdraft accounts and term deposits, corporate loans are negotiated products. Terms of the loan agreement are generally customized to match specific situations and conditions, addressing both the customer's capital needs and the bank's profit and risk concerns. Hence, the time required to initiate a corporate loan transaction can be significant, and fulfillment and maintenance requirements are long-lived. In contrast, standardized financial product transactions can be initiated more quickly, because there is no negotiation and the product parameters are limited.

As background for exploring the solution considerations of corporate lending, it is useful to first examine the key characteristics of corporate loans. Fundamentally, making use of different loan characteristics helps banks manage their risks. By determining who will receive credit, which loan products will be offered, and the constituent attributes of the loan products, banks are able to ensure that risks match returns, and that customers are incentivized to behave in a way that does not jeopardize the bank's interests.

Table 8-1 lists common attributes that banks use to create loan products. How banks choose to utilize and combine these attributes will be based on the customers they serve, past lending experience, and economic conditions. Beyond these basic parameters, in some countries, banks have also become creative in constructing complex home loan product structures. For instance, in the United States, besides fixed rate and adjustable rate mortgages (ARM), banks also offer convertible ARM, hybrid option ARM, interest only, and graduated payment mortgages, as well as many others.

One advantage of lending to corporations is that financial information is readily available from the company's management accounts. Furthermore, financial accounts from several years' business operations can be evaluated to determine trends and the overall health of the firm. When a company engages an independent accounting firm to audit its financial statements, the veracity of the financial

Table 8-1 Common loan attributes

Attribute	Description/Examples
Loan type	Personal, business expansion, mortgage, educational, and so on
Tenure	Duration of the loan
Secured versus unsecured	Whether physical assets or securities are provided as collateral (for example, house, automobile, equipment, and jewelry)
Covenants	Conditions and restrictions that the borrower must abide by as part of a commercial loan
Amount/credit limit	Value of the loan or limit of the credit facility
Repayment schedule	Dates and amounts of the loan repayment
Rates and fees	The fixed or floating interest rate, possibly linked to an index such as the London Interbank Offered Rate (LIBOR for short), and fees that may be charged up front and during the lending term
Penalty clauses	Additional fees that the bank may charge in cases where the customer fails to meet contractual obligations of the loan, such as when late payments are received or if the loan is repaid before its maturity.

information provided will be better assured. However, more complicated due diligence processes are required that may not be easy to automate. Or if they can be automated, the processes may require information to be integrated from a range of diverse sources. Extensive **anti-money laundering (AML)**, also referred to as **know your customer (KYC)**, checks must also be implemented when lending to corporate customers to ensure that funding is not provided to known criminals or used for illicit purposes.

The transaction value of corporate loans is also significantly greater than for retail transactions, and the number of transactions is smaller. This favors a quality-over-quantity approach. Where the pool of loans is smaller, the impact of a single default will be greater. Hence, the effort to perform detailed investigation and analysis on companies' ability to repay loans is worthwhile. Likewise, due diligence checks are necessary to ensure that there is no misrepresentation.

Additionally, tracking and enforcing counterparty limits are vital. If two loans are made to the same company and the company fails, then from a risk perspective, the two loans are effectively one aggregated exposure. While this may seem obvious for simple cases, it becomes more difficult to keep track of when different geographic branches of a bank independently make loans to a customer's subsidiaries that reside in different regions. Similarly, loans may be made to two seemingly different companies that turn out to be subsidiaries of the same parent corporation; bankruptcy of the parent could, in turn, put loans to both subsidiaries at risk.

8.1.2 Retail Banking Context

This subsection discusses unsecured and secured credit in the retail banking context. It is important to note, however, that many of the points identified also have relevance for corporate banking, particularly for small- and medium-sized enterprises. In general, retail products are more standardized—that is, they involve little, if any, negotiation and, thus, less time and effort are required to initiate these transactions. Consumer loans and credit cards in many market are approved within a few days and, in some cases, in less than a day or even immediately after the application is submitted.

8.1.2.1 Unsecured credit

Over the past several decades, unsecured consumer credit has grown tremendously. In developed markets, credit card debt and personal loans are a source of major lending business for banks and are the basis for a large proportion of retail payments. In 2016, over 42% of US customers used credit card accounts as a revolving credit facility [2]. In some markets, other forms of unsecured credit, besides credit cards, are used. For example, in the United Kingdom, overdraft facilities are a standard feature of current (chequing) accounts.

In contrast to corporate loans and secured consumer credit, the exposure to individual customers is relatively small, and the number of exposures is relatively large. Default by any one customer will have little effect; the problem is when individuals begin to default en masse. Hence, there are different strategies to help prevent losses. One is for the lender to limit the amount of credit offered to each individual, which helps minimize losses when they do occur. Another is to offer credit to a large diversified pool of individuals. Alternatively, credit may be offered to a select set of creditworthy customers. The most creditworthy customers, though, are less likely to require loans and expect better terms when they do, potentially making loans to them less profitable.

Generally, the interest rates charged on unsecured credit are many percentage points higher than those charged for secured lending. This represents the expectation of a relatively large number of defaults with limited potential for recovery of funds. Likewise, fees are an important means of generating revenue with unsecured credit. Customers who regularly incur late payment and over-credit-limit fees likely represent higher risk of default. Without the prospect of fee revenue, it may not be cost effective to offer them credit.

In developed markets, credit information about individuals applying for unsecured loans is typically obtained from credit bureaus. Credit score information, in conjunction with other supporting documentation, is then used to analytically determine if credit should be granted and, if so, for what amount. Unlike corporate lending, detailed analysis of each account is not economical.

8.1.2.2 Mortgages and other secured credit

Secured lending in the form of mortgages and automobile loans comprises a large proportion of retail lending. In some countries, the norm is to have secured loans that have a fixed rate for the entire term. In other countries, only floating rate loans are available. More recently, hybrid mortgage structures have become popular in many countries. Hybrid adjustable-rate mortgages establish the interest rate for a fixed, upfront time period and allow it to float thereafter.

Mortgage refinancing is also a major business. When interest rates drop, it is often most practical for customers to pay off an existing mortgage that was financed at a high fixed interest rate and refinance it with a new mortgage that is fixed at a lower rate or, alternatively, an adjustable rate mortgage. Likewise, second mortgages may be purchased when customers have built up significant equity in their property.

Like unsecured lending, the profitability of secured lending is to a large extent dependent on the creditworthiness of the customers. However, in case of default, the collateral serves as a cushion for losses, thereby reducing the banks' overall risk of financial loss. Because the risk of financial loss is lower for secured lending, the cost of borrowing for the customer is usually lower than that for unsecured loans.

For the loan collateral to provide an effective risk cushion, it is critical that the value of the collateral be determined accurately and that the right "**haircut**" is then applied. For example, if a property is correctly valued at US$500,000, the bank might apply a 20% haircut and, hence, provide a loan of up to US$400,000 against the property as collateral. The size of the haircut will be dependent on the volatility of the collateral's value, the liquidity of the asset, the expected depreciation of the asset, and the cost of disposal. Likewise, where it is difficult to accurately assess the value of an asset or its valuation is changing rapidly, it is prudent to increase the amount of the haircut to account for potential valuation error (Case Study 8-2). Furthermore, banks must reassess the value of the loan collateral on

---

Case Study 8-2
Challenges in Measuring Collateral Value

The housing market boom of the 2000s was ripe for fraudulent transactions, with an estimated US$10 billion in suspicious deals taking place in Florida alone. House "flipping," that is, buying a property and then quickly selling it at a profit, was a common way to speculate in the market, and banks' eagerness to originate mortgages fueled this practice. While many of the gains were made through legitimate sales, there were other cases where prices were manipulated to favor buyers and sellers at the expense of banks.

One fraud strategy was to artificially inflate house prices by arranging purchases by friends, family, and business associates. Fraudsters would buy houses or condominiums and then sell them to someone they knew to boost the prices. The buyers of the properties would then use the inflated prices to get banks to loan them money to cover the purchases, in excess of what the properties were actually worth. The buyers and sellers would then split the profits on the transactions.

In the inevitable housing bust, many banks, both large national lenders and small community banks, suffered losses with loan defaults on properties where the collateral was worth a fraction of the loan amount. In many cases, it was due to their own bad lending practices and inefficiencies. Banks continued to provide loans on properties whose apparent values were rapidly increasing even though prices in the broader market were flattening out and starting to decline. Likewise, sloppy credit management practices compounded problems caused by shifts in the market. For example, Washington Mutual made a US$2 million loan to an individual that it had foreclosed on three months earlier. It subsequently became the largest bank failure in the history of the United States.

Sources: Braga, Michael, Chris Davis, and Matthew Doig, "'Flip That House' Fraud Cost Billions," *Herald Tribune* (Sarasota, FL), July 19, 2009, http://www.heraldtribune.com/article/20090719/ARTICLE/907191031; Braga, Michael, Chris Davis, and Matthew Doig, "Lenders Failed to Heed Red Flags," *Herald Tribune*, July 23, 2009, http://www.heraldtribune.com/article/20090723/ARTICLE/907231072.

---

a periodic basis to help manage their risk. If the value of the collateral has shrunk significantly so as to be insufficient to cover the amount of the loan principle, by the terms of the loan agreement the bank may require the borrower to post additional collateral to cover the shortfall.

A number of factors can complicate secured lending processes. The client-facing activities may be performed by agents, such as mortgage brokers or automobile dealerships, which serve as a sales channel for the bank. Agents may also be used to assess the value of collateral. For example, in the United States, home appraisers are commonly used to obtain independent valuations for properties. Other servicing activities—such as collections, insurance verification, and inspections—may also be outsourced, particularly if the loans are securitized or sold, as opposed to being kept on the bank's balance sheet.

8.2 OPPORTUNITIES

Given that loans, along with deposits, are one of the most common financial products offered by banks, competition is rife. This section considers some opportunities that banks have to improve their lending business. In particular, diversifying banks' loan portfolios provides a way of reducing overall risk and the impact of loan defaults. Taking advantage of unique knowledge about markets and customers and creatively using information technology are also ways that banks can improve their competitiveness.

Loan portfolio diversification is achieved by having a large pool of customers whose likelihood of repaying is not identical. Ideally, the factors influencing the repayment of each loan should be as diverse as possible. This strategy helps guard against substantial losses occurring at the same time. For example, a bank may lend to a discount department store chain and to a vacation resort. Depending on economic conditions, one or the other may be favored, but it is unlikely that there will be a situation where both would default simultaneously. While this is an overly simple example, the approach becomes more practical when there are thousands, or even millions, of different loans that have different business and economic dependencies. Loans to customers in different geographic regions also provide some diversification benefit.

Diversification strategies clearly favor larger institutions because they have the capacity to acquire more loans, and thus, greater heterogeneity. Smaller institutions typically have to compete using unique market positioning or knowledge. Small- and medium-sized banks can focus more effectively on market niches and compete more effectively in those areas. Advantages may come from geographical location, partnerships, industry expertise, or other specialized analytics. For instance, a small- or medium-sized bank in Silicon Valley might benefit from its physical proximity to the headquarters of technology firms. Likewise, it might take advantage of its relationship with venture capital firms in the area. Most importantly, by narrowly focusing on a small range of products, it can determine the most effective business parameters to operate within based on detailed analysis of the profitability of historical transactions.

Information technology (IT)-based solutions can enable banks to provide innovative pricing for credit products. Risk-based pricing is common, but there is also the opportunity to use customer profitability as a basis for pricing. For example, banks can help retain highly profitable customers by offering them preferred borrowing and savings rates. However, to take advantage of profitability-based pricing, banks must be able to calculate and integrate customer-specific profitability information into relevant pricing processes and IT systems. Product bundling can also be used as a basis for customizing deposit and credit pricing. For instance, a bank could reduce the credit card interest rate for customers who maintain a specified minimum current account balance. Hence, besides creditworthiness, banks can also use customer profitability and product bundling structures to come up with competitive rates for customers.

Banks can use technology to streamline lending processes to gain a competitive edge in the market. By providing self-service platforms—where there is little, if any, human intervention by bank staff is required from the time of application to funding—banks have the opportunity to improve customers' experience and at the same time lower processing costs. Self-service platforms enable customers to adjust various loan parameters themselves during application process and see the effects. They can also upload and electronically sign documents, avoiding the need to visit a branch or mail paper documents. In some cases, loan applications may be able to be approved immediately by the platform. Alternatively, the status of applications that take longer to process can be monitored by customers using the online platform, eliminating the need for customers to call a loan officer or a customer service agent. A 2015 study found that consumers who were able to view and sign documents electronically as part of the mortgage closing process felt more in control and found the process more efficient than those using paper documents [3]. This technology-driven approach can also significantly reduce the time required to complete the mortgage closing process; for example, bringing it down from 90 to 15 minutes.

Moreover, there are large parts of the world population that have very limited or no access to credit. Often it is not practical for banks to service these markets because the loan amounts are often too small to be cost effective to originate or service. However, as demonstrated by marketplace and microcredit lenders, by leveraging technology to reduce origination and servicing costs, expenses can be lowered so as to make new market segments profitable (Case Study 8-3). Likewise, new business models and risk analysis techniques may be required to overcome the limitations of existing approaches to lending.

Case Study 8-3

The Emergence and Development of Microcredit

The concept of microcredit, which is the provision of small loans to individuals and small-business entrepreneurs, was formally initiated in the 1970s. It gradually developed into a full-fledged business model in the 1980s and 90s, and began to accelerate significantly in the early 2000s. It is estimated that 80% of the population in developing countries are not served by commercial banks and, thus, microcredit services can potentially serve hundreds of millions of people. Typically, microloans will range from US$10,000 to US$25,000 and have repayment terms of up to two years. They provide capital for small shop owners to improve their premises, for education that can help poor people develop higher-value working skills, and for farmers to improve their agricultural practices, such as through the addition of irrigation systems.

One of the complications with microcredit is that traditional credit risk management tools such as credit history checks and pledging of collateral are not applicable to the target customer population, that is, those who have no credit histories and no collateral. Hence, traditional loan agreement enforcement and collection mechanisms are impractical for microcredit. As an alternative, many microcredit schemes have taken advantage of group-lending structures to help reduce risk. With group lending, each member of the group serves as a guarantor for the other members of the group. This way, peer pressure is used as a mechanism for helping to ensure loan repayment. Individuals who are suspected or known to be untrustworthy are less likely to be included in lending groups. Another complication with microcredit is that transaction costs must be kept low; otherwise, they would dwarf the value of the loan. Accordingly, successful microcredit operations tend to be based in emerging market countries where operating costs are low and regulatory compliance requirements are relatively uncomplicated.

For some time, the institutions that provided microcredit were relatively low-technology operations. Since the services were provided in developing countries, human resource costs were low. Likewise, often the availability of IT workers was limited. However, industry growth and the entrance of new competitors have driven microfinance institutions (MFIs) to make greater use of IT. As with traditional lenders, technology can support scalable growth, provide greater cost efficiency, reduce operational risk, and extend services to a broader range of customers. In cases where many potential customers live in remote rural areas, the logistics of handling and delivering cash payments is problematic and, thus, mobile electronic payment facilities have great potential to support microlending activities.

While microcredit has experienced strong growth, it has had to overcome a number of challenges. First, new entrants to the microcredit market have been exerting pressure on existing MFIs to improve their efficiency and governance so that they can remain competitive. Second, in some cases, regulators have introduced more regulatory requirements for MFIs. For instance, in 2010, Andhra Pradesh, a state in India, banned MFIs from collecting loan repayments on a weekly schedule, which is standard practice in microfinance, and only allowed monthly collection. Likewise, in 2011, the Reserve Bank of India announced new regulations for MFIs that capped the interest rates they could charge at 26%. Third, as banks and other for-profit firms have begun to enter the microcredit market (many MFIs are nonprofit institutions), the microfinance industry has faced accusations of profit-seeking at the expense of customers they are meant to be helping, and of coercive debt collection tactics.

Nonetheless, microcredit has achieved impressive results. As of 2015, over 130 million borrowers worldwide participated in loans valued at a total of $96 billion. IT can help the microcredit industry to continue to grow by enabling more efficient delivery of services, improved credit decision making, and better monitoring of customers in remote locations. For example, in parts of Africa, microlenders have leveraged mobile payment and wallet technology, such as M-PESA which is discussed in Chapter 9, eliminating the need to distribute cash to and collect cash from borrowers. This strategy lowers operational costs, reduces the risk of theft and robbery, and enables the entire process—including the loan application, approval, funding, and repayment—to be performed by customers on their mobile phones quickly and conveniently. Implementation of similar types of solutions in other geographic market could make microcredit ubiquitous and significantly enhance its standing as a financial product.

Sources: "The Determinants of the Success of Microlending: A Comparison of Iraq and the United States," *International Journal of Entrepreneurship* 14 (2010): 59–70; Kauffman, R. J. and F. J. Riggins, "Information and Communication Technology and the Sustainability of Microfinance," *Electronic Commerce Research and Applications* (2012), http://dx.doi.org/10.1016/j.elerap.2012.03.001; Kazmin, Amy, "Payment Ruling Knocks Microfinance Shares," *Financial Times*, November 18, 2010, http://www.ft.com/cms/s/0/5fb54082-f33a-11df-a4fa-00144feab49a.html; Kazmin, Amy, "SKS in Red after India's Microlender Purge," *Financial Times*, May 7, 2011, http://www.ft.com/cms/s/0/7c153d2c-7837-11e0-b90e-00144feabdc0.html; "Your Inflexible Friend," *Economist*, October 8, 2016, http://www.economist.com/node/21708258/; "Cash Call," *Economist*, October 8, 2016, http://www.economist.com/node/21708254/.

8.3 CHALLENGES

At first glance, lending money may seem like a simple business for banks. However, there are a number of factors that make implementation complicated. Here are a few aspects that can contribute to overall complexity:

- **Variable attributes.** Loan products can include a wide range of attributes and structural considerations that may result in a large number of permutations to be supported. Different interest rate calculations may be used, payment and repayment cash flows may vary by product and by individual agreement, and various forms of collateral may or may not be accepted for different product types.

- **Variable approval structures.** Credit approval decisions may be objective and easily automated, or may be subjective, requiring one or more person's approval. Rules regarding approval may be based on transaction size or customer segment and may vary for each type of loan product. The required approvals could be performed sequentially or in parallel. An example of sequential approval would be as follows: if the manager approves, then forward it to the senior manager for approval. Alternatively, a parallel approval process would be as follows: forward to managers A, B, and C and wait for one (or possibly all) of them to approve. Furthermore, special rules, for example, if loan request is from customer X, manager D must also approve, may also be instituted.

- **Integration with external parties.** Information provided by the customer, external ratings agencies, appraisers, insurers, and government agencies may need to be integrated into the banks' order capture, fulfillment, and maintenance processes. This information may come through paper documents, phone conversations, faxes, email, and computer files.

Lending processes are also affected by country-specific considerations. When granting credit, the assessment process is highly dependent on the transparency of information. Most developed countries have fairly rigorous regulatory requirements in place to ensure that information reported by corporations is accurate. Also, credit rating agencies, such as Moody's and S&P, provide independent ratings of companies' credit risk. While these safeguards are not foolproof, they provide many benefits compared with countries where corporate financial transparency is very limited.

Likewise, the strength of a country's legal system is crucial when it comes to taking possession of collateral in cases of loan defaults and bankruptcy. In some developing nations, bankruptcy procedures may not be well established. Likewise, if a country's judiciary is not entirely independent, a lender may have difficulties recovering funds in cases of default, due to inefficiencies in the legal system. Hence, in some countries, it may not be practical to offer certain types of loan products as they may require significant modifications to avoid undue risk.

Compliance with lending and debt collection regulations is a major challenge for many financial institutions. For example, in the United States, banks must comply with laws addressing Unfair and Deceptive Acts and Practices (UDAP) that apply to all retail customers. At the same time it must also abide by laws, such as the Servicemembers Civil Relief Act, which only apply to a subset of retail customers, such as active military personnel and their families. The business processes that underlie lending, and the technology solutions that support them, are riddled with complexities and special conditions that stem from regulations. These factors often make financial products and technology solutions that were designed for use in one country to not be impractical to use in other countries, because their regulations differ.

Banks also face rising competition from Fintech marketplace lending services, as discussed in Case Study 8-1, that link borrowers directly with investors. Web and mobile phone applications have enabled marketplace lenders to offer cost-effective services that can reach a wide audience of potential borrowers and investors. Marketplace lending services rate borrowers based on their credit history and enable individuals to loan funds directly to a single borrower, or distribute their lending across a pool of borrowers. These services have been most useful to individuals and small businesses that cannot qualify for traditional bank loans. Since marketplace lending services only act as intermediaries that help source and originate the loan, the financing activity does not hit their balance sheets and they are not directly exposed to credit default risk. Thus, they compete on a different playing field from banks. Moreover, regulators in some countries, such as United Kingdom, have welcomed the entrance of marketplace lending as an alternative to traditional banks [4]. In many cases Fintech lenders have been able to operate in a regulatory environment that is less stringent than the one that banks operate within.

In the United States, marketplace lending represents a small fraction of loans made to consumers, less than 1% as of 2016. However, by providing customers with alternative financing choices, marketplace lenders have begun to compete more directly with banks. For example, one motivation for customers to borrow using marketplace lending services is to consolidate credit card debt—i.e., pay off debt owed on one or more credit cards with a marketplace loan financed at a lower interest rate. Marketplace lenders have also begun offering refinancing of auto loans. However, such competition may be limited; as marketplace lenders' size and reach grows, regulatory scrutiny will follow. In 2017, the Consumer Financial Protection Bureau is expected to begin supervising the largest US-based marketplace lenders, and the US Congress began investigating whether the way marketplace lenders are using artificial intelligence to make decisions about lending could lead to discriminatory practices. Likewise, in 2016 regulators in China introduced new rules for marketplace lenders to help reduce fraud and improve risk management.

8.4 MANAGING COUNTERPARTY CREDIT RISK

It is a foregone conclusion that banks will at some point suffer losses due to counterparties failing to meet their debt obligations (Case Study 8-4). Therefore, rather than focusing on absolute prevention, counterparty risk management is about controlling that risk and finding ways to mitigate it. It is critical for banks to accurately estimate their risk exposure and ensure that it does not exceed the level at which the bank's capital would be insufficient to cope with credit-related losses. For banks, counterparties typically fall into two categories: customers and other banks. This section will review the types of counterparty credit risk that banks face and how they can use credit limits to manage that risk.

8.4.1 Forms of Counterparty Credit Risk

Banks' counterparty risk exposure to individual retail customer defaults is minimal, but their exposure to broad groups of customer defaults is a concern. Counterparty credit risk for consumers is managed using scoring models to determine which customers a bank will provide credit to and using formulas to determine customer credit limits. Credit risk management is also largely dependent on a bank's collection abilities. Recovery of all or some of the outstanding credit amounts helps to minimize losses. To some extent, a bank's collection recovery rates are determined by its ability to locate delinquent customers, communicate with them, and negotiate repayment terms.

Banks often have sizable exposures to specific corporate customers. Counterparty credit risk exposure may stem directly from corporate customers' borrowing activities or indirectly through trade finance, foreign exchange (FX), and derivatives transactions. A common challenge for banks is accurately measuring counterparty credit risk across all product types and business lines, corporate customer entity structures, and across different geographies. Counterparty credit risk may exist directly with an individual corporation as well as its parent corporation(s). Accordingly, significant complexity is involved with setting limits and tracking counterparty risk exposure for large corporations that have complicated legal structures.

Banks also have credit risk exposure to other banks that serve as trading partners, particularly for transactions that have extended **settlement** periods, such as FX outright forwards and interest rate swaps (discussed in Chapters 11 and 12). The payment obligations with other banks resulting from such transactions may extend for months or years. Hence, if the counterparty bank were to become bankrupt or default on payments during that period, losses could occur. The failure of Barings Bank in 1993 and Lehman Brothers in 2008 are two examples of when other banks who were their trading partners faced the threat of potential counterparty credit losses.

The architecture used to aggregate the information necessary to calculate counterparty credit risk is much the same as the architecture used to support **market risk** management, as discussed in Section 18.7. Credit exposure information must be consolidated from all transactional systems in all countries to determine the bank's total counterparty credit risk. The rest of this section will focus primarily on how credit limits are implemented and managed.

8.4.2 Approaches to Counterparty Credit Risk Management

Banks manage counterparty credit risk primarily by establishing and enforcing counterparty credit limits. Limits should be defined for all counterparties of a bank before any transactions are performed and should be reviewed and adjusted on a regular basis. Processes for detecting and managing credit limit breaches must also be implemented. **Presettlement credit limits** and **settlement credit limits** should be defined. Presettlement limits are based on the expected risk of transactions during the validity period of the contract. Settlement limits cover the total difference between gross outbound and inbound payments with a given counterparty during the settlement cycle, usually between one and a few days.* It is necessary to ensure that transactions will not breach either limit.

There are two main approaches to managing credit limits across business lines and geographies: distribution of partial limit allocations and pretransaction limit checks using a central limits management system. The first approach is the simplest approach from an IT systems standpoint. A bank's risk management function will determine the acceptable overall credit limits for all its counterparties. These limits will be maintained in a credit risk and limits management system. The total limit amount for a customer will then be divided into portions that will be allotted to different lines of business such as lending, trade finance, and treasury. These credit risk limit allocations will then be communicated to the relevant IT systems that support each of the business functions, and each downstream IT system will be responsible for ensuring that its limit allocation is not exceeded. As depicted in Figure 8-1, each individual business line may then further divide its allocation into portions that will be allotted to an individual country's business operations, which may also have their own IT system. Alternatively, limits may be allocated first to geographies and then divided by business lines.

In some cases, the downstream IT systems' credit limit management implementations will translate notional transaction amounts into credit, that is, loan, equivalent amounts for the purposes of calculating limit utilization. For example, unlike a loan, the credit risk that a bank would face as a result of entering into a one-year US\$1 million FX forward with a corporation would not be the **notional amount** of US\$1 million. Rather, the counterparty credit risk for the contract would be its current replacement cost, that is, current market value, plus the potential change in value during the remaining portion of the contract duration. The potential change in value for derivatives contracts can either be calculated using simple formulas based on a percentage of the notional value and time left on the contract or more accurately by using advanced statistical methods.

The approach of dividing and distributing notional counterparty credit limit amounts is simple from an integration standpoint because risk limits can be fed into downstream systems on an overnight basis and imported as part of the systems' batch upload processes. The distribution of limit information is unidirectional and occurs only once a day. However, the downside of using this approach is that limits will never be optimally distributed and, thus, some lines of business and/or countries will have customer transactions that hit their counterparty limits, while other lines of business and/or countries have surplus limit allocations that they do not utilize. Note that it is possible to "borrow" or transfer limit allocations between business units and systems. For example, Bank A's Tokyo office may want

---

* Settlement limits are not relevant when a central counterparty is used (discussed in Chapter 14), and can be reduced using netting agreements so that gross payments are not required (discussed in Chapter 9).

to transact with Bank B but has reached its local limit with Bank B. In this case, Bank A's Hong Kong office could "lend" some of its allocated limit for Bank B to Bank A's Tokyo office. While this approach works, it can lead to complicated operational processes that are slow and inefficient to implement. If transaction volumes are high, manual reallocation of limits may be problematic.

Alternatively, banks may choose not to divide and delegate limit management to downstream systems, and instead implement limit-checking functions as part of a central limits management system. In this case, as illustrated in Figure 8-2, downstream systems make interactive requests to a central limits management system to determine if there is sufficient counterparty credit available. The downstream system will pass information related to the counterparty, the transaction type, amount, and settlement dates(s) to the limit management system. In return, it will receive a status reply indicating if the transaction will cause a limit breach and the limit that would be affected. As part of a credit limit check, the downstream system usually reserves the limit required by the transaction, and either confirms the limit utilization once the transaction has been executed, or if the transaction is not completed, releases the limit reservation. The limit reservation is necessary to prevent race conditions whereby another transaction utilizes the entire available limit between the time of the limit check and the time of the transaction.

Centralizing counterparty credit limit management enables more optimal limit utilization and provides many benefits from a business standpoint. It also simplifies operational processes by eliminating the need for operational staff to manage limits differently in multiple systems. However, it is often difficult technically to implement a fully centralized limits system. The transaction workflow logic of downstream systems must be able to bypass their own internal credit limit checking mechanisms and make a call out to an external system. While providing such a function may not sound technically difficult, it may not be easy to add to **legacy systems** (for example, mainframe-based systems), and adding such capabilities to existing applications may not be a priority for IT system vendors. Hence, in practice, it is not unusual for hybrid solutions to be implemented, whereby some downstream systems are provided with static limit allocations while others make credit limit availability requests to a central limit management server. Whether banks choose to divide up limits or manage them centrally will depend on the

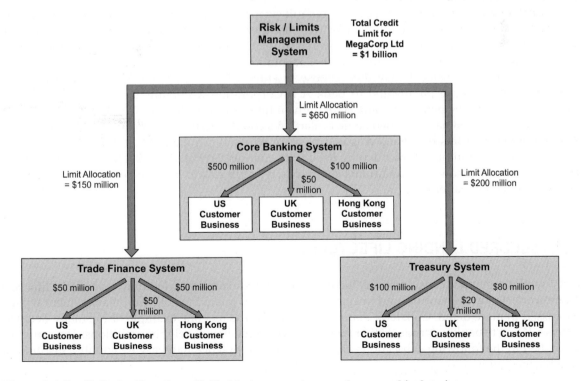

Figure 8-1 Credit limit allocations divided between systems and geographical regions

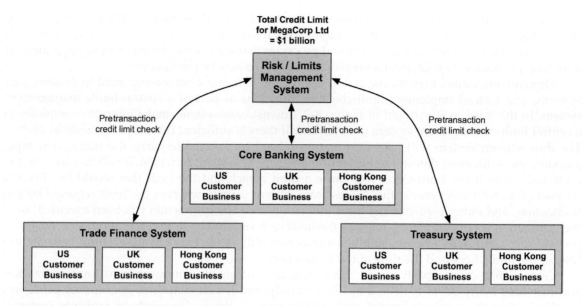

Figure 8-2 Centralized credit limit management with pretransaction checks

benefits that will be achieved through centralization, in comparison to both the technology and staff costs involved with each of the two approaches. Generally, larger banks use the centralized management approach.

Besides applying counterparty credit limits, banks also use collateral and bilateral netting agreements to help manage counterparty credit risk. Netting agreements take into account the gains and losses associated with multiple transactions that occur during the same period so that only their total net difference is calculated as the basis for counterparty risk exposure. The concept of netting is discussed in more detail in Chapter 9.

Additionally, derivatives, that is, credit default swaps (CDS), can in some cases be used to hedge counterparty risk. A CDS is an agreement with another party that effectively provides insurance against the default of a corporation or sovereign government. For example, consider the case in which Bank A does extensive business with Corporation X and reaches its counterparty risk limit with Corporation X. Bank A may then choose to enter a CDS agreement with Bank B whereby Bank B agrees to make payment(s) to Bank A if Corporation X defaults on its credit. In return, Bank A will make payment(s) to Bank B for a given time period so long as Corporation X does not default. Thus, Bank B has offloaded some of Bank A's counterparty risk exposure to Corporation X. Having transferred this risk, Bank A is in a position where it can make additional credit available to Corporation X without overburdening itself with counterparty credit risk. However, in this case, Bank A would also now have additional counterparty credit risk to Bank B; hence, this approach is not without complications.

8.5   SECURED LENDING LIFECYCLE

This section reviews considerations related to secured corporate lending using the lifecycle framework (Figure 8-3) introduced in Chapter 6. Activities related to collateral management will be discussed in more detail. Collateral management is taken as just one example of the many detailed facets relating to banking products that must be addressed when developing solutions. The activities described in the following subsections are generic, and in practice will vary by country, institution, and business unit.

Case Study 8-4

When Counterparty Limits Matter

In 2009, Dutch-based chemical company LyondellBasell placed 79 of its subsidiaries, including its US operations and a European financing division, under bankruptcy protection. The bankruptcy was caused by too high a debt load and a reduced demand for its products. The bankruptcy led a number of banks, including UBS, Royal Bank of Scotland, and Goldman Sachs, to record significant loan losses.

The headline grabber, though, was Citibank's gross exposure of US$2 billion, of which US$1.4 billion was recorded as a loss in its fourth quarter results. In fact, Citibank's exposure had been even larger. However, in 2008, Citibank had sold US$1.9 billion of LyondellBasell debt to a private equity group for less than 90 cents on the dollar to help lower the bank's exposure.

Under normal conditions, the benefits provided by counterparty limits are not measurable; however, when things do go wrong, they are enormously important. Besides banks' counterparty exposure to their customers, counterparty limits are equally important for banks' exposure to other banks and customers' exposure to banks. When Lehman Brothers failed, banks around the world were rushing to assess their potential loss exposure. Likewise, the San Mateo county government in California faced potential losses of US$150 million related to its holdings of Lehman debt securities, that is, corporate bonds and commercial paper.

Sources: Guerrera, Francesco and Julie MacIntosh, "Citi Exposed to $1.4 Billion Loss over LyondellBasell," *Financial Times*, January 9, 2009, http://www.ft.com/cms/s/0/68b9a448-dde3-11dd-87dc-000077b07658.html; Sender, Henry and Francesco Guerrera, "Goldman Stands Apart over Lyondell Losses," *Financial Times*, April 16, 2009, http://www.ft.com/cms/s/0/4c2b3406-29e5-11de-9e56-00144feabdc0.html; Doyle, Jim, "Lehman Brothers Bust Hit San Mateo County Hard," *San Francisco Chronicle*, October 19, 2008, http://www.sfgate.com/bayarea/article/Lehman-Bros-bust-hit-San-Mateo-County-hard-3265442.php.

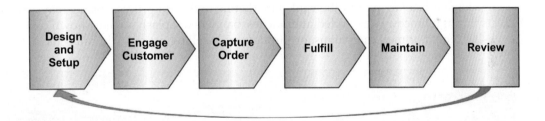

Figure 8-3 Transaction and services lifecycle model

8.5.1 Design and Setup

Design and setup of secured lending products will be performed far in advance of transaction execution. The bank's business units will determine what types of products they want to offer and what specific attributes will be provided as part of those products. The bank will also determine the channels through which to provide the product combinations. For example, a bank may choose to offer a secured lending product that takes corporate-owned properties, equipment, or vehicles as collateral to customers only through the bank's branch network.

Product setup typically requires the definition of data records (for example, customers) and configuration of templates (for example, product data entry screen definitions) in the core banking system. Common data entities that must be defined include:

- **Customer information:** customer accounts, name, contact details, relationships with other corporate customer entities (that is, subsidiaries), and signature authority

- **Product information:** type of product, minimum and maximum amounts, payment schedules, and documentation required

- **Limit information:** total exposure limits, group/subsidiary limit structures, daily settlement limits, and limits on collateral

- **Fee information:** product fees, channel fees, customer-specific fees, volume adjustments, and bundling adjustments

- **Product attributes:** calendars, cash-flow schedules, and acceptable collateral

When a transaction is initiated, these data elements will be linked together during the order capture and fulfillment process. For example, a customer record will be linked to an instance of a specific loan product, which will be validated based on the limit and information linked to that customer, and appropriate fees will be applied based on the product, customer, and channel. If the product requires collateral, then collateral details will need to be provided and associated with the information records associated with both the customer and the instance of the loan product.

Furthermore, when designing financial products, it is critical that legal and regulatory compliance steps are followed. As a case in point, in the United Kingdom, Lloyds Banking Group had to reimburse a total of £500 million to around 300,000 customers because one of its subsidiaries did not adequately disclose how much interest those customers were paying on their mortgages [5]. Confusing wording in the loan offer documentation mistakenly led some customers to believe that they would benefit from terms that capped the variable interest rate, when in fact they would not. Thus, while being able to roll out a new financial product quickly is critical for competitiveness, it must be balanced by rigorous validation and review to ensure that no unexpected operational risk is created.

8.5.2 Engage Customer

Customer engagement is a key part of the bank's marketing and sales process. Banks may advertise their products through brochures provided at branches, banners or splash screens shown on Internet banking websites, email or mail campaigns, or through cross-selling activities in call centers. Once a

Figure 8-4 Face-to-face interactions are common for lending (© Standard Chartered Bank. Reprinted with permission.)

customer has shown interest, in most cases, a **relationship manager (RM)** or loan officer will meet with the customer to understand his or her business and finance needs (Figure 8-4). Specifically, the bank will need to work with the customer to determine the loan amount required. Inexperienced borrowers may overestimate or underestimate their funding requirements; this is where banks' experience and expertise in understanding customers' borrowing needs can be of benefit to the customer.

The purpose of the loan and potential means of repayment will be explored. Future cash flows will be assessed as a source of repayment. Options will also be explored with the customer as to what collateral is potentially available to secure the loan as a secondary source of repayment. For instance, corporate-owned property, vehicles, plant equipment, or potentially a related party's personal possessions may be deemed acceptable as collateral. With this understanding, the bank staff can most effectively advise customers on their eligibility for products and which are most suitable.

Besides avoiding potential losses due to credit default, when lending, banks must also consider their legal obligations to customers and investors who buy the loans bundled into securities. Lawsuits and regulatory fines related to mis-selling of financial products can do significant reputational damage and lead to losses related to operational risk. For example, leading up to 2007, a number of lenders and mortgage advisers did not adequately assess the plausibility of the information that customers provided in relation to their ability to repay loans. In many cases, the customers were unable to afford the loan repayment amounts and, thus, became delinquent and defaulted at high rates. Several years later, in the United States, the Federal Housing Finance Agency sued 17 global financial institutions for billions of dollars for allegedly having made materially false statements about the quality of mortgages they bundled and sold as mortgage-backed securities. Hence, banks may still suffer when due diligence to evaluate customers' creditworthiness has been neglected, even when they do not directly hold the credit risk associated with the loans.

Case Study 8-5

The Importance of Due Diligence in Lending

The importance of performing due diligence checks throughout the transaction lifecycle to prevent potential loss from fraud cannot be emphasized enough. Inadequate procedures and skipping of steps can easily lead to losses. Besides the risk of bank employees and customers committing fraud, lack of due diligence by the individuals involved in the lending process also present risks.

In 2004, four banks lent over US$80 million to Asia Pacific Breweries (APB)—or at least they thought they did. APB is a listed company, and is one of the largest beer makers in Asia; thus, by itself the lending would have probably been a good **credit risk**. Unfortunately for the banks, the finance manager of APB's Singapore unit secured the loans for his own purposes, without the authorization of ABP. He used the money to support a gambling problem and had some funds transferred directly to a casino.

Two European banks took the case to court in Singapore, claiming that APB should be responsible for the actions of its finance director. The courts rejected the claims, partially on the basis that the banks "had made themselves 'easy prey' by disregarding their own manuals and normal banking procedures." Some of the oversights that were cited included failing to verify the authenticity of signatures on corporate resolutions authorizing the loan, failing to investigate discrepancies in documentation, and failing to question why the finance director was the only person at APB involved in the transaction for a loan of that size.

This case is not unique. In 2009, another case where a bank lent over US$700 million to a prominent property developer went to court in China. The company's chairman allegedly secured the loans with the help

(Continued)

(Continued)

of a senior executive at the bank, and then absconded with the money. The company's shareholders had no knowledge of the loans, and as a result of the fraud, the trading of its shares was halted indefinitely.

Even if it is to obtain a high-profile customer in an emerging market or through arrangements based on personal trust, it is critical that best practices not be sidestepped in the process of securing that business. The banks that lent the amounts had to book losses related to **operational risk**, and likely spent considerable effort afterwards to enhance their processes to ensure that rigorous due diligence steps would be followed without fail in the future.

Sources: Lim, Kevin, "SEB, HVB Lose Claim Versus Singapore's Asia-Pacific Breweries," *Reuters*, September 1, 2009, http://www.reuters. com/assets/print?aid=USSIN33031220090901; "Banks Missed 'Red Flags' Waved by Chia," *Business Times*, September 3, 2009; Anderlini, Jamil, "China Suffers Largest Suspected Bank Fraud," *Financial Times*, August 5, 2009, http://www.ft.com/cms/s/0/82c175f6-81f2-11 de-9c5e-00144feabdc0.html.

8.5.3 Capture Order

The "order" for a loan product is, in most cases, received in the form of a paper-based loan application. Subsequently, detailed credit evaluation and verification steps are performed. Credit evaluation involves qualitative review, that is, understanding the company's business and the trends of its business environment, and quantitative review, that is, analysis of its financial statements. Credit evaluation processes are discussed in more detail in Section 8.7. Verification can include activities such as the investigation of the terms and restrictions of other loan agreements that the company may already have in place. Likewise, it would be necessary to obtain and verify legal documentation, such as memorandum and articles of association, corporate resolutions approving the loan transaction, financial statements, proof of collateral ownership, and verification of the signatories' employment status. Other requirements would include due diligence steps, such as inquiries related to verifying the intended use of the funding. As illustrated by Case Study 8-5, failing to perform adequate due diligence can lead to dire consequences.

Detailed negotiations related to payment terms, fees, and covenants may also be required. Loan covenants that protect the interests of the bank may be viewed as overly restrictive on the company's business operations so compromise may be necessary. Where collateral is used to secure a loan, it may be necessary to inspect and appraise the value of the collateral and determine the loan-to-value ratio, that is, the amount the bank is willing to lend against the collateral. Specific terms and conditions related to the collateral such as restrictions on use, maintenance requirements, and insurance requirements may also be defined.

Furthermore, preparation of the contractual documentation will be required so that all the necessary terms and conditions are specified in sufficient detail. The customer's legal support, internal or external, will likely need to be involved to review and revise the terms and conditions of the agreement. A bank's legal department may also need to review and determine the steps necessary to place liens and debentures or to take ownership of collateral. Banks will generally use their own standard legal agreement templates as a base and then modify them as necessary to address the transaction's specific details.

8.5.4 Fulfill Transaction

Fulfillment of the loan will include verification of signatures, sending transaction advice to the customer, generation of account entries, and disbursement of proceeds to the customer. Where collateral is involved, physical handover, legal transfer of ownership, or the registration of a lien may be required.

Depending on the institution and the nature of the transaction, fulfillment may ultimately lead to the loan being securitized or sold to another institution. In this case, the servicing of the loan, that is, the transaction maintenance, may continue to be performed by the bank or may be performed by another party.

8.5.5 Maintain Transaction

Given the potentially long tenure of loan transactions, significant transaction maintenance effort is usually required. Repayments will need to be processed and monitored to ensure that they correspond to the schedule and amounts defined by the loan agreement. Late payments may incur additional fees and interest and potentially trigger collections or loan foreclosure processes. The customer may default or go bankrupt, requiring legal recovery actions by the bank (Case Study 8-6). Also, if the loan agreement permits, the bank may have to accommodate early loan repayments.

Additionally, for corporate customers, it may be necessary to monitor their activities to ensure that loan covenants are not broken. Financial statements will need to be obtained and reviewed, any discrepancies investigated, and follow-up actions taken with the customer, as necessary. Changes in the customer's ability to fulfill loan covenants may lead to cancelation or amendments to the credit agreement. For example, a loan covenant may stipulate that a company's capitalization must remain above a fixed amount, for example, US$30 million. Various accounting events, such as an impairment write-down, may lead to a breach of covenant. In some cases, credit facilities may need to be reapproved on an annual basis, and the borrower may have to accept revised terms and conditions.

In cases where loan agreements are secured by collateral, periodic inspections and insurance verification may be required. Reassessment of collateral value may trigger changes to the loan provision amount or topping up of collateral to fulfill the loan's requirements. Likewise, customers may also choose to withdraw or replace the collateral from time to time.

Banks also get involved with remedial management of loans. Legal action may be taken against companies to enforce guarantees. Foreclosure on property and subsequent sale or auction of the property may be necessary as part of the funds recovery process. Creditors may participate in the restructuring of companies to help ensure that they can generate the cash flows necessary to repay their loans. Alternatively, when finances of companies cannot be salvaged, banks may take part in the winding up or bankruptcy receivership process.

Case Study 8-6

Invasion of the Robo-signers

As part of banks' standard practices, specialized business functions will manage the foreclosure of properties in cases of mortgage default. However, the surge of defaults due to the large volume of subprime mortgage securities that were issued in the United States between 2003 and 2006 overwhelmed the foreclosure processing capabilities of many banks. By 2010, there were over 6.5 million distressed properties and over 2 million homes in foreclosure status. This glut led to concerns that bank employees were rubber-stamping foreclosure documents without checking their accuracy, effectively acting as "robo-signers." Allegedly, at one bank in the United States, a vice president, on behalf of the bank, signed up to 500 foreclosure-related documents a day, approximately one per minute during business hours.

Investigations of banks by state attorneys-general and federal regulators led lenders to review their procedures and internal controls. Some of the largest home mortgage lenders suspended their foreclosure

(Continued)

(Continued)

proceedings, and in the case of one bank, foreclosures were halted for over a year. In February 2012, five of the top lenders in the United States agreed to a US$26 billion legal settlement related to foreclosure abuses. Banks are expected to face more fines and legal settlements related to improper foreclosure processes in the coming years as well and, as highlighted in Case Study 8-7, robo-signing has not been limited to mortgages.

Some banks tried to address the growing backlog of mortgage foreclosures by automating their foreclosure processes, but these attempts were largely abandoned. The time required to analyze existing processes, define requirements, design, implement, and test an IT solution would likely have taken many months or, more likely, longer than a year to complete. As an alternative, banks hired more staff, most of whom did not have experience in this business area, to accommodate the excessive volume of paperwork. While many areas of banking, such as payments, are almost completely automated using **straight-through processing (STP)**, other areas, such as foreclosure processing, are still very much manual, paper-based operations. From a processing cost perspective, in many cases, it is not practical to automate these functions. However, automation enables increases in volume and demand spikes to be accommodated more easily, thus reducing operational risk. Automation can help avoid human errors that occur more frequently during high-pressure crunch periods. Nonetheless, these benefits of automation are often not appreciated until a crisis unfolds, when it is already too late.

Sources: "Robostop," *Economist*, October 14, 2010, http://www.economist.com/node/17257787; Kapner, Suzanne, "Wells Adds to Crisis over Home Seizures," *Financial Times*, October 14, 2010, http://www.ft.com/intl/cms/s/0/ed4aa856-d70b-11df-9cd5-00144feabdc0.html#axzz1z9Dse3Ms; Kapner, Suzanne, "US Banks Seek Foreclosure Experts," *Financial Times*, November 2, 2010, http://www.ft.com/intl/cms/s/0/d620ed3a-e6c3-11df-99b3-00144feab49a.html#axzz1z9Dse3Ms; Braithwaite, Tom, "Foreclosure Practices under Intense Scrutiny," *Financial Times*, October 25, 2010, http://www.ft.com/intl/cms/s/0/0173d6b4-e039-11df-9482-00144feabdc0.html#axzz1z9Dse3Ms; Schwartz, Nelson D. and Shaila Dewan,"States Negotiate $26 Billion Agreement for Homeowners," *New York Times*, February 8, 2012, http://www.nytimes.com/2012/02/09/business/states-negotiate-25-billion-deal-for-homeowners.html?pagewanted=all; Nasieipour, Shahien, "HSBC Foreclosures Halted for More Than a Year," *Financial Times*, February 27, 2012, http://www.ft.com/intl/cms/ s/0/00f4a038-616b-11e1-94fa-00144feabdc0.html; Silver-Greenberg, Jessica, "As Foreclosure Problems Persist, Fed Seeks More Fines," *New York Times*, April 1, 2012, http://www.nytimes.com/2012/04/02/business/fed-targets-eight-more-firms-in-foreclosure-probe.html.

8.5.6 Review

Ongoing reviews are required to monitor and evaluate various factors that may affect corporate customers' ability to repay loan obligations and the banks' overall risk exposure. Corporate activities, such as mergers and acquisitions, must be monitored to determine how they will affect a customer's financial position and the credit limit structures used for the parties involved. For example, a merger could simultaneously weaken the financial standing of the acquirer, as was the case with the Royal Bank of Scotland's purchase of ABN AMRO, and increase their creditors' aggregate exposure to default by a single entity. That is to say, a default by either entity after the merger would result in a default by both.

Besides mergers and acquisitions activities, banks need to monitor customers' risk profiles and behavioral patterns. Financial statements will indicate if income levels are increasing or decreasing, and how the balance sheet is changing. Revenue and spending patterns may be steady or volatile. Late payments may increase, causing the customer to enter several stages of delinquency. The customer may default on obligations to other creditors. These considerations will be factored into customers' ongoing internal credit ratings, leading to increases or decreases in credit limits or changes to the interest rate and fee structures that are offered. In some cases, the bank may need to make provisions for bad debt in advance of default.

Economic conditions, both macro and sector-specific, must also be reviewed regularly by banks. The state of the economy may impact both the reliability of loan repayment and the realizable value of collateral. Changes in economic conditions may lead a bank to reduce the volume or amount of loans made to a specific segment of the market, increase eligibility requirements, or adjust rates. As a case in point, during the recession that lasted from 2007 until 2009, there was a marked reduction in the willingness of banks to refinance loan obligations to corporations. In cases where they were willing to finance corporate debt, the interest rate spreads offered in many cases greatly exceeded government benchmark rates.

8.6 LIFECYCLE FOCUS: CREDIT EVALUATION

This section reviews, in greater depth, the activities involved in the credit evaluation processes of banks for commercial and consumer loans. Typically, credit evaluation will be performed during the customer-engagement and order-capture stages of the transaction lifecycle. Banks use both qualitative and quantitative information to assess customers' creditworthiness. Banks that primarily provide **transactional banking** services, which focus on selling high volumes of standardized products, rely more on quantitative measures that can be assessed quickly and with minimal effort. On the other hand, banks that are involved in **relationship banking**, which is characterized by a tighter connection between the bank and the customer, make greater use of qualitative information that they have or can obtain about their customers. Figure 8-5 shows the activities typically involved in the credit evaluation process for a commercial loan,* which incorporates both qualitative and quantitative information.

Qualitative evaluation factors are considerations that are not necessarily straightforward to determine and may have to be assessed subjectively. For example, evaluating the character of the

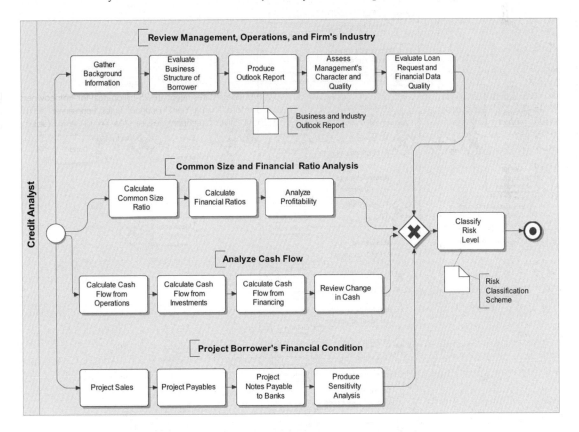

Figure 8-5 The credit evaluation process for a commercial loan

---

* Figure 8-5, Figure 8-6, and their related descriptions provided in this section summarize the explanations provided by the chapters "Evaluating Commercial Loan Requests" and "Managing Credit Risk and Evaluating Consumer Loans" in *Bank Management: A Decision-making Perspective* (ISBN: 978-981-4416-13-9).

firm and its management is one such consideration. Such evaluations are extremely important when providing credit, but they are difficult to quantify and may be assessed differently by different individuals. Similarly, determining the purpose for a loan may not be obvious and will have to be

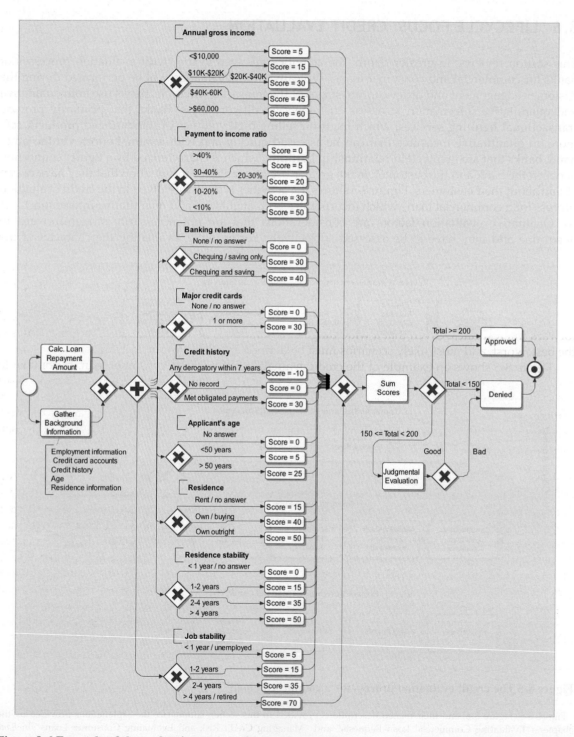

Figure 8-6 Example of the evaluation process for a consumer loan

assessed subjectively. For instance, funds borrowed for additional working capital could potentially be used for other purposes, such as staff bonuses.

Alternatively, quantitative evaluation factors are based on clearly measurable information. The customers' management accounts, credit scores, and transaction history are examples of information that can be utilized for quantitative analysis. For example, cash-flow analysis is a core area where quantitative analysis is used for credit evaluation. It is necessary to ensure that customers have, or will be able to generate, sufficient cash flow to support their repayment of the loan.

Whereas qualitative evaluation processes are highly reliant on investigation and observation by people, quantitative analysis processes are more readily supported by software solutions, such as spreadsheets. For example, information from customers' balance sheets and income statements is used to calculate ratios such as the current ratio, quick ratio, and sales-to-asset ratio. These performance statistics can then be compared from one year to the next and with benchmarks for the company's industry. Likewise, customers' return on equity, return on assets, and sales growth can be calculated to help assess their financial health.

Reported net income is often different from available cash flows; hence, extensive cash-flow analysis is also required. It is possible for a company to be profitable from an accounting standpoint, but also to run out of money due to poorly managed cash flows. Reported cash-flow activities are separated into components related to operations, investing activities, and financing activities. Information related to the cash flow from operations will then be used to help determine how much of the company's operational cash is available to support additional borrowing.

Forward financial projections are also performed as part of the credit evaluation. For example, sales projections are used to estimate sales growth; historical averages, such as the number of days that accounts receivable are outstanding, are used to help calculate expectations for related balance sheet items at future dates; and interest due on floating-rate debt need to be estimated based on forecasts of forward interest rates. Given that a wide range of assumptions need to be made during the analysis, the best, worst, and most-likely scenarios must be defined and their outcomes evaluated.

Figure 8-6 shows an example of the credit evaluation process for a consumer loan. In contrast to the commercial loan evaluation process, this process is more quantitatively oriented. Only in cases where the calculated score is between the automatic approval and the denial ranges will a credit officer get involved to investigate further and make a judgmental evaluation. Qualitative factors that may be taken into consideration are customers' extended employment history, the amount of their loan downpayment, and their overall relationship with the bank.

IT can benefit quantitative credit analysis immensely. It can help improve the efficiency of calculations, standardize and codify evaluation procedures, reduce manual calculation errors, and manage historical information. While spreadsheets are commonly used for analysis purposes, they are not considered ideal tools for quantitative analysis for several reasons. First, although spreadsheets are good for displaying information, they are not designed to enforce process. Important steps may be accidentally missed or intentionally skipped for purposes of simplicity. Second, when significant automation is built into spreadsheets, they can become difficult to maintain and debug. Third, spreadsheets do not natively support the centralized management of data, for example, in a database. Customized client-server applications, **business process management (BPM)** workflow systems, and rule-engine-based solutions are all more robust alternatives for implementation. Furthermore, data warehouses can be used to combine data about scorecard decisioning and subsequent loan repayment behavior that supports analysis of scorecard effectiveness and tuning of scorecard rules.

8.7 ARCHITECTURE CONSIDERATIONS: DEBT COLLECTION TECHNOLOGY

When banks extend credit to customers, a key objective is to ensure that the debt can and will be repaid. Unfortunately, there will be situations where that is not the case. A number of factors can affect customers' debt repayment abilities. To a large extent, economic conditions determine the ability of both businesses and consumers to repay debt. Likewise, specific factors, such as loss of customers for businesses or the loss of a job or severe illness for individuals, can lead to default on repayment of a loan. In particular, Millennials living in the United States have high debt levels, with 56% estimated to be living paycheck-to-paycheck [6]. Furthermore, as of 2015, some 77 million people in the United States had debt that was in the collection process [7]. This section reviews the business context along with the approaches and technologies that are used for collections of unsecured lending, e.g., credit card debt.[*]

8.7.1 Business Context

In the context of unsecured credit in the United States, the collections process is triggered when a customer fails to make an agreed payment. At that point, the delinquency period, which is measured in days, begins. For the period up to 180 days past due, using in-house or external collectors, banks will attempt to rehabilitate the account so that it is once again current. Typically the longer the account has been delinquent, the more difficult it is to rehabilitate it and recover funds. For example, a customer that is less than 30 days delinquent may have the funds available, but have forgotten to pay. On the other hand, a customer who has missed several payments is more likely to be suffering financial distress. Accordingly, the approach used for collections for the various stages of delinquency will differ.

After 180 days of delinquency, banks are required by federal regulations to charge off, i.e., treat as bad debt, the amount due on the account. At this point, the account is considered to be in collections status, as opposed to being past due. Banks may choose to continue trying to collect using in-house or external collection agencies, or it may sell off the charged-off account at a steep discount to a debt buyer who will then try to collect. Throughout this process, banks will send letters to customers regarding their past due and collections status. Additionally, banks may report status to credit bureaus the delinquency status when the account is 30, 60, or 90 days past due and when an account goes into collections.

8.7.2 Approaches

Banks that have loans in default have several options for recovering funds. The first is to perform debt collection in-house. The second is to outsource debt collections to a third party that typically works on a commission basis. The third option is to sell the debt at a discount to a third party that will collect on the debt on its own behalf. The fourth is to write off the debt. Banks may use some or all of these options in combination. For example, banks may choose to use their own collection operations for accounts that they think are more likely to be recoverable, and sell off or outsource those that they believe are less likely or will be more work to recover. While outsourcing debt collection provides some advantages, it also comes with risks. Banks have less control over how outsourced debt collectors operate. If a third-party debt collection agency uses abusive practices, it can come back to haunt the bank that engaged them. Likewise, a bank can face regulatory fines if it provides inaccurate information to an outsourced collector that causes the collector to unwittingly try to collect on debt that has already been repaid.

Collection of debt from delinquent borrowers is more complex than just calling a customer to tell them that their payment is 30 days overdue. Often other creditors may be trying to collect delinquent debt from the same customer, which creates competition as to which institution will receive what limited funds the customer may have for repayment. Likewise, customers in financial hardship may be difficult to contact; they may have had to move their place of residence or may avoid answering calls that they think may be from debt collectors. Hence, debt collection strategy is important. The first

---

[*] The process for secured debt has the additional dimension of repossession or foreclosure, which has its own myriad of complications.

and most important strategy consideration is the ability to contact customers who have delinquent payments. This requires having up-to-date contact information and also multiple ways to communicate with the customer, e.g., home phone, mobile phone, post, email, through the Internet banking website, etc. The second key element is being able to provide options that help facilitate current and future repayment. Payment due dates may be rescheduled, and the end goal is to bring the customer out of delinquency and back into good credit standing. Accordingly, debt payments may be restructured or rescheduled to accommodate a customer's short-term financial troubles, such as the loss of a job.

While the strategy for debt collection is fairly straightforward, the tactics are more complicated. Once contact is made with customers, it is often difficult to engage them in discussions about their finances and getting commitments for payment. Collectors may try different scripted dialogs as well as improvised conversations to get past these challenges. When encouraging customers to repay their debt, it is important that collectors do not say something that is not compliant with regulations, such as threatening legal action. Hence, it is crucial that bank management trains and monitors collectors to avoid compliance violations. Likewise, there are regulatory constraints on how debt payments can be restructured. For instance, in some cases, recurring repayment amounts that have been negotiated must be sufficiently large so that they offset the recurring interest charges so that the total amount owed does not continue to grow.

There are many different regulatory rules that debt collection operations must comply with. For example, in the United States, the Fair Debt Collection Practices Act (FDCPA) prohibits debt collectors from engaging in activities such as harassment, making false statements, applying unfair practices, and calling at inconvenient times. Figure 8-7 shows a snapshot from 2015 of customer complaints related to FDCPA violations. Likewise, communications with delinquent debtors may be limited by other communication regulations. As a case in point, in the United States the Telephone Consumer

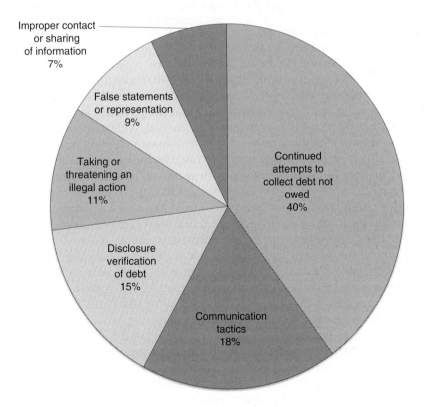

Figure 8-7 Debt collection complaints by type of issue

Protection Act (TCPA) limits the use of automatic telephone dialing system to call customers' mobile phones unless the caller has expressed prior consent to make such calls from the called party. TCPA violations can cost a bank up to $1,500 per call, so that a thousand errant autodialed calls could result in a fine of over a million dollars. Likewise, as highlighted in Case Study 8-7, the penalties for fair debt collection violations can be very severe. Hence, it is essential to have processes and technology in place that help support and ensure compliance.

8.7.3 Technology

While much of the debt collection process involves human interaction, technology is critical to supporting collection activities. For banks that perform in-house collections, key components of the technology architecture include collection management, payment, customer channel communication, automated dialer, and call recording and monitoring.

Collection management. Collection management functions typically involve:

- monitoring and managing the status of delinquent accounts;

- tracking interactions with customers;

- maintaining customer contact information;

- calculating customer-specific payment options that can be offered by collectors;

- recording and tracking customers' promises to pay on future dates; and

- generating reports that can be used for financial, audit, and compliance purposes.

These functions may be provided by one or more standalone applications or integrated into other platforms. Collection management functions are often integrated with core banking, payment, communication channel/CRM, and predictive dialer systems.

Payment. Successful collection efforts result in payments that, ideally, will be processed immediately by the bank doing the collection. Time is of the essence to determine whether the payment information provided from a customer is valid and also to ensure that the payment is completed while the funds are still available. Rather than wait for a cheque to be mailed, collectors will see to obtaining funds more quickly using other payment channels such as automated clearing house (ACH) or debit card transactions. Hence, collection management systems often include or are integrated with the payment systems banks have in place for other purposes, such as branch or online banking.

Customer communication channels. While telecommunications is the main channel that debt collection operations use to reach customers, other channels such as letters, email, mobile phone text messages, and websites may also be leveraged. For legal compliance purposes, letters are sent to customers about their delinquency and collection status. Email and text messages may be used to spur customers to call the bank or login to its Internet banking website get information about the status of their accounts and/or engage in a discussion with a collector. In recent years, automated web-based collection systems have begun to be used in parallel with call-center collection operations. The idea behind such systems is that some customers may be less comfortable talking to a collector about their financial situation and more comfortable interacting with a system to determine what repayment options they may have available. Likewise, automated collection is less costly for banks, since it does not require salary payments, desk space, or management supervision. On the other hand, online systems may not be as persuasive as the collector in person, and, thus, not as effective.

Predictive dialer. Sizable debt collection operations generally use predictive dialers to initiate calls to customers. The dialer is fed a list of telephone numbers of delinquent borrowers that it automatically dials and, if a connection is made, will route the call to a call center agent who handles debt collection.

Predictive dialers maximize the likelihood that an agent will be available to answer a connected call by analyzing the time spent by collectors on and waiting between calls and adjusting the rate at which outbound calls are made accordingly. Eliminating the need for call center agents to manually dial numbers greatly increases call center efficiency, enabling more calls to be made with fewer people. Likewise, ensuring that collectors are available when customers are connected to by phone reduces the chance that customers will hang up because they have been called and then immediately put on hold or hear silence. Dialers may be configured to handle multiple outbound call lists, where the lists divide the customers to be called into groups based on their stage of delinquency, e.g., 30 or 60 days past due. Calls connected from each list are routed by the dialer to a different group of collectors, who are trained for and/or best skilled at collecting at that the associated stage of delinquency.

Call recording and monitoring systems. Recording customer calls is important for collection operations for several reasons. First, call recordings can be used by managers to evaluate individual collectors' skills and, combined with training, to improve their skills. Second, it enables the checking and auditing of whether collectors are complying with regulations such as UDAP. Third, it provides a record that can be used to assess the validity of, and counter, unsubstantiated customer complaints. Call recording systems may be integrated with screen recording technology so that those reviewing or monitoring collectors' activities can see what collectors were doing on their workstation while having discussions with customers.

Case Study 8-7

The Perils of Bad Debt Collection Practices

Banks face a number of risks with their debt collection practices, and outsourcing collection activities does not eliminate those risks. In fact, it can increase them. As a case in point, around 2011, Citibank had a total of 22 branch offices and 105 automated teller machines (ATMs) in Indonesia, where it offered retail, corporate, and wealth management services. Citigroup ran into trouble with its business there when Indonesian authorities investigated a potential homicide, where a Citibank Indonesia client died under mysterious circumstances after being questioned by third-party debt collectors that the bank used.

The fallout from this scandal was immense and was worsened by the arrest of a senior vice president of the bank for embezzling US$1.7 million of Citibank Indonesia customers' money. Indonesia's central bank suspended Citi's acquisition of premium banking customers for one year and barred it from issuing credit cards for two years. Furthermore, Indonesia's central bank conducted 40-day "fit-and-proper tests" for Citibank executives after it found the bank's standard operating procedures to be noncompliant with regulations related to wealth management and debt collection. Bank executives who failed the tests could lose their jobs and be banned from the banking industry in Indonesia for several years (it was reported that a few had, in fact, failed the evaluation). Besides the regulatory sanctions, the ongoing negative press reports also damaged the bank's reputation.

While this case was clearly extreme, it is not uncommon for banks to be penalized for improper collection practices. In another example, in 2015, JPMorgan agreed to pay more than $200 million in refunds to customers and regulatory penalties for wrongful collection practices on its customers' credit card debt. The bank also agreed to permanently halt collections on more than half a million accounts. Regulators accused JPMorgan of providing erroneous information when it sold accounts to third-party debt collectors. Problems with the information included debts being associated with the wrong person, incorrect amounts, and previously discharged debt. Moreover, the bank had signed large quantities of documents without verifying the information, i.e., robo-signing was involved. As a result, JPMorgan also agreed to overhaul its

(Continued)

(Continued)

practices for selling debt to third-party collectors, including verification of customer account information on an individual basis.

Sources: Tucker, Sundeep, "Citigroup Flags Asia Revenue Growth," *Financial Times*, February 3, 2010, http://www.ft.com/cms/s/0/2dd8be2e-10a3-11df-975e-00144feab49a.html; Citibank Indonesia press release, October 7, 2010, https://www.citibank.co.id/IDGCB/APPS/portal/loadPage.do?tabId=kartu+kredit&path=/info/ det/news/news-07oct10.htm; "Citibank Indonesia Senior Vice President Arrested for Embezzlement," *Jakarta Post*, March 31, 2011, http://www.jakartaupdates.com/1299-03/citibank-indonesia-senior-vice-president-arrested-for-embezzlement; Deutsch, Anthony and Francesco Guerrera, "Citi Barred from New Indonesia Accounts," *Financial Times*, April 6, 2011, http://www.ft.com/cms/s/0/991ac 348-6076-11e0-9fcb-00144feab49a.html; Samboh, Esther, "Citibank Executives May Lose Careers If They Fail BI Test," *Jakarta Post*, May 10, 2011, http://www.thejakartapost.com/news/2011/05/10/citibank-executives-may-lose-careers-if-they-fail-bi-test.html; Golson, Jennifer, "Ex-CitigroupVP Admits Embezzling over $22 Million," *Reuters*, September 6, 2011, http://www.reuters.com/article/2011/09/06/ us-citigroup-embezzlement-idUSTRE7854P320110906; Nangoy, Franceska, "Top Citi Execs Tripped Up by Tests, BI Says," *Jakarta Globe*, June 29, 2011, http://www.thejakartaglobe.com/home/top-citi-execs-tripped-up-by-tests-bi-says/449846; "JPMorgan to Pay $136 Million to Settle Debt Collection Case," *New York Times*, July 8, 2015, http://www.nytimes.com/2015/07/09/business/jpmorgan-to-pay-dollar136-million-to-settle-debt-collection-case.html?partner=rss&emc=rss; Witkowski, Rachel, "JPMorgan to Pay More Than $200M for Faulty Card Collections," *American Banker*, July 8, 2015, http://www.americanbanker.com/news/law-regulation/jpmorgan-to-pay-more-than-200m-for-faulty-card-collections-1075280-1.html?zkPrintable=true.

8.8   SOLUTION CONSIDERATIONS

This section will elaborate on how IT can help improve the lending function within banks. The use of technology to support multistage loan approvals, loan application processing and monitoring, and internal and external data integration will be studied.

8.8.1 Multistage Loan Approval

Instituting multiple review and control points is a risk management strategy applied by banks across many different products. In its simplest and most generic form, the maker/checker division of labor reduces the chances of operational mistakes, and serves as a fraud-prevention measure. In the context of lending, where many subjective factors may influence lending decisions, multiple approvals can be used to help ensure that due diligence is adequately completed, and that a "second set of eyes" is used to verify that the evaluation process is complete and not biased.

Loan approvals require one or more managers or peers to sanction the transaction. The determination of who must approve transactions and under what conditions, is usually defined by a set of business rules based on considerations such as the loan amount, interest rate offered, fees applied or waived, and unusual terms that are provided for in the loan agreement. For example, a US$100,000 loan may only require peer review and approval, whereas a US$1 million loan may also require a manager's approval, and a US$10 million loan may require a manager's and division director's approval.

The approval-process logic may be relatively simple and fixed, with a limited number of approvers and levels of escalation. These types of static requirements work well with hardcoded process IT solutions. For example, a core banking system may be able to easily support three levels of loan approvals, but not ten. Supporting ten may be feasible technically, but the cost of customization to meet this and other types of special requirements is often prohibitive.

Alternatively, the approval workflow may be complex and/or flexible (that is, ad hoc). An example of a more complex business process may be where special approval by the chief financial officer is required if the transaction is to be completed during the last week of the financial quarter. An example of a flexible workflow is where one approver can dynamically choose the next person to review and approve the transaction. Complex and flexible approval workflows are easier to implement where paper-based loan files are being physically passed around because there are no strict rules governing their handling. However, these workflows can be problematic for traditional IT solutions, where routing logic usually cannot be changed on the fly.

Ultimately, it is up to each bank to determine if its loan-approval process can be brought in line with the capabilities of an existing solution, if a custom solution must be developed, or if some hybrid of the two approaches is more practical. A hybrid strategy may be to develop customizations or provide workflow facilities around an existing lending solution. Where complex or flexible requirements are common, implementing solutions on top of a **business process management system (BPMS)** can provide significant benefits (as discussed in Chapter 2).

8.8.2 Loan Application Processing and Monitoring

Historically, loan application processes were managed as stacks of paper that moved between people's desks, and different review and data enrichment activities were performed each step of the way. In many financial institutions worldwide, this is still how they are handled. Paper-based systems have a number of problems. First, there are logistical issues. Paper files must be physically moved to each location where they are processed, and can only be at one place at a time. This is less relevant if the transportation is between multiple desks in the same room; it is a more serious consideration when some of the processing is done in another building or another country. Another problem with paper is that it tends to get lost. One possibility is that files may get physically lost, for instance, falling behind a desk or getting stuck to the back of another document. Another is that they may get stuck somewhere in the processing chain. For example, they may end up on a desk of someone who is out sick or off-duty for several weeks.

When working with paper, it is difficult to monitor the present status of an application, measure process efficiency, and ensure that **service-level agreements (SLAs)** are met. If a customer calls the bank's contact center or the relationship manager to check on the status of his or her application, the only way to track it is to contact each person in the processing flow to find out if they have the file. When there is no automated solution for monitoring application processing in place, this type of manual tracking is required, which is extremely inefficient and troublesome for all the people involved.

There are a number of ways to tactically address this issue. A common approach is to implement a shared spreadsheet or small departmental database that is used to capture information on which transactions are being worked on by people in the relevant group or department. However, while this poor-man's management information system (MIS) solution may be practical, it is problematic in that it requires additional ongoing support and maintenance, is prone to manual input errors, and is siloed and not available to other groups. In addition, it may not be in compliance with IT or audit policies. It is also important to note that this approach does not improve the overall workflow; all the other paper-processing problems still remain.

There are a number of other more strategic technology-based solutions that could be applied. A simpler, but less effective approach is to leverage existing technology, such as the bank's CRM IT system, to track application status. If application-processing staff is granted access to the CRM system, they can then enter in the customer record the stage of application processing reached. While this sounds straightforward, implementing this approach can lead to complications, such as the cost of providing CRM system user licenses to back-office employees and the availability of network connectivity between departments. It also may increase issues involving internal control, whereby back-office staff can access front-office customer information. Likewise, issues related to handling paper applications would still remain.

A more robust solution is to use a workflow or BPM platform to manage application processing. In its simplest form, it could provide application-processing status management, determining who should be processing each application and, based on business rules built into the solution, where the application should go next. This approach can help alleviate problems when an application gets stuck on an empty desk—the solution can detect the processing delay and reallocate the work activity to someone else. Also, a side benefit of status management is that it is much easier to monitor application-processing performance in aggregate, calculate average processing times for all loan applications, and track SLAs for individual applications. Given the availability of low-cost and open-source BPM platforms, this is a practical and cost-effective approach to begin with.

Although the foregoing approach solves the monitoring and work-allocation problem, paper-based application problems will still persist. To resolve them, a typical approach is to scan application-related documents at the source (for example, the branch) and create a digital file that can be accessed by all the participants as part of the workflow. This resolves many of the logistical issues inherent in paper processing and can also provide a more robust audit trail for tracking changes to the application documentation.

To be most effective, the BPMS and document scanners should be integrated. When a document is scanned, it can automatically be assigned to a new or existing workflow. When a user accepts a new application for processing from the BPMS, the scanned images related to that application should be immediately accessible through the same interface. Moreover, to support customer information requests, contact-center staff need to have access to the BPM monitoring information, ideally presented through integration with their main CRM system interface.

Being able to access scanned documentation and customer information, and invoke banking system functions from consolidated web-based BPMS interfaces helps streamline processing by providing a single interface that can be used to execute multiple different processing operations. In contrast, without such facilities, it is often necessary for processing staff to access multiple different banks' IT system interfaces, some of which may not be accessible from remote locations where processing is performed. BPM also enables manual processing to be routed to remote operation centers and extended to third parties, supporting business process outsourcing. BPMS can automatically allocate processing activities to different locations depending on the operating centers' working-hour availability, loading, and operating costs. Providing a single web-based interface simplifies solution deployment, that is, multiple back-end server components do not need to be installed remotely. Likewise, there are fewer security risks since customer data is only displayed temporarily at the processing locations and is not stored there.

8.8.3 Internal and External Data Integration

Besides the integration with document scanners that was described in the previous section, other internal and external integration is also required to improve efficiency. Customer information that is maintained internally, such as existing loans that are outstanding, internal credit scoring, and credit limits, need to be accessed to process the loan application. External information, such as customer earnings and balance sheet details, credit rating scores, and third-party collateral appraisal information, also need to be accessed. In a paper-based environment, this information will be obtained from multiple applications, printed out, and then added to the application file. Relevant details from those printouts will then be manually entered into the credit evaluation or core banking systems. For example, in Singapore, when opening an account or applying for a loan, the bank processing staff must verify the current status of the company's directors who have authorized the transaction. The Singapore Accounting and Corporate Regulatory Authority provides an Internet-based service to allow this information to be accessed in real time for a small fee. In many cases the loan officer will use the website to access the information and print out the relevant details for inclusion with the transaction file.

There are a number of issues with the approach of manually accessing the website before using the printed copy to support processing. First, it is inefficient—the time and effort taken to access the system is significant on the whole and is non–value-adding work that slows down the application and increases personnel processing effort. Second, it is complicated—bank staff need to be trained on how to use the different systems to access the information required. Third, it is error prone—transcription errors can easily occur when the information is copied or reentered into the necessary systems, adding operational risk.

Providing better systems integration is the ideal solution for addressing these problems. However, it is usually impractical, from budget and time perspectives, to integrate all systems and information flows. Hence, analysis is required to determine the answers to questions such as:

- What information is available via electronic interfaces?

- How often is the information used?

- How often can transmission (entry) errors occur, and what is their risk significance?

- Will the information that is captured digitally also be of benefit for MIS purposes?

Answers to these questions will help determine the costs and benefits of integrating different types of information into the application-processing business process. There is no one set of correct answers; the analysis will be contextual and organization specific. On the one hand, a small bank that is focused primarily on payments may process a relatively small number of applications, making it impractical from a cost-benefit perspective to do much, if any, integration. On the other hand, a large bank that is focused on lending may realize major benefits from system integration, easily justifying the cost of the effort required. Moreover, a bank in a country that has low labor costs will have less economic incentive for integrating IT systems to reduce manual processing effort, but may still benefit from doing so to reduce operational risk and improve customer service by providing bank staff with easier and faster information access.

8.9   SUMMARY

This chapter covered:

- differences between corporate and retail lending products and practices;

- the lifecycle activities involved with secured lending to corporate customers;

- the practices and technology that support loan payment collection; and

- how business processes, core banking systems, and information integration are interrelated as part of a lending transaction.

The next chapter will review payment services that banks provide to customers.

FURTHER READING

Books

Koch, MacDonald, and Duran, *Bank Management: A Decision-making Perspective* (Singapore: Cengage Learning Asia, 2013) (ISBN: 978-981-4416-13-9), chapters on

- Overview of Credit Policy and Loan Characteristics

- Evaluating Commercial Loan Requests and Managing Credit Risk

- Evaluating Consumer Loans

Papers

Greene, W. H., "A Statistical Model for Credit Scoring," in *Advances in Credit Risk Modelling and Corporate Bankruptcy Prediction*, eds. S. Jones and D. A. Hensher, pp. 14–43 (New York, Cambridge University Press, 2008).

Mason, S. P. and S. L. Roth, "Note on Bank Loans," *Harvard Business School*, 9-291-026, 1993, http://hbr.org/product/note-on-bank-loans/an/291026-PDF-ENG.

"2016 Small Business Credit Survey: Report on Employer Firms," *Federal Reserve Bank of New York*, April 2017, https://www.newyorkfed.org/smallbusiness/small-business-credit-survey-employer-firms-2016.

Rosenberg, R., Gaul, S., Ford, W. and Tomilova O., "Microcredit Interest Rates and Their Determinants," *CGAP Access to Finance Forum*, No 7, June 2013, http://www.cgap.org/publications/microcredit-interest-rates-and-their-determinants.

Turner, M. and Agarwal, A., "Using Non-traditional Data for Underwriting Loans to Thin-file Borrowers: Evidence, Tips and Precautions," *Journal of Risk Management in Financial Institutions*, Vol 1, 2 165–180.

"Leveraging Technology to Empower Mortgage Consumers at Closing," *Consumer Financial Protection Bureau*, August 2015, http://files.consumerfinance.gov/f/201508_cfpb_leveraging-technology-to-empower-mortgage-consumers-at-closing.pdf.

Web

Federal Trade Commission Staff Commentary on the Fair Debt Collection Practices Act, https://www.fdic.gov/regulations/laws/rules/6000-1325.html.

"Opportunities and Challenges in Online Marketplace Lending," U.S. Department of the Treasury, May 10, 2016, https://www.treasury.gov/connect/blog/Documents/Opportunities_and_Challenges_in_Online_Marketplace_Lending_white_paper.pdf.

"A Temporary Phenomenon? Marketplace Lending," Deloitte, 2016, https://www2.deloitte.com/content/dam/Deloitte/uk/Documents/financial-services/deloitte-uk-fs-marketplace-lending.pdf.

ENDNOTES

1. McLannahan, B., "Tech Companies Invade Banks' Territory with Customer Loans," *Financial Times*, June 8, 2017, https://www.ft.com/content/b45c0008-4bc1-11e7-919a-1e14ce4af89b?mhq5j=e3.

2. Passy, J., "Embrace the Digital Mortgage as a Competitive Advantage," *American Banker*, January 10, 2017, https://www.americanbanker.com/news/embrace-the-digital-mortgage-as-a-competitive-advantage.

3. "Credit Card Market Monitor," American Bankers Association, May 2016.

4. Moore, E., "Peer-to-peer Lenders Gain Traction," *Financial Times*, March 30, 2012, http://www.ft.com/cms/s/0/81f595d8-78c8-11e1-9f49-00144feab49a.html.

5. Goff, S., "Lloyds Agrees to Pay £500 Million Mortgage Refunds," *Financial Times*, February 21, 2011, http://www.ft.com/cms/s/0/9aa1d810-3dc5-11e0-ae2a-00144feabdc0.html.

6. "2014 Wells Fargo Millennial Study," Wells Fargo.

7. "Fair Debt Collection Practices Act—CFPB Annual Report 2016," US Consumer Financial Protection Bureau.

— — —

8. Financial Services Authority, "FSA Finds Poor Practice by Intermediaries and Lenders within Subprime Markets," press release, July 4, 2007.

9. Braithwaite, T., K. Scannell, and D. McCrum, "Banks Sued over Mortgage Deals," *Financial Times*, September 3, 2011, http://www.ft.com/cms/s/0/c3656efc-d57c-11e0-9133-00144feab49a.html.

10. Moore, E.,"Loyal Customers Receive Tailored Rates," *Financial Times*, June 10, 2011, http://www.ft.com/cms/s/2/a33c9750-9386-11e0-922e-00144feab49a.html.

11. Kennard, M. and S. Bond, "Interest Soars in US Peer-to-peer Lending," *Financial Times*, November 24, 2011, http://www.ft.com/cms/s/0/2345e94a-0bb1-11e1-9a61-00144feabdc0.html.

12. Comptroller of the Currency, US Treasury, "Risk Management of Financial Derivatives, Comptroller's Handbook," 1998.

13. Witkowski, R., "JPMorgan to Pay More Than $200M for Faulty Card Collections," American Banker, July 8, 2015, http://www.americanbanker.com/news/law-regulation/jpmorgan-to-pay-more-than-200m-for-faulty-card-collections-1075280-1.html.

14. Crosman, P., "BBVA Automates Debt Collection," *American Banker*, September 1, 2012, http://www.americanbanker.com/btn/25_9/bbva-automates-debt-collection-1052165-1.html.

15. Thessin, J., "When Can I Call My Customer?" *ABA Banking Journal*, October 28, 2016, http://bankingjournal.aba.com/2016/10/when-can-i-call-my-customer.

16. Buhayar, N., "LendingClub's New Pitch? Refinance Your Pricey Car Loan with Us," *Bloomberg Markets*, Oct. 25, 2016, http://www.bloomberg.com/news/articles/2016-10-25/lendingclub-s-new-pitch-refinance-your-pricey-car-loan-with-us.

17. Witkowski, R., "Consumer Finance Watchdog Plans to Supervise Marketplace Lenders," *Wall Street Journal*, April 27, 2016, http://www.wsj.com/articles/consumer-finance-watchdog-plans-to-supervise-marketplace-lenders-1461794493.

18. Wildau, G., "China P2P Lending Regulations Target Hucksters and Risk-takers," *Financial Times*, August 24, 2016, https://www.ft.com/content/5b179264-69e0-11e6-a0b1-d87a9fea034f.

19. Clozel, L., "Is Your AI Racist? A Lawmaker Wants to Know," *American Banker*, June 30, 2017, https://www.americanbanker.com/news/is-your-ai-racist-a-lawmaker-wants-to-know.

20. McLannahan, B., "Amazon to Ramp Up Lending in Challenge to Big Banks," *Financial Times*, June 8, 2017, https://www.ft.com/content/78755202-4bb6-11e7-919a-1e14ce4af89b?mhq5j=e3.

9 Payments

In ancient times, transfer of livestock was one of the first forms of payment. Gradually, payment technology evolved to support more portable forms of currency, including seashells, and around 1000 BC metal money and coins came into use. With these forms of currency, payment was achieved through physical transfer between parties. The next major leap in payment technology came in the 16th century when prototypical banks accepted gold deposits and provided receipt notes to the depositors that were negotiable, i.e., could be transferred to other parties. Thus, transfer of notes could be used as a means of payment, rather than the transfer of the underlying assets they represented.

This system further evolved to the point where banks would bilaterally accept notes from other banks, so that funds deposited at one bank could be withdrawn from another, and the banks themselves would settle and transfer funds between each other. Over time, concerns such as settlement risk and managing a large number of bilateral agreements that had to be maintained led to the formation of central clearing banks. The clearing bank served as a common central payment transfer facility with which all banks held accounts. This eliminated the need for having many different bilateral agreements and reduced the participants' counterparty risk to be limited to just the central clearing bank.

Basic payment technologies and the systems that support them were developed over thousands of years. In contrast, today, payment innovation is occurring around the world on a continuous basis, and payment services are one of the fastest growing areas in financial services. In contrast to lending, which is primarily about financial products and risk management, services are the foundation of banks' payments businesses.

The advent of new customer communication channels has been a driving force for changes in payments. Payments made through Internet banking are one example of how new channels have revolutionized the payment process. For example, electronic payments have eliminated the need for:

- customers to handle paper, as is necessary with cheques;

- customers to travel to branches, as is required for transfers using cash notes; and

- banks to perform manual processing for routine payment transactions.

These changes have produced major benefits for both customers and banks. Customers have benefited from increased convenience, reduced transaction times, and better information about the status of incoming and outgoing funds. Banks have benefited from reduced processing costs and the ability to support larger volumes of transactions. Higher capacity enables banks to service more customers and helps ensure that customers receive consistent levels of service as transaction volumes grow.

In recent years, nonbank Fintech companies have been driving change in the payments world, challenging traditional financial institutions. Unencumbered by legacy systems and strict regulatory oversight, new startups and established technology firms have been able to push the payments industry into areas such as peer-to-peer and mobile payments. By catering to Millennials' needs and expectations, Fintechs have taken the lead in providing new technology-related services. Accordingly, banks have had to play catch-up to avoid losing customers and/or being disintermediated, i.e., having another party acting as a middleman between the bank and its customers.

Banks have also had to adapt to changing payment infrastructure as well. Many domestic payment systems have been or are going to be revamped to move from processing payments once a day in a batch, which causes settlement to span multiple days, to near real-time processing. Often regulators have had to press banks to make this change, since customers, rather than banks, are the main beneficiaries. Likewise, cross-border payment services, which have for many years been a lucrative business for banks, are also coming under pressure from new market entrants. In particular, digital currencies have provided mechanisms for individuals and businesses to transfer funds between countries and at lower costs compared to the transactional services that banks offer. The advent of distributed ledgers has also provided new payment infrastructure that banks may benefit from.

Nonetheless, banks have a number of advantages they can leverage in the battle against new market entrants. One is inertia. Changing customer behavior to use new payment methods, as highlighted in Case Study 9-1, is a major challenge that plays in banks' favor. Likewise, existing mechanisms for managing payment risk, controlling fraud, and handling customer disputes are well understood and have been proven over time. These factors provide a level of comfort to customers that must be overcome by new payment service providers and those using recently developed payment technologies.

This chapter explores payments, also commonly referred to as remittances, from the business, process, architecture, and solution points of view. First, the concepts that underlie payment systems are presented. Next, common payment technologies are reviewed. Then, uses of payment services by business and retail customers are explored. Given this context, the opportunities and challenges that banks face with providing payment services are reviewed. Following that, the core activities in the transaction lifecycle of a payment are examined. Finally, process and solution considerations related to payments are surveyed, and architecture issues related to batch and real-time processing are explored. Topics such as digital currencies, e.g., Bitcoin, and distributed legers, i.e., blockchain, could logically be included in this chapter; however, because of the large volume of information contained herein, they are discussed instead in Chapters 7 and 20, respectively.

Case Study 9-1
Mobile Payment Challenges

Many countries have struggled to get consumers to make merchant payments using their mobile phones. Examining various attempts in the United States to achieve this goal provides insights into the many challenges that must be overcome. Most large mobile payment initiatives have focused on using mobile phones as mobile wallets that store credit- and debit-card information and having them communicate directly with merchants' POS terminals. Many of these implementations use tokenization technology so that the wallet transmits a proxy account identifier, rather than the account number itself.

Softcard, which was originally called ISIS, was of the first major initiatives and was driven by a joint venture of three large telecommunication network operators. It was designed for NFC-enabled smartphones running the Android operating system and was offered to the general public starting in 2013, and then discontinued in 2015. It encountered several challenges, including a relatively small number of NFC-enabled phones being available and purchased by consumers, lack of NFC-enabled POS terminals at merchants, and the inconvenience of having to enter a PIN code on the phone to complete transactions. Softcard had limited support for credit cards and also required a special SIM card to be used in the phone, making setup relatively complicated.

Google Wallet was launched around the same time and used a similar approach to Softcard, supporting card transactions using NFC-enabled phones running the Android operating system. Its success was limited by some of the same factors as for Softcard, plus it was hampered by the fact that it competed with Softcard and, thus, the mobile telecommunication carriers were unwilling to sell phones with Google Wallet installed on them. Ultimately, when Softcard closed down, Google bought some of Smartcard's technology and the carriers behind Smartcard agreed to preload Google's wallet applications onto Android smartphones newly purchased by customers. Subsequently, Google shifted NFC-based mobile payments into another service called Android Pay and reserved the use of Google Wallet for peer-to-peer payments.

Apple Pay was launched in 2014 shortly before Android Pay, and addressed some of the usability challenges that its predecessor had encountered. One big difference with Apple Pay was that prior to the launch, Apple had enlisted hundreds of banks, including some of the largest, to support and promote the service. Another difference was that Apple had simplified the card enrollment process for users. It also leveraged the fingerprint recognition capability of its newest phones to authorize transactions at POS terminals, reducing the time and effort required, compared with having to type a PIN on the phone to authorize transactions. Unlike the Android NFC implementation that provided applications with access to the phones' secure element and NFC capability, Apple restricted access to these components on its phones to only the Apple wallet and Apple-owned applications. That is to say, no third-party mobile wallets were able to use the phones' NFC capabilities. Banks whose cards were enrolled into Apple Pay also had to pay interchange fees, which were assessed on each card transaction, to Apple.

In 2015 Samsung launched Samsung Pay which used Magnetic Secure Transmission (MST) technology included in its newer model phones. MST allowed the phone to be placed near the POS terminal and transmit the card account information to its magnetic stripe reader. Thus, it could work with the vast majority

(Continued)

(Continued)

of existing merchant POS terminals, and did not require them to be NFC enabled. However, Samsung Pay only was supported by a subset of Samsung's smartphones.

Separately, a consortium of major US-based merchants pulled together to create its own mobile payment service called CurrentC that would link to customers' bank accounts, rather than card accounts. This approach would enable the merchants to avoid having to pay interchange fees to credit and debit card issuers on CurrentC transactions. Two years after its launch and following a beta test, the CurrentC service was discontinued. Prior to CurrentC's demise, one of its major retail backers, Walmart, launched its own mobile payment application called Walmart Pay. Walmart Pay used the mobile phones' camera technology to capture a picture of the QR code displayed on the POS register display, making it compatible with both iOS and Android devices and eliminated the need for those devices to be NFC enabled. Also, it could be linked to multiple payment methods, such as credit, debit, prepaid, and gift cards.

More recently, banks have also moved into the mobile wallet space, with Wells Fargo launching its own Android-based mobile wallet solution that uses NFC technology. JPMorgan Chase also launched its own Chase Pay mobile payment application that uses QR codes and could be used at a number of large US merchants.

Clearly, there has been a lack of cooperation between the major market participants, which has led to fragmentation of the mobile payments market in the United States. The complexity and differing objectives of the participants in the mobile payments ecosystem make it difficult for any one solution to gain sufficient critical mass to provide ongoing growth. Key areas of conflict between participants include how revenue for mobile payments will be divided and who controls the relationship with consumers. It has yet to be seen whether, at least in the near term, mobile payments in the United States will gain sufficient traction or will fizzle out. Banks' and other institutions' investment in mobile payments may end up being a way to defend against other competing initiatives, rather than having a chance to become successful in their own right.

The lack of clear direction in the market has not in any way helped mobile payments move toward large-scale adoption. A 2015 survey of North American consumers found that only 18% of consumers made a mobile payment on a weekly basis and that usage had declined from the previous year at large retailers, grocery stores, restaurants, and convenience stores. Furthermore, mobile payment services such as Apple Pay, which were initially launched in the United States, have also faced challenges expanding into other countries. It is uncertain where mobile payments are headed but lack of a dominant solution, an uncertain business case, and a lack of compelling reasons to use them, are ongoing problems that have yet to be overcome.

Sources: Metz, Cade, "Why Android Pay Will Succeed Where Google Wallet Failed," *Wired,* June 2, 2015, https://www.wired.com/2015/06/android-pay-will-succeed-google-wallet-failed/; Pogue, David, "How Mobile Payments Are Failing—and Credit Cards Are Getting Better," *Scientific American,* February 1, 2015, https://www.scientificamerican.com/article/pogue-how-mobile-payments-are-failing-and-credit-cards-are-getting-better/06.02.15; Heun, David, "Some Bankers See Apple Pay As a Threat," *American Banker,* October 22, 2014, file:///Users/red/Research/Web%20Scrapbook/data/20160319135527/index.html; "Mobile Payment App Backed by Target and Walmart Shuts Down," *Fortune,* June 8, 2016, http://fortune.com/2016/06/08/target-walmart-mobile-payments/; Tabuchi, Hiroko, "Walmart Prepares to Enter Mobile Payments Business," *New York Times,* December 10, 2015, http://www.nytimes.com/2015/12/10/business/walmart-prepares-to-enter-mobile-payments-business.html?partner=rss&emc=rss; www.walmart.com; Siegel, Matt, Jeremy Wagstaff, and Eric Auchard, "Early Days, but Apple Pay Struggles Outside U.S.," *Reuters,* June 2, 2016, http://www.reuters.com/article/us-apple-pay-idUSKCN0YN61U, www.wellsfargo.com, www.chase.com.

Questions

1. What factors could drive consumers to increase their use of mobile payments?
2. What would the business case be for small- and mid-sized financial institutions to enter the mobile payments market? What approaches might they use?
3. Outside of the United States, how might governments intervene to help mobile payment initiatives avoid market fragmentation and consumer adoption problems?
4. How could generational changes affect consumers' adoption of mobile payments?

9.1 CONCEPTS

This section reviews key concepts related to payments and **settlements**. Three main activities occur sequentially when banks process payments:

1. **Payment instruction generation**—specification by the payer of the fund transfer details, such as the amount, payee, payee's account, and any intermediary bank information.

2. **Clearing**—the process whereby, prior to settlement, banks transmit and exchange the payment instruction information to a **clearing house** to be matched, reconciled, and in some cases, netted.

3. **Settlement**—the transfer of cash, or securities, such that the transfer is final from a legal standpoint.

The clearing cycle is the period of time between the date a payment instruction or cheque is submitted for clearing and its settlement date, that is, when the funds are received in the recipient's account. For securities transactions, the **settlement** cycle (also referred to as the settlement period or settlement interval) refers to the period of time between the trade date and the settlement date.

As part of this process, clearing houses commonly aggregate settlement information and calculate counterparties' net exposures. In some cases, clearing houses may also serve as a **central counterparty (CCP)**. In this capacity, they act as an intermediary for interbank settlement, whereby the CCP assumes the risk of default by any individual bank and, thus, eliminates the banks' risk exposure to one another. Clearing and central counterparties are discussed in greater detail in Chapter 14.

9.1.1 Settlement

Banks may participate in many different types of settlement activities, including interbank same-currency settlement, multicurrency foreign exchange (FX) settlement, and securities (for example, stocks and bonds) settlement. This section focuses on settlement in the context of same-country, same-currency interbank settlement. In this case, usually a government- or central bank-related payment system serves as an intermediary that manages the transfer of funds between banks.

In some cases, multiple payment systems may function in the same country, providing different services for large and small value payments. For example, the United Kingdom has five different national payment systems: Bacs Payment Schemes Limited (Bacs), Faster Payments Service (FPS), Cheque & Credit Clearing Company (C&CCC), CHAPS Clearing Company Limited (CHAPS), and LINK. Bacs handles low-value direct debits and credits, such as monthly utility bill giro and salary payments, and has a three-day clearing cycle. FPS is designed to support low-value person-to-person payments, which are initiated over the Internet or telephone banking channels, and standing payment instructions; FPS settles three times per day. The C&CCC system handles clearing and settlement of personal and **cashier's cheques**, with a three-day clearing cycle. The CHAPS payment system is used for high-value business-to-business transactions and supports real-time settlement. Lastly, the LINK system supports automated teller machine (ATM) transactions with a one-day clearing cycle, that is, they settle the following business day. Figure 9-1 shows the average daily transaction volumes and total value of payments handled by several of these systems.

In the United States, the automated clearing house (ACH) handles low-value electronic payments, Fedwire is used for large-value time-critical domestic payments, and the Clearing House Interbank Payments System (CHIPS) is used for international interbank transactions. Similarly, in Singapore, the Singapore Automated Clearing House (SACH) and the Monetary Authority of Singapore Electronic Payment System (MEPS+) facilitate low- and high-value settlements, respectively.

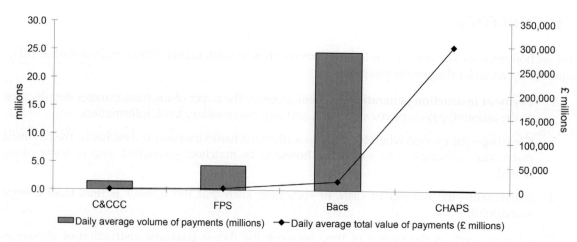

Figure 9-1 Daily average payment statistics for UK payment systems in 2016
Source: **"Annual Summary of Payment Statistics 2016,"** *Faster Payments Scheme Limited.*

The requirements to be a **clearing member** of a national payment system vary by country and system. In some cases, smaller financial institutions and foreign banks may not qualify, or it may not be financially practical for them to be a clearing member. In this case, they will use another financial institution that is a clearing member as their **settlement agent**, which can clear and settle its own transactions as well as transactions for its customers.

The frequency and timing of settlement will vary with the payment system. The settlement may span multiple days, or occur the next day, the same day, or within some specified number of hours or minutes. The **settlement lag**, that is, the delay between the acceptance of the payment instruction and its final settlement, will depend on the type and purpose of settlement, the underlying technology used to implement the payment system, and the capabilities of banks and other financial institutions that utilize the payment system.

9.1.2 Settlement Risk

Settlement risk arises from settlement lag. Settlement lag can be caused by time zone differences, and clearing and confirmation delays. During settlement lag, settlement obligations accumulate, increasing the amount to be settled at the end of the settlement cycle. The risk is that when the time comes to settle, a bank's counterparty may fail to meet its settlement obligations. This is a type of counterparty **credit risk**, as is discussed in Chapter 8. In cases where **gross settlement**, that is, settlement of individual payment instructions, is used and transaction volumes are high, the settlement risks can be significant. Take, for example, the case where over the course of one day, Bank X has a total of US$800 million worth of payments due to settle with Bank Y, and Bank Y has US$900 million worth of payments due to settle with Bank X. At the end of the day, Bank X transfers the money associated with its payments. Now, before Bank Y makes its payments to Bank X, Bank Y becomes insolvent. This means that besides missing out on the US$900 million that Bank X was due to receive, it also has effectively lost the US$800 million that it transferred during the settlement process.

Settlement risk is not just theoretical—it has occurred several times in practice. The first and most famous case involving settlement risk related to FX transactions was when Herstatt Bank collapsed in Germany in 1974. During European business hours, Herstatt Bank was paid in Deutsche marks, but it failed to settle its US dollar obligations because it defaulted prior to US trading hours. As a result, financial institutions in the United States that were due to receive US dollar funds from Herstatt incurred losses when it failed to make the payments. This is why settlement risk is also sometimes referred to as Herstatt risk.

More recently, another German bank, KfW, incurred settlement risk-related losses when Lehman Brothers collapsed in 2008. In this case, on the day that Lehman Brothers became insolvent, KfW made a €300 million payment to Lehman Brothers related to the settlement of an FX swap, but never received the US dollars that Lehman owed it as part of the swap transaction. This case actually involved both settlement risk and **operational risk**. KfW mistakenly allowed the automated fund transfer to occur even though it was already public knowledge that Lehman had collapsed; hence, the settlement risk could have been avoided. Ultimately, several years later, the bank was able to recover about two-thirds of the amount it had sent to Lehman. Nevertheless, two of the bank's senior executives lost their jobs as a result of the mishap.

Banks typically control their settlement risk by instituting limits on their intraday exposures to counterparties (as discussed in Chapter 8). Implementing netting agreements, rather than gross settlement, also helps reduce settlement risk exposure by reducing the amount to be settled between counterparties. In the first example of Banks X and Y, if a netting agreement were in place, Bank X would not have needed to transfer any money—the settlement obligation would have been for Bank Y to pay Bank X a net amount of US$100 million (US$900 million – US$800 million). Netting is explained in more detail in the next subsection.

Using central counterparties or intermediary entities for clearing and settlement can eliminate settlement risk between banks. For example, the Continuous Linked Settlement (CLS) Bank began operations in 2002 to facilitate cross-border FX settlement for banks, and it handles settlement for around 50% of global FX trades. The CLS Bank receives and matches trade settlement information from both counterparties in real time, and then calculates the net amounts due in each currency. The counterparties deliver to the CLS Bank the currencies they owe to other counterparties on a daily basis. The CLS Bank will only release payments to a bank once it matches all of the bank's settlement instructions with its counterparties' instructions and receives the offsetting currency amounts the bank owes to its counterparties. It is important to note that the CLS Bank does not operate as a CCP, that is, it does not take responsibility for any of the counterparties' settlement obligations. Rather, it acts as a trusted intermediary that helps ensure the synchronous transfer of funds between counterparties.

CLS provides a **payment versus payment (PvP)** mechanism that ensures that the settlement of foreign currencies occurs simultaneously. A similar mechanism used in relation to securities settlement is **delivery versus payment (DvP)**. DvP ensures that the cash transfer associated with a securities transaction occurs simultaneously with the delivery of securities. DvP is discussed further in Chapter 14.

9.1.3 Netting

Netting agreements enable banks to offset their obligations to one another by calculating the net settlement positions that result from a series of payments or trades. If settlement flows are unidirectional, netting will have little effect. On the other hand, if settlement flows are bidirectional and of similar amounts in each direction, netting will significantly reduce the amount that is settled. Netting also decreases the number of transactions and accounting entries required for interbank settlement.

As illustrated in Figure 9-2, gross settlement requires bidirectional payments so that the number of payment flows necessary will be twice the number of counterparties. While the diagram shows only banks as the counterparties, in practice, netting agreements can be put in place by banks with customers and other types of financial institutions. As an alternative to gross settlement, counterparties may agree to bilateral netting. In this case, they will calculate the net amount due on a periodic basis, often daily, so that only the counterparty with a net amount due will be required to make payment. Bilateral netting reduces the number of payment flows to one per counterparty pair, but more importantly, as discussed in the previous subsection, it reduces the settlement risk that stems from the inexact timing of bidirectional payments.

Counterparties may also agree to multilateral netting arrangements, where the payment flows between multiple counterparties, not just individual counterparty pairs, are taken into consideration during the netting process. The left side of Figure 9-3 shows the payment cash flows for the previous example when multilateral netting is applied. In this case, Bank A no longer needs to make a payment to Bank C, and instead pays the US$20 million for the settlement with Bank A, thereby reducing the amount Bank C needs to pay to Bank B. However, when counterparties settle directly with one another, multilateral netting has an undesirable side effect of reallocating counterparty credit risk. For example, when gross or bilateral net settlement is used, Bank B has a US$30 million exposure to Bank A, but when multilateral net settlement is used, its exposure to Bank A increases to US$50 million. Hence, this approach may only be suitable when credit risk is not a significant concern, such as between subsidiaries of the same parent corporation. Instead, a CCP may be used to act as an intermediary for the settlement process.

A CCP serves as a trusted intermediary between the counterparties, and acts as a clearing house for settlement. Multilateral netting through a CCP is a common mechanism used by financial institutions for reducing settlement risk. It is used for interbank cash settlements within countries, such as the Bacs system in the United Kingdom and the ACH system in the United States. Netting is also implemented by clearing corporations that provide settlement services for transactions involving securities.

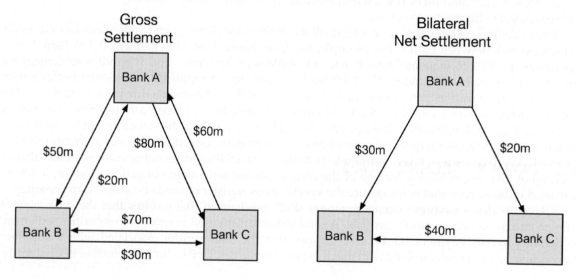

Figure 9-2 A comparison of cash flows for gross settlement and bilateral netting

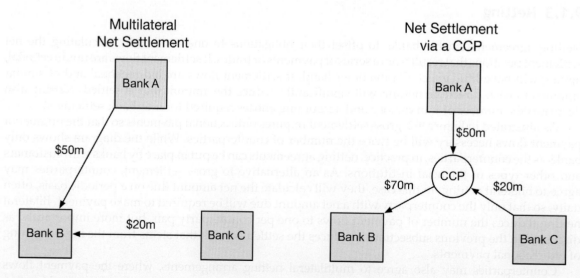

Figure 9-3 Cash flows for multilateral netting with and without a CCP

In some cases, over-the-counter (OTC) derivatives transactions may also be settled through a CCP (discussed more in Chapter 14).

Within large corporations, a centralized treasury function may act as the clearing house and CCP to settle transactions performed between subsidiaries. Subsidiaries in different countries will settle net amounts in their own currencies with the centralized treasury based on a pre-agreed timing cycle. Some banks help their corporate customers implement multilateral netting by providing solutions that help calculate net settlements and facilitating inter-account settlement transfers.

9.1.4 Real-time Gross Settlement

Netting helps reduce payment flows, but it requires that there be a settlement lag, that is, a period during which individual settlements are aggregated and netted. The need for a settlement lag is suboptimal for a few reasons. First, it increases settlement risk; the longer the lag, the greater the risk. Second, it delays the availability of funds for the receiver of the payment. Third, it is typically implemented using end-of-day batch processing, which may become overloaded as transaction volumes grow. Accordingly, periodic intraday settlement is preferable to overnight settlement, and real-time settlement is even more desirable.

Banks use **real-time gross settlement (RTGS)** to settle money or securities transactions as they are processed without any settlement lag. Gross settlement is required in this case because there is no time period during which netting may occur. Typically, national payment systems, such as CHAPS in the United Kingdom and Fedwire in the United States, manage settlement in real time across multiple banks' accounts. RTGS also helps improve banks' liquidity since they have faster access to funds.

9.2 PAYMENT TECHNOLOGIES

This section examines several common technologies used to facilitate payments. First, intranational ACH payment transactions are reviewed. Next, the SWIFT platform, which is used to send payment messages internationally, is discussed. Finally, the technology considerations related to card payments are examined. With the exception of SWIFT, these payment technologies will be reviewed primarily in the context of the payment environment in the United States. Readers should keep in mind that the information provided is a summarization and that many details have been excluded or glossed over for brevity.

9.2.1 Automated Clearing House Transactions

Bank-to-bank Automated Clearing House (ACH) transactions began in the United States in the 1970s, providing a mechanism for electronic money transfer that supported both debits and credits, from and to different types of bank accounts. ACH payments are governed by the National Automated Clearing House Association (NACHA), which sets and enforce rules for ACH payments. Besides falling under the NACHA rules, ACH payment transactions are also covered by federal regulations and laws governing commercial transactions (discussed more in Chapter 19). Keep in mind that the ACH payment network is used for clearing transactions; no funds are transferred through it. Banks settle with one another via the Federal Reserve Bank.

Several participants are or may be involved in ACH transactions:

- **Originator**—an individual or company that initiates the debit or credit of funds to a receiver's account;

- **Originating Depository Financial Institution (ODFI)**—a bank or other financial institution that receives payment instructions from an originator and sends them to an ACH operator;

- **ACH Operator**—a central clearing facility that sets the settlement date, sorts, and routes ACH entries to the corresponding receiving depository financial institutions;

- **Receiving Depository Financial Institution (RDFI)**—a bank or other financial institution with which the receiver of an ACH payment maintains an account; and

- **Receiver**— an individual or company that is the counterparty to the originator.

One example of an ACH payment is where a company, the originator, pays its employees directly to their bank account via direct deposit. First, the company will need to put in place an agreement with the employees to directly credit paycheques to their bank accounts and obtain their account details. When payroll is being processed, the company will prepare an ACH file with ACH entries that correspond to the payment details for each employee bank account to be credited. The company would then send the file to its bank, the ODFI. The bank would then send the company's payment instructions, along with those of other customers, to an ACH operator, either the Federal Reserve (FedACH) or the Electronic Payments Network (EPN). Based on NACHA rules, the operator would set the settlement date and then aggregate the originator's payroll ACH entries along with other ACH entries in a file that would be provided to the employees' banks, the RDFIs. The employees' banks would then retrieve these files, process them, and credit the accounts of the employees, the receivers, as per NACHA rules.

Another example is where a public utility company receives authorization from one of its customers to debit his chequing account for the monthly bill amount. The utility company, the originator, would send a debit ACH entry to its bank, the ODFI, who would then forward the entry to the ACH operator. The operator would set the settlement date and route the entry to the customer's bank, the RDFI, who would then debit the checking account of the customer, the receiver. Note from this example that it is not the direction that money flows that determines who the originator is; rather it is who generates the payment instruction and initiates the transaction with the ODFI.

The ODFI is the party that is financially responsible for instructions sent through the ACH payment network. Accordingly, it must have exposure limits for each originator and ensure that the transactions it sends on behalf of originators have the appropriate authorizations, i.e., for debit transactions, the originator has authorization from the receiver to withdraw funds. Likewise, the ODFI must ensure that ACH entries are accurate and submitted in a timely manner.

ODFIs are obligated to serve as RDFIs for their customers in cases where their customers end up being receivers of ACH transactions. To illustrate this point, consider from the first example, the situation where the company is receiving invoice payments from other companies via ACH. In this case its bank will serve as an RDFI. An RDFI must accept all types of ACH entries and ensure timely and accurately posting of funds to receivers' accounts on the settlement date specified in the ACH entries. According to NACHA rules, ACH entries are considered to be received by an RDFI on the day it was made available by the ACH operator. Furthermore, in the case where both the originator and the receiver are customers of the same financial institution, that institution can make the transfer directly in its systems without sending the ACH entries to an ACH operator.

Currently, the US ACH network is a store and forward payment system. ACH files created by the originator—or a third-party acting on its behalf, such as an external accountant or payroll processor—are received by the ODFI and then forwarded to the ACH operator. The operator verifies that the formatting is correct and sets the *settlement date* value in the ACH entry based on the date of submission and time of receipt in relation to daily cutoff times, according to NACHA rules. The ACH entries are extracted from the files submitted by the ODFIs, sorted, and grouped according to the destination RDFI. Then, four times a day, the operator generates ACH files and makes them available for download by the RDFI.

Within the ACH entry record, a number of fields make up the payment instruction, including information such as the amount of the payment, the RDFI's transit routing number and receivers' account number. Additionally, the originator uses the *effective date* value in the ACH entry record to specify the date that it would like the settlement to occur. In some cases, the settlement of credit entries can be specified up to a few days after the submission date. Besides the effective date, the originator will specify a *standard entry class (SEC)* code to identify the type of payment—e.g., whether the entry is for a corporate credit or debit, and whether the transaction is being performed as a merchant POS or card-not-present transaction. The *trace number* is a 15-digit identifier used to identify each ACH entry, with the first eight digits identifying the ODFI and the remaining seven digits specified by the originator. The *transaction code* is a two-digit number that specifies the type of account—e.g., chequing, savings, general ledger, or loan—the payment is destined for and whether the entry is a credit or a debit. An *addenda record* may also be included with the ACH entry to provide additional payment information to the receiver, such as the invoice number with which the payment is associated.

Until recently, the US ACH payment system has been a next-day payment system. That is to say, the earliest settlement would occur on the next business day after the payment instructions have been received by the ACH operator. In September 2016, as part of a three-phase plan, NACHA changed it rules to enable same-day processing and settlement. This revision still maintains the batch-oriented, store-and-forward mechanism used for next-day settlement. However, it provides two new clearing windows, with deadlines at 10:30am ET and 2:45pm ET that settle by 1:00 pm ET and 5:00 pm ET, respectively, on the same day. Furthermore, as of 2017 a task force put together by the Federal Reserve was evaluating proposals for supporting immediate payment transactions between US-based banks, which is likely to be implemented in the coming years. Solution considerations related to immediate payments will be discussed in Section 9.9.

9.2.2 International Payment Messaging

The SWIFT* network was launched in 1977 by a cooperative of over 200 banks from 15 countries, as a replacement for the Telex messaging platform, to communicate payment information across international borders. The SWIFT messaging platform routes messages between financial institutions based on a standard set of message types and identifiers for participating parties. SWIFT was designed to enable fully automated and secure communications between computer systems. As of 2016, the SWIFT platform processed, on average, over 25 million messages per day.

SWIFT has various message types defined to support different transactional activities. They are categorized by numbers grouped by hundreds. Table 9-1 shows the categories of messages associated with each hundred range of messages. Within each hundred series, not all of the sequences are used; rather, only a few dozen messages may be defined. An example of a SWIFT message is the MT 103 message, Single Customer Credit Transfer, which is commonly used to effect cross-border company-to-company payments. The payment instructions included within the message would include information such as the receiving company's name, bank and account number, payment amount, payment currency, and notes about the purpose of the payment (e.g., the associated invoice number). Payment instruction details are discussed in more depth in Section 9.8 in the context of order validation. Likewise, a detailed example of the structure and format of a SWIFT message is provided in Chapter 11.

Financial institutions that send and receive funds on behalf of customers are uniquely identified in SWIFT messages using an eight- or 11-character Business Identifier Code[†] (BIC). SWIFT maintains the directory of BICs. BICs are an example of reference data that banks must store and maintain to support straight-through processing. The formation of new financial institutions or mergers between institutions can lead to changes in the BIC directory. Because most banks will only synchronize their

---

* SWIFT is an acronym for the Society of Worldwide Interbank Financial Telecommunication. It was formed in 1973 and has its headquarters in Belgium.

† BICs are defined by the ISO 9362 standard and may be used to identify nonfinancial institutions.

Table 9-1 Major SWIFT message series categories

Series	Categories
MT 100	Customer Payments and Checks
MT 200	Financial Institution Transfers
MT 300	Treasury Markets: Foreign Exchange and Derivatives
MT 400	Collections and Cash Letters
MT 500	Securities Markets
MT600	Treasury Markets: Precious Metals and Syndications
MT 700	Documentary Credits and Guarantees
MT 800	Traveler's Cheques
MT 900	Cash Management and Customer Status

list of BICs with SWIFT's on a periodic basis, they may occasionally get payment instructions to a recipient that is not listed in their reference data, triggering an exception process that quite probably would require checking the BIC code using SWIFT's website through a manual procedure.

It is important to keep in mind that SWIFT is a messaging platform, not a clearing or settlement system. If the sending and receiving financial institutions involved in the payment transaction cannot settle the currency directly, i.e., they are not clearing members of the national payment system associated with the payment currency, they will need to route the transaction through one or more **correspondent banks** that are able to settle the specified currency.

Banks will send and receive SWIFT messages using gateways that are usually modules of core banking payment systems or standalone components that are integrated with the core-banking platform. SWIFT must certify gateway components before they can connect to the SWIFT network. The security of the SWIFT network and the gateways that connect to it are paramount since falsified payment instructions could lead to fraud-related losses. As a case in point, cybersecurity breaches related to SWIFT connectivity led to the theft of funds at several financial institutions (discussed in more detail in Chapter 17).

9.2.3 Payment Cards

Payment card transactions represent a major portion of consumer payments in many countries. Figure 9-4 shows the use of payment cards, measured by overall transaction value, across several developed markets, as of 2014 [1]. There is wide variance in level and type of card used by country. Note that when card use is measured by transaction volume, the overall percentages of use are lower, reflecting the fact that cash transactions are still favored for low-value consumer payments. Card payments, especially credit cards, tend to be used for higher value transactions. For instance, in Australia the average transaction amount for cash transactions is around (US)$15, whereas the average for debit-card transactions is close to $43, and for credit card transactions it is about $60. The proportion of these averages is representative for many other countries as well.

The card payment ecosystem is complex both with regards to the number of participants involved and the broad mix of technologies that are used. This subsection provides an overview of payment card fundamentals and the technologies that underlie card payments.

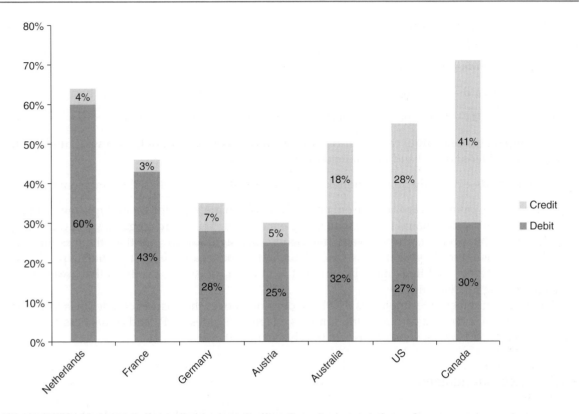

Figure 9-4 Payment card share of consumer transactions, by transaction value

9.2.3.1 Overview

There are several participants in the card-processing ecosystem, including the card associations, card issuers, transaction acquirers, merchants, and payment processors. Card associations are organizations, such as MasterCard and Visa, which provide the underlying payment network infrastructure and sets the rules governing card transactions. Card issuers are banks, other financial institutions, or merchants that typically offer branded cards to their customers, also referred to as cardholders. Card transaction acquirers are banks or other institutions that work with merchants to process card transactions on the merchants' behalf. Small- and medium-sized banks may choose to outsource certain issuer and acquirer functions to payment processors, who can achieve better economies of scale. Typical issuer functions that are outsourced to payment processors include card plastic manufacturing and distribution, hosting and maintenance of the core banking system that supports card transactions, and transaction fraud monitoring and response.

To help illustrate how the participants work together to complete a card transaction, consider the following example. A customer at a coffee shop chooses to pay with a credit card. The coffee shop owner will have a POS terminal that reads the account information from the credit card and is linked to the transaction acquirer, in this example a bank. The acquirer sends a transaction authorization request to the issuer via the card association network to determine if funds are available for the transaction. The issuer responds with a transaction approval or decline that is routed back over the card association network to the transaction acquirer and ultimately to the POS terminal. Assuming the authorization request was approved, posting of the actual transaction would follow the same flow. If the issuing bank used a payment processor to host its core banking system for credit cards, the authorization and transaction requests would be routed from the card association to the payment processor, which would provide the transaction responses on the issuing bank's behalf.

There are several types of cards that are used for payments; simplified descriptions of common payment card types are:

- **Credit cards**—draw upon a revolving credit facility;

- **Charge cards**—draw upon a credit facility that must be settled on a monthly basis;

- **Debit cards**—draw upon funds held in a bank demand deposit accounts;

- **Prepaid (stored value) cards**—draw upon funds held in an account loaded with funds by the cardholder and held and maintained by the card issuer; and

- **Gift cards**—typically non-reloadable prepaid cards that are purchased via merchants.

Furthermore, payment cards can be either *open loop*, which are accepted by multiple merchants, or *closed loop*, which are designated for use with a single merchant. The **interchange fees** that card issuers receive from debit, prepaid, and gift card transactions are significantly less than the fees for credit and charge cards. Accordingly, in many cases debit and prepaid cards are not profitable products in themselves for banks, and thus, must be bundled with other, profitable products that create a cost-effective offering in their entirety.

There are a number of technologies that have developed over the past several decades to support card transactions, including card account numbers, magnetic stripes, EMV and contactless cards, and tokenization. The following subsections will briefly examine these.

9.2.3.2 Account number

At the heart of card transactions is the account number, which identifies the source of the funds for payment. As shown in Figure 9-5, 16-digit card account numbers are composed of three parts: the bank identification number (BIN), the account identifier, and a checksum.

The BIN identifies the issuer and is used by card association networks to route authorization and transaction requests. A single financial institution may have multiple BINs assigned to it by a card association. The first few digits in the BIN to some extent identify the industry or card association that the account is associated with. For example, account numbers beginning with the number four are Visa branded cards and those starting with numbers between 51 and 55 are MasterCard branded cards. The account number is unique and is defined by the card issuer. The checksum digit at the end is a value that is dependent on the other digits in the account number and is specified so that the entire card number, including the checksum, will pass validation when it is input into the modulus 10 formula calculation, which is also referred to as the Luhn algorithm. This validation is useful for detecting if an account number has been incorrectly communicated or if one or more of the digits have been transposed. This check is usually performed prior to submitting a transaction for processing, avoiding an error condition occurring further downstream when the transaction is being processed by the card association network or by the issuer.

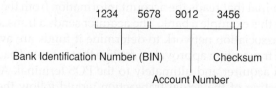

Figure 9-5 The structure of 16-digit payment card account numbers

9.2.3.3 Magnetic stripe

The magnetic stripe, also referred to as the magstripe, was added to credit cards in the 1980s, enabling paper-based transaction records to be replaced by electronic ones. This change greatly increased the speed and efficiency of transaction authorization and processing. The account holder name, account number, expiration date, and a card verification value (CVV) are stored in the magstripe using the ISO/IEC 7813 standard. Magstripe technology has several advantages: it is inexpensive to produce, it enables transactions to be processed quickly, and it is able to be read ubiquitously by merchant POS terminals around the world.

Unfortunately, the fact that magstripe data is easily readable also turned out to be a major security weakness for the technology. A common tactic for criminals is to attach "skimming" devices to ATMs and merchants' POS terminals, which are disguised to appear to users as part of the ATM or POS device. Skimming devices capture the credit card information when the card is swiped and criminals use that information to create counterfeit cards or perform card-not-present purchases over the phone or Internet. Magstripe technology made it relatively easy and low cost for fraudsters to skim legitimate cards and then produce counterfeit cards. This problem has been a bane of the industry for many years and led to the switch to EMV technology.

9.2.3.4 EMV

EMV is a technical standard based on ISO/IEC 7816 and is managed by EMVco.* Unlike magstripe technology, which simply stores the account information electronically on the card, EMV technology uses a microprocessor, i.e., a computer chip, on the card to run software applications and communicate with merchants' POS terminals. While not foolproof, this mechanism provides a number of security benefits for card payments. First, unlike magstripe technology, the information in the EMV chip cannot be easily accessed physically or read by commercially available card readers. Second, EMV chips and EMV-enabled POS terminals prevent the use of counterfeit cards by using public-key encryption techniques to verify the card's authenticity. Third, to help limit losses related to lost and stolen cards, EMV cards support the ability to store the card PIN information in the chip so that **two-factor authentication** can be used to authenticate the transaction, without requiring an online connection to the issuer to perform PIN verification.

Besides using encryption, EMV supports a number of sophisticated capabilities. For example, an EMV chip may host more than one payment application, and POS terminals can access multiple payment software applications on the card, if they are available. For example, a single EMV chip card could host applications that provide access to both credit and debit accounts. Accordingly, the EMV chip on the card and the EMV-enabled POS terminal may need to negotiate which application should be used to perform a transaction, based on a set of predefined rules or possibly requiring the cardholder to make the selection.

EMV supports two different authentication modes: offline and online. Offline authentication supports cases where the POS terminal does not have an active connection to the card association network. Alternatively, online authentication is used when connectivity is available. Cardholders can verify EMV transactions either by entering a PIN into the POS terminal or with a signature. The EMV chip card will specify which methods are supported and the conditions in which they may be used. While PIN-based transactions are more secure, it is not uncommon for EMV-based credit card transactions to be verified using signature instead of a PIN. Often, when cardholders are migrated from magstripe to EMV cards, the issuers may choose not to require consumers to change their

---

* EMV is an abbreviation that stands for Europay, Mastercard, and Visa, which are the companies that were the pioneers for the technology. Today, other card associations also support the standard.

behavior and to have to select, remember, and use a PIN when making purchases. Hence, signature verification continues to be used with EMV, even though it is less secure.

EMV payment cards continue to have magstripes for backward compatibility with POS terminals that do not support EMV. Conversely, EMV POS terminals support magnetic stripe transactions to process transactions for payment cards that are not EMV-enabled. However, if both the POS terminal and payment cards support EMV, transactions will have to be processed using the EMV mechanism rather than via the magstripe.

While some countries, mostly in Europe, were quick to adopt EMV technology, others in Asia and North America, the United States in particular, have been laggards in switching from magstripe to EMV technology. A key challenge with migration is getting support from a sufficient number of participants in the ecosystem to give the migration sufficient momentum, i.e., getting the network effect working. Significant cost and effort are required to support the use of EMV payment cards. Issuers must reissue existing magstripe cards, replacing these with more expensive chip-based cards. Merchants must upgrade their terminals to support EMV cards. Core card processing systems must be upgraded to support EMV configuration parameters. Consumers must be educated on how to use EMV cards. Moreover, EMV transactions are slower to process than magstripe transaction at the point of sale, causing longer waiting time for customers. Thus, if few banks are issuing EMV payment cards, there is little reason for merchants to invest in EMV-enabled terminals, and vice versa.

In the United States, these barriers were finally overcome by the card associations setting a date for when fraud liability would shift to the party, the merchant or the issuer, who did not have EMV capabilities in place. Despite this incentive, several months after the date of the liability shift, many issuers had not upgraded significant portions of their cardholders to EMV and a large proportion of merchants had yet to upgrade their POS terminals to support EMV. In some cases the migration was hindered by limited delays in delivery of certification of merchants' EMV POS terminals. Nonetheless, this move was enough to get a sufficient number of participants to make the change and get the conversion moving forward.

Markets that have switched to EMV cards have experienced significantly lower levels of card-present transaction fraud at the point of sale. However, levels of card-not-present fraud have increased. When payments are made by phone or over the Internet, EMV technology provides no advantage. Likewise, EMV technology does not prevent card account information from being obtained as a result of security breaches where cybercriminals are able to access merchants' IT systems and download cardholder account information. Tokenization has been developed as a way to help address this concern.

9.2.3.5 Tokenization

While fraud caused by card skimming had an impact on the card payment industry, its impact was limited. Only a relatively small number of customers will use any given POS terminal that has been compromised. The greater concern has been breaches by hackers of merchants' databases that contain card information and the IT systems that manage the POS terminals. These types of cyberattacks can, in the worst case, provide fraudsters with card account information for all of the merchants' customers, both past and present. As a case in point, between November 27 and December 15, 2013, cyberthieves stole card payment information on 40 million customer accounts from a major retailer based in the United States [2]. It is estimated that the cost, not including losses due to fraud, for banks to reissue cards to customers as a result of this breach was over $200 million. While this was one of the largest card data breaches, keep in mind that it is only a fraction of the total reissuance cost due to breaches, since it is not uncommon for dozens of them to occur annually.

Tokenization was designed to help minimize the impact of merchant breaches and also to make it easier and less costly for merchants to comply with the Payment Card Industry Data Security Standard (PCI DSS). It is also designed to help protect card account information for card-not-present transactions, where EMV technology cannot be used. The principal behind tokenization is that prior to performing an online or a mobile transaction, the POS software will send the cardholder account information to a token vault, which in return, provides a proxy account identifier, also known as a token, that can be used in place of the card account information when transacting. The token vault keeps a record as to which tokens are associated with which customer account information. The POS software uses the token, instead of the real account information, to process the transaction. The merchant presents the token information to the acquirer and the acquirer presents it to the payment network. The payment network provides the token to the payment vault and retrieves the customer account information, which is then provided to the issuer so that it can fulfill the transaction.

The benefit of this approach is that the merchant only has access to tokens, which resemble and can be stored in place of the card account number, rather than the actual account information. Hence, if a data breach were to occur, cybercriminals would steal the token information, rather than the account information. If a token were to be compromised, the token vault could quickly invalidate it and create a new token that would be used for future transactions. In this case, the underlying card account information would still be secure, eliminating the need for the card to be reissued. Furthermore, compared with account numbers, tokens have rich functionality in that they can be configured to be valid for only a certain time period, for fixed dollar amounts, or be linked to a specific merchant.

It is worth noting that as of 2017, tokenization is still relatively new and its level of adoption within the industry is unclear. Factors that are likely to affect its use will include the fees charged by token vaults as well as security concerns about providing cardholder account information to a third party, i.e., the token vault provider, for safekeeping.

9.2.3.6 Contactless payments

While contactless payments have been prevalent for many years in mass transit—e.g., the Oyster card in London, the Octopus card in Hong Kong, and the EZLink card in Singapore—contactless credit and debit card payments have had less exposure and success. Dual interface chip cards contain both an EMV chip that, as is normally the case, requires physical contact with the POS terminal to be read, as well as an interface that has a radio frequency antenna that uses near field communication (NFC) protocols. These proximity cards use electromagnetic induction to draw electrical power from the POS device and can also communicate with it at distances of up to several centimeters. ISO/IEC 14443 is the standard used for contactless payment cards.

To refer to this technology as "contactless," is somewhat of a misnomer since typically the procedure for using them was for the cardholder to tap them against an NFC-enabled POS terminal, as opposed to having them hover or wave the card close to the terminal. Nonetheless, this interaction is faster than having to dip an EMV card into a POS terminal and wait for the transaction to be authorized. A challenge for broad adoption of this technology was that, at least historically, relatively few merchants have POS terminals that support NFC communications. Without a large number of cardholders that had contactless cards, merchants had little incentive to invest in upgrading their POS terminals to support contactless transactions. Conversely, with few merchants supporting contactless payments, issuers and cardholders were not motivated to provide or use contactless cards.

Contactless cards have not had a major impact on the debit and credit card market, but they did help pave the way for contactless payments via smartphones. Major smartphone vendors used the same NFC communication technology that was used by contactless cards for communication to POS terminals. However, the two main smartphone operating system vendors chose to tackle the storage of account credentials differently. Apple iOS chose to implement the card emulation approach of embedding a *secure element*, much like an EMV chip on a contactless card, in its phones to store account information and communicate with the POS terminal. Alternatively, Google Android focused its efforts on providing host card emulation (HCE), where applications on the mobile device are able to emulate the functions of an EMV chip and communicate with the POS terminal using NFC.

With HCE, account credentials are typically stored in the cloud and accessed by the mobile application over the Internet. As discussed in Case Study 9-1, card-based mobile payments have had limited success so far and will likely continue to evolve in the coming years.

9.2.3.7 Display cards

Payment cards have also seen technological changes that enable them to incorporate user interfaces into the physical card devices. In some cases, small liquid crystal display readouts have been added, often with one or more touch-sensitive buttons that the cardholder can push to interact with the card. Display cards have several potential applications. One application is to have the display card serve as a second factor authentication device. By having the cardholder enter a card-specific PIN code, the microprocessor can generate one-time passwords that can be used to verify online banking and other transactions. Another application is to access information, such as a dynamic CVV number or the current account balance, which is stored on the card. There have also been some fairly novel prototype applications such as storing information for multiple debit and credit accounts on the card and enabling the user to select which one to use at the time of purchase by pressing buttons on the card. In this case, the card then displays the associated account number, and uses those credentials to complete transactions via magstripe or EMV.

To date, there has been limited adoption of display cards by banks, most likely because of the high cost, compared with basic plastic cards. However, the economics are more practical in markets such as Singapore, where two-factor authentication has been mandated as a regulatory requirement. From a convenience standpoint, having the authentication token integrated with a payment card eliminates the need for customers to keep track of another bank-issued device.

9.3 CORPORATE BANKING CONTEXT

Payments are an integral part of corporate transactions—they control the flow of funds out of companies' accounts and facilitate the inward flow of goods and services that is necessary for ongoing business operations. Banks provide several facilities for payments, including paper cheques, interbank fund transfers, domestic electronic payments, and **telegraphic transfers (TTs)**. Payments are usually made directly to and from customers' accounts. Cashier's cheque and demand draft facilities, however, are payments that are secured by a bank's account rather than a customer's account. Issuance of cashier's cheques is an example of a value-added service that banks provide on a fee basis.

Domestic interbank fund transfers and electronic bill payments are normally implemented through a national payment system, such as the MEPS+ in Singapore and ACH in the United States, managed by the relevant country's central bank. Alternatively, payments that cross international borders are typically accomplished via TTs, also referred to as wire transfers, using the SWIFT network.

Banks also offer other payment-related services, such as standing instruction and bulk-payment facilities. Standing instructions allow customers to make single or recurring payments on future dates. Bulk payments enable customers to issue multiple payments, by electronic payments or by cashier's orders or cheques, with a single payment instruction. For example, bulk payment services are commonly used for processing companies' payrolls. Corporate customers upload a file containing salary payment details for its employees, and the bank then issues cheques to the employees or credits their bank accounts electronically.

Banks' merchant-payment services enable businesses to accept credit and debit card payments. Merchant services typically include the provision of card readers that perform payment authorization checks and capture card-based transactions. These devices connect to the bank via phone or Internet connections. The bank then performs the clearing and settlement of the card transactions in conjunction with the card providers, after which the corporate customer will receive the funds directly in its bank account.

Additionally, banks can provide services that help prevent fraud such as positive pay services. In many countries, cheques are still very much a means of payment for companies to their employees or to other companies. One of the weaknesses of paper cheques is that they can be lost, stolen, modified, or duplicated. Hence, cheque fraud is a serious concern for both businesses and financial institutions. Accordingly, cheques have a number of built-in safeguards to help prevent fraud. One example is the use of magnetic ink for printing of the account and routing information at the bottom of cheques, which is read electronically by banks. The sale of this ink is restricted to financial institutions. Another example is the background pattern on cheques that is used to make alterations more easily detected. Yet, such mechanisms are not foolproof.

In contrast to cheque fraud prevention measures that involve the physical cheque, positive pay is a service-based facility offered primarily by banks in the United States. Bank customers regularly provide the bank with reports of cheques that they have issued. These reports are usually transferred electronically to the bank as files and include details of the cheque numbers, cheque amounts, dates issued, and beneficiaries. The bank then reconciles this list with cheques presented for settlement and flags any discrepancies. This process helps prevent copied, altered, or counterfeited cheques from being cashed. This value-added service helps corporate customers avoid fraud losses while providing fee-based revenue for banks.

9.4 RETAIL BANKING CONTEXT

Payment services in the retail banking context are quite similar to that for corporate banking, but are generally simpler. One-time or recurring transfers to the bank accounts of other parties via ACH or GIRO are fairly standard services that banks offer. Online bill payment is also a common retail payment service provided by banks. Additionally, many banks also support cross-border wire transfers. This section examines some of the retail payment trends and innovations that have gained ground in recent years. Specifically, it focuses on how mobile peer-to-peer payments have developed in different markets.

In Europe, Barclays Bank launched PingIt, the first account-to-account mobile money transfer service offered by a bank in Europe. The PingIt smartphone application was free to download, and enabled Barclays' customers to transfer funds, up to £300, to other mobile phone customers that have registered their UK-based current account and mobile phone number with Barclays. Funds could be transferred between accounts in as little as 30 seconds. The service was initially provided to retail customers, and later extended to business customers, that is, merchants, who could both send and receive payments using PingIt. Other UK banks' customers could only receive payments via PingIt after having registered with Barclays.

In the United States, Fintech firms led the charge into mobile peer-to-peer payments. Venmo, now owned by PayPal, has been one of the most successful peer-to-peer payment services, processing more than $17 billion worth of payments in 2016 [3]. It combines social networking with payments and has been popular with Millennials. Users can make payments to friends through a mobile application and include notes about the payment that can also be viewed by a broader audience that uses Venmo. Major US banks have countered Fintech's foray into peer-to-peer payments by forming a joint venture called clearXchange, which was later rebranded as Zelle. It enables their customers, after registering, to make person-to-person payments to one another by specifying a mobile phone number as the payment destination identifier, rather than a bank account number. Generally, peer-to-peer payment services have been a loss leader. They are provided for free with the aim of acquiring customers and engaging them to hopefully use other revenue generating services as well. Banks have also invested in peer-to-peer payment platforms to prevent any one solution, such as Venmo, from gaining overall dominance.

In China, the largest mobile payment market, the popular social media service WeChat has been gaining ground in peer-to-peer and mobile payments. It is thought to have one of the largest payment systems in the world, with over 750 million active users and annual transactions totaling over $500 billion. Rather cleverly, it promoted a "red packet" service that replaced the traditional small red envelopes with money inside that are given out during Chinese New Year with digital payments instead. Furthermore, WeChat users are able to purchase retail goods and services with the WeChat Pay service.

Looking beyond peer-to-peer payments, following a model similar to M-PESA discussed in Case Study 9-2, banks in the United Kingdom and the United States offer services whereby customers can use the banks' mobile application to generate a code that can be entered into their ATMs to withdraw cash. Likewise, a major ATM vendor has also begun supporting withdrawals that use a mobile phone rather than an ATM card. In this case, the ATM screen displays a barcode that is scanned by the mobile phone's camera. A mobile banking application installed on the phone then uses the barcode to identify the ATM's location and validate the transaction.

Other types of innovations in the mobile payment space have emerged. For example, mobile phone hardware add-ons that can read the magnetic strip of a credit card and perform merchant transactions using an application on the phone have become popular in some market segments. These devices are well suited to individuals or small businesses that want to take credit card payments while on the go or do not want to invest in or maintain traditional POS systems.

9.5 BUSINESS OPPORTUNITIES

An attractive feature of offering payment services is that it generates fee-based revenue. Yet, unlike lending, these services do not have a material impact on the bank's balance sheet and, hence, do not require the bank to raise additional regulatory-mandated capital. Payment services also produce little, if any, credit, market, and interest-rate risk.

Fee structures offered to customers can vary depending on customers' needs, banks' marketing objectives, customers' cost sensitivities, and the ways banks optimize their services. Table 9-2 shows the charges commonly associated with TT service. Some or all of these charges may apply, depending on the particular bank and customer.

Besides the revenue that payment fees generate, the support that payment capabilities provide for corporate cash management services (discussed in Chapter 7) can also produce indirect benefits for banks. For instance, the value that centralized cash management produces for corporate customers incentivizes them to consolidate their business with just a handful of

Table 9-2 Common types of TT fees

Fee Type	Fee Structure
Handling fee	1) Percentage of payment amount, with minimum and maximum fee limits (e.g., 0.1% of payment amount, with a minimum of US$10 and a maximum of US$50) 2) Increased fees or limits for nonaccount holders
Wire transfer charge	Fixed amount (e.g., US$25)
Foreign currency handling charges	1) Percentage of payment amount, with minimum and maximum fee limits (e.g., 0.1% of payment amount, with a minimum of US$10 and a maximum of US$50) 2) Cash-handling fees as a percentage of the payment amount depending on currency (e.g., 1% for USD, 1.5% for TWD)
Standing instruction sign-up fee	Fixed amount (e.g., US$10)
Standing instruction amendment fee	Fixed amount (e.g., US$5)

banks. Hence, the banks that provide these services will see increased transaction volumes, which will in turn lead to increased revenue. Additionally, providing payment services can also supply banks with detailed information about customers' cash flows. Insights into a company's accounts receivable can potentially improve the quality of credit-related decisions [4].

Banks have a major opportunity to help customers migrate from manually intensive payment methods, such as cash notes and cheques, to automated payment methods, such as Internet banking, that support **straight-through processing (STP)**. Similarly, getting customers to enter payment transaction details electronically, rather than using paper-based forms, can greatly reduce banks' operational costs, transaction processing times, and error rates associated with manual processing. Typically, banks will incentivize customers to use more efficient payment methods by discounting the fees charged on those methods and over time, slowly increasing the fees charged for less efficient payment methods.

Moreover, emerging markets often have unique characteristics that provide opportunities for innovation. Often financial, technical, or physical infrastructures may be lacking, limiting the applicability of payment solutions that have been designed for developed markets. Likewise, the economics of providing services may be substantially different in poorer countries. Case Study 9-2 highlights how these types of constraints can be overcome.

Case Study 9-2

Mobile Payments in Developing Markets

Mobile phones have a much greater penetration rate than Internet connections in many countries and, thus, have great potential for delivering electronic banking services. The fact that people keep their mobile phones with them wherever they go make these devices ideal for facilitating both person-to-person and person-to-merchant payments. However, the migration to mobile phone-based payments has been slow worldwide, partially due to adverse network effects—if not enough people are using the payment platform, it is not worthwhile to join. One of the most successful mobile payment initiatives is M-PESA in Kenya.

Launched in 2007, M-PESA was introduced by Safaricom, a mobile telecommunications operator in Kenya. M-PESA enables customers to access stored value and make mobile payments from their mobile phones. To exchange electronic value for cash or vice versa, customers can go to any one of the 28,000 retail stores that act as Safaricom agents. Customers can also transfer funds to pay merchants or individuals who are not Safaricom customers. Registering for an M-PESA account and making deposits are free, but customers pay US$0.30–0.40 for payments and withdrawals. Customers receive no interest on their deposits. The retail stores that serve as Safaricom's agents are paid a fee by Safaricom for providing liquidity, that is, exchanging electronic value for cash. Customers can also withdraw money from ATMs provided by banks that are partners with M-PESA. No bankcard is required for ATM transactions; instead, the customer receives a one-time authorization code on their mobile phone that is entered into the ATM to withdraw cash.

To begin using M-PESA, customers must register at an M-PESA retail outlet where they are then assigned an electronic money account. Customers can then access their M-PESA account, which is tied to their mobile phone number through an application that is resident in their mobile phone SIM cards. The M-PESA application can be quickly launched from the mobile phone's main menu. This application enables M-PESA customers to transfer money to anyone with a GSM-based mobile phone in Kenya by entering basic information, such as the mobile phone number of the recipient, the amount, and a personal identification number. After the user confirms the transaction, which is limited to a maximum of around US$800, its details are sent using a single encrypted short message service (SMS) text message to an M-PESA server. The M-PESA server then

(Continued)

(Continued)

immediately sends an SMS message with the details of the transaction to the customer. This message also serves as an electronic receipt and helps confirm that the money was sent to the correct recipient. M-PESA then debits the customer's account and sends the recipient an authorization code via SMS, which can be used to obtain cash at any of the retail stores that act as M-PESA agents.

In less than five years since it was introduced, M-PESA has been adopted by 68% of Kenya's adult population. It processes over US$415 million worth of fund transfers per month, although the average size of a payment transaction is about US$33. Approximately 20% of the electric utility bills in Kenya are paid using M-PESA. While it is designed to serve as a payment facility, M-PESA also provides a means for customers to maintain savings, particularly for the unbanked living in rural areas.

New payment networks, such as M-PESA, face a number of challenges during their startup phase. For one, sufficient scale must be achieved quickly so that the benefits of positive network effects can be gained. That is to say, if people are to be attracted to join a particular payment network, enough users must already be on it. M-PESA addressed this concern by initially targeting Safaricom's existing mobile phone customers, co-opting retail shops that already sold Safaricom airtime, and allowing fund transfers to mobile phone users who are not Safaricom customers. Likewise, Safaricom had already established a position in the market that enabled it to make large upfront investments to get the service going, and its existing relationships with customers helped it overcome trust concerns. Regulatory hurdles are also often a limiting factor for new service growth. In this regard, M-PESA was fortunate that the Central Bank of Kenya allowed it to operate as a payment system that was not subject to banking regulations. However, to gain this provision, M-PESA had to deposit customer funds in a regulated bank and forego "float" interest earned on those funds. Accordingly, M-PESA's revenue is derived from transaction fees, averaging around US$0.30 per transaction.

Probably, the greatest factor in M-PESA's success was that from the beginning, it was able to address an important customer need—domestic payments. M-PESA initially targeted workers in urban areas who needed to send money back home to their families living in rural areas, which is a large market segment in Kenya. By using M-PESA to transfer money, users could avoid the high costs and risks associated with delivering money to remote locations. This benefit provided consumers with a compelling reason to use M-PESA. In many cases, customers who used M-PESA to send money already had traditional bank accounts, but those accounts were not designed to support remittances to rural areas. M-PESA would later expand its services to address the needs of a much larger market: the unbanked poor and rural people in Kenya. Also, as the microcredit market developed (discussed in Chapter 8), M-PESA turned out to be an efficient and effective means for distributing funds to borrowers.

Moreover, for all its benefits, M-PESA is not practical to use in many rural areas where mobile phone service is not available. To tackle this challenge, a team of academics has developed a prototype system that enables money to be transferred between mobile phones without requiring mobile phone connectivity. Instead, a thin electronic component that contains a microchip is inserted into transacting phones over the SIM chip and used to authenticate and authorize transactions offline. When a mobile signal is available again, it will upload the transactions to the mobile payment service. Innovations like this provide the potential for extending mobile payment services to an even broader set of customers.

M-PESA was just the beginning of mobile money solutions in Africa. Within a number of years, phone companies, banks, and independent startups began providing similar services across a number of different countries including Zambia, Malawi, Senegal, and Mozambique. Clearly, the technology solution that M-PESA innovated addressed a pervasive problem. Also, its simple design, which addressed a range of stakeholders needs, proved to be a robust one. Taking note of these basic success factors would be of benefit to mobile payment solution providers in developed markets as well.

Sources: Mas, Ignatio and Dan Radcliffe, "Mobile Payments Go Viral: M-PESA in Kenya," *Journal of Financial Transformation* 32 (August 2011): 169–182; Hodson, Hal "Souped-up SIM Allows Mobile Payments Where There's No Network," *New Scientist*, October 26, 2016, https://www.newscientist.com/article/2110566-souped-up-sim-allows-mobile-payments-where-theres-no-network; "Cash Call," *The Economist*, October 8, 2016, http://www.economist.com/node/21708254/; "A different approach to mobile money in Africa," *Economist*, April 12, 2017, http://www.economist.com/news/finance-and-economics/21720624-startup-takes-banks-and-mobile-operators-different-approach-mobile.

9.6   BUSINESS CHALLENGES

While payment services offer benefits to both the bank and its customers, factors such as price competition, processing efficiency, and operational risk are crucial concerns. Processing efficiency, which underlies price competitiveness, requires that only a minimal amount of manual processing be performed so that large transaction volumes can easily be supported. That is to say, STP is necessary to ensure low transaction costs and high levels of customer service. Having economies of scale is important to make investments in payment infrastructure and STP cost effective. This dynamic favors large institutions over small ones when it comes to offering payment services.

Regulators may periodically introduce market-wide changes that have a major impact on banks. In some cases, they may mandate the transition from overnight batch-based payments to real-time payments. This was the case when the Faster Payments Service was launched in the United Kingdom in 2008. UK banks were required to support same-day fund transfers to other UK banks for online, phone banking, and branch-based transfers of up to £100,000. Likewise, in Europe, the Single Euro Payments Area (SEPA) initiative, which began in 2004 and was completed in 2014, affected banks across the continent. SEPA simplified cross-border payments and debit/credit card usage for customers, reducing the need for having multiple accounts and cards in different countries. As a result, banks had to adapt, test, and convince users to adopt new SEPA products and services. SEPA affected both how banks interacted with one another and how they interacted with their customers. Moreover, by lowering national barriers for payments, SEPA increased competition between banks operating within Europe.

Operational risk is another factor that determines the profitability of cash management and payment services. A major area of potential operational risk relates to regulatory penalties that may be incurred when banks do not comply with **anti-money laundering (AML)** practices. Extensive scrutiny is required both when on-boarding customers and remitting customers' funds to third parties to ensure that no AML rules are broken. The case of Barclays Bank highlights the consequences of having inadequate AML procedures. In 2010, it was fined US$298 million by the US government for facilitating payments on behalf of countries that were under economic and trade sanctions from the US government. In the same year, Wachovia Bank in the United States agreed to pay US$16 million in relation to charges by the US Justice Department that the bank's lax controls had enabled drug gangs to launder money through foreign currency exchange and cross-border payment operations near the US-Mexico border.

Another form of operational risk, monetary loss due to processing errors, is also a major concern for banks. A payment business that is marginally profitable under normal conditions will likely produce losses if operational failures occur. There are a number of things that can go wrong with payments processing. For example, payments may be lost or delayed, thereby causing settlement failures for the payees and causing customers to incur late or failed payment fees. Another possibility is that payments may be mistakenly effected twice, which can cause liquidity problems for the customers making payments and lead to fund-recovery concerns for the bank. Moreover, where manual processing is necessary, human error is likely to occur. Amounts may be mistyped or misread, and processing steps may be forgotten or accidentally repeated. When processing errors occur, in many cases, the bank will have to waive processing fees and possibly compensate customers for any direct costs that were caused by the error. Regulatory penalties may also be incurred.

Besides unintentional operational failures, fraud is also a major risk concern for payments. A 2012 study of financial institutions in the United States found that debit cards, cheques, and credit cards were the top payment types contributing to fraud losses [5]. Figure 9-6 shows the top fraud schemes used in conjunction with payments by or on behalf of customers. While external actors, working by themselves, were identified to represent 75% of the perpetrators, in many cases, acts of fraud are committed from within or with help from inside the organization. Accordingly, internal operational and technical security must be carefully controlled and maintained to ensure that fraud-related losses are minimized. Typical internal controls that help prevent fraud losses include:

- periodic internal and/or external audits;

- verifying that controls are applied as designed through audit or management review;

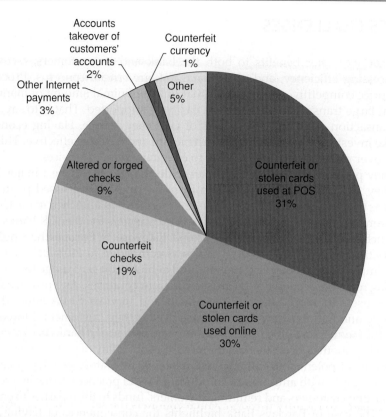

Figure 9-6 Common fraud schemes involving customer payments

- quickly addressing exception items;

- applying transaction limits for payment disbursements;

- applying authentication and authorization controls within payment processes; and

- controlling physical and logical access to payment networks and applications.

Technology solutions can also help reduce fraud losses. In many cases, fraud detection software that looks for abnormal behavior patterns can help prevent or limit the financial impact of payment fraud. Fraud information databases and alerting services can also be used to identify potential perpetrators. Counterfeit detector pens—that make a mark on paper used for counterfeit cash notes, but not on the special paper used for legitimate government-issued notes—are also used to prevent fraud. Moreover, educating bank staff and customers about the methods used to perpetrate payment fraud is also a powerful tool to help mitigate fraud risk.

9.7 TELEGRAPHIC-TRANSFER SERVICE LIFECYCLE

As shown in Figure 9-7, the transaction lifecycle that was defined in Chapter 6 is not only applicable to financial products, but can also be used to describe financial services. The main differences are that instead of fulfilling product delivery, service provision is required, and maintenance is not of an account or transaction but, rather, it involves the artifacts that support the service delivery process.

To help illustrate how the lifecycle framework applies to services, the following subsections will explore the lifecycle activities that are part of a high-level process, in this case, TT payments. To get

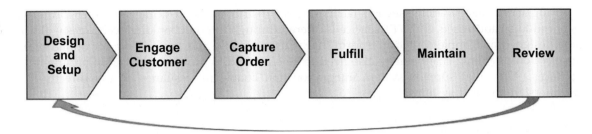

Figure 9-7 Transaction and services lifecycle model

a better sense of some of the intricacies involved, a low-level activity will also be examined, namely, the capture of payment instructions. This is the process followed when a bank receives payment instructions from a customer.

9.7.1 Design and Setup

Setting up a financial service such as TT has a number of prerequisites. The service's terms and conditions will need to be defined, reviewed, and approved by the bank's legal and compliance departments. The service fee structure will also need to be defined. Which fees are charged or not charged will be driven by the bank's marketing strategy, as well as competitive pressure. Fee structures may be simple or complex, involving many different customer and transaction parameters. It will also be necessary to identify through which channels the service will be provided.

A TT's terms and conditions would likely stipulate that the customer is responsible for any loss due to incorrect details provided in payment instructions. Likewise, it will be important to make customers aware that payments received after a particular cutoff time will be processed the following day. Fees may be determined by the transfer amount, with minimum and maximum fee limits. Additional fees may also be charged for using certain channels, such as the branch. The allowed access channels could be defined as branch, mobile, and Internet banking, but not call center or by mail.

A further consideration during the design of both products and services is the languages in which they will be supported. For example, in parts of North America, it may be advantageous to provide forms in both English and Spanish. In Hong Kong and Singapore, English as well as Cantonese or Mandarin are commonly supported by banks. Large multinational banks will need to support a large number of languages. Moreover, language support goes beyond paper forms. Electronic channels must also provide for the supported language, and call center and support staff must have multilingual capabilities.

9.7.2 Engage Customer

Once the service parameters have been defined, the service must be marketed to customers so that they are both aware of the service availability and are given incentives to use it. This marketing could be implemented using letters, emails, or mobile text messages sent to customers. The Internet banking website could also display a "splash" screen upon login that advertises the service or small graphic advertisements to the side of the main display area. To help increase the initial take-up, customers may be offered fee waivers or other benefits to encourage use of service.

Beyond the definition of which channels will provide access to the service during the design and setup stage, channel configuration and tuning are also necessary when the customer is engaged. For example, if a TT application is going to be accepted at branches, an application form must be designed, and branch staff will need to be trained to instruct customers on how to fill out the form.

Other logistical considerations, such as facilitating the distribution and storage of paper forms, will also need to be addressed. If the TT service is offered through Internet banking, webpages will need to be designed and implemented in a form that is user-friendly and appropriate for online access. The electronic banking channel may also need to be enhanced to provide application programming interfaces (APIs) that support system integration and enable the issuance of TTs directly from customers' in-house IT systems.

9.7.3 Capture Order

Capturing the payment instruction will involve information validation, and possibly multistage approvals. Information validation will verify that the customer has provided all necessary information (more details provided in Section 9.8). Besides validating transaction details, other security and AML checks will be required. The payee will need to be checked against blacklists provided by various governments and regulators. If a match occurs, the transaction will need to be managed using special workflows, which would most likely involve manual processing.

Approval and signature verification is another stage of verification that may occur in both the order-capture stage and the service-fulfillment stage. Signature verification at the order-capture stage of the transaction may only involve the receiver, for example, the branch staff, to verify that the signature is original. Alternatively, TTs that are captured via the Internet business banking channel can involve the customer assigning separate maker and approver roles that are built into the order-capture processing workflow. One role may prepare the payment instruction and then forward it through the bank's online application to another role, the signatory, for approval using a digital signature.

Also, as part of order capture, timestamps will be recorded physically on the application form when the bank receives it. If the instruction is placed using an electronic channel, a timestamp will be added digitally to the payment instruction record. This timestamp may be used as evidence as to whether cutoff times have been met, as well as for service-level measurement and tracking.

9.7.4 Fulfill Service

Once a TT has been captured, additional verifications may be performed. For example, where the signature may have only been verified as being original, as opposed to a photocopy, at the time of capture, it would be checked again during fulfillment to further verify that the signature on the TT form matches the signature on the bank's record. Additionally, checks may be necessary to determine if multiple signatories are required and under what conditions, for example, if the transaction is over a certain dollar amount.

Once all of the required validation steps have been completed, the transaction will be entered into the core banking system and accounting entries can be generated. Functional components that handle clearing and settlement will manage connectivity to payment gateways. In the case of TTs, the transaction may then be routed to external payment networks, such as SWIFT. These functions may be either modules of the core banking system or separate components that are integrated with the core banking system.

In many cases, the clearing of TTs may require additional work. If an intermediate bank involved with the transfer rejects the payment instruction, it may be necessary to correct the payment details, reprocess the payment, and notify the customer about the payment delivery status. Customers may also inquire about the status of payments that have not been received by the payee, requiring the bank to track down and verify the payment's processing status, possibly necessitating interaction with a correspondent bank.

Moreover, if the remitter agrees to pay for all the fees associated with the payment, determining the amount of transaction fees to charge the customer is more complicated. In this case, the remitter's bank will need to determine the fees charged by all the banks involved with the payment processing, including intermediary correspondent banks, and then aggregate those charges with the bank's own fee before charging the customer. It may be the case that the fees incurred can only be known after the the funds have been delivered to the recipient's bank, which may take several days to complete.

9.7.5 Maintain Service

Maintenance activities associated with TTs will include daily reconciliation between payment gateways and the core banking system. Static data such as fees structures and standard settlement instructions will also need to be revised from time to time. Destination codes for banks over various payment networks will need to be kept up to date. Also, if payment networks change their messaging formats or interfaces, solutions will need to be enhanced or upgraded to meet the new requirements.

9.7.6 Review

One example of a review for TT payment processing is the monitoring of how well **service-level agreements (SLAs)** are being met. Similarly, it is critical to capture information related to why transactions must be handled manually and the level of effort involved to process them. This information can be analyzed to determine ways to reduce the need for manual processing and to determine how to minimize the effort that is required when it is necessary (Figure 9-8). Transaction volumes may also be monitored to help forecast future operational resource requirements, and when processing capabilities may be increased or decreased based on developing business or seasonal trends.

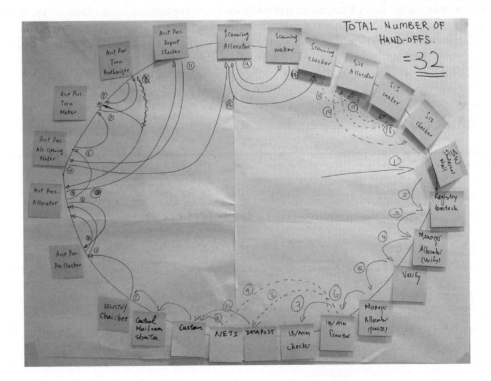

Figure 9-8 Analyzing where processing handoffs occur can help improve efficiency (© DBS Bank. Reprinted with permission.)

9.8 LIFECYCLE FOCUS: ORDER VALIDATION

From a high-level perspective, payment processing may appear quite straightforward. However, as always, things are more complicated than they seem on the surface. As highlighted in Section 9.6, the effectiveness and profitability of banking services is largely a function of how well exceptions are managed. Accordingly, this section will examine in greater depth some exception cases that can occur during order capture of TTs.

A good starting point for considering failures is the acquisition of payment instructions. As discussed in Chapter 8, paper-based channels are particularly prone to error. There is the possibility of losing the paper form at various points in the processing chain. If the customer mails the form to the bank, it may be lost in the mail, or the instructions may become damaged and illegible. Also, paper instructions received by the bank may be lost or mishandled before the information is captured into the processing system. Papers that are stacked together may get stuck to one another, leading to documents being missed during processing.

Even when payment instructions are properly received, the information that is provided in the instructions may cause exceptions. Table 9-3 shows information that is typically required from a customer to process a TT.

Most of this information is necessary to process the payment instruction. Hence, missing information on a TT application can easily result in a processing exception. One approach for minimizing exceptions related to incomplete information is to perform completeness checks as early as possible. For example, if the paper form is submitted at a branch, the teller who receives it can verify that all fields have been filled out before accepting the form. Similarly, if the instruction is entered online, the webpage that captures the information can verify that all required fields have valid values before allowing submission of the web form.

In cases where banks accept payment instructions from customers by written letter, the payment processing staff will need to manually extract relevant payment information from the content of the letter. One letter may contain multiple payment instructions. Furthermore, the letter may be ambiguous regarding certain details; thus, it may require further clarification. Due to the manual and complex nature of this task, there is a significant risk that the bank's staff may erroneously interpret or translate information contained in the letter when capturing it to the bank's payment system.

Table 9-3 Payment instruction details

Category	Details required
Applicant	Company name, company identifier, address, and contact number
Beneficiary	Name, account number, and address
Beneficiary's bank	Name, address, country SWIFT code, and branch or clearing code
Payment details	Currency and amount, source account, processing date. FX forward contract reference, and FX rate
Fee assignment	All fees paid by applicant, all fees paid by beneficiary, and split fees
Payment details	Free text to provide additional instructions such as beneficiary's bank routing instructions for intermediary correspondent banks
Signature	Signatory's approval
Other	Special instructions to bank for processing

Some exception cases caused by incorrect information may be identified immediately, but others may not. In some cases, invalid payment details may only be validated and detected at later stages of processing. For example, an error such as a mismatch between the beneficiary's bank name and the SWIFT code may only be detected when an exception is generated during the clearing process. Alternatively, if an invalid beneficiary bank account number is specified, the error will not be identified until the payment instruction has been sent to the beneficiary's bank.

There are also a whole host of exceptions that can occur when TT payments are routed through correspondent banks. When the payee's bank requires the use of a correspondent bank to process the payment, often, the correspondent bank is the destination of the payment instruction and details of the end-beneficiary's bank and account number will be specified in the special instructions field of the TT form. Because a freeform text field is used to convey this information and there is no standard way of specifying the end-beneficiary details, errors commonly occur. For example, the information may not be clear, may be incomplete, or may be misspelled, and can thus cause confusion. Such errors may lead to payments being held up, sometimes seeming temporarily lost, by correspondent banks.

9.9 SOLUTION CONSIDERATIONS

This section discusses the solution considerations related to real-time and batch processing and discusses an example that relates to payment systems. Historically, most transaction processing systems were batch-oriented. When only paper was used, transactions would be recorded on slips of paper and then recorded in account ledgers at the end of the day. Now, most transactions are recorded electronically during the day, but processing is not completed until end-of-day batch processing is performed after hours. When batch processing is used, a cutoff time for entering transactions is required, after which time transactions entered will be included in the next day's batch. In contrast, when transactions are processed in real time, they are processed individually and without delay.

Batch processing activities usually have a time period, or "window," assigned to them, for example, between 1:00 am to 4:00 am. Different batch activities may be dependent on one another, such that each batch must complete its processing within its own specific time window so as not to impede the processing of other dependent batches. Transaction volume increases will often lead to longer batch processing times. It is not uncommon for increases in transaction volumes to reach a point where they cause the batch processing times to exceed the allocated window, limiting the system's scalability. Alternatively, technical and operational problems can also cause the processing window to be breached. As highlighted in Case Study 9-3, when batch processing cannot be completed within its designated time window, the follow-on impact can be severe. Another issue with batch processing is that when used to process payments, it creates settlement lag, delaying the availability of funds for customers, and affecting their cash-flow and funding needs.

Customers' increased use of real-time service channels, such as Internet and phone banking, has also led to higher demand for real-time settlement services. Immediate payment services that Fintech companies offer have also raised the bar for the payment services that financial institutions provide. Hence, regulators in many countries pushed forward with upgrading national payment systems so that banks can provide immediate payment services to customers. This capability requires that both banks and national payment systems are able to process payment transactions in real time, rather than batch mode. Accordingly, changing from end-of-day settlement to near real-time settlement is a massive, industry-wide exercise. In particular, requiring financial institutions to upgrade core legacy systems, which were designed for batch-mode processing, to newer systems that support real-time processing, requires significant time, testing, and expense.

An example of such a migration was when the United Kingdom introduced the Faster Payments Service (FPS). FPS was created to provide a faster alternative to Bacs for making low-value payments.

Using Bacs was free, but it had a three-day settlement cycle. On the other hand, CHAPS provided same-day settlement, but was intended for high-value payments and was relatively expensive to use for low-value payments. FPS was designed to settle small-value payments, less than £100,000, within two hours and to be available 24 hours a day, seven days a week.

When migrating from batch settlement to quasi-real-time settlement, a number of concerns had to be considered. One concern was the ability to meet target SLA. For example, FPS requires banks to provide a response within 15 seconds confirming whether a payment is accepted or rejected. Processing delays caused by IT systems, communication links between systems, or IT system failures can easily cause this time threshold to be exceeded. Thus, business applications, IT infrastructure, and resilience architecture designs must all be closely aligned so that SLAs can be consistently met.

Besides the technical concerns, a number of operational concerns must also be addressed. First, a 24/7 operation may require bank staff to work longer hours. Second, additional application and infrastructure monitoring may be required to ensure that system disruptions are detected quickly and do not cause SLAs to be exceeded. Likewise, when IT system problems are detected, escalation and resolution processes must be fast and efficient. Where possible, processes should be fully automated to avoid delays and mistakes that may result from human error. Moreover, extensive testing and validation of real-time message flows, as opposed to end-of-day file transfers, will be required during the transition.

Fraud detection processes and how they are implemented must also be considered when moving from batch to real-time payments. In many cases, batch processing of payments allowed suspicious transactions to be identified and analyzed manually over a course of many hours or even days. In contrast, immediate payments require fraud detection decisions to be made in seconds. Accordingly, technology must be used to automate the analysis of potentially fraudulent transactions.

Support for immediate payments varies by country. A number of other countries have implemented immediate payment systems, including Singapore (FAST), India (IMPS), China (IBPS), Norway (Instant Payments), and Sweden (BiR). Some of these have only recently been implemented. For instance Singapore's FAST system, which enables individuals and firms to make low-value transfers between accounts held at local banks, was launched in 2014. Other countries are in the process of upgrading their payment infrastructure to support immediate payments. Australia plans to support immediate payments in 2017. Also, as of 2017, a task force set up by the US Federal Reserve was

Case Study 9-3

How Things Can Go Wrong with Payment Processing

News headlines regularly provide a sample of payment-related problems that are significant enough to be noticed by the press; many more are known to only those within the banks and affected customers. A few of the more visible cases are highlighted here.

In 2008, a man in the United States attributed the US$175,000 that was deposited in his and his wife's bank account to divine providence. In fact, the deposit was the result of a bank error. What should have been a US$1,772.50 deposit to the account was recorded as US$177,250. Instead of notifying the bank of this error, the customers simply withdrew the money, quit their jobs, and moved to Florida. It was unclear how much, if any, of the money the bank was able to recover.

Also in 2008, an Australian bank encountered problems with its business banking service that precluded corporate customers from processing bulk payment files that were used to pay employees. Moreover, the problem created a backlog of payments that could not be processed quickly. As a result of the outage, the bank's customers had to try to fulfill their payment obligations to their employees by various means, which included making large cash withdrawals so that cash payments could be made and also manually setting up individual electronic payments. The bank offered to reimburse any fees that corporate customers, or their employees, incurred due to the outage. The bank faced more trouble in 2010, when technical problems with its payment processing delayed payments for several days. Not only did the outage affect the bank's customers, it also impacted the customers of multinational banks that used the bank as their settlement agent for Australia's national payment system. To help compensate for the mess, the bank kept over a hundred branches open over the weekend and promised to reimburse customers for any penalties that they incurred that resulted from delayed payments.

In 2012, a problem with a software upgrade at one of the largest UK banks delayed the overnight batch from being processed on schedule. This delay created a huge backlog of payments that took days to finish processing, affecting millions of customers. The bank extended the opening hours of over a thousand branches, doubled the number of call center staff, and stayed open on Sunday to help deal with the debacle. The problem was expected to cost the bank at least £100 million. The bank offered to waive fees incurred by its customers, but it was unclear if payees who were not customers of the bank but were financially affected by late payments would also receive compensation. Furthermore, there was public concern as to whether the customers' credit histories would be tainted in cases where they were unable to repay their loans as a result of the payment outage.

Sources: "Pa. Man Considered Bank Error 'A Gift from God'," *Associated Press*, January 23, 2009, http://www.msnbc.msn.com/id/28793620/ns/us_news-weird_news/t/pa-man-considered-bank-error-gift-god; "Software Error Cripples NAB," *Australian IT*, July 30, 2008, http://www.theaustralian.com.au/australian-it-old/software-error-cripples-nab/story-e6frganf-1111117058388;"NAB Glitch Continues to Cause Trouble," *Herald Sun*, November 28, 2010, http://www.heraldsun.com.au/money/banking/nab-glitch-continues-to-cause-trouble/story- e6frfh5o-1225962277946; Moore, Elaine, "Customers Face Fallout from RBS Failure," *Financial Times*, June 29, 2012, http://www.ft.com/cms/s/0/13ea4bc2-c136-11e1-8eca-00144feabdc0.html; "RBS CEO Hester to Waive Bonus after IT debacle," *Reuters*, June 29, 2012, http://www.reuters.com/article/2012/06/29/rbs-hester-bonus-idUSL6E8HTD2J20120629.

reviewing proposals for creating a new nationwide system that supports immediate payments. Given that there are over 10,000 financial institutions providing retail banking services in the United States, migrating all of them to support near-real-time payments will be a substantial challenge.

9.10 SUMMARY

This chapter covered:

- key concepts related to payment systems;
- how businesses and retail customers use payment services;
- the opportunities and challenges that banks face when providing payment services;
- the key activities involved in the transaction lifecycle of a payment; and
- process and solution considerations related to payments.

The next chapter examines the products, services, and technologies involved with banks' trade finance operations.

FURTHER READING

Books

Nakajima, M., *Payment System Technologies and Functions: Innovations and Developments* (Pennsylvania: IGI Global, 2011).

Journals

Journal of Payments Strategy & Systems, Henry Stewart Publications, https://www.henrystewartpublications.com/jpss.

Papers

Cotteleer, M. J., C. A. Cotteleer, and A. Prochnow, "Cutting Checks: Challenges and Choices in B2B E-payments," *Communications of the ACM* 50 (2007): 56–61. http://216.27.81.122/treasuryresources/PDF/PSR-BriefingAug06.pdf.

"Strategies for Improving the U.S. Payment System," US Federal Reserve System, January 26, 2015, https://www.federalreserve.gov/newsevents/press/other/20150126a.htm.

"Payment Systems in Singapore," Bank for International Settlements, CPMI Papers No. 47, November 2001, http://www.bis.org/cpmi/publ/d47.pdf.

"Payment Systems in the United States," Bank for International Settlements, CPSS—Red Book 2003, https://www.bis.org/cpmi/paysys/unitedstatescomp.pdf.

Greene, C., M. Rysman, S. Schuh, and O. Shy, "Costs and Benefits of Building Faster Payment Systems: The U.K. Experience and Implications for the United States," Federal Reserve Bank of Boston, Current Policy Perspectives No. 14-5, February 24, 2015, https://www.bostonfed.org/-/media/Documents/Workingpapers/PDF/economic/cpp1405.pdf.

"Merschen, T., "Fraud Dynamics in the Card Payments Industry: A Global Review of the Realities of EMV Deployment," Journal of Payments Strategy & Systems Volume 4 Number 2, http://www.ingentaconnect.com/content/hsp/jpss/2010/00000004/00000002/art00006.

"The U.S. Path to Faster Payments," Faster Payments Task Force, January 2017, https://www.federalreserve.gov/newsevents/press/other/US-path-to-faster-payments-pt1-201701.pdf.

"Technologies for Payment Fraud Prevention: EMV, Encryption and Tokenization," Smart Card Alliance Payments Council, October 2014, http://www.smartcardalliance.org/wp-content/uploads/EMV-Tokenization-Encryption-WP-FINAL.pdf.

"The 2016 Federal Reserve Payments Study," Federal Reserve Board, https://www.federalreserve.gov/newsevents/press/other/2016-payments-study-20161222.pdf.

"2017 Payments Strategy Survey," American Bankers Association, http://www.aba.com/Tools/Function/Payments/Documents/2017-Payments-Strategy-Survey.pdf.

Web

"Continuous Linked Settlement: The Great FX Fix—Case Study," http://www.cls-group.com/SiteCollectionDocuments/Case%20Study%20-%20The%20Treasurer.pdf.

"Payment Systems—Handbooks in Central Banking No. 8," http://www.bankofengland.co.uk/education/ccbs/handbooks/ccbshb08.htm.

"NACHA File Layout Guide," Regions Bank, https://www.regions.com/virtualdocuments/nacha_file_layout_guide.pdf.

ENDNOTES

1. Bagnall, J., D. Bounie, K. P. Huynh, A. Kosse, T. Schmidt, S. Schuh, and H. Stix, "Consumer Cash Usage a Cross-Country Comparison with Payment Diary Survey Data," European Central Bank Working Paper No. 1685, June 2014.

2. Chaudhuri, S., "Cost of Replacing Credit Cards after Target Breach Estimated at $200 Million," *Wall Street Journal*, February 18, 2014, http://www.wsj.com/articles/SB10001424052702304675504579391080333769014.

3. Rudegeair, P., "Why Apple and J.P. Morgan Are Chasing Venmo," *Wall Street Journal*, June 26, 2017, https://www.wsj.com/articles/why-apple-and-j-p-morgan-are-chasing-venmo-1498469401.

4. Nakajima, M., *Payment System Technologies and Functions: Innovations and Developments* (Pennsylvania: IGI Global, 2011): 1–28.

5. "2012 Payments Fraud Survey Summary of Results First District," Federal Reserve Bank of Boston, November 2, 2012.

— — —

6. Sheppard D., "Payment Systems," *Bank of England Handbooks in Central Banking* no. 8 (1996): 18–35.

7. Hughes, Jennifer, "Lessons on Running a Smooth Settlement System," *Financial Times*, August 20, 2009, http://www.ft.com/cms/s/0/aed5c154-8da7-11de-93df-00144feabdc0.html# axzz1z9Dse3Ms.

8. "Germany's KfW to Get Back Lehman Millions," *Reuters*, December 12, 2012, http://www.reuters.com/article/2009/12/12/financial-lehman-germany-idUSGEE5BB05X20091212.

9. Nakamura, L., "Monitoring Loan Quality via Checking Account Analysis," *Journal of Retail Banking* 14 (1992–1993): 4.

10. "Faster Payments," http://www.fasterpayments.org.uk/faster_payments.

11. European Central Bank, "The Single Euro Payments Area (SEPA)," 2009, http://www.ecb.int/pub/pdf/other/sepa_brochure_2009en.pdf.

12. Goff, Sharlene, "Barclays Fined $298m over Sanctions Breach," *Financial Times*, August 17, 2010, http://www.ft.com/intl/cms/s/0/6918f646-a96b-11df-a6f2-00144feabdc0.html#axzz1z9Dse3Ms.

13. Carter, Emma, "Considering the Continuity of Payments for Customers in a Bank's Recovery or Resolution," *Bank of England Quarterly Bulletin* (2012 Q2): 147–153.

14. Lieber, Ron, "Why It's So Hard to Transfer Cash to Your Friends," *New York Times*, February 24, 2012, http://www.nytimes.com/2012/02/25/your-money/why-its-so-hard-to-transfer-cash-to-your-friends-your-money.html.

15. Adams, John, "Wells, B of A and JPM Look to Shake Up P-to-P Payments," *American Banker*, May 25, 2012, http://www.americanbanker.com/issues/177_102/ClearXchange-debuts-P2P-app-seeks-more-bank-members-1049646-1.html?zkPrintable=1&nopagination=1.

16. "Banks and Vendors Make Moves on Mobile/ATM Integration," *Banking Technology*, June 14, 2012, http://www.bankingtech.com/bankingtech/article.do?articleid=20000225561.

17. "Singapore Banks to Deploy Improved Electronic Payments System," *Channel News Asia*, June 29, 2012, http://www.channelnewsasia.com/stories/singaporebusinessnews/view/1210532/1/.html.

18. SWIFT Message Type Reference, https://docs.oracle.com/cd/E19509-01/820-7113/6nid5dl2r/index.html.

19. All About Payment Cards, MasterCard, https://www.mastercard.com/us/company/en/docs/All_About_Payment_Cards.pdf.

20. Credit Card Validation - Check Digits, https://web.eecs.umich.edu/~bartlett/credit_card_number.html.

21. EMV Specifications, http://www.emvco.com/specifications.aspx.

22. Ramamoorthy, A., "How Positive Pay Deters US Check Fraud," *Gtnews*, October 25, 2004, http://www.gtnews.com/Articles/2004/ How_Positive_Pay_Deters_US_Check_Fraud.html.

23. Merschen, Toni, "Fraud dynamics in the card payments industry: A global review of the realities of EMV deployment," *Journal of Payments Strategy & Systems*, Vol. 4 No. 2, 2010, pp. 156–169 Henry Stewart Publications, 1750–1806.

24. Abrams, Rachel, "Chip-Card Payment System Delays Frustrate Retailers," New York Times, Mar 22, 2016, http://www.nytimes.com/2016/03/23/business/chip-card-payment-system-delays-frustrate-retailers.html.

25. Android Developer Guide, https://developer.android.com/guide/index.html.

26. "Tokenization Technology," American Bankers Association, https://www.aba.com/Tools/Function/Technology/Documents/Tokenization-Infographic.pdf.

27. Ali, Robleh, Barrdear, John, Clews, Roger, and Southgate, James, "Innovations in payment technologies and the emergence of digital currencies," Bank of England Quarterly Bulletin 2014 Q3. http://www.pbs.org/wgbh/nova/ancient/history-money.html.

28. "The History of Money," NOVA, http://www.pbs.org/wgbh/nova/ancient/history-money.html.

29. Savvas, Antony, "Barclays Opens PingIt Mobile Payment System to All Businesses," *Computer World UK*, May 23, 2012, http://www.computerworlduk.com/news/mobile-wireless/3359500/barclays-opens-pingit-mobile-payment-system-to-all-businesses

30. Brignall, Miles,"Barclays Launches PingIt Money-sending Service for Smartphones," *Guardian*, February 16, 2012, http://www.guardian.co.uk/money/2012/feb/16/barclays-pingit-money-sending-smartphone;

31. Gillette, Felix, "Cash Is for Losers!," *Bloomberg*, Nov. 21, 2014, https://www.bloomberg.com/news/articles/2014-11-20/mobile-payment-startup-venmo-is-killing-cash.

32. Demos, Telis, "Citigroup Teams Up With Rival Banks to Fight Venmo," *Wall Street Journal*, Sep. 28, 2016, http://www.wsj.com/articles/citigroup-teams-up-with-rival-banks-to-fight-venmo-1475084844.

33. "WeChat's world," *Economist*, Aug 6th 2016, http://www.economist.com/node/21703428.

34. Lee, Yimou and Carsten, Paul, "WeChat payments rocket as China's Tencent rides gaming wave," *Reuters*, Mar. 17, 2016, http://finance.yahoo.com/news/chinas-tencent-q4-revenue-beats-094419211.html.

35. Osawa, Juro, "China Mobile-Payment Battle Becomes a Free-for-All," *Wall Street Journal*, May 22, 2016, http://www.wsj.com/articles/china-mobile-payment-battle-becomes-a-free-for-all-1463945404.

36. "World Payments Report 2015," Capgemini.

37. "2013 NACHA Operating Rules & Guidelines," NACHA.

38. https://www.nacha.org/

39. Crosman, P., "Faster ACH Payments Strain Bank Anti-fraud Systems," *American Banker*, December 29, 2016, https://www.americanbanker.com/news/faster-ach-payments-strain-bank-anti-fraud-systems.

10 Trade Services and Finance

In the 12th and 13th centuries, banking and money markets became a central part of international trade. Family-run banks in Venice and other major cities in Europe facilitated cross-border transfers and payments for merchants and travelers. Financial instruments, such as bills of exchange, enabled payments to be drawn from banks in remote locations, currencies to be exchanged, and credit to be provided. They also helped avoid conflicts arising from religious restrictions that existed during those times which prohibited charging of interest on loans. Medieval bankers bore several risks when providing these services, including default by counterparties and losses from exchange rate fluctuations and payment disputes that would potentially be settled in courts of law. To offset these risks, the effective interest rate charged on bills of exchange then was often in excess of 14%.

Over the centuries that followed, trade expanded and merchant bankers rose to prominence in London and parts of Europe. Firms such as Hambros, Barings, Warburgs, Lehman Brothers, and Rothschilds provided financial support for international trade. These firms funded business ventures by providing trade services and issuing securities on behalf of companies, and they also traded securities on their own accounts. Later, in the 1900s, investment banks replaced merchant banks in bringing securities to market and secondary market trading. Likewise, commercial banks rose to support the finance of international trade.

During the early years of trade finance, many core financial products and processes, which continue to be used today, were developed. Bills of exchange, **letters of credit (L/Cs)**, banks' **nostro** and **vostro accounts**, and the exchange of discounted credit instruments were all established many centuries ago. Up until the introduction of electronic communications, there would be little change to how trade finance was implemented by banks and trading partners. Yet, even with the availability of advanced technology, automation of trade finance has continued to lag behind other areas of banking. Streamlining the international trade finance process has been an uphill battle. Significant progress was made in this regard in the mid-1900s by standardizing rules that govern trade finance agreements.

Acceptance of standard rules by trading partners was relatively simple; the rules could be adopted by including reference to them in trade finance agreements. However, streamlining other aspects, such as documents' formats and their modes of transmission, has been more difficult to achieve. In many cases, it would require firms to adopt and put up money for new technologies. Besides, streamlining interactions between partners has come up against network-effect issues. If only a few trading parties agreed to support standardization and automation, there would be little incentive for other trading parties to take part. Gains would be limited by the small number of participants and, thus, the effort and cost of upgrading would outweigh the benefits. The challenge still remains as to how technology can be used effectively to modernize a centuries-old business that today represents a $4 trillion industry [1]. As shown by Figure 10-1, trade finance is still very much driven by manual processes, and relatively straightforward solutions have struggled to gain acceptance (Case Study 10-1). Yet, new technologies such as blockchain have renewed interest in leveraging technology to improve the efficiency of trade finance transactions and reduce their risk.

This chapter reviews the basic concepts that underlie trade finance and the services that banks provide in international trade. The principle flows between importers, exporters, and their banks are

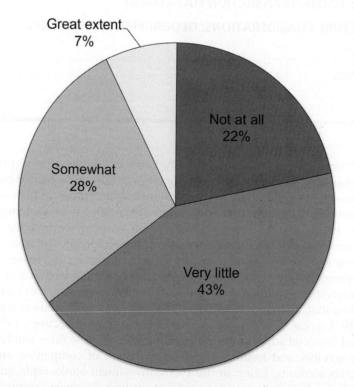

Figure 10-1 Extent to which banks' trade finance transaction processes are digitized
Source: ICC Global Survey on Trade Finance 2016

presented first. Following this, a more detailed examination of documentary collections is provided, covering the opportunities, challenges, and technologies used by banks to support this financial product. Finally, architecture considerations related to the geographic distribution of business operations and IT systems will be explored.

Case Study 10-1

The Struggle to Dematerialize Shipping Documents

In international trade, handling paper documents, such as bills of lading, is problematic both for banks and trade participants. Often, banks must compare shipping documents delivered through trade finance arrangements with seaborne shipping documents that arrive with the goods in port. However, sending, receiving, and processing delays can cause trade-related documentation to arrive later than the shipment. Problems then arise because ships can remain in port for a limited time only, and the necessary documents may not arrive in time. Much of the delay can be eliminated if electronic messages were used in place of paper documentation. Furthermore, the use of electronic shipping documentation would support automated processing, saving time, reducing costs, and decreasing error rates.

Several initiatives have attempted to dematerialize, that is, eliminate the paper form of, negotiable bills of lading. The SeaDocs program was launched in the 1980s, but did not get past the first phase of implementation. One of several problems that SeaDocs faced was that many banks were concerned that a competitor, Chase Manhattan Bank, had exclusive control of the registry. Ultimately, SeaDocs was unable to gain enough support to be financially viable. CMI Rules was another more open initiative that was promoted by the Comité Maritime International in 1990. Unfortunately, legal concerns, security concerns, and concerns about its lack of central administration prevented CMI Rules from gaining sufficient momentum to launch.

In 1998, SWIFT and the Through Transport Club, a mutual insurance association that included several thousand transport operators, launched the Bolero initiative. Two years later, the project acquired additional financial support from venture capitalists. Bolero aimed to replace paper trade documents, such as bills of lading, with an electronic title transfer facility. The Bolero platform provided three functions: it provided an electronic messaging platform (built on top of SWIFT's infrastructure), served as a certificate authority, and acted as a title registry. These capabilities enabled electronic messages and data records in the title registry to replace paper bills of lading.

Bolero's messages could be transmitted over public or private networks and use encryption to secure communications. Open interfaces were provided to Bolero so that users could connect through a variety of different channels. However, for all its virtues, Bolero's initial incarnation had limited success. It failed to gain support from banks, which had doubts about the legal governance that applied to Bolero's paperless transactions.

Banks relied on having full title to bills of lading so that they could use the shipped goods as collateral to back L/Cs. Hence, doubt over ownership of the goods would undermine the security backing banks' transactions.

In 2003, Bolero replaced its management team and shifted its focus to multibank trade finance applications, which supported trade-related processes between banks, corporate customers, and commodity traders. These new services could be deployed as either traditional software applications or as software-as-a-service (SaaS) web-hosted applications. In 2010, Bolero migrated its core infrastructure off of SWIFT's infrastructure to a commercial hosting facility.

Despite the benefits that electronic bills of lading provide, they have been difficult to put into practice. Diverse objectives and long-standing practices of banks, corporate customers, and shippers create significant

(Continued)

barriers to change. Likewise, the variance and ambiguities of different countries' legal jurisdictions also create barriers to adoption. In recent years, Bolero has begun to gain traction with markets in Asia Pacific, particularly, China and Australia. However, there is still a long way to go before the use of this technology becomes widespread.

Questions

1. What incentives or assurances might Bolero have used to encourage banks to get past their concerns about the legality of paperless transfer of title?
2. Why would Bolero choose to use SWIFT's infrastructure to begin with? Why would it elect to migrate off of that same infrastructure some ten years later?
3. Why would Bolero continue seeking new business approaches, whereas SeaDocs and CMI Rules had much shorter lifetimes?
4. If a bill-of-lading dematerialization initiative is launched again today, what implementation or delivery strategies might improve its chance of success?

Sources: Laryea, Emmanuel T., "Bolero Electronic Trade System—An Australian Perspective," *Journal of International Banking Law* 16, issue 1 (2001): 4–11; Dubovec, Marek, "The Problems and Possibilities for Using Electronic Bills of Lading As Collateral," *Arizona Journal of International & Comparative Law* 23, issue 2 (2006): 437–466; Bolero website, http://www.bolero.net; "Bolero: Dancing to a Different Tune," *Treasury Today*, September 2013, http://treasurytoday.com/2013/09/bolero-dancing-to-a-different-tune; "Cargill Australia Migrates to Bolero for South Korea Shipment," *Finextra*, April 4, 2016, https://www.finextra.com/pressarticle/63815/cargill-australia-migrates-to-bolero-for-south-korea-shipment.

10.1   CORPORATE BANKING CONTEXT

This section examines the structure of international trade flows and the concerns of corporate customers when importing or exporting goods.

10.1.1 International Trade Interactions

The growth of international trade has revolutionized the world economy and provided companies with a means of growing beyond the size of their own domestic markets. Be that as it may, international trade is more complex than the domestic sale of goods. Business practices and laws differ across countries and regions and the creditworthiness of trading counterparties is often less certain. **Credit risk** and fraud are often of greater concern with international and trade-related transactions. For instance, in 2014, several international and Chinese banks faced hundreds of millions of dollars in losses when a Chinese trading company pledged the same metal stocks as collateral for multiple loans by using duplicate storage receipts.

One of the challenges of understanding trade-related banking services is that most people are not familiar with the processes that underlie importing and exporting and the complications that can arise. This section provides abridged background information about international trade that will serve as a foundation for further discussion on trade-related banking services.

10.1.1.1 Participants and flows

The types of participants involved in international trade vary from one transaction to the next. Many of them can be ignored for the purposes of understanding banking trade services. For illustration purposes, only five of them will be considered: the importer, the exporter, the carrier of the goods, the importer's bank, and the exporter's bank. The high-level activity flow of these participants for a simple international trade scenario is shown in Figure 10-2. For the purposes of this discussion, it should be assumed that the importer and its bank are in one country and the exporter and its bank are in another.

There are three primary flows between the participants: payment for goods, delivery of trade-related documents, and delivery of goods. To help illustrate the general concept, Figure 10-2 shows the payment as a continuous flow from the importer to the exporter via their banks; however, in practice, the immediate, trade-related flow would be from bank to bank, transferring funds from the importer's bank account to the exporter's bank account. As discussed in Section 10.2.1, this transfer may not be direct or immediate.

When goods are shipped, the exporter delivers the goods to the carrier for shipment to the importer. When the exporter hands the goods over to the carrier, the carrier will provide trade-related documents to the exporter that will later have to be presented by the importer to receive the goods. Hence, the exporter must deliver these trade documents to the importer as soon as possible so that the importer will have them in time to claim the goods when they arrive.

10.1.1.2 Trade-related documents

There are a number of different shipping documents that banks may handle in the provision of trade-related financial services. Table 10-1 provides a list of common shipping documents and their purpose in international trade.

Bills of lading are important when container ships are used as the means of carriage. They provide evidence of the contract between the exporter and the shipping company that specifies the terms and conditions for carrying the goods, and serve as a receipt. A bill of lading also provides the consignee with title, that is, ownership, to the goods. Normally, bills of lading are negotiable; the consignee may transfer ownership of the goods to another party by endorsing the bill. The importer must produce the original copies of the bill of lading to take possession of the goods. Hence, they are often a key component of trade documents delivered to the importer.

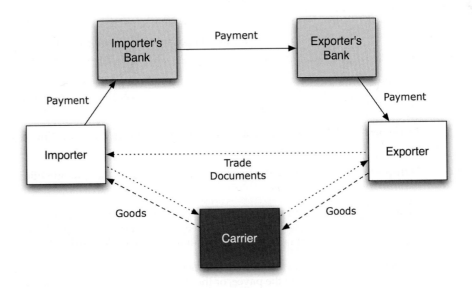

Figure 10-2 Participants and flows in simple trade payment scenarios

10.1.2 Banking Customer Needs

In trade agreements, the terms of payment and delivery of goods are crucial; they are one of the underlying risks of the business venture. On the one hand, the importer faces the risk of loss if the goods purchased are not delivered, are not delivered on schedule, or if the goods received are of inferior quality; on the other hand, the exporter faces the risk of loss if the importer does not pay for the goods as promised or delays payment. Likewise, both parties face risks related to the damage or loss of goods in transit.

The timing of payments and delivery of goods also affects both the importer's and the exporter's cash flows and ultimately determines who will finance the transaction. Ideally, the importer would like to delay payment until the goods have been received and resold. Alternatively, the exporter would like to receive payment before the goods are produced and shipped. In the former case, the exporter may provide financing to the importer by providing trade credit. In the latter case, the importer may provide the exporter with working capital by making payment in advance.

In light of these concerns, importers and exporters may choose from several options when specifying the terms of delivery and payment as part of the commercial agreement.

Table 10-1 Common trade-related documents

Document	Type	Purpose
Commercial invoice	Commercial	Provides a statement of the amount due to be paid. Includes the names of buyer and seller, description of goods, unit prices, and payment terms, for example, 30 days.
Packing list	Commercial	Provides a detailed list of the goods shipped.
Certificate of inspection	Commercial	Documented results of an inspection of the goods before shipment by a recognized third-party inspection agent
Certificate of origin	Official or commercial	A statement signed by a third party that provides evidence of the goods' origin
Insurance certificate/policy	Insurance	Provides evidence of insurance on the exported goods. Insurance may cover considerations such as damage, theft, and delay.
Bill of lading	Transport	Issued by the carrier for container goods delivered by ship. Provides receipt of goods, serves as the contract, and gives title to the goods.
Airway bill	Transport	A receipt for shipment by air. Does not provide title to the goods.
Rail consignment note	Transport	A receipt for shipment by train. Does not provide title to the goods.
Bill of exchange	Financial	An unconditional order drawn by the payee instructing the payer to pay the payee, or the bearer of the bill, a sum of money immediately or at a specified future date
Promissory note	Financial	An unconditional order drawn by the payer promising to pay the payee, or the bearer of the note, a sum of money immediately or at a specified future date.

Cash-in-advance and open account arrangements only require banks to facilitate payments. With cash-in-advance payment, the importer pays the exporter in advance of receiving the goods. This arrangement represents the highest risk for the importer because it has no guarantee and little leverage to ensure that the goods will be received as agreed. Likewise, the importer must have sufficient **liquidity** or must arrange financing to support its cash-flow requirements during the time that the payment is made to the exporter, and when the goods are received and are subsequently resold.

Alternatively, goods may be purchased under an open account arrangement. The exporter ships the goods, provides the trade documents (for example, the bill of lading), and invoices the importer on pre-agreed payment terms (for example, 30 or 90 days). In this case, the exporter bears the risk that the importer may not pay for the goods as promised. It also must have sufficient liquidity or obtain financing to support the cash-flow requirements of producing and shipping the goods until the payment is received.

With both cash-in-advance payments and open account terms, there may be legal recourse to recover in the case of loss. However, depending on the counterparty's country of origin, it may not be practical to pursue. Significant time and cost may be involved when pursuing legal remedies. Additionally, the legal system in the counterparty's home country may not be reliable or efficient. Even if there is a swift and favorable judgment, enforcing the judgment for recovery purposes may be difficult.

The use of cash-in-advance and open account arrangements depends on the regions, countries, industries, and companies involved in the trade transactions. In North American and European trade, open account arrangements are common. Alternatively, in emerging markets or in cases where the importer is financially weak or resides in an unstable country, the exporter may require cash in advance.

10.2 BANKING TRADE SERVICES

In simple trade scenarios, such as those described in the previous section, banks' involvement in the trade process is primarily limited to facilitating payment. However, in many cases, banks are more involved in the trade process. They can provide services that help reduce the importer's and the exporter's risks. The trade counterparties may choose to use banks to support the collection process or to provide payment guarantees. Many banks provide documentary collection services and documentary credits, commonly referred to as L/Cs, to address these needs. Figure 10-3 shows how these financial services can be viewed from the risk perspective of the importer and the exporter in relation to cash-in-advance and open account payment arrangements.

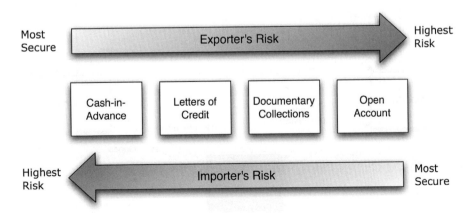

Figure 10-3 Payment risk spectrum

The following subsections review the services provided by banks to support international trade, including basic payment services, documentary collections, and L/Cs. The explanations provided have been simplified to help highlight the underlying concepts and to hide the process and terminology variations that can be distracting for the novice reader. References to detailed explanations of **bills of exchange**, collection services, and documentary credits can be found in the Further Reading section at the end of this chapter.

10.2.1 Payment Services

With cash-in-advance or open account arrangements, banks' involvement with the trade process is primarily limited to facilitating payments. Invoices and bills of exchange presented by the exporter and accepted by the importer initiate the payment process. Bills of exchange, also referred to as trade bills, are commonly used as a written order from the exporter to the importer or importer's bank for the **settlement** of international trade. It is similar to a cheque or promissory note, but is drafted by the exporter, rather than the importer. By accepting a **bill of exchange**, the importer takes on a legally binding obligation to pay. This obligation may either be immediate, that is, a sight bill, or at a future date, that is, a term bill. Like cheques, bills of exchange can be endorsed by the payee and passed on as negotiable instruments. While cheques are commonly used for clearing domestic payments, they are problematic for international payments. They often take several weeks to process and involve relatively high bank processing fees. Hence, **telegraphic transfers (TTs for short)**, which were introduced in Chapter 9, are the primary means of effecting international payments, that is, to settle amounts due from invoices or bills of exchange.

10.2.2 Collection Services

Banks help facilitate international trade by providing documentary collection services. With documentary collections, the exporter's bank collects payment in cooperation with another bank, the collecting bank, in the importer's home country. As shown in Figure 10-4, the exporter's bank

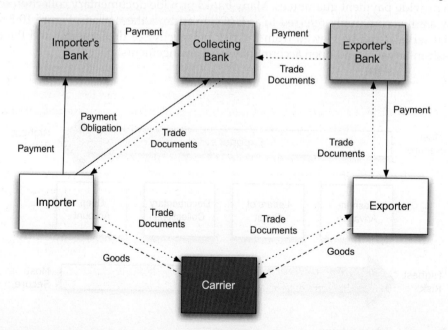

Figure 10-4 Participants and flows for documentary collections

manages the delivery of the trade documents instead of having the exporter send them directly to the importer. The exporter's bank forwards the trade documents (for example, a bill of lading) and financial documents (for example, a bill of exchange) to the collecting bank. The collecting bank then allows the importer to examine the trade documents. If the importer is satisfied with the documents, it arranges for immediate payment, provides a promissory note, or accepts a bill of exchange with a future date of payment in exchange for the documents. The importer's bank then facilitates settlement with the collecting bank, which then settles with the exporter's bank.

Documentary collections provide benefits for both the exporter and the importer. The exporter retains control over the goods up to the point when the importer makes payment or provides a legal obligation to pay by accepting a bill of exchange or issuing a promissory note. Likewise, after a bill of exchange is accepted, the exporter may be able to use the bill as security to obtain financing. In this case, the exporter's counterparty payment risk is reduced, compared with requesting payment against an invoice. The importer also benefits from documentary collections by being able to examine the trade documents in advance of payment, and gains another means of obtaining short-term financing.

While documentary collections provide many benefits, they do not address all trade-related concerns. The exporter faces the risk that when presented with the trade documents, the importer may refuse to pay or accept a bill of exchange. The exporter can retain control of the goods in this case, but will have to dispose of or ship back the goods. The importer also faces the risk that even if the trade documents are in good order, the shipment may not be delivered as expected after the payment obligation is made. Furthermore, the fees charged by the banks to provide the documentary collection service must be borne by the exporter or factored into the price included in the commercial agreement.

10.2.3 Trade Finance Services

Irrevocable documentary credits, commonly referred to as irrevocable L/Cs, go further to reduce the exporter's risk by using one or more banks to guarantee payment to the exporter. As part of the commercial agreement, the exporter may require the importer to have a bank issue an L/C to the exporter on the importer's behalf. The L/C is presented by the importer's bank to the exporter's bank, which advises the exporter of its issuance. The L/C guarantees payment to the exporter on the condition that it provides the required trade documents within a given time frame, as specified by the L/C. Figure 10-5 shows the participants and high-level flows for an L/C transaction.

The exporter presents the trade documents to its bank, which then verifies that the documents are exactly as required by the L/C and forwards them to the importer's bank. The trade documents will typically include a bill of lading as well as a bill of exchange drawn upon the importer's bank, as illustrated in Figure 10-6*. The importer's bank then examines the documents to ensure that they match the L/C specifications and if so, will make payment immediately or at a future date stated in the bill of exchange. Next, the importer's bank will deliver the trade documents to the importer and collect payment. Figure 10-7 shows, in more detail, the main process flows in an L/C transaction.

L/Cs reduce the exporter's risk by providing a bank guarantee that the exporter will be paid, as long as it complies with the requirements stipulated in the L/C, as illustrated in Figure 10-8. Accordingly, the L/C advice that the exporter receives can be used to secure local preshipment finance. L/Cs also help the importer by enabling it to fix a date by which the exporter must ship to comply with the terms of the L/C. Furthermore, the security provided by issuing an L/C enables the importer to get a longer term of credit, via a term bill of exchange, than it might normally get without the guarantee provided by an L/C.

Although there are many benefits to using L/Cs, those benefits are limited in several ways. First, payment of the L/C is linked only to the presentation of the required documentation; it is not

---

* Figure 10-6 and other examples of trade finance-related documents in this chapter are fictitious and do not relate to actual companies or banks.

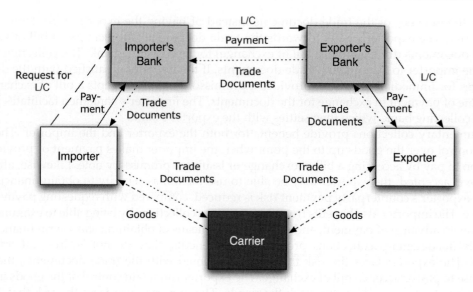

Figure 10-5 Participants and flows for L/Cs

$100,000   Singapore
                                            January 20, 2017

At 90 days after the date of this exchange, pay to the order of Wool World Pty Ltd the sum
of one hundred thousand US dollars.

Drawn under Irrevocable Documentary Credit number XYZ3334442 of
Dragon Bank Ltd, Singapore, dated December 1, 2016.

To: Dragon Bank Ltd   For and on behalf of
        30 Robinson Road   Wool World Pty Ltd
        Dragon Bank Tower
        Singapore 048882
        Republic of Singapore   (signature here)

Figure 10-6 Example of a bill of exchange linked to an L/C

dependent on the delivery of the goods or their condition when delivered. Third-party inspection may be required as a condition of the L/C to help mitigate this concern, but it comes at an additional cost. Second, to obtain an L/C, the importer must have a line of credit with its bank, or have sufficient funds to deposit as security for the L/C. Third, the cost of the L/C, which is higher than that of documentary collection, will be borne directly by the importer and is dependent on its credit rating.

There are many variations of L/Cs, two examples being revolving L/Cs and confirmed L/Cs. Importers may arrange revolving L/Cs with their bank, which allows them to draw upon a predefined line of credit that is allocated for L/C issuance on an ongoing basis. This credit line is replenished as each L/C is closed out (that is, the goods are delivered and all payments are completed). This facility helps minimize the overhead of applying for new L/Cs for each shipment when it is known that L/Cs will be required on a recurring basis to match regular shipments of goods. Alternatively, with confirmed L/Cs, the exporter's bank will also guarantee the payment so that the exporter draws payment on its bank, and the exporter's bank bears the counterparty risk if the importer's bank does not fulfill its payment obligation.

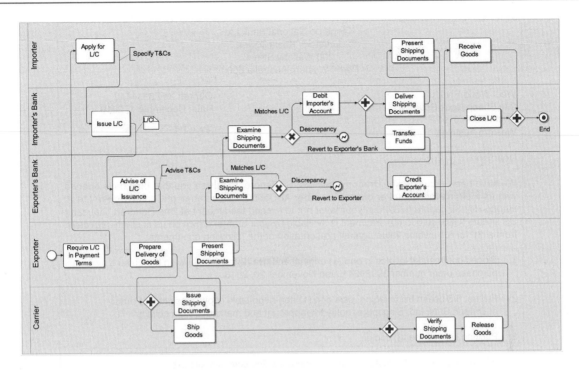

Figure 10-7 L/C process model

10.2.4 Trade Finance

Financing of corporate customers' trade activities is similar to other bank lending activities and is complementary to trade services provided by banks. This section explores three common forms of finance that banks provide to support corporate customers' trade activities: working capital finance, discounting purchase of term bills, and **factoring**. These activities are discussed at a macro level, leaving out many of the complicated details and variants to help make it easier to understand the basic concepts. Further details can be found in the references listed in the Further Reading section at the end of this chapter.

10.2.4.1 Finance of working capital

It is common for commercial banks to provide lending facilities to their customers that provide them with additional working capital to support the purchase, production, and delivery of goods. These lending facilities are usually dependent on the customer's need for trade-related financing and require documentation that demonstrates that there is an underlying transaction that the loan will support. Additionally, other financial requirements may need to be met, such as profitable business operations for a year or more. Exporters may need to borrow funds when they provide open account payment terms to importers and do not have sufficient working capital to pay for the production of goods prior to receiving payment. Likewise, importers may need credit to fund purchases that are made on cash-in-advance payment terms.

Credit may be provided either as individual short-term loans or as revolving credit lines. Individual loans may be granted for periods from three months up to one year, and will often be linked to specific transactions. Alternatively, revolving credit facilities can be provided when regular shipments are expected or when funding for smaller, less predictable transactions is required. Revolving credit lines

---

Kangaroo National Bank Ltd
Level 35, Koala Tower
200 Wallaby Street
Perth, Western Australia 6000

Wool World Pty Ltd
234 Sheep Neck Road
South Perth 6151
Western Australia

Our ref: XYZ3334442
Date: December 1, 2016

Dear Sirs:

We have been requested by Dragon Bank Ltd, Singapore, to advise you that they have opened with us their irrevocable letter of credit number ABC5550391 on behalf of CoatsRUs Pte Ltd, 1 Jurong Hill, Singapore 628920 in your favor not to exceed the amount of One Hundred Thousand US Dollars (US$100,000.00). Payment is available by your draft(s) drawn on us at ninety (90) days from sight for full invoice value against presentation of the following documents:

1. Signed commercial invoice in one (1) original and two (2) copies showing the buyer's purchase order number 3992994 dated November 20, 2016.

2. Full set 3/3 ocean bill of lading, plus one (1) non-negotiable copy, consigned to order of Dragon Bank Ltd, Singapore, notify the applicant and marked "freight collect."

3. Packing list in three (3) copies.

4. Insurance policy in duplicate for 110% of invoice value covering all risks.

5. Inspection certificate in one (1) original and two (2) copies issued by Hawk Ltd

that cover: 8,000 kg Halfbred Ewe & Wether Cast Light Arable Fleece Wool
              grade number 346

Shipment from Perth, Australia to Jurong Port, Singapore
Partial shipment: not permitted
Transshipment: not permitted

All charges outside of Singapore are on applicant's account.

Documents must be presented for payment within ten (10) days after the date of shipment.

We confirm this credit and undertake that all drafts drawn under and in compliance with the terms of this credit will be duly honored upon delivery of documents as specified, if presented on or before January 8, 2017.

Yours faithfully,

(signature)

Figure 10-8 Example of an L/C

enable customers to overdraw their current accounts in variable amounts and at variable times, up to a predefined limit.

To help ensure repayment of working capital loans, banks may place liens on customers' equipment, raw materials, inventory, or accounts receivable. Use of trade-related credit reduces the overall credit that a customer has available with his or her bank; likewise, use of other lines of credit will reduce the credit available for trade finance. In some cases, a bank may only provide trade finance credit facilities on condition that the customer obtains export credit insurance to protect against the risk of nonpayment by the importer.

10.2.4.2 Term bill discounting

Where L/Cs are used to secure trade payments, they can also be structured so that they can provide finance facilities. Such financing is possible after the exporter has shipped the goods and presented the trade documents to the bank, and the importer has accepted a bill of exchange against the L/C. A negotiable bill of exchange that is payable only after a fixed period of time, that is, term bill, represents a security that can be sold at a discount to raise funds immediately. The discount factor will be based on the time to maturity, reference interest rates, and the credit rating of the bank that provides the payment obligation. Because payment of term bills linked to L/Cs are drawn against the exporter's bank, rather than the exporter, they carry considerably less credit risk and, thus, are attractive for third parties to purchase as money market instruments.

Discounting of term bills can be an attractive option for exporters who would like to offer trade credit to their customers but have difficulty in obtaining bank loans to do so. This financing arrangement provides benefits for both the importer and exporter. The importer receives a period of trade credit that allows it to generate proceeds from its purchase before making payment to the exporter. Likewise, the exporter receives immediate payment. However, the discounting factor, costs related to securing the L/C, and other processing fees will all weigh on the profitability of the trade transaction. These costs must be factored into the commercial transaction to determine if sufficient profit will be generated.

10.2.4.3 Export factoring

Export factoring is another form of trade finance that can be used by exporters who have difficulty securing bank lines of credit, such as small and medium enterprises. Under a factoring arrangement, a factor pays cash for the legal right to receive payments associated with the exporters' invoices or accounts receivable. In return, the factor pays a portion of the invoice amounts to the exporter in advance of receiving payments from the importer. Hence, there is no need for the exporter to obtain an L/C or sell a bill of exchange. When the factoring is without recourse, the factor assumes the risk that the importer does not pay. Thus, a factoring arrangement can both improve the exporter's cash flow and reduce its counterparty credit risk. Factoring without recourse also does not require debt to be added to the exporter's balance sheet.

The amount paid for short-term foreign accounts receivable, that is, less than 180 days, is the face value of the amounts due, less a discount. The amount of the discount will depend on prevailing interest rates, the amount advanced, the date that the receivable is due, and also the likelihood of nonpayment by the importer. Typically, the factor will only advance a certain percentage of the discounted amount upfront, and hold the remainder until the payment is received from the importer. Because the risk in factoring is dependent on the importers' creditworthiness rather than the exporter's creditworthiness, it can be an important option for exporters that cannot obtain other forms of bank lending credit. Some banks and other nonbank finance companies provide export-factoring services.

An export-factoring agreement between an exporter and an export factor will typically also involve an import factor, which acts as a correspondent in the importer's home country. Before the export factor agrees to purchase invoices or accounts receivable from the exporter, the import factor will investigate the credit of the importer. The outcome of this investigation will determine the viability of factoring and its cost to the exporter. As part of the factoring agreement, once the exporter has shipped the goods, it will assign the export factor as the payee of the invoice and in exchange for a cash advance on the invoice amount. The export factor then passes the invoice to the import factor, which collects locally from the importer and forwards the proceeds, less the import factor's fees, to the export factor. Next, the export factor will deliver the amount collected—less the advance paid, the interest charges, and fees—to the exporter.

10.3   BUSINESS OPPORTUNITIES

Trade finance can be improved greatly by standardization. The International Chamber of Commerce (ICC) has drawn up a common set of rules for trade finance that are used by most international banks. The ICC's Uniform Rules for Collection govern documentary collections, and the Uniform Customs and Practice (UCP) for Documentary Credits govern documentary credits. Yet, as discussed in Section 10.4, lack of standardization of financial and trade documents makes processing L/Cs very labor intensive. For example, the wording and structure of L/Cs may vary from bank to bank, bills of lading vary from country to country, and invoices vary by suppliers.

There have been ongoing attempts to standardize and automate the processing of trade. Although hosted multibank, multicorporate Internet portals, such as Bolero, have been developed to streamline trade document processing, they have met with limited success. Differences in legal frameworks from country to country have made standardization efforts difficult. SWIFT has made significant progress in standardizing and automating trade finance-related communications between participants. For instance, the SWIFT MT700 series messages are commonly used to facilitate electronic processing of L/Cs. However, even when SWIFT is used, physical delivery of supporting trade documentation is still required.

Another potential area for growth is in transitioning customers from using documentary collections and L/Cs to open accounts (Case Study 10-2). Open account arrangements enable the importer's bank to directly pay into the exporter's bank account, thereby eliminating the need for the exporter's bank to participate in the trade transaction, as is required with L/Cs. Likewise, the exporter does not need to have a credit line with its bank. Eliminating intermediation by the exporter's bank reduces transaction costs and processing delays, and improves cash flow for both the importer and the exporter.

Open account arrangements are well suited for large corporations that import from a large number of exporters to support their supply chain. The large number of suppliers and transactions makes it cumbersome and costly to issue L/Cs for each and every transaction. From a bank's perspective, as importers, these large corporates are often cash-rich and have strong credit. Hence, the bank can help transition from L/Cs to open accounts by providing a blanket guarantee of payment to exporters. If the importer accepts the documents, the bank will guarantee the invoice payment. Likewise, standardization of and support for electronic delivery and matching of invoices, as provided by SWIFT's Trade Services Utility, can also streamline and automate open account processes.

Moreover, banks that have large trade finance operations have the opportunity to provide white-labeled trade finance services to banks that have smaller operations. As part of a **white-labeling** arrangement, as discussed in Chapter 4, the smaller institution would outsource its trade services delivery to a larger institution. However, the smaller institution would still brand trade services as its own, and customers would generally be unaware of the outsourcing arrangement.

Despite the advantages that open account arrangements provide, the **Global Financial Crisis** of 2008 recreated demand for the security that L/Cs provide to trading partners. Hence, there is renewed interest in promoting documentary collections and L/Cs. However, because of the inherent challenges in providing trade finance services, as discussed in the next section, banks providing these services benefit from economies of scale. Accordingly, white labeling can make sense for banks, both large and small.

Fintech companies have also begun providing solutions related to receivables and supply chain financing. Using online platforms, they have streamlined interactions with customers and enabled them to gain access to financing more quickly and from a broader range of sources. Automation and low transaction overhead are essential for providing services to smaller businesses, which are often underserved by banks.

Moreover, there are also opportunities to leverage emerging technologies such as distributed ledgers, i.e., blockchain, and smart contracts (discussed further in Chapter 20). Distributed ledger technology has the potential to reduce duplicate fraud, record and verify ownership of assets and goods, and improve the operational efficiency of trade finance transactions. Smart contracts could be used to automate the execution of transactions. For example, a smart contract could be designed to automatically release a payment to an exporter immediately upon verification that the goods have been delivered. Not surprisingly, a number of banks and Fintech startups have been testing and developing proof-of-concept IT solutions that demonstrate the application of these technologies in the context of trade finance.

Case Study 10-2

Bridging the Way from Letters of Credit to Open Accounts

Linking supply chain management with finance and payment activities can significantly reduce costs and improve business visibility. Integrated trade finance solutions can enable corporations to better forecast and optimize the management of working capital. The transition from L/Cs and documentary collections to open account terms could make achieving these benefits more important, and vice versa. Seeking to capitalize on this opportunity, SWIFT launched its Trade Services Utility (TSU) in 2007 to help banks automate open account trade processing. The goal of TSU is to help banks and their corporate customers lower costs by automating payables and receivables management.

TSU enables banks to exchange and match standardized trade document information with other banks. Information is extracted from trade documents and shared using SWIFT's messaging infrastructure. TSU also provides a matching engine that automatically compares purchase order, invoice, transport documentation, and certification information. This automated matching reduces the time required to process payments and identifies discrepancies at an early stage of processing, thus, helping to avoid payment delays. Furthermore, banks can use matched transactions to initiate payments or offer financing to importers and exporters.

Unlike other portal-based solutions, TSU does not extend its reach to end customers. Rather, it provides a backbone for bank-to-bank services and leaves it to the banks to provide channel connectivity and supply chain-related financial services to their customers. Hence, each bank can implement its own method for transferring trade information to and from its customers and apply its own processes for managing trade information discrepancies. With TSU, many of the processes required for L/Cs that are related to document creation and auditing can be avoided.

Moreover, TSU seeks to provide a standard set of rules governing open account arrangements that can be adopted by market participants, much like the UCP provides a set of standard market practices for L/Cs. As part of these rules, SWIFT has introduced a Bank Payment Obligation (BPO) function. A BPO states that when TSU matches an importer and an exporter's electronic documents, the importer's bank provides a payment guarantee to the exporter's bank for the underlying transaction. This facility can help reduce the risks banks face when offering pre- and post-shipment finance, serving a function similar to an L/C.

There is great potential for TSU in Asia, where L/Cs are prevalent. In 2009, the Bank of China and the Bank of Tokyo Mitsubishi UFJ agreed to create a direct bank-to-bank connection through SWIFT's trade services utility. However, as of 2010, TSU trade volumes in Asia were light. Banks faced difficulties getting their customers to understand the benefits of using TSU. Nonetheless, new opportunities have emerged for TSU. Within China, TSU BPO service agreements may be positioned to supplant domestic L/Cs. The vast majority of domestic L/Cs are for intrabank transactions, and more than half of them are paper-based transactions. Thus, banks in China may be able to unilaterally adopt TSU and still achieve significant gains by automating their internal processes.

Sources: Broens, Herbert, "Standardized Confirmation of Receivables TSU," *Business Credit* 112, issue 8 (September/October 2010): 48; Conn, Christopher A., Julie Hazen, and George Hoffman, "Shift from Letters of Credit to Open Account Using Electronic Supply Chain Management Tools," *AFP Annual Conference 2009*, http://www.afponline.org/pub/conf/2009/sessions/ed_global_html.html; Russell, Edward, "Swift Pushes to Commercialise Trade Services," *Finance Asia*, May 11, 2010, http://www.financeasia.com/News/173439,swift-pushes-to-commercialise-trade-services.aspx; "Enhancing Domestic Trade with the BPO," *Trade Finance* 13 (October 2010): 77.

10.4   BUSINESS CHALLENGES

As discussed in the previous section, standardization of the rules that govern trade finance and electronic delivery of trade documents has greatly helped improve the efficiency of trade finance. Even so, processing L/Cs can still be very manual, requiring specialized skills and expertise. While electronic formatting helps to separate and tag key information such as the expiration date, amount, and applicant in the L/C, much of the information is maintained in free-form text. As shown in Figure 10-9, critical information such as the documents required (field 46A), additional conditions (47A), and payment instructions (78) can be specified uniquely in each and every L/C. Also, because some countries do not recognize electronic transactions, supporting paper copies must still be maintained.

To provide trade finance services, banks must employ people who are well versed in trade documentation and can understand and interpret the content of L/Cs and trade documentation. These specialists must carefully read the terms and conditions of L/Cs and verify importers' compliance. To avoid monetary losses, this detail-oriented and labor-intensive process must be executed flawlessly. Human errors, such as overlooking a requirement in an L/C, may lead the bank to release funds in error, potentially resulting in financial loss for the bank.

Managing the credit and recovery risk is also critical when providing L/C services. The importer's bank must continually monitor and assess the importer's ability to fulfill its payment obligations. Also, in the case of nonpayment, the importer's bank may retain the goods, but the recovery rate can vary greatly depending on the type of goods. In particular, the value of perishable goods will decrease with time and may be impacted by shipment delays. Liquidation of nonperishable goods will incur storage and transportation costs and may not find ready demand, leading to sales at greatly discounted prices.

Fraud has also been a persistent problem in trade finance. Forged L/Cs may be fraudulently presented to banks, for example, falsely stating that they have been issued by a particular bank along with either legitimate or fraudulent trade documentation. Loss due to fraudulent L/Cs can be avoided by verifying the authenticity of the L/C with the drawee, that is, the bank having the payment obligation, referenced in the L/C. There is also a risk that the L/C is legitimate, but the importer and exporter have colluded to provide forged or falsified trade documents. To avoid this concern, banks may require unknown or untrustworthy parties to deposit the full amount of the L/C for the bank to facilitate the transaction, rather than providing credit terms.

10.5   LETTER OF CREDIT LIFECYCLE

In this section, we will use the six-stage transaction lifecycle framework shown in Figure 10-10 to discuss the activities banks engage in when processing L/C transactions. The descriptions are generalized, and in practice will vary by country, institution, and customer.

10.5.1   Design and Setup

To begin with, the types of L/Cs that will be offered to customers must be defined, along with the variations that will be supported within each type. The forms of customer communication that will be provided and SWIFT message types that will be used must be configured and connected with relevant customer communication channels.

Fee structures must also be established. Processing costs will need to be estimated to determine fee structures, as shown in Table 10-2. Fees for services provided to importers (for example, opening of the L/C) and exporters (for example, advising of the L/C) must be defined. Also, general fees related to handling of documents must be communicated to customers and incorporated into the information technology (IT) systems that calculate and debit fee amounts.

{1:F01ABCBUS33AXXX3728156193}	*header information*
{2:O3001139050822XYZBUS33AFXO29169650200508221139N}	
{3:{108:FC003405ded7970a}}	
{4:	
:27:1/1	*seq number / of total*
:40a:IRREVOCABLE	*type of credit*
:20:XYZ3334442	*reference number*
:31C:161201	*issue date*
31D:170108	*expiry date and location*
:50:COATSRUS PTE LTD, 1 JURONG HILL, SINGAPORE	*applicant*
628920	
:59: WOOL WORLD PTY LTD, 234 SHEEP NECK ROAD SOUTH	*beneficiary*
PERTH 6151, WESTERN AUSTRALIA	
:32B:USD100000, 00	*currency and amount*
:39B:NOT EXCEEDING	*maximum credit amount*
:41A:ANY BANK BY NEGOTIATION	*payable by*
:42C:90 DAYS SIGHT FOR 100 PCT INVOICE	*when payable*
:42A: DRAGON BANK LTD, 30 ROBINSON ROAD, DRAGON BANK	*drawee — importer's bank*
TOWER, SINGAPORE 048882, REPUBLIC OF SINGAPORE	
:43P:PROHIBITED	*partial shipments*
:43T:PROHIBITED	*transshipment*
:44A:PERTH, AUSTRALIA	*from port*
:44B/JURONG PORT, SINGAPORE	*to port*
:45A:8, 000KG HALFBRED EWE & WETHER CAST LIGHT	*description of goods*
ARABLE FLEECE WOOL GRADE NUMBER 346	
:46A:+SIGNED COMMERCIAL INVOICE IN ONE (1) ORIGINAL	*documents required*
TWO (2) COPIES SHOWING THE BUYER'S PURCHASE ORDER	
NUMBER 3992994 DATED 20 NOVEMBER 2016.	
+FULL SET 3/3 OCEAN BILL OF LADING, PLUS ONE (1)	
NON-NEGOTIABLE COPY, CONSIGNED TO ORDER OF DRAGON	
BANK LTD, SINGAPORE, NOTIFY THE APPLICANT AND	
MARKED "FREIGHT COLLECT".	
+PACKING LIST IN THREE (3) COPIES.	
+INSURANCE POLICY IN DUPLICATE FOR 110% OF INVOICE	
VALUE COVERING ALL RISKS.	
+INSPECTION CERTIFICATE IN ONE (1) ORIGINAL AND TWO	
(2) COPIES ISSUED BY HAWK LTD	
:47A: THIS CREDIT IS SUBJECT TO THE ICC UCP600.	
:48: DOCUMENTS MUST BE PRESENTED FOR PAYMENT WITHIN	*additional conditions*
TEN (10) DAYS AFTER THE DATE OF SHIPMENT.	*presentation period*
:49: WITH	*confirmation requirement*
71B: ALL CHARGES OUTSIDE OF SINGAPORE ARE ON	*charges*
APPLICANT'S ACCOUNT.	
:78: ALL REQUIRED DOCUMENTS ARE TO BE SENT TO	*instructions to pay*
DRAGON BANK LTD, 30 ROBINSON ROAD, DRAGON BANK	
TOWER, SINGAPORE 048882, REPUBLIC OF SINGAPORE, IN	
ONE SET, VIA COURIER CONFIRMING THAT ALL TERMS AND	
CONDITIONS HAVE BEEN COMPLIED WITH.	
}	
{5:{CHK:97BE21F29A78}}	*checksum*

Figure 10-9 Example of an L/C sent as a SWIFT MT700 message

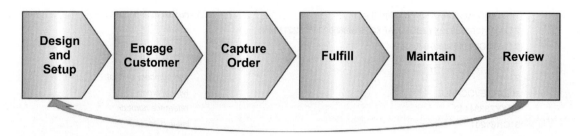

Figure 10-10 Banking transaction lifecycle model

Table 10-2 Types of fees paid by importer for an L/C

Fee Type	Fee Structure
Opening fee	1. Percentage of credit amount, with minimum fee limits (e.g., 0.2% of first $100 and 0.1% on the remaining balance, with minimum fee of $50) 2. Extra fees may be charged for lengthy or complex instructions (for example, $20 for each page over 3 pages)
Amendment charge	1. For increase in the L/C amount or significant extension in validity, fees may be identical to those for opening an L/C 2. Other amendments at a fixed amount (e.g., $25)
Cancellation	Fixed amount (e.g., $25)
Cable charges	Fixed amount per message (e.g., $10 for opening and each amendment)
Postage charges	Fixed amount or variable amounts depending on delivery mechanism (e.g., $5 for airmail and variable rates for courier delivery)

Application forms for L/Cs must also be created to capture transaction details both on paper and electronically. Application forms should make it easy for customers to use standard terms and conditions by providing check boxes and fill-in-the-blank values where possible. Likewise, standard templates that contain bank-specific L/C terms and conditions must be created along with placeholders for customer- and transaction-specific details. The L/C templates can either be stored in a core banking or dedicated trade finance IT system or in word processing files, depending on the capabilities of the IT system used.

10.5.2 Engage Customer

Before L/C services are offered to customers, **antimoney laundering**-oriented know your customer (KYC) checks must first be performed. Additionally, the corresponding bank must be vetted to ensure that it is not associated with political corruption or illicit activities. It is not necessary, though, for the importer's bank to check the credentials of the beneficiary of the L/C, that is, the exporter, because the exporter's bank bears this responsibility.

Applicants for L/Cs are usually existing customers and, thus, credit limits should have already been established. However, in some cases, banks may issue one-time L/Cs on behalf of importers who are not regular customers. In such cases, deposits must be secured in lieu of a credit line to cover the bank's risk exposure for providing the L/C.

10.5.3 Capture Order

Applications for L/Cs may be received in paper or electronic form. The application will typically capture the following details that are to be included in the L/C:

- beneficiary name and address

- applicant name and address

- currency and amount

- expiry date

- delivery mode: registered mail, courier, or SWIFT/Telex

- payable on sight or for term and term length

- documents required, for example, commercial invoice, clean bill of lading made out in importer bank's name, insurance policy

- delivery location

- loading port

- discharge port

- latest acceptable shipment or delivery date

Besides the KYC checks involved with on-boarding customers, additional checks must be performed when an application is received. For instance, the bank must verify that the port of delivery and the transit ports are not in countries that have been blacklisted, for example, on the US Treasury Department Office of Foreign Assets Control's (OFAC) sanction list. Also, the bank must verify that there are no government prohibitions against the goods being shipped, for example, that they are not black-market weapons shipments. Likewise, if the exporter is not already a customer, the correspondent bank that advises the exporter of the L/C must perform KYC checks on the exporter.

10.5.4 Fulfill Transaction

The fulfillment process for L/Cs typically spans 90 to 180 days. As shown in Figure 10-11, L/C fulfillment consists of four stages. To begin with, opening an L/C involves the importer's bank accepting the importer's application and issuing the L/C to the exporter's bank. The exporter's bank then advises the exporter of the L/C.

After the L/C has been opened, the importer may choose to apply for one or more amendments to the L/C. For example, delays in production or shipping may require the terms and dates of the L/C to be changed. With the exporter's agreement, the importer could extend the expiry or latest shipping date, adjust the amount of the L/C, modify the trade documentation requirements, or change beneficiary's details.

Receipt and verification of the trade documents will then trigger the importer's bank to make payments according to the instructions in the L/C. When all the required payments have been remitted to the exporter and all documents have been delivered to the importer, the L/C can be closed. After the L/C is closed, it will no longer affect the importer's credit line. Section 10.6 will further examine how banks verify trade documentation as part of the fulfillment process.

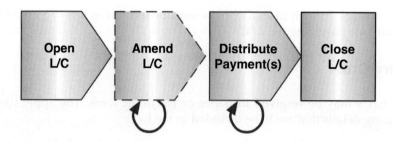

Figure 10-11 L/C high-level fulfillment activities

10.5.5 Maintain Transaction

Periodically reviewing customers' credit lines is the primary maintenance activity required for L/Cs. Credit limit reviews may occur on an annual basis for financially stable customers, and on a more frequent basis for less mature companies or those that are experiencing financial stress.

10.5.6 Review

Review activities include evaluation of the profitability of the L/C products offered to customers. The revenue achieved from fees, commission, interest float, and securitization of L/Cs will be assessed and compared with the operational costs of running the business. Banks may also analyze which customers would benefit from other trade services that the bank offers, such as working capital financing that support open account trade arrangements.

10.6 LIFECYCLE FOCUS: TRANSACTION FULFILLMENT

When banks process L/Cs, effective verification of trade documentation is crucial. On the one hand, a bank may erroneously delay payment to the exporter leading to a penalty interest claim by the beneficiary. On the other hand, if the bank erroneously makes payment before all the terms of the L/C have been fulfilled, it may not be reimbursed, leading to financial loss. L/C processing mistakes may also cause reputational damage and subsequent loss of business. Accordingly, banks must ensure that trade-related documents are carefully examined [2].

First and foremost, banks must ensure that an L/C includes reference to a current version of the UCP for Documentary Credits, that is, currently UCP 600, and is compliant with that set of rules. Other typical documentation checks for L/Cs include verifying the following:

- that the documents presented relate to the L/C;

- that documentation was presented before the expiry date;

- original L/C and amendment documents, if required;

- endorsements, transfers, or assignments; and

- that the documents are in compliance with accepted amendments.

Internal procedures must be established and implemented consistently to ensure that all relevant documents are examined thoroughly. A best practice is to use checklists or workflow tools that determine the order in which documents will be examined, provide standard wordings, and look for common discrepancies. Besides checking for document completeness, it is also necessary to verify that the trade documents are consistent with one another. Both the importer's and exporter's banks must perform their own set of detailed checks; they should not assume that the other bank's checks are sufficient. Identifying discrepancies earlier, rather than later, will minimize the amount of rework that is required by all parties.

Documentation received by the importer's bank must be reviewed within a reasonable timeframe after receipt, usually not more than seven working days. If the trade documents are found to be compliant with the L/C terms within this period, the importer's bank will accept the documents and make payment to the exporter's bank. Alternatively, if the documents are not compliant, the importer's bank may pursue one of two options. If the documents appear to be compliant in principle, but not in letter, the bank may contact the exporter to seek a waiver. Otherwise, the importer's bank may refuse the documents and inform the presenting party that they have not been found to be in compliance with the L/C. The full set of procedures for dealing with document discrepancies and waivers are defined in UCP 600 Articles 13 & 14.

10.7 ARCHITECTURE CONSIDERATIONS: GEOGRAPHIC DISTRIBUTION

L/C processing is complicated by the logistics involved in handling and processing physical documents. L/C processing may be decentralized or centralized. With fully decentralized processing, L/C applications and documentation are processed at the location where they are received, either at the branches or local service centers. This minimizes unnecessary transport time and routing of the documents prior to processing. However, this approach is not efficient from a resource perspective. Each location must have at least one bank officer—or more likely, two for process resilience—who has been trained for and is capable of performing all the required checks. Decentralized processing also makes it difficult to optimize resource utilization because the L/C processors in one location may be underutilized some of the time and overloaded at other times. Work cannot easily be shared between processors in different locations.

On the other hand, when processing is fully centralized, the workload can be efficiently distributed among all available resources but logistical delays will likely be encountered. Time is required to aggregate and transport trade documentation within or between countries to a centralized processing center. In the extreme case, a multinational bank might have a single processing center in just one country and ship trade documents from exporters around the world to that location for processing and then back out again to the importers' banks. For instance, a European bank that issued an L/C for a commercial transaction between an importer in Singapore and an exporter in China might route the trade documents from China to Germany for processing and then to Singapore. Hence, the goods shipment might arrive in Singapore before the paperwork was delivered from Germany.

In practice, hybrid strategies are used to process L/C documentation. Multiple regional processing centers, ideally in low-cost locations, may be used to improve economies of scale and reduce processing costs. Also, instead of waiting for the physical documents to arrive at central processing centers, electronic copies that are scanned at the location where they are received can be transmitted more quickly to regional centers and be used to begin processing. Ideally, common scanning and **business process management (BPM)** platforms, as discussed in Chapter 2, can be used to manage the capture and routing of trade finance documents as well as paperwork that is required for other types of bank transactions, such as loan and TT application forms. At the central processing center, trade finance-specific workflows would be triggered when the scanned images are captured, and the workflows would interact with application functions provided by the bank's trade finance IT system. Depending on the scale of their operations, banks may either use trade finance functionality that is included in its core banking system, or use an IT system that has been designed specifically for trade finance. Banks that have relatively small trade finance operations may choose to use their core banking system's capabilities to avoid the additional complexity and integration required to use a separate system. However, the functionality available will be more limited. For example, a core banking system might not provide facilities for creating and managing L/C templates for individual customers, requiring L/C customization to be performed manually outside of the core banking system.

Alternatively, using a separate trade finance IT system can help streamline operations by providing workflows and administration capabilities that have been designed specifically for trade finance. In this case, manual processing can be minimized, but extensive integration will be required with other bank systems, as shown in Figure 10-12. The procurement and maintenance of a separate trade finance system and integrating it with other relevant IT systems would only be cost effective in cases when large volumes of transactions are being processed. **Business process management systems (BPMS)** can also be leveraged to help manage and track manual processing of exception cases that are not catered for by the trade finance system. For instance, processing an L/C transaction that triggers a credit limit breach may require special approval outside of the bank's trade finance business unit.

The deployment of trade finance IT systems may also be geographically centralized or distributed both logically and physically. Common configurations include the following:

- **Fully centralized**. A single trade finance IT system instance, most likely physically located at the bank's headquarters, processes the trade finance transactions for all of the bank's international operations. Country-specific business rules and workflows are configured within the trade finance IT system.

- **Centralized multi-instance**. Multiple instances of the trade finance IT system are run in parallel, one for each country served (or possibly for a small group of countries). Each IT system instance is configured to match the specific requirements of the countries that it serves. All of the application instances are run in one physical location, usually at the bank's headquarters.

- **Distributed multi-instance**. Multiple instances of the trade finance IT system are run in parallel, and each instance is physically located within the country that it serves. Each IT system instance is configured to match the specific requirements of the country that it serves.

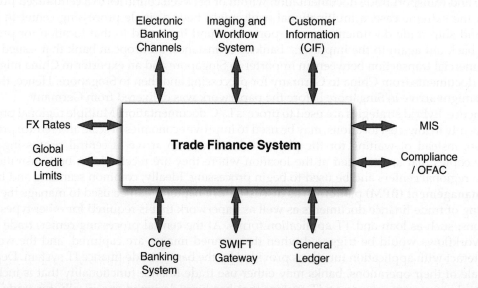

Figure 10-12 Trade finance system integration

A further level of complication can occur with the multi-instance cases. The instances may all be based on the same IT software application or may use different applications. It is generally preferable to have all the instances use a common application to simplify management and reduce maintenance costs. However, as a result of mergers and acquisitions, banks sometimes end up with different types of software applications providing similar or identical services in multiple locations. However, even when the same software application is used, the particular software versions being run may vary and some application instances may have special customizations that make them distinct from the rest.

10.8 SUMMARY

This chapter covered:

- the key participants and flows in trade finance transactions;
- the business processes that underlie L/C transactions;
- the opportunities and challenges associated with providing trade finance services;
- the service lifecycle activities that support L/C transactions; and
- centralized and distributed processing strategies and trade-offs.

The next chapter discusses how banks support corporate customers' treasury needs by providing financial products related to foreign exchange.

FURTHER READING

Books

De Roover, R., *Rise and Decline of the Medici Bank, 1397–1494* (Massachusetts: Harvard University Press, 1999).

Kouladis, N., *Principles of Law Relating to International Trade* (New York: Springer, 2006).

Wechsberg, J., *The Merchant Bankers* (New York: Pocket Books, 1968).

Papers

Bergami, R., "Risk Management in Australian Manufacturing Exports: The Case of Letters of Credit to ASEAN," PhD dissertation, Victoria University Melbourne, Australia, March 2011.

Herath, G., "Supply-chain Finance: The Emergence of a New Competitive Landscape," *McKinsey on Payments*, October 2015.

Klapper, L., "The Role of Factoring for Financing Small and Medium Enterprises," *Journal of Banking & Finance* 30 (2006): 3111–3130.

Mullineux, A. W. and V. Murinde, "Settlement and Finance of International Trade," in *Handbook of International Banking*, pp. 259–282 (Gloucestershire: Edward Elgar Publishing, 2003).

"Why Discrepancies?" *Trade & Forfaiting Review*, April 29, 2004, http://www.tfreview.com/feature/deals/why-discrepancies.

Vance, D. E., "Asset Based Lenders and Factors," in *Raising Capital*, pp. 69–88 (New York: Springer, 2005).

Zheng, Q., S. Li, Y. Han, J. Dong, L. Yan, and J. Qin, "E-commerce and International Trade," in *Introduction to E-commerce*, ed. Q. Zheng, pp. 375–408 (New York: Springer, 2009).

Web

Bank of Nova Scotia, *Documentary Letters of Credit—A Practical Guide*, http://www.scotiabank.com/images/en/filesbusiness/1180.pdf.

Barclays, "Corporate Trade Tutorial," http://www.business.barclays.co.uk/BRC1/jsp/brccontrol?task=channelgroup&site=bbb&value=3387&menu=2875.

International Chamber of Commerce, "2017 Rethinking Trade & Finance," https://iccwbo.org/publication/2017-rethinking-trade-finance/.

International Trade Administration, *Trade Finance Guide: A Quick Reference for US Exporters*, 2008, http://trade.gov/media/publications/abstract/trade_finance_guide2008desc.html.

SWIFT for Corporates, "Standards MT Message Implementation Guidelines, Trade Standards Extract," http://www.swift.com/solutions/factsheet_downloads/SWIFT_Trade_Extract_Standards_Messages_Implementation_Guidelines_200811.pdf.

Toronto Dominion, *A Guide to Letters of Credit*, http://www.tdsecurities.com/tds/pdfs/TDS3.3.6.1PDF1.pdf.

US Treasury Department, "OFAC Sanctions Programs Listing," http://www.treasury.gov/resource-center/sanctions/Programs/Pages/Programs.aspx.

ENDNOTES

1. Burton, M., "Metals Trading Has a Paper Fraud Problem," *Bloomberg*, July 3, 2017, https://www.bloomberg.com/news/articles/2017-07-03/paper-trail-on-metal-loans-ended-in-fakes-as-banks-lose-millions.

2. Citigroup Global Transaction Services, "The Art and Science of Letter of Credit Document Examination," presentation, 2006, http://www.citigroup.com/transactionservices/home/trade_svcs/trade_u/docs/eng_master.pdf?lid=artsciengpdf.

— — —

3. Watson, A., *Finance of International Trade*, 6th ed. (New York: Hyperion Books, 1998).

4. Hume, N., "Qingdao Fraud Case Taints Commodity Financing," *Financial Times*, December 19, 2014, https://www.ft.com/content/b3cc4dc4-86ba-11e4-9c2d-00144feabdc0.

5. Perez, B., "Hong Kong's Monetary Authority Unveils Trade Finance Platform Based on Blockchain Technology," *South China Morning Post*, March 30, 2017, http://www.scmp.com/tech/innovation/article/2083536/hong-kongs-monetary-authority-unveils-trade-finance-platform-based.

6. Dab, S., Ramachandran, S., Chandna, R., Hanspal, R., Grealish, A., and Peeters, M., "Digital Revolution in Trade Finance," Boston Consulting Group, August 30, 2016, https://www.bcg.com/publications/2016/digital-revolution-trade-finance. "Applying Cryptotechnologies to Trade Finance," Euro Banking Association, *Version 1.0*, May 2016, https://www.abe-eba.eu/downloads/knowledge-and-research/EBA_May2016_eAPWG_Applying_cryptotechnologies_to_Trade_Finance.pdf "ICC Global Survey on Trade Finance 2016," International Chamber of Commerce, https://iccwbo.org/publication/icc-global-survey-trade-finance-2016/.

11 Treasury and Exchange

Equity markets typically garner the most media attention; however, foreign exchange (FX) markets are much larger by comparison and make up the largest segment of the financial markets. In April 2016, the Bank for International Settlements estimated the average daily turnover of the FX markets to be over five trillion dollars, many times the value that is traded on the world's stock exchanges. Behind this great difference in scale are the purposes that these markets serve. Equities and fixed-income instruments are issued by companies to raise capital and are purchased by investors to generate investment income. FX markets, on the other hand, are a byproduct of international trade. They support the purchase and sale of foreign goods and help companies manage their currency exposures. Globalization and free-trade initiatives have increased international trade. Consequently, FX has become an integral part of the banking and financial services markets. Raw materials may be sourced in countries such as Canada or Australia; products may be manufactured in Mexico or China and then sold to consumers in the United States or Europe. Besides the logistical challenges related to shipping the goods, there are also financial complications related to cross-currency payment obligations associated with such arrangements.

For international businesses, there is an ongoing need to deliver payments in foreign currencies. Buyers may amass holdings in foreign currencies when making or receiving payments. If these funds are maintained in the foreign currency, their value will fluctuate according to exchange rates. These fluctuations may result in realized or unrealized gains and losses. When currency prices are volatile, the financial risks involved can be substantial. If the foreign currency is to be converted into local currency, then an exchange agent or market must be available to buy and sell the relevant currencies.

Hence, there is an opportunity for banks to provide services that address these needs. One fundamental service that banks provide is multicurrency deposit accounts that enable customers to maintain their own currency reserves. Banks also serve as dealers and **market makers,** providing **liquidity** to end customers so that they can easily exchange currencies (Case Study 11-1). They also provide derivative products that help customers hedge the risks related to currency price fluctuations. Additionally, banks may offer FX management advisory services to customers.

Banks are in a unique position to provide these services because, collectively, they effectively constitute the FX marketplace. However, both business and technological advances are changing the landscape in which they operate. For instance, the rise of digital currencies (discussed in Chapter 7) has led to specialized exchanges that provide conversion services between digital currencies and sovereign currencies. For the most part, banks have chosen not to provide these types of services. Also, up and coming Fintech companies have begun providing FX money transfer services that compete head on with bank's services, leveraging new technology that enables them to charge significantly lower fees.

This chapter examines corporate treasury services provided by banks, with an emphasis on FX. First, different types of basic FX and money market transactions are discussed in the context of corporate and retail customers' business needs. Next, the opportunities, challenges, and fundamental processes involved with banks' FX trading operations are presented. Then, product lifecycle considerations are reviewed in relation to one type of treasury product, forward FX swaps, with special focus on how trade confirmations are managed. Finally, FX-related architecture and solution considerations are explored.

Case Study 11-1
The Evolution of FX Trading

Advances in technology have revolutionized how both sell-side financial institutions and their buy-side corporate customers trade FX. Up until the early 1990s, FX transactions were executed via phone conversations. Interbank trading would be executed by traders who would call one another to buy and sell large blocks of currencies, typically greater than US$5 million. Individual banks would specialize in providing liquidity for specific currency pairs. Corporate customers would call dealers at their bank to perform smaller-scale transactions, with the banks serving as intermediaries to the interbank market. Banks would effectively hold currency inventories that their customers could tap when required for currency conversions.

The first major advance that information technology enabled was to facilitate electronic conversations between interbank traders. Instead of making phone calls, chat sessions could be initiated using software and networks provided by solution vendors Reuters and EBS. By shifting the transaction conversations from phone to chat sessions, it was easier to spot miscommunications, capture an audit trail, and begin to automate the capture of transactional information. These electronic platforms also provided streaming indicative rate information that reduced the need for interbank traders to call one another to determine current market prices.

A further advance in the interbank market occurred when the interbank trading electronic chat facilities were enhanced so that bank traders could express interest in trading specific currency pairs, and the system would then match parties who had complementary interests. This enhancement eliminated the trial-and-error approach of trying to find the counterparty that would offer a good price for a trade. It was the first major step in creating an exchange-like environment, specifically for banks, for FX and money-market transactions.

By the mid-1990s, electronic trading became the dominant form of **interbank FX** and today, over 90% of interbank trading for major currency pairs is executed electronically.

The technology advances that improved banks' FX transaction capabilities were slower in reaching corporate customers and only began to enter the mainstream in the late 1990s. Initially, banks offered their own proprietary autodealing platforms, also referred to as single dealer platforms (SDPs), to customers. These systems quoted margin-adjusted rates to customers without requiring any human intervention. Customers could also execute transactions, based on the automatically quoted rates, and receive deal confirmations using the bank's autodealing platform. While corporate FX dealers were still involved in exceptional cases and were still contactable by phone, a large proportion of corporate FX transactions could be automated within the bank's environment, enabling **straight-through processing (STP)** to the bank's other systems. However, single dealer platforms only allowed customers to see rates available from the bank that provides the system. Thus, to compare different banks' rates electronically, customers needed to install and use multiple different SDPs.

Autodealing has continued to evolve, with much of the focus on expanding customers' access to multiple banks through a common FX trading platform. Individual banks, consortiums of banks, and independent solution providers have established multibank FX trading portals where numerous banks are able to offer liquidity, and corporate and institutional customers are able to trade on that liquidity. This arrangement has provided customers with more transparency with regard to market prices and easier access to trading facilities with multiple banking counterparties. It has also provided banks with a means of reaching more existing and potential customers without having to purchase or develop their own technology platforms.

Some parts of the FX market have also begun to adopt structures similar to the equity markets, where electronic commerce networks (ECNs) provide an order-driven market for FX trading.[*] ECNs enable banks to act like **agency brokers** that route customers' orders to be executed on an ECN and take responsibility for the clearing and **settlement** of the executed trades. Furthermore, banks may choose to either execute orders in the market that offset the transactions that they execute with customers or internalize the customers' orders and fill them from the banks' own in-house positions.[†]

The availability of electronic execution venues has also led to increased participation in the FX market by the professional trading community, including **hedge funds** and proprietary traders. These participants trade for profit and seek to take advantage of market inefficiencies. However, they add more liquidity and in some cases may serve as independent market makers. As of 2016, hedge funds and proprietary trading firms accounted for 8% of the foreign exchange market turnover. High-speed computer-driven algorithms are used for much of this trading, much like in the listed equity and exchange traded derivatives markets.

Sources: Gallaugher, John and Nigel Melville, "Electronic Frontiers in Foreign Exchange Trading," *Communications of the ACM* 47, issue 8 (2004): 81–87; Barker, William, "The Global Foreign Exchange Market: Growth and Transformation," *Bank of Canada Review* (Autumn 2007): 3–12. Bank for International Settlements, "Triennial Central Bank Survey—Foreign Exchange Turnover in April 2016," September 2016, http://www.bis.org/publ/rpfx16.htm.

Questions

1. What are some of the benefits that can be realized from migrating from phone-based trading to electronic trading?
2. What challenges might have been faced with trying to get users to switch from phone-based conversations to electronic channels?
3. What advantages would autodealing solutions offer to corporate customers and banks? What disadvantages or threats might they lead to?
4. How might the advent of multibank FX portals affect banks' business strategies?
5. What are some of the technological and operational challenges that would need to be addressed to support the migration from phone dealing to autodealing?

---

[*] ECNs are discussed in more depth in Chapters 13 and 14, and order-driven markets are explained in Chapter 14.
[†] FX order internalization is explained in Chapter 15.

11.1   TREASURY INSTRUMENTS

Banks offer a variety of products that help customers manage their FX risk. This section discusses some of the more common and straightforward products. Details regarding the structure and pricing of FX instruments are well covered in many other texts and are, therefore, not included in this chapter. Readers who are interested in learning more about these financial products can refer to the Further Reading section at the end of the chapter. FX spot will be discussed briefly, and FX forward and forward FX swap products will receive more emphasis. In particular, forward FX swaps are more complex and, thus, provide a more interesting basis for examination. But first, to round out the discussion on treasury instruments, money market products are briefly covered.

11.1.1 Money Market Instruments

One default option for generating returns on surplus cash is simply to have it in an interest-earning deposit account. However, other higher-yielding alternatives may be more beneficial. Higher account balances may be invested in money market instruments such as fixed deposits, certificates of deposit, short maturity bonds, treasury bills, commercial paper, and floating rate notes. Although money market instruments provide higher yields than bank accounts, they may not be as liquid and they require funds to be tied up for a longer period. They may also expose the depositor to additional risks such as counterparty **credit risk**, since unlike savings deposit accounts in some countries, money market instruments are not backed by any government guarantee.

11.1.2 Foreign Exchange Instruments

This section briefly reviews the basic types of FX products, including FX spot, FX forwards, and forward FX swaps. For all of these instruments, the settlement date, that is, the date when foreign currencies are actually exchanged, is also referred to as the value date. Alternatively, the trade date is the date on which the FX transaction is recorded as executed. Also, when trades are executed late in the day, after a specified cutoff time, the trade date will be recorded as the next business day.

11.1.2.1 FX spot

FX spot is the standard FX product for near-term trading of currencies. As shown in Figure 11-1, for most currency pairs, spot is defined for most currencies as transactions settled two days after the trade date (t + 2).* That is to say, a spot deal is transacted on the current business day, and then the currencies must be delivered and settled two business days later. It is important to note that weekends and public holidays, observed by the financial markets in the countries whose currencies are being traded, may

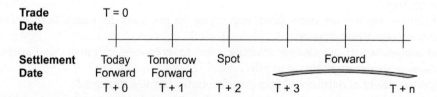

Figure 11-1 Settlement dates for FX spot and forward products

---

* The most notable exception being the US dollar traded against the Canadian dollar (USD/CAD), which has a settlement date of t + 1.

cause the value date to be more than two calendar days in the future. See Chapter 6 for the discussion on the complexities related to determining valid settlement dates for different currency pairs.

In the context of market rates, it is the spot price that is commonly quoted as the current FX price for trading purposes. The spot price also serves as the underlying basis for pricing forwards and forward FX swaps. FX spot trades do not go through an exchange; rather, they are bilateral agreements between parties to trade **"over-the-counter" (OTC) products**. OTC agreements between banks and customers or banks and other banks are legally binding agreements, but are subject to the risk that for some reason the counterparty may not settle the trade. This is a type of counterparty credit risk and is discussed more in Chapter 8.

11.1.2.2 FX forwards and futures

Forward FX contracts are OTC agreements to exchange currencies on a date other than the spot value date. Typically, forwards are used to lock in exchange rates for currency needs at some point further in the future, for example, two weeks, one month, or on a specific date. Forward contracts can also be used to transact earlier than the spot settlement date. As shown in Figure 11-1, a "today" forward will have the same value date as the trade date, and a "tomorrow" forward will have the value date t + 1.

As an example of how FX forward contracts are used, take the case where an importer has agreed to purchase raw materials from another country in a foreign currency, and the payment is due 60 days after the purchase. The purchaser may want to use a forward contract to lock in the current exchange rate to ensure that monetary loss is avoided due to shifts in the rate between the time the purchase is agreed upon and the time when the payment is due. In this case, the purchaser can obtain a forward FX contract for the transaction amount with a value date matching the intended payment date.

FX forward contacts are priced in terms of **forward points**, which is an adjustment amount that is applied to the spot rate to determine the pricing of the **forward rate**. For example, if the US dollar (USD)/Singapore dollar (SGD) spot rate was 1.3800 and the forward rate was calculated to be 1.3820, the forward would be quoted at a rate of 20 forward points. The forward rates are calculated based on the interest rate differential of the two currencies. Details on the theory and mechanics of this calculation can be found in the materials referenced in the Further Reading section at the end of this chapter.

Banks may advertise and distribute indicative rates to customers for fixed amounts on fixed time intervals for common currency pairs (for example, 50 **basis points** for three months on volume > US$500,000). However, because forwards have variable amounts and value dates, pricing for specific transactions are usually quote-driven. In other words, a customer would specify the deal parameters for the forward contract and the bank would then provide an FX rate quote. When quotes are provided electronically, they will be valid for only a short period of time, that is, seconds or minutes, depending on the volatility of the underlying currency pair. Alternatively, the quotes may be continuously updated, that is, streaming, so that they can be traded on at any time using the currently quoted price.

Another type of FX forwards is nondeliverable forwards (NDF). NDFs are cash settled, that is, only the amount of profit or loss is exchanged between the counterparties, and the **notional amounts** are never settled. On the fixing date for an NDF, the settlement amount for the contract is determined by the difference between a benchmark NDF rate and the spot rate. NDFs are popular for FX transactions involving countries that have FX controls, such as China and India, that inhibit forward FX trading. Because NDFs are cash settled for only the net gain or loss, rather than the full notional value of the contract, they are popular for trading on expected FX rate movements where FX speculation is restricted by local market regulations. It is estimated that speculative trading accounts for between 60% and 80% of NDF volume [1]. Not to be confused with FX forwards, FX futures are exchange-traded instruments. While futures and forwards achieve similar results, forwards can be customized to meet specific risk hedging needs and, hence, are more appropriate for most corporate customers. The fixed size and delivery dates that characterize FX futures make them unwieldy for using to offset the risk of specific foreign currency cash flows. Likewise, the daily ongoing cash flows associated with

Table 11-1 A comparison of FX forwards and futures

Characteristic	FX Forwards	FX Futures
Trading mechanism	Over the counter	Exchange traded
Contract terms	Variable amounts, variable delivery dates, wide range of currency pairs	Standardized contract size, fixed delivery/ expiry dates, limited currency pairs
Counterparty risk	With bank or customer	With exchange clearing house
Settlement cash flows	Notional amounts settled on value date	Cash settlement on contact expiry with daily margining
Revaluation	Based on quote from bank	Market-driven pricing

margining requirements for futures can significantly complicate cash management and accounting. Furthermore, where many banks offer FX forward products to their corporate customers as OTC products, FX futures often will need to be traded through a broker who is a **clearing member** of a futures exchange. Table 11-1 summarizes the differences between FX forwards and FX futures.

11.1.2.3 Forward FX swaps

A forward FX swap is used to exchange currencies for a fixed period of time at a predetermined rate. Typically, the near "leg" of the swap will be a spot trade or a near-dated forward. The "far" leg of the trade, which reverses the near-leg transaction, will be a longer-dated forward transaction. For instance, a forward FX swap could be structured as a conversion of US$1 million to Japanese yen (JPY) with a spot value date (t + 2) and then the conversion of the same amount back from JPY back to USD three months later. The price of the swap will be quoted as forward points and will be calculated based on the interest rate differentials between the swapped currencies.

Forward FX swaps are used for a variety of purposes, including funding, hedging, position management, and speculation. One important function of forward FX swaps is to allow corporate banking customers to exchange currencies temporarily without incurring the risk that the exchange rate of the currencies could move adversely leading up to the settlement date of the far leg of the swap. However, in the long term, it does not change their currency exposure. Forward FX swaps can also be used to neutralize the FX risk of borrowing in foreign currencies.

The following example illustrates how forward FX swaps can be used to hedge FX risk. A company may have an ample supply of its base currency, SGD, and may want to keep little or no USD. As part of its normal business, it may buy US$1 million worth of software payable immediately in USD, and then sell the software for US$1.1 million, to be received 60 days later in USD. One option would be for the company to do a spot transaction to convert SGD to USD to fund the purchase and another spot transaction two months later to convert back the payment received. In this case, it would be subject to risk of loss or gain due to FX movements over that two-month period. Alternatively, when the business transaction occurs, it could do the spot transaction covering the purchase and also a forward transaction covering the receivable. In effect, a forward FX swap is combining these two transactions into one operation for convenience.

Note that forward FX swaps are different from cross-currency interest-rate swaps (IRS). Their common shortened names of "FX swaps" and "currency swaps," respectively, can cause some confusion. Cross-currency IRS usually involve the periodic exchange of floating- and fixed-interest payments as a core part of the transaction. In contrast, forward FX swaps do not require periodic payments and have no cash flows directly associated with interest. IRS are discussed further in Chapter 12.

11.1.2.4 Other FX forward instruments

There are also country- and region-specific variations on standard FX forward instruments, especially in the Asia-Pacific region. Some examples of nonvanilla instruments are step-rate "option" forwards, prorata forwards, and historical rate rollovers. These instruments often represent ways of agreeing in advance on the pricing for early settlement of forwards or the costs of extending forwards for longer periods of time. Although such highly customized instruments can be convenient from the customers' standpoint, they can be problematic for banks, whose processes and systems must also be customized to handle these nonstandard instrument types.

11.2 CORPORATE BANKING CONTEXT

11.2.1 Corporate Treasury Investment

Besides managing working capital and liquidity to support business operations, a company's treasury function is also responsible for maximizing returns on working capital. Cash management facilities (discussed in Chapter 7), such as account sweeping, help ensure that cash balances are aggregated so that larger balances can be invested in the money market.

11.2.2 Corporate Treasury Risk Management

Risk management is another core function of corporate treasury. Corporations are intrinsically exposed to financial risk by transactional cash flows that are variable and may be dependent on external market factors. In certain industries, companies have significant exposures to commodity prices. For example, companies that provide or are heavily dependent on transportation are significantly impacted by changes in the price of oil. More common, however, is the situation where companies are exposed to price fluctuations of currencies due to cross-border transactions. Typically, corporate customers will use FX forwards to hedge against FX rate fluctuations that may affect their accounts payable and accounts receivable, that is, the payments that they are obligated to make and expect to receive in the future, respectively.

   The need to perform FX hedging is driven by the volatility of the currencies involved and the capacity of the company to absorb fluctuations. For example, in cases where the FX rate is fixed—as is the case with the Hong Kong dollar versus the USD—or has low volatility, there is little reason to hedge. On the other hand, for cases where there may be large, short-term swings in currency prices, as with the JPY versus the USD, hedging becomes much more relevant. For instance, in the year 2008, it was not uncommon for the JPY/USD exchange rate to fluctuate over 10% within a period of several weeks. More recently, the decision in 2016 by the United Kingdom to exit the European Union caused the British pound's value versus the US dollar to drop by more than 17%. Companies' abilities to absorb external market volatility will be largely driven by their profit **margins** on transactions and expectation about the volatility of their earnings. Consider first the impact of currency fluctuations in relation to profit margins. The impact of a 5% currency price movement will be more significant to a company that has a 3% profit margin on a transaction than to a company that has a 15% margin. In the former case, the currency movement may be greater than the profit itself and has the potential to result in a net loss on the transaction; thus, not to hedge in this case would be imprudent. In the latter case, a 5% swing in the FX rate could result in either a 10% or a 20% profit margin on the transaction; the decision to hedge will depend on management and shareholders' preference depending on whether to minimize earnings volatility or achieve higher average returns by avoiding hedging costs.

   Besides reducing the bottom-line impact of currency fluctuations, hedging helps ensure that a firm's core financial performance is not overshadowed by gains or losses driven by risk factors that could have been controlled. For example, a company whose operational profit margin is 12% may exceed its competitors' average of 10%. However, in a given year, FX losses may result in a total profit of 8%. In this case, the total annual profit would make the company's management appear to be underperforming in comparison to its competitors. However, this is not the case; the negative performance difference is due to bad luck in the currency markets, not poor business capability. In another year, the currency exposure effects may be just the opposite, resulting in overperformance in comparison to industry benchmarks or similar firms' performance.

It is important to understand that hedging of FX risk negates both potential losses as well as potential gains. If the assumption is made when there is an equal chance of currency movement in either direction and the volatility can be absorbed, over time the fluctuations in different directions may balance each other out. Since hedging involves costs, for example, bank fees and the spread between the buy and the sell price, avoiding hedging can sometimes be a reasonable course of action.

There are also some indirect alternatives to outright hedging, such as revenue currency **diversification** and cost-sales currency matching. If a company can balance the revenue it generates across a range of non- or inversely-correlated currencies, their price movements will help offset one another, thereby reducing the volatility of the valuation of firm's aggregate portfolio of foreign currency assets. Likewise, if related purchases and sales are executed in the same currencies, the exposure will be limited to the net difference between the actual buy and sell amounts rather than the notional transaction amounts. For example, if a Singapore-based company with a base currency in SGD buys raw materials from Thailand for US\$10 million and sells processed goods to Japan for US\$11 million, the exchange risk exposure between SGD and USD would only be the net difference of US\$1 million. Alternatively, if the goods were purchased in Thai baht (THB) and sold in JPY, the risk exposure would be to the gross THB/SGD and JPY/SGD amounts, thus increasing the risk exposure and hedging costs significantly.

11.3   RETAIL BANKING CONTEXT

FX conversion and hedging have less relevance in the retail banking context. The transaction amounts are significantly smaller, and the processing cost per transaction is proportionately higher. The four main areas where FX is relevant to retail customers are exchange of foreign-currency notes, conversion of foreign-currency payments, foreign-currency deposits, and speculative foreign-currency trading. The relative importance of these different offerings will depend on the country or region. For example, it is rare for retail banks to offer foreign-currency deposits in the United States, whereas it is quite common in Singapore and Hong Kong.

Some banks provide services to buy and sell specific currency notes, primarily to facilitate traveling to and spending in foreign countries. Such services are more difficult to manage than financial services that do not require physical delivery of currency notes. Logistical concerns include maintaining sufficient inventory in the currencies offered and avoiding counterfeit notes. Furthermore, the currency stock sold to customers must be from a current, easy-to-negotiate issue. For example, the Bank of England withdrew some of the older Series E pound sterling denominations in 2003. Foreign banks that held stocks of those notes and sold them to customers after their withdrawal dates were effectively providing currency that many UK-based businesses would not accept, which required the notes to be exchanged at a UK bank for the newer Revised Series E or Series F notes. Another example is, in 2016, the Indian government abruptly announced that in a matter of months, the 500-rupee note would no longer be legal tender.

Like corporate customers, retail customers may also make or receive payments in foreign currencies. In contrast to corporate customers, however, it is less likely that retail customers will have a foreign currency account to which such payments could be deposited to or withdrawn from. Hence, foreign currency payments will typically need to be converted to local currency when they are delivered to or transferred from a retail customer's account.

In some countries and regions, banks offer retail customers the ability to open savings and chequing accounts and time deposits in foreign currencies. Such accounts are often used as a way of hedging currency exposure, particularly where local currencies are highly volatile. For example, between 1998 and 2008, the Indonesian rupiah fluctuated between 7,000 and 14,000 to the USD. For Indonesians, holding savings in foreign currencies during this time would have helped reduce the impact of such fluctuations on the purchase of foreign goods and commodities that had prices that were more or less fixed in dollar terms.

Foreign-currency deposits can be used for speculative purposes as well. Customers may choose to put their savings in foreign currencies with the hope of obtaining higher interest rates or capital gains due to appreciation of the currency. This activity is similar in purpose to foreign-currency trading, which is also provided by some banks and brokerages to retail customers. In contrast to foreign-currency deposits, however, FX trading is typically leveraged and is oriented toward more frequent trading.

11.4 FOREIGN EXCHANGE PROCESSES AND SYSTEMS

This section discusses the participants, front office IT systems, and activities involved with booking customer FX transactions and managing FX-related risk. First, **voice dealing** and interbank trading processes are explained to provide historical context and introduce the basic concepts. Then, online interbank FX trading and online customer dealing are discussed. Fully automated risk management and interbank trading are explained in Chapter 15 in relation to FX trading internalization. The level of electronic trading and automation used will depend on the size of the bank, the geography it operates in, and its market positioning. Note that the voice dealing process described here is very similar to the processes that are still used to trade less liquid OTC derivative products.

Figure 11-2 shows the participants and IT systems involved in voice-based FX rate quoting and voice execution of FX transactions, commonly referred to as voice dealing, because the primary means

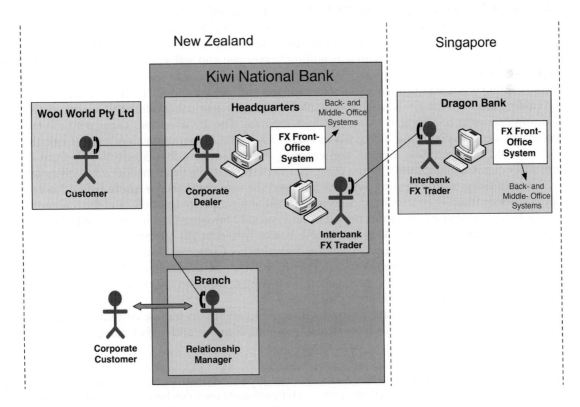

Figure 11-2 Phone-based FX transaction interactions

of communications is by telephone.* The customer is typically an individual who is responsible for managing treasury functions for a corporation. The bank's corporate dealer has a sales role and is responsible for quoting tradable rates and capturing the customer's order. A **relationship manager (RM)** may help capture customer orders at a bank branch. The FX front office system records the customer order details and calculates the bank's FX position, that is, the amount and value of different currencies that it holds, based on the sale and purchase of currencies by the bank and by customers. The interbank FX trader is responsible for monitoring and managing the bank's position in one or more currencies. Interbank FX traders manage FX positions by buying foreign currencies from or selling foreign currencies to interbank FX traders at other banks also using voice-based trading. Note that these are logical roles, and there may be many people at a bank providing the same function or a single person who performs multiple functions. For example, banks with small FX business units may have the same person act as both the corporate dealer and the interbank trader.

For a voice dealing transaction, the customer would begin by calling a dealer at the bank or going to a branch, in which case an RM would call the dealer on the customer's behalf. The customer would request a price to buy and sell a pair of foreign currencies in specific amounts on a specific date. The corporate dealer would check the current market rate, add a **spread**, and then quote the rate to the customer. Then, the customer could accept the rate and complete the order, reject the rate and abort the transaction, or try to negotiate a better rate. If the transaction proceeds, the corporate dealer would verify that the transaction would not cause the customer's counterparty credit limits to be breached, enter the transaction in the FX front office system, and then confirm the details verbally over the phone.

The bank deals with customers using its own inventory of foreign currencies. As a result of the bank's transactions with customers, it may accumulate excess inventory in certain foreign currencies and low supply in others. In turn, these imbalances must be dealt with, especially the excess positions, which contribute to the bank's **market risk**. For instance, if a bank in Brazil holds a large position of JPY, it could suffer losses if the yen were to weaken against the Brazilian real. Banks manage their FX positions by having their interbank FX traders find liquidity in the market, source the best rate, and reduce excessive positions by selling foreign currency and buying foreign currency to replace low inventory. Hence, an interbank trader at the Brazilian bank could contact a number of interbank traders at Japanese banks to check who was willing to buy yen and sell real in the quantities required and at the best rates.

Voice dealing predated the use of modern computing technology and the Internet. The transition to online trading began in the 1990s when interbank FX traders began using interbank dealing networks to communicate with one another instead of by telephone. The advancement came with the launch of automated dealing platforms, as shown in Figure 11-3. The corporate dealers' role of calculating spread adjusted rates, quoting a price, and entering the transaction details into the FX front office system was not particularly difficult for a computer to perform; thus, this function was well suited for automation. Initially, **online dealing systems** followed the same **request for quote (RFQ)** interaction model as voice dealing. They calculated rates when customers requested a quote, and the rate provided was valid for execution for some short period of time, usually measured in tens of seconds. Over time, as network and hardware technology advanced, banks would begin offering customers streaming tradable rates that were continuously updating in real time. Customers could access banks' online dealing systems remotely from their offices over the Internet or leased lines. Alternatively, RMs at bank branches could access the system on behalf of customers using an interface of the online dealing system that is designed for use by branch staff.

Automating corporate FX dealing provided several benefits to banks. Automating simple FX transactions enabled dealers to focus their efforts on selling complex and higher margin products, and

---

* Note that voice brokering is different from voice dealing. Voice brokers are intermediaries who act as agents for banks, traditionally using voiced-based technologies, to help them anonymously search for buy or sell interest with other banks. Banks typically use brokers to help disguise their activities in the market, particularly when they have a large position that they need to unload, and knowledge of their intention to buy or sell in the market could adversely affect the trade's execution price.

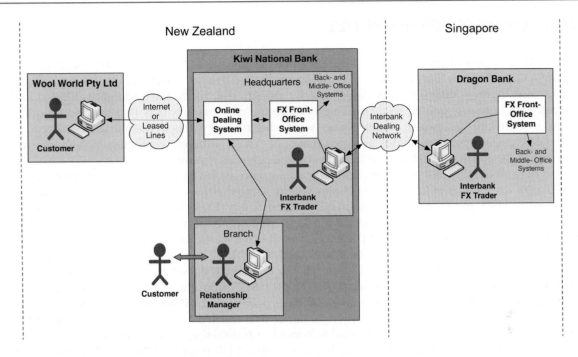

Figure 11-3 Automated FX transaction interactions

providing more value-adding services. Even though this service was mostly automated, dealers continued to be occasionally involved in the workflow for simple FX transactions. Manual intervention could be required when a customer order triggered a credit limit breach or when customers wanted to negotiate the rate for larger deal amounts. Nevertheless, the vast majority of corporate FX transactions were executed using STP. Another benefit of automating the dealing process was that it became practical for banks to offer FX dealing services to smaller companies that traded FX in small volumes and small amounts. While processing large numbers of small transactions would not have been cost effective with voice dealing, the marginal cost for handling additional transactions with automated dealing was relatively low.

Corporate customers also benefited from increased transparency of foreign exchange rate pricing that automated dealing provided. To get current FX rate information with voice dealing would have involved calling several banks to check their prices, whereas with automated dealing, the prices of several banks could be compared simultaneously with the click of a button. Corporate customers also received more consistent rates, since the spreads charged by the bank were calculated using an algorithm, as opposed to being open to the discretion of a corporate dealer. Customers also benefited from lower transaction fees, which banks were able to offer because of the cost savings that they achieved by automating transaction processing.

The transition from voice dealing to automated dealing did not happen quickly. Many corporate customers, dealers, and traders who were familiar with voice trading were not eager to change. Hence, along the path to online dealing, hybrid-trading models emerged where customers and traders would source rate information electronically, but then execute trades over the phone. There were several reasons why customers would choose to place the order over the phone instead of electronically. First, when computers were relatively new, many trading veterans, who had for many years only participated in voice dealing, lacked familiarity with and confidence in them. In some cases, there was also the belief that by speaking with someone on the phone a better rate could be obtained. Moreover, in cases where a customer or trader made a mistake while executing a transaction, with electronic orders, they could no longer claim that the other party had made a mistake.

11.5   BUSINESS OPPORTUNITIES

Like cash management and payments, corporate treasury products and services can provide lucrative business opportunities that have minimal impact on banks' balance sheet and capital requirements. Banks' fees are more difficult to assess because the margin charged to the customer is hidden in the bid-ask spread that is quoted to them. This is more the case for products that have low liquidity, where it is difficult to compare a quoted price with other offered prices in the market. Banks can also internalize customer orders, that is to say to match or "cross" different customers' orders internally, and realize the entire spread between the buy and sell prices as revenue.

To help illustrate these concepts, consider a company based in the Netherlands that has sold US\$20,000 worth of services to a customer in the United States. When the company receives payment in USD, they then need to sell USD and buy euro (EUR) to fund their local salaries and operations. To perform this transaction, their bank may quote rates of USD/EUR 0.8591 (USD 1 = EUR 0.8591) to buy USD and USD/EUR 0.8661 to sell USD. At the same time, the bank may be able to buy and sell USD for USD/EUR 0.8625 and USD/EUR 0.8627, respectively, on the interbank FX market. Hence, if the customer were to buy USD at USD/EUR 0.8661 from the bank and the bank immediately bought the same amount at USD/EUR 0.8625 from the interbank market, in a **back-to-back transaction**, the bank would make a 50 basis point gain (0.5%) transaction.* Moreover, if at about the same time the bank had another customer that wanted to sell the same amount of USD, the bank could internally cross the two sales instead of transacting them on the interbank market. In this case the bank would make the full spread, USD/EUR 0.8661 − USD/EUR 0.8591 = 0.007, around a 1% gain on the transaction.

This may sound like good business, but with so many banks providing services in this FX market, margins have been whittled away over time. Commodity products like FX spot and forwards have become less lucrative, and profits are largely driven by operational efficiency. At the same time, new higher-margin FX products have been developed. For instance, **dual currency investments (DCIs)** enable customers to achieve higher rates on deposits by taking a chance that their principal may be returned in another currency, depending on the movements on FX rates over the term of the investment.

This complex investment structure is actually achieved by combining a fixed-term deposit with an FX option, but these products are packaged in a way that the underlying components are hidden from the customer. This approach provides a simpler way for customers to make use of complicated products, like options, that they would not normally purchase. The bundling of products also makes it harder for the customer to measure the margins and fees associated with the product.

11.6   BUSINESS CHALLENGES

Banks' margins on commodity products, such as FX spot, forwards, and swaps, have been reduced through competition. Likewise, because of the increased availability of market price information, which is widely available for free on the Internet, banks' spreads on commodity products have become more transparent to customers. For many years, a customer would have to call multiple banks to compare rates; now, such information is readily available on FX trading portals, as discussed in Case Study 11-1. Accordingly, banks have had to adapt to a rapidly changing market environment and invest in electronic trading platforms and STP. As shown in Figure 11-4, in the United Kingdom as of 2016, the majority of the FX turnover was through electronic execution methods [2]. Of that, there was more turnover through banks' own proprietary platforms than through multibank FX trading portals. Just three years earlier, earlier multibank portals had been the dominant electronic execution method.

---

* Transaction spreads, commissions, and profit margins are often discussed in terms of basis points, increments of $1/100^{th}$ of 1.

During this period, banks began internalizing more customers' FX transactions so as to reduce the frequency which they had to actively trade in the external market. Likewise, banks needed to adapt their electronic pricing and risk management algorithms to better handle "flash crashes" which have become more frequent in the FX markets.

Trading of commoditized products in FX markets favors larger institutions because they are able to benefit from economies of scale. On a per-transaction basis, the cost associated with fixed investments in technology and operations is lower when transaction volumes are higher. Also, internal crossing of customer orders is more likely when handling larger numbers of orders. Moreover, lower per-transaction costs can help lower the price spreads offered to customers, leading to more business and increased volumes. While this model creates a virtuous circle for large institutions, it makes it difficult for other smaller ones to compete.

In contrast to commoditized products, when banks move into new, specialized product areas like DCIs, other challenges arise. One challenge is that hybrid products may not be readily accommodated by existing IT systems. For example, the underlying components of a DCI would likely be booked as a deposit in the core banking system and an FX option in the treasury system because neither system is designed to specifically handle a DCI product. Hence, there is a need to coordinate the booking, cash-flow events, and reporting between the two systems. This may likely require a third system that manages the specific transaction lifecycle considerations of DCIs and integrates with the other product booking systems.

Purchasing or building systems to process specialized products may address an immediate need, but it is not practical in environments where new products are rapidly being developed on an ongoing basis. The number of systems will proliferate quickly, raising costs or increasing complexity to a point where it is no longer manageable. Likewise, enhancing existing systems to support new products may involve considerable cost and time. For such situations, a useful approach is to ensure that the core-banking systems that process FX transactions are designed to be easily extended, both with respect to products' definitions and their lifecycle workflows.

In the retail and corporate banking context, new competition from Fintech startups is another challenge that banks are facing with regards to money transfers involving foreign exchange. It is

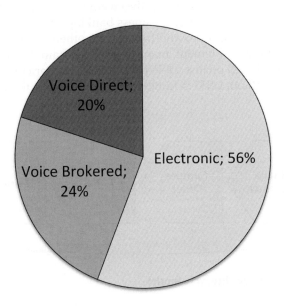

Figure 11-4 FX turnover by execution method in the United Kingdom

not uncommon for retail banks to charge between 1.5% and 3% in combined fees and exchange rate markups to convert and transfer a few thousand dollars overseas [3]. On the other hand, their Fintech competitors offer to transfer the same amounts for net cost of 0.5%, or in some cases, no fees at all. Fintech companies have been able to reduce costs by pioneering new technology strategies for implementing international payments and FX conversions. One Fintech company, Transferwise, uses an approach that is similar to the centuries-old hawala money transfer system (see the Further Reading section for more background on hawala). Another company, Circle, uses blockchain technology and generates its revenue from trading digital currencies, rather than assessing fees on FX transfers. While the use of these new FX services is still quite limited, they have the potential to disrupt a major business area for many banks.

11.7 FORWARD FOREIGN EXCHANGE SWAP SERVICE LIFECYCLE

To help illustrate how banks' business processes function in the context of FX products, this section will review the product lifecycle of a forward FX swap (Figure 11-5). Additionally, the transaction-fulfillment stage will be examined in more detail.

11.7.1 Design and Setup

As with other financial products, such as loans, the design and setup stage for FX-related products involves determining which types of products will be offered to customers and what features those products will provide. First, the tradable currency trading pairs must be defined for forward FX swaps. Next, the service features that need to be supported through the banks' processes and solutions must be identified, such as early and partial settlement of transactions. Rules regarding which customers will be able to access the forward FX swap product will also need to be defined. Certain service characteristics, such as streaming tradable rates, may be provided to some customers and not to others. Rules may also be defined to require the intervention of an FX dealer in certain cases.

Fee structures will also need to be defined and implemented. As discussed in Section 11.4, fees are usually reflected as a margin or spread quoted on top of interbank rates. Fee structures can be based on multiple factors such as transaction size, the customer's total deal volume, the currency pair, and the deal execution channel, e.g., Internet business banking. It may be decided that fee amounts are to be negotiable under some conditions and fixed under others. The resulting fee "matrix" can be multidimensional and difficult to implement, manage, and maintain. Hence, it is common to simplify fee structures to be calculated based on just a few parameters, with pricing based on fixed increments, for example, less than US$1 million, US$1–5 million, and so on, rather than on a continuous scale.

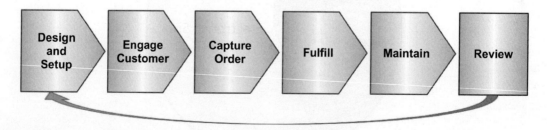

Figure 11-5 Transaction and services lifecycle model

11.7.2 Engage Customer

When banks engage the customer, they need to decide which channels customers will be allowed to use to place orders for forward FX swaps. Accordingly, support for activities such as FX rate distribution, deal capture, and order validation will need to be implemented within those channels. For example, a bank may need to deliver streaming prices to Internet banking customers, provide automated electronic quotations to corporate customers' treasury systems, and train branch staff to call the dealing room to obtain prices for walk-in customers.

Engaging the customer may also involve the setup of "static data" that will support the underlying transactions. Specific currency pairs may be enabled on a per-customer basis, with standard settlement instructions defined for each currency pair. The use of standardized settlement instructions (SSIs) is a banking best practice that simplifies deal capture and helps to reduce exceptions. To set up SSIs, customers must provide the details of their settlement accounts in advance of dealing so that the account information can be referenced automatically when transacting.

11.7.3 Capture Order

As with most types of transactions, deal capture for forward FX swaps begins with validation of the deal parameters. Limit checks are an important part of order processing as they determine if the bank should allow the transaction to be completed. Some of the limits that may be verified include:

- counterparty credit limits;

- daily settlement limits;

- overall settlement limits;

- total transaction size limits; and

- channel limits (for example, maximum size for online transactions).

As discussed in Chapter 8, counterparty limit checking may require integration with external, often global, credit limit management systems. Customers' credit limits are utilized by outstanding loans, lines of credit, and trade finance facilities, as well as FX transactions.

Besides validation, the order capture process may also involve a dealer. For example, for large-value transactions, customers may want to negotiate fee spreads directly with a dealer either over the phone or via online chat sessions over electronic channels. In other cases, credit limit breaches may trigger dealer intervention. Limit breaches may be allowed in some cases, after having undergone additional review and approval.

Once an FX swap transaction has been validated and accepted, it will be decomposed for booking and fulfillment purposes inside the bank's treasury system. Decomposition of a forward FX swap will involve allocating the spot portion of the deal to the bank's spot "book", i.e., trading account, and the forward portion to the forward book. Similarly, currency pairs will be broken down, booked to accounts, and processed by their cross-currency components. For example, an SGD/THB deal will be split into its SGD/USD and USD/THB components to simplify accounting and facilitate further downstream processing. Subsequent interbank trading of the positions created will only be traded between SGD with USD and THB with USD.

11.7.4 Fulfill Transaction

Fulfillment of a forward FX swap requires the two counterparties to send confirmations to one another, which are then matched and reconciled. It may be the case that each party sends out two sets of confirmations: one set of confirmations is sent when the transaction is booked in the front-office system and another set is sent from the back-office system for settlement. The back-office system's confirmations are the "official" ones used by the bank's system of reference, while the front-office confirmations are used to help detect discrepancies early on, thereby reducing the cost of correction. Deals that are booked manually are more prone to errors due to miscommunication and data entry mistakes.

For example, when different foreign accents are used over the phone, the number quoted as "22" by one party may be mistakenly heard as "23" by the other party. Alternatively, it may have been heard correctly, but mistakenly typed as "33" by one side when the transaction is entered. Front-office confirmations can help identify such mistakes quickly so that they can be corrected before back-office processing begins.

In the front-office system, customer transactions will also be aggregated over time so that the bank's resulting net positions can be calculated. Trades on the interbank market are then typically used to offset, or "square," the net positions. In the back office, funds are recorded for accounting purposes and then settled in customers' accounts on the specified settlement dates. In cases where settlement instructions were not provided when the order was captured, it will be necessary to follow up with the customer or dealer to get the necessary details prior to settlement.

11.7.5 Maintain Transaction

Maintenance of forward FX swaps primarily relate to supporting customer actions on the far leg of the trade. After the near leg has settled, the outstanding part of the transaction is equivalent to an outright forward. As with forwards, customers may choose to have early and possibly partial settlement, commonly referred to as "take ups," of the far leg to match immediate payable or receivable settlement needs. For instance, a customer may know that his or her obligation for funding in a foreign currency may be necessary for up to three months. However, this need may end sooner depending on external factors such as the timing of the receipt of payment from a third party. In this case, the customer could enter into a three-month FX swap agreement with the bank. If after two-and-a-half months the funding requirement was no longer necessary, the customer could request an "early take up" so that the transaction will settle prior to the originally agreed settlement date.

Customers may also choose to cancel or amend the deals. A cancelation will be reflected as an event that simply reverses the original deal's cash flows. Amendments may appear as changes to the original deal from the customer's view, but they may be treated differently within the bank's systems. Amendments are often booked as a cancelation followed by a new deal that corresponds to the amended terms. The cost of reversing and booking of the new transaction will be reflected to the customer as the cost of making of the adjustment. An example of an amendment to a forward FX swap would be if the customer wanted to extend the settlement period of the far leg. This "rollover" case is the opposite of an early take up. To the customer, the rollover may look like an extension of the original deal; however, in the bank's system, it may be implemented as a second FX swap that only covers the extension period. The settlement of the second leg of the original FX swap will be offset by the first leg of the new FX swap, and the new swap's second leg will correspond to the extension date. This approach is complicated from an IT systems perspective because multiple internal transactions need to linked with what appears to be a single transaction for the customer.

Case Study 11-2
No Free Lunch at the Foreign Exchange Table

To a large extent, FX transactions' market risk can be passed on to the interbank market. However, banks must still manage counterparty and residual market risk. As a case in point, PT Bank Danamon Tbk, Indonesia's fifth largest lender, faced serious concerns toward the end of 2008 when the Indonesian rupiah was very volatile and commodity market crashed. The first problem that Danamon faced was exposure to FX derivatives, which made large movements under volatile conditions. The second problem was that many of the bank's counterparties were commodities exporters whose ability to service forward FX contract obligations was jeopardized by economic conditions.

To effectively manage these types of risks, it is critical for banks' systems to be able to generate reports that show risk concentration across a number of different dimensions. Likewise, building in exposure limit rules—by currency, counterparty, and sector—into business processes can also help control these risks. Furthermore, simulation and "what if" analysis can be used to assess the potential financial impact of various economic scenarios. Needless to say, all of these tools will be of limited value if a bank's management is unable to quickly make decisions and take action once this information is available.

Source: "Shares in Indonesia's Danamon Rebound on FX Hopes," *Reuters*, January 22, 2009.

11.7.6 Review

With regard to forward FX swaps, the bank's management will want to evaluate a number of areas on an ongoing basis. Profitability considerations are one such area. The profitability of the products offered, customers' use of those products, and the profitability of negotiated transactions will drive changes to offerings, pricing, and fee structures. For instance, if there are very few forward FX swaps on certain currency pairs, support for trading those currencies may be dropped. Alternatively, if customer-negotiated transactions are found to be unprofitable, rules may be put in place to allow negotiation only under certain conditions or only for specific customers.

Risk exposure created by open FX positions and exposure to counterparties must also be monitored on a regular basis. The bank may choose to hedge these risks when they reach an excessive level or to reduce its exposure by decreasing limits. In this regard, it is crucial that banks have aggregated risk information available on a timely basis. During the 1998 Asian Currency Crisis, many banks found that they were unable to determine their aggregate risk exposures across specific corporate groups, countries, and currencies quickly enough to take corrective action (Case Study 11-2). Even in cases where the systems had the necessary reporting capabilities, often the data aggregation process, especially across global business operations, was done manually, leading to long delays in reporting and potentially providing out-of-date risk information.

11.8 LIFECYCLE FOCUS: CONFIRMATIONS FOR FOREIGN EXCHANGE TRANSACTIONS

To help better understand the details and complexities involved with fulfilling FX transactions, this section will examine the mechanics of back-office confirmations. Historically, paper confirmations would be sent by mail or fax between counterparties and manually reconciled. Needless to say, this

Tag	Field Name	
	Message Begin	
	Mandatory Sequence A General Information	
15A	New-Sequence	
20	Sender's-Reference	
21	Related-Reference	
22A	Type-of-Operation	
94A	Scope-of-Operation	
22C	Common-Reference	
17T	Block-Trade-Indicator	
17U	Split-Settlement-Indicator	
82a	Party-A	SWIFT Sender
87a	Party-B	SWIFT Receiver
83a	Fund-or-Beneficiary-Customer	
77D	Terms-and-Conditions	
	Mandatory Sequence B Transaction Details	
15B	New-Sequence	
30T	Trade-Date	
30V	Value-Date	
36	Exchange-Rate	Forward Rate
	Mandatory Subsequence B1 Amount Bought	
32B	Currency, Amount	Sender Buy Currency & Amount
53a	Delivery-Agent	
56a	Intermediary	
57a	Receiving-Agent	
	Mandatory Subsequence B2 Amount Sold	
33B	Currency, Amount	Sender Sell Currency & Amount
53a	Delivery-Agent	
56a	Intermediary	
57a	Receiving-Agent	
58a	Beneficiary-Institution	
	Optional Sequence C Optional General Information	
15C	New-Sequence	
29A	Contact-Information	
24D	Dealing-Method	
84a	Dealing-Branch-Party-A	
85a	Dealing-Branch-Party-B	
88a	Broker-Identification	
71F	Broker's-Commission	
26H	Counterparty's-Reference	
21G	Broker's-Reference	
72	Sender-to-Receiver-Information	
	Optional Sequence D Split Settlement Details	
15D	New-Sequence	
17A	Buy-(Sell)-Indicator	
32B	Currency, Amount	
53a	Delivery-Agent	
56a	Intermediary	
57a	Receiving-Agent	
58a	Beneficiary-Institution	
16A	Number-of-Settlements	
	Message End	

Shaded fields are mandatory

Figure 11-6 Specification of the MT-300 FX confirmation message

Source: Foreign Exchange Committee, EMTA, Inc. and the FX Joint Standing Committee, *Guide to Economic Terms in SWIFT MT 300 Format for Non-deliverable Forward FX Transactions*, June 29, 2007, http://www.newyorkfed.org/fxc/2007/fxc062907b.pdf.

was terribly labor intensive. Hence, the evolution of high-speed communication networks enabled FX confirmations to be transmitted and matched electronically, thereby increasing processing efficiency and the volume of transactions that can be handled.

The best practice is for both parties involved in the transaction to send confirmations to one another as soon as possible after finalizing the deal. This is usually done within two to three hours. Subsequently, confirmation matching is used to detect trading errors. The goal is to catch exceptions as early in the trading process as possible. The cost of correcting mistrades after settlement is significantly greater than before settlement. Processing of clearing confirmations is performed in the back office, independently of front-office operations to reduce the chances of fraud. This **separation of duties** is recognized as an international best practice. Furthermore, when bank divisions or booking centers trade with each other, it is not uncommon for them to send confirmations between the units, as they do with external transactions.

As discussed previously, mismatched confirmations may occur for a number of reasons. Where deals are conducted over the phone, one side may accidentally key in the wrong amount or currency pair. This case is easily resolved by checking with front-office staff to determine which party made the mistake. Alternatively, there may be a misunderstanding between the two trading parties. This case will involve more complicated resolution processes. Mismatched deal confirmations can also identify when software, hardware, or communication network problems cause trade information to be incorrectly relayed or lost. Most FX deals are confirmed electronically using SWIFT MT300 series messages.* Electronic confirmations may be routed between banks or branches using SWIFT's proprietary network, or internally using the banks' own network. Figure 11-6 shows the data dictionary and message format of an MT300 confirmation message, and Figure 11-7 shows sample message content for a FX forward confirmation. SWIFT messages use a tag-delimited format

```
{1:F01ABCBUS33AXXX2768156193}
{2:O3001139050822XYZBUS33AFXO29569620200508221139N}
{3:{108:FC001105ded7970a}}
{4:
:15A:
:20:REF123
:22A:NEWT
:22C:XYZB334209ABCB33
:82A:KIWINATXX
:87A:DRAGONBKZ
:15B:
:30T:20120422
:30V:20120513
:36:1,2481
:32B:USD100000,00
:57A:SOMCEFTZKD
:33B:SGD124810,00
:53A:COFMCAN1
:57A:NOMCDATMLQ
:15C:
:24D:BROK
:88D:FTF-LN}
{5:{CHK:84BEA3F26A24}}
```

Figure 11-7 A sample MT-300 message

Source: **Foreign Exchange Committee, EMTA, Inc. and the FX Joint Standing Committee,** *Guide to Economic Terms in SWIFT MT 300 Format for Non-deliverable Forward FX Transactions,* **June 29, 2007, http://www.newyorkfed.org/fxc/2007/fxc062907b.pdf.**

---

* An introduction to SWIFT messaging is provided in Chapter 9.

whereby field identifiers and separators are used to identify message content. For example, the tag in an MT300 message "33B:" identifies the string that follows as the currency and amount of the currency sold. Only a subset of the fields available will be used for most confirmations and various message types are defined for confirmations of different financial product types: MT300 is used for FX confirmations, MT305 is used for foreign currency option confirmations, and MT320 is used for fixed loan/deposit confirmations.

Machine-readable electronic confirmations have been a great improvement for the financial services industry. Be that as it may, the SWIFT format and its message types are relatively complex and are not simple to construct and parse. Quite often, third-party adapters are used for this purpose. Likewise, specialized components are used to match SWIFT confirmations and generate exception reports for further action by bank staff.

11.9 ARCHITECTURE CONSIDERATIONS: MARKET DATA DISTRIBUTION

This section discusses the distribution of real-time market prices and rates, which is crucial for the operation of FX and capital market trading systems. **Market data** is information related to current market prices, publicly reported trades, and trading volume that is distributed directly by exchanges and other financial institutions or by vendors who serve as data aggregators and specialist information providers. First, market data usage and FX rate distribution are reviewed in the context of banks' FX trading requirements. Next, the architecture that is used for distributing market data within banks is explained, along with the strategies used to implement load balancing and resilience. Then, the complications of streaming real-time tradable rates to customers are discussed. Finally, market data architecture patterns are examined using the channel-services architecture framework that was introduced in Chapter 3.

11.9.1 Context

As discussed in Section 11.7.2, distributing tradable FX rates to customers is a key part of engaging the customer. Historically, when dealing was done primarily over the phone, a customer would call the dealing room and ask for a quote to buy or sell currency pair—spot, forward, or swap. The dealer would get the current price from data feeds from vendors, such as Reuters and Bloomberg, which were disseminated through the bank's market data distribution system. The dealer would then add on a profit margin and quote the adjusted rate to the customer, who would then have some limited number of seconds to decide whether or not to complete the transaction. Sometimes, customers would call to get rate information without transacting; this was especially the case if the customer was shopping around several banks trying to find the best quote.

With the introduction of automated dealing, this process was improved by enabling corporate customers to request rates from the bank's online dealing system over leased lines or the Internet. In the early stages of automated dealing, the automated rate quotation process was almost identical to the manual one. A pricing engine component would generate margin-adjusted prices on demand and provide them to the customer as tradable rates within a short period of time, usually less than a minute, to protect the bank from losses due to currency fluctuations (pricing engines are discussed more in Chapter 15). Price distribution further evolved so that indicative streaming prices were delivered to the customer. Indicative pricing could be streamed to customers on an ongoing basis and deal-specific, margin-adjusted prices would be streamed upon request. Another advancement came when instead of streaming indicative rates, tradable rates continuously streamed. These rates could be traded upon at any time and, thus, a specific validity period was no longer required.

Besides needing to stream real-time rate information to customers, banks also need to distribute market data internally. For example, traders need market data to make decisions about market transactions and pricing engines need it to calculate margin adjusted rates.

11.9.2 Internal Market Data Distribution

Internal market data distribution is a universal requirement for almost all financial institutions. If traders and dealers do not know what the current market conditions are, they cannot trade in the market or quote rates and prices to customers. In the early 1990s, distribution of market data shifted from analog video screens to elementized data feeds. Since that time, the amount of data has proliferated and market data distribution has posed significant challenges for financial institutions. In the 1990s, the main challenge was managing the distribution of large volumes of real-time prices across the banks' internal networks and between systems. Many of these challenges were related to the performance of the workstation hardware and networks of the time. System performance has since improved greatly, but users' requirements have also changed and their expectations have grown. For instance, real-time distribution to additional communication channels, such as the Internet browsers and mobile devices, emerged as requirements.

An unusual characteristic of market data is that it is asynchronous and unidirectional. Unlike client-server interactions that follow a point-to-point, request-reply model, market data is typically broadcast from one producer to many consumers. Market data usually is generated when a price change occurs in the market, then flows to financial institutions via market data vendors to data feeds within the bank, through the bank's market-data distribution system and then out through relevant channels to internal and external consumers of that data. Distribution management is a major function in these systems. Whereas it may be the case that many consumers of data will receive the same price updates for the EUR/USD spot price, only one consumer may need updates for the Uruguayan peso, and no consumers may require updates for the Congolese franc. To utilize network and IT server resources effectively, market data should be filtered so that subscribers only receive the information they are interested in.

It is important to appreciate that this use case does not fit well with the traditional client-server, request-reply architecture designs. Periodic client-to-server polling for current prices is not scalable for large numbers of users. Likewise, the polling interval leads to potentially stale data. If the polling interval is reduced to increase the timeliness of delivery, the distribution becomes less scalable as the volume of network traffic and server load increases. To avoid rate update delivery **latency** and enable scalable delivery to large numbers of users, publish-subscribe models and technologies are used for market data distribution systems. Likewise, alternatives to point-to-point communication protocols, that is, broadcast and multicast network communication protocols, are commonly used for market data communications because they inherently support one-to-many data distribution.

Figure 11-8 shows the high-level design of a three-tier market data distribution platform.[*] Banks will typically source data from multiple market data vendors, who serve as aggregators, or directly from exchanges or **broker-dealers**. Each market data provider provides its own data "feed" that provides current value and price update information in its own proprietary format. Hence, feed handler components are required to decode data vendors' communication protocols, extract the relevant pricing information, and forward it for distribution to subscribers. However, not all downstream consuming applications will require all of the market data provided by each feed, so a subscription and distribution management component (often referred to as a "ticker plant") is required to cache,

---

[*] Although the connections shown between the components in Figure 11-8 are depicted as direct point-to-point connections for simplicity, in practice they would likely use an information bus platform that supports multicast distribution for intercomponent communication.

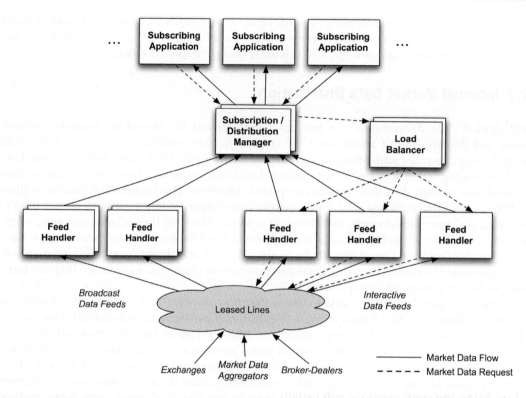

Figure 11-8 A three-tier market data distribution architecture

filter, and distribute market data to subscribing applications. The types of applications that subscribe to market data will vary from one financial institution to another; however, they typically include "terminal" display applications used by traders and dealers and IT systems, such as FX front-office systems and pricing engines.

Market data architectures are complicated by the fact that there are two primary types of data feeds: broadcast and interactive. Broadcast feeds continuously distribute price information for every instrument that they provide. They typically are provided by sources that have a relatively small instrument universe, such as stock exchanges, which have at most several thousand tradable equities. On the other hand, interactive feeds only distribute price information for instruments requested by the feed handlers to which they are connected. Market data aggregators, which aggregate and distribute data from multiple exchanges and market, usually provide interactive feeds.

From an architecture perspective, broadcast feeds can be easily accommodated. The subscription and distribution management component filters the broadcast data stream and only distributes relevant price information to subscribing applications. However, supporting interactive feeds is more complicated, because subscription request information must be routed from the subscribing applications to the data feeds. Furthermore, interactive feeds usually have limited capacity—where capacity is measured by the maximum number of instruments for which they can distribute market data information—so multiple feeds are required to support medium and large-sized trading operations.

For example, consider a bank whose dealing floor requires price and rate information for 3,000 instruments from a market data aggregator that delivered its information using interactive feeds. If each interactive data feed can deliver 1,200 instruments, the bank would need at least three feeds. However, it is more likely that four feeds would be used so that if one feed fails, the remaining three could continue to service a full set of instrument subscriptions. A load balancer component is required to allocate instrument requests to the available interactive feeds and manage reallocation of active instrument data distribution in cases of feed failures.

Two common architecture patterns that are used in market data distribution systems to provide scalability and resilience are static and dynamic load balancing. These approaches are examples of **horizontal scaling** techniques, that is, adding additional servers incrementally to achieve higher **throughput**, and support larger volumes and/or larger numbers of users.

11.9.2.1 Static load balancing

Static load balancing divides the processing load across multiple servers by having each server manage a predefined subset of the services provided. Figure 11-9 shows how a static load balancing could be implemented by subscription and distribution manager components in a market data architecture. If the instrument universe subscribed to is larger than the capacity of a single server's ability to distribute, then the delivery function must be distributed across multiple servers. Multiple subscription and distribution components would be required, and each set will perform caching and manage distribution of the market data for a subset of the instruments. For resilience, each server would need to be run in a **hot standby configuration,** represented in the Figures 11-9 and 11-10 by two stacked boxes. Thus, if the distribution and subscription management service needs to be partitioned across three servers, a total of six servers would be required to provide resilience.

Static load balancing is simple from a design perspective, but the load on the servers will be nonoptimal under varying client usage conditions. For example, on some days there may be more subscription requests for instruments having symbols in the range H through R, and fewer for the range A through G. As a result, some servers may be overutilized while others are underutilized. The static load balancing configurations will usually be structured to try to achieve the best results under average usage conditions. By their nature, the partitioning of "static" load balancing configurations is not intended to be changed frequently.

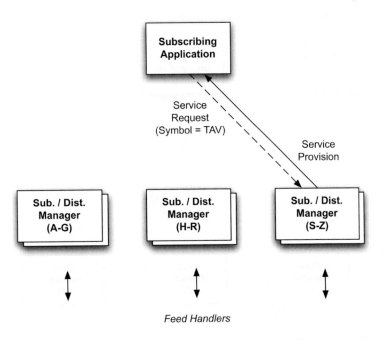

Figure 11-9 A static load balancing configuration

11.9.2.2 Dynamic load balancing

In contrast to static load balancing, dynamic load balancing uses an intermediary component, a load balancer, to distribute requests between available service or data providers (Figure 11-10). This approach is often used in market data architectures for managing interactive data feeds. Load balancers may use simple work allocation strategies, such as round robin. Alternatively, they may use algorithms that have complex rules and also may need to maintain state information related to each service provider to determine which of them is best suited to support inbound requests.

Dynamic load balancing is generally more efficient than static load balancing because the load balancer can cater to changing request patterns and service source availability situations. This configuration is also more efficient from a resilience standpoint because it does not require each service provider to have a hot standby. In cases of a feed failure, the load balancer can automatically reallocate subscriptions that the failed feed was servicing to other available feeds. In such cases, the load balancer manages the recovery from feed failures, rather than the service requester.

11.9.3 Streaming Real-time Rates

Many of the architectural concerns that relate to internal distribution of market data also relate to external distribution of prices and rates. A key difference is that distribution over external networks usually requires the use of point-to-point connections, which is much less efficient than broadcast or multicast data delivery. Platforms that distribute market data externally must also cater for a wide range of variability in data recipients' available network bandwidth and hardware processing power. Slow network links can become saturated and old hardware may be overloaded.

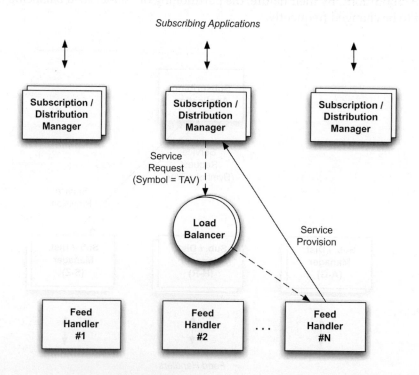

Figure 11-10 A dynamic load balancing configuration

Moreover, the number of unique data streams that need to be distributed can be very large. For example, consider the requirements for streaming live FX rates to 100 corporate customers each having ten users. If 20 currency pairs were distributed to those 1,000 users with an average update rate per currency of two updates per second, the distribution platform would need to be able to distribute 40,000 updates per second.

11.9.4 A Channel-services Architecture View of Market Data

This section discusses how market data distribution systems can be mapped onto the channel-services architecture framework introduced in Chapter 3. The architecture shown in Figure 11-11 is representative and is intentionally presented at a high level. The details of implementation in banks will vary considerably depending on the business environment and technology vendors used. For brevity, only a subset of the components is presented; in practice, the operating environment would be more complex. The following subsections examine the information flow and components involved in the data services, business services, and channel layers.

11.9.4.1 Data services layer

The data services layer will largely be made up of data-feed handlers. Feed handlers serve as adapters that take price information from vendors, such as Reuters and Bloomberg, and map them to formats that can be used by other components in the bank's architecture. Besides taking data from vendors, pricing information may be sourced from other internal systems that may, for example, represent the bank's estimation of forward interest rate or volatility curves. Historical market data may also be captured and stored in databases and provided as a data service. Historical data is commonly used by components in the business services or channel layers in calculations and charting.

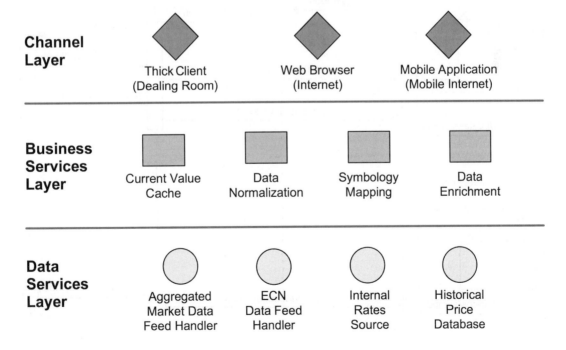

Figure 11-11 A channel-services architecture view of market data distribution

11.9.4.2 Business services layer

In the business services layer, the real-time data cache is a primary component. A common requirement for market data distribution is that when consumers subscribe to an instrument, such as the EUR/USD spot rate, they will want to retrieve the current value, rather than having to wait for the next price update. A real-time data cache component fulfills this requirement by storing recent market prices in memory and making them available to new consumers. The cached record that is provided as the initial value to the subscriber will have all of the data fields for the instrument, whereas subsequent updates usually only include information for the fields that have changed. Figure 11-12 shows the interactions between various components when market data from an interactive data feed is subscribed to by an front-end application.

Other components in the business services layer will depend on the bank's business requirements. Where multiple data vendors are used, data normalization and symbology mapping may be required. For example, the USD/SGD rate may need to be requested using the symbol "SGD=" from one data vendor and the symbol "USDSGD" from another. Likewise, data enrichment at the business layer can eliminate the duplication of effort across multiple channels in the channel layer. For example, some market data sources may provide "hints" for how market data should be displayed: the USD/SGD rate should be displayed to four decimal places and the USD/KRW need

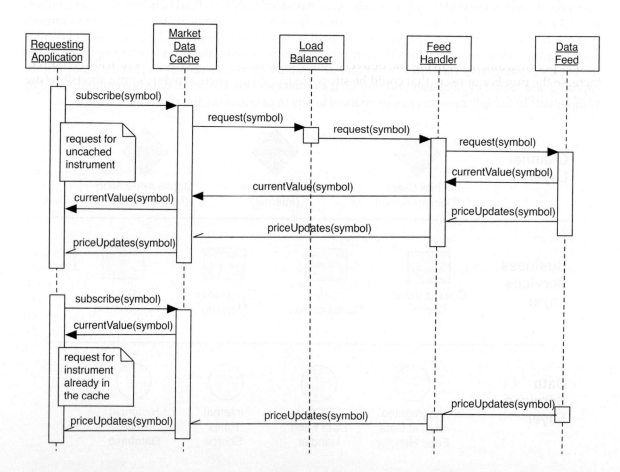

Figure 11-12 Sequence diagram of a subscription to market data from an interactive data feed

only be displayed to one decimal place. For other sources that do not provide hints, a business layer component could be implemented to enrich the data to provide display hint information. Implementing this logic in the business layer eliminates the need to incorporate it into all of the channel layer components.

11.9.4.3　Channel layer

As shown in Figure 11-11, multiple channels may be supported by a single market-data distribution platform, where the business and data services layers constitute the platform. Each channel may include specialized data-distribution management facilities that correspond to the requirements and limitations of the channel. Functionality specific to the data flow and presentation characteristics of each channel are embedded in each of the relevant channel-delivery components. For example, market data delivered to the dealing room may be presented using proprietary vendor data formats, whereas market data delivered over the Internet may be formatted in Internet standards such as HTML and XML. Prices distributed over mobile channels may also need to be able to accommodate low bandwidth connections and variable connectivity.

Flow control of data delivery is a major consideration with regard to performance and scalability. For example, distribution of prices to the dealing room is usually optimized for performance, with an emphasis on high-volume and low-latency delivery of data to a relatively small number of users. On the other hand, data distribution over the Internet is typically optimized for scaling to a larger number of users and providing resilience under a wide range of conditions. To this point, the rate of price updates distributed over the Internet may be throttled back to only one update every second per instrument. Slowing the delivery rate would reduce the network bandwidth required, increase the number of users that could be supported, and help accommodate applications that are slow consumers of data.

11.9.4.4　Communication and distribution management

While the framework decomposition shown in Figure 11-11 portrays modular and separate components, this is often not the case in real-world implementations. For example, the logical services depicted in Figure 11-11 are combined within the components shown in Figure 11-8. Caching and symbology mapping is usually handled by the distribution and subscription manager, and data normalization is often implemented in market data feed handlers.

An alternative to the architecture shown in Figure 11-8 is a two-tier market data architecture where the data feed handlers distribute data directly to subscribing applications. This architectural approach is less scalable but performs better. With fewer layers of processing, there is less latency, that is, delay, between the time that data is received and it is processed. While saving milliseconds or microseconds may not have much relevance for human traders, it is a major concern for automated high-frequency trading. In two-tier market data architectures, the feed handlers usually perform the data normalization and caching functions. Often, symbology mapping and data enrichment functions are eliminated because they introduce unwanted delay.

11.10　SOLUTION CONSIDERATIONS

In recent years, there has been a push to outsource hosting and management of banks' market data platforms to managed service providers. This strategy is driven by the fact that most banks derive relatively little competitive advantage from market data and that it is, for the most part, a commodity service. Yet, banks spend significant sums on sourcing market data, managing it, and reporting on its usage. Vendors that provide market data as a shared service to multiple customers can achieve economies of scale that banks would never be able to achieve by themselves. And, better economies of scale should translate into lower costs for banks.

Looking beyond market data services, **white labeling** is another approach that some banks use to reduce the cost of providing transactional services to customers and other banks use to generate income. Consider for example, a hypothetical small bank in New Zealand, NZ Farmers Bank, that wants to provide online FX dealing capabilities to its corporate customers. Given its small customer base, the costs of buying or building and operating an online dealing system would probably be prohibitive (they can easily cost hundreds of thousands or even millions of dollars). It would also be impractical for it to provide trading in all currency pairs and across all time zones. Furthermore, another large hypothetical New Zealand bank, Kiwi National, already has large-scale FX trading operations and has made a major investment to implement an online dealing system for its customers. Ideally, it would like to find additional ways to recoup its investment and offset ongoing operational costs.

By providing a white-label online dealing service to NZ Farmers Bank, Kiwi National could address the objectives of both banks. As illustrated in Figure 11-12, the white-label service could be run as a separate instance of Kiwi National's online dealing software in Kiwi National's data center, managed by Kiwi National staff. The additional software instance would be set up to display NZ Farmers' logo and would be loaded with its customer information. Thus, when NZ Farmers' customers connect to it, they would think they are using NZ Farmers' system, and not Kiwi National's. Presumably, the fees that NZ Farmers Bank would pay Kiwi National for the white-label service would be more cost effective than NZ Farmers Bank buying and operating its own online dealing system.

The arrangement for booking FX transactions via white-label systems varies. For the case shown in Figure 11-13, Kiwi National only operates the online dealing system; the transaction lifecycle and risk management is handled by NZ Farmers Bank. Alternatively, if NZ Farmers Bank did not have its own FX dealing system and interbank trading operation, it could arrange to have a **back-to-back transaction** with Kiwi National for each customer deal it receives so that it holds no market risk. Kiwi National would be responsible for managing the resulting positions. The back-to-back transaction would be another deal between NZ Farmers Bank and Kiwi National for the opposite amount of the transaction that NZ Farmers Bank did with its customer, less any fees and markups that NZ Farmers Bank applied to generate revenue on the transaction. Thus, the two transactions made by NZ Farmers Bank, one with the customer and the other with Kiwi National, offset each other.

As part of this arrangement, NZ Farmers Bank acts as an FX liquidity retailer and specializes in managing the end customer counterparty risk. Conversely, Kiwi National serves as a wholesaler that provides liquidity to NZ Farmers Bank and manages the market risk for its end customer transactions. This arrangement enables NZ Farmers Bank to cost effectively provide comprehensive services to its customers. Likewise, Kiwi National is able to reach customers that it would normally not serve without having to deal with concerns over their individual creditworthiness.

Some banks may find that white-label FX services are only provided by competitors, and thus, it might seem like a bad idea to make use of a competitor's services. However, it may be the lesser of two evils—the alternatives of not providing any online FX service to customers or spending significant sums of money so as to incur losses are probably worse. In general, smaller banks have had difficulty keeping up with the rate of technology change. Particularly with FX order execution, the largest banks have made substantial investments and, as a result, have captured a large share of the market.

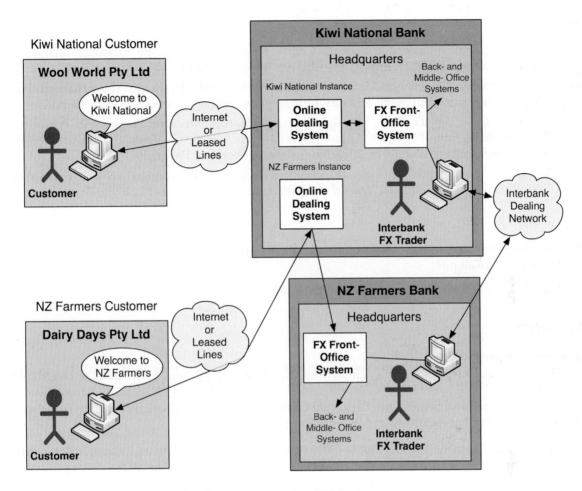

Figure 11-13 A white-label solution for corporate online FX dealing

11.11 SUMMARY

This chapter covered:

- basic FX products and the purpose for which they are used;
- opportunities and challenges that banks face with respect to treasury products;
- product lifecycle considerations for basic FX instruments;
- architectures used for real-time market data delivery; and
- white-label solution implementation strategies.

The next chapter will review the processes and technology related to treasury derivative products that banks offer to customers.

FURTHER READING

Papers

Bank for International Settlements, "Triennial Central Bank Survey—Foreign Exchange Turnover in April 2016," September 2016, http://www.bis.org/publ/rpfx16.htm.

Jost, P. and Sandhu, H., "The Hawala Alternative Remittance System and its Role in Money Laundering," United States Department of the Treasury, http://www.nmta.us/assets/docs/hawala.pdf.

King, M. R., C. Osler, and D. Rime, "Foreign Exchange Market Structure, Players and Evolution," Norges Bank Working Paper 10, August 14, 2011, http://m.norges-bank.no/Upload/English/Publications/Working%20Papers/2011/Norges_Bank_Working_Paper_2011_10.pdf.

Pantzalis, C., B. J. Simkins, and P. A. Laux, "Operational Hedges and the Foreign Exchange Exposure of US Multinational Corporations," *Journal of International Business Studies* 32 (2001): 793–812.

Web

"Foreign Exchange and Money Market Transactions," http://www.ibb.ubs.com/Individuals/files/brochure/booken.pdf.

"PACIFIC Exchange Rate Service," http://fx.sauder.ubc.ca.

ENDNOTES

1. Lipscomb, L., "An Overview of Non-deliverable Foreign Exchange Forward Markets," Federal Reserve Bank of New York, May 2005, http://www.bis.org/publ/cgfs22fedny5.pdf.

2. Bank for International Settlements, "Triennial Central Bank Survey—Foreign Exchange Turnover in April 2016," September 2016, http://www.bis.org/publ/rpfx16.htm.

3. Williams, A., "Payment App Revolut to Offer Free Money Transfers Abroad," *Financial Times*, May 16, 2017, https://www.ft.com/content/45c6bbae-38bd-11e7-821a-6027b8a20f23.

4. Bank of England, "Withdrawn Banknotes," http://www.bankofengland.co.uk/banknotes/Pages/withdrawn/default.aspx.

5. Davies, R., P. Richardson, V. Katinaite, and M. Manning, "Evolution of the UK Banking System," *Bank of England Quarterly Bulletin 50 (2010): 321–332.*

6. Barker, W., "The Global Foreign Exchange Market: Growth and Transformation," *Bank of Canada Review* (Autumn 2007): 3–12.

7. Rodionova, Z., "Pound Sterling Slump: The Key Moments in Six Charts-and How Low It Could Drop," *Independent*, January 16, 2017, http://www.independent.co.uk/news/business/news/pound-sterling-slump-drop-key-moments-four-charts-graphics-how-low-could-it-go-a7529136.html

8. Kelly, J. and Irrera, A., "Goldman-backed Startup Circle Launches No-fee Foreign Payments Service," *Reuters*, June 15, 2017, http://www.reuters.com/article/us-fintech-payments-circle-idUSKBN19539X.

12 Treasury Derivatives

Chapter Overview

Over the past two decades, derivatives and their use by financial institutions have often been unfairly maligned. Besides being linked with the failure of Barings Bank in the late 1990s and the **Global Financial Crisis** in 2008, financial derivatives have been the source for many other smaller but significant financial woes for banks and their customers. Politicians and businessmen alike have called for tighter controls on derivatives usage and, in some cases, completely banning their use. Yet, despite all their apparent dangers, the use of derivatives by banks and corporations grew precipitously but has leveled off over the past decade, as shown in Figure 12-1. As of June 2016, the Bank of International Settlements estimated that the **notional amount** outstanding for over-the-counter (OTC) derivative contracts was more than US$544 trillion [1].*

When used wisely, derivatives are powerful financial tools that can help manage risk and be used to synthesize new financial instruments. A useful analogy might be to think of them as explosives—they can be used for constructive purposes, but can also cause catastrophic disasters when mishandled.

---

* The notional values of outstanding derivative contracts has dropped in recent years due to the "compression" of contracts, as discussed in Section 12.4, rather than from diminished usage. Trading volumes for OTC derivatives have remained steady.

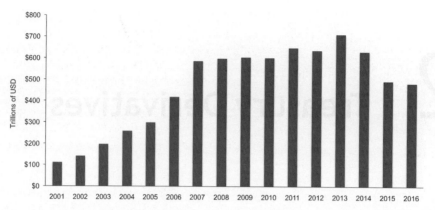

Figure 12-1 Notional amounts outstanding for major OTC derivatives contracts
Source: **BIS Statistics Explorer, http://stats.bis.org/statx/toc/DER.html**

The popularity of derivatives is due to their ability to help manage exposures to a wide range of risk concerns. Unfortunately, the criticisms of derivatives far surpass the number of praises they have received. Despite their dangers, explosives have not been banned; however, access to them is controlled. In recent years, derivatives have experienced a similar fate and their use has been moderated.

For banks, derivatives represent one of the last frontiers of innovation. Many of the other business areas in which banks compete have become commoditized; however, derivatives still provide opportunities for banks to customize products and adapt them to very specific customer needs. Customized OTC derivative products present banks with opportunities to provide high-value services to customers. Whereas the profit on payment transactions and other commodity services are measured in dollars and sometimes cents, the profit on a single, complex derivatives transaction could be measured in hundreds of thousands or millions of dollars.

As attractive as the derivatives business may sound, it is not simple to implement. Bank staff, from the sales desk to the chief executive, need to understand the potential risk that comes with using these products. Comprehensive risk management facilities and controls are necessary. The information technology (IT) systems that support derivatives transactions can be difficult to understand and complicated to set up and manage to implement and manage. Where manual processing is involved, scaling up derivatives processing operations to handle higher volumes can also be challenging. Seemingly minor implementation concerns, such as how reference data is sourced and managed, can have major impacts on a bank's business and operations. Moreover, users of derivatives have had to make major adjustments to how they buy and sell these products to stay in line with changing regulatory requirements (Case Study 12-1).

Case Study 12-1

The New Age of Electronic Swap Trading

Imprudent use of OTC derivatives was one of the factors that contributed to the Global Financial Crisis. Compared to exchange-traded derivatives, voice-traded OTC derivatives had much less transparency and oversight. After several large financial institutions required government bailouts because of massive financial losses on their OTC derivative holdings, OTC derivatives trading was targeted for a regulatory overhaul. In particular, new laws in the United States and Europe were introduced to make the OTC swaps market more transparent and tightly controlled. One area of concern was how OTC derivatives were cleared and settled, and another was how they were traded. Because of the chaos that ensued after Lehman Brothers collapsed, there was little debate as to whether commonly traded OTC derivatives contracts should be cleared through a **central counterparty (CCP)** to help reduce systemic risk. However, reaching a consensus on how swaps transactions should be matched, executed, and reported going forward was another matter altogether.

Since OTC derivatives are traded globally, there is no single regulatory body to define and enforce trading rules. In the United States, interpretation and implementation of the Dodd-Frank Act was split between the Commodity Futures Trading Commission (CFTC) and the Securities and Exchange Commission (SEC). The CFTC regulates interest rate, currency, commodity, and credit default swaps, whereas the SEC regulates swaps related to securities, for example, credit derivatives on individual companies. In Europe, three sets of legislation—Markets in Financial Instruments Directive (MiFID), Markets in Financial Instruments and amending Regulation (MiFIR), and the European Markets Infrastructure Regulation—were the driving force behind the changes to OTC derivatives trading.

In the United States, the CFTC's mandated changes that required standardized swaps to be traded on existing exchanges or on a new type of trading venue called a swap execution facility (SEF). The Dodd-Frank Act required SEFs to provide a trading platform that enables users' orders to be electronically matched with bid and **offer prices** provided by multiple market participants. This trading method effectively shifted interactions from being a one-to-one relationship between the parties involved in voice-executed transactions to a many-to-many relationship. As a result, swap prices would be more accessible and, thus, lead to greater competition. The introduction of SEFs would also increase the transparency into the trading process by providing an electronic audit trail of how transactions were originated and executed.

In Europe, on the other hand, lawmakers created a new category of trading platforms called organized trading facilities (OTF). The approach taken with OTFs was more flexible and was not limited to electronic trading, and voice execution was also allowed. Lawmakers and regulators took the view that voice execution was beneficial for trading illiquid and large-value swap transactions, which could easily overwhelm electronic marketplaces that only had small trading volumes. While standardized swap contracts can be readily traded electronically, there are other swaps that are illiquid and are not well suited for open markets. Also, other types of derivatives, beside swaps, could be traded on OTFs.

Many countries have yet to outline the requirements for swap execution, **clearing**, and **settlement**, and some of those that have proposed guidelines have taken approaches different from those of the US and European models. In Singapore, for example, the Monetary Authority of Singapore proposed centralized clearing and settlement for some common OTC derivatives contracts, but did not require that they be traded on an electronic platform or an exchange. In Asia, voice trading is the dominant form of swap trading.

These regulatory changes threatened many banks' and interdealer brokers' long-established business models. For others, it provided new opportunities. Consider, for example, ICAP, one of the largest interdealer brokers with a long history of voice trading operations. In 2003, it purchased BrokerTec, a company that provided an electronic trading platform for fixed income trading. Then, in 2006, it purchased EBS, which was one of the two dominant electronic FX trading platform providers. In 2010, ICAP launched an electronic platform for trading interest rate swaps called iSwap. It quickly gained traction and cannibalized some of ICAP's **voice dealing** business, and also drew transaction volume away from its competitors' voice dealing units. In 2012, ICAP agreed to purchase a small-cap stock exchange, providing it with a UK exchange license that enabled it to offer listed derivatives in Europe and compete with established exchanges. ICAP provides an example of how a financial institution can transform itself to accommodate market changes.

As a result of the regulatory changes, exchanges and other types of financial institutions also were provided with opportunities to move into OTC derivatives markets. In 2008, Inter Continental Exchange (ICE), which operates derivatives exchanges in the United States and the United Kingdom, purchased interdealer broker Creditex, which specialized in credit default swaps (CDS) and other credit derivatives. Through its Creditex

(Continued)

(Continued)

subsidiary, ICE was able to offer a hybrid trading, which included both voice and electronic execution models for CDS. Likewise, State Street, a firm that provides global custody and investment management services, launched a swap execution facility in 2015. For its SEF offering, SwapEx, State Street leveraged the same technology it used to implement its electronic trading platforms for FX, Currenex, and for US government bonds, GovEx.

As of 2017, these regulatory changes had been fully implemented in many markets. Over half of interest rate derivatives were traded on SEF, and around 75% of interest rate swaps were cleared through central counterparties. However, one of the largest regulatory reforms, MiFID II, had yet to come into effect. The original date for MiFID II's implementation had been scheduled for January 2017, but the European Commission chose to extend the deadline by a year to provide more time for market participants and regulators to prepare for the multitude of business process and IT system changes that were required.

Sources: Spencer, Michael, "ICAP Wins Fight to Create Trading Colossus," *Telegraph*, April 22, 2006, http://www.telegraph.co.uk/finance/2937296/Icap-wins-fight-to-create-trading-colossus.html; Serdarevic, Masa, "ICAP's Swap Platform Exceeds Expectations," *Financial Times*, April 1, 2011, http://www.ft.com/cms/s/0/98526a30-5b9c-11e0-b965-00144feab49a.html; Mackenzie, Michael, "Swap Execution Facilities: Industry Hopes Longer Delays Will Mean Looser Rules," *Financial Times*, November 3, 2011, http://www.ft.com/cms/s/0/38cd2bb4-f8c6-11e0-ad8f-00144feab49a.html; Grant, Jeremy, "Europe: New Trading Venues Aim to Provide Choice of Structures," *Financial Times*, November 3, 2011, http://www.ft.com/cms/s/0/571dc016-0234-11e1-a0fa-00144feabdc0.html; Lim, Kenneth, "MAS Lays Down Rules for OTC Derivatives," *Business Times*, February 14, 2012; Weitzman, Hal, "ICE in $625m Deal to Buy Creditex," *Financial Times*, June 3, 2008, http://www.ft.com/cms/s/0/6a5880be-317f-11dd-b77c-0000779fd2ac.html#axzz20qYKyOAT; Stafford, Philip and Simon Mundy, "ICAP Secures Plus Exchange License," *Financial Times*, May 18, 2012, http://www.ft.com/cms/s/0/fbcce840-a0fd-11e1-aac1-00144feabdc0.html; Grant, Jeremy, "State Street Plans OTC Derivatives Platform," *Financial Times*, February 15, 2012, http://www.ft.com/cms/s/0/7dbca282-57c5-11e1-ae89-00144feabdc0.html; "OTC Derivatives Statistics at End-June 2016," Bank for International Settlements, November 2016, http://www.bis.org/publ/otc_hy1611.pdf; Stafford, P., "No More MiFID II Delays–European Markets Regulator," *Financial Times*, June 7, 2017, https://www.ft.com/content/663b3629-c764-34de-892d-50c62d515643; "Trends in IRD Clearing and SEF Trading," International Swaps and Derivatives Association, December 2016, https://www2.isda.org/attachment/OTAzMA==/Trends%20in%20IRD%20Clearing%20and%20SEF%20Trading1.pdf.

Questions

1. Why would financial institutions choose to buy firms that have existing electronic trading platforms rather than implement those platforms themselves?
2. What incentives would swap users have for migrating their trading to electronic platforms?
3. What are the benefits and drawbacks of implementing electronic swap trading solutions prior to the new regulations being finalized?
4. What advantages does voice-based trading offer over electronic trading?

In the previous chapter, basic foreign exchange (FX) products were introduced. This chapter will continue by exploring more complex derivative instruments, which are commonly used by corporate customers to help manage risk. First, the characteristics and usage of common derivative instruments will be presented. Next, the challenges and opportunities that banks face when offering derivative products are discussed. Then, the product lifecycle for an interest rate swap will be examined. Finally, the performance characteristics of architectures will be reviewed in the context of derivatives and **credit risk** management IT systems.

12.1   COMMON OTC DERIVATIVES

The vast majority of outstanding OTC derivatives contracts are related to interest rates and FX (Figure 12-2). As discussed in Chapter 11, **OTC products** are traded bilaterally between dealers, which are typically banks, and customers. OTC derivatives are usually tailored to meet specific customer needs. For example, it is possible for a customer to vary the notional principal amount of an interest rate swap over the term of the agreement. Interest rate futures and other standardized financial products do not offer the same level of flexibility. This section discusses OTC derivatives commonly used by

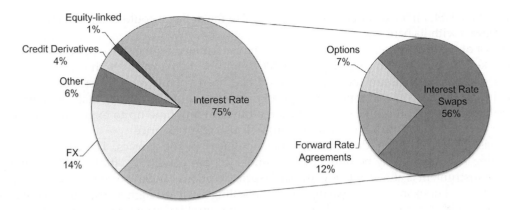

Figure 12-2 Types of OTC derivatives outstanding as measured by notional amount, December 2016
Source: BIS Statistics Explorer, http://stats.bis.org/statx/toc/DER.html

corporate treasurers and institutional customers to manage risk. Specifically, FX options, interest rate swaps, and structured products will be covered.

12.1.1 Hedging FX Risk with FX Options

As discussed in Chapter 11, forward FX contracts are relatively simple financial products that can be used to hedge current and future currency exposures. Alternatively, options are a more flexible type of financial instrument that are used across many asset classes. They allow hedging against price movements in just one direction and for movements within a specific range, as well as speculation. Call and put options give the buyer the right, but not the obligation, to purchase or sell the underlying instrument at a pre-agreed price, that is, the strike price. In many ways, purchasing options can be compared to purchasing insurance. The buyer pays a premium that provides protection against adverse price movements of the underlying instrument that the option is based upon, up through the expiry date of the option.

As an example, consider the case of a service provider in the United States who has agreed to provide services to a firm in Japan for a total of ¥105 million over a six-month period. At the current exchange rate of ¥105 to the US dollar (USD), the deal is worth US$1 million in the service provider's base currency. The risk is that the USD/Japanese yen (JPY) rate may fluctuate over the next six months and the deal could be worth significantly less than expected. For instance, if the USD/JPY exchange rate moved to 115, the service provider would incur a US$86,957 reduction in income due to FX losses, which is over 8% of the overall deal value.

To hedge the risk, the service provider could use a forward FX contract to lock in the six-month **forward rate**, which is determined by current spot and interest rates. However, the supplier might hold the view that the JPY rate would most likely stay the same or strengthen, in which case, the USD/JPY rate would decrease, over the next six months. In this case, hedging with a forward FX contract would eliminate all gains in the case of the JPY strengthening. It could, therefore, be more advantageous if options are used to hedge this exposure. If the service provider wanted to protect itself against FX

Current spot FX rate:	USD/JPY = 105.00 Purchase type: buy
Contract type:	call
Notional amount:	¥105,000,000
Expiry:	6 months
Strike price:	107.00
Cost of premium:	¥1,050,000 (US$10,000)

losses when the USD/JPY exchange rate exceeds ¥107 to the dollar, it could enter into the following FX option contract with its bank.

The cost of the option premium would largely be determined by the strike price and the volatility in the market. An option with a strike price of 106 would be more expensive than an option with the strike price of 107. Likewise, if the option market had been volatile recently or was expected to be volatile during the term of the option, the option premium would be greater than in times of steady prices. Whether an option can be exercised by the buyer at any time up to expiration (an American option) or only at expiration (a European option) will also affect its price.

Options, like most other derivatives, have nonlinear payoff curves. Hence, their properties as a hedging instrument may be only effective under certain conditions, that is, if the value of the underlying instrument is above or below the strike price. Options can be combined to achieve complex payoff strategies. For example, purchasing a call and selling a call at a higher strike price could be used to hedge only within a specific range. In the example, this strategy might be used to provide a hedge that offsets price movements between 107 and 112. Such a combination could be appropriate if the hedger thought it unlikely that the rate would exceed 112 and wanted to reduce the cost of the hedging transaction accordingly.

There are a number of ways to price options; the Black-Scholes equation is a standard way of calculating the value of an option based on its parameters. However, in practice, banks use more complex techniques to price options. These techniques take into account forecasts of future volatility and expectations that the distribution of the underlying instrument's price movements will not correspond to a normal distribution. Options are complex; there are many books that cover option usage strategies and pricing in depth (refer to the Further Reading section).

Besides "vanilla" American and European options, there are many other types of options that have their own unique features. For instance, barrier options only become active, or are deactivated, when the underlying instrument goes above or below a specific price, that is, the barrier. Barrier options are less expensive to purchase than a vanilla option with the same strike price and expiration date that does not have the barrier feature. Corporate customers often choose to use barrier options if they want to achieve some level of protection, but not at the full cost of paying for a standard option.

Another type of option is an Asian option. Pricing and settlement of an Asian option is based on an average of the underlying instrument's price during a specified time period, rather than on the price at the time of expiry as with a European option. Asian options are less expensive than European options and are also beneficial when hedging multiple exposures that are spread across extended periods, as opposed to a single exposure that falls on a specific settlement date. Besides Asian and Barrier options, there are many other common types that banks offer to customers through their dealing floors (Figure 12-3).

12.1.2 Hedging Interest Rate Risk with Interest Rate Swaps

Besides FX risk, many corporations and institutional customers need to hedge their exposure to fluctuations in interest rates. Interest rate swaps (IRS) are the most common type of interest rate derivatives used by corporations to hedge fixed or floating rate commitments. For instance, a customer may have taken a loan at a variable rate, but may want to fix the amounts of the payments due. Alternatively, the objective could be to fix the rate of return on a variable rate deposit. Besides hedging, IRS provide a means for banks and other financial institutions to speculate on interest rate movements.

Vanilla fixed-float interest rate swaps are structured so that one of the parties involved agrees to exchange floating interest payments for fixed, and the other party agrees to exchange fixed payments for floating. The size of the cash flows involved is proportional to the notional transaction amount; however, the notional amount is not exchanged as part of the swap transaction. The fixed payment rate is referred to as the swap rate. The floating payment rate will usually be based on a reference rate, such as the London Interbank Offered Rate (LIBOR), plus some adjustment factor. Only the net difference between the payments due will be settled.

Figure 12-3 Banks' treasury dealing floors primarily focus on sales and trading of derivatives (© DBS Bank. Reprinted with permission.)

For example, consider a company that is taking out a two-year, variable-rate loan for US$100 million that requires payments every three months, starting October 1, 2012. It can choose to fix its interest rate exposure by entering into an interest rate swap agreement with its bank or other counterparty with the following parameters:

Direction:	Sell/be the Payer—fixed rate is paid
Trade date:	Aug 22, 2017
Commencement date:	Oct 1, 2017
Notional principle:	US$100,000,000
Term:	2 years
Floating payment frequency:	Quarterly (Jan 1, Mar 1, Jul 1, and Oct 1)
Reset dates:	2 business days prior to settlement
Floating rate:	3-month LIBOR + 2%
Fixed rate payment frequency:	Semiannual (Jan 1 and Jun 1)
Fixed rate:	5%
Compounding:	None
Averaging:	None
Day count convention:	30/360
Reset date:	2 days prior to payment date
Upfront fee:	US$500,000
Initial reset rate:	3%

The payment dates and rates for the floating rate payments would be structured to correspond to the rate and schedule of the company's loan payment obligations. The initial reset rate, that is, the floating interest rate for the first three months of the agreement, is typically set at the time the swap deal is executed and, thus, the floating payment amount due on October 1 would be:

$100,000,000 \times 0.03$ (reset rate) $\times$ 90/360 (quarterly) = \$750,000, and

the fixed rate payment that would be received on January 1 would be:

$100,000,000 \times 0.05$ (fixed interest rate) $\times$ 180/360 (semiannual) = \$2,500,000.

Figure 12-4 shows a simplified view of the cash flows associated with this example, where the solid lines show the upfront fee and fixed rate amounts paid and the dashed lines show the floating rate amounts received. As highlighted in the figure, the amount of the floating rate payments that follow the initial accrual period are initially unknown; they will be determined on the **reset date** when the benchmark interest rate is recorded and used to calculate the payment amount.

If the two counterparties have a netting agreement in place, the payments due on January 1 and July 1 will be netted off one another so that only one payment is required. For example, if the three-month LIBOR rate was 0.5% two business days prior to January 1, the floating rate payment on that day would be 2% + 0.5% and the amount due calculated to be:

$100,000,000 \times 0.025$ (reset rate) $\times$ 90/360 (quarterly) = \$625,000,

which, if netted against the fixed payment due of \$2,500,000, would result in a single payment from the company to the bank of \$2,500,000 − \$625,000 = \$1,875,000 on that date. Alternatively, if **gross settlement** were used, the company would pay \$2,500,000 and would receive \$625,000 from the bank separately.

It is also possible to conduct IRS across different currencies. This practice is referred to as a cross-currency swap and enables companies to borrow in one currency at a variable interest rate, convert its repayment obligation to another currency at a fixed interest rate, or vice versa. It may be the case that an IRS is required because a company cannot borrow cost effectively at a fixed rate in a particular currency or market.

Swaps involve less counterparty risk than other underlying instruments such as bonds because, generally, the principal amount is not transferred. In the case of default, the potential loss is the value of the swap, which may be positive or negative depending on the interest rate environment. Furthermore, it is common for bilateral IRS trades to include a Credit Support Annex (CSA) that requires margin collateral to be posted to help minimize losses in case of default by a counterparty.

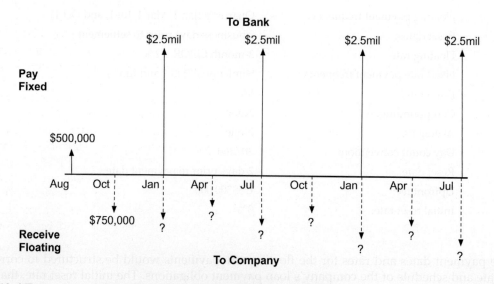

Figure 12-4 Example cash flows for a fixed-floating interest rate swap

In addition to IRS, other types of interest rate derivatives can be used to hedge interest rate exposures, including:

- caps, floors, and collars;
- swap options ("swaptions");
- interest rate options; and
- forward rate agreements (FRAs).

Except for FRAs, all of these instruments involve optionality, that is, their valuation is dependent on a contingent event, such as a benchmark interest rate reaching a particular level. For example, payment for a cap will only be required within a given accrual period if the benchmark rate exceeds a predefined strike price (rate). The buyer will pay an upfront premium and will only receive a payment from the seller if the agreed payout criteria are met.

Like swaps, these instruments vary in terms of their tenor, that is, the length of time they are active, and their frequency of settlement. Some instruments, such as caps, floors, collars, and IRS, may have tenors that extend for several years and usually have intermediate settlements that mirror the cash flows of the underlying instrument they are meant to hedge, for example, a bond. Intermediate settlement also reduces the credit risk exposure between the counterparties by preventing the amount owed between the counterparties from potentially ballooning over the lifetime of the contract.

12.1.3 Hedging Other Risks with Structured Products

Some banks offer customized derivatives, referred to as structured or synthetic products, to address specific customer needs. In some cases, corporate or institutional customers will want products that provide complex payout structures or hedge-specific risk exposures. In these cases, the customer will typically call the structured products desk at a bank and explain their requirements. It will then be up to the bank to formulate a product that addresses those needs, assess its risk and cost to manage, and then price the product accordingly. Some structured products can be constructed by combining existing products available in the market, such as bonds, exchange traded futures, and options. In other cases, the bank may have to find other means of managing or offloading the risk associated with a structured product. For example, in some Asian markets, banks' institutional customers may want to buy an option on a basket of equities; however, exchange-listed options may not be available for the underlying equities or if a listed option is available, the market may not be sufficiently liquid to support the size of the trade. In these cases, the bank could provide a structured product that achieves the customers' objectives. To manage its risk, the bank would likely need to delta hedge* its position over the lifetime of the product. Pricing and processing structured products require advanced business skills, IT systems, and operational capabilities. Hence, only a limited number of banks offer structured products to customers. Accordingly, banks have less competition in this area and a greater opportunity to achieve high margins. This is especially true since, due to its complexity, product pricing is mostly opaque to the customer. However, the costs and risks associated with offering customized derivatives are also high. Whereas the International Swaps and Derivatives Association (ISDA) has determined a common set of definitions, provisions, terms, and conditions that are commonly used as a basis for swap transactions, structured product transactions generally cannot leverage standard agreements. Thus, they require specialized legal documentation to be drafted. Likewise, IT systems and internal processes that are designed to support common financial products may not readily cope with custom-made products.

---

* Delta hedging involves buying and selling the underlying instruments as their prices move to offset the corresponding option's price movements so as to control the risk exposure.

Most of the processing, such as confirmation validation and price revaluation, must be performed manually and may require a detailed understanding of the contract agreement.

12.1.4 Managing Bank Risk as Over-the-counter Derivatives Dealers

As discussed in Chapter 11, when banks act as dealers for OTC securities, they take on the risk associated with the other side of customers' transactions. The bank may hold the inventory, or position, risk until it is able to perform a similar transaction in reverse with another customer that, for the most part, offsets that risk. Alternatively, the bank can perform a transaction with another dealer in the interbank market, also referred to as the interdealer market, or using interest rate futures. The availability of liquid markets for hedging the interest rate risk that banks take on as dealers makes it practical for them to provide IRS **liquidity** to customers. In cases where banks take on large positions when they deal with customers, it may take them several days to offset the risk [2].

Transactions performed in the interbank market will involve commonly traded contract types that do not cater to customization. For example, to be liquid, vanilla IRS contracts traded between dealers will have standard contract parameters and common term periods, such as two or five years, and will have fixed start and end dates. Thus, even when a bank is able to roughly match customer IRS transactions with one another or offset their interest rate risk in the interbank market, it will still have residual interest rate risk, which results from this mismatch, that it must monitor and manage.

12.2   RETAIL BANKING AND WEALTH MANAGEMENT CONTEXT

Given their complexity and risk characteristics, derivatives are not generally suitable as retail banking products. That said, in some markets, hybrid products have been offered to retail customers that combine deposit and derivatives products. **Dual currency investments (DCIs)** are one such instrument. A DCI is a form of deposit whereby funds are deposited in one currency but potentially returned in another currency at the end of the deposit term depending on exchange rate fluctuations. The customer faces the risk that the amount returned, when converted, may be less than the original deposit amount. However, for accepting this risk, the deposited amount yields interest at a higher rate.

In practice, DCIs can be decomposed into deposit and FX option components. The premium yielded by the option is incorporated into the DCI's interest rate. This type of packaging can make investing in derivatives simpler and more attractive (less scary) for retail customers. Likewise, the complexity of the structure hides the banks' margin, making these types of products attractive to banks. It is important to note, though, that unlike normal deposit products, customers who purchase DCIs may realize losses as well as gains. Hence, such products are often limited to high-net-worth customers, who are viewed as being in a position to tolerate the potential losses.

There are many other flavors of structured investment products that are based on derivatives offered to retail customers. Equity-linked investments are another example, where deposits are linked to performance stocks rather than currencies. Even more complex structures may be marketed to private banking customers. For example, accumulators, a product sold to high-net-worth customers in Asia, involve the purchase of a stock at a fixed price at regular intervals and also include a knockout option [3]. Accumulators became less popular with customers after they resulted in significant losses during the market crash of 2008.

Derivatives can also be used to construct retail and wealth management investment products that guarantee a minimum return, but also provide additional upside that is tied to a particular market or returns on an underlying asset. For example, as an alternative to investing pension savings in the stock markets, "capital protection" products are offered that provide a low guaranteed minimum payout on funds, for example, 1%, but with higher returns provided a particular stock market index increases substantially. These types of products can be attractive when interest rates are low and investing the money in savings or an annuity would yield small returns, and when customers are concerned about the potential of incurring losses if the money is invested in stocks, and the markets are going down. Typically, guaranteed return products are constructed by combining a zero-coupon bond and equity futures or an equity swap. Options are also employed to limit losses or cap gains in structured investment products.

12.3 CORPORATE BANKING CONTEXT

Ninety-four percent of the world's 500 largest corporations use derivatives to manage risks, with large corporations in developed economies making the most use of derivatives [4]. Among industry sectors, the financial services sector was, not surprisingly, the greatest user of derivatives, be it interest rate, FX, commodity, credit, or equity derivatives. On the other hand, most other industry sectors were only active users of interest rate and FX derivatives. Outside of financial services, the basic materials, services, and utilities sectors are the three largest users of commodity derivatives. Companies in all sectors used small amounts of equity derivatives, and banks were the primary users of credit derivatives.

Several factors determine the type of instruments used by corporate customers. Some of the primary drivers are as follows:

- **Purpose/strategy**. The size, skills, and remit of the corporate treasury will largely determine whether simple instruments, such as forwards, or more complex derivatives are used. Where treasury units have the latitude to take views on currency exchange and interest rates based on their forecasts, they may be more inclined to choose option-based products, which support directional hedging.

- **Accounting treatment**. Derivatives' effects on companies' financial statements can be as important as their hedging effects on cash flows. Since the objective of hedging is to reduce cash-flow and earnings volatility, accounting treatment of hedging instruments' gains and losses becomes a critical consideration. The preference is that gains and losses from hedging transactions should not show up in the companies' profit and loss statement; if they do, they should be matched with offsetting gains or losses from the underlying exposure that is being hedged.

- **Taxation**. How gains and losses are taxed for different types of hedging transactions is also a significant concern. The effect of taxes can affect both the cost and effectiveness of hedging, as well as how well the hedge matches the underlying exposure. Taxation on the use of different types of financial instruments varies by country.

- **Documentation requirements**. For some types of instruments, to qualify for special accounting and/or tax treatment, it may be necessary to maintain documentation that clearly relates the hedging transaction to the underlying exposures that they hedge. The effort required to document hedging transactions, and the risks involved with doing it incorrectly, may also determine firms' appetite for using different types of instruments.

- **Internal controls and reporting capabilities**. Leveraged directional instruments, such as options, can involve risk because they can be used to speculate as well as hedge. Overleveraged speculative trades can lead to financial ruin. Hence, it is critical that corporations have sufficient internal controls and reporting capabilities to ensure that hedging activities are within approved parameters and can adequately monitor the exposures created by derivatives trades.

For many years, some customers viewed the costs associated with using derivatives to hedge risk like buying insurance—it was unlikely to provide much benefit, but was necessary. However, the volatility of financial markets, currencies, and business environment that was brought about by the Global Financial Crisis and the sovereign debt crises in Europe, have brought a new appreciation for the risk management benefits that derivatives provide.

12.4 BUSINESS OPPORTUNITIES

Banks' derivatives businesses provide them with many opportunities for providing unique and profitable products and services to their customers. Furthermore, because the requisite skills and infrastructure to support derivatives to customers take substantial time and resources to develop, this creates a natural barrier to entry for many institutions. Where some banks struggle to remain competitive in markets that have become commoditized, others position themselves on the leading edge, taking advantage of new profitable derivatives product niches. Profits are driven by transaction volume, rather than being dependent on interest rates and economic cycles. Hence, derivatives can counterbalance banks' more traditional lending business.

Historically, the margins associated with OTC derivatives have been substantial; as a result there has been less focus on automating and streamlining the related business and operational processes. However, as highlighted in Case Study 12-1, regulatory and competitive pressures have been driving changes in how OTC derivatives are traded and processed. Hence, banks have an opportunity to implement more **straight- through processing (STP)** of OTC derivatives products. STP helps reduce error rates and per-transaction processing costs and support increased volumes. The banks that engage in this strategy sooner can offer more competitive prices and better service to customers, helping them gain market share. Moreover, automated processing can help reduce the operational risk associated with miskeying and other human errors that occur with manual processing. As a case in point, in 2015, a major investment bank mistakenly made a $6 billion payment to one of its hedge fund customers, when a junior staff member keyed in the gross settlement amount instead of the net settlement amount [5].

There is also an opportunity for banks to apply derivatives in new and creative ways to address market needs. For example, exchange traded funds (ETFs) have gained popularity as retail and institutional investment vehicles, increasing from around one trillion dollars in 2011 to over four trillion dollars in 2017 [6, 7]. As they grew, ETFs progressed from being relatively simple investment structures that purchased and held the underlying stocks in an equity index, such as the S&P 500, to complex products that incorporate commodities, fixed income, and FX exposures. Some ETFs are also leveraged such that their price movements are a multiple, for example, twice that, of an index. Others may have performance characteristics that mimic the inverse performance of an index, so that if the price of the underlying index goes down, the price of the ETF will go up. OTC derivatives have enabled much of this innovation by eliminating the need for fund managers to buy and sell the underlying products to achieve an ETF's target performance objectives. Instead, synthetic ETFs enter into swap or structured product agreements with banks, whereby the bank will provide the desired ETF performance characteristics through a derivatives product.

Moreover, some markets participants have been able to lower operational and regulatory costs by reducing the number of outstanding derivatives contracts that they hold through a process referred to as trade compression. This process replaces multiple gross contracts with a single one that provides the same net financial exposure. Reducing the number of contracts makes it easier to discern overall risk exposure, and having fewer large notional positions is more favorable from a regulatory standpoint. Some interdealer brokers have begun offering services related to trade compression to help their customers benefit from this tool.

12.5 BUSINESS CHALLENGES

Probably the most significant challenge related with derivatives is measuring and managing their many associated risks. Overexposure to derivatives is a major concern. Since derivatives' gains or losses are driven by market events, their effects may seem benign one month and catastrophic the next.

As a case in point, Barings Bank collapsed because of excessive index future and option trades, and American International Group's (AIG's) insurance business was all but brought down by the credit derivatives positions that it had taken on. In both cases, the losses were amassed by the firms' overseas derivatives trading units. Banks' customers have also been stung by derivatives positions that went wrong, and in some cases, have blamed the financial institutions that sold them the products for their losses (Case Study 12-2).

Besides overexposure, the inherent complexity of derivatives also makes them difficult to assess and manage. Managers of trading desks and business heads may not have advanced degrees in mathematics or financial engineering and, thus, may not be in a position to fully understand the level of risk that the traders working for them have taken on through complex derivatives transactions. Similarly, those in middle-office risk-review positions may not have sufficient knowledge to evaluate

---

Case Study 12-2
Derivatives Mis-selling Risk

Even when a bank manages its financial risk effectively, it must also sometimes be concerned about losses that its customers may incur from the misuse of derivatives. Although banks may not have fiduciary responsibilities to corporate and institutional customers, it does not bar legal suits from being brought against banks when substantial losses do occur. Mis-selling of financial products may be alleged, leading to regulatory complications, reputational damage, and possibly monetary damages. As a case in point, after losing over US$1 billion due to bad bets on derivatives positions in 1994, Orange County sued its principal broker and eventually settled for over US$400 million.

Unfortunately, Orange County was not the end of banks' troubles with selling derivatives to city governments. Again, 18 years after the Orange County debacle, several multinational investment banks would go on to settle a lawsuit with the city of Milan in Italy. In this case, the banks provided **investment banking** services to Milan for its sale of €1.7 billion worth of bonds in 2005 and then entered into an interest rate swap agreement so that the city would pay a floating interest rate, rather than the higher fixed interest rate. One of the features of the swap transaction was that it had a "collar" provision that required Milan to pay more if rates fell beyond a particular level. So, when interest rates fell precipitously in the years following the Global Financial Crisis, the city found itself losing out as a result of the collar provision. The city claimed that it was misled into believing that it would benefit from the arrangement more than it did, and also that the banks charged it €101 million in hidden fees. Ultimately, in 2012, the banks agreed to settle the civil lawsuit for €455 million.

Milan was not the last European city to make claims against banks. In 2012, the town of Cassino, Italy, also reached a settlement with JPMorgan over an interest rate swap deal in which it had lost money. Likewise, the German city of Pforzheim, which lost €57 million on swaps, settled a legal claim against the bank. Clearly, tighter controls and better transaction validation are required on the side of local governments to ensure that they understand the consequences of the transactions into which they have entered. However, banks also would benefit from clearer disclosure and documentation covering the potential risks and worst-case outcomes of the products they are offering. As a result of doing so, they may not win the customer's business, but at least they will not have to clean up the mess afterward.

Sources: "Orange Country Value-at-Risk Case," http://merage.uci.edu/~jorion/oc/case.html; "Municipalities and Derivatives: Cities in the Casino," *Economist*, May 28, 2010, http://www.economist.com/node/15731538; Bertacche, Marco and Elisa Martinuzzi, "Milan Settles Derivatives with UBS, Deutsche Bank, JPMorgan," *Bloomberg*, March 23, 2012, http://www.bloomberg.com/news/2012-03-22/city-of-milan-reaches-accord-with-banks-to-settle-derivatives.html; Martinuzzi, Elisa, Lorenzo Totaro, and Veron Silver, "JPMorgan Cassino Settlement Shows Derivatives Failed Taxpayers," *Bloomberg*, April 20, 2012, http://www.bloomberg.com/news/2012-04-11/jpmorgan-cassino-settlement-shows-derivatives-failed-taxpayers.html; "2 JPMorgan bankers charged over Pforzheim swap sale," *Business Times*, February 9, 2015, http://www.businesstimes.com.sg/banking-finance/2-jpmorgan-bankers-charged-over-pforzheim-swap-sale.

or question the positions taken by front-office traders. Even when the intricacies are understood, small implementation errors in complex pricing or risk models may be difficult to identify. Hence, "model risk" can also lead to unexpected losses.

Moreover, one of the most significant regulatory changes that have come about since the Global Financial Crisis was the requirement for banks that trade OTC derivatives to hold more capital to account for the risks associated with derivatives. Likewise, new rules related to clearing and settling OTC derivatives reduce counterparty risk, but also increase the cost of trading derivatives. Particularly in fragmented markets, such as Asia, the cost of complying with each country's regulatory requirements related to clearing and settlement may be prohibitive. Hence, these changes have reduced the profitability of banks' derivatives trading businesses, and caused some banks to abandon their derivatives operations in certain markets. Additionally, a number of jurisdictions began requiring participants in OTC derivatives transactions, such as financial institutions and their customers, to report those trades to regulators on a near real-time or daily basis. The technology solution considerations related to OTC derivatives trade reporting are discussed in Chapter 19.

12.6   INTEREST RATE SWAP PRODUCT LIFECYCLE

To help illustrate how banks' business processes function in the context of derivative products, this section will review the product lifecycle of an interest rate swap (Figure 12-5). To help illustrate basic concepts, voice-based execution processes are described, and activities involving electronic matching and clearing are not covered.

12.6.1 Design and Setup

Before initiating an interest rate swap, it is necessary to define and set up the allowable parameters, such as the currencies that will be supported, the minimum and maximum tenors, the limit structures, and the allowable variations to basic deal types. For example, a variant of the standard interest rate swap structure, which exchanges fixed and floating cash flows, could exchange two different floating interest rate payments streams, commonly known as a "basis" swap. The benchmark interest rates that can be used—such as the LIBOR for USD, the Singapore Interbank Offer Rate (SIBOR) for SGD, and the Bank-Bill Swap Rate (BBSW) for Australian dollars—must also be configured. The source of the market rates that are used to construct the interest rate curves used for pricing will also need to be defined.

The derivatives front- and back-office system vendor may provide off-the-shelf configurations that can be used as the basis of the core setup and conforms to industry best practices. However, it is usually the case that each financial institution will have its product and process variants and restrictions that it will want to implement.

Part of what determines which instruments and variations on instruments that will be supported is the bank's ability to handle and support them in the front, middle, and back offices. In particular, pricing of derivatives, especially exotics, is much more difficult than pricing simple instruments, such as spot, forwards, stocks, and bonds. Complex algorithms may need to be implemented and, in some

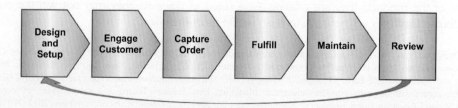

Figure 12-5 Transaction and services lifecycle model

cases, Monte Carlo simulation may be necessary. These pricing techniques are usually complex and computationally intensive and, thus, expensive to implement. Implementation cost may result from having to recruit people with the requisite math and modeling skills to determine the best pricing method and then build and validate the pricing models. In production, a single server may be utilized for hours just to compute a derivative's price using some techniques. Alternatively, multiple servers can be utilized in parallel to achieve faster computation times, but this requires additional investment in hardware and leads to increased maintenance costs.

12.6.2 Engage the Customer

Like most OTC products, the terms and conditions for individual interest rate swaps are based on an ISDA Master Agreement (for example, the ISDA 2006 Definitions) that defines the general terms and conditions that apply to the transactions. CSAs, which specify the collateral agreements between the two parties, may also be attached to the agreement. Use of collateral deposits provides each of the counterparties with some security in case the other counterparty defaults. After these agreements have been put in place, IRS trades can be executed between the counterparties.

There are two main markets for trading interest rate swaps: corporate and institutional customers, and other banks. Thus, the voice execution process for IRS is similar to that shown for foreign exchange in Figure 11-2. Unlike FX forwards, which are now executed mainly over electronic channels, nonstandard IRS and other complex derivatives are more likely to be transacted through the corporate dealing desk (that is, over the phone), and daily transaction volumes are more likely to be in the hundreds, rather than millions for most financial institutions. Wherever possible, standard settlement instructions should be set up to help ensure that exceptions do not occur during the fulfillment stage of the transaction.

Derivatives, such as options and IRS, are complicated from an electronic price distribution standpoint due to the multitude of instruments that can be generated. In the case of options, the strike price and expiry dates may vary, so that for each expiry date there is a range of option put and call prices potentially available that correspond to the available strike prices (Case Study 12-3). For IRS, the tenor, settlement dates, swap rates, currencies, payment frequencies, rate compounding options, and rate averaging options can create many combinations. This makes precomputation of prices, for distribution to customers, impractical and, therefore, real-time pricing capabilities that can fulfill requests for on-demand price quotations are required.

12.6.3 Capture Order

By nature of being OTC instruments, interest rate swaps are privately negotiated between counterparties. Typical order capture activities will include determining the transaction parameters, pricing the transaction, negotiation of fees, limit verification, and potentially reserving a portion of the credit limit for the pending deal. Pricing the transaction will require the net present value (NPV) to be calculated, based on interest rate curves. Since IRS are OTC transactions, banks must be concerned about the counterparty credit and settlement limit exposures. However, it is important to note that the risk involved is related to the potential net settlement amounts, not the notional value of the transaction.

12.6.4 Fulfill Transaction

As part of the transaction fulfillment, confirmation will be sent between the parties and then reconciled. If the SWIFT network is used for confirmations, the SWIFT MT360 message type is used to confirm interest rate derivatives involving only one currency, and the MT361 is used for multicurrency interest rate swaps. Alternatively, other electronic confirmation services, MarkitWire for trade confirmations, and, in some cases, fax or email may also be used. Whereas the net settlements for IRS are likely to be scheduled for some future date, transaction fees may be immediately payable and, thus, require near-term settlement. Initial accounting entries will be generated, and the required documentation will be stored, as required by the accounting treatment that is utilized. Depending on the regulatory jurisdiction where the trade is booked, trade reporting may also be necessary.

12.6.5 Maintain Transaction

Because interest rate swaps require ongoing, periodic settlement, transaction maintenance will involve periodic calculation of the cash-flow amounts due, based on the value of predefined benchmark rates, and the net settlement of those cash flows. Accounting entries will also be required to match these settlements. Maintenance activities will be discussed in more detail in Section 12.7. Additional maintenance may also be required if the swap is terminated early through another transaction.

If an IRS agreement has a Credit Support Annex attached, the counterparties must regularly review the value of collateral posted. If the value of the collateral value does not fulfill the terms of the CSA, additional collateral will need to be posted to address the shortfall. Also, customers may also request to change the terms of their IRS, such as asking for early termination of the swap. If the customer requests to terminate an IRS before the maturity date, the bank would need to recalculate the value of the IRS, in which case the customer may be subject to additional costs or rebates to exit the swap agreement, depending on current interest rates.

Moreover, banks themselves are required to maintain minimum credit ratings to act as counterparties to derivatives transactions. Many swap agreements have a clause that allows a swap to be settled immediately and terminated if either party's credit is downgraded. Thus, if a bank's credit rating is downgraded below the acceptable level of an IRS contract, the counterparty of the swap may substitute it with another bank [8].

12.6.6 Review

Besides mark-to-market revaluation and limit monitoring, both corporate customers and banks may perform market sensitivity analysis on existing swap obligations. This analysis could involve adjusting parts or all of an interest rate curve to reflect potential changes in market conditions. Repricing of IRS based on adjusted curves will produce new NPV that reflects the change in value of the derivatives contract. Depending on the parameters of the transaction, its sensitivity to changes in different parts of the interest rate curve will vary.

12.7 LIFECYCLE FOCUS: OTC DERIVATIVES TRANSACTION MAINTENANCE

The maintenance portion of the trade lifecycle begins after the deal has been executed and the initial settlements have been completed. At that point, the transaction will be idle until the next settlement is due, and the reset date, also known as the fixing date, for the floating rate is reached. The rate-reset dates will be determined when the deal is executed. They may be designated as some number of days prior to settlement, for example, two days, or possibly at the time of the previous settlement. The rate-reset process specifies the floating rate that will be used to calculate the amount due for the floating rate portion of the swap settlements.

As shown in Figure 12-6, each day, the fixing process is performed for the swaps that have a rate reset scheduled.* However, before the process can begin, validated reference rates must be available. Usually, a separate, middle office group will be responsible for sourcing, validating, and storing the reference rates in a common repository or distributing them to downstream IT systems. Once the reference rate is available, then either the amount due or the amount payable to the counterparty can be calculated based on that rate. Then, if the bank is paying the floating rate, it will send payment advice and make payment to the

---

* Even though settlement usually occurs at the end of the accrual (coupon) period, the rate used for calculating the settlement (the reset) is often determined prior to the start of the accrual period.

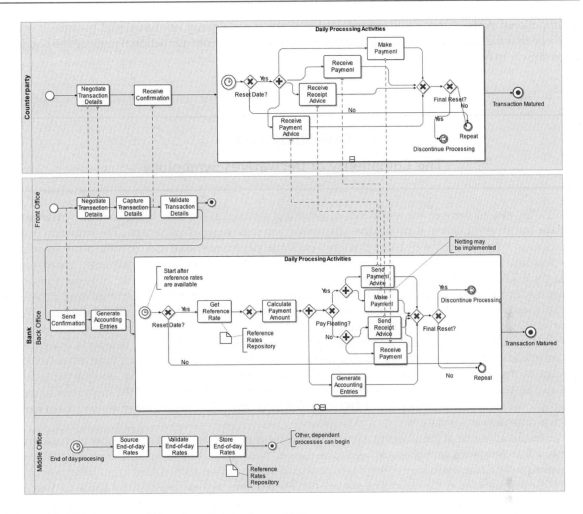

Figure 12-6 Maintenance lifecycle activities for an IRS

counterparty using the bank's normal settlement facilities. Alternatively, if it is paying the fixed rate, it will send receipt advice and receive the floating payment. Accounting entries would also be generated during each fixing and passed to the bank's **general ledger (GL)** system. The process model shown in Figure 12-6 is a simplified version of the interest rate swap process for illustration purposes. It assumed that there is no early termination and no exchange of principle, that is, the notional amount of the transaction, and only shows the counterparty's corresponding actions to the banks' actions. In practice, the counterparty would also perform its own full rate reset process similar to the bank's process. Also, if the two parties' rates or calculated interest amounts do not match, they would then need to reconcile the differences.

On the last payment date, the transaction would transition to a mature state. If collateral was exchanged initially, it would be retuned and final payment advice, settlement instructions, and accounting entries would be generated to complete the transaction. In practice, multiple operational groups, with designations such as "trade support" and "payment processing," would perform the functions shown in the back-office swim lane shown in Figure 12-6.

12.8 ARCHITECTURE CONSIDERATIONS

Performance is one of the nonfunctional areas that are fundamental to solution architecture. Whereas system accuracy could be considered as a performance need from the business perspective, for the purposes of this discussion, accuracy will be considered a functional requirement, and not a nonfunctional performance requirement. Performance is considered nonfunctional because it could easily be that the solution does exactly what it is supposed to do from a functional perspective but does it too slowly to be effective.

Case Study 12-3

The Complexity of Derivatives Symbology

It is often easy to overlook the importance of things that are used all the time. In the context of **market data** and IT, one example is symbology—the naming and referencing of instruments. The institution that creates an instrument or the exchange that lists it usually defines the reference code or name of the financial instrument. Spot FX is fairly standardized and is referenced based on the currency pair being traded, for example, USD/SGD. Equities usually have a pneumonic symbol, or a numeric code for languages that do not readily translate into ASCII characters, such as Japanese. Referring to a bond and other fixed income instruments is more complicated; a unique alphanumeric code is assigned to each individual issuance. The symbology for derivatives is even more complex.

As a case in point, consider exchange-traded options in the United States. For decades, a five-letter system was used as the basis for referencing options. The base code contained in the first three letters would relate to the underlying instrument, the fourth letter would indicate the expiry month, and the last letter would be associated with a specific strike price. For example, the option symbol XOMAP might refer to the January call option at the strike price of $80 for Exxon Mobil stock. This naming scheme worked, but had many drawbacks and limitations.

For instance, one of the problems with this naming structure was that the limited number of characters meant that the options symbols would need to be recycled from one year to the next. References to options expiring in the future would have different base codes and the symbol would then need to be "rolled over" to the current year code as the expiry time drew nearer. For example, the next year's July call option for Exxon Mobil stock might start out as XAQFP, but at some point it would be transitioned to XOMFP to represent the current year's option. Likewise, corporate actions, such as stock splits and unexpected dividends, could lead to multiple option symbols with the same expiry month and strike price.

To address these and other shortcomings, as well as to help support growth of the derivatives industry, broker dealers, exchanges, vendors, and the Option Clearing Corporation launched the Option Symbology Initiative (OSI) in 2005. The OSI's mission was to develop a new symbology that would eliminate the need for symbol rollovers, minimize the impact of corporate actions on the naming scheme, and help reduce front-, middle-, and back-office errors. The new 21-character codes have six characters reserved for the base symbol, and include the year, month, and day of the expiration as well as a call/put indicator. Hence, with the new system, a January call option with a strike price of $80 for the Exxon Mobil stock would look like ODU110122C00080000.

The impact of such a change should not be underestimated. All market participants were affected including the exchanges, **clearing houses**, brokers, vendors, as well as institutional and retail customers. Participants' IT systems, that is, security master databases, analytic systems, **order management systems (OMS)**, and clearing and settlement systems, all had to support the new symbology. Worse yet, the data size requirements for option symbols were increased significantly. Hence, databases and display entry screens that had arbitrary size limits, such as 20 characters, would potentially need to be retrofitted and redeployed. Moreover, even if systems' existing designs were able to handle the new option symbols, extensive end-to-end testing would be required to ensure that new exception cases were not encountered.

Over a four-year period, the symbology specification was refined, extensive testing was undertaken, and in February 2010, the option symbol conversion was complete. While the new system will make things easier going forward, the previous symbology is likely to haunt historical data stores for years to come. Moreover, imagine the effort that could have been saved, both coping with the limitations of the old naming system and adapting to using the new system, if a more robust symbology had been defined and used from the start. The symbology used for OTC derivatives has benefited from lessons learned the hard way by their listed counterparts.

Sources: The Options Clearing Corporation (OCC) website, http://www.optionsclearing.com; "The Option to Change," *Westwater,* February 2008, http://download.microsoft.com/download/7/6/e/76ed5263-d2ab-41c2-b580-4a7bb1ed2d24/Westwater_Whitepaper.pdf.

12.8.1 Context

Due to the competitive and time-sensitive nature of financial transactions, performance is often a critical concern for solutions. The first and most important consideration is to define what performance is and how it will be measured. Two primary means of describing performance are (1) **throughput**—how many transactions per unit of time can be processed, and (2) **latency**—the time required to complete a single transaction.

For example, in the case of derivatives, the speed at which the pricing of exotic options is completed can be critical to the effectiveness of solutions that provide this function. "Speed" may be measured by throughput. The system may need to be able to process over 100 transactions per second to handle peak customer loads. If throughput is slower, inbound transactions may be queued, delaying their execution and negatively impacting the users' experience. Throughput would be relevant where there is a large number of users accessing the solution simultaneously or where a large number of derivatives needs to be priced together to value a combined portfolio.

In this example, latency may be measured as the time it takes between starting the pricing computation and generating the price. This time could be measured in seconds, milliseconds, or microseconds depending on the business needs. Low latency is usually a requirement for trading applications that realize gains from arbitrage opportunities, i.e., disparate prices for the same instrument in different markets. This strategy requires that minimal delay be incurred between the time market conditions that create an arbitrage opportunity occur and the time that the trades are executed.

Derivatives pricing, especially Monte Carlo simulation-based methods, can be computationally expensive and require extended time to complete. Hence, this need provides a good backdrop for discussing how performance considerations can be addressed by solution architectures.

12.8.2 Defining Performance Requirements

The first and probably most important consideration, with regard to performance, is to make sure that performance requirements are clearly defined in advance of design and implementation. Business requirements regarding performance are often not explicit or are vague, leading to confusion and disputes during user acceptance testing. Given that performance is a nonfunctional requirement, it is something that business analysts may easily overlook when capturing and preparing the solution requirements. It is, therefore, necessary for the solution architect to ensure that these requirements are adequately thought through and documented.

Quantifying performance targets is not as easy as it appears. A simple statement of requirements, such as "the transaction must take less than 500 ms to complete," is not always useful or clear. Is 500 ms the maximum time a transaction should take or the time it should take on average? Is it allowable for transactions to take a longer time during periods of peak load on the system? The answers to these questions will greatly affect the performance characteristics of the solution produced, as well as its implementation cost. As part of requirements analysis, both the minimum acceptable and average performance requirements should be specified. Ideally, performance under various loadings and the associated allowable performance variance should also be defined.

12.8.3 Designing for Performance

Besides addressing current performance needs, future needs must also be considered. It is often the case that expectations increase over time with regard to the speed at which transactions should be completed and the volumes that must be handled. Solutions should be architected in such a way that there is a clear path to improving performance as future needs develop. It should not be necessary to redesign the solution in the future to support incremental performance increases. Redesign is costly and usually requires significant time to complete.

The same techniques used to support the expansion of the capacity of IT systems, **vertical** and **horizontal scaling** (discussed in Chapter 3), can also be used to support high or increasing throughput requirements. Vertical scaling, where the hardware capacity of a single server is increased to address performance needs, can usually be achieved by adding processors or using faster processors. Software components that have been effectively designed for multithreading environments may not need any modification in this case. Horizontal scaling distributes processing across multiple servers, and usually requires the solution software to be designed for this configuration.

Hardware configurations have some bearing on latency-related performance requirements, but transaction processing pipeline efficiencies are often more important. Ensuring that the time required at each stage of the transaction processing is minimized is a core design consideration. Minimizing the transition time, for example, interprocess or network hops, between processing stages is another. It is also necessary to verify that the processing rates of the various pipeline components are matched so that one stage is not waiting idly while another stage is running at full capacity ahead of it, causing the transaction flow to back up.

For the most part, during normal operating conditions, throughput and latency can be thought of independently. However, during peak loading, when transaction volumes exceed the system's maximum throughput rate, transactions will be queued, resulting in increased latency times. This consideration is critical, as it relates the average and maximum latency with expected loads and overall system throughput. The more often peak loads exceed system throughput capacity, the higher the average latency. Similarly, the longer peak loads exceed system throughput capacity, the higher the maximum latency.

12.8.4 Performance Trade-offs—Cost/Benefit Analysis

While everyone would usually like to have the highest performance possible, this goal will be limited by available budgets and other needs, such as resilience, that share the budget. It is, therefore, necessary to analyze, during the architecture phase, the practicality of implementing various levels of performance and the associated trade-offs. For example, by forgoing resilience or paring down security-related requirements, extremely high performance may be achieved, but these trade-offs may not be acceptable to the solution stakeholders.

It is important to note that for high-performance systems, as performance increases linearly, implementation costs can increase exponentially, as illustrated by Figure 3-9 in the chapter on Solution Architecture. Where it may cost US$100,000 to implement a system that processes transactions with a latency of 1 second, it may cost US$500,000 to implement a system that processes transactions with a latency of 0.5 seconds, and US$5,000,000 for a system with a latency of 0.1 seconds. Whereas the business may say that they want 0.5-second performance, if the overall budget is only US$200,000, they may need to adjust their expectations. It is the architect's role to consider all the options and explain these concepts so that effective compromises are reached.

12.9   SOLUTION CONSIDERATIONS: SOLUTION EVOLUTION

The evolution of banking systems tends to follow a consistent pattern. New, innovative products are developed and traded in small volumes initially. Often, for new financial products, the front-office "IT system" that is used to calculate pricing, record transactions, and keep track of positions will be implemented and maintained as spreadsheets, and back-office clearing will be driven by paper-based or unstructured electronic messages, for example, email. Most of the processes will be manual. Although this approach is time intensive and error prone, the low volumes do not justify the development of more robust IT systems.

In the early days, such implementations may make sense. However, there will come a point when increases in volumes cause manual possessing and weak IT systems to buckle under pressure. For instance, in their early days, manual processing caused interest rate swaps to have estimated trade-booking error rates of more than 10%, and the rate for credit derivatives was 20% [9]. Manual processing backlogs also caused, in some cases, swap confirmations to remain unprocessed by banks' back-office operations for up to two weeks. As products mature, back-office processes must evolve to use more robust and automated clearing methods, which support automated confirmation matching and settlement netting. Likewise, front-office technology must be redesigned to be more efficient and scalable so that larger transaction volumes can be supported. Trade information will need to be integrated in real time to help provide a comprehensive and accurate view of positions' risk and profitability

Unfortunately, it takes time to design and implement robust business processes and also to build the IT systems that support them. Revamping existing processes can be disruptive and negatively impact short-term business. The last thing that businesspeople want to do is to reduce their business capacity by making changes when sales are booming despite the fact that they may have to pay a greater price to make improvements at a later time. Where the necessary improvement discipline is not enforced at an organizational level or an industry level, regulatory intervention or a crisis may be required before such growth problems are addressed (Case Study 12-4).

Nevertheless, a number of solutions have been developed to help standardize and streamline the post-trade processing of OTC derivatives. Whereas years ago, large stacks of papers represented unprocessed derivatives transactions, today much of the process is being handled electronically, enabling higher levels of automation. In particular, solutions that match derivatives confirmations have been developed to reduce the cost and **operational risks** associated with manual reconciliation processes.

One example of a solution that has evolved to address the issues related to derivatives post-trade processes is SwapsWire.* The SwapsWire platform was launched in 2002 and was formed by a number of major banks with the aim of streamlining the downstream processing of swap transactions. SwapsWire addressed two key concerns: the need for a central utility that facilitates trade confirmation and confirmation matching, and a standard way of communicating confirmation information. SwapsWire utilized the Financial products Mark-up Language (FpML) to help standardize how counterparties would share information with one another. Leveraging FpML helped to eliminate the effort required to integrate varying data representation standards and proprietary interfaces used by different banks.

---

* SwapsWire was renamed MarkitWire after its acquisition by Markit Group Limited in 2008.

Case Study 12-4   Credit Default Swap Back-Office Chaos

Credit default swaps (CDS) gained great popularity over a short period of time, and by 2007, the notional value of outstanding CDS was estimated to be over US$60 trillion. Whereas CDS began as tools that allowed banks to hedge their exposure to large corporate customers, they became instruments used by many different market participants for speculative purposes, thereby fueling their growth. Being OTC instruments, there was no central counterparty for CDS trades and, consequently, counterparty risk became a major concern. Sadly, they became a major source of distress during the financial crisis of 2008 when Lehman Brothers failed and AIG was on the brink of insolvency.

Besides the widespread concern over CDS counterparty risk, the absence of a mature clearing system and inefficient back-office processing were also major problems. These areas had been largely neglected and became a bottleneck as the market grew. For instance, there was no mechanism that allowed offsetting CDS contracts to be netted off and closed out. Such netting would decrease the number of outstanding contracts so as to reduce operational costs and complexity, and make trading exposures easier to discern. While many of the operational problems related to CDS were apparent from the outset, serious effort to tackle them was only undertaken after the industry was shaken by a financial crisis.

A solution to the counterparty risk concerns has been the introduction of CCPs for OTC derivatives transactions. CCPs typically require collateral from their members that provide a capital base that helps protect them in the case of failure of another member. Centralized clearing organizations can also help standardize the terms and conditions that govern derivatives agreements. Despite the benefits that CCPs provide, they are also a source of risk themselves, particularly when they are clearing less liquid instruments. When Lehman Brothers failed, the CME, the world's largest futures exchange, faced new challenges when dealing with Lehman Brothers in its last days, and then disposing off Lehman's positions after its collapse. While the CME came through the turmoil unscathed, it became more apparent that CCPs could face serious problems when derivatives markets become upset.

Sources: "The Great Untangling," *Economist*, November 6, 2008, http://www.economist.com/node/12552204; Brettell, Karen, "ICE, CME Clearing Membership Rules Challenged for CDS," *Reuters*, March 10, 2010, http://www.reuters.com/article/2010/03/10/cmclearing-swaps- idUSN1040509320100310; Meyer, Gregory and Aline van Duyn, "Lehman Report Raises Derivatives Clearing Fears," *Financial Times*, May 15, 2010, http://www.ft.com/cms/s/0/ae6da736-306d-11df-bc4a-00144feabdc0.html.

12.10 SUMMARY

This chapter covered:

- the purpose, structure, and fulfillment process for interest rate swaps;
- how retail and corporate customers use derivatives;
- the opportunities and challenges that banks face with derivatives;
- performance-related architecture concerns and design patterns; and
- how solutions must be adapted as financial products grow and mature over time.

This chapter ends Part Two and the coverage of banking-specific topics. The following chapter begins the next part, which focuses on topics related to capital markets.

FURTHER READING

Books

Hull, J. C., *Options, Futures and Other Derivatives*, 6th ed. (New Jersey: Prentice Hall, 2005).

Simmons, M., *Securities Operations: A Guide to Trade and Position Management* (West Sussex: John Wiley & Sons, 2006).

Taylor, F., *Mastering Derivatives Markets: A Step-by-Step Guide to the Products, Applications and Risks* (Essex: Financial Times/Prentice Hall, 2006).

Papers

Bank for International Settlements, "Triennial Central Bank Survey—OTC Interest Rate Derivatives Turnover in April 2016," September 2016, http://www.bis.org/publ/rpfx16ir.pdf.

Brown, G. W., "Managing Foreign Exchange Risk with Derivatives," *Journal of Financial Economics* 60 (2001): 401–448.

"Dispelling Myths: End-User Activity in OTC Derivatives," International Swaps and Derivatives Association, August 2014, http://www2.isda.org/attachment/Njc2Nw==/ISDA-Dispelling%20 myths-final.pdf.

Grahl, J. and P. Lysandrou, "Sand in the Wheels or Spanner in the Works? The Tobin Tax and Global Finance," *Cambridge Journal of Economics* 27 (2003): 597–621.

Merton, R. C., "You Have More Capital Than You Think," *Harvard Business Review* (November 2005): 85–94.

"OTC Derivatives Market Reforms Tenth Progress Report on Implementation," Financial Stability Board, 4 November 2015, http://www.fsb.org/wp-content/uploads/OTC-Derivatives-Market-Reforms-Eleventh-Progress-Report.pdf.

Popova, I. and Simkins, B., "The Value of OTC Derivatives: Case Study Analyses of Hedges by Publicly Traded Non-Financial Firms," International Swaps and Derivatives Association, March 2014, http://www2.isda.org/attachment/NjQzOQ==/FINAL%20-%20Betty%20Simkins%20 Paper%20.pdf.

Web

"Bloomberg Open Symbology Whitepaper," http://bsym.bloomberg.com/sym/pages/bsym-whitepaper.pdf.

"Derivatives: SEFs-Opening Bell Sounds," http://www.pwc.com/en_US/us/financial-services/ regulatory-services/publications/assets/fs-reg-brief-derivatives-sefs-opening-bell-sounds.pdf

"Financial Derivatives—Handbooks in Central Banking No. 17," www.bankofengland.co.uk/ education/ccbs/handbooks/ccbshb17.htm.

Official FpML website, http://www.fpml.org.

"Policy Perspectives on OTC Derivatives Market Infrastructure—Federal Reserve Bank of New York Staff Reports," http://www.newyorkfed.org/research/staff_reports/sr424.pdf.

"Understanding Interest Rate Swap Math Pricing," http://www.treasurer.ca.gov/cdiac/publications/ math.pdf.

ENDNOTES

1. Bartholomew, H., "Swaps Notional Jumps to US$544trn in First Half—BIS," *Reuters*, November 11, 2016, http://www.reuters.com/article/idUSL8N1DB7LU.

2. Smyth, N., "Trading Models and Liquidity Provision in OTC Derivatives Markets," *Bank of England Quarterly Bulletin 2011 Q4*, http://www.bankofengland.co.uk/publications/quarterlybulletin/qb1104.pdf.

3. Santini, L., "Accumulators Are Collecting Fans Again," *Wall Street Journal*, August 31, 2009, http://online.wsj.com/article/SB125166464377570481.html.

4. International Swaps and Derivatives Association, "ISDA Research Notes: ISDA Derivatives Usage Survey," 2009, http://www.isda.org/researchnotes/pdf/ISDA-Research-Notes2.pdf.

5. Arnold, M. and Martin, K., "Deutsche Bank in $6bn 'Fat Finger' Slip-up," *Financial Times*, October 19, 2015, http://www.ft.com/cms/s/0/0546944a-7682-11e5-a95a-27d368e1ddf7.html.

6. "Exchange-traded Funds: From Vanilla to Rocky Road," *Economist*, February 25, 2012, http://www.economist.com/node/21547989.

7. Wigglesworth, R., "Global ETF Assets Reach $4tn," *Financial Times*, May 10, 2017, https://www.ft.com/content/89c18106-3591-11e7-bce4-9023f8c0fd2e.

8. Alloway, T. "Counterparties Feel Effect of Bank Downgrades," *Financial Times*, June 29, 2012, http://www.ft.com/cms/s/0/030aebbe-c153-11e1-8eca-00144feabdc0.html.

9. Struye, K., "Driving Over-the-counter Derivatives Security," *Journal of Corporate Treasury Management* 1 (2007/08): 362–365.

— — —

10. Armstrong, R., "Asia's Derivative Reforms Set to Heap Pain on Banks," *Reuters*, April 18, 2011, http://in.reuters.com/article/2011/04/18/idINIndia-56405320110418.

11. Masters, B., "Banks Face Tougher Trading Capital Rules," *Financial Times*, May 3, 2012, http://www.ft.com/cms/s/0/fb273f5c-9505-11e1-ad72-00144feab49a.html.

12. Rennison, J., "OTC Derivatives Shrink to Lowest Level Since Financial Crisis," *Financial Times*, May 5, 2016, https://www.ft.com/content/dbc08ae2-1247-11e6-91da-096d89bd2173.

13. Stafford, P., "Interdealer Broker BGC Targets Swaps Compression Services," *Financial Times*, July 17, 2017, https://www.ft.com/content/ecffc45a-6ad7-11e7-b9c7-15af748b60d0.

PART THREE
FINANCIAL MARKETS
TECHNOLOGY

13 Capital Markets Contexts

Chapter Overview

13.1 CAPITAL MARKETS PARTICIPANTS

13.2 BUY-SIDE CONSIDERATIONS

13.3 LIFECYCLE FOCUS: TRADING STRATEGY IMPLEMENTATION

13.4 ARCHITECTURE CONSIDERATIONS

13.5 SOLUTION CONSIDERATIONS

13.6 SUMMARY

FURTHER READING

ENDNOTES

While lending activities and foreign exchange (FX) practices have been in existence for thousands of years, the rise of capital markets is a relatively recent development. Organized markets for trading debt can be traced back to Italy in the 1100s, and trading equities can be traced back to Holland in the 1600s. Capital markets have since evolved to provide companies with various means of raising capital and providing an alternative to bank lending. Likewise, capital markets have provided investors with more choices of investment vehicles, including higher return and higher risk alternatives to bank deposits.

For the past several hundred years, equity and debt securities, that is, stocks and bonds, have dominated the capital markets. Equities have provided investors with a means of participating directly in the profits and losses of corporations. On the other hand, debt securities have provided governments and corporations with lower-cost funding, and investors with a means of achieving more predictable, but limited, returns.

Securities are traded in both primary and secondary markets. Primary markets focus on the sale of newly issued securities. Typically, investment banks underwrite new stocks and bonds offerings, that is, they take to market and sell these securities directly to investors. Secondary markets allow investors to trade securities they already own with other investors and securities dealers. Just as banks are at the center of the FX markets, the secondary securities markets revolve around stock exchanges and other public trading venues.

In parallel with the development of equity and debt instruments, that is, capital markets, the commodities markets were the driver for the development of derivatives contracts (futures and options). Commodity producers, consumers, and middlemen used these instruments to limit the impact of commodity price fluctuations. Use of commodity futures ushered in trading of financial futures. Stock index, government bond, and currency futures quickly gained in popularity. Public derivatives markets provided investors and speculators with an efficient means of hedging and assuming risk across multiple asset classes. Subsequently, the line between securities and derivatives markets has become blurred and increasingly homogeneous. As these markets have grown and evolved, regulators have struggled to adapt the rules governing transactions and protecting markets participants (Case Study 13-1).

Over the past several decades, the structure of the capital markets has undergone many changes. New market segments and participants have emerged, and existing ones have had to change and adapt to a rapidly changing market environment. This chapter will provide an overview of capital markets participants, their functions, and the business models on which they are based. The focus of this chapter and the two chapters that follow will be mainly on secondary markets for equities, that is, securities trading markets. The goal is to provide readers with a high-level understanding of and appreciation for the needs and roles of the different market participants. This will provide a context for more detailed analysis of the processes and technologies that support trading activities in capital markets.

Case Study 13-1

MiFID II—The Next Generation of Financial Market Regulation

Brought into effect in 2007, Markets in Financial Instruments Directive (MiFID) was designed to increase competition and further the provision of cross-border financial services within Europe. Besides making it easier for financial institutions to conduct business across Europe, MiFID also had a major impact on European financial markets. First, it supported the creation of alternative venues for share trading in the form of multilateral trading facilities (MTFs) and systematic internalizers (SIs). MTFs provided share traders with an alternative to established exchanges. As SIs, financial institutions were allowed to match customer orders internally against their own proprietary positions rather than forwarding them to an exchange for matching. MiFID also increased market transparency. Brokers were required to define and disclose their **best execution** policies, that is, when orders would be internalized and how they would be routed to available execution venues. MiFID increased competition and reduced transaction costs for investors, but there were many considerations that it did not address. Hence, European regulators proposed its enhancement, commonly referred to as MiFID II, in October 2011.

MiFID II imposes new restrictions and requirements on fund managers, traders, banks, MTFs, and exchanges. For fund managers and independent investment advisers, it aims to prevent conflicts of interest by prohibiting monetary gains from third parties, for example, banks promoting specific financial products. MiFID II also places additional restrictions on how investment advice is provided and how complex financial products are offered.

MiFID II also targets how traders operate in the markets, specifically with regard to their use of algorithmic (that is, automated trading) and high-frequency trading strategies. The goal of the new regulations is to help maintain market **liquidity** and prevent **algorithmic trading** from increasing market volatility and causing excessive price swings. Financial firms engaging in algorithmic trading will be required to implement controls and make certain that their systems are resilient enough to help ensure that trading system faults would not disrupt the market. Furthermore, on an annual basis, traders will be required to provide regulators with information about the algorithmic strategies used, the risk controls implemented, and the testing performed.

Organized trading facilities (OTF) are a type of execution venue that is included in the MiFID II regulatory framework that support fixed income and derivatives trading. MiFID II requires some over-the-counter (OTC) derivatives contracts, such as interest rate swaps, to be exchange traded, either on a regulated market, an MTF, or an OTF. Brokers' internal crossing systems and interdealer brokers' trading platforms may be categorized as OTF. Unlike SIs, OTF cannot match orders against a financial institution's internal positions.

There are many other changes that MiFID II introduces. Commodity derivatives traders will be required to report whether or not their positions are speculative. Brokers who provide **direct market access (DMA)** services will be required to implement additional controls for customer orders sent via that channel. Additional price reporting will also be required for bond, structured product, and derivatives markets.

After over two years of negotiation between the European Parliament and the European Union member states, MiFID II was adopted by the parliament in 2014, and its implementation scheduled for January 2017. Later, the implementation deadline was extended by one year to January 2018 to allow more time for regulators and market participants to prepare. Given the broad scope of changes and the large number of market participants that are affected by these regulations, it was not surprising that more time was required. Over the next few years, the full effects of the MiFID II regulation will begin to be understood.

Sources: "Miffed with MiFID," *Economist*, November 16, 2006, http://www.economist.com/node/8131795; European Commission, "New Rules for More Efficient, Resilient, and Transparent Financial Markets in Europe," press release, October 20, 2011, http://europa.eu/rapid/ pressReleasesAction.do?reference=IP/11/1219; "The MiFID Review—European Commission Consultation," *Linklaters*, October 21, 2011, http://www.linklaters.com/pdfs/mkt/london/A12814778.pdf; Stafford, Philip, "FSA Warns on MiFID Review Proposals," *Financial Times*, January 30, 2012; Stafford, P. "No more Mifid II delays—European markets regulator," *Financial Times*, June 7, 2017, https://www.ft.com/content/663b3629-c764-34de-892d-50c62d515643; "MiFID (II) and MiFIR," European Securities and Markets Authority, https://www.esma.europa.eu/policy-rules/mifid-ii-and-mifir.

Questions

1. Why might the issues addressed by MiFID II not have been a part of the original MiFID implementation?
2. Which market participants are likely to benefit from the changes that come as a result of MiFID II?
3. What sort of safeguards could be implemented in **algorithmic trading strategies** to help prevent market disruption?
4. What steps could financial institutions take in advance of the final agreement of the MiFID II rules to prepare for upcoming changes?

13.1 CAPITAL MARKETS PARTICIPANTS

For the purpose of discussion, it is useful to categorize the different participants in the capital market ecosystem by function. However, in practice, a single entity, such as an investment bank or a stock exchange, may perform multiple functions. Figure 13-1 illustrates a logical view of the interrelationship between participants. The following subsections review each function.

13.1.1 Capital Markets Customers

While most people can associate with the role of retail customers in capital markets, they represent a relatively small proportion, by dollar volume, of exchange transactions in developed markets. In most developed markets, institutional customers provide a much larger proportion of transaction volume, especially when measured by dollar value. Hence, this section focuses on institutional customers, commonly referred to as the "buy side" because they are the ones buying financial products.

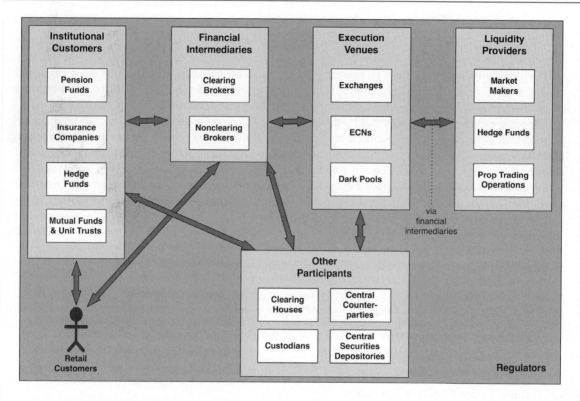

Figure 13-1 Secondary market participants for equity trading

13.1.1.1 Types of customers

Retail customers are large in number, but, for the most part, they trade infrequently and perform small transactions. Likewise, the assumption is that retail customers have little understanding of market dynamics and trading experience. Regulators have, therefore, in many cases incorporated restrictions into the market structure to help protect retail customers from abuse.

On the other hand, there are relatively few institutional customers, but they trade large volumes. As professionals, institutional investors are presumed to have sufficient knowledge to handle themselves in the market. Hence, less regulatory protection is provided for institutional customers. **Pension funds, insurance companies, mutual funds**, and **hedge funds** are examples of institutional customers.

Pension funds are funds set up by large corporations or public entities to collect, invest, and distribute retirement pensions to employees. For instance, the Japanese Government Pension Investment Fund is the largest pension fund in the world. It manages over one trillion dollars' worth of assets. Because of the extended duration over which retirement benefits must be paid, pension funds have long investment time horizons and are less sensitive to short-term volatility in their portfolios. Accordingly, besides investing in liquid assets such as stocks and bonds, they also invest in illiquid asset classes, such as hedge funds, private equity, and forestry.

Like pension funds, insurance companies are private corporations that have both short- and long-term payment obligations to customers. The largest insurers in the world will each hold trillions of dollars' worth of assets. When the future payment requirements are predictable, as with fixed annuities, insurers will invest in fixed-income products, such as long-term government bonds. When future payment requirements are not fixed, as with variable annuities, insurers can take advantage of a broader range of investment options, including equity and nongovernment debt instruments.

Mutual funds and unit trusts enable investors to pool their funds to take advantage of economies of scale and access to professional managers. There are thousands of mutual funds, investing in different asset classes, geographies, and investment styles. Small mutual fund houses may manage less than a hundred million dollars of assets, whereas large funds can manage assets worth over a hundred billion dollars. Unlike pension funds and insurance companies, mutual funds are subject to continual inflows and outflows of customers' capital. It is not uncommon for mutual funds to see large outflows in times of market turbulence. Consequently, mutual funds maintain some of their assets in cash to satisfy redemption requests. If existing cash holdings are not sufficient, investment assets may need to be liquidated.

Hedge funds are similar to mutual funds, but are not open to retail investors and typically use alternative investment strategies. The majority of mutual funds are "long only," that is, they cannot short-sell securities, and are bound to a particular investment style, such as investing in large capitalization domestic stocks or stocks from a particular geographic region or business sector. On the other hand, hedge funds may take long, short, or market-neutral positions, and may vary their investment style and focus depending on market conditions. Furthermore, hedge funds often have time restrictions on customers' withdrawal of capital from the fund. A hedge fund's customers may only be able to withdraw their money at certain times of the year or with an advance notice of a certain number of days or months.

The relationship between institutional customers may intersect and overlap. For instance, pension funds may invest in mutual funds and hedge funds. Similarly, insurers may offer customers the option of investing in variable annuities that are based on third-party mutual funds. Hedge funds can also invest in mutual funds or other hedge funds, that is, offer themselves as a "fund of funds." Moreover, there are also other types of institutional customers, for example, central banks, sovereign wealth funds, and independent investment firms.

13.1.1.2 Institutional customer needs

Institutional customers are often challenged by the fact that the equity markets are, to a large extent, designed to support the needs of retail investors. The typical transaction size for an institutional customer can easily exceed 200,000 shares. In contrast, during the latter half of July 2017, the average trade size on the New York Stock Exchange was fewer than 400 shares, and less than two percent of trades exceeded 2,000 shares [1]. While trading in small share quantities has little impact on retail customers' orders, which are typically also small in size, an institutional order may require 200 separate transactions to be fully executed.

A major concern for large orders to buy or sell securities is that size of the order will affect the execution price. As the market becomes aware of the order and gains knowledge about the shift in demand for a security, the underlying price may move adversely prior to or while the order is being filled. This situation is referred to as **price slippage**. Larger orders and longer execution times lead to increased slippage. Consider the simplified example where:

- the best **bid price** for a stock is 1,000 shares at $30.50;

- the next best bid is 1,000 shares at $30.48; and

- the remaining shares available are 50,000 bid at $30.00.

An institutional investor selling 200,000 shares of the stock would, ideally, want to sell them all at or near the current bid price of $30.50. In the existing market conditions, achieving this goal would be difficult because only 1% of the total order (2,000 shares) is available for purchase around that price. Furthermore, if the market gets wind that there is an outstanding order to sell a large quantity of the stock, bid prices will likely fall in anticipation of the selling activity. If the institutional investor sold 2,000 shares to all the available buyers at $30.50 and $30.48, other buyers might suspect that there was more of the order outstanding and, thus, the bid to buy 50,000 shares could quickly drop to $29.50. Accordingly, the trade's average execution price could end up being much lower than the beginning market price of $30.50.

Trading losses due to slippage can quickly erode investing profits, so minimizing slippage is critical. When placing orders, institutional customers try to remain hidden from the market and mask their intentions so as to avoid moving the market. Another concern is that the broker an institutional customer uses to execute a trade may try to trade in the market ahead of the order so as to make gains at the expense of the customer. This practice, called **front running**, is illegal in most countries, but remains a concern. Even if the broker does not trade on information about an order, there is also a concern that the broker may leak information to other market participants who can then trade with advance knowledge of the order.

To avoid front running and information leakage, institutional investors may slice up large orders into smaller orders and allocate the component orders to different brokers for execution (Case Study 13-2). Alternatively, the order may be divided into multiple parts that are sent to a broker for execution over several hours or days. Institutional customers also use nonexchange execution venues and crossing services to gain access to additional liquidity and obscure the size of the order. These venues, such as dark pools, attempt to opaquely match large buy orders with similar-sized sell orders; they are discussed further in Section 13.1.3.

13.1.2 Financial Markets Intermediaries

Brokers, commonly referred to as the "sell side" because they sell financial services to other market participants, are the main intermediaries in the equity markets. They act on behalf of customers and route trades to one or more exchanges. Brokers also benefit exchanges by helping to consolidate and manage customer order flow. Brokers must usually be **clearing members** of an exchange in order to

---

Case Study 13-2

Migrating Trading Capabilities from Brokers to Asset Managers

Historically, asset managers concentrated on acquiring and managing funds. As part of this arrangement, buy-side managers relied upon brokers to manage the execution of their trades. More recently though, execution management has become a priority for buy-side managers. Concerns related to execution costs, information leakage, and tighter regulations have changed how institutional customers utilize brokers.

Some institutional customers have purchased IT systems that perform functions similar to those provided by brokers. These systems perform algorithmic execution of orders, decide which execution venues to route orders to, and analyze transaction costs. With these capabilities, asset managers are able to more easily shroud their activities and compare the effectiveness of different brokers' execution services.

For all the benefits that directly managing order execution provides to buy-side managers, there are also associated complications. Asset managers must purchase different systems to support different functions, leading to significant integration, support, and maintenance requirements. By using brokers to manage order execution, asset managers avoid these concerns. However, as the buy-side execution management requirements become better understood, systems vendors should be able to provide more comprehensive solutions and single-system implementations. Likewise, hosted and cloud computing solutions that provide execution management services to customers may be another approach that provides the best of both worlds. Asset managers can have full control over execution management without the burden of managing the IT systems.

Source: Curley, Peter, "The Buyside and the Three Phase-Evolution of Electronic Trading," *The Journal of Trading* 2, issue 1 (2007): 103–106.

trade directly on it. As a clearing member, a broker is required to deposit upfront **margin** collateral with a **central counterparty (CCP)** and post additional collateral to meet the **settlement** obligations of its outstanding positions. From the CCP's perspective, a clearing broker is responsible for settling the trades of its customers as well as its own trades. If a customer fails to settle a trade with the broker, the broker is still obligated to settle with the CCP.

Nonclearing brokers must place orders on exchanges through clearing brokers. In many cases, nonclearing brokers are smaller firms that do not have the financial scale to fulfill what is required to be a clearing member. Alternatively, nonclearing brokers may be local branches of foreign brokerages. Some brokers also provide off-exchange, negotiated trade services to customers for large-block transactions. They contact other potential customers to determine if there is "natural" interest from another market participant to take the other side of the trade. These bilaterally negotiated off-exchange transactions are referred to as OTC block trades and must be publicly reported through standard exchange facilities. Alternatively, in some markets, brokers may internalize orders against their own trading books, that is, proprietary positions. In Europe, such brokers are referred to as SIs. Financial intermediaries are covered in depth in Chapter 15.

13.1.3 Execution Venues

The purpose of exchanges is to provide a managed trading environment, ensure that companies issuing stock meet listing criteria, and monitor and report price and trade information for listed companies. For many years, stocks could only be traded on the primary exchange where they were listed. Over time, stocks were listed on multiple stock exchanges, providing multiple venues for trading the same instrument. Separating **clearing** and settlement functions out from exchanges and into independent entities helped enable purchases performed on one exchange to be offset against sales performed on another exchange.

In the 1990s, alternative trading networks emerged. These execution venues are referred to as electronic communication networks (ECN) in North America, MTFs in Europe, and proprietary trading systems (PTS) in Japan. Alternative trading networks enabled investors to match their trades outside of traditional exchanges, often providing advantages such as extended trading hours and smaller tick sizes, that is, the smallest increments by which the price of securities can change.

By making the prices and volume on offer to buy and sell securities visible, execution venues enable participants to determine the liquidity that is available, that is, the amount of buy and sell demand. For example, the best bid of a particular stock on its primary exchange may be to buy 10,000 shares at $14.80. However, the same stock may be bid at 1,000 shares at $14.81 on an ECN. Based on the quantity and price offered on different exchanges, traders can decide to which execution venue to route their orders. A retail customer who only wants to buy 500 shares may route their order to the ECN, whereas an institutional customer who needs to buy 8,000 shares would likely route it to the primary exchange to increase the likelihood that the order would be executed in its entirety at the current market price.

Stock exchanges and alternative trading networks are commonly referred to as **lit pools** or lit venues. They make information regarding outstanding buy and sell orders publicly available and, thus, are "lit up" for market participants to see what liquidity is available. **Dark pools**, on the other hand, are execution venues where information related to open orders is not divulged prior to execution. Typically, institutional customers will attempt to opaquely match large orders with other orders placed by other market participants by routing them to dark pools. Dark pools enable orders to be matched, or attempt to be matched, without exposing customers' buying or selling intentions to the broader market prior to the trade's execution.* Dark pools may be set up as separate exchange-like trading venues or may be offered as proprietary services by brokers. Exchanges and execution venues

---

* Orders sent to dark pools are only hidden during the order submission and matching process. Once an order has been matched and executed, it must be publicly reported like other trades executed on lit venues. However, reporting delays may occur with trades executed on dark pools.

13.1.5 Other Market Participants

Clearing houses are centralized facilities that coordinate communication of instructions related to the payment of funds or delivery of securities between market participants. CCPs often participate in clearing and settlement processes to reduce counterparty risk. In some cases, clearing house and CCP functions will be combined in the same business entity. Clearing houses facilitate the clearing and settlement process between clearing members of an exchange, and CCPs serve as a firewall, or buffer, between the trading counterparties. Even if one of the counterparties defaults, the CCP will ensure that the settlement obligations are fulfilled to the other counterparty. Having a central counterparty reduces **settlement risk** for the member brokers, thereby helping to increase confidence in trading activities.

The failure of Barings in 1995 provides an example of CCPs' value. Barings Futures was counterparty to trades with many brokers executed on the futures exchange in Singapore. When Barings collapsed, its trading counterparties were protected from the concern that Barings would fail to meet its settlement obligations because the CCP was their counterparty for settlement purposes, not Barings. Clearing houses and CCPs will be discussed further in Chapter 14.

In markets where securities are **scripless**, that is, they have no physical form, **central securities depositories (CSDs)** maintain official record of share ownership and facilitate the transfer of securities between counterparties by recording the changes as computerized accounting entries, commonly referred to as **book entry system**. **Custodians** are financial institutions that provide safekeeping and transfer of securities such as stocks and bonds. They may also collect dividends and payment coupons for securities held on behalf of their owners. Custodians will notify securities owners of corporate actions, such as stock splits and rights issuances, and other shareholder-related activities. They take instructions from the owner regarding elective choices and notify the security issuer. For example, under a custodial agreement, a nominee company may be listed as the registered owner of shares on behalf of the actual owner of the shares. When the nominee/custodian receives shareholder resolution voting materials for the company whose shares are held, the custodian will forward them to the actual owner for action.

Exchanges, clearing houses, and custodians may be wholly separate entities or combined. For example in the United States, the New York Stock Exchange (NYSE) provides exchange-matching services for equities, and the Depository Trust & Clearing Corporation acts as a clearing house, CCP, and CSD. Alternatively, in Singapore, the Central Depository Pte Ltd is a wholly owned subsidiary of the Singapore Exchange and acts as both a clearing house and a CSD for Singapore-listed equities. In both the United States and Singapore, various local and multinational banks provide custodial services.

13.1.6 Regulators

Regulators are responsible for establishing and maintaining safe, fair, and efficient markets. Achieving this goal on an ongoing basis is challenging, given the wide range of participants and interests involved. Furthermore, the fact that the markets are continually changing means there will always be new problems to consider and challenges to address. For example, in recent years, regulators have had to introduce new regulations to address the complexities brought on by the introduction of new types of execution venues, for example, dark pools.

Brokers can often choose where to route customers' orders. Thus, regulators have defined rules to help ensure that brokers provide their customers with the best execution for their trades. These regulations obligate brokers to route orders to the execution venue that is "best" for the customer, rather than to a venue that provides the broker with monetary incentives for order flow, or in which the broker has a beneficial interest. Best execution rules vary across markets because they are governed by different regulatory bodies.

In the United States, Regulation NMS (Reg NMS) requires brokers to route orders to the trading venue with the lowest price. This approach excludes considerations such as where the execution would occur most quickly or which venue has the most liquidity. Alternatively, in Europe, MiFID and MiFID II provide more flexibility. It requires brokers to define and disclose the policy by which best execution is determined. This policy sets out the relative importance of various considerations, such as execution price, speed of execution, likelihood of execution, and cost, or the process by which their importance is determined. It is then the brokers' responsibility to demonstrate that they have routed customer orders according to the policy that they have defined.

13.2   BUY-SIDE CONSIDERATIONS

The rest of this chapter focuses on buy-side considerations. This section begins by examining basic concepts that are relevant to institutional customers, as well as their general needs and concerns.

13.2.1   Concepts

The distinction between investing and trading can sometimes be unclear and may overlap. Typically, trading refers to implementing short-term speculative strategies, whereas investing refers to applying longer-term strategies that usually rely upon expected long-term positive returns from specific markets, that is, equities and fixed income.

Trading in many ways is similar to gambling. With gambling, in the long run, profits can only be expected if the gambler has some advantage over the casino, which has the games' odds set in its favor. Similarly, investors and traders must find some competitive edge, commonly referred to as just "edge" in trading contexts, that provides them with an advantage in the market (Case Study 13-4). Gamblers must also carefully manage their financial resources to ensure that no single bet or string of bets will wipe them out. Traders and investors face the same concern, particularly those that use leverage, that is, borrow money to invest more and magnify their returns.

Asset managers attract customers by offering returns that are superior to the market, provide lower risk, or both. Thus, measurement of fund performance is critical to judging performance. Benchmarking is done on a relative basis as compared to general market performance or predefined metrics. For instance, the performance of a fund manager whose focus is on the UK equity market might be measured against the performance of the FTSE 100 index. If over the course of a year, the return of the index was −3%, a return of −2% by the fund would be seen as overperforming the benchmark. Likewise, if the index return was 8% and the fund's return was 6%, the fund would be seen as underperforming its benchmark.

Performance measurement is often more complex than just gauging relative returns. For instance, volatility of returns, that is, the magnitude of increase or decrease of the portfolio value over time, is also a common consideration. For instance, if a fund achieves a 1% greater return than its benchmark index but is twice as volatile, its performance would be worse than another fund that achieved the same 1% return, with half the volatility as the benchmark index. Moreover, investing strategies that span across asset classes may be difficult to measure against a single index. Hence, a target such as 2% over the risk-free interest rate, that is, LIBOR or the US federal funds rate, may be used.

Common terms used when discussing fund performance measures are **alpha** and **beta**. While a very simple description of these terms is provided here, a detailed explanation of these terms can be found in the texts mentioned in the Further Reading section at the end of the chapter. In simple terms, the measurement of alpha represents the excess return of a trading strategy over a specific benchmark. Positive alpha outperforms the market, whereas negative alpha underperforms. Alpha is often equated with the fund manager's skill.

Alternatively, beta measures the level of the fund's volatility, or risk, that is directly attributable to movement of the market. The performance of a fund manager whose holdings exactly matched the composition benchmark index would be expected to have a beta of 1.0. Alternatively, a fund manager

---

Case Study 13-4

Gaining from Understanding Other Traders' Behavior

Financial markets are, for the most part, vast and anonymous; when stocks are bought or sold, the counterparty may be one of many different individuals or firms. However, for stocks that trade in low volumes, only a few investors and market makers may be trading at any one time. In this environment, trading is less anonymous and trading patterns and behavior can be more readily examined.

In 2010, two day traders based in Norway through observation reverse engineered the algorithm that a US-based market maker's computer system used and could predict how it would react to specific trading patterns in low-volume stocks. Using this information, they were able to design their own trading strategy that took advantage of the algorithm's limitations, and were able to realize gains from making a series of trades that led the algorithm to trade unprofitably.

Unfortunately for the traders, the Oslo stock exchange identified irregular trading patterns and notified Norway's financial regulator, which convicted them of market manipulation. Its view was that they were unduly influencing the price of low-volume stocks by giving false signals about their supply and demand. The traders countered that although they learned how the computer would react to price changes, they were not responsible for the computer's behavior. In the end, the traders were given suspended prison sentences and were fined for the approximate amount of their gains, which amounted to tens of thousands of dollars. When finding an edge in the market, it is also important to ensure that it does not fall afoul of regulators.

Source: Ward, Andrew, "Norwegians Convicted for Outwitting Trading System," *Financial Times*, October 13, 2010, http://www.ft.com/cms/s/0/f9d1a74a-d6f3-11df-aaab-00144feabdc0.html.

---

who invested in less volatile stocks might have a beta of 0.9. That is to say, if on a given day, the market went up or down 1%, the fund's value would be expected to change by only 0.9%. On the other hand, if a fund invested in more volatile stocks or used leverage to invest, its beta would be greater than one, and its performance would be more volatile than the benchmark.

Adding further complexity to performance measurement is the need to measure results over time. For example, a gambler cannot gauge, in games where skill is involved, his or her performance from the results of just a few bets. Winnings may be the result of a string of lucky hands rather than the player's skill. Typically, a longer series of events will need to be evaluated to determine if the result, that is, achieving net gain or loss, is statistically significant. Similarly, fund managers' long-term performance is what counts. Having above-average returns one year and the next may be purely related to the investment strategy being temporarily aligned with current market conditions, rather than being attributable to manager's skill. If the market changes, the strategy may no longer be profitable, and may in fact generate losses.

In many cases, trading, and in some ways asset management, can be seen as a zero-sum game—for every winner there will be a loser. Even where the market, such as the equity market, has a positive bias for investors, performance relative to the benchmark, which represents the market average, will be a zero-sum game. Gains for investors that outperform the market index will be matched by losses for investors that underperform the market. Furthermore, the index does not reflect the cost of trading, that is, trading commissions, management costs and fees, and paying the bid-ask spread when buying or selling. Investors and buy-side firms enter the market with the odds stacked against them. Not surprisingly, index-based investing has become a popular investment approach, because it minimizes costs related to trading and management fees and, by nature, eliminates the risk of underperforming the index. Unless traders and fund managers find a unique advantage, or edge, it will be difficult for them to prosper or even survive.

13.2.2 Opportunities

For all the challenges that buy-side firms face, it is still a very lucrative business. Wealth has increased substantially in markets such as Asia and Latin America, providing a ready source of funds for investment. At the same time, low global interest rates have driven money from cash deposits to other asset classes, and for many asset classes, such as bonds, equities, and commodities, the most effective way to diversify holdings and/or reduce transaction costs is to invest in a mutual fund, unit trust, exchange traded fund, or hedge fund.

Likewise, there are many new investment vehicles that can be utilized by asset managers and traders. Equity markets around the world are becoming more accessible, providing new sources of profit and **diversification**. Likewise, the availability of exchange traded derivatives, that is, futures, has enabled investment, trading, and hedging on a wide range of commodities and composite instruments, such as stock indices. OTC derivatives and structured products go one step further by allowing customized "bets" to be made on any measurable concern, such as the default of a company or country on its debts, the rate of global warming, and the expected return on a basket of stocks.

Another opportunity that buy-side firms have is to improve their trading capabilities and take better advantage of market efficiencies. Historically, and it is still the case in some markets, institutional customers would have to blindly trust their broker and human-driven exchanges to get the best execution price for their transaction. For example, in the 1980s, a fund manager in the United States would have had to call their broker to buy a half-million shares of a stock and hope that the broker would discretely execute the order, and that other brokers and traders at the exchange, as illustrated in Figure 13-3,* would not detect the buying activity and push up the price in advance of or as the order was being filled.

Today, institutional customers can directly control the market impact of large orders using trading algorithms, which are discussed in Chapter 15. Likewise, transaction cost analysis, that is, measuring the effectiveness of trade execution strategies and brokers' efficiency, is becoming prevalent. By being

Figure 13-3 Financial markets in the 20th century (© NYSE Group, Inc. Reprinted with permission.)

---

* The photograph shown may not contain the most up-to-date information; the current NYSE materials can be found at http://www.nyse.com/images/about/NYSETradingFloorCrowds.jpg.

able to measure and achieve efficient trade execution, buy-side firms can reduce the amount of market "friction" that they must overcome and, thus, reduce the amount of edge they must find to produce adequate returns.

13.2.3 Challenges

Institutional customers, especially mutual funds and hedge funds, face many challenges. The first is finding a way to consistently outperform the benchmark, given that market friction costs (that is, market spreads, commission fees, and slippage) and the costs of operating the fund will reduce the overall return. For example, consider the case in which an actively managed fund investing in US equities finds a trading strategy that returns on average 2% more than the S&P 500 index. If its operating and trading costs shave off 1.5% of the fund's return, the net return that investors would receive would only be 0.5% greater than the S&P 500 index benchmark. Given the small difference, investors may instead choose to invest in a passively managed index fund that tracks the index, rather than going with a fund that tries to beat the index, but only can by a small margin, and may not do so consistently.

Because a large portion of a fund's operating costs is fixed, while fund returns are proportional to the size of the assets under management, economies of scale are very important to investment funds. Continuing with the example of the equity fund, its costs may represent a drag on returns of 1.5% when it manages a portfolio of $10 million, but 0.8% if its portfolio size is $100 million, and perhaps only 0.1% with $1 billion of assets under management. Whereas a net return, with high overhead costs, of 0.5% over the benchmark may not be particularly attractive to investors, a return, with low overhead costs, of 1.9% would be. Unfortunately though, it is usually only possible to start small. Fund managers face a "chicken and egg" problem—investors only want to invest in funds that have a strong and long track record, and it is difficult to achieve a good track record without sufficient investments to make the fund size cost effective.

Besides being too small, funds also face problems when they get too large. Market inefficiencies may be exploited to yield sizeable returns for a small portfolio, but may not scale, and produce only limited returns for a large portfolio. For example, a hedge fund that generates returns by investing in "frontier" markets, such as freshly developing markets in Africa and Asia, may find that when it reaches $300 million, the fund size is greater than the stock market capitalization of the countries in which it is investing. Accordingly, funds investing in some sectors may choose to stop accepting investments from new investors at a certain point to limit their growth and help maintain the level of their returns. Another problem that large funds face is increased market impact. At a size of $10 million, a fund investing 10% of its assets in a particular stock may require it to buy 400,000 shares. If the fund size is $1 billion, to invest 10% of it in a stock would require buying 40 million shares, which may represent a significant portion of the available float of the stock in the market. Hence, it would be difficult to buy or sell such a large position undetected and, thus, the fund would expect to see price slippage when buying or selling its position. This slippage would reduce the overall returns of the fund's investment strategy.

Traders and fund managers also have to comply with extensive regulatory requirements that vary from one market to another, and may change from year to year. For example, hedge funds must report short selling to regulators in many jurisdictions, and global hedge funds that have US-based customers must be registered with the Securities and Exchange Commission in the United States. Moreover, changes to market rules made by regulators may also affect buy-side firms' investment or trading strategy. For instance, a prop trading firm that uses a market-neutral strategy of buying shares of companies it thinks are undervalued in the market and short selling the shares of companies it thinks are overvalued may be adversely affected when regulators place temporary bans on short selling of specific stocks or across the entire market.

Moreover, both sell-side and buy-side firms have had to contend with Fintech companies that provide robo-advisory services, as discussed in Chapter 6. These services pose threats to financial institutions in several ways. First, they can become substitutes for investment advisory services that banks' financial advisers provide, eliminating revenue from fees related to advisory and money management services. Second, robo-advisers can intermediate banks' relationships with their customers. Third, robo-advisory services tend to recommend investments in passive mutual funds and exchange traded funds, rather than actively managed funds. This approach results in less business for active fund managers, who are already fighting the trend for investors to move to passive investment vehicles, such as index funds.

13.3 LIFECYCLE FOCUS: TRADING STRATEGY IMPLEMENTATION

A high-level view of the trading lifecycle is shown in Figure 13-4. The same lifecycle would apply to investing, as opposed to trading; the main difference would be in the types of strategies used. Trading strategies typically would have shorter timeframes and more frequent transactions than investing. Trading strategies are often based on technical analysis, that is, expectations of future prices based on recent or historical price movements, or on the relative value between different financial instruments. On the other hand, investing strategies are usually driven by analysis of market fundamentals, such as the financial health and future prospects of a company, industry, or country.

This section will focus on reviewing the high-level process that buy-side firms engage in during strategy conception, the first stage of the trading lifecycle. Figure 13-5 shows the typical activities that are involved when developing a trading or investing strategy. The rest of this section will discuss in more detail each of the activities shown.

13.3.1 Idea Generation

Idea generation drives the strategy conception process. Traders and fund managers must use their imagination and powers of observation to come up with ideas for strategies that can be used to take advantage of market inefficiencies. The more unique a trading strategy is, the less likely that other traders will also take advantage of it and dilute its profit potential. Ideas that have widespread adoption are likely to be less effective, because as more people try to take advantage of the idea, the more efficient the market will become and, thus, there will be less room for profit.

For example, take the case where a trader identifies that there is a historical correlation between the price of gold and the Swiss franc. He or she might then develop a strategy to buy gold and sell francs when gold appears undervalued compared to the franc, and vice versa when the franc appears undervalued compared to gold. In theory, if a large number of traders follow the same strategy or if a few traders apply a large amount of money to the strategy, the profit opportunity will decrease, or even disappear. When the franc starts to become undervalued compared to gold, there will be enough buying pressure owing to traders' strategies to drive up the exchange rate and, thus, the franc never reaches a fully undervalued level, reducing the opportunity for the strategy to profit. Hence, it is

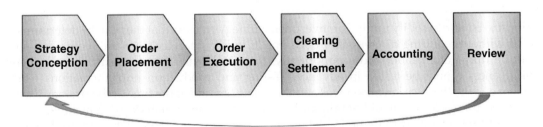

Figure 13-4 Trading lifecycle

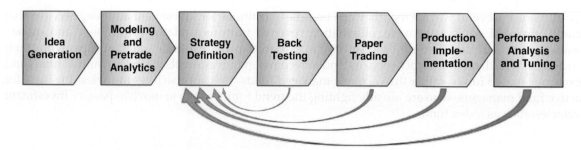

Figure 13-5 Strategy conception and implementation process

usually best to leverage strategies that are not widely followed. Traders and fund managers are often very secretive about their strategies since knowledge of them by other market participants could cause them to be less effective.

The basis for trading strategies varies. Many trading strategies that use technical analysis are designed around **mean reversion**. The expectation is that the price of a financial instrument will temporarily fluctuate around its true market value, and profits can be made from trading on the temporary fluctuations. Traders may trade multiple financial instruments and take advantage of differences in their relative value, as illustrated by the gold/Swiss franc example in the preceding paragraph. On the other hand, investment managers might analyze the fundamentals of a company or market to determine if particular instruments, that is, equities, bonds, and currencies, are undervalued, and invest accordingly.

Ideas for trading strategies can come from a variety of sources. A trader or fund manager may get ideas from observing market behavior over time. New trading strategies promoted by market "gurus" may be adopted in pure or modified form. Alternatively, current academic research may be used as the basis for developing new trading strategies.

13.3.2 Modeling and Pretrade Analytics

Any number of tools, such as spreadsheet, statistical analysis, and charting tools, may be used to help investigate and refine ideas. Access to historical data, that is, hourly, daily, or monthly time series data, is often required. In some cases, tick-by-tick historical data, which provides exact details of every change in price and every trade execution over a given time period, may also be required. Most analysis tools will provide graphical representations of the data, in the form of price and trading volume charts. Pretrade analysis will try to determine which financial instruments are relevant to a particular trading or investment idea, and what market conditions are necessary to support a particular strategy. The objective of this stage of the strategy conception process is to provide the initial validation of ideas and refine their scope.

13.3.3 Strategy Definition

It is critical to be able to codify trading or investment strategy rules so that they can be deterministically executed without requiring discretionary decisions. If judgmental decisions are required, a strategy will not be fully automatable. More importantly, though, it will not be repeatable and, therefore, its effectiveness cannot be tested in advance. Testing and production implementations would be dependent on who the decision maker was and their state of mind at the time of the strategy execution. Hence, most strategies try to avoid or minimize dependencies on human decision making.

The outcome of strategy definition will be a set of rules, that is, an algorithm, for trading that can identify when and how to enter and exit positions. The rules may incorporate technical data indicators,

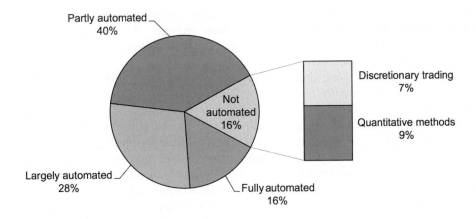

Figure 13-6 Level of buy-side trading automation (© Automated Trader Ltd. Reprinted with permission.)

such as moving averages, or statistical calculations. The order generation rules may be fully automated for algorithmic trading strategies and high-frequency trading, or manually executed for some low-frequency trading and long-term investment strategies. Even where strategies are manually executed, it is still good practice to have a predefined set of rules based on quantitative methods that are followed for two reasons. First, it is necessary that the strategy can be repeated consistently so that its success or failures are not arbitrarily determined by how it is implemented each time. Second, consistent strategy execution enables evaluation of its performance over different conditions over time so that the strategy can be corrected and improved. Alternatively, **discretionary trading** relies on the traders' judgment, the quality of which may vary from one day to the next. Figure 13-6 shows the automation level of buy-side firms based on a 2011 survey of over 180 responses [3].

Generally, simple strategies are preferred over complex ones. At first glance, using complex strategies might appear to be beneficial because they would be harder for others to replicate. However, complex strategies are much more difficult to design, test, and execute. Determining which part of a complex strategy is faulty or causing problems can be difficult. Typically, the strategies themselves will be relatively simple, but will be dependent on a number of static input parameters that control the algorithm behavior. Often the input parameters used are as critical as the algorithm that is defined. Back testing is used to determine the optimal values of these parameters, and they can be further tuned during paper and production trading.

13.3.4 Back Testing

A strategy may look good in theory but, for many reasons, it may not be practical to implement. Rather than directly testing the idea in the market and risk losing money on an unworkable idea, it is prudent to first perform an in-depth analysis. It is important to determine if the strategy would have been profitable had it been used in the past. Having said that, there is no guarantee that a strategy that would have been profitable in the past will also be profitable in the future. However, if a strategy is found to have been unprofitable in the past, then it is quite likely that it will be unprofitable in the future and, thus, should be avoided.

Back testing runs historical **market data** through the strategy trading rules simulating when positions would have been entered and exited, and calculating the profit and loss and risk characteristics of the strategy. Other statistics, such as the maximum drawdown, may also be calculated, which identifies the necessary amount of capital required to support trading. Based on the results of back testing runs, strategy input parameters will be adjusted and additional back testing runs performed to determine the effect of those changes. Back testing may determine the optimal set of input parameters or, alternatively, may determine that a strategy is unprofitable and therefore should not be implemented.

Back testing is performed using data from different periods. An **out-of-sample data** set that is closest to the current time is usually reserved for final validation of the back-tested strategy. A key concern with tuning strategies through back testing is that the resulting algorithm has been optimized specifically for the test data, but that implementation may be poorly suited for other market conditions. Testing with out-of-sample data, which has not been used to tune the strategy, can help determine the strategy implementation's ability to perform under different, and near current market conditions.

Back testing makes many assumptions and, therefore, is not foolproof. Assumptions must be made about transaction fees, slippage, and the ability to achieve order executions at quoted prices. For example, the historical data may show that a strategy trigger price was temporarily available for trading, but in practice, the price may have changed by the time the fund's order was received at the exchange. Likewise, historical data may not include special events such as "gap ups" and "gap downs" in the market, when the market suddenly jumped from one price range to another, making it impossible to trade at a price in between the two ranges.

Besides back testing using recent market data, traders and fund managers may stress test their strategies by either using market data from periods when the market was highly volatile or generating market data for testing that simulates potentially new market conditions. Stress testing can help identify a scenario's sensitivity to different market and economic conditions, such as interest rate shifts, changes in volatility, fluctuating market liquidity conditions, and variable execution timing.

Back-testing platforms may be purchased and installed locally, accessed from hosted solution providers, or accessed through a broker who provides a hosted back-testing service as part of its offering. The technology behind back testing itself is not particularly complex. Rather, it is acquisition and maintenance of "clean" historical data that is troublesome. Often, historical market data that is purchased from vendors can have flaws that distort and, thus, invalidate back testing results. The cost of purchasing sufficient historical market data to support back testing, especially for strategies that involve multiple asset classes, may be impractical for smaller funds. Hence, hosted services are often popular to use since the data sourcing costs and maintenance effort can be shared among a larger number of users.

13.3.5 Paper Trading

Only after back testing has been completed, the algorithm been tuned, and its performance and risk characteristics understood based on backward-looking information, can preproduction testing, or "paper trading" begin. Paper trading refers to the implementation of the strategy on an ongoing basis using current market data, but only recording transactions on paper or electronically rather than executing them in the market. This additional testing phase helps validate that the strategy behaves as expected in current market conditions as well as historical conditions. Based on the results of the paper trading stage, further strategy tuning may be performed to improve performance.

13.3.6 Production Implementation

The technology used to implement a strategy will vary by the type of strategy, the technology available, and backgrounds of the implementers. Small firms and firms that do low- to medium-frequency trading, that is, a few trades a day or a week, will often use spreadsheets to implement strategies. A spreadsheet may identify a trading signal that a person then executes or may be integrated directly with a broker's application programming interface (API) so that orders can be sent directly from the spreadsheet to the broker electronically. Automation is generally preferred since it minimizes order execution delay and reduces the chances of errors introduced by manual operations.

Alternatively, medium- and high-frequency trading strategies are more likely to use **complex event processing (CEP)** engines (discussed in more detail in Section 15.5.2) or customized programs as the implementation platform. The logic defined in these tools is usually more straightforward to debug and maintain, compared with spreadsheets, and can be more readily shared and reused. Likewise, these technologies are designed to provide higher performance and reliability.

Based on positive outcomes following back testing and paper trading, a strategy can be run in live market conditions so as to production test the strategy. Often, the production implementation will start with a small capital allocation and be gradually increased over time. By starting small, losses due to flaws in the design of the strategy or its implementation will be minimized. Further tuning may be performed to take into account actual processing time and market impact that is observed, and could only be estimated during back testing and paper trading. Based on the demonstrated success of the strategy in live market conditions, the capital base may then be increased gradually or in step increments.

Gradually increasing the monetary size of the strategy also helps test its scalability. The maximum size of a trading strategy may be limited by the market impact of its trades. For example, a currency-based strategy that trades US dollars versus euros would likely be able to handle billions of dollars because the foreign exchange (FX) market for these two currencies is very liquid. Alternatively, a strategy that trades shares of a stock with a small market capitalization might only scale to tens of millions before the market impact of the trades makes the strategy unprofitable. The technology used may also limit scalability. A strategy that involves just a few stocks and is implemented with spreadsheets may be viable for millions or tens of millions of dollars. However, to scale up to hundreds of stocks and handle hundreds of millions of dollars, a spreadsheet "farm" may be required, and the **operational risk** of using that hardware and software configuration may be unacceptable for the amount of capital at risk, and, thus, may warrant investment in a better technology architecture and infrastructure.

A key source of risk for trading firms is operational risk. A strategy may be profitable if executed flawlessly, but may be subject to major losses in cases when operational errors occur. Manual trade entry may be delayed. Communication links between systems or to brokers may be interrupted. Brokers systems may be slow or inaccessible. Applications and servers may crash. An exceptional case, such as an erroneous market data value being received and triggering a divide by zero error, may be handled badly by the strategy implementation. Hence, robust implementation and execution of a strategy is as important as having a good design.

13.3.7 Performance Analysis and Tuning

Once a profitable strategy has been deployed in the market, significant work is still required to monitor its performance and behavior and make adjustments as necessary. The initial set of parameters that were used to control a strategy's behavior will need to be modified as market conditions change from those used for back testing and paper trading. Even when tuned, a strategy may gradually become less effective over time, and it may reach a point where it is no longer cost effective to run. In this case, the strategy will need to be replaced with a new strategy idea. Hence, several streams of the strategy conception process, as shown in Figure 13-5, must be run staggered, in parallel so that as one strategy is retired, another is ready to begin production implementation.

Strategies must also be adapted over time to handle new market rules and events. For example, when regulators introduce new rules related to trading curbs and circuit breakers, discussed in Chapter 14, strategies may need to be modified to take into account that they may not be able to trade for certain periods of time, or may face a gap down in prices when the market resumes. Also, when short selling is banned on certain stocks in certain market, strategies may need to be adjusted if they are no longer able to use short positions in those stocks to hedge long positions in other stocks or as part of arbitrage strategies.

Ideally, strategies will be well thought out and should be able to cope with a wide range of market conditions. However, new and unforeseen events occur regularly and, hence, no strategy will be completely foolproof. Therefore, investing and trading strategies usually have the equivalent of a "panic button" that can be used when conditions exceed the worry threshold of their managers. The panic button may be as simple as a rule to stop trading or close out all open positions.

The danger of using the panic button is that second guessing the strategy in times of emotional stress can lead to losses. During the Flash Crash, discussed in Chapter 15, when there was a never-before-seen rapid and dramatic drop in US equity market prices, many managers faced the dilemma of whether or not to hit the strategy panic button. Those who did may have realized losses that would have been regained if they allowed the strategy to continue to trade when the market bounced back up.

However, those managers who stayed in the market may have faced losses due to trades that the strategy made that were subsequently "busted" by the exchange, that is, orders that were matched, but that the exchange did not require or allow the counterparties to fulfill because they were deemed as being outside of reasonable market operating conditions.

Being a buy-side manager is harder than one might imagine. Having a brilliant trading idea or investment strategy is not enough. Significant work must go into validating, implementing, optimizing, and monitoring it. Even then, there is no assurance of profitability. A strategy's risk profile may result in the profits made over two years being wiped out by a single day's trading in adverse market conditions. Alternatively, a money-making strategy may end up going outside the boundaries of market rules or regulations (Case Study 13-5). Traders and fund managers come and go, achieve fame, and then often face rapid downfalls. Given the challenges that professional fund managers equipped with substantial

---

Case Study 13-5

Algorithmic Trading Order Spoofing Leads to Jail Time

Trading strategies often require orders to be changed or canceled in response to market movements. However, there are cases where market participants may place orders and subsequently change or remove them to create the appearance of buying or selling demand. Their goal is to manipulate the market so that they can profit from other participants who act on that false information. The practice of rapidly placing orders without the intent of actually filling them, then canceling them before they can be executed as trades, is referred to as order spoofing.* Exchanges and other authorities have for many years disallowed this practice; however, in 2010, it became a criminal offence under the financial reforms set out by the Dodd–Frank Wall Street Reform and Consumer Protection Act. This law explicitly prohibits "bidding or offering with the intent to cancel the bid or offer before execution."

The first criminal prosecution in the United States for order spoofing came in 2015 when a high-frequency trader was found guilty of using algorithmic trading techniques to submit large buy orders for commodity futures, such as copper and gold, that were subsequently canceled and never filled. Simultaneously, the trader would place smaller orders to sell, which would execute when other firms drove up prices in response to his false buy orders. Over the course of just a few months in 2011 he was able to generate profits of over $1 million using this strategy.

---

* In the technical context, spoofing generally refers to sending something under false pretenses or a false identity. Network IP addresses can be spoofed to make it look like network packets are coming from somewhere other than their true origin. Likewise, email messages can be spoofed to look like they were sent from a false or fictitious email address.

In itself, placing orders and subsequently cancelling them is not an uncommon practice in financial markets. Some estimates are that over 90% of orders are not filled. Even so, the convicted trader went beyond normally acceptable practices by designing his algorithms to combine simultaneous larger orders placed in one direction that were canceled in less than half a second with small orders placed in the other direction that were executed. Hence the trader's guilt rested on the fact that since the algorithm was designed to have this structure, he never intended for the canceled orders to be filled.

Ultimately the trader was sentenced to three years in prison; the jury only took one hour to decide the verdict. It probably did not help that the trader chose to testify in his own defense and stated that he "absolutely wanted to fill every order." He was also subject to over $3.5 million in settlements for civil charges and regulatory fines. Moreover, for other high-frequency trading firms, this was an earth-shaking event, causing them to consider whether the strategies they use are likely to come under the same type of scrutiny.

Sources: Scannell, Kara and Gregory Meyer, "Trader Faces Criminal 'Spoofing' Charges," *Financial Times*, October 2, 2014, http://www. ft.com/intl/cms/s/0/9bf94196-4a53-11e4-b8bc-00144feab7de.html#axzz3F5T1Pq9P; Henning, Peter, "Conviction Offers Guide to Future 'Spoofing' Cases," *New York Times*, November 9, 2015, http://www.nytimes.com/2015/11/10/business/dealbook/conviction-offers-guide-to-future-spoofing-cases.html?partner=rss&emc=rss&_r=0; Hirtzer, Michael and Tom Polansek, "First U.S. Trader Convicted of Spoofing Sentenced to Three Years in Jail," *Reuters*, July 13, 2016, http://www.reuters.com/article/us-court-spoofing-sentence-idUSKCN0ZT232.

training, tools, and experience face achieving consistent profitability, it is hard to imagine that amateur stock pickers or currency traders would be able to outperform them in the long term.

13.4 ARCHITECTURE CONSIDERATIONS

In many cases, cost is the primary driver of architecture decisions. This is especially the case for buy-side firms in relation to the architecture choices for implementing their trading platforms. Sell-side firms and exchanges often require sizeable capital bases to support their business activities, which can also be used to help fund the purchase of core IT infrastructure. On the other hand, buy-side firms, such as hedge funds and prop trading operations, tend to start small and grow over time. Hence, they may only have limited resources available in the early days of operation to fund the purchase, support, and maintenance of core IT systems.

Buy-side firms typically deal with funding restrictions by initially leveraging their broker's trading platform infrastructure. Many brokers provide portfolio, order, execution, and risk management IT system capabilities as well as market data distribution as part of their service customer offerings. For example, the only software that a small buy-side firm may choose to purchase is spreadsheets to use for quantitative analysis. It may remotely access its broker's online trading platform via the Internet to view market prices, enter orders, initiate order execution algorithms, monitor positions, and calculate margin requirements. The broker's platform may not provide every desired feature and will tie the buy-side firm to that broker's services; however, it is a cost effective option. Usually, brokers will not impose any direct costs for using their platforms. Rather, they will recoup the cost through commission, float, and interest charges associated with the customer's use of its trading services.

As a buy-side firm grows and has more financial resources, it may redesign its architecture to rely less on brokers' systems. For example, it may choose to implement its own **order management system (OMS)** that can route trades to multiple brokers and obtain market data from its own dedicated terminal or data feed. However, buy-side firms may continue to use advanced capabilities provided by brokers, such as the implementation of order execution algorithms (discussed in Chapter 15). Only the largest buy-side firms will find it cost effective to use in-house implementations for all trading platform components.

Another option for sourcing and implementing trading system components is to use capabilities provided by an independent third party, such as market data aggregators and private cloud service providers. This arrangement is advantageous in that it provides a platform that is broker neutral while avoiding large upfront expenditures. Typically, fees for such services will be charged on a monthly basis and may also be calculated based on the number of users and transactions performed.

Besides avoiding upfront costs, this arrangement also eliminates the costs and support concerns related to the operation and maintenance of the trading platform software and IT systems. Due to economies of scale, it is more cost effective for a third party to provide services on a shared basis for many customers than for individual firms to manage it in-house. The additional scale provided by shared service arrangements can also enable greater investment in platform resilience and performance.

Furthermore, using hosted software platforms also eliminates the need to perform software upgrades and testing. This is especially important when regular upgrades are required to take advantage of improved business functionality, such as new order execution algorithms, or to comply with changing regulatory requirements.

13.5   SOLUTION CONSIDERATIONS

There are similarities in the technology needs of traders and fund managers. Both use systems to record and review their trading activity and positions. However, where traders' short-term view requires them to monitor real-time prices and position values, fund managers typically work more with end-of-day prices and have more static, but more extensive, reporting requirements. Typically, fund managers' reporting requirements are more onerous because they are directly responsible for other people's and institutions' money. Depending on the jurisdiction a fund manager operates in, he or she will have to provide reporting information to many different parties, such as the investors in the fund, the fund's management and shareholders, and regulators.

While spreadsheets can be used to track simple portfolios, they lack the more advanced capabilities required to generate flexible reports, validate transactions, and accurately measure performance. Likewise, they have no built-in audit trail facility, which is required to help track down data entry errors and prevent fraud. Typically, portfolio management systems will support the accounting and review stages of the trading lifecycle shown in Figure 13-4. However, depending on the application used, it may also be the case that order capture and execution capabilities are integrated into or directly linked with the portfolio management system. The following sections will review common functions provided by portfolio management systems.

13.5.1 System Information Setup

When capturing transactions, a number of values must already be defined in the portfolio management system so that the transaction can be correctly and richly described to make extensive reporting possible. Table 13-1 shows the parameters that are commonly defined initially and maintained over time.

13.5.2 Trade Blotter

The trade "blotter" is an essential information management tool that is used by traders and fund managers. It captures a record of the trades executed and will include details such as the time and date, security, bought or sold, price, quantity, and fees associated with the transactions*. Transactions may be entered into the blotter through deal capture screens, which provide entry fields for the different parameter values or may be entered into a tabular representation where each row represents a buy or sell transaction, and each column represents a detail of the trade. Alternatively, transactions may be fed in from another system, such as a front-office trading system or from broker's electronic trade confirmations.

Multiple blotter operations may be entered together as a single atomic transaction so that several transaction additions, amendments, and deletions in the trade blotter will either all be recorded or none at all. For example, if one transaction fails validation, none of the other transactions being "posted" in the blotter will be entered into the portfolio transaction database. This approach helps prevent inconsistent views, where only part of a multileg transaction is captured in the system. Transactions may fail validation for many different reasons, such as missing **reference data** for a new option symbol that has not been traded before or trying to enter a sell transaction for a security that is not held in the portfolio (possibly due to a mix up as to which portfolio a trade should be posted to).

Table 13-1 Portfolio management system setup information

Setup Information	Purpose
Industry groups/sectors	Enables each holding to be associated with an industry group or sector so that holdings by sector/group can be generated
Security types	Describes the type and characteristics of each security, for example, symbol, asset class, dividend dates, yield, maturity/expiration date
Asset classes	Defines the different types of asset classes that can be associated with a security, for example, equity, fixed income, future, option, commodity
Split dates	Defines the dates that an equity has corporate action stock splits so that portfolio share quantities can be adjusted accordingly
Withholding taxes	The withholding taxes that may be applied by foreign governments to dividends and/or capital gains on securities held in those countries
Currencies	The currencies used in the system for cash accounts and securities transactions
FX rates	The FX rates for dates that transactions occur on or for reporting dates
Country	The country that a security is associated with used for reporting holdings' exposure to individual countries
Exchanges	Exchanges that securities are traded on or may be used for reporting purposes
Brokerages	Brokerages that are used to execute transactions or may be used for reporting purposes
Bond revenue sources	For US municipal bonds, the revenue source may determine if dividends are taxable and must thus be captured for tax-reporting purposes
Commission purpose	Identifies the purpose of fees paid to brokers, for example, execution or research, for reporting and allocation purposes

---

* The term "trade blotter" goes back to a time before computers were invented when traders would write down trade details on their blotters, large pads of blank paper that covered their desks. Today, spreadsheets serve as trade blotters for casual investors, whereas professionals typically use specialized software applications for this purpose.

An audit trail monitor will enable users to review, but not modify, the operations performed through the trade blotter. Deleting a transaction will usually be shown as a special transaction that reverses the original entry. Likewise, trading-oriented systems may also provide a position blotter that shows the open quantity, current price, average cost of the position, and profit or loss. The position blotter may allow the user to drill down on individual holdings to look at the previous transactions, buy and sell, that led to the current quantity and average cost. Whereas traders often require interactive position blotters that are updated with real-time prices, static reports may be sufficient for fund managers, who have a longer-term focus.

13.5.3 Portfolio Reports

Portfolio reports are critical analytical tools for helping fund managers analyze their holdings and communicate the portfolio information to the fund investors. Common reports that are generated are listed in Table 13-2.

13.5.4 Performance Reports

Besides analyzing and reporting portfolio state information, a portfolio management system will provide performance reports for aggregate holdings, individual portfolios, or performance of specific asset classes or securities. Likewise, reports showing gains and losses for specific

Table 13-2 Common portfolio reports

Report Type	Purpose
Summary	Aggregate portfolio holdings as well as segmentation by security, asset class, country, and industry segment
Realized/unrealized gain/loss	Realized gains/losses for securities bought and sold, unrealized gains for open positions valued at current market prices
Income and expenses	Income generated by portfolio (e.g., deposit interest and dividends) as well as expenses (e.g., fees, margin interest, and security borrowing costs)
Cash ledger	Cash held in the portfolio account(s) and cash transaction history
Securities held longer than holding period	Securities that have been held for longer than periods required to meet advantageous capital gains tax treatment (e.g., long-term gains tax treatment requires holding of at least one year in the United States)
Upcoming maturity/expiration	Bonds that will mature and options that will expire in a specified upcoming time period
Change in market value	Change in market value of securities within a given period of time
Commissions	Fees incurred by portfolio over a given period; can be segmented by purpose, broker, or exchange
Management fees	Management fees charged by the fund manager or submanagers over a given period of time

periods, such as quarterly, year-to-date, or five years, will be provided. Historical performance statistics and charts may be provided showing trends and comparing performance to market benchmarks.

Information from portfolio and performance reports may be incorporated into fund investors' monthly statements and reviewed by managers to determine what decisions to make regarding managing the fund holdings. For example, reports that show the portfolio allocation to different countries, industry sectors, or individual securities may be used to decide how best to rebalance the portfolio. Besides portfolio and performance reports, a portfolio management system may also have the capability to generate periodic holding and end-of-year tax statements for investors, as well as specialized reports required by auditors and regulators.

13.6   SUMMARY

This chapter covered:

- key financial markets participants and their roles;

- the business considerations of buy-side firms;

- the process through which trading strategies are implemented;

- how cost considerations determine buy-side firms' trading platform architecture; and

- the core functions provided by portfolio management systems.

The next chapter discusses in more detail how exchanges and execution venues support order matching, and the clearing and settlement process for equity trades.

FURTHER READING

Books

Bodie, Z., A. Kane, and A. Marcus, *Essentials of Investments* (New York: McGraw-Hill/Irwin, 2005), Chapter 3: How Securities Are Traded.

Groot, M., *Managing Financial Information in the Trade Lifecycle: A Concise Atlas of Financial Instruments and Processes* (London: Academic Press, 2008).

Kissell, R. and M. Glantz, *Optimal Trading Strategies: Quantitative Approaches for Managing Market Impact and Trading Risk* (New York: AMACOM, 2003).

Lewis, M., *Flash Boys: A Wall Street Revolt* (New York: W. W. Norton & Company, 2015).

Lowenstein, R., *When Genius Failed: The Rise and Fall of Long-term Capital Management* (New York: Random House, 2001).

Schwartz, R. A. and R. Francioni, *Equity Markets in Action: The Fundamentals of Liquidity, Market Structure & Trading* (New Jersey, John Wiley & Sons, 2004), Chapter 2: Institutional Order Flow.

Thulasidas, M., *Principles of Quantitative Development* (West Sussex: John Wiley & Sons, Inc., 2010).

Papers

Nuti, G., M. Mirghaemi, P. Treleaven, and C. Yingsaeree, "Algorithmic Trading," *IEEE Computer* (November 2011): 61–69.

Periodicals

Automated Trader, http://www.automatedtrader.net.

Journal of Financial Markets, http://www.sciencedirect.com/science/journal/13864181/16/4?sdc=1

Journal of Portfolio Management, http://www.iijournals.com/toc/jpm/current

Journal of Trading, http://www.iijournals.com/toc/jot/current

Web

Committee of European Securities Regulators, the, "Best Execution under MiFID, Questions & Answers," http://www.cesr.eu/popup2.php?id=4606.

"Financial Markets with Professor Robert Shiller," http://oyc.yale.edu/economics/financial-markets. "Regulation NMS," http://www.sec.gov/rules/final/34-51808.pdf.

"Singapore's Securities and Futures Act," http://statutes.agc.gov.sg/non_version/cgi-bin/cgi_retrieve.pl?actno=REVED-289&doctitle=SECURITIES%20AND%20FUTURES%20ACT%0A&date=latest&method=part.

World Federation of Exchanges Market Highlight, https://www.world-exchanges.org/home/index.php/statistics/market-highlights.

ENDNOTES

1. NYSE Markets Data Volume Summary, http://www.nyxdata.com/Data-Products/NYSE-Volume-Summary

2. Miller, R. and Shorter, G. "High Frequency Trading: Overview of Recent Developments," Congressional Research Service, April 4, 2016, https://fas.org/sgp/crs/misc/R44443.pdf.

3. The source of the data used in Figure 13-6 is "Automated Trader 2011 Algorithmic Trading Survey Presentation & Panel Discussion," © Automated Trader Ltd. 2011.

— — —

4. "Government Pension Investment Fund, Japan," http://www.gpif.go.jp/eng/index.html.

5. Mooney, A., "Fintech Lures Millennial Investors Away from Asset Managers," *Financial Times*, January 19, 2017, https://www.ft.com/content/0bb9f8ce-d330-11e6-b06b-680c49b4b4c0.

14 Exchanges and Execution Venues

For hundreds of years, stock exchanges operated with the help of little or no information technology (IT). Stock exchanges were formed by groups of brokers and traders and, in many cases, were initially run in public places, often outdoors. Direct participation was limited to members of the exchange who agreed to abide by its rules. The primary means of trading was open outcry. Exchange members would announce their customers' orders or the amounts and prices that they were willing to directly buy and sell individual stocks at by shouting out prices. Bid and **offer prices** would be written on a blackboard, which served as the main means of real-time price distribution. Each party would record trades on sheets of paper, referred to as trade tickets. Trade tickets would later be matched and recorded into trading books.

Over time, the exchanges became more organized and modernized. For many decades, stock exchanges and brokers were limited by the technology of that time. **Market data** and order instruction delivery for many years required physical messages to be passed in person or by carrier pigeon. The invention of the telegraph made it possible to transmit stock prices over telegraph lines, giving rise to ticker tape machines. Later, the telephone would revolutionize the speed at which customers could place orders with their brokers, who were then able to relay those orders to the stock exchange. The invention of television led to the use of analog video displays to show price information to market users and digital wallboards replaced blackboards for displaying stock prices at exchanges.

Computers and digital networks further enabled modernization and efficiency gains. Initially, only deliveries of order instructions, order confirmations, and order fills were performed electronically. For many years, stock traders manually used open outcry to match and execute trades at the exchange. In the 1970s, all-electronic stock markets, which used computers to match and execute trades between brokers and **market makers**, came into existence. Gradually, many traditional exchanges did away with the open outcry system and adopted electronic matching engines to cross trades (Case Study 14-1). This change often coincided with the demutualization of exchanges, shifting their ownership from the member brokers to being publicly listed entities.

Today, many of the old traditional exchanges have merged and consolidated, while at the same time, new alternative trading venues have proliferated. Changes in technology and regulation have required centuries-old institutions to radically change their business models. These changes have occurred at different rates and in different ways in different parts of the world.

This chapter reviews the exchange market structure and the driving forces behind it. Some of the processes, data, and IT systems that support exchanges will also be examined. Henceforth, the term "exchange" will be used to generically refer to an execution venue, for example, a stock exchange, an electronic communication network (ECN), or a **dark pool**. Also, in some locales the "offer price" is also referred to as the "asking price"; accordingly, the terms "bid-offer" and "bid-ask" can be used interchangeably.

Case Study 14-1

Automating Open Outcry Trading

Today, electronic matching and execution underlie almost all stock exchanges. Automation of the order matching process has enabled exchanges to perform billions of transactions per day, each performed within a fraction of a second. In hindsight, it seems like the obvious implementation strategy for exchanges. However, leading up to and during the conversion process, there was considerable debate regarding the comparative merits of using people rather than computers to perform exchange trading functions. In many places where floor trading still exists, the debate continues. Key concerns of exchanges in this regard include their ability to attract order flow and maintain their profitability.

There are a number of obvious benefits of automation including lower transaction costs, faster execution, and the ability to support higher volumes. Electronic trading also reduced the number of exceptions that had to be resolved. "Out trades," that is, different details reported by floor traders for the same trade, were very common in open outcry markets. On the other hand, arguments for human-based open outcry trading have focused on the supposed ability of floor traders to better understand the market's state and dynamics because of their physical proximity to the trading activity. Likewise, proponents of open outcry trading have argued that automated trading would lead to lower **liquidity**. Since they have better market visibility, floor traders would be more likely to participate in a wide range of market conditions.

With the migration from manual to automated trading over the past few decades, it was possible to begin measuring some of the actual effects of automation. In 1989, the Singapore Stock Exchange, now called the Singapore Exchange (SGX), transitioned to computerized systems and closed their floor trading operations. Analysis of trades done before and after the automation determined that after automation, the trading volume increased for all stocks, as did the overall liquidity, calculated as the ratio of volume to volatility. However, there were also slight increases in bid-offer spreads.

Another transition occurred in 2006 when the New York Stock Exchange (NYSE) migrated from a floor-trading environment to a hybrid market that included automated trading. This change was designed to address both competitive and regulatory pressures. The new model reduced the average trade execution time from several seconds to less than one second, bypassing floor traders most of the time. After the migration, the effects on market quality were measured. Specifically, the hybrid market reduced the bid-offer spreads, trading costs, and execution time. While overall market quality appeared to have improved, the business models of the floor traders and "specialist" market faced significant challenges as a result of automation. Their role of managing the execution of larger trades was largely taken over by computer algorithms.

Interestingly, both the Singapore Stock Exchange and NYSE had run pilot systems that provided automated trading services in the years prior to their conversion. However, these pilot systems had restrictions that limited the amount of transaction volume that they would handle. In the case of NYSE's pilot system, only **limit orders** were supported and the order size had to be less than 1,100 shares. Likewise, only one order could be placed in any 30-second period.

While there are still some islands of manual order matching and filling in the exchange world, they are fast shrinking. One of the last bastions for open outcry trading is the listed options markets in the US where, as of 2017, thirteen percent of transactions were executed through floor trading. In fact, one options exchange is bidding to open a new floor-trading operation, one of the first to launch in decades, to complement its electronic platform. The Box Options Exchange has one of the smallest market shares in US options, and believes that it can expand its business by offering open outcry trading. Hence, the debate over where people really add value to the order execution process is set to continue.

Questions

1. If automation increases volumes and increased volumes generate more revenue for exchanges, why would exchanges resist automating their matching and execution functions?
2. From a regulatory perspective, which would be preferable: automated or manual trade execution?
3. Why would an exchange make the investment to create an automated trading pilot system that ran in parallel with floor trading operations, but then cripple the automated system by placing excessive restrictions on its operating parameters?
4. In the trading ecosystem, what human capabilities are superior to computers, and how can they best be applied in the capital markets ecosystem?

Sources: Naidu, G. N. and S. Rozeff, "Volume, Volatility, Liquidity, and Efficiency of the Singapore Stock Exchange before and after Automation," *Pacific-Basin Finance Journal* 2 (1993): 23–42; Storkenmaier, A. and R. Riordan, "The Effect of Automated Trading on Market Quality: Evidence from the New York Stock Exchange," *Enterprise Applications and Services in the Finance Industry, Lecture Notes in Business Information Processing* 23 (2009): 11–30; Banerji, G., "Plan for New Trading Pit Triggers Feud in U.S. Options Market," *Wall Street Journal,* July 9, 2017, https://www.wsj.com/articles/plan-for-new-trading-pit-triggers-feud-in-u-s-options-market-1499605202.

14.1 MARKET STRUCTURES

Exchanges bring together buyers and sellers, establish and communicate market prices, and match orders. They define and enforce rules related to market interactions and structure to help ensure that their functions are provided fairly and consistently. This section will review quote driven, order driven, and hybrid market structures, which are the primary mechanisms used by financial exchanges.

14.1.1 Quote Driven Markets

In a quote driven market, registered market makers, also referred to as dealers, are required to continually provide two-way quotes, for both buying and selling, for the specific securities they trade.

Market makers' bids to buy and offers to sell are displayed on an exchange's order book and can be viewed by other market participants to determine the tradable amounts that are available at different prices. For less liquid instruments, such as some options, indicative prices may be provided and tradable quotes given only on demand.

Quote driven markets are guaranteed to be liquid, but may have wider bid-offer spreads than order driven markets. Institutional investors may also negotiate large trades directly with market makers to achieve trading prices that are better than the indicated best bid or offer. Individuals and firms are often provided with incentives, such as special stock borrowing privileges and exemption from some fees and taxes, to serve as market makers. Alternatively, firms may pay exchanges to be market makers and in turn be guaranteed a proportion of the execution volume. NASDAQ, the NYSE, and the London Stock Exchange were all originally purely quote driven markets, but have over time migrated to hybrid structures.

14.1.2 Order Driven Markets

Order driven markets are based on a continuous auction system. Limit orders from investors and brokers provide liquidity to the market and determine the bid-offer **spread**. Orders are managed, matched, and executed manually on an exchange floor or, more commonly, automatically by computer. Under normal conditions, bid-offer spreads may be lower on order driven markets. However, it may also be possible for the spreads to widen dramatically if a stock becomes illiquid. Because there is no requirement for any participant, such as a market maker, to continuously offer to buy or sell, there may be times when there are no other market participants readily available to take the other side of a trade. The Tokyo Stock Exchange (TSE) is an example of an order driven exchange.

14.1.3 Hybrid Structures

Hybrid markets have evolved to address the weaknesses and limitations of quote and order driven markets. For instance, the limited transparency of quote driven markets led to concerns that the visibility floor traders and market makers had with regard to supply of and demand for securities gave them an unfair advantage over other market participants. Order driven markets, on the other hand, were very transparent but were subject to large price swings or high volatility in times of uncertainty. There was no guarantee that buyers or sellers would be available to take either side of a trade, buying or selling.

Hybrid market structures use the limit order book structure of an order driven market, but also have designated market makers, thus enabling traders to access the liquidity provided by both the market makers and public limit orders. They provide the benefits of guaranteed liquidity, increased liquidity and, in some cases, reduced bid-offer spreads.

14.2 EXCHANGE PROCESSES AND DATA

In order to understand how exchanges work, it is necessary to examine the underlying interaction types, processes, and data structures. This section reviews concepts relating to how orders are managed and matched within a limit order book.

14.2.1 Order Messages

To begin with, it is useful to review basic order messages that are exchanged between brokers and exchanges related to orders and executions. Customer orders will typically begin as new order messages that indicate whether the order to buy or sell should either be executed at the current market price or at a specified limit price. **Market orders** will be executed immediately at the best bid or offer price, whereas limit orders may or may not be filled depending on whether the best bid or offer price reaches the specified limit price.

After accepting a new order message, the exchange will send an acknowledgement message confirming that the order has been accepted for processing. The acknowledgement will include an order identifier (ID) that will be used as the reference for subsequent messages related to the order. The broker may send messages requesting to amend or cancel an order, identifying the order by its order ID in the request. When the exchange matches an order, it will send one or more messages to the broker with information reporting the details of the order execution. When executed, an order may be filled in its entirety or only partially. Thus, multiple **partial fill** messages may be sent indicating the portion of the order that has been matched. For example, a limit order to buy 1,000 shares might be matched against other sell orders for 500, 200, and 300 shares, causing the exchange to send three partial fill messages to the broker.

14.2.2 Order Book and the Tape

The order book is the core technology component that is used by order-driven exchanges. When individual orders are received, they are either matched against resting orders in the order book or added to the order book. Typically, one order book will exist for each security that is traded. The order book represents the current state of outstanding orders and will be updated continuously during trading hours. It will show the depth of the market in terms of the volume of buy or sell orders at different prices for each security. The buy and sell orders that are closest to each other are the best bid and best offer, and they will be the first to be crossed with incoming market orders or limit orders that match their prices.

Figure 14-1 presents a simplified example of an order book for a single security. It maintains information about the price, quantity, and counterparty of each order. Actual order books would also track the order types and other attributes. As shown in Figure 14-1, the best price bid to buy the security is $43.54 and the best price offered to sell the security is $43.55. The "tick size," that is, the minimum price change increment, for this security is $0.01. The bid-offer spread, the difference between the best bid-offer price and best **bid price**, in this example is $43.55 − $43.54 = $0.01. In this case, the bid-offer spread is as small as it can be—only one tick difference.

When viewing the quote information for a security, retail investors will usually only see the best bid and offer prices and volumes, sometimes referred to as level 1 market data. Alternatively, the entire order book, also known as level 2 market data, may be viewed, although exchanges often charge higher prices for this in-depth market information. In some cases, exchanges may only distribute partial order book information as market data to conserve network bandwidth and reduce the processing load that data recipients need to handle. Unlike the order book that the exchange maintains, the depth of market data that is provided to market participants does not indicate the identity of the brokers who have placed the orders resting in the order book and will only show the aggregate order volume at each price level. For example, in the order book shown in Figure 14-1, the market data received from the exchange would only indicate that a total of 1,400 shares were bid at a price of $43.50. Note that the orders associated with each broker in the order book are usually orders that they placed on behalf of their customers. Hence, they may show up multiple times and at different price levels within the order book.

The other critical market data generated by exchanges is the stream of information related to trades executed. This information is often referred to as "the tape," in reference to when it was actually printed on ticker tape. Similarly, execution of trades is sometimes referred to as the trades being "printed." Figure 14-2 shows an example of what the tape might look like for the order book shown in Figure 14-1. The unshaded rows represent trades executed showing their price, size, and time of execution. The shaded rows indicate when the best bid and offer prices changed and their new values. This information is normally included with the trade execution information so that trade prices can be compared with the current market prices at the time of execution. When exchanges or market data aggregators distribute this information, it is typically referred to as "time and sales" data.

Buying Counterparty	Shares	Limit Price	Shares	Selling Counterparty	
		44.00	5,000	Broker A	
		44.00	1,000	Broker B	
		43.65	400	Broker C	
		43.63	200	Broker B	Offers
		43.62	100	Broker B	to sell
		43.60	700	Broker A	
		43.60	1,000	Broker B	
		43.58	10,000	Market maker	
		43.56	200	Broker B	
		43.55	300	Broker C	←Best offer
Best bid → Broker A	100	43.54			
Broker B	500	43.54			
Market maker	10,000	43.53			
Broker B	200	43.51			
Bids Broker B	300	43.50			
to buy Broker A	1,000	43.50			
Broker B	100	43.50			
Broker D	400	43.49			
Broker B	600	43.46			
Broker C	100	43.46			

Figure 14-1 An example of an order book

43.52	43.54	10:14:21
43.54	100	10:14:22
43.52	400	10:14:22
43.52	100	10:14:22
43.54	200	10:14:22
43.52	100	10:14:22
43.54	1000	10:14:23
43.54	200	10:14:23
43.53	43.54	10:14:23
43.53	43.55	10:14:23
43.53	100	10:14:23
43.54	43.55	10:14:23
43.55	100	10:14:23
43.54	300	10:14:23

Figure 14-2 Time and sales market data—"the tape"

14.2.3 Order Types

There are two fundamental types of securities orders: market orders and limit orders. Market orders are executed immediately at the best available trading price at the time they are received by the exchange's matching engine. As the best bid or offer may change between the time an order is placed and the time that it is executed, the price that a market order will be executed at is not fixed or determined when it is placed. Market makers' quotes may shift during that time span, and liquidity held in the order book may be taken up by other orders that are received earlier.

Limit orders, on the other hand, are designated to trade only at a specific price, or better. A limit order to buy will be immediately matched if it is at a price that is greater than or equal to the lowest resting offers, that is, orders to sell, on the exchange. If the price of the limit order to buy exceeds the best offer currently in the order book, the best offer price will be used as the execution price, rather than to the price of the incoming order. For example, if an order to buy 100 shares at $43.60 was sent to the exchange and the best offer was for 100 or more shares at $43.55, the incoming order would be executed at $43.55. Alternatively, if the buy order is lower than the best offer, it will be placed in the order book as one of the resting bids. The converse is true for the orders to sell, which will be matched against the resting bids.

Orders may be specified with a validity period as to when the order may be executed. Some examples of order validity times include:

- immediate or cancel;
- good until canceled;
- good for the day;
- at market open; and
- at market close.

Additionally, a minimum fill quantity may be specified as part of an order. For instance, an immediate-or-cancel order is a type of limit order that has no minimum fill requirement and specifies that, if possible, all or part of an order should be executed immediately when it reaches the market and that any unexecuted part of the order will be canceled. Alternatively, a fill-or-kill order is like an immediate-or-cancel order, but specifies the minimum fill quantity that is usually total order size. A fill-or-kill order must be matched as soon as it reaches the exchange, but only if it can be matched with another order that is as large or larger than the minimum fill quantity specified for the order. If the minimum fill quantity cannot be matched, the entire order will be canceled.

Over time, exchanges have introduced new order types to better meet diverse customer needs. For instance, a mid-point order defines the order price as the current mid-price between the best bid and best offer prices. Similarly, a pegged order defines the order price as the current best bid or offer, with an optional offset. The price of pegged and mid-point orders can change over time when the best bid and best offer prices change. Alternatively, a hidden order allows some or all of an order's quantity to be maintained in the order book, but not to be displayed to market participants. Often, hidden orders will have lower priority for execution than normal market and limit orders. An iceberg order is a type of hidden order where only a part of the overall order is held in the order book at any given time. When that amount has been matched and executed, another portion of the order is made available for execution.

14.2.4 Matching Process

Incoming orders will be matched with market makers' quotes or limit orders in the order book based on a set of precedence rules that are defined by the exchange. Generally, "price time priority" rules will be applied. For matching purposes, resting orders in the order book are first prioritized by the orders' prices, and then by their time of arrival. When market orders and crossable limit orders arrive, they will be matched with resting bids and offers, based on the resting orders' priority status in the order book. Limit orders that are not immediately matched will be positioned in the order book according to their price time priority. Other factors that may be incorporated into prioritization rules include:

- **Order size**: larger or smaller order sizes may be given higher priority

- **Public orders versus floor orders**: public orders may be given priority over designated market makers' or floor dealers' orders at the same price

- **Displayed versus hidden orders**: order types that are partially hidden may be given lower priority than those that are fully visible

The matching process may be quite complicated, especially when complex order types are supported. For instance, when processing an iceberg order, once the visible part of the order has been matched, the next portion that is made available must be placed at the bottom of the priority queue at that given price level. While this does not sound complex by itself, it requires significant computing resources when managing hundreds of thousands of orders simultaneously.

14.2.5 Brokered Matching

Some markets may allow brokers to match large block trades bilaterally between counterparties outside of the exchange. This may be appropriate because market makers are unwilling to provide liquidity for large trade volumes at a fixed price and there is insufficient liquidity in the **central limit order book** to fill the order at a desirable price. Likewise, if a large limit order is placed in the order book, it may serve as a signal to other market participants and cause the market price to move away from the order, resulting in slippage, that is, the order being executed at a suboptimal price. Accordingly, for large block orders, brokers may actively search for other market participants who are interested in and willing to take the other side of the trade. Bilaterally negotiated off-exchange transactions are referred to as over-the-counter (OTC) block trades and must be publicly reported through standard exchange facilities. These trades are sometimes referred to as "upstairs trades" and are, to some extent, similar to the services that dark pools provide.

14.2.6 Circuit Breakers

In times of great uncertainty or high volatility, it is critical to have clear guidelines that determine under what conditions trading will be suspended and the duration of the suspension. Market "circuit breakers" are special rules and procedures instituted by exchanges to temporarily halt trading or, in some cases, limit the price range if there are excessive movements in market prices. They have been instituted to help dampen price volatility and, in extreme cases, prevent liquidity from being exhausted, which could lead to even greater volatility. Circuit breakers are also intended to improve investor confidence and prevent free-fall price declines. Typically, trading is temporarily suspended or, under extreme circumstances, the market may be closed early, before the end of the normal trading session.

For instance, the NYSE's Rule 80B defines its circuit-breaker levels and procedures [1]. Trigger levels for market suspension are set at drops of 7%, 13%, and 20% of the S&P 500 index. These percentages are translated into a specific number of index points daily, based on the previous day's closing price for the S&P 500 index.

The length of time that trading is halted under circuit breaker conditions are dependent on both the size of the drop and the time of day. Table 14-1 shows the Rule 80B circuit breaker rules as of 2017 for regular scheduled close days. It is important to note that circuit breakers are often specific to individual exchanges. That is to say, multiple execution venues trading the same instruments may not always follow the same circuit breaker rules.

Besides exchange-wide circuit breakers, trading curbs on individual stocks may also be instituted. Beginning in 2010, a pilot program went into effect in the United States to halt trading of any stock in the S&P 500 and Russell 1000 indexes for five minutes if it varies by more than 10% within a five-minute period. This strategy can help reduce the volatility of individual stocks, particularly when erroneous trades cause large price movements. For instance, an order that was mistakenly placed and executed outside of the normal market price range might create a large shift in the price. Other traders and trading algorithms that see the price movement and expect that the trend will continue may immediately place similar orders, further magnifying the price movement. Large price movements may trigger resting stop-loss limit orders to execute, further exacerbating the price movement.

Trading curbs are designed to help provide a cool-down period that allows market participants to better understand what has caused major price changes. If it is determined that the initial price movement was due to a mistaken trade, the price may revert to its original state more quickly, thus, reducing volatility. However, they could also have a negative impact. Because trading curbs and circuit breakers create discontinuities in trading, during the halt they may introduce uncertainty about what the market behavior will be following resumption of trading. This uncertainty, in turn, may increase volatility.

14.2.7 Surveillance

In order to fulfill their responsibility to create fair and orderly markets, it is necessary for exchanges to monitor market participants' activities. The market surveillance function within exchanges tracks the actions of market participants and the effect of those actions. Exchanges will verify that market participants are complying with the exchange's rules, and are not gaining an unfair advantage. It is not uncommon for brokers or investment firms to be reprimanded, fined, or banned from trading activities for manipulating markets for various ends.

Some common examples of trading activities that market surveillance will watch for include:

- broker trades coming just ahead of customer orders, also known as "**front running**";

- trades made just prior to corporate announcements or the release of broker research that could be based on insider information;

- feigned activity, where orders are submitted and then canceled before they can be executed;

Table 14-1 NYSE market circuit breaker Rule 80B

Type	Amount of Drop	Timing	Effect
Level 1	7%	9:30 am–3:25 pm	15 minute halt
		after 3:25 pm	no halt
Level 2	13%	9:30 am–3:25 pm	15 minute halt
		after 3:25 pm	no halt
Level 3	20%	any time	close for rest of day

- inflated trading volume, where trades executed generate little or no profit;

- extraordinary shifts in the spread between best bid and best offer for an instrument; and

- other unusual instrument price behavior, for example, trades executed at prices outside of the observed or implied bid-offer spread.

Typically, the exchange will have a dedicated group responsible for surveillance, with systems that are designed specifically for identifying potential market abuses.

14.3 EXCHANGE SERVICES

Today, largely due to competition and demutualization, exchanges provide a variety of services. By way of illustration, Figure 14-3 shows the proportions that different services contributed toward the SGX's revenue in the financial year 2016 [2]. The types of services that are provided and their relative importance will vary from one exchange to another. However, trading, market data, and market access services are technology-intensive services provided by all exchanges. The previous section explored trading; in this section, we will examine market data and market access services.

14.3.1 Market Data Services

Trading is dependent on market data. Without accurately knowing the current price and demand for an instrument, few will want to trade that instrument. Market data must be both accurate and timely. Trading on stale market or erroneous market data can easily lead to losses. Since exchanges are the primary source of market information, market data services are an important part of their service offerings.

Exchanges may provide many different types of market data offerings. They may provide simple feeds of best bid, best offer, and last traded price information; or for a higher price, they may provide full market depth information, that is, most details about the order book. Market participants may

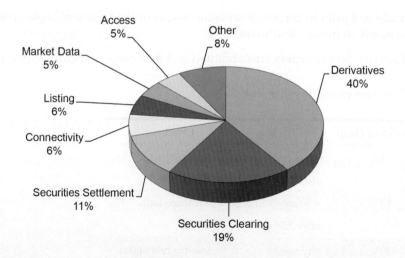

Figure 14-3 SGX's revenue breakup (FY2016)

receive exchange data directly from the exchange's feed or may receive the market data via an aggregator, such as Bloomberg or Reuters. Even when market participants receive market data through an aggregator, they still must pay fees to the exchange for using that data. Usually, the data aggregator will be responsible for collecting data usage fees from customers and forwarding the proceeds to the relevant exchanges.

In the US market, which is highly fragmented, regulators require orders matched by nonexchange execution venues, such as ECNs, dark pools, and brokers, to be reported to a **trade reporting facility (TRF)** so that market participants can see all the trades executed across different execution venues on a "**consolidated tape**."* Some exchanges, such as NYSE and NASDAQ in the United States, offer TRF services to other market participants. Similar requirements are included as part of MiFID II for European execution venues.

The volumes of market data can be enormous, especially when the full depth of market information is involved. Every addition, cancelation, or change in price in the order book must be sent out as market data. Optimizations are used to try to reduce the overall volume of data that is transmitted. For example, a standard practice is to send the entire market data record only once at the beginning of a session and, subsequently, to only send the fields that have changed, such as the last trade price. When market data records have dozens or hundreds of fields, this optimization is extremely beneficial for reducing the amount of data that must be distributed and processed by receivers. Of course, such optimizations also complicate the software architecture (see Chapter 11 for more a detailed discussion of market data distribution architectures).

Similarly, the communication interfaces used to distribute market data may be optimized for performance. While delivering market data in an easily processed, self-descriptive format such as XML would be beneficial from a programming standpoint, the resulting large message sizes would put a heavy burden on the distribution infrastructure. Hence, market data is often distributed in highly efficient, but proprietary formats that are specific to each exchange.

14.3.2 Market Access Services

Market access services enable brokers and other exchange members to connect to the exchange, send orders, and receive order status information. The connectivity interface provided by the exchange may be a proprietary one that is defined by the exchange or one based on a standard interface protocol. The Financial Information eXchange (FIX) protocol is the most common way that exchanges and execution venues provide access to their services.

Exchanges will provide a protocol specification that describes the message types that the exchange supports along with details about specific fields within the message. Typical categories of FIX messages that exchanges support include:

- connection and session management;
- standard orders, for example, new, cancel, status requests;
- order variations—post-trade allocations and multileg orders (that is, spread trades and buy-write/covered call trades);
- execution reports; and
- administrative messages.

---

* Some jurisdictions have similar reporting requirements for OTC derivative trades; however, they have been put in place for regulatory governance purposes rather than to provide market transparency. Trade reporting, in the context of OTC derivative transactions, is reviewed in Chapter 19.

FIX also supports delivery of market quotes, for quote driven markets, and market data. However, these features are not commonly used by equity and derivative exchanges (the FIX protocol will be discussed in more depth in Chapter 15).

14.4 BUSINESS STRATEGIES

Exchanges have undergone tremendous change in recent decades. In many markets, competition from alternative trading networks and dark pools have forced exchanges to dramatically alter their business models. There has also been a wave of mergers and consolidation in the industry. Consider, for example, NYSE Euronext, which is one of the largest exchanges in the world. It was formed from the union of the NYSE Group and Euronext in 2007. As shown in Figure 14-4, the NYSE Group was, in fact, a conglomeration of the Pacific Exchange, the Archipelago ECN, and the NYSE.* Likewise, Euronext was formed from mergers of the Lisbon Exchange, the London International Financial Futures and Options Exchange, the Paris Exchange, the Brussels Exchange, and the Amsterdam Exchange. However, the consolidation trend may be losing momentum. In 2011, the European Commission blocked the proposed merger between NYSE Euronext and the Deutsche Börse Group, which would have created the largest equity and derivatives exchange in the world. Then, in 2013, the Intercontinental Exchange (ICE) acquired NYSE Euronext, and subsequently divested Euronext through an initial public offering. The following subsections will discuss the business strategies of different types of exchanges and execution venues.

14.4.1 Established Exchanges

The business model of established exchanges has typically been focused on revenue earned from listing services, provision of market data, trade-matching services, and, in some cases, **clearing** services. Also, while many exchanges are commonly thought of for their stock trading, commonly referred to as **"cash equities"** market services, in many cases, futures trading comprises a large proportion of the transaction volume and revenue of exchanges. Innovation in the exchange-traded derivatives markets has, therefore, become a major area of interest. While regulators have been pushing banks to match standardized OTC derivative trades using exchanges or electronic trading platforms, for the most part, established exchanges have not elected to provide these services, leaving it to banks and **broker-dealers** to address this requriement. Many exchanges have begun looking outside their national market to provide listings for foreign companies. This strategy has been especially important for countries such as Singapore and Hong Kong that have relatively small numbers of local corporations that are eligible for listing.

Established exchanges have also become more aggressive about monetizing existing nontangible assets such as the information that they generate. Accordingly, market data services have been expanded and enhanced. To further increase data-related revenue, many exchanges have expanded their services to include historical data services and direct market data feeds that minimize data delivery latency, which are useful to high frequency traders. Furthermore, competition from alternative trading networks has led some incumbent exchanges to expand and improve the services that they offer to customers (Case Study 14-2).

---

* The figure shown may not contain the most up-to-date information; the current NYSE materials can be found at http://www.nyse.com/pdfs/NYSEEuronextTimeline-web.pdf.

NYSE Group

2006
NYSE and Archipelago merge to form NYSE Group, Inc., which begins trading publicly on March 8.

2005
Archipelago acquires the Pacific Exchange.

PACIFIC EXCHANGE

2001
Archipelago Exchange (ArcaEx) becomes a regulated facility of the Pacific Exchange.

1976
The Pacific Stock Exchange launches its options trading business.

1957
The Pacific Coast Stock Exchange is created by the merger of the San Francisco and Los Angeles Stock Exchanges.

1938
The San Francisco Curb Exchange is acquired.

1883
The Los Angeles Oil Exchange (later the Los Angeles Stock Exchange) is organized.

1882
The Stock and Bond Exchange is established in San Francisco.

ARCHIPELAGO

2004
Archipelago Holdings, Inc. Initial Public Offering launches on August 19.

2001
Archipelago Exchange (ArcaEx) is launched.

2000
Arca acquires PCX Equity Trading Business.

1997
Arca Electronic Communications Network (ECN) is launched.

NEW YORK STOCK EXCHANGE

2004
NYSE's regulatory function, dedicated to strengthening market integrity and investor protection, is placed within an independent operating structure.

1972
The Securities Industry Automation Corporation (SIAC) is established to provide data processing services to the NYSE.

1869
NYSE merges with the Open Board of Brokers and the Government Bond Department.

1863
Name is shortened to New York Stock Exchange (NYSE).

1817
New York brokers form the New York Stock & Exchange Board (NYS&EB).

1792
Twenty-four brokers and merchants sign the "Buttonwood Agreement," agreeing to trade securities on a commission basis and laying the basis for securities trading in New York City.

Figure 14-4 Evolution of a stock exchange (© NYSE Group, Inc. Reprinted with permission.)

14.4.4 National Markets

In the past, exchanges had a clear association with a city, region, or country. Today, however, territorial boundaries of exchanges are less clear. For instance, for several years NYSE Euronext listed companies and provided a secondary market for financial products originating in several different countries on two continents. Asian markets and exchanges are quite the opposite, though, and are still quite segregated by country. Regulatory structures vary widely across the Asia-Pacific region, with competitive market frameworks set up in some countries, and outright or quasi-monopolies being supported in others. In some cases, there is cross-border competition between exchanges to list foreign companies and to create or dominate certain derivative products.

14.5 CLEARING AND SETTLEMENT

The primary purpose of exchanges and execution venues is to match orders from trading counterparties. The actual exchange of securities and cash is handled independently of the matching process by different functional entities. Clearing and settlement functions are closely linked with trade execution, and these services may be provided by a subsidiary of an exchange, as is the case in Singapore, or by an entirely separate entity, as is the case in the United States. The clearing and settlement model will vary by financial product type, by countries or region, and potentially across different exchanges within the same country. This section will begin by reviewing the basic concepts of clearing and settlement, in the context of OTC derivatives trades (for example, interest rate swaps) that are negotiated directly between counterparties. Then, a more complex process will be discussed in relation to the clearing and settlement of cash equities for trades processed by brokers on behalf of institutional customers.

To begin with, it is useful to review the terminology related to clearing and settlement. Clearing refers to the process of communicating and reconciling security transfer and payment instructions prior to settlement. Settlement is the actual process of transferring funds and securities to fulfill trade execution obligations. A **clearing house** is a centralized facility that coordinates communication of instructions related to funds or securities between market participants. **Central counterparties (CCPs)** are often involved in the clearing and settlement process to reduce counterparty risk. In some cases, clearing house and CCP functions will be combined in the same business entity.

14.5.1 Over-the-counter Derivatives Clearing and Settlement

While exchanges have not rushed to provide execution facilities for OTC derivatives, they have introduced clearing and settlement services for these instruments. This subsection will first briefly explain how, historically, OTC derivatives have been cleared and settled bilaterally. It will then go on to explain the relatively new role of CCPs in clearing and settlement of OTC derivatives. Background information about OTC derivatives and how they are traded is covered in Chapters 11 and 12.

14.5.1.1 Bilateral clearing and settlement

To understand the different entities and their roles in the clearing and settlement process, it is easiest to first begin with a simple example and review the complications that it presents. Figure 14-5 shows the trade participants and their interactions if they were to settle bilaterally, that is, directly with one another. To keep the discussion focused, interactions with central depositories, custodial banks, and settlement banks are not included. In practice, these entities would also be involved in the clearing and settlement processes.

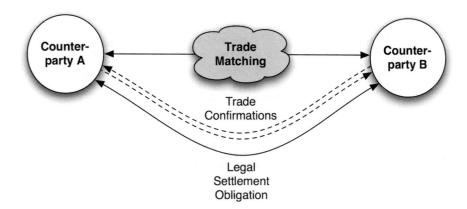

Figure 14-5 Bilateral clearing and settlement

First, the counterparties would match their orders in the front office, either via an execution venue or possibly by phone, in the case of an OTC derivative trade. Then, the counterparties would send one another trade confirmations forming a legal settlement obligation between the two entities, referred to as clearing. Cleared trades have been approved and accepted for settlement. Finally, as stipulated by the trade agreement, cash payments or securities would be transferred between the counterparties, referred to as settlement.

While this arrangement is relatively simple, it presents several concerns. One problem is that up until the point of final settlement, each of the counterparties faces the risk that the other counterparty might default on their trade settlement obligations. In cases where the trade settlement obligations may extend out over months or years, as with FX forwards and options, this concern is more material and, thus, may limit the amount of business that can be conducted with a specific counterparty. For example, Counterparty A's risk management group may decide that the largest credit exposure that can be safely maintained to Counterparty B is $5 million. This would be the greatest potential loss that would be borne if Counterparty B were to go bankrupt. However, it also means that if the credit limit is reached, no more trades can be carried out with Counterparty B until some of the outstanding settlement obligations have been fulfilled. Alternatively, market conditions (that is, prices) may change, reducing the counterparties' credit exposure and, thus, less of their counterparty limit allocation is utilized. Counterparty **credit risk** is discussed in greater depth in Chapter 8.

Another concern is **settlement risk**. Because the transfer of funds and securities will not happen at the exact same instance, the party that sends first may find that the other party does not fulfill their obligation in return. For example, the day that the trade is due to settle, funds may be wired by Counterparty A to Counterparty B to complete a stock purchase at 9:00 am, but Counterparty B might go bankrupt at noon and then not deliver the securities as promised by the end of the day. Settlement risk is discussed further in Chapters 9 and 13.

14.5.1.2 Centralized clearing and settlement

Settlement through a CCP or clearing house can help address the issues identified with bilateral settlement in Section 14.5.1. Chapter 9 discusses the concepts behind netting of settlement cash flows; this subsection builds on those concepts and explains the processes behind centralized clearing for settlement and the role of clearing houses. Figure 14-6 shows the functional entities involved in centralized clearing of OTC products and their relationships. Often, a trade registration service is

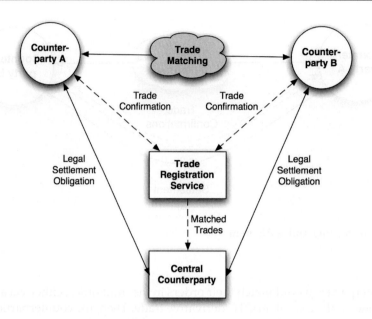

Figure 14-6 Centralized clearing and settlement

used to facilitate the clearing process, and a central clearing counterparty intermediates the settlement process between both counterparties.

In this case, after the two counterparties have matched their orders, they will send the confirmations, in the form of electronic messages, to the trade registration service. The trade registration service will verify that corresponding confirmations are received from both parties for the trade and that the trade details included in the confirmations are consistent. Mismatched trades will be flagged to the counterparties as exceptions for further action, and matched trades will be forwarded to the CCP for processing. Trade details cannot be modified once the trade registration service has forwarded them to the CCP for settlement.

After verifying that the counterparties have sufficient collateral deposited with the CCP, the CCP can act as an intermediary for the counterparties' settlement agreements. In this case, the initial contractual relationship between the two counterparties is replaced with two separate contractual relationships, that is, between each of the counterparties and the CCP. Through this process, the two counterparties no longer bear credit risk of the other defaulting; they only require that the CCP remains solvent. For example, in this arrangement, even though Counterparty A executed the trade with Counterparty B, for settlement purposes, Counterparty A's obligations and credit risk are with the CCP, not Counterparty B. Hence, if Counterparty B were to default, Counterparty A would not be affected—the CCP would bear any credit or settlement losses caused by Counterparty B's default.

For a central clearing arrangement to be effective, the CCP must be financially stable and be able to sustain defaults by individual counterparties. To ensure the CCP's solvency, it will typically require counterparties that it serves, its **clearing members**, to contribute to a default fund, also referred to as clearing fund. Likewise, clearing members will be required to post **margin** collateral for the positions that they enter into a settlement arrangement with the CCP. The amount of margin collateral that is required will depend on the risk exposure created by the underlying instrument traded, and will vary over time as the value of the instrument changes (Case Study 14-3).

Case Study 14-3

Ensuring the Solvency of the Central Counterparty

For the CCP model to be effective, it is critical that the CCP itself is never at risk of becoming insolvent. It is, therefore, necessary for the CCP to receive sufficient margin collateral from its members to ensure that their positions can be closed without loss in case of default or general inability to meet the margin requirements for their position. For example, to purchase one Nikkei 225 index futures contract, which represents a **notional amount** of ¥4,500,000, might require that initially ¥600,000 of margin collateral be posted by the counterparty involved in the trade. If the futures price were to decline significantly, additional margin payments would be necessary to cover the additional risk exposure.

The method used to determine the amount of margin required, both up front and also in case of unrealized losses, is not obvious. If too little margin collateral is received, then the CCP may become financially unstable if their counterparties default. On the other hand, collecting too much margin would unnecessarily limit the total value of customer trades that the clearing house would support. That is to say, requiring clearing members to post excess capital, handicaps the market and unfairly burdens market participants.

In 1988, the Chicago Mercantile Exchange (CME) developed the SPAN margining system to calculate margins for futures and options contracts that were traded on the exchange. SPAN calculates margin requirements by simulating possible changes in value of the positions held based on 16 different scenarios that evaluate the effect of relatively simple changes in the price and volatility of the underlying instrument or index that the derivative is based upon. The worst loss amount that results from the different scenarios is used as the basis for determining the amount of margin collateral that is required. When more than one instrument is held by a counterparty, scenario losses are calculated for each instrument and then summed across all instruments for each scenario. The maximum aggregated loss across all 16 scenarios is then used in conjunction with a number of other calculations to determine the margin collateral requirement. The CME went on to license the SPAN margining system to third parties, and a number of financial institutions have adopted the SPAN methodology.

While SPAN has been effective for calculating the margin collateral requirement for futures and options, it is quite dated and is unsuitable for the next generation of clearing requirements. CCPs for OTC derivatives must support more complex instruments such as foreign exchange (FX) forwards, interest rate swaps, and credit derivatives. SPAN was not designed for determining the margin collateral required for these types of instruments and more advanced risk management calculation methods are necessary. **Value at risk (VaR)**, which is discussed in Chapter 18, is a more suitable method for calculating the margin collateral requirements for OTC derivatives.

Calculation of VaR uses significantly more computational resources than SPAN calculations and requires different types of business applications. Thus, existing exchanges and CCPs must make substantial changes to be able to provide OTC derivatives clearing services. The SGX implemented VaR for clearing interest rate swaps (IRS) starting in 2010, and cleared around US$80 billion worth of IRS transactions within eight months. It further extended its OTC clearing services to cover FX forwards in 2011.

Sources: Knott, Raymond and Alastair Mills, "Modelling Risk in Central Counterparty Clearing Houses: A Review," in *Financial Stability Review Regulatory Structure Articles 2002*, http://www.bankofengland.co.uk/publications/Documents/fsr/2002/fsr13art11.pdf; "Singapore to Offer Clearing on OTC Derivatives," *Financial Times*, April 21, 2010; Enriquez, Millet "SGX to Clear Asian FX Forwards," *Channel News Asia*, June 1, 2011, http:// www.channelnewsasia.com/stories/singaporebusinessnews/view/1132559/1/.html.

A secondary, but important, function that the CCP provides is to generate regulatory reports on the total outstanding exposures of clearing members. These reports help provide regulators with a clear view of the risk exposures that individual institutions have outstanding in the market. For example, Singapore regulators raised concerns with Barings Bank's management about its exposures, as discussed in Case Study 19-1, based on the reports that the futures exchange's clearing house had provided. Unfortunately, those warnings went unheeded by Barings.

Obtaining a view of counterparties' market exposure is more difficult without a CCP. Each party would have to report its exposure to all its counterparties, and it would then be necessary for the regulator to aggregate these reports to determine the overall market exposure to a particular counterparty. For instance, this concern was realized when Bear Stearns and Lehman Brothers collapsed in 2008 and 2009, respectively. Regulators struggled to determine the exposure that other financial institutions had to these two banks through OTC derivatives trades that were settled bilaterally, rather than through a CCP. Hence, regulators, such as the European Central Bank, have made efforts to mandate that all standardized OTC trades are settled via a CCP, and all OTC derivatives trades are reported to a trade repository (discussed further in Chapter 19).

14.5.2 Exchange-traded Equities Clearing and Settlement

In the context of exchange-traded equities, clearing and settlement processes are well established, but the structure and roles of the entities involved vary by country and region. Furthermore, clearing and settlement processes become more complicated when unique institutional customer needs must be addressed. This section examines the process of clearing and settling an institutional equity trade executed by a broker, and provides a simplified explanation of the clearing and settlement model used in the United States.

Figure 14-7 shows the trade execution and clearing process for a block trade where an institutional customer is buying shares. It is not uncommon for an institutional customer to have its broker execute a large block order to buy or sell a stock and request to have the executed trade settled against many different accounts. For example, a large fund management company may decide that it no longer wants

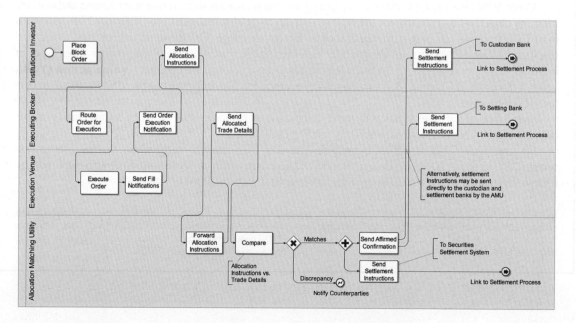

Figure 14-7 Clearing process for an institutional customer cash equities trade

to have exposure to a particular stock in any of its **mutual funds** and, thus, may instruct its broker to execute a block trade to sell all its holdings. However, the trade settlement, that is, the security and fund transfers, will need to be applied to the bank and custodial accounts of multiple mutual funds. Typically, the customer, that is, the fund manager in this case, will instruct the broker to allocate the trade settlement to individual fund accounts after the trade execution. This process is referred to as **blocking and allocation**.

In some cases, allocation instructions may be sent directly from the customer to the broker. The broker will then provide the trade allocation details to the customer, and the customer must review and confirm that the trade allocations are correct. Alternatively, an **allocation matching utility (AMU)**, which plays a similar role to the trade registration service discussed in the previous section, may act as a clearing house for the allocation instructions and allocated trade details. The AMU compares the allocation instructions and trade details that are provided by the institutional customer and the broker. Once the AMU has successfully reconciled the clearing information, it delivers the settlement details to the participants of the settlement process. The matching utility provides real-time automated matching capabilities that speed up the clearing process, reduce errors, and provide economies of scale.

In markets where securities are **scripless**, that is, having no physical form, as is the case in this example, the **central securities depository (CSD)** maintains the official record of share ownership, and facilitates the transfer of shares between counterparties by recording the changes as accounting entries, commonly referred to as **book-entry system**. The **securities settlement system (SSS)** is an IT system that typically the CSD operates to manage and maintain electronic securities transfers. The CCP, clearing member, and the customer must either have their own accounts with the CSD or, alternatively, use a **settlement agent** who has its own account with the CSD. Custodian banks often act as settlement agents.

Settlement is usually required at two levels: (1) between the CCP and the clearing member and (2) between the clearing member and its customer. In Figures 14-7 and 14-8, the executing broker is also a clearing member. As part of the settlement process, each party sends settlement instructions, possibly via its settlement agent, to the SSS.* Aggregation and netting may be implemented between the CCP and the clearing members so that significantly fewer settlements will be required, compared with the number of trades. For allocations matched by the AMU, the AMU will provide allocation information to the broker's and the customer's respective settlement agents and the agents will send the settlement instructions to the SSS on their customers' behalf.† When the SSS receives the settlement instructions, it effects transfer of the security on the CSD's accounting books, and receives payment from and makes payment to the settlement and custodian banks, as shown in Figure 14-8.

As part of the settlement process, the SSS typically provides for the simultaneous legal transfer of securities (that is, change of ownership) and payment, which is commonly referred to as **delivery versus payment (DvP)**. This settlement model minimizes principal risk—the risk that one counterparty completes one half of the settlement while the other counterparty does not. Settlement between CCP and clearing members, and between brokers and institutional customers, is usually carried out on DvP basis. Alternatively, settlement between brokers and retail customers is usually completed on free-of-payment (FOP) basis, where the delivery of securities is not directly linked to receipt of a payment. However, matched DvP settlement instructions between brokers and customers may also be guaranteed by a CCP, but the CCP used between brokers and customers need not be the same CCP as the one used to settle transactions between clearing members. For example, in Japan, Japan Securities Clearing Corporation (JSCC) guarantees transactions between clearing members, whereas JASDEC DVP Clearing Corporation (JDCC) is the CCP for matched DvP settlement instructions between brokers and institutional customers.

---

* The settlement instructions may be sent to the SSS via a presettlement matching utility (PSMU), which is usually separate and independent from the AMU.

† There are some cases where it is not be necessary to match the parties' settlement instructions. For example, clearing members may give standing authorization to the CSD allowing the CCP to settle directly into their accounts.

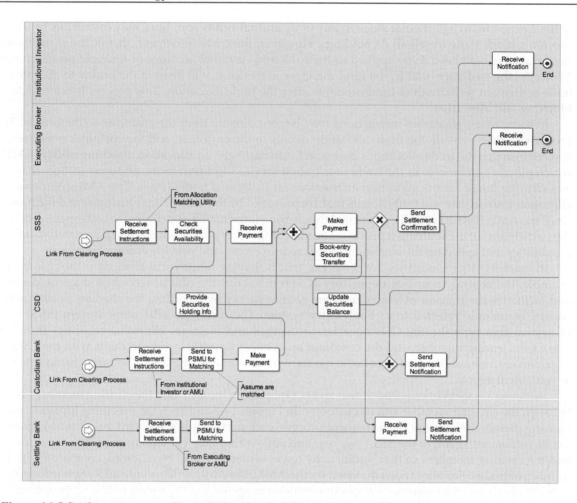

Figure 14-8 Settlement process for an institutional customer cash equities trade

Depending on the market, the clearing and settlement functions and roles may be performed by completely separate business entities or provided by closely linked organizations. For example, in the United States, there is a wide separation, from a corporate ownership point of view, between the execution venues, the matching utility, and the CCP used for cash equity trading. On the other hand, in Singapore, all of these functions, including the guarantee of matched DvP settlement instructions between clearing members and customers, are closely linked with the SGX and are provided by its subsidiary, the Central Depository (Pte) Ltd (commonly referred to as the CDP). The Singapore CDP allows end customers, including retail customers, to open and maintain accounts with it. Other CSDs do not, and only provide accounts to clearing members.

14.6   EXCHANGE TECHNOLOGY

Having reviewed the functions, structure, and mechanics of exchanges, it is practical to review their technology considerations. This section will explore the key business and technical considerations that underlie the design of exchange information technology systems.

14.6.1 Business Considerations

The IT systems that exchanges operate are the core of the capital markets, and it is critical that they operate effectively; hence, reliability and resilience are major concerns. If a broker's systems are down, only its customers will be affected, but if an exchange's systems are down, the entire market will be affected, and the situation will come to public attention very quickly. Case Study 3-2 highlighted the importance of exchanges' systems being robust and avoiding unexpected downtime. Likewise, accuracy is critical. As the **system of record**, if the exchange provides inaccurate market data or trade execution information, market participants may lose confidence in its integrity, causing long-term damage to the market.

Capacity is also a major business concern and is determined by the technology platforms used. Exchanges usually have fixed transaction processing capacity and cannot easily limit the number of trades they receive in any given time period. In the case where trading activity exceeds the order handling capacity of an exchange, market disruption can occur. For example, in 2006, a major exchange had to close the market early due to a surge of orders received. The concern was that the total number of orders received that day would exceed the limit of the exchange's IT systems [3].

Likewise, changes to market rules and parameters can have a significant impact on message volumes and put stress on exchanges' IT systems. Exchanges' reduction of the minimum price change increment, referred to as the tick size, is one such case. For example, in the 1990s, the Stock Exchange of Singapore (now the SGX) reduced the minimum tick size for some stocks from SG$0.50 to SG$0.10. In the United States, there was a transition from trading in fractional units, for example, one-sixteenth, to trading in decimals, which effectively reduced the minimum tick size from US$0.0625 to US$0.01. A reduction of tick sizes has generally led to increases in order placement and cancelation by market participants, significantly increasing the rates at which price update information is generated and must be distributed to customers. Hence, changes in one business area, for example, trading, may require technology changes in another business area, such as market data distribution.

Another major business concern for exchanges is pre- and post-trade risk management. Although brokers are responsible for ensuring that the orders they submit on behalf of their customers or themselves are valid, in practice, a trader may mistype, or "fat finger," an order, adding an extra zero or mixing up the price and quantity. Similarly, a high-frequency trading algorithm may go haywire and blast thousands of buy or sell orders into the market erroneously. In either case, there is a risk that executing these trades may exceed a broker's clearing limit and/or detrimentally impact market prices on the exchange. For example, in 2005, a trader at a brokerage firm in Japan erroneously entered a trade to sell 610,000 shares of a newly listed stock at ¥1 each, rather than 1 share at ¥610,000 [4]. This order size was more than 40 times the number of outstanding shares in the stock and caused the price to temporarily drop more than 16%. Moreover, some exchanges allow customers to route orders to the exchange through the broker, bypassing the broker's pretrade risk checks to minimize order processing latency. Instead, the clearing broker is required to perform post-trade risk management checks almost in real time, that is, just after the order has been submitted. However, some exchanges have implemented their own pretrade risk filters that brokers can use to limit customers' trading activities.

Exchanges must take into account the needs of a wide range of market participants' technical capabilities. On the one hand, an exchange may need to put in place safeguards against automated trading algorithms that send too many orders in quick succession and overwhelm the exchange's systems. On the other hand, the change may need to accommodate small brokers' systems that are unable to keep up with the rate of market data or trade execution information that is sent to them. In general though, exchanges and execution venues have been actively working to address more of the high-end technology requirements. The following sections will examine technology strategies used by exchanges for addressing these needs.

14.6.2 Architecture Considerations

Historically, specialized hardware was used to provide ultra-high availability for stock exchange systems. Today, hardware, operating systems (OS), and software architectures have reached the point where highly proprietary designs are no longer required. Commodity hardware can be used to achieve both high reliability and high performance, although in many cases, some customization may be necessary to enhance performance.

As discussed in Case Study 14-4, low **latency** and high **throughput** has become an important selling point for execution venues. Generally, exchanges measure trade latency as the time between when the exchange receives an order, its matching engine processes it, and the confirmation status of the order is sent back to the sender of the order. Trade latency is commonly measured in milliseconds or microseconds and may be quoted as the average or maximum latency, or by certain percentiles of latency variability, for example, less than five milliseconds 99.9% of the time. Trading throughput is the volume of orders and execution that the exchange can process in a given period of time, for example, 40,000 orders per second.

Supporting high throughput is especially critical for stock exchanges in countries with large populations, such as India and China, where the volume of retail trades can be enormous. As a case in point, during January 2012, the National Stock Exchange in India matched over 130 million trades in its electronic order book, with an average of over 6,000 trades per second [5]. Moreover, the number of orders per second that must be accommodated will actually be much higher than the average number of trades, that is to say order fills, since many orders may be placed, amended, and canceled for every trade that is executed. Likewise, the trading volumes during the day will not be even and, thus, the peak throughput rate is usually many times the average rate.

The speed at which an exchange can match orders will largely depend on the efficiency of its matching engine software and the speed of the hardware that it runs on. However, as throughput requirements increase, other software design considerations will come into purview. For instance, an exchange's software architecture may be designed to minimize the number of software processes and servers that an order must flow through when it is processed to minimize end-to-end processing time. Likewise, distributed processing techniques may be used to divide up the matching engine's processing load across multiple servers so that the load never exceeds any server's processing capacity. However, there are some fundamental limitations on how software components can be implemented on hardware architectures. For instance, the operations performed on an individual security's order book must be single threaded to ensure fairness and predictability of order processing. Thus, parallel computation hardware architectures will provide limited benefits for individual order book implementations.

In addition to optimizing the software architecture, hardware optimizations may also be implemented. Central processing units (CPUs) with large numbers of processor cores may be used to reduce the number of servers required and minimize the need for communication between servers over networks, which is slower than intraserver communications. Data persistence may be shifted from disk-based storage to redundant copies that are stored in random-access memory (RAM) to provide faster access time. Alternative network designs, which minimize network segmentation so that messages do not get slowed down while passing through network routers, may also be used. Furthermore, physical distances may be minimized to reduce the time it takes for electrical signals to travel between system components. Hence, the colocation of customer servers in or near the exchanges' data centers has become a lucrative business for many exchanges.

14.6.3 Design Approaches

Figure 14-9 shows the logical components involved in order execution in an exchange. Order messages are received by the exchange, validated, and then routed to a matching engine for processing. Order confirmation messages are sent asynchronously in response to the broker, and fill messages are sent to the broker when all or part of an order is matched. Besides providing remote connectivity to brokers and other members, many exchanges also provide data feed and exchange order access connections to their colocation facilities (colocation configurations are discussed in Chapter 15).

To provide scalability and segregate customer network traffic, an exchange will run multiple instances of the same trading system components. Each instance will provide similar services, but may run on different hardware servers to ensure that it provides acceptable response times, throughput, and latency. This is an example of **horizontal scaling** (discussed in Chapter 3). For example, multiple exchange access gateways and data feed components may be run in parallel to provide high-performance service to multiple customers and ensure that activities related to one customer do not directly affect another customer. Usually, exchange access gateways will have predefined throughput (also referred to as "throttle") limits that specify how many orders per second will be accepted to avoid overloading their processing capacity. Hence, a single exchange customer may require connections to multiple exchange access gateways to support high levels of order throughput.

Similarly, multiple instances of the matching engine component may be run on different servers. In this case, however, the matching engines provide identical services. Instead, the order books and matching functions for all the securities supported by the exchange would be partitioned across different matching engines. Each matching engine would be assigned to a specific set of securities. For instance, matching engine number one could provide services for securities starting with letters A through AM, matching engine number two could provide services for securities starting with letters AN through AU, and so on. This is an example of static load balancing, as discussed in Chapter 11. In extreme cases, dedicated hardware and matching engine software components may be allocated to single, highly liquid security. An order routing component directs inbound orders to the appropriate matching engine, as shown in Figure 14-7. In the diagram, the order router, data consolidation, and market data distribution components are shown as single boxes for simplicity. However, in practice, they would be implemented in an active-active, hot-standby resilience configuration (see Chapter 7 for discussion on resilience configurations).

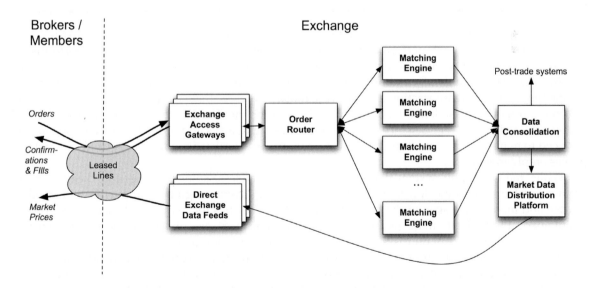

Figure 14-9 Exchange software order management component architecture*

---

* For simplicity, the components necessary to support clearing and settlement activities are not shown in the diagram. Also, the term "leased lines" in the diagram refers to dedicated telecommunications links, which may be implemented using any number of technologies, such as Multiprotocol Label Switching (MPLS for short) networks.

Case Study 14-4
The Need for Speed

In recent years, a major focus for exchanges has been to reduce the time required to place orders and execute trades, largely to accommodate the needs of customers that use high frequency trading (HFT) techniques. Particularly in emerging markets, HFT provides a major opportunity for growth. For instance, on the SGX, the percentage of trades generated by HFT over a two-year period in the derivatives market increased from 10% to 30%. In developed markets, HFT can account for over 50% of the traded volume.

High frequency traders use computer algorithms to receive market data, evaluate trading opportunities, and place trade orders automatically. HFT systems can generate thousands of orders per second. While there has been some ethical debate over the fairness of HFT, it is attractive to exchanges because it can help increase trading volume and overall market liquidity. In turn, increased liquidity can help lower trading costs and attract additional investors. Fast execution services also help promote other exchange services, such as colocation and direct data feeds, which avoid delays that are incurred with feeds provided by market data aggregators.

Upgrading the IT systems of exchanges to minimize trading time can be a major undertaking. For instance, in 2011, the SGX launched a new trading platform that reduced its trade execution time from 16 milliseconds to 90 microseconds, creating one of the fastest exchange trading platforms in the world at that time. At a certain point, though, further increases in performance can become much more difficult and require significantly greater cost to achieve relatively small improvements in performance. The expected cost of SGX's upgrade was expected to be around US$180 million, which is quite a large outlay, even for exchanges.

Source: "Spread Betting," *Economist*, August 12, 2010, http://www.economist.com/node/16792950.

While request-reply client server-based software designs are prevalent in many industries, they are not appropriate for high-performance trading and order matching systems. Trading platforms are designed to send and receive asynchronous messages related to orders and executions, rather than synchronously requesting information from or submitting information to a database. Furthermore, the components processing transaction messages are mostly stateless, that is, they do not have to maintain information about transactions after their processing is complete. The stateless approach can be equated to "process and forget." For instance, the exchange access gateways and order routing components do not need to maintain state and, thus, follow a receive-process-forward model, as opposed to a request-process-reply model.*

While many trading system components will be stateless, some will need to keep track of accumulated current state information. For example, matching engine components will need to update and manage the state of the order books for the securities they support. Where state must be maintained, it is typically managed using in-memory databases, as opposed to relational databases that maintain their storage on disks. Disk input/output (I/O) is much slower than code execution, RAM access, and network communications. Hence, high performance systems will avoid database and disk access whenever possible in the main processing execution path. That is not to say that database disk storage is never used but, rather, that it is used in an asynchronous mode that does not require the main processing flow to wait for data to be written before processing can continue.

---

* In some cases, for example, with exchange access gateways, components may reply to acknowledge receipt or acceptance of order messages, but do not wait to reply with the final result of the transaction. The transaction status will be sent separately at another point in time.

14.6.4 Measuring and Tuning Performance

It is critical to design performance characteristics into the solutions from the outset. Performance needs will drive decisions regarding which hardware, software, and network components can be used. Likewise, it is best that performance measurement and debugging facilities be designed into the system, rather than considered separately. Obtaining precise and accurate performance metrics usually requires the integration of performance testing facilities into the solution components. One fundamental concern is to determine how performance should and can be effectively measured within and across components. Table 14-2 lists some of the techniques available for measuring performance that support performance tuning.

Table 14-2 System performance measurement techniques

Approach	Benefits	Drawbacks	Tools
Build timing measurements into source code	Requires no special tools or skills.	Requires coordination by developers and access to code. Measurement can affect performance. May not measure performance impact of libraries or OS.	printf() getlocaltime()
Network packet sniffing/timing measurement	Measures performance including effects of all layers, including OS. Noninvasive.	Requires special tools and skills to perform measurements. Requires understanding of intercomponent network communication protocols.	ethereal, TCPdump, hardware-based network packet sniffers
Multithreading performance analysis	Ensures that program code is effectively making use of multithreading hardware.	Only applicable to multi-core servers and CPU-bound applications.	truss/strace/ktrace, vmstat/mpstat
Java Virtual Machine (JVM) performance analysis	Ensures that configuration parameters of the JVM are optimally set to support maximum performance.	Only applicable to Java-based applications.	jconsole, jstat, jstack
Operating system performance analysis (CPU, net I/O, disk I/O)	Ensures that configuration parameters of the OS are optimally set to support maximum performance. Determines where OS-level bottlenecks are occurring.	Does not help when performance issues are fundamentally application related.	kernel settings, top, vmstat, iostat, taskmgr
Database performance analysis	Useful when database access is a bottleneck point. Can help identify type of database issue (i.e., design vs. indexing).	May require that sufficient numbers of database records be used for testing before results are meaningful.	database specific

Besides determining where and how to measure performance, it is also possible to perform design-level analysis to determine where performance bottlenecks would likely be expected. Common bottleneck points are data storage and access, transactional data writes, and WAN communications. A theoretical, paper-based exercise is a good starting point to help identify the locations of potential performance bottlenecks and related improvement opportunities. However, it is often the case that performance issues arise in unexpected places when systems go into production; hence, comprehensive end-to-end measurements should also be performed to validate assumptions that have been made regarding system performance.

Prototyping and load tests that simulate end-to-end performance can help validate assumptions and gain an empirical understanding of the environmental performance characteristics. This is ideally something that should be done in parallel with the architecture design. This verification can also serve to assess the performance characteristics of specific hardware and/or software platforms that may be considered for use within the architecture. However, it is important to keep in mind that it may not be possible to effectively simulate loads that will be encountered with real-world usage. Even when past transactions are "replayed" to do load testing, the speed of the replay mechanism may not replicate the original transactions' traffic patterns with sufficiently high fidelity.

14.7 SUMMARY

This chapter covered:

- the three main types of market structures;

- the purpose of a central limit order book and how limit and market orders are processed;

- clearing and settlement concepts and processes;

- the technology design approaches for exchange trading systems; and

- performance measurement and tuning techniques.

The next chapter examines the functions and technologies that brokers, as financial intermediaries, provide to capital markets customers and how they interact with exchanges.

FURTHER READING

Books

Bodie, Z., A. Kane, and A. Marcus, *Essentials of Investments* (New York: McGraw-Hill/Irwin, 2005), Chapter 16: Futures Markets.

Lewis, M., *Flash Boys: A wall Street Revolt* (New York: W. W. Norton & Company, 2015).

Loader, D., *Clearing, Settlement, and Custody* (Masachusettes: Butterworth-Heinemann, 2002). Schwartz, R. A. and R. Francioni, *Equity Markets in Action: The Fundamentals of Liquidity, Market Structure and Trading* (New Jersey: John Wiley & Sons, 2004), Chapters 6, 7, and 10.

Papers

Ahn, H. J., K. H. Bae, and K. Chan, "Limit Orders, Depth, and Volatility: Evidence from the Stock Exchange of Hong Kong," *Journal of Finance* LVI (2001): 767–788.

Chung, K. H. and C. Chuwonganant, "Tick Size and Quote Revisions on the NYSE," *Journal of Financial Markets* 5 (2002): 391–410.

Duffie, D., A. Li, and T. Lubke, "Policy Perspectives on OTC Derivatives Market Infrastructure," *Federal Reserve Bank of New York Staff Reports*, Staff Report no. 424, January 2010 (revised March 2010), http://www.newyorkfed.org/research/staff_reports/sr424.html.

Ende, B. and J. Muntermann, "Opacity and Exclusivity in Electronic Securities Trading: The Case of Dark Pools," *Multikonferenz Wirtschaftsinformatik* (2010): 35–44.

Hasbrouck, J., G. Sofianos, and D. Sosebee, "New York Stock Exchange Systems and Trading Procedures," NYSE Working Paper #93-01, 1993.

Jain, P., "Improving Liquidity through Efficient Stock Market Structure and Operational Design," *Journal of Financial Transformation 18 (2006): 151–159*.

Kauffman, R., Hu, Y. and Ma, D., "Will High-frequency Trading Practices Transform the Financial Markets in the Asia Pacific Region?" *Financial Innovation* (2015): 1:4.

Meyer, D. R. and Guernsey, G., "Hong Kong and Singapore Exchanges Confront High Frequency Trading," *Asia Pacific Business Review*, Volume 23, Issue 1 (2017): 63–89.

Moise, C. and Flaherty, P., "Limit Up-Limit Down" Pilot Plan and Associated Events," U.S. Securities and Exchange Commission, March 2017.

Periodicals

Focus: The World Federation of Exchanges monthly newsletter, http://www.world-exchanges.org/news- views/focus.

Web

"ASX New Order Types," http://www.asx.com.au/professionals/pdf/asx_trade_new_order_types.pdf.

"ASX SPAN Margining," http://www.asx.net.au/professionals/clearing/operations/span_margining.htm.

"B/View," http://pages.stern.nyu.edu/~jhasbrou/BView/launch.html.

"CME Clearing Financial Safeguards," http://www.cmegroup.com/clearing/files/financial safeguards.pdf.

"Guide to TSE Trading Methodology," http://www.tse.or.jp/english/rules/equities/dstocks/guide.pdf.

"NASDAQ Time and Sales Data," http://www.nasdaq.com/aspx/nlstrades.aspx?symbol=AAPL&selected=AAPL.

"National Futures Association Margins Handbook," http://www.nfa.futures.org/nfa-compliance/publication-library/margins-handbook.pdf.

"NYSE Arca Order Types," http://www.tradearca.com/traders/order_types.asp.

"Tokyo Stock Exchange," http://www.tse.or.jp/english/about/history/floor/index.html. "World Federation of Exchanges," http://www.world-exchanges.org.

ENDNOTES

1. NYSE Trading Information, "Circuit Breakers," https://www.nyse.com/markets/nyse/trading-info#Circuit_Breakers.

2. "Singapore Exchange Annual Report 2016," http://files.shareholder.com/downloads/ABEA-69RPAC/0x0x906184/6F03DAA5-806B-4CAB-B163-2A231C967BD1/SGX-Annual-Report-2016-.pdf.

3. "Selling Panic Closes Tokyo Market," *BBC News*, January 18, 2006, http://news.bbc.co.uk/2/hi/business/4623076.stm.

4. "Probe into Japan Share Sale Error," *BBC News*, December 9, 2005, http://news.bbc.co.uk/2/hi/business/4512962.stm.

5. World Federation of Exchanges, "Number of Trades in Equity Shares–Electronic Order Book Trades," World Federation of Exchanges, accessed May 9, 2012, http://www.world-exchanges.org/focus/2012-02/m-5-11.php.

— — —

6. Barker, A., J. Grant, and J. Wilson, "Deutsche Börse-NYSE Merger Blocked," *Financial Times*, February 1, 2012, http://www.ft.com/intl/cms/s/0/3615546a-4cb7-11e1-8b08-00144feabdc0.html.

7. Dabous, F. and F. Rabhi, "Information Systems and IT Architectures for Securities Trading," in *Handbook on Information Technology in Finance*, International Handbooks Information System, eds. D. Seese, C. Weinhardt, and F. Schlottmann, pp. 29–50 (Berlin: Springer-Verlag, 2008).

8. DTCC, "Following a Trade," accessed May 8, 2012, http://www.dtcc.com/downloads/about/Broker_to_Broker_Trade.pdf.

9. Securities and Exchange Commission, "Interpretation: Confirmation and Affirmation of Securities Trades; Matching," Securities and Exchange Commission, accessed May 8, 2012, http://www.sec.gov/rules/interp/34-39829.htm.

10. European Central Bank, "Glossary of Terms Related to Payment, Clearing and Settlement Systems," December 2009, http://www.ecb.int/pub/pdf/other/glossaryrelatedtopayment clearingandsettlementsystemsen.pdf.

11. Michie, R. C., "The London and New York Stock Exchanges, 1850–1914," Journal of Economic History 46 (1986): 171–187.

12. Comerton-Forde, C. and J. Rydge, "The Current State of Asia-Pacific Stock Exchanges: A Critical Review of Market Design," Pacific-Basin Finance Journal 14 (2006): 1–32.

13. Naidu, G. N. and M. S. Rozeffb, "Volume, Volatility, Liquidity, and Efficiency of the Singapore Stock Exchange before and after Automation," Pacific-Basin Finance Journal 2 (1994): 23–42.

14. Akhtar, S., ed., Demutualization of Stock Exchanges—Problems, Solutions and Case Studies (Manila: Asian Development Bank, 2002).

15 Financial Markets Intermediaries

Chapter Overview

15.1 BUSINESS ACTIVITIES

15.2 TRADING SYSTEM ARCHITECTURES

15.3 ORDER FLOW INTERNALIZATION

15.4 ALGORITHMIC ORDER EXECUTION

15.5 ARCHITECTURE CONSIDERATIONS

15.6 SUMMARY

FURTHER READING

ENDNOTES

Like exchanges, the business models and technology platforms of brokers have undergone major changes over the past few decades. Transactions have gradually migrated from voice-based execution to electronic trading, and at the exchange, from floor trading to automated matching. Trading volumes have multiplied and low **latency** trade execution services have become competitive offerings. One of the main drivers behind these changes has been the shift in asset managers' responsibilities and expectations. Over time, the performance of asset managers has come under greater scrutiny. Since transaction costs can be a major drag on overall investment performance, brokers' fees and their quality of trade execution became a major concern. Likewise, the widespread availability of real-time **market data** has provided "buy-side" traders with better visibility into market activity.

At the same time, the orientation of sell-side firms has also changed. Automated trading platforms enable a single customer to send out thousands of orders per second to their broker. A new breed of buy-side firms emerged that were focused on algorithmic and high-frequency trading. For these customers, it was important to minimize the delay, or latency, between when the broker received the order and when it was delivered to the exchange. Moreover, these customers were attractive in that they tend to trade in large volumes and, thus, generated large amounts of commission fees. However, to acquire and retain them, brokers' technology infrastructure had to be retrofitted and continually enhanced to keep up with ongoing changes in hardware, software, and trading markets.

Besides updating their IT systems, brokers began offering additional services to help attract new, and retain existing, buy-side customers. Some brokers extended the availability of their in-house trading and portfolio management systems to their customers. **Prime brokerage services**, including centralized securities lending, financing, and global custody services, were another offering provided to customers. Brokers also ramped up their own **proprietary trading (prop trading)** operations, that used the broker's own capital to trade in the market. Unlike the business of handling customer orders, prop trading was the equivalent of having a private **hedge fund** embedded within the broker.

These changes occurred over an extended period and some financial intermediaries responded faster than others. This uneven growth also led to many technology-related challenges. The migration from phone calls, faxes, and paper confirmations to entirely electronic system-to-system communications required participants to simultaneously support all communication methods. Likewise, from the outset, there was no standard way for the sharing of electronic trade information between buy-side firms, sell- side firms, exchanges, **clearing houses**, and depositories.

This chapter examines the business functions, trading processes, and technology of financial markets intermediaries, which include independent brokers and investment banks for securities as well as commercial banks for foreign exchange (FX). It builds upon the concepts introduced in Chapter 13, specifically the roles and objectives of financial services providers and other market participants. Concepts presented in Chapter 14, such as order types and states, are also referenced.

Case Study 15-1

Evolution of a Communication Standard for Trading Systems

As financial markets have become more automated, facilitating electronic communications between market participants has become an important concern. The SWIFT protocol and communication network (as discussed in Chapter 11) was developed in the 1970s and was quickly adopted for clearing transactions between back offices in banks. In contrast, a standard for communicating securities orders and execution information between asset managers and brokers evolved more slowly. In the early stages of automation, each broker provided its own proprietary interface for electronic order submission. A software interface component had to be implemented and supported to enable communication with each individual broker, which was a cumbersome task for asset managers who dealt with multiple brokers.

The Financial Information eXchange (FIX) protocol got its start in the early 1990s when Fidelity, a large asset management firm, and Salomon Brothers, then a large broker dealer, used it to share equity trade information. Unlike SWIFT, which provided a messaging protocol and a secure communications network, FIX only defined the messaging standard. It was left to the sender and receiver to determine how the FIX messages would be transmitted. Following the initial pilots, FIX gained rapid popularity around the world, and in 1999, the FIX Protocol Ltd Company was formed to help guide the protocol development.

FIX was originally designed for communicating equity trade information. However, over time, it was enhanced to support exchange-traded derivatives, FX, fixed income, and over-the-counter (OTC) derivative instruments. These new capabilities increased the complexity of the protocol. In FIX's early incarnations, only 17 message types were supported, whereas FIX version 4.4 supported 80. Likewise, the number of fields that were defined by the standard jumped from around 100 to over 900.

The scope of where and how the FIX protocol was used also increased. Initially, it was only used in the front office to facilitate electronic trading between brokers and their customers. It then began to be used for communication with exchanges and clearing houses. To better support these post-trade interactions, the base structure of FIX protocol was adapted and a new protocol, FIXML, was created. FIXML, which was designed to be an eXtensible Markup Language (XML) version of FIX, was fully self-describing and provided improved flexibility and extensibility. Because FIXML included embedded XML tags, FIXML messages are significantly larger and slower to process than standard FIX messages. Hence, FIXML was not in a position to supersede the standard FIX protocol for front-office use.

Moreover, FIX has gone beyond supporting order and trade information and now also supports the distribution of price information, that is, market data. The FIX Adapted for Streaming (FAST) protocol was created to support market data's efficiency requirements—support for ultra-high volumes with minimal processing delays. Standard FIX and FIXML encoded data as text, whereas FAST used binary encoding. Binary data can be processed more efficiently by computer systems and reduced message sizes. FAST addressed many of the concerns that limited FIX's use in super-high-performance implementations.

Questions

1. Given that encoding formats for FIX, FIXML, and FAST vary, what do they still have in common?
2. What is the potential downside of increasing the number of fields so significantly?
3. Which market participants would benefit from FIX standardization? Who would not benefit?
4. Compared to SWIFT, why might it have taken so long for the FIX protocol to be developed?

Sources: "The FIX Protocol Organization," http://www.fixprotocol.org; Maguire, F., "FIXing Derivatives—The Need for Standardization," *Derivatives Use, Trading Regulation* 11, no. 2 (2005): 157–161.

15.1 BUSINESS ACTIVITIES

A financial markets intermediary may be involved in a single business activity or many different activities. For instance, a financial institution might only provide equity brokerage services as a member of a single exchange. On the other hand, another financial institution might provide equity brokerage services in multiple geographies, support trading of listed derivatives, provide investment research, make markets in FX, as well as provide **investment banking** services. Figure 15-1 shows proportion of revenue generated by business unit for the ten largest investment banks [1]. The following subsections will examine the common services that are engaged in by financial intermediaries. To help narrow the scope of discussion, this section will focus primarily on the activities of **agency brokers** and **broker-dealers** in the context of equity trading (financial intermediaries' involvement with foreign exchange and OTC derivatives trading are discussed in Chapters 11 and 12). Specifically, this section covers customer-focused services, prop trading, market making, and risk management.

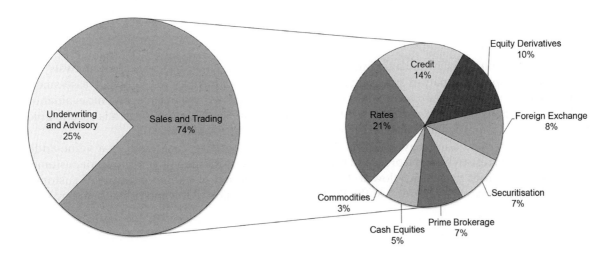

Figure 15-1 Investment banking revenue by business unit (2013)

15.1.1 Customer-focused Services

The types of customer services provided by a financial intermediary vary depending on the institution. Even so, there are brokerage-related services, such as order management, research, and advice, that are prevalent across many institutions.

15.1.1.1 Order management and execution

Due to capital and regulatory requirements, it is impractical for most buy-side firms to be exchange members. Hence, order management and execution are primary services that agency brokers provide to customers. Agency brokers act as agents for their clients, performing transactions on customers' behalf and without serving as a counterparty in the transaction. Many agency brokers are exchange members. Alternatively, an agency broker who is not a member may execute customer orders via another broker who is a member of the exchange.

Buy-side customers typically use nonmember brokers to help disguise their trading activity. For example, an asset manager may be concerned about leakage of information that a large order is pending in the market, if it is placed with a single broker. Therefore, it might choose to split the order and send the different parts to multiple brokers to manage the execution. Distributing the order helps obfuscate the source of the trading, and no single intermediary will know the scale of the overall transaction. Likewise, the "footprints" in the market left by the order's execution will appear to be from multiple unrelated sources.

Common services related to order management that agency brokers provide include:

- order execution—routing orders to execution venues;
- position tracking and reporting;
- algorithmic order execution; and
- smart order routing.

With regard to position tracking and reporting, a "position" is the value, that is, the product of the quantity and price, of a cash or security holding. A small quantity of a high-priced asset can represent a large position, as can a large quantity of a low-priced asset. Algorithmic order execution and smart order routing are discussed in Section 15.4.

15.1.1.2 Research

Many financial intermediaries have internal research teams, including securities analysts and economists, who provide analysis and opinions on a range of investment topics. Valuation assessments of companies, expectations for currency and interest rate movements, and macroeconomic evaluations of countries, regions, and markets are some of the areas that may be covered. Research is used to guide trading and asset allocation for financial intermediaries' investments and trading.

Financial intermediaries may also distribute research reports to customers as a value-added service. Typically, research will be provided to customers without charge as an incentive for customers to send some or all of their order flow to the broker. An Internet link to an example of customer-oriented broker research is provided in the Further Reading section at the end of this chapter.

15.1.1.3 Advice

Besides research, some financial intermediaries provide advisory services. Advice may be targeted at broad or detailed levels. For example, a financial intermediary may make high-level

---

Case Study 15-2
The Danger of Not Giving Advice

It is not unusual for customers to protest when they are given poor advice by their brokers. However, brokers may also encounter problems when they neglect to offer advice. As a case in point, arbitrators ordered Citibank to pay $3 million in a case where a brokerage customer claimed that Smith Barney, a unit within Citibank, failed to recommend appropriate risk-management strategies.

The customer lost $70 million on holdings of Washington Mutual stock. Washington Mutual Bank had high exposure to the US mortgage market and was placed into receivership in 2008. Between 2007 and 2008, the price of Washington Mutual stock dropped from over $30 per share to being worthless. The customer complained that Smith Barney should have advised her to diversify her holdings so as to have a less concentrated position.

Of course, if Smith Barney had recommended **diversification** into other banking stocks, such as Bear Stearns or Lehman Brothers, that also suffered severe losses, it could have been accused of offering poor advice instead.

Source: Giannone, Joseph A., "FINRA Orders Citi to Pay $3 Million over Client's Losses," *Reuters,* December 1, 2010, http://www.reuters.com/article/2010/12/01/us-citigroup-arbitration-idUSTRE6B0394201012011.

---

recommendations about allocation percentages across a range of asset classes such as domestic equities, international equities, government bonds, and cash. Alternatively, they may make a specific recommendation about the valuation of a company's stock and issue a rating for it: buy, sell, or hold.

Banks and brokers also provide advice that takes into account customers' existing holdings and specific needs. In particular, customers may benefit from guidance on which financial instruments can help them achieve specific investment or risk hedging objectives. Financial intermediaries have begun, more recently, to recommend the use of specific algorithms to customers that execute large orders. Such advice may be based on in-depth knowledge of the algorithms' design and behavior in various market conditions. Likewise, customers may need direction on how to set an algorithm's parameters so as to achieve optimal results.

Despite the fact that advisory services are intended to help customers, they have come under scrutiny. One concern has been that financial institutions' investment banking relationships with companies have led to the provision of biased investment ratings on those companies. Another concern is that the advice provided to customers has been motivated and influenced, to some extent, by brokers' goal of getting customers to buy products and services rather than addressing customers' needs. Consequently, there have been numerous lawsuits around the world that have accused financial intermediaries of mis-selling products to customers.

Financial markets intermediaries have tried to address concerns regarding their advisory services in several ways. Lengthy legal disclaimers have been added to banking agreements and research reports to help protect against lawsuits. Banks and brokers have also provided more training on regulatory requirements and client obligations to customer-facing staff, that is, front-office employees who interact directly with customers. Furthermore, some financial institutions have implemented stricter internal controls for business activities that provide financial advice or product recommendations to customers. In some cases, **business process management systems (BPMS)**, discussed in Chapter 2, have been used to help ensure that **relationship managers (RMs)** and brokers actually execute the processes as intended.

15.1.1.4 Other services

Besides the core services described above, brokers offer a variety of services to address specific customer needs. Prime brokerage services are service packages designed to support smaller fund managers, especially hedge funds. Common services provided as part of and in conjunction with prime brokerage arrangements include:

- securities lending;
- centralized **clearing**;
- global custody;
- provision of trading and order management systems (OMS);
- operational support and consulting services; and
- leasing of office space.

Many of these services may not have visible fees associated with them. Instead, the bank or broker will generate revenue indirectly from interest charges on customers' **margin** account and fees related to the customers' trading activity. However, other services, such as leasing and consultancy, may be billed on a monthly basis.

Prime brokerage arrangements are attractive to customers, particularly new and smaller funds, because it provides a "one-stop shop" that enables them to get going quickly, with a minimal amount of overhead. Likewise, the per-transaction cost model minimizes the need for hedge funds to obtain upfront capital to set up infrastructure for their business operation.

15.1.1.5 Customer relationship management

Brokering and customer relationship management (CRM) are often not thought of as being closely related. In many countries, securities brokering requires certification and extensive training compared with working as a branch teller or call center agent at a bank. Also, historically, brokers had one-to-one relationships with their customers, making CRM less of a concern.

Over time, retail brokerages adopted many of the CRM techniques used in banking. Centralized call routing, multichannel delivery capabilities, and CRM systems are all now commonly used by retail brokers. However, brokers who provide services to institutional customers have been slower to apply CRM techniques. Business entertainment of buy-side customers has often been the focus of relationship management, and dedicated RM interaction models are common.

Even where front-office interactions have been streamlined, back-office support interactions may not be efficiently managed. For example, corporate actions, such as rights issuances and stock splits, may occur at any time. Brokers' back-office staff will need to monitor for these events, notify their customers about corporate actions that relate to their security holdings, and, in some cases, take instructions regarding the action, that is, whether to subscribe to a rights issuance. The timeliness of the customer service that is provided in these cases can vary widely, depending on the broker and its CRM capabilities. Whereas some brokers may simply post the information in the mail, others may use email channels or notify the front office to call the customer directly if a response has not been received by a certain cutoff time.

15.1.2 Proprietary Trading

Besides providing the customer services discussed in Section 15.1, another type of broker, a broker-dealer, also trades in the market on its own account. The function within a financial institution that trades purely for the purpose of making a profit is referred to as prop trading. Prop trading desks will typically take views on the relative valuation or direction of prices and take short or long positions accordingly. Like hedge funds, prop trading desks may perform speculative trading in a wide range of asset classes and use leverage to magnify returns.

Following the **Global Financial Crisis**, concerns that banks' prop trading operations were putting depositors' savings at risk led lawmakers and regulators to impose additional restrictions on banks' trading activities. Even so, there has been debate as to whether banks' market-making activities in OTC derivatives, which are still allowed by regulators, could be used as a vehicle for circumventing these restrictions [2]. Because market making often requires maintenance of financial product inventory, as is the case with bonds, or positions, as is the case with OTC derivatives, there may be some ambiguity as to whether the holdings and positions are purely necessary for market-making activities or if they are being used to bet on expected price movements.

15.1.3 Market Making

In contrast to prop trading, the aim of market making is not to profit from speculation, but instead to profit from the difference between financial instruments' bid and ask prices, that is, taking the **spread**. A **market maker** may place **limit orders** in a market to buy at the **bid price** and sell at the ask price. In an ideal scenario, the instruments traded will not trend in one direction or the other, and the market maker will be able to buy and sell equal quantities so that no net position will be held.

For example, a market maker might place limit orders on an exchange simultaneously to buy and sell 10,000 shares of General Electric at the current market best bid and best **offer prices**—buying at $25.50 and selling at $25.55. For the purposes of this example, assume the market makers' orders are first in line for execution in the exchange's order book. When a **market order** arrives at the exchange to buy 1,000 shares, the market maker will sell 1,000 shares at $25.55. Later, when another market order arrives to sell 3,000 shares, the market maker will buy 3,000 shares at $25.50. The broker would make a profit of $50 [($25.55 − $25.50 = $0.05) × 1000] on the two transactions. The broker would, however, still have an outstanding short position of −2,000 shares that it will need to eventually close out, preferably by filling additional market orders to buy stock. It also faces the risk that the price may move adversely before the position can be closed out, potentially creating a loss greater than the profit realized on the initial transactions.

Because market makers' per-transaction profit is small, their transaction costs must also be small. In this regard, large financial intermediaries are well suited for market making. Banks and brokers already have the resources in place to execute, clear, and settle customers' orders; hence, the marginal cost of processing additional trades that support market making activities is small.

Financial intermediaries may perform market-making activities on exchanges or deal directly with their customers, or both. For instance, a bank could place limit orders to buy and sell in FX electronic communication networks (ECNs), similar to the example above, while simultaneously acting as a dealer directly with its corporate customers, providing them with tradable rates to both buy and sell currencies.

15.1.4 Risk Management

Different types of business activities that financial intermediaries engage in require different types of risk management. In situations where a customer has a margin trading account with a financial intermediary, risk management involves calculating available margin, making margin calls, and closing out positions if the calls are not met. On the other hand, risk management for market making focuses on managing the size of net exposures and/or inventory of securities.

While market making is meant to be, for the most part, a market-neutral trading strategy, large net exposures can create trading positions that are sensitive to market direction. Reduction of net exposures can be achieved by skewing the prices offered in the market, that is, providing a more favorable bid or offer price to help reduce the size of the position. Alternatively, the financial intermediary can become a market user, placing market orders that offset the unwanted position in a currency or security. However, this approach directly eats into gains that were made by acting as a market maker.

Risk management for prop trading is similar to risk management for asset management. Setting and managing trading limits is one key area of concern, as are managing aggregate exposure to specific factors, such as volatility, and avoiding overallocation to any one security or industry sector.

Based on an understanding of the common business activities performed by financial intermediaries, the following sections examine some of the technology-centric services they provide.

15.2   TRADING SYSTEM ARCHITECTURES

Over time, the development of equity order routing systems have followed different paths. Initially, **high-touch order management systems** were built to support manual order execution that requires people to be involved. For example, a fund manager might call his broker to ask the broker to manually "work" an order on the market to get a good execution price or to execute it using one of the broker's algorithms. More recently, though, low-touch order routing platforms have become popular. In the low-touch case, a buy-side trader or an IT system that implements an **algorithmic trading** system would send orders straight into a **direct market access (DMA)** trading platform. The execution of these orders would then be managed electronically, and without human intervention.* This section examines the functional components commonly used by banks and brokers to route and manage customer orders for exchange traded instruments. Two common service delivery configurations, DMA and colocation, are also reviewed.

15.2.1 Order Routing System Components

Order routing systems support the delivery and processing of orders as they flow from the end user to an execution venue. As shown in Figure 15-2, a number of functional components may be involved. OMS are one of the most common systems used by both brokers and their customers. OMS were originally designed to perform electronic recordkeeping for orders placed over the telephone. Order-capture and position screens replaced paper order tickets and position blotters in the front office. By managing trade information in a database, OMS were also able to support back-office functions such as accounting, reporting, and reconciliation.

Execution management systems (EMS), on the other hand, were designed for electronic trading, where trading volumes are much higher and execution speed is critical. EMS manage the execution of orders electronically and with no manual intervention, sometimes by using algorithms to execute orders over an extended period of time. There is some debate over whether, ultimately, the functionality of OMS and EMS will merge, and that it will not be necessary to choose between the two types of systems. However, it may be the case that certain specialized capabilities cannot be provided by a "one size fits all" implementation, and that demand for such features will support the continued existence of both types of systems.

Connectivity gateways provide interfaces, often based on standard protocol such as FIX, that enable customers to send orders electronically to the broker. The risk management system verifies that the customer orders will not exceed their margin or cash limits. Smart order routers determine to which execution venue(s) orders should be routed.

Market access gateways, also referred to as line handlers, connect and communicate orders to different execution venues. Each connection, or "line," to the exchange will have a limited capacity that is commonly referred to as its "throttle" limit. For example, a single connection to the

---

* Human intervention may be required occasionally to handle processing exceptions, but the expectation is that these occurrences should be minimal.

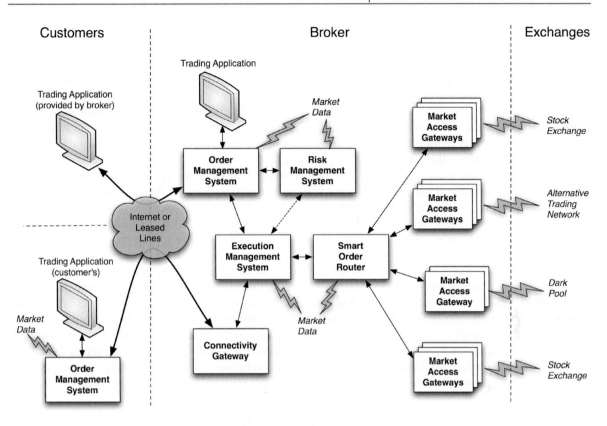

Figure 15-2 Order routing architecture implemented by brokers

exchange may support up to 100 messages per second, which includes messages related to orders, acknowledgements, and fills. Hence, to handle a peak processing rate of 250 orders per second, a broker would require multiple exchange connections. Alternatively, if only one line were used, orders and responses would queue up at peak times and be subject to processing delays, that is, latency. Even if **throughput** was not a concern, typically, at least two exchange connections would be maintained to provide resilience— if one telecommunication link to the exchange were to fail, the other would continue to provide connectivity, preventing service interruption.

The connectivity between components may be achieved in a number of different ways. Components can communicate with one another directly over the network using relatively low-level TCP/IP communication protocols. Alternatively, in higher-performance environments, specialized middleware messaging products may be used to implement scalable, low-latency network communications. In ultra-high performance configurations, multiple components may be run within the same server and communicate with one another using interprocess communication (IPC) mechanisms, such as shared memory communication. Using IPC avoids the delay involved with sending messages over the network, often reducing latency by an order of magnitude.

In all the figures in this chapter, the cloud images that show "leased lines" refer to dedicated telecommunications links, which may be implemented using any number of technologies, such as multiprotocol label switching (MPLS) networks. Likewise, multiple stacked boxes indicate where multiple instances are run for load balancing purposes, as is the case with the market access gateways shown in Figure 15-2. It should be assumed that some form of active-active, hot-standby resilience, discussed in Chapter 11, is used for all of the components, even though a single box is shown in the diagrams.

15.2.2 Direct Market Access

DMA is a service whereby customer orders are sent electronically to the broker, who then routes the order to the relevant exchange with minimal interruption. In Figure 15-2, DMA orders begin their journey in the lower left-hand corner, flow through a connectivity gateway, and are then routed by an EMS to execution venues. To minimize delay, DMA orders circumvent the broker's OMS on their way to the execution venue. Also, DMA orders are not visible to the broker's front office prior to execution because they do not have access to monitor order flow through the EMS. After execution, the trade details will be reported by the EMS to the OMS. Allowing the financial intermediary's staff to only access post-trade information diminishes the chance of information leakage, that is, other market participants gaining knowledge of the order and making trades in advance of or in parallel with the customer.

Brokers compete on the speed at which their DMA platforms can deliver orders to execution venues, and every microsecond counts. As a case in point, a broker has claimed as part of its public marketing one-way latencies of between 200 and 600 microseconds to various Asian stock exchanges [3]. Specialized order routing components designed and tuned to deliver high performance are used to implement DMA. To avoid delays, these components only perform basic risk validation and compliance.

For example, whereas an OMS would retrieve current margin or credit availability information from the risk management system as part of the pretrade validation process, calls to an external system would introduce a very long delay for DMA. Alternatively, the components used for DMA could retrieve customer risk information at the beginning of the day and only perform pretrade risk checks that approximate the customer's current risk position based on their intraday transactions. While the latter method is less accurate, it significantly reduces the interaction between systems and, thus, the processing time. To help compensate for the reduced accuracy, risk-limit thresholds could also be lowered.

15.2.3 Exchange Colocation and Proximity Hosting

Most trading strategies will place orders when instrument prices reach specific levels, with the expectation that the trade execution prices will be close to the same price that triggered the order. However, the price that is available to trade when the order reaches the market may differ substantially. The longer the time gap between when the price information is sent from the exchange to the time the corresponding order is received by the exchange, the greater the likelihood that the price will have shifted. Trading strategies that are based on making small gains very frequently are particularly sensitive to delays; small price movements can wipe out profits and potentially lead to losses.

Hundreds of milliseconds can pass between the time the price changes in the market, the market data is received by an automated trading system, the system generates the order, the broker receives the order and forwards it to the exchange, and the exchange places the order into the order book. Much of this delay is attributable to the time it takes the electronic information to travel between locations. The physical distance is one concern, as it increases the time it takes information to travel through fiber optic telecommunication cables between the customer and the broker, and the broker and the exchange. Another concern is delay added by computer systems and network components that process the information en route.

Colocation minimizes both the physical distance and the number of systems involved. The end customer will install its systems in a server rack in an exchange's colocation facility, that is, the exchange's data center. As shown in Figure 15-3, with colocation, the customer's trading system receives market data directly from an exchange data feed in the colocation center, uses automated algorithms to determine when to trade, and then sends orders to an exchange access gateway that is also in the colocation center. The customer's automated trading platform will also forward order information to the Broker's OMS. The customer's interactions with the colocation setup are for the initial installation and ongoing remote management of the software components.

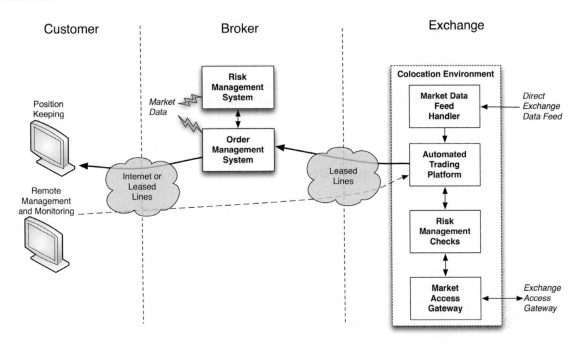

Figure 15-3 An exchange colocation order management architecture

Even though a customer's trading systems may be located at the exchange, the customer is not a direct counterparty to the trade as far as the exchange is concerned. Buy-side customers are not exchange members and, therefore, a broker, who is a member, must represent them. Accordingly, brokers should implement risk management checks for all orders that they or their customers send to exchanges. In colocation environments, simplified risk checks, linked to order size or daily transaction dollar amount limits, may be used to avoid delays associated with communications with the broker's risk management system. Customer orders that originate in a colocation center may either be sent to the exchange via the broker's exchange access gateway in the colocation center or may be sent directly to the exchange's gateway, but be identified as being attributable to the broker. Either way, the exchange's time and sales data will record the broker as the counterparty to the trade. When the broker receives the order execution information from the exchange, it will clear and settle the trades for the customer.

Proximity hosting is similar to colocation, but instead of locating trading components at a single exchange, they are hosted at an external data center that offers low latency connectivity to multiple trading venues. Proximity hosting, which is usually less expensive than exchange colocation, may be used for multiple reasons. Proximity hosting can be more cost effective using trading algorithms that are time sensitive, but not so much that they require exchange colocation. Likewise, trading strategies that involve multiple markets, for example, taking advantage of differences in prices of equivalent futures contracts traded at exchanges in Singapore and Japan, may not gain much advantage from being colocated in just one of the execution venues and, therefore, be better served by a proximity hosting center that has high speed network connections to both markets.

15.3 ORDER FLOW INTERNALIZATION

Internalization of order flow occurs when a financial intermediary crosses orders internally instead of routing them to an execution venue for matching. There are two forms of internalization. In the first form, the financial intermediary is not a counterparty in the transaction, as is the case with agency brokers. Customer orders are crossed with orders received from other customers or market participants. In the second form, the financial intermediary will act as a counterparty in the transaction, as is the case with broker-dealers. The intermediary fills customer orders without having corresponding orders from other customers to take the opposite side of the trade.

The following subsections discuss both forms of internalization in more detail. First, internalization will be examined in the context of equity order crossing, where brokers do not act as counterparties. Next, FX trading will be reviewed, where banks and brokers internalize customer order flow by acting as counterparties.

15.3.1 Internal Crossing of Equity Orders

With equity order flow internalization, customer orders can be crossed internally with other customers' orders before being routed to public execution venues or **dark pools**. For instance, if the broker received market orders to buy a security from one customer and a market order to sell the same security from another customer within a short time frame, the broker could internally cross the two orders at the midpoint between the market best bid and best offer prices. This action would generate price improvement for both customers. If the order was routed to an execution venue, the market orders to buy and sell would be filled at the best offer and best bid prices, respectively. If the market bid-offer prices are $25.10 and $25.20, respectively, the buy order would be matched at the exchange at $25.20 and the sell order will be matched at $25.10. However, with internal crossing at the mid-point, both orders would be filled at $25.15.

Besides providing price improvement, crossing customer orders internally results in faster executions and lower transaction costs. Note, however, that orders must be crossed at prices equal to or better than the best prices quoted in the market at the time of execution. Internally crossed trades must also be reported to the security's primary exchange and cleared and settled the same way as if they had been executed on an exchange.

Furthermore, brokers may enable other market participants to place orders that can be matched with the broker's internal order flow. In this case, the broker effectively creates its own dark pool execution venue, as shown in Figure 15-4. Hence, many dark pools are sponsored by brokers and are extensions of their order routing platforms.

From a systems perspective, a **crossing engine** component, also referred to as a matching engine, maintains an internal order book and matches customer orders. This functionality is logically separate from the functions that an EMS performs and is typically implemented as a separate component. Connecting a FIX gateway to the crossing engine can provide external connectivity, that is, a dark pool interface that accepts orders from other market participants.

The concept of internal crossing of equity orders is simple in theory, but is complicated in practice. Execution rules and regulatory reporting requirements vary between geographic markets. In the United States and Europe, regulation and management of the equity markets has consolidated to a large extent. In Asia, however, many different market structures and restrictions must be accommodated.

15.3.2 Internalization and Pass-through of Foreign Exchange Orders

Unlike agency brokers that facilitate trading of exchange traded equities and derivatives, market makers for other types of instruments usually deal from and must manage the inventory of the financial instruments that they trade. Market makers' inventory may accumulate purely from investment and market-making activities, as is the case with bond dealers. Alternatively, their inventory may derive from other activities such as lending and providing foreign currency exchange services, as is the case with banks' foreign exchange positions.

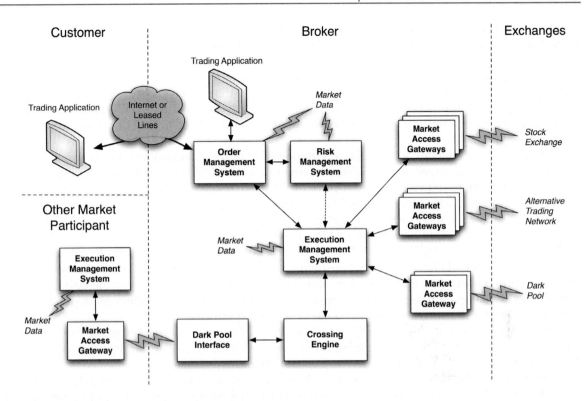

Figure 15-4 Equity order flow internalization architecture

The simplest and most straightforward design for broker-dealer trading operations is to separate customer-dealing order flow from interbank-trading order flow. As discussed in Chapter 11, excess inventory, or positions, that is accumulated through customer dealing is eliminated through interbank trading. The disadvantage of this approach is that the dealer acts as a market user in the interbank market and, thus, must pay the bid-offer spread on those transactions. More complicated internalization and market pass-through trading strategies help avoid this concern.

Historically, banks that dealt with currencies only filled customers' orders from their own inventory; no external execution venues existed. Interbank counterparties would typically trade in volumes many times those of customer orders, so they were not a suitable destination to route individual customer orders to. However, in the early 2000s, FX electronic commerce networks and bank-sponsored FX **liquidity** pools emerged. Thus, banks and brokers were able to add margins to prices quoted by external venues and match individual customer orders as "back-to-back" trades with those venues. When it makes a back-to-back trade, the bank does not take on any risk from rate fluctuations because other market participants take on the risk position produced by fulfillment of the customer order. However, because the bank is counterparty to an ECN for the customers' trades as well as to the customer, it bears double the risk that either of the counterparties may default on settling the transaction.

Skewing the prices quoted to customers is another approach used to manage inventory. During the rate aggregation process, the banks' positions may be viewed as another source of liquidity. If the bank quotes prices for its own inventory that are as good as or better than the market's top-of-the-book prices, customer orders will be matched with internal positions, rather than those offered by external parties. Prices offered to customers from the bank's inventory should match or improve upon competitive market prices. Therefore, internalization should not adversely impact customers and may, in fact, benefit them.

To help illustrate how FX internalization, pass-through routing, and skewing works, consider a bank that had a long position in Japanese yen that it wanted to reduce. The prices in this example are quoted as yen per US dollar, so a higher rate represents a cheaper price for buying yen and vice versa. If the best bid and offer prices received from ECNs and other liquidity pool providers were ¥104.238 and ¥104.234, respectively, the bank could skew the rates it provides to customers by selling yen at ¥104.235, a slightly better rate to sell than the market price of ¥104.234. Because it does not want to add to its existing position, the bank would fulfill customer orders to sell yen through a corresponding **back-to-back transaction** with an ECN or another bank. However, if it received a customer order to buy yen, it would book the order against its own inventory and sell yen to help decrease the size of its position.

Alternatively, if the bank had to act as a market user in the interbank market to reduce its yen position, it would have to sell at the market's buying rate of ¥104.238. Thus, by internalizing customer order flow, it is able to sell yen at a better price of ¥104.235. Likewise, the bank's customer is able to buy at a better than market price of ¥104.235. At market prices, the customer would have had to pay ¥104.234. For simplicity, this example has ignored the pricing effects of the margin spread that the bank would normally add to the FX prices offered to customers.

Figure 15-5 shows a logical view of the functional components involved in internalization and pass-through routing of FX trades for end customers. The dashed lines between components represent rate and quote information flow, and the solid lines represent order flow from the customer. The components are shown separately in the diagram to help explain functions, although in practice they may be collapsed into a single server or process to optimize performance.

As shown at the bottom of the diagram, the bank subscribes to market prices from foreign exchange ECNs and tradable quotes from other banks. A rate aggregator component collects the rates and constructs a consolidated view of available liquidity, similar to an order book. A pricing engine component then receives the "top of the book," that is, best bid and best offer prices, currency and interest rates from the aggregated rate feed. When the pricing engine receives rate updates, it

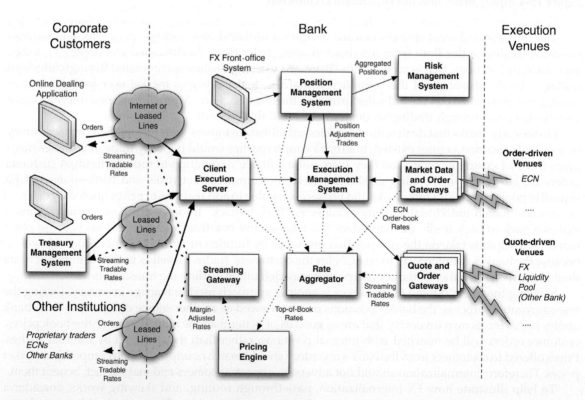

Figure 15-5 FX order internalization rate and order flows

calculates forward and option prices and adds customer-specific margins to the instruments' base price. A streaming gateway component then distributes tradable quotes to customers and other market participants offering to buy and sell **FX spot**, forwards, and options across a range of currency pairs.

When customers place an order to buy or sell a quoted instrument, the client execution server determines if the exchange rate included in the order is still acceptable. If an order is received from a customer too long after the original quote was sent out to them, that is, more than half a second for fast-moving currencies, the order may be rejected. Criteria for accepting and rejecting an order will depend on the agreement that is in place with the customer and the volatility of the underlying market rates. If the order is accepted, the client execution server will determine whether to internalize the order or send it to an external execution venue. If it is internalized, the position management system will book it against the banks' own position; otherwise, the execution management system will execute the customer order against an external venue. The execution management system also handles orders that the bank places in the interbank market to adjust its positions, that is, manage risk.

The position management system may also send orders to the execution management system to adjust, or autohedge, when the bank's positions produced by nontrading activities grow unacceptably large. Also, if the financial intermediary has prop trading operations, they may also take advantage of internalization to adjust their positions. Typically, the position management system will send aggregated position information to the bank's risk management platform on a daily or periodic intraday basis.

15.3.3 Comparing Equity and Foreign Exchange Trading Architectures

The primary difference between FX and equity trading is that FX trading is dominated by quote driven pricing. In some cases, quotes may only be provided when a **request for quote (RFQ)** is received. In other cases, tradable prices may be streamed continuously to market participants.

From a technology perspective, the RFQ method is more efficient in terms of the amount of data that is distributed, but is more complex to implement because it requires an interactive communication protocol to be used. The streaming approach is simpler in terms of the number of interactions that must be supported, but may involve the distribution of large volumes of price information. However, streaming rates are time sensitive and are valid for only a short period. Delays in transmitting prices or orders in response to prices received can cause an order to be rejected because the quoted price that they specify as the buy or sell price is no longer valid.

In general, equity and FX order routing architectures are gradually converging. While their functional components differ, common underlying technologies are used, that is, high performance **messaging middleware**, the FIX protocol, and external connectivity gateways. Likewise, algorithmic order execution and smart order routing technologies have also been utilized in a similar manner for trading of both equities and FX.

15.4 ALGORITHMIC ORDER EXECUTION

As discussed in Chapter 13, institutional investors, such as pension, mutual, and hedge funds, must achieve sizable positions in individual equities, which makes it difficult for them to achieve preferable execution prices. If an institutional investor submits a large market order, just a small portion of it may take up all available liquidity at or near the current market price. The part of the order that cannot be filled by the available liquidity may be executed at suboptimal prices. Alternatively, placing a large limit order, instead of a market order, could signal the intention to buy or sell a large quantity of the security, thereby leading other market participants to react quickly and drive the market price in an unfavorable direction. Therefore, in practice, large orders are sliced into smaller orders and executed over a period of time. Historically, people at brokerages did this manually. In recent years, it has

TWAP order's size to impact the price, and then sell after the order raised the price. Therefore, in practice, TWAP algorithms have been adapted to include variation and randomization to help avoid this problem.

15.4.3 Volume-weighted Average Pricing Algorithms

In contrast to TWAP algorithms, VWAP algorithms are a type of volume participation algorithm that incorporates trading volumes into the order size calculations. VWAP order sizes are proportional to the expected trading volume during the given time period. Larger orders will be placed during time periods that have higher volumes traded. Figure 15-7 shows how a VWAP algorithm would distribute orders to buy a total of 150,000 shares over the course of the trading day. Since 150,000 shares would be 30% of the stock's hypothetical daily volume (500,000 shares), a VWAP algorithm would target to buy approximately 30% of the traded volume during each thirty-minute period.

VWAP addresses the shortcomings of TWAP by placing orders for variable percentages of the intraday trading volume rather than fixed amounts. Even so, VWAP has a problem of its own—determining what the trading volume will be over the course of the day. The total volume traded will vary every day and the actual trading volume for each time period during the day may only be known after the fact. VWAP algorithms deal with this problem by using historical data to estimate the expected daily volume and its temporal distribution. If the trading volume has consistently followed a similar pattern over the previous month, the assumption is made that the pattern will hold for the current day. Consider the case where a stock's average trading volume between 9:30 am and 10:00 am was 12% of its total daily volume over the past 20 trading days. Based on this information, a VWAP algorithm would execute 12% of the total order during the same time period.

VWAP algorithms are well suited when performance is measured using a VWAP benchmark. However, because price is not factored into either TWAP or VWAP algorithms, they may continue to trade into sharp spikes or drops in the market, leading to a poor execution price and further exacerbate price movements. Incorporating parameters into the algorithm that set trading price limits can help address this concern.

VWAP algorithms are also problematic if the market moves in the wrong direction for the trade, that is, when the market drops steadily throughout the day as a large sell order is being executed. The portions of the order that are reserved for execution in the middle and at the end of the day will execute at a substantially worse price than those orders at the beginning of the day. In this situation, it is better to execute most, if not all, of the order early in the day, even if it temporarily perturbs

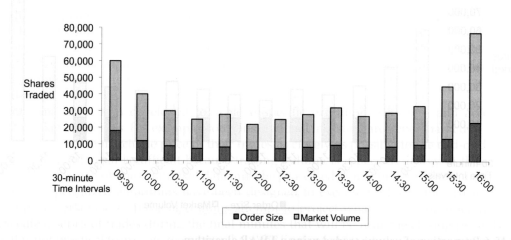

Figure 15-7 Proportion of volume traded using a VWAP algorithm

the market. Hence, VWAP is best applied in flat market conditions as opposed to when there is directional trending.

VWAP algorithms have been popular despite their drawbacks. VWAP is also a common benchmark used to gauge traders' performance and, thus, using a VWAP algorithm helps ensure that an order's execution price is in line with the benchmark. Likewise, VWAP algorithms help ensure that the size of trades in any given time period will not stand out.

15.4.4 Liquidity-seeking Algorithms

TWAP and VWAP algorithms are two relatively simple methods used to execute orders. Other more complex trading algorithms are more dynamic and take available liquidity into consideration. Rather than mechanically slicing up and executing orders, liquidity-seeking algorithms use **depth-of-market information** to decide the timing and size of orders. Such algorithms often place market orders to try to immediately fill as much of the order as possible without substantially moving the price. The algorithm may then attempt to fill the remainder of the order "passively" using limit orders. Alternatively, new orders may be placed when additional liquidity becomes available within a target price range.

To illustrate how liquidity-seeking algorithms work, consider a simple example of an order to buy 100,000 shares of a stock. Based on the depth-of-market data, as shown in Figure 15-8, the algorithm would initially place a market order to buy 30,000 shares to try to purchase the available shares for sale at $14.60 and $14.65. Additional liquidity is available in the exchange's order book; however, purchasing the remaining shares at $15.00 would adversely affect the average execution price for the order. Instead, the algorithm might place a limit order to buy 10,000 shares at $14.55. When the limit order was filled, the algorithm would place new child limit orders until the entire parent order was filled. The algorithm might also place market orders to buy when shares were on offer again in an acceptable price range, for example, for sale at or below $14.70.

	Shares Bid	Price	Shares Offered	
		15.00	100,000	
		14.65	18,000	
		14.60	12,000	←Best offer
Best bid→	7,000	14.50		
	9,000	14.45		
	100,000	14.00		

Figure 15-8 An example of available stock liquidity shown by depth-of-market data

---

Case Study 15-3
Algorithmic Trading and the Flash Crash

In May 2010, the US equity and futures markets experienced an unprecedented intraday drop in prices and loss of liquidity. Subsequently, this event was commonly referred to as the Flash Crash because the price drop was severe, but brief. The S&P 500 futures fell over 5% and hundreds of equities dropped more than 60% in

(Continued)

a matter of minutes. During the peak of the crisis, a number of stocks traded at prices of one penny or less. However, by the end of the day, prices had recovered to their precrisis level.

Not surprisingly, regulators and the public were very concerned by this event. There was speculation that an automated trading strategy had "gone wild" and was responsible for the crash. In fact, an official report issued by regulators found that a complex set of events contributed to the crash. The report attributed the trigger of the crash to a large order, worth over US$4 billion, that was entered by a fund manager to sell 75,000 S&P 500 E-mini futures contracts. The fund manager chose to execute the order using a volume participation algorithm that was set with the execution rate to be 9% of the trading volume observed over the previous minute without regard to price or time.

Unlike TWAP and VWAP algorithms, volume participation algorithms do not attempt to fill an order over a set time period. Instead, they generate orders in quantities that are proportionate to the trading volume observed in the market. This strategy's advantage is that an order can be executed more quickly if there is sufficient trading volume to conceal the order while, ideally, minimizing the order's market impact. The danger, however, is that it assumes that high trading volume reflects abundant liquidity.

The day the Flash Crash occurred, the market was highly volatile and there was reduced liquidity. As prices dropped and market participants' anxiety set in, trading volumes rose. Increasing volume led the algorithm used by the fund manager to sell at a faster rate, thus compounding the problem. Consequently, the algorithm executed the entire order of 75,000 contracts within 20 minutes, triggering a sell-off. There were not enough buyers to meet the sellers' demand, causing prices to decline rapidly and trading volume to increase as panic selling engulfed the market.

While it might be easy to blame algorithmic trading for the Flash Crash, in reality it was just one of many contributing factors. Moreover, the algorithm behaved as intended. Several months earlier, the fund manager used the same algorithm to execute an order of similar size over a period of five hours, with negligible market impact. In the case of the Flash Crash, poor use of the algorithm combined with specific market conditions was really to blame. Had price or time limit parameters been specified or had a VWAP algorithm been used, that order would not have triggered the crash. As with automobiles, the vehicles are usually not the cause of accidents.

Sources: Demos, Telis, "'Flash Crash' Blamed on Computer, but Not Error," *Financial Times*, November 2, 2010, http://www.ft.com/cms/s/0/c0604048-e607-11df-9cdd-00144feabdc0.html; US Commodity Futures Trading Commission and US Securities & Exchange Commission, "Findings Regarding the Market Events of May 6, 2010, Report of the Staffs of the CFTC and SEC to The Joint Advisory Committee on Emerging Regulatory Issues," September 30, 2010, http://www.sec.gov/news/studies/2010/marketevents-report.pdf.

This example was simplified to help explain the general concept. In practice, such algorithms can be quite complex and may take into account liquidity that is potentially available but not displayed in the market depth information, that is, hidden and iceberg orders. Hybrid algorithms, which mix liquidity-seeking and benchmark-tracking strategies, are also available. Algorithms may also make use of liquidity that is available across multiple execution venues, taking advantage of a trading system's smart order routing capabilities, if they are available.

15.4.5 Smart Order Routing

Smart order routing is applicable when an order can be executed on more than one execution venue. In North American and European markets, multiple exchanges and dark pools are available to trade highly liquid stocks. A simple order routing approach would consistently send orders to a single venue or require the person placing the order to designate the target venue. Alternatively, smart order routing evaluates a number of factors and then decides how much of an order to send to different execution venues so as to achieve the optimal execution price.

The best available price at each venue is one factor used to route orders, but this consideration is complicated by price information that may not be publicly available, such as hidden orders on lit execution venues and orders sitting in dark pools. Available liquidity is another factor to be considered. If the venue that has the best price only has a small amount that is available for trading at that price, it may not be the best routing destination. The likelihood of execution on different venues will also be relevant. For instance, the greater the time lag between when the price information is received from an execution venue and the time the order is processed by the venue, the greater the chance that the price will have moved by the time the order is received. Based on these and other considerations, a smart order routing component could decide to route an order to one or multiple execution venues, either sequentially or in parallel.

Algorithmic trading may also incorporate smart order routing to optimize performance to handle situations where the available liquidity is fragmented across multiple venues. For instance, a liquidity-seeking trading algorithm might initially fill part of an order by sending child market orders to a subset of lit execution venues, exchanges, and ECNs. The order quantity sent to each venue would depend on the availability of shares at that venue within a specific price range. Then, the remaining amount of the parent order could be divided and placed using passive limit orders on both lit and dark execution venues.

15.5 ARCHITECTURE CONSIDERATIONS

This section examines two architecture considerations that are important for order routing systems: application-level communication standards and **complex event processing (CEP)**.

15.5.1 Application-level Communication Standards

Case Study 15-1 highlighted the need for standards to support interparty communication of orders and execution status information. The FIX protocol is a real-time message communication standard that has become the predominant standard for communication between asset managers', brokers', and exchanges' trading systems. FIX is also commonly used for communications between components within a trading system, such as between the connection gateways, OMS, EMS, and market access gateways. Besides FIX, other proprietary protocols exist. In some cases, components may support both FIX and a proprietary protocol. Whereas FIX provides simple "plug-and-play" connectivity, accommodating proprietary protocols will typically require additional integration effort, but may also provide better performance. As a case in point, the Singapore Exchange supports trading access both via a FIX gateway as well as using its own proprietary API, whereby the proprietary API provides lower latency.

FIX supports a wide variety of transaction types, such as the generation of new orders, cancelation of orders, and communication of execution reports. FIX messages are sent between market participants' order and execution management systems. SWIFT messages, on the other hand, are primarily used for back-office communications within banks, as discussed in Chapter 11. Like SWIFT, FIX is encoded using a text-based ASCII format. Even so, FIX is unlike SWIFT in that FIX does not provide a network for message communication. FIX is independent of any specific transport layer communications protocol. Message transfers are usually implemented on top of TCP/IP, but are also sent over other protocols, such as Java Messaging Standard implementations or tunneled through Secure Sockets Layer encrypted connections.

15.5.1.1 The FIX protocol

Like many other communication protocols, the FIX protocol is defined by its:

- **Message structure**—every FIX message has three parts: a header, a body, and a trailer. The FIX header includes the version of the FIX message, the length of the message body, and the message type. The content contained within the message body will vary depending on the message type. The trailer primarily consists of a checksum that is used to verify the integrity of the message.

- **Data dictionary**—consists of field and message definitions, and acceptable field values. For example, FIX version 4.0 defines message type "D" as an "Order—Single" message that contains eight mandatory fields and 29 optional fields. One of the mandatory fields in the message is field number 54, which is the "Side" field. FIX 4.0 defines the valid values for the Side field to be 1, 2, 3, 4, 5, and 6, which correspond to buy, sell, buy minus, sell plus, sell short, and sell short exempt, respectively.

- **Encoding format and syntax**—define how field and message values are represented as physical messages. Within the header, body, and trailer of a FIX message, field values are encoded using tag-value pairs, for example, "54 = 1" (tag = field value). The tags are integer values whose meaning the FIX data dictionary defines. Some tag values are reserved for private use between the sending and receiving parties and can be used to extend and customize the protocol. Field values are delimited using the nonprintable ASCII 01 <SOH> control character.

- **Interaction semantics**—describe valid message communication sequences. FIX provides two levels of interaction semantics: one at the session level and another at the application level. Session-level semantics define the valid sequence of logon, logout, heartbeat, and other message exchanges that are not business related. FIX relies upon sequence numbers to ensure that messages are not lost or duplicated. Session-level semantics define how the sender and receiver should recover dropped messages, while application-level semantics define the valid responses for specific message types, such as orders and cancelation requests.

Figure 15-9 shows an example of an order message encoded using FIX protocol version 4.2. This message represents a single order sent from a fund manager to a broker. The message shown represents an order to buy 50,000 shares of General Electric common stock at a limit price of $25.50 that is good until end of day. In this example, the ASCII 01 field delimiters are represented using the "^" symbol. The Side field of the trade, shown highlighted, corresponds to the 15th field in the message and it is set to the Buy value, which is represented by the number "1." The other fields and their values can be determined by referencing a FIX dictionary, such as the online one referenced in the Further Reading section at the end of this chapter.

15.5.1.2 FIX versions

While FIX is a standard, several versions of the standard are actively used. Common versions of the FIX protocol that are used include FIX 4.0, 4.1, 4.2, 4.3, 4.4, and 5.0. The encoding format and data dictionary are consistent between the FIX versions. The available list of fields, message types, and valid values has been expanded with each new version of the protocol. For example, field 54—defined by FIX as the "side of an order," such as buy, sell, short sell, and cross—has nine valid values in FIX version 4.2, whereas in FIX version 4.4 sixteen different values are valid. The interaction semantics have also changed between protocol versions.

```
8=FIX.4.2^9=202^35=D^49=BUYSIDEID^56=SELLSIDEID^34=132^52=2010
0905-14:34:25^11=999999^1=123456^63=0^64=20100908^21=3^110=500
0^111=10000^55=GE^48=369604103^22=1^54=1^60=20100905-13:34:51^
38=50000^40=1^44=25.50^15=USD^59=0^10=127
```

Figure 15-9 Example of a FIX message

FIX protocol destinations, such as brokers and exchanges, will advertise which FIX version(s) they support. For example, Saxo Bank, an equities, futures, and FX broker, supported FIX versions 4.3 and 4.4 (as of 2017), and the London Stock Exchange supported FIX 5.0 (as of 2017).

15.5.1.3 FIXML and FAST

FIXML and FAST are two standards that are derivatives of the FIX protocol. FIXML is an XML-based standard version of FIX that is defined by document type definition (DTD) schemas. FIX was originally designed to be compact so as to minimize transmission and processing overhead, which is important for time-sensitive pretrade processing. After the FIX standard was developed, XML became a popular means of encoding data. Use of XML was advantageous because it was flexible and widely supported. The disadvantage of using XML, however, was that XML-based messages were long and required more processing time. Accordingly, FIXML was developed to support post-trade activities that were less time sensitive, such as clearing functions.

Figure 15-10 shows an example of a FIXML message represented using the FIX 4.4 Schema Version [4]. While the FIXML version is easy to read, it is larger than the FIX message with content similar to that shown in Figure 15-9.

FAST, on the other hand, was adapted to make the FIX protocol more efficient to transmit and process. FAST uses implicit tagging so that the tag values can be omitted from the message; instead, message templates are used. Also, certain fields can be left out of a message. The value of an omitted field can be inferred by the message receiver to be a default value, defined in the message template, or the value of the field that was sent in a previous message of the same type. FAST also encodes the message in binary format instead of text format. This results in both shorter messages and messages that are more easily processed electronically.

FAST was designed to provide a FIX-based binary protocol for streaming market data. Traditionally, market data distributors and exchanges have had their own proprietary protocols for delivering market data, making it difficult for market participants to connect to multiple data sources. Extending the FIX protocol to support market data could provide a common standard, but using text-based FIX was too inefficient for high volume market data. Hence, FAST was developed to address these concerns. By encoding information in binary form, FAST reduces the transmission overhead and eliminates the processing time required to convert from human readable text format

```
<FIXML>
    <NewOrdSingle ClOrdID="999999"
                  Side="1"
                  TransactTm="2010-09-05T13:34:51-05:00"
                  OrdTyp="1"
                  Px="16.50"
                  Acct="123456">
        <Hdr Snt="2010-09-05T14:34:25-05:00"
             PosDup="N"
             PosRsnd="N"
             SeqNum="132">
            <Sndr ID="BUYSIDEID"/>
            <Tgt ID="SELLSIDEID"/>
        </Hdr>
        <Instrmt Sym="GE"
                 ID="369604103"
                 IDSrc="1"/>
        <OrdQty Qty="50000"/>
    </NewOrdSingle>
</FIXML>
```

Figure 15-10 Example of a FIXML message

to computer readable binary format. FAST is used by a number of exchanges, ECNs, and financial intermediaries to provide direct market data and rate feeds.

15.5.1.4 FIX Engines

Like most systems used in financial markets, it is not necessary to build systems to send and receive FIX messages; there are a number of off-the-shelf systems that provide this capability. In fact, it is generally impractical to build FIX parsing and encoding functionality. This subsection has provided a simplified view of the FIX protocol for ease of understanding. In practice, however, much more complexity must be handled. For instance, the FIX message structure allows for nested groups of repeating field groups, and FIX has specific rules about how encryption should be applied to FIX messages. There are dozens of available FIX engines, both commercial and open source, available that have already addressed these concerns.

FIX engines are software components that do the following: manage the network connectivity of the FIX session, encode and parse the FIX messages, perform validation of the FIX messages received, and automatically handle the session interaction semantics, that is, sequence number tracking, message loss recovery, and sending periodic "heartbeat" messages to show that the session is active. A FIX engine acts as a gateway for applications to communicate with other market participants outside the organization using standardized FIX formats. FIX engines may come as components that are already integrated into an OMS. Alternatively, standalone FIX engines may be used, and then must be integrated with other OMS and EMS components.

Typically, FIX engines will support encryption, persistence, multiple messaging transports, monitoring tools, and simultaneous sessions that use multiple versions of FIX. Additionally, high-availability configurations may be available along with prebuilt interfaces to ECNs and other market participants. For some market participants, such as high-frequency traders, performance of the FIX engine may also be a key consideration. To this end, there are some FIX engines that have been implemented using customized hardware to maximize performance, as opposed to software running on commodity server hardware.

15.5.2 Complex Event Processing

Many activities in the financial markets can be processed as event streams. Events, such as price changes for a financial instrument, may be monitored and actions taken when specific criteria are met based on a set of predefined rules. Criteria can be used to correlate different events from single or multiple event streams. CEP engines have been developed to support this process. CEP is also referred to in different contexts as event stream processing (ESP) and business event management (BEM), although their exact definitions vary. The term BEM tends to be used in conjunction with business activity monitoring (BAM). BEM provides real-time event processing, and BAM complements BEM by providing a means of visualizing the event information and communicating it to business users. Within this section, CEP, ESP, and BEM will be considered to be equivalent, and only CEP will be referenced.

CEP engines provide a platform for building applications that monitor, correlate, and then act upon large volumes of real-time events. By looking for event patterns and running predefined rules when patterns are detected, CEP engines can accelerate the implementation and operation of event processing applications. In contrast to general-purpose **rules engines**, CEP engines do not rely upon relational databases for rule execution; they maintain all of the information in memory that is required to perform filtering and matching operations.

CEP provides a number of useful constructs for constructing applications:

- **Events**—low-level abstractions that correspond to specific data attributes that are processed by the CEP engine. A bid-price update for a specific instrument, an order, and a partial order fill are all examples of events that can be monitored. Also, a specific time of day, such as market opening, can be defined as an event.

- **Event patterns**—abstractions that define criteria for filtering event streams. They define explicit thresholds that events must match, for example, the bid-price for a specific instrument increasing by a certain percentage. Likewise, they may define a specific time or a time window, for example, within the last minute.

- **Rules**—abstractions that act on events by taking action when matching event patterns are detected. Depending on the CEP technology used, event patterns and rules may be closely interlinked. There may be a rule that is defined for each outcome of an event pattern: matched or not matched.

Figure 15-11 provides a simplified example of how a trading algorithm could be defined using CEP abstractions.

Using event-processing abstractions helps to separate processing elements so that they can be easily recombined for other purposes. CEP engines are configuration driven so that low-level programming can be avoided for the most part. These benefits help reduce development time and make it easier to understand and maintain event-processing applications.

In contrast to stream processing applications that have been built from scratch, CEP engines provide ready-made functionality that has been tested and can be used for a range of application needs. Out-of-the-box CEP engines can provide flexibility, high-performance, and resilience capabilities. They often have ready-made connectivity to common sources of market data and have inbuilt FIX protocol connectivity. CEP engines are available from vendors and as open source implementations. High-end commercial versions can cost hundreds of thousands of dollars, whereas open source versions are available for free. Some CEP engines provide graphical environments for defining event patterns and rules. Other engines use proprietary scripting languages or variants of SQL to perform queries on real-time event streams.

Examples of financial markets applications that use CEP include [5]:

- **Market data enrichment**—calculating the implied volatility or "Greeks"—i.e. measures of the sensitivity of an option's price to various factors—for an equity option based on price updates received for the underlying security from an exchange. Calculated values are added to the market data and forwarded to downstream applications.

- **Algorithmic trading strategies**—correlating events, calculating values, and monitoring time windows to generate trading signals to take advantage of short-term market inefficiencies (as illustrated in Figure 15-11).

- **Algorithmic order execution**—monitoring trades on a security, tallying the volume traded, and then periodically sending slices of a large order in small increments that are proportional to the total market volume that has been traded.

Event_1:	update on JPY/USD foreign exchange rate
Event_2:	update on EUR/USD foreign exchange rate
Pattern_1:	Event_1 increases more than 0.01%
Pattern_2:	Event_2 decreases more than 0.01%
Pattern_3:	events occur within a 5 second sliding time window
Action_1:	buy EUR 100,000 and sell JPY 100,000 * JPY/EUR rate
Rule_1:	if (Pattern_1 and Pattern_2 and Pattern_3) then execute Action_1

Figure 15-11 Example of CEP abstractions used to implement a trading strategy algorithm

- **Order book aggregation and smart order routing**—aggregating prices from multiple exchanges and then determining which exchange(s) to send orders to based on the price and available liquidity at each exchange.

- **Pretrade risk management**—performing simple risk checks, such as maximum order size and daily position change thresholds, on inbound orders before routing them to execution venues. CEP engines are suitable risk management tools in DMA order flows because CEP is designed to handle high volumes and also enables the risk rules to be more easily adapted to address new regulatory requirements.

- **Market surveillance**—monitoring changes in an exchange's order book and matching order placement and cancelation patterns that characterize market manipulation. Alternatively, CEP can be used to monitor designated market makers to verify that they are fulfilling their obligations related to instrument pricing and liquidity provision.

Additionally, some of the FX trading components discussed in Section 15.3 can be implemented using CEP engines. CEP engines can subscribe to currency spot rates and interest rates, and then perform forward pricing calculations on each update received so as to serve as a pricing engine. CEP engines can also be used to implement crossing engine components. Furthermore, execution of customers' FX orders can be automated, verifying that they fall within the required parameters, using CEP so as to provide client execution server capabilities.

Besides capital markets, CEP is also used in retail and **commercial banking**. Fraud detection and prevention is one common application. While many software applications are designed to detect specific types of fraud, CEP technology can look for patterns across multiple channels, for example, automated teller machine (ATM), branch, Internet banking, credit card, or point of sale. For instance, when a credit card transaction occurs in a foreign country, a fraud detection algorithm in a credit card processing system might flag it as a potential fraud situation. A CEP engine could monitor the credit card processing system as an event and correlate its events with other events, such as ATM usage in the same country, to determine whether to suspend the card account.

Moreover, CEP can be used to enhance CRM applications. Real-time events related to customers' transactions and channel interactions can trigger RMs to take specific actions. In contrast to capital markets applications, in retail and commercial banking, the correlation capabilities of CEP engines are more relevant than processing speed. Whereas a half-a-second processing delay could mean the difference between a profitable and a loss-making trade, it will have negligible effect on a CRM interaction. Hence, different CEP engines are often designed to cater to specific business use cases.

15.6   SUMMARY

This chapter covered:

- services provided by financial intermediaries, specifically equity brokers;
- key trading platform architecture components;
- order flow internalization;
- how algorithms are used to execute large orders;
- the background and usage of the FIX protocol; and
- how CEP engines can be used to build and support financial markets solutions.

The next five chapters will cover financial institutions' cross-functional capabilities and will begin by reviewing service delivery channels and customer relationship management.

FURTHER READING

Books

Chandy, K. and W. Schulte, *Event Processing: Designing IT Systems for Agile Companies* (New York: McGraw-Hill, 2009).

Johnson, B., *Algorithmic Trading and DMA: An Introduction to Direct Access Trading Strategies* (London: Myeloma Press, 2010).

Kim, K., *Electronic and Algorithmic Trading Technology: The Complete Guide* (Massachusetts: Academic Press, 2007).

Papers

FIX Protocol Ltd, "FIXML 4.4 Schema Version Guide," January 9, 2004, https://www.fixtrading.org/packages/fixml-4-4-schema-version-guide/.

Mangkorntong, P. and F. A. Rabhi, "A Domain-driven Approach for Detecting Event Patterns in E-Markets: A Case Study in Financial Market Surveillance," in *Web Information Systems Engineering—WISE 2007, Lecture Notes in Computer Science* Vol. 4831, eds. M. Weske, M.S. Hacid, and C. Godart, pp. 147–158 (Berlin: Springer, 2007).

Web

"Apache Flink Stream Processing Framework," https://flink.apache.org/.

"Esper Complex Event Processing," http://www.espertech.com/.

"Marketcetera," http://www.marketcetera.com.

"Online FIX Dictionary," https://www.onixs.biz/fix-dictionary.html.

"QuickFIX," http://www.quickfixengine.org.

"SASE Complex Event Processing," http://avid.cs.umass.edu/sase.

ENDNOTES

1. Balluck, K. "Investment banking: linkages to the real economy and the financial system," *Bank of England Quarterly Bulletin* (Q1 2015); 4–22, http://www.bankofengland.co.uk/publications/Pages/quarterlybulletin/2015/q1.aspx.

2. Lewis, M., "Proprietary Trading Goes Under Cover," Bloomberg, October 27, 2010, http://www.bloomberg.com/news/2010-10-27/wall-street-proprietary-trading-under-cover-commentary-by-michael-lewis.html.

3. Credit Suisse, "Credit Suisse Launches AES® Velocity in Australia," November 1, 2010, https://www.credit-suisse.com/news/en/media_release.jsp?ns=41625.

4. FIX Protocol Ltd, "FIXML 4.4 Schema Version Guide," January 9, 2004, https://www.fixtrading.org/packages/fixml-4-4-schema-version-guide/.

5. DeLoach, D. and J. Wootton, "Applying Event Processing to Electronic Trading," *Journal of Trading* 4, issue 3 (Summer 2009): 56–58.

— — —

6. Schmerken, I., "Deutsche Bank Algo to Help Buy Side Navigate the Close," *Advanced Trading*, June 26, 2012, http://www.advancedtrading.com/algorithms/240002724.

7. "The Fix Protocol Organization," http://www.fixprotocol.org.

8. "MIT 202 - FIX Trading Gateway (FIX5.0)," London Stock Exchange, Issue 11.6.1, 15 June 2017, http://www.londonstockexchange.com/products-and-services/millennium-exchange/ millennium-exchange-migration/mit202-issue103v5.pdf.

PART FOUR
CROSS-FUNCTIONAL
CONSIDERATIONS

16 Channels and Customer Relationship Management

Chapter Overview

16.1 FINANCIAL SERVICES CONTEXTS

16.2 CONCEPTS

16.3 BUSINESS OPPORTUNITIES

16.4 BUSINESS CHALLENGES

16.5 PROCESS CONSIDERATIONS

16.6 ARCHITECTURE CONSIDERATIONS

16.7 SOLUTION CONSIDERATIONS: MOBILE BANKING

16.8 SUMMARY

FURTHER READING

ENDNOTES

For many years, customer relationship management (CRM) processes were relatively simple for banks. The only customer service delivery channel was the bank branch, and CRM was largely determined by the branch staff's friendliness, efficiency, and knowledge about customers. Customer loyalty was often associated with the interpersonal relationships that were developed through regular interaction. Today, financial services CRM is very different and much more complex. Customers use digital channels extensively, which in most cases do not involve direct interaction between customers and financial institutions' **relationship managers (RMs)**. Nevertheless, a customer's experience is largely determined by the quality of the service delivery channels that he or she uses and the effectiveness of the institution's business processes.

Ideally, channels and CRM should be customer centric, that is, focus first and foremost on customer needs, and then consider how technology and business processes can be best designed to meet those needs. By nature of a bank's organization and business objectives, it is easy for customers' priorities to be subordinate to those of a bank's management and shareholders. Furthermore, as part of the banking experience, customers are rarely interested in the technology itself, but rather the experience that it provides for them. Hence, much of the effort involved with implementing banking channels and CRM is related to concealing technology service delivery concerns, covering up divisions and disconnections between internal groups or systems, designing digital channels to be intuitive to use, and molding business processes to fit customers' needs. Achieving a positive customer service experience depends on hiding the inconsistencies and discontinuities between channels, processes, technologies, and business units.

Delivery channels' strengths and weaknesses along with customers' usage patterns need to be taken into consideration. Increasingly, customers want to decide how they interact with delivery channels, in some cases, switching between multiple channels over the course of a single transaction. They may be happy to use self-serve digital channels for simple transactions. At the same time, they may want to quickly shift to interactive channels that provide direct communication with a bank representative to address more complex transactional needs. Technologies such as online chat, voice over Internet, and online video communication provide the potential for integrating human interaction into digital channels.

While customer experience is a driving factor behind service delivery and CRM, cost efficiency and technological change are also major considerations. Improved cost efficiency has helped advance the use of new channels—the costs of customer transactions performed over digital channels, such as the Internet, are much lower than those performed at branches. The customer "self-service" mentality that has evolved across many industries has also supported the use of digital communication channels by financial services firms. Technologies, such as the networks and devices that support online transactions, have made it possible to transact remotely, largely eliminating the need for customers to visit bank branches and use automated teller machines (ATMs).

Service delivery channels, CRM, and business intelligence (BI) are interrelated functions that are driven by and support banks' marketing and customer service functions. Marketing strategy should determine the type of products and services to offer and the channels over which to provide them. The choice of the channels to support will be driven by the needs of the bank's customer base and its competitive strategy. While channel needs may vary to some extent by product or business unit, channel and CRM capabilities are best established at an enterprise level to maximize scalability and cost efficiency.

In practice, however, these capabilities are often implemented independently by different business units as part of tactical solution deliveries, leading to duplicate and segregated functionality. Hence, the effectiveness of banks' enterprise-level architecture strategy and its implementation will affect the level of benefit that channels and CRM provide. Fragmented architectures create challenges for providing good customer service. Moreover, the changes required to rationalize and consolidate disparate implementations after they have been deployed is a painful exercise, both for banks and customers.

This chapter will explore the opportunities and challenges that financial institutions face with regard to channels, CRM, and BI (Case Study 16-1). The goal is to provide an introduction to the core concepts and then relate them to specific banking examples and process, architecture, and solution considerations. Many books have been written about CRM and BI. Readers interested in learning more about these topics can find references to more in-depth information in the Further Reading section at the end of this chapter.

Case Study 16-1

Leveraging Big Data Analytics to Gain Competitive Advantage

Ever increasing amounts of information are available about customers, the business environment, and financial markets. Many financial institutions have invested in channel, CRM, and **business process management systems (BPMS)** that can capture huge volumes of information related to customer interactions and how transactions are processed at every step of fulfillment. Furthermore, the ability to capture and analyze voice and video recordings also adds a new dimension and greater scale to the information available. Firms that can effectively make use of this wealth of information have the opportunity to develop deeper insights about their customers and identify business opportunities, so as to gain a competitive edge. However, dealing with the enormous quantities of data available is not easy. Managing and analyzing what is commonly referred to as "big data" or excessively large volumes of information, some of which may be unstructured, has emerged as a contemporary technology and business challenge.

Leveraging big data enables financial firms to gain unique insights and, thus, a competitive advantage that cannot be easily replicated by competitors. Analyzing information from diverse sources that produce similar conclusions supports evidence-based management. Basing business decisions on quantitative evidence from a diverse range of sources and applying rigorous statistical analysis of the information available can lead to better and more consistent management decisions, especially when compared to relying on gut feelings and anecdotal evidence, as is often the case. Big data can also help predict potential problems, thereby enabling them to be proactively addressed. Take, for example, the massive amounts of real-time information generated by telemetry systems of racing cars about the vehicles' operation; such detailed information can help predict, for instance, when the car brakes are in danger of overheating. Similarly, the information generated by IT systems of banks can provide information regarding which transactions are delayed and likely to exceed service-level thresholds.

Collecting, aggregating, and analyzing customer information are not new concepts, but applying these techniques to big data has created new challenges. One challenge is the logistical and organizational challenge of collecting and aggregating data across internal groups and systems, as well as from external sources. Financial institutions often struggle with integrating customer and transactional data from their core systems to support straight-through transaction processes. Integrating data from a large number of new information sources to support big data analysis would only further exacerbate this problem. Another challenge is validating the vast quantity of data collected so that the results generated are accurate and trustworthy. Obsolete, duplicated, incomplete, and erroneous records must be found and removed, and ways to relate data sets must be identified. Quality assurance processes must be implemented to ensure the integrity of the data used and the results produced.

Moreover, the greatest challenge is that big data can overload the IT processing capabilities of financial institutions. The volume of data that must be processed has been increasing steadily; hence, IT infrastructure that is adequate at one point in time may not suffice a year later. Networks can be inundated and data storage facilities overwhelmed by the volume of data that can be captured. Databases and software applications used for BI may have fundamental limitations that restrict the size of the operable data sets. Furthermore, generating results for big data analysis using existing computing hardware may require days or weeks, whereas answers may be needed in hours or minutes. Hence, new processing, storage, and analysis technologies are commonly required to support big data. Distributed in-memory databases are one technology that is used to manage big data storage. For instance, Hadoop is a technology that enables distributed applications to perform ad hoc analysis of both extremely large structured and unstructured data. By enabling a high degree of parallel processing, Hadoop can help perform big data computations very quickly. As a case in point, the time required to process 73 billion transactions using traditional methods might easily take one month; Hadoop can complete the task within minutes. Cloud computing is also an attractive option for processing big data. It allows many computational processing resources to be sourced quickly and for a short period of time to support parallel processing technologies, such as Hadoop.

Hiring personnel with the analytical skills that are necessary for working with big data is also a concern. Business analysts and technologists who have a good understanding of statistics and have experience integrating, managing, and manipulating excessively large volumes of data are in short supply. It is also difficult to find people with the requisite knowledge who are also able to effectively communicate the complex concepts associated with big data to the rest of the organization. Furthermore, business and IT managers must have an appreciation of the potential provided by and limitations of quantitative analysis techniques.

(Continued)

(Continued)

Even when financial firms are able to effectively analyze big data, taking advantage of the insights discovered presents other types of challenges. Many existing business processes, ranging from cross-selling and delivery-channel management to fraud control and risk management, must be adapted to achieve benefits. Often, the greatest challenge resides in convincing business users, operations staff, managers, and technologists to change the existing way of doing things. Moreover, actual use of big data analytics is still relatively small. A 2014 survey on analytics related to fraud prevention and detection showed that while 72% of respondents believed that big data technology could be of benefit, only 2% were actually using it.

Sources: Davenport, T. H., "Competing on Analytics," *Harvard Business Review* (January 2006): 99–107; "A Different Game," *Economist*, February 25, 2010; http://www.economist.com/node/15557465; Ernst & Young, "Global Banking Outlook 2015: Transforming Banking for the Next Generation," 2015.

Questions

1. What are some nontraditional sources of customer and market information that financial institutions could incorporate into existing analysis techniques?
2. What strategies could financial institutions implement to ensure that the data used for analysis is accurate?
3. What challenges might a financial institution encounter when trying to use technologies that support big data analysis, such as hadoop and cloud computing services?
4. Why might internal stakeholders be skeptical about the conclusions generated by big data analysis? What steps could be taken to get past their concerns?

16.1 FINANCIAL SERVICES CONTEXTS

Channels, CRM, and BI are functional considerations that are common concerns across all lines of business. However, in cases where financial institutions are organized around vertical lines of business, these functions are usually embedded separately within each business unit. For example, the credit card lending division of a bank may have robust and well-tuned channel and CRM delivery capabilities, whereas the mortgage lending division may have much more limited facilities. Likewise, larger institutions may have groups that are dedicated to these functions and serve multiple business units.

Effective management of customer relationships is relevant to all types of financial services, including **retail banking, commercial banking**, retail brokerage, and **investment banking.** These considerations are most often visible in the context of retail banking, where there are large numbers of customers that must be managed, and where customer turnover rates may be high. With retail customers, relationship management is complicated by differing customer expectations and preferences, which often relate to generational differences. Older customers may want personal interaction when transacting, whereas younger customers may be more comfortable with using self-service digital channels (Figure 16-1). The relevance of different channels may also depend on customers' geographical locations. For instance, it could make sense for a bank to simultaneously close branches and shift customers to digital channels in a developed market to reduce operational costs while increasing the size of its branch network in an emerging market to gain market share.

Supporting operational efficiency is more relevant when delivering services to and managing relations with commercial banking customers. The provision of different banking services must be integrated and supported over multiple channels, both physical and electronic. When corporate customers receive large payments, their bank may notify them via phone, fax, email, or a digital message sent directly to the customer's treasury management system. Customers' business processes

Figure 16-1 ATMs—the original self-service digital channel (© Standard Chartered Bank. Reprinted with permission.)

and technology infrastructure will determine the types of services that can be offered and the channels over which they will be delivered. Corporate channel connectivity often involves bank-to-customer IT system integration. Accordingly, some banks have dedicated digital channel management groups that support the setup and management of integration with customers' IT systems.

In the context of CRM, identifying the customer is more complicated when dealing with corporations. Often, different employees will interact with the bank on behalf of the corporation, and the individuals who are involved may change over time. Hence, a hierarchical structure that relates a corporate customer and its representatives must be incorporated into commercial banking CRM processes and IT systems. For example, a corporate customer's chief financial officer would be authorized to perform more types of transactions and use a broader range of channels than its payments processing clerk. Corporate hierarchies can also overlap, as in the case of conglomerate corporations. A single individual may transact on behalf of multiple corporations. Accordingly, a single user login to a corporate Internet banking website may provide access to the accounts of multiple companies.

Retail brokerages were pioneers in shifting customers from phone-based relationships with dedicated RMs, that is, the brokers, to self-serve digital channels. "Low-touch" channels, such as the Internet, were introduced to support common transaction types in conjunction with traditional phone-accessible brokerage desks. Services provided through low-touch channels can be processed without human intervention, which significantly reduces the cost of pre- and post-trade processing. These cost savings were, in turn, passed on to customers in the form of lower commission fees. Lower commissions were particularly attractive for retail investors because broker commission fees were high, relative to the overall size of their share purchases.

CRM for investment banking applies to two different areas. First, in their role of bringing securities to market, investment banks operate more like law or accounting firms. Relationships are at a personal level, and communications are likely to be face-to-face, over the phone, or via email. In this case, it is important to capture and analyze the information conveyed through these channels. BI tools can help find and show the connections between different investment bankers and corporate executives.

Such information may be used strategically to gain a foothold or garner support in investment banking sales situations.

Second, in their role as financial markets intermediaries and **liquidity** providers, which facilitate the purchase and sale of securities, it is important to provide customers with effective operational support. This is especially true where large volumes or high-value transactions are performed over digital channels. Although it does not fit into the traditional sales-oriented view of CRM, helping customers handle exceptions is an important part of maintaining good customer relations. Efficient handling of customer problems is important when onboarding customers and fulfilling their transactions. An example of a transaction-oriented CRM system is the Bombay Stock Exchange's Short Message Service (SMS) Alert & Complaint Tracking (SACT) system that was launched in 2011. The system enables the exchange's customers to track support queries via text messages on their mobile phones. SACT is integrated with the exchange helpdesk's Complaint Management System and an Internet website that allows customers to check the status of complaint tickets [1].

16.2   CONCEPTS

Planning business strategy without effective CRM and BI is like driving a car at night without headlights. The driving speed will be slow and the driver may often veer in the wrong direction. Collection and analysis of customer channel information can help identify usage patterns, thereby enabling banks to plan ahead more effectively. The sections that follow provide an overview of how channels, CRM, and BI interrelate from a banking perspective. Figure 16-2 provides a visual representation of how banking channels, CRM, and BI interrelate.

16.2.1   Channels

This section examines common channels used for providing banking and other financial services. First an overview of the channels used is provided, followed by a more in-depth look at three dominant channel categories: branches, contact centers, and digital channels.

16.2.1.1   Overview

In financial services, delivery channels underpin marketing, customer acquisition, product distribution, and service delivery functions. Over time, many different channels have evolved. Table 16-1 compares the attributes of some common channels. While channels are critical to CRM and customer service

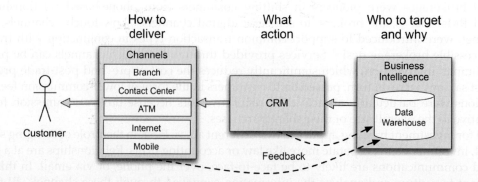

Figure 16-2 Channels, CRM, and BI interrelationships

experience, being able to steer customers towards lower-cost channels is also important from a financial management perspective.

In general, customer interactions can be viewed as either routine or exploratory. For routine interactions, such as withdrawing cash or making payments, efficiency and speed of execution are of primary importance for channel implementations. On the other hand, the depth of information available and the quality of its presentation are more relevant to exploratory interactions, such as shopping for financial products. Accordingly, service delivery should be matched with specific channels based on the channels' capabilities and customers' preferred usage patterns. For example, ATMs are well suited for routine transactions such as withdrawing cash, but not for exploring new product offerings. Thus, technology solution implementations for ATMs should be optimized to minimize hassle and transaction times. Alternatively, Internet banking can be used for both routine and exploratory transactions; thus, routine Internet banking functions should be designed such that they are easy to access and simple to use, whereas other features may be designed to support more complex and time-consuming interactions.

Besides providing new routes for performing transactions and delivering services, the introduction of new channels has also altered the usage patterns of pre-existing channels. For example, in many countries, the purpose and function of bank branches have been transformed over the past few decades. As mundane transactions, such as deposits, withdrawals, and checking of account balances, have been migrated to other channels, bank branches have had to adapt to maintain their relevance.

Table 16-1 A comparison of banking channels

Channel	Strengths	Weaknesses
Branch	• Face-to-face conversations • Verification of ID and original documents • Supports complex interactions • Physical delivery of currency, notes, and other products • Comprehensive access to products and services	• High delivery cost • Limited geographical coverage • Difficult to share resources across locations • Costly to scale up services
Regular mail/post	• Delivery of physical materials (e.g., cards and statements) • Asynchronous notifications • Low cost to deliver • Highly scalable • Universal access	• Reliability • No confirmation of receipt or opening • Non-interactive
Fax	• Asynchronous notification • Low cost to deliver • Highly scalable	• Reliability receipt • No confirmation of reading • Non-interactive • Becoming less common in retail context
Contact center	• Supports complex interactions • Asynchronous notification • Extensive product and service access	• Medium delivery cost • Requires specific language skills • Not easily scalable

(Continued)

Table 16-1 A comparison of banking channels (Continued)

Channel	Strengths	Weaknesses
Interactive voice recognition (IVR)	• Moderately scalable • Low per-transaction cost	• Slow interaction speeds
ATM/Kiosk/ITM	• Physical delivery of currency, notes, and other products • Moderately scalable	• Limited interactive capabilities • Medium cost to deliver
Internet—web	• Supports some interaction • Highly scalable • Low per-transaction cost	• Bank cannot initiate contact • Must support a variety of browsers
Internet—online chat	• Interactive communication • Low cost to deliver • Can span multiple time periods and user sessions • Interactions can be automated using artificial intelligence	• Limitations as to the type of information that can be delivered (e.g., documents) • Lower bandwidth than interactive voice communications (i.e., telephone conversations)
Mobile—SMS	• Asynchronous notification • Ubiquitous access • Highly scalable • Low cost to deliver • Interactions can be automated using artificial intelligence	• Minimal interactive capabilities • User interface limitations
Mobile—web	• Supports some interaction • High level of accessibility • Highly scalable • Low cost to deliver	• Bank cannot initiate contact • User interface limitations • Must support a wide range of device configurations and browsers
Mobile applications	• Asynchronous notification • Location awareness • Supports some interaction • Can leverage other phone capabilities (e.g., camera) • Highly scalable • Low cost to deliver	• Requires multiple application implementations for different handset operating systems • Must support a wide range of device configurations • Limited customer take up

16.2.1.2 Branches

With the rise of digital channels, it might seem as though branches' days are numbered. In fact, at least in the United States, they are hanging on rather well. From the peak, in 2009, to 2015, the number of branches fell only 6%, with over 90,000 open at the end of that period [2]. Even though the cost of operations for branches is high, between $2–4 million to open and $200,000-400,000 annually to operate and maintain, they are still the preferred channel for certain types of business. In particular, branches play a key role in customer acquisition and are best suited for selling mortgages and providing investment advisory services. They are also still commonly used for cash and cheque deposits. Hence, by closing branches, banks run the risk of causing revenue to go down more than the reduction in expenses would offset. In comparison with other countries, the United States has reduced branches, in relative terms, more than Canada, France, and Germany but less than Greece, Ireland, Italy, and Spain.

To help maintain their relevance and presence, branches have adapted in recent years. One trend has been to shift from a small number of large branches to a large number of small branches that are strategically placed. In many cases, mini- and micro-branches are set up in other retail establishments, such as grocery stores. Likewise, some banks have redesigned branches' physical layouts and staff interaction models to follow more of the approach that retail stores use. This leverages their strength of close personal interaction, which most other communication channels cannot fulfill. At the same time, banks have also incorporated new technologies into branches that customers can use by themselves or with the assistance of branch staff.

One technology that banks have been experimenting with at branches are "video teller" kiosks, also referred to as interactive teller machines (ITMs), that connect to bank staff at other locations, typically contact centers. These ATM-like machines are equipped with video and audio, cash deposit and withdrawal, cheque deposit, and signature pad capabilities. While they can accommodate many of the same activities as a branch teller, they are usually not used to apply for a loan or open a bank account. It may seem strange that customers at a branch would want to talk to someone through a kiosk rather than a real person; however, typically customers who visit branches expect quick services. Hence, if there is a long line to reach live tellers at a branch, and a video teller machine is free, customers may opt to use the latter. This is particularly true of younger customers, who have higher expectations regarding the time that it takes to transact and are more technology oriented.

Technologies such as video tellers are unlikely to displace branch staff in the near term. Account opening, product sales, and advisory services are usually best provided as face-to-face interactions. That said, video tellers are a useful tool for enabling excess branch demand to be shifted to contact centers.

16.2.1.3 Contact center

Historically, contact centers primarily handled phone calls from customers. Over time their scope has broadened to include direct customer communication via digital channels such as email, online chat sessions, and ITMs. Accordingly, in this book and across the industry, the terminology has shifted from "call centers" to "contact centers." Younger customers, in particular, are more apt to communicate with contact center staff though digital channels.

Like branch traffic, customer phone calls to contact centers have also decreased over time with the shift of interactions to Internet and mobile channels. Yet, contact centers remain the centerpiece of banks' interactive channels. While contact centers do not provide face-to-face contact like branches, they do not have the limitations of geographic scope that branches have and offer a wider range of services than digital channels. Likewise, as discussed in Chapter 1, contact centers fall into the middle ground in terms of cost, with contact center transactions costing at about half that of those executed in branches, but around ten times more than those performed using digital channels.

While much of the technology that is used in contact centers has been around for many years, existing technology has been extended and new solutions have been developed. One change has been the integration of web chat capabilities into telecommunication systems such as phone switches. Web chat capabilities can be easily implanted independently as part of Internet banking platforms; however, integrating it with voice communication systems takes advantage of these systems' load-balance capabilities. Phone switches are able to determine which contact center agents are currently handling calls and which are available to handle customer chat sessions and route chat traffic accordingly. Also, speech analytics technology, which can automatically extract information from real-time and prerecorded voice streams, has begun to be used in contact centers. This information can be used to trigger workflows and alerts as well as categorize and search through call recordings. The latter capability is particularly useful for reviewing that contact agents' conduct was appropriate and verifying that they provided the necessary disclosures.

The telecommunications and other technology infrastructure, as discussed in Chapters 5 and 8, that is required to operate contact centers involves significant investment to put in place and maintain. Equipment such as phone switches, automated dialers, interactive voice recognition systems, voice recording systems, and telecommunication lines, all must be redundant to provide high availability. Likewise, maintaining the correct level of contact center staffing is an operational challenge, given that customer contact demands vary from hour to hour and day to day. Hence, migrating these activities to digital channels provides major cost advantages.

16.2.1.4 Digital Channels

Clearly, digital channels provide many advantages for banks and their customers. They provide greater convenience, around-the-clock service, consistent delivery of services, and are less expensive to operate and maintain, compared with branch and contact center channels. For a long time, website, email communication, and text messages to mobile phones have been the primary digital channels used by financial institutions. In more recent years, however, as mobile devices have gained prominence, it has become more important for banks to provide mobile-friendly websites and native mobile applications to customers. Technology solutions for mobile devices are discussed at length in Section 16.7.

The technology infrastructure that supports digital communications is vast and complex. Chapter 5 discusses the many components involved. Something seemingly as simple as email communication with customers comes with many complications. Delivery of some email messages may have to be tracked and verified for regulatory compliance purposes. Email content needs to be designed for and test-viewed on various types of desktop and mobile devices. Legal and compliance functions will have to review and approve email content. Email gateways need to be integrated with multiple transactional systems. Email distribution components may need to be patched or upgraded to address newly discovered security weaknesses. Third parties may erroneously block email communication, believing that it is spam. Each type of digital channel requires its own particular care and feeding; hence, migrating customers to digital channels provides benefits, but also leads to a new set of challenges.

While digital channels can provide standalone service to customers, as highlighted in Case Study 16-2, this is the exception rather than the rule. Customer communication channels are best when they complement one another.

16.2.1.5 Omni-channel communication

Customer interactions may migrate between channels over the course of a transaction. For example, a transaction may begin with the bank emailing or sending an SMS text message to a customer about a new credit card offer, which directs them to the Internet banking website to obtain more information. The customer may then ask a question about the product via web chat or by calling the contact center, and apply for the card at a branch. The card may be mailed to him or her, and then activated via a call to the bank's interactive voice recognition system. For the transaction experience to appear seamless from the customer's perspective, interactions across all of the channels must be integrated in real time with the bank's CRM system. In contrast, an example of poor channel integration, which results in poor customer service, occurs when a representative at a contact center or branch is unable to view or modify recent transactions that have been performed by customers using digital channels, and vice versa.

Case Study 16-2
Digital-only Banking

With the popularity of ATMs, phone banking, Internet banking, and, most recently, mobile banking, one may wonder about the relevance of physical branches. There would be many cost savings if bank branches could be made obsolete. The maintenance of bank branches is associated with significant overhead costs, high per-transaction costs, and the ability to only serve a limited set of customers that transact in the branch's local area. To this end, some banks have been set up with a digital-only business model. One example is Egg Plc, which was launched in 1998 by the insurer Prudential in the United Kingdom.

Egg's value proposition was largely based on providing highly competitive interest rates to customers, which would be cost effective because of the bank's lower operating cost. Egg offered its best interest rates to customers who have agreed to only access services using the Internet and rates that were not quite as good, but still than its branch-based competitors for customers who used its phone-banking service. A high proportion of its customers chose the Internet-only option. Egg also expanded its services to include a facility that aggregated customers' account information from different banks' Internet banking web sites and provided a single consolidated view.

Cross-selling was also a core part of the bank's competitive strategy. The bank gradually expanded its product portfolio to include deposit accounts, personal loans, credit cards, mortgages, insurance services, and online equity trading capabilities. Credit cards were by far Egg's most successful offering. As of 2001, three years after the bank's launch, Egg had over 1.7 million customers, of which about 65% held credit cards, 36% had deposit accounts, and 5% had personal loans. A third of its customers held at least two of its financial products. In 2004, the bank had over 3.2 million customers.

Egg had a unique and interesting business model. However, it struggled to achieve and maintain profitability, and was sold to Citibank in 2007, which then sold Egg's credit card portfolio to Barclays and its mortgage and savings portfolio to Yorkshire Building Society in 2011. Other pure-play Internet banks, such as ING Direct and E-Trade Bank, faced other challenges. One problem was growth of deposits outpacing the growth of lending, which led to an asset-liability imbalance that made it difficult to generate adequate returns on customer deposits. Digital-only banking also does not support collection and use of "soft" information about customers, such as their general appearance and state of mind, which can sometimes be valuable when making lending decisions. Hence, digital-only banking still has some way to go before becoming a mainstream business model for retail banking.

Sources: "Online Banks Scramble for Customers," *BBC*, May 26, 2000, http://news.bbc.co.uk/2/hi/business/764180.stm; "Egg Edges Towards Profitability," *BBC*, July 24, 2001, http://news.bbc.co.uk/2/hi/business/1453327.stm; "Prudential Sells Egg to Citigroup," *BBC*, January 29, 2007, http://news.bbc.co.uk/2/hi/business/6309731.stm; Egg website, http://www.egg.com; Arnold, I. J. M and S. E. van Ewijk, "Can Pure Play Internet Banking Survive the Credit Crisis?" *Journal of Banking & Finance* 35 (2011): 783–793.

16.2.2 Customer Relationship Management

In bookstores and libraries, books relating to most banking topics are usually found in the finance or technology sections, while CRM books are generally found in the marketing section. Accordingly, there is a need to consider both viewpoints to effectively apply CRM. Whereas much of the attention in banks is focused on CRM IT systems, aligning CRM processes with the bank's marketing strategy is critical. Since banks cannot survive without customers, developing and maintaining good relationships with customers is a foundation of their business strategy. Hence, CRM focuses on many nonfunctional, "soft" considerations such as usability and customer experience, which are often afterthoughts for many IT projects.

CRM is many things to many people, but its essence is the process of acquiring and retaining customers and satisfying their interaction and relationship needs so that they will generate greater business volume. These objectives contribute to the broader business goal of increasing revenue. How these objectives are achieved depends on a financial institution's products, services, and competitive landscape, and the customer segments that it serves.

Some mass-market segments, such as retail banking, may be best served by short-lived anonymous customer service relationships. The information related to these customers may be relatively simple and easily stored in a bank's databases. Other customer segments, such as private and institutional banking, may rely more on developing closer, long-term relationships through dedicated RMs and sales executives. For these customers, detailed knowledge may be acquired over an extended period of time and not be easily captured as structured data that can be easily categorized and searched. Alternatively, for corporate customers, tight integration with their business processes and systems may be more relevant to CRM than personal interactions.

As one might expect, on average, banks with superior CRM capabilities perform better than their competitors. However, it is important to identify which CRM capabilities are the most critical. Also, how CRM is implemented is generally more important than the specific technology infrastructure that is used to deliver CRM services [3]. While IT is necessary to support CRM functions, it is more important to first ensure that business processes are aligned with customer needs and behaviors. Transaction fulfillment processes should be aligned with marketing and sales objectives. Likewise, organization structures must be designed such that they facilitate, rather than thwart, customers' experiences. For example, even the best CRM IT system can do little to alleviate the frustration experienced by customers when they are shuttled between bank departments to complete a single service request.

To take full advantage of CRM tools and techniques, financial firms should use a strategy-driven, top-down approach, rather than a technology-driven, bottom-up approach. Accordingly, business processes' designs should be aligned with high-level CRM goals. Likewise, as with all solutions, all of the different stakeholders' needs must be taken into consideration. If the CRM system does not provide sufficient benefits for sales people to offset the overhead of them using it, the net value that it produces may be negative from the perspective of sales staff and the customers, two very important stakeholders.

CRM systems are instrumental in aggregating and centralizing access to customer information. The quality of information in a CRM system is more important than the quantity. The benefits derived from using the system will be reduced if the presentation of information is poor, or the information itself is inaccurate or outdated. Similarly, it may be difficult to analyze customer data when the information that RMs capture about customers is mostly unstructured, for example, information entered as free-form text notes as opposed to predefined fields and enumerated values.

16.2.3 Business Intelligence

BI is commonly used in financial services to support CRM, management of risk, and compliance, and to improve operational efficiency. This chapter will limit the discussion of BI to its role as an analytical extension of CRM. CRM analytics are used to identify customer segments, support business decision making, target customers more effectively, and predict customer behavior. For example, based on specific transaction and channel usage patterns, BI can be used to help determine if a customer is shifting his or her banking activities to another institution. Likewise, BI can help optimize the products and services that are offered to different customer segments.

BI can also analyze customer, product, and channel profitability. Banks often use BI to identify "low value" customers, and apply strategies to improve these customers' profitability. Besides evaluating customers' current value, BI techniques may also try to estimate and take into account customers' future potential or overall "lifetime value" to the bank. For instance, college students may not be a high-profit segment initially; however, this segment will become more profitable over time. Capturing customers at an early stage in their lifecycle and then retaining them may be more cost effective than trying to compete for their business at a later stage. BI can also help financial institutions shift from reacting to observations related to past events to using information analysis to predict customer behavior so that they can implement proactive measures (Case Study 16-3). For instance, financial institutions often take remedial steps aimed at retaining customers when they request to close their accounts. Alternatively, predictive BI, which analyzes customer complaint and account activity patterns, can enable actions, such as offering to waive certain fees, to be taken before customers decide to move their business to another financial institution.

BI can help financial institutions fine-tune product and service offerings and the structuring of offerings. If BI determines that a subset of customers regularly performs low-value transactions using high-cost channels, the bank can design bundled product and service offerings that help ensure profitability under those conditions. For example, free ATM usage might only be offered in conjunction with a minimum balance of $2,000 in a noninterest-bearing chequing account—the float interest earned by the customers' deposits would offset ATM servicing costs. Alternatively, fee structures and customer acquisition and retention strategies could be altered to achieve profitability.

In contrast to using spreadsheets to assess the results of database queries, BI focuses on finding patterns that are hidden in large volumes of structured and unstructured data. Advanced mathematical and statistical techniques provide the foundation for BI analysis. Regression and cluster analysis are two common techniques that are used in BI. Expert rules, decision trees, and neural network analysis techniques are also used. While many software tools provide BI functions, in-depth knowledge of statistical techniques is necessary to effectively utilize these tools. Skill and experience are required to determine what information should be used as input and what analyses to perform. Once the initial analysis is complete and a set of results obtained, it is then necessary to determine if the observations may be coincidental or are statistically significant. Likewise, statistical techniques must be used to determine if related events or behavior are merely correlated, that is, they both happen at the same time, but do not directly affect one another, or whether a causal (one event triggering another) relationship exists.

Determining the granularity of measurement and interpreting the analyzed results are often more of an art than a science. Due to the mathematical and analytical nature of BI, financial institutions often have dedicated groups focused on this function. An understanding of BI and access to the underlying tools may be limited to a niche group within the BI group. Often, front-line managers, who are best placed to validate the approach and results and determine the best use of the intelligence that has been gathered, may only be on the fringes of the BI efforts. In such cases, the potential value of BI can be lost when translating the needs and results between the BI group and other parts of the bank.

It is often the case that financial institutions' BI functions will analyze historical data. However, it is also possible to perform real-time BI analysis that leverages both current and historical information. The ability to generate real-time BI can be incredibly valuable when companies can quickly act upon the insights that are produced. **Complex event processing (CEP)** platforms (discussed in Chapter 15) can be combined with historical analysis BI tools to enable real-time detection and reaction.

Moreover, financial institutions have the opportunity to perform ongoing experiments that, in conjunction with BI, can improve their understanding of customers. For instance, attempts may be made to contact customers at different times of the day via different channels. Measuring and analyzing the result of these attempts can determine channel effectiveness and help optimize ongoing channel usage. Alternatively, a subset of customers may be offered a product at a reduced fee to assess price sensitivity.

Such experiments must be carefully designed and have a control group that can be used for comparison so that the effects of a change can be differentiated from other effects brought about by unrelated factors. The end goal of performing such experiments is to better understand, from both a marketing and operational perspective, how the bank's actions can trigger or influence customers' behavior.

Case Study 16-3
Evidence-based Customer Relationship Management Strategy and Operational Management

Even though the trend has been for customers to shift to self-service channels, they still occasionally need to speak to customer service representatives (CSRs). Banks' contact centers support complex customer interactions. Contact centers are often managed and optimized according to metrics such as the average time taken to answer customer calls and the conversion rate for cross-selling products to customers. The latter is important as it generates revenue and can help turn the contact center, which is usually an operational function as opposed to a line of business, from a cost center to a profit center for the bank.

Most financial institutions do not offer customers the option of canceling services or closing their account using self-service channels; instead, they must communicate directly with a bank representative. This strategy enables CSRs to inquire why customers are seeking to abandon the bank's products or services and to attempt to retain their business. This function of customer retention is vital for competitive business areas that experience high customer turnover, such as credit card businesses in many markets.

Customer retention is especially important for subscription-based financial products, where customers are continually charged a monthly or annual fee for the service. For these types of products, the cost of losing a customer is equal to their expected future subscription revenue, which may be several years' worth of income. Assurant Solutions is an example of an institution engaged in this type of business. Assurant Solutions is a multinational financial services provider that sells and provides customer service for credit insurance and debt protection products. To help improve customer retention rates, the company undertook a major BI effort that used analytical techniques to help redesign how calls were handled in the contact center. By making better use of the information it already had, the company was able to increase its retention rate from 16% to over 30%.

Assurant's analytics effort achieved gains by optimizing two considerations: automatically routing specific customers to specific agents and changing the time taken to answer calls. Previously, customer calls were routed to the first available agent, or to agents who were assumed to have the most relevant skills for the customer service requested. This policy was abandoned. Instead, customers were segmented into many small clusters based on their historical transaction and interaction behavior. CSRs' interaction histories with customers were also analyzed. CSRs were then rated based on their retention effectiveness when dealing with different customer segments. Based on the results of these analyses, customer calls were routed based on customer segment to the CSRs that had the best statistical chance of success.

However, this strategy had a downside. The "best" CSRs for a particular customer may already be engaged and not be available when the customer's call arrives, potentially increasing customer wait times. This problem led Assurant to analyze how customer satisfaction was affected by wait times. They discovered that, contrary to popular belief, customers' satisfaction was not significantly affected when the wait time was doubled from 20 seconds to 40 seconds. Hence, Assurant Solutions could use the additional time to wait for a CSR with the best matching profile to become available.

In summary, effective use of BI enabled Assurant Solutions to improve retention rates by taking the counterintuitive step of increasing customer wait times while maintaining customer satisfaction levels.

Source: Hopkins, Michael S. and Leslie Brokaw, "Matchmaking with Math: How Analytics Beats Intuition to Win Customers," *MIT Sloan Management Review* 52, issue 2 (Winter 2011): 35–41.

16.3 BUSINESS OPPORTUNITIES

Improving banks' channel and CRM capabilities can lead to new business opportunities. Making more effective use of channels can reduce costs, improve convenience for customers, and make it possible to service new customer segments. For example, in the context of corporate banking, using the Internet channel made it cost efficient for banks to provide corporate treasury services to smaller customers. Previously, it was impractical to provide pricing information and transactional services via the bank's corporate dealers due to the cost and limited **throughput** of phone-based transactions. Hence, using the Internet channel helped to expand banks' overall customer base in this market.

Improving companies' ability to cross-sell products and services is a benefit commonly touted for CRM. Cross-selling is when additional products of a company are sold to its existing customers. To effectively cross-sell, it is necessary to aggregate information regarding demographics and behavior patterns, the products customers already have, and other products that have attracted their interest. By analyzing this information, IT systems can predict the best products to try to cross-sell. This information can then be provided to RMs or be used to directly market specific products to customers.

In general, channels and CRM enable financial institutions to capture additional information about customers and to gain more benefits from the information that is gathered. For example, business processes used by the contact center and branches can be designed to make periodic inquiries to capture information regarding customer interests and preferences. Likewise, capturing information about how and when customers use different channels can provide clues about changes in their employment status or geographic location. Increasing banks' "wallet share" of existing customers, that is, the proportion of customers' aggregate business transactions across all of the banks that they use, is also an important strategy for increasing revenue. Hence, capturing information related to customers' relationships with and holdings at other financial institutions is of particular interest to banks.

In this regard, banks that offer Internet-based account aggregation and personal financial management services, discussed in Chapter 7, can more easily determine how much of customers' business they are capturing. Account aggregation provides customers with a consolidated view of the financial products they have across different financial institutions. This helps customers see their overall financial position without having to access multiple banks' websites or statements. While this service is valuable to customers, it also supplies useful information to the bank by providing information about customers' relationships with other banks. This knowledge supports better segmentation of customers, incorporating how much more wallet share could potentially be gained, and allows marketing to be targeted more precisely toward products areas that customers hold at other financial institutions.

Other technologies, such as video cameras, have the potential to be used in new and creative ways. Video surveillance in branches and at ATMs can be used to monitor the frequency of customer traffic, measure queue lengths, and determine how many people choose to abandon queues and, thus, not transact. Online video chat enables better and more dynamic conversations with contact center representatives, bringing the contact center closer to being a virtual branch. Besides video, artificial intelligence (AI) technology can also be used to simulate human interactions for online chat sessions so that the customer does not realize that they are interacting with an artificial intelligence, rather than a person. Although using AI to service customers might seem a bit farfetched, a number of financial services firms are already using this technology.* Automated online assistants, also known as "bots,"

---

* It is difficult to find any public disclosures that banks are using AI to respond to online chat. Presumably, they are concerned that customers may not be comfortable knowing that they are not actually communicating with a real person during their customer service inquiries.

can provide faster responses, better consistency, and more correct spelling and grammar. Furthermore, AI can automatically improve its answers to questions based on feedback from customers on their level of satisfaction with its past responses.

New technology has also breathed new life into old channels, such as ATMs, contact centers, and branches. As a case in point, one of Russia's largest retail banks, Sberbank, has experimented with next-generation ATMs that have advanced technological capabilities, such as voice analysis, the idea being that voice analysis could be used to help determine if customers are lying about their financial status when applying for credit at an ATM. Voice analysis technology has been used in contact centers to gauge customers' hostility levels during phone calls, enabling supervisors to better determine which conversations may be contentious so that they can monitor them and intervene when necessary. Sberbank has also experimented with facial scanning and recognition that can be used by ATMs and at branches to identify customers [4].

Many banks are still in the early stages of using social media as a communication channel and have the opportunity to expand the ways in which they use it. More specifically, social media can be helpful for promoting a company's brand, attracting new customers, addressing customer complaints, and for recruiting. Some US-based banks have had some hesitation about using social media because regulators may potentially view it as advertising. Accordingly, legal and compliance review of social media content is an important part of the content management process. Specialized software can be used to manage and monitor content and help address compliance concerns.

While it is not cheap or easy to develop good channel, CRM, and BI capabilities, banks that are successful in implementing these capabilities will gain a competitive advantage. Success, though, does not require banks to have the strongest competencies in each of these areas. It is more important that they are developed to satisfactory levels and that they are well integrated and aligned with strategic goals. As with football/soccer, having a team full of star players who only play well as individuals may be less effective than good players who play together superbly as a team.

16.4 BUSINESS CHALLENGES

With respect to CRM, one of the greatest challenges that financial institutions face is having unrealistic expectations regarding CRM IT systems' capabilities. Fundamentally, business strategy should drive CRM, and business processes must implement CRM. IT only supports execution of business processes; it cannot be substituted for a CRM-oriented business strategy and will not in and of itself align business processes with CRM goals. There are many documented cases of failed and underachieving CRM implementations (see Case Study 16-5), where the IT system implementation was taken as the end goal, rather than viewed as being just part of the means by which CRM benefits would be achieved. Moreover, when CRM IT systems are poorly integrated with business processes, they can actually decrease efficiency and worsen customer relationships.

Growth in the number of available service delivery channels has also created a number of challenges for financial institutions (Case Study 16-4). Initially, the introduction of new banking channels was advantageous for both banks and customers. For banks, however, supporting multiple channels has become burdensome as the number of channels has grown. First, the costs of developing support for and maintaining each channel are substantial. Second, enabling a wide range of banking products and services to be delivered through multiple channels can be difficult from a technical perspective. For example, development of channels by individual business units can lead to channel implementations that are closely linked to specific business functions, as shown in Figure 16-3. As a result, each business function may choose to develop its own channel implementation for expediency, which leads to a silo-based system architecture. Lastly, developing an enterprise-wide channel delivery strategy, that is, deciding which products and services should be delivered over which channels, requires considerable focus and coordination.

Case Study 16-4
Improving Customer Relationship Management with System Integration

A mid-sized bank in Greece faced a number of customer service challenges. Most transactions took place at its 64 branches, which were overloaded by customers and had long lines. The high volumes seen at branches were, to some extent, due to limitations in the bank's contact center. Customer waiting time for phone-based service was often 20 minutes or more, and the only transaction that could be performed, presumably because of IT system limitations, was to check their account balance. Hence, branches were inundated with customer transactions. Customer and employee satisfaction was low, and the cost of providing service was high. Furthermore, operational costs were dragging down the bank's profitability.

To address these problems, the bank chose to deploy a CRM system. Its goal was to lower the cost of service delivery and improve customer service. A key feature that the CRM solution provided was a single interface so that contact center staff could access the many IT systems that supported customer transactions. Having a single interface for accessing customer interfaces and performing common transactions provided several benefits. First, it made it easier for new staff to learn how to perform the basic functions they needed to serve customers. Second, it was simple to use, which enabled bank representatives to focus more on the service that they were providing to customers. Third, it allowed the contact center to support customer transactions for a wider range of financial products.

At the core of the solution architecture was the CRM system and a central **operational data store (ODS)**. Contact center personnel accessed customer information using CRM application screens, and computer telephony integration was used to link the bank's phone switch to the CRM system. The phone switch and other back-office systems were also integrated with the ODS. This integration enabled the ODS to serve as a central repository of information, which could be accessed through the CRM system's user interface. Hence, the solution enabled customer service staff to easily access a wide range of customer information without having to interact with multiple IT systems. The new system also enabled contact center employees to view customer activities that were performed via different channels, such as branches, ATMs, and the automated phone banking system.

The CRM solution made it possible to perform more customer transactions at the contact center, thereby reducing operational costs. Call volume in the contact center increased by around 40%, customer waiting times were reduced tenfold, and the conversation time required to perform transactions decreased by 50%. Moreover, the cost that the bank incurred to provide services using an employee in the contact center was half the cost of providing them using an employee at a branch. Reducing the volume of routine transactions that branches had to process also enabled customer-facing staff at branches to focus on developing customer relationships and supporting more complex, higher-value products. Contact-center staff could spend more time on sales-related activities and less time on IT system navigation.

As illustrated by this example, it is not unusual for major CRM initiatives to be focused more on improving customer service processes than on improving CRM system functions. For CRM to be effective, disparate systems must be easily accessed and aggregated. Hence, wide-scale integration efforts are often driven by customer service-related business initiatives, such as CRM. CRM systems themselves cannot provide a "**single view of the customer**"; extensive back-end integration is required to make this goal a reality.

Source: Blery, Evangelia and Michalis Michalakopoulos, "Customer Relationship Management: A Case Study of a Greek Bank," *Journal of Financial Services Marketing* 11, issue 2 (2006): 116–124.

Besides the problems that architecture **silos** create, business process silos are also an impediment to CRM. Inefficient or failed communication handoffs between departments or divisions can cause delays and negatively impact customers' service experiences. For example, when a customer contacts a

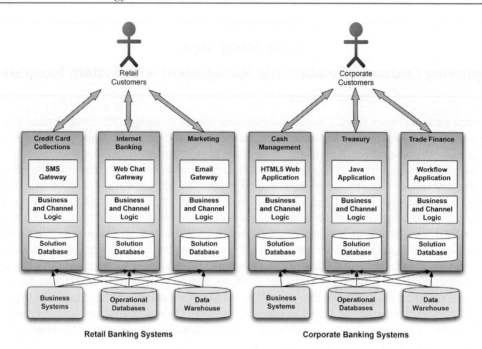

Figure 16-3 A business silo-oriented implementation of multiple channels

bank's contact center with a problem, a siloed organization will often require one or more call transfers between different departments to reach the person who can resolve it. Each time the customer is transferred, he or she may need to re-explain the problem, thereby resulting in time wastage. Furthermore, if a particular department in the chain is unavailable to answer the call at the time of the transfer, the whole process may come to a halt and have to begin all over again later. Ideally, a financial institution should hide these divisions by having the contact center representative navigate through these complications and coordinate as necessary, shielding the customer from potential frustrations. However, transferring customers' frustration onto RMs is not particularly helpful for improving the level of service they provide, either. Hence, it is preferable to try to better integrate the underlying processes.

There are also many challenges with developing an effective BI function. BI is highly dependent on the consolidation of information from many different source systems into the bank's **data warehouse**. Faulty communication links, poor data mapping, inadequate data models, and ineffective operational monitoring can all lead to poor data quality in the data warehouse. The need to coordinate with many different business units to integrate data from their systems can be onerous. With so many dependent factors, it is not surprising that there are many examples of failed data warehousing projects [5] where incorrect or inconsistent information has undermined BI goals.

Additionally, the limitations of existing systems, especially core banking systems, present challenges for CRM and BI. Many retail and corporate banking systems provide file-based interfaces that can only be accessed through end-of-day batch processes. In these environments, CRM strategies that are designed to provide real-time notifications to customers may not be feasible; the underlying systems will only be able to provide transaction event information overnight when the batch processes are run. Furthermore, the central data entity of many banking systems is the account, whereas CRM and BI often focus on the customer level. This disparity can be problematic for CRM and BI when a single customer has multiple accounts in the same system, when multiple customers share the same account, or when a customer has multiple accounts spanning different systems. Typically, additional software systems and/or databases are necessary to keep track of these relationships.

Case Study 16-5

Grappling with Customer Relationship Management System Implementation

As CRM systems became standard components of enterprises' architectures, stories emerged of multiyear CRM solution implementations that consumed millions of dollars but had not produced the promised business benefits. These reports were substantiated by an article in *Harvard Business Review* that was published in 2002, warning business managers of the dangers that awaited CRM solution implementations and providing prescriptions on how to minimize the risks.

Supported by market research statistics, the authors claimed that 55% of CRM projects at that time failed to produce results. According to the authors, one of the main reasons was that the executives sponsoring the CRM initiatives did not understand the actual concept of CRM. The executives believed that software tools alone could address all of the firms' CRM needs, and that these tools could do so independently from the firms' marketing strategy. Presumably, CRM system vendors' marketing efforts helped perpetuate this belief.

Another reason that the authors identified for CRM project failures was that executives did not understand the scale of the project delivery effort required. Budget and time expectations were grossly underestimated, leading to disappointment when overruns occurred. The number of organizational and business process changes that were required to use a CRM platform was also not fully appreciated. Because CRM involves front-line employees, customers, and management, many different people were affected. Accordingly, an effective change management program was necessary to build support and gain acceptance from all of the participants involved.

A common misconception is that CRM can be encapsulated in a product. In fact, it is more about corporate strategy, business processes, IT system integration, and changing employee mindsets. If CRM initiatives are not aligned with corporate strategy, or vice versa, CRM is unlikely to be successful. Likewise, changing employees' mentalities to be customer-oriented takes significant time and effort to achieve. In cases where service staff have been acting in a certain way for decades, it is unlikely that they will want or be able to change their behavior radically within months. For all that, technology is also a major contributor to failure in CRM initiatives.

Some of the technology challenges that companies encountered with enterprise CRM platforms helped give rise to cloud-based CRM platforms. The cloud-based Software as a Service (SaaS) model provides firms with another CRM implementation option that can greatly reduce the time and delivery risks associated with CRM platform deployment. The lower upfront costs of the SaaS provisioning model can also be used to help manage the expectations of management and users. Furthermore, individual departments can utilize SaaS CRM offerings without having to wait for purchasing decisions to be made at an enterprise or divisional level. Nevertheless, using an SaaS platform can limit the level of customization that is possible. However, some would argue that this limitation could actually be a benefit, since it is not uncommon for business users to ask for more customization than is really necessary, which can lead to higher costs and longer delivery timelines.

Sources: Rigby, Darrell K., Frederick F. Reichheld, and Phil Schefter, "Avoid the Four Perils of CRM," *Harvard Business Review* (February 2002): 101–109; "Universal Service?" *Economist*, April 20, 2006, http://www.economist.com/node/6838606.

16.5   PROCESS CONSIDERATIONS

Channels, CRM, and BI are relevant at all stages of the banking transaction lifecycle. While earlier sections focused on these activities in the context of front-office activities, such as engaging the customer and capturing orders, this section will examine them in the context of other stages of the transaction lifecycle such as design and setup, transaction fulfillment, transaction maintenance, and review (Figure 16-4).

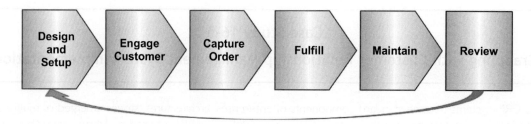

Figure 16-4 Transaction and services lifecycle model

During the design and setup stage, the channels used to deliver different products and services should be defined based on considerations such as customer convenience, delivery cost, channel effectiveness, and security. Decisions regarding which channels will be used should be largely driven by the BI information that is generated during the review stage of the process. Figure 16-5 illustrates what the channel-services delivery matrix might look like for a retail bank. In practice, however, the limitations that a silo-based architecture and lack of integration impose, as discussed in Section 16.4, may restrict the channels used to deliver specific services.

Besides defining which channels should be used to deliver services, business rules must also be defined and implemented within business processes to manage which channels are used by banks to deliver information to customers. These rules are, to a large extent, based on customer preferences, each channel's cost, and different channels' effectiveness in reaching customers. For example, if communications sent by email are as effective as communications sent by post and email is more cost effective, then a bank could encourage customers to switch to email notifications if it matched their usage preferences. Nevertheless, the effectiveness of channels may change over time and regulatory restrictions may, in some cases, determine which channels are used.

While channels and CRM are typically associated with front-office sales activities, they are also relevant to back-office functions such as transaction fulfillment and maintenance. Customer satisfaction is affected by financial institutions' ability to effectively manage exceptions, such as missing information that may be required to complete a transaction. Timely and streamlined communications regarding exceptions and other processing events can reduce transaction cycle times and improve operational efficiency. For example, if supporting documents that were required to process a customer's loan application were missing, email and SMS text messages could be sent to the customer asking him or her to provide the required documentation. This strategy would be faster than sending a letter, more cost effective than calling the customer, and much better than taking no action and waiting for the customer to call to find out why he or she had not yet received his or her credit card.

By measuring and analyzing the effectiveness of individual channels as part the review stage of the transaction lifecycle, it is possible to optimize a bank's contact strategy. Some of the ways to measure a channel's effectiveness are as follows:

- using surveys to gather information about customers' channel preferences;

- measuring phone call conversation duration and frequency;

- using promotional codes or unique identifiers to determine which channel marketing campaign information is received and acted upon;

- using web bugs, that is, objects that are embedded in emails to determine if the email message has been viewed; and

- tracking customers' access of web links embedded in email or SMS text messages.

Services	Branch	Internet			Phone			Post
		Web Site	Secure Web Email	Cust's Email	Contact Center	IVR	Mobile (SMS)	
Account opening								
Request application	✓	✓	✓	✓	✓	✓		✓
Submit application	✓							✓
Customer inquiries								
Account balances	✓	✓	✓		✓	✓	✓	✓
Transaction history	✓	✓	✓		✓	✓	✓	✓
Card min. payment due	✓	✓	✓		✓	✓	✓	✓
Card total credit limit	✓	✓	✓		✓	✓	✓	✓
Card available credit limit	✓	✓	✓		✓	✓	✓	✓
Card payment due date	✓	✓	✓	✓	✓	✓	✓	✓
Request statement	✓	✓	✓		✓			✓
Request to have an agent call		✓	✓	✓			✓	✓
Customer notifications								
Over card credit limit		✓			✓		✓	✓
Card payment due soon					✓		✓	
Card payment overdue		✓			✓		✓	✓
Card payment received					✓			
Transaction > $ amount occurred				✓	✓		✓	
Fraud alert		✓	✓	✓	✓		✓	✓
Card sent			✓	✓	✓		✓	
Account balances (periodic update)				✓			✓	
Avail. credit limit (periodic update)				✓			✓	
Change of cust account details			✓	✓			✓	✓
Card activation pending reminder				✓	✓		✓	✓
Account service requests								
Address change request	✓	✓			✓			✓
Name change request	✓				✓			✓
Credit limit increase request	✓				✓			✓
Credit limit decrease request	✓							✓
Close account request	✓				✓			✓
Report lost or stolen card	✓				✓			✓
Change I'net banking pwd. request		✓						✓
Issue new pwd. for forgotten request	✓				✓	✓		✓
Create or change card PIN						✓		

Figure 16-5 A channel services delivery matrix

Capturing this information and storing it in a data warehouse for BI use enable customer communication strategies to be fine-tuned. Communication improvement may be achieved across the entire customer base, within specific customer segments, or even for individual customers.

Channel feedback can also be used to improve the effectiveness of individual channels. For instance, the relative effectiveness of different marketing copy and graphic messages used to deliver information via the web, email, or post can be tested so that the most effective message form is used. Likewise, the skills of different CSRs can be compared so that customers can be connected to a CSR within a contact center or branch with the most relevant skills, as discussed in Case Study 16-3.

16.6 ARCHITECTURE CONSIDERATIONS

This section presents an architecture model for managing customer communications over multiple channels; briefly reviews data warehousing in the context of channels, CRM, and BI; and discusses how digital channels are used in the context of commercial banking.

16.6.1 Multichannel Delivery

To rationalize channel implementations that are tightly coupled to business functions, as described in Section 16.4, it is necessary to identify a target architecture that can serve as a better alternative. Figure 16-6 shows how a multichannel delivery architecture can be built on top of the information bus and process orchestration building blocks, which were discussed in Chapter 2. Within this architecture, the information bus provides a central and standardized means of connecting to back-end systems. The process orchestration layer manages and executes business rules that determine which channels will be used for different business functions. These rules may be related to specific business functions, for example, loan application submissions may not be available over the mobile phone channel. Alternatively, they may be linked to individual customer preferences; for example, Lisa prefers to receive transaction alerts via both email and SMS.

A key question with regard to Figure 16-6 is: "Where is the CRM system?" Practically, the CRM system may be involved in many different functions within the architecture. For example, it could be used as part of the branch and contact center channel interfaces that capture notes related to RMs' discussions with customers. Likewise, the CRM system might serve as or integrate with the common ODS so that customer information captured through automated channels would be available along with the information captured through people-based channels. Alternatively, it could be a standalone back-end IT system that is used as a repository for information collected from **business process management (BPM)** and business process orchestration systems that handle the bulk of both people-based and automated customer interactions.

One benefit of using a multichannel delivery platform is that channel-specific considerations can be decoupled from business logic. For example, the core retail-banking system could send a notification to the channel delivery layer that an ATM withdrawal transaction has occurred. The channel management layer could then determine the best ways to notify the customer, for instance, via email and SMS channels. The channel management layer would also determine how to present

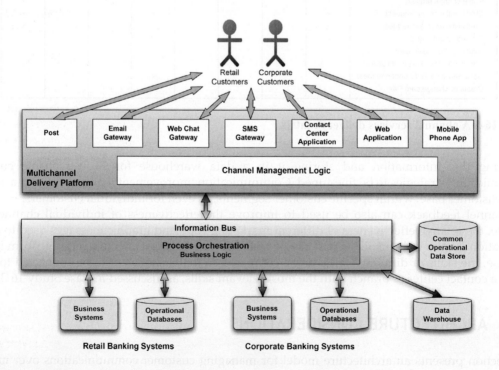

Figure 16-6 A multichannel delivery architecture

the alert information using those channels, and format the information accordingly. The emails may include detailed explanations and graphics, whereas the SMS messages would be terse, so as to keep within the 160-character limit.

Another benefit of using a multichannel delivery platform is that a channel delivery platform enables business applications to access different channels via common interfaces. Channel interface management logic and exception handling functions can be centralized and reused. Likewise, common channel-related business rules, such as the time at which different channels may be used, can be managed within the channel delivery platform, rather than being coded in business systems. For example, such rules may enforce government-mandated restrictions regarding the time of day that outbound phone calls may be made to customers. Alternatively, channel management rules may handle customer responses requesting to opt out of receiving messages in the future for email and SMS channels.

Moreover, as can be seen by comparing Figure 16-3 with Figure 16-6, using multichannel delivery capabilities helps simplify banks' system architectures. The addition of business units and new channels will be relatively painless. Alternatively, if silo-based channel architecture is used, for each addition, one of the existing silos must be retrofitted to handle new requirements or a new silo must be built. System maintenance also becomes easier when common functions are centralized and shared. Rules governing channel behavior can be cleanly separated from business logic, reducing the impact of changes to either area.

16.6.2 Data Warehousing

Data warehousing is integral to both CRM and BI—it aggregates, manages, and provides access to a financial institution's information assets. The data warehouse serves as the nexus for all customer information and provides the foundation upon which BI tools operate. Data warehouses differ from centralized ODS in that they are usually not updated in real time, nor do business systems access the data warehouse to support processing of customer transactions. Also, data warehouses will hold more data than an ODS. For operational support purposes, only a year or a few months of transaction information may be kept in an ODS, whereas a data warehouse may hold many years' worth of data to support BI activities.

Data warehouses provide users with a clean and consistent view of business information. Different business systems and operational databases may hold overlapping information and provide inconsistent views of that information, leading to confusion over which values are correct. In contrast, a data warehouse aggregates information from different systems and determines which data will be accepted as the master version. The data warehouse then provides this "single version of the truth" to downstream business applications. Furthermore, data cleansing is applied to information coming into the data warehouse to ensure that erroneous data does not get distributed and missing information is procured.

At a high level, data warehouse architectures consist of:

- **Data sources**. Information is received from different business systems, extracted from application databases, flat files, and application programming interfaces (APIs).

- **Extract, transform, load (ETL) tools**. Software tools provide connectivity to data sources to extract the information required by the data warehouse. Transformation facilities are also provided to map the raw source data into the structures and formats required by the data warehouse. Typically, ETL tools extract data on an end-of-day basis in batch mode.

- **Databases**. One or more databases may be used for preparation and staging of source data, aggregation of the information into a single data model, and construction of customized views ("data marts") for client applications of the data warehouse. The data warehouse's data model is usually domain specific, for example, designed for retail banking, and will be customized to address customer-specific needs.

- **User applications**. BI and other reporting tools access the information in the data warehouse. Operational data stores may also be consumers of information from the data warehouse, which makes it available to business applications for transaction fulfillment purposes.

More often than not, data warehouse implementation projects are major endeavors that take years to complete and cost millions of dollars. Acquiring or developing a data model that is comprehensive enough to handle the data from all the different source systems is a major concern. Another challenge is getting business users to be sufficiently involved during the requirements planning, implementation, and testing phases of the project. Users must validate that the information made available by the data warehouse will adequately support the needs of the business.

16.6.3 Digital Channel Integration

As discussed in Chapters 7 and 9, to facilitate cash management and payment transactions, commercial banks need to integrate with corporate customers' internal systems using digital channels. Unlike other types of channels, online banking channels are designed to implement **straight-through processing (STP)** that involves little, if any, human interaction. For instance, email can be used for communicating simple information to retail customers, such as credit card transaction notifications, but it is not a good digital channel for communicating with corporate customers. Email can be lost or corrupted, is not secure, and often requires human intervention to process. Hence, banks generally prefer to use more robust digital channels, including:

- website access (that is, Internet banking);

- file upload/download facilities; and

- direct host-to-host communications (that is, back-end system integration).

Ideally, a single corporate digital banking channel solution will support multiple lines of business, such as cash management, **remittances**, trade finance, and treasury services. However, this is not always the case. Different business divisions within the same bank may have built or purchased separate digital banking solutions at various times for various reasons. Using disparate solutions to support digital channel communications is inefficient to operate and maintain. Likewise, the inconsistencies and complexities introduced by using multiple systems can degrade customers' experiences. Thus, consolidation of digital channel implementations is an important goal for some financial institutions.

Security is paramount for corporate digital banking channels because of the high-value nature of corporate transactions and the connectivity between the customers' and the bank's systems. Second-factor authentication (discussed in more detail in Chapter 17), such as smart cards and password tokens, are commonly used to secure online banking sessions. Furthermore, digital channels often provide complex authorization schemes that enable customers to control which information and transactional facilities users are able to access over each channel. Solutions that implement corporate digital banking channels also need to produce access and usage reports for auditing purposes.

Besides providing secure connections, it is necessary for digital banking channels to support common electronic data interchange (EDI) standards and other proprietary formats. These standards facilitate sharing of information between the bank and different types of customer systems. Simple unstructured standards such as comma-delimited text files may be supported, along with more sophisticated standards, such as proprietary EDI formats used by enterprise resource planning (ERP) systems. Depending on the size of the bank, the size of the customer, and the nature of their relationship, the onus may be on the customer to adapt to the bank's communication channel standards, or vice versa.

Message transformation and process-orchestration platforms are commonly used to support connectivity and integration for corporate online banking solutions. Functions that these tools support are shown in Table 16-2. Off-the-shelf digital channel platforms provide support for a variety of

Table 16-2 Corporate electronic banking channel communication functions

Function	Usage	Examples
Connectivity	Extract or deliver transactional information directly from or to IT systems	• SFTP • SWIFTNet • SAP XI
Flow control	Manage information transfer scheduling, queuing, and recovery, in case of failures	• end-of-day transfers • periodic intraday transfers • resend entire file in case of broken connection • manage according to specific connectivity protocol standards
Transformation	Interpreting and formatting data contents for use in other systems' native formats	• CSV file parsing and generation • HTML or XML reports • mapping to and from FIXML, X11, EDIFACT, and/or TWIST formats
Security	Performing end-user authentication and encryption functions	• managing login and session information • encrypting files and communication streams • encryption key management
Monitoring	Tracking status of information transfers and generating alerts when exceptions occur	• communications dashboard • daily or monthly reports • email and SMS alerts on failure conditions

protocols and communication methods. For example, they can simultaneously support communication with one customer by transmitting simple comma-delimited files over the Internet using the secure file transfer protocol (SFTP), and with another customer using SWIFT's message format, protocol, and network.

16.7 SOLUTION CONSIDERATIONS: MOBILE BANKING

Of all the channels currently available, mobile devices provide financial institutions with the most potential for interacting with customers in new and innovative ways. At the same time, mobile technology is continuously developing and the ecosystem of participants is complex. Mobile technology advances every few years, sometimes every year, providing little time to implement solution strategies, achieve widespread customer adoption, and realize adequate returns on investment. Accordingly, banks have faced many complications when charting a course forward for their mobile-banking channel strategies. This section will examine the evolution, technology challenges, and opportunities of mobile banking technology solutions.

16.7.1 Historical Evolution

Many readers may not be aware of it, but browser-based mobile banking began in the early 2000s with solutions built upon the Wireless Application Protocol (WAP) and WAP browsers that ran as applications in mobile phones. This phase occurred prior to the introduction of modern smart phones with touch-screens. WAP-based banking services enabled customers to access their account information and perform rudimentary transactions. Unfortunately, WAP-based banking services were not user friendly and had other problems that ultimately led to their demise. Specifically, WAP connection times were slow and would often time-out user requests, and the screen-based interaction model of WAP was confusing and difficult to navigate. It did not help that relatively few phones had WAP connectivity and WAP-enabled browsers. Furthermore, mobile phone operators often tried to act as intermediaries for WAP services, controlling the sites that users accessed. Limiting the services available over WAP inhibited user uptake of the platform. Based on the failure of this technology, many banks were discouraged by their initial attempts to implement mobile banking.

After the failure of WAP, mobile banking shifted away from browser-based technologies toward text messaging, that is, SMS. Mobile text messages were used to trigger simple transactions, such as balance enquiries and account status alerts. As higher speed 3G networks became available and standard HTML-based browsers were supported on more handsets, many banks began to offer scaled-down versions of the Internet banking sites that were designed for small-screen mobile-phone access. Then, over time, as smart phones, tablet computers, and mobile applications gained in popularity, native mobile banking applications that are downloaded to and run on mobile devices have become commonplace.

The growth and evolution of mobile banking solutions vary by region. Mobile device usage patterns differ significantly among Asia, Europe, and North America, as does the ecosystem of financial institutions and other market participants. Hence, mobile banking solutions in countries such as Singapore and the United States evolved at different rates and went in different directions. On the one hand, Singapore has a concentrated population that is oriented toward mobile technology and has a small financial services and telecommunications industry. Likewise, Singapore's government is actively involved in developing and promoting the use of standards that help address some development and adoption challenges. On the other hand, the United States has a more geographically distributed and technologically diverse population and has thousands of banks that need to be accommodated and coordinated. Furthermore, the US government has very much taken a hands-off approach and provided little support or direction for banks' mobile banking technology strategy.

16.7.2 Mobile Banking Challenges

The plethora of mobile devices and rapid introduction and advance of software development platforms have made it challenging to implement mobile banking strategy. Device screen size is a limiting factor for the types of services that can be offered through mobile phones. However, the introduction of tablet computers and hybrid, notepad-sized mobile devices has greatly increased the possibilities. Also, many unknowns, such as user uptake of new technologies and the potential moves by competitors, further complicate the picture. Accordingly, mobile banking strategies must be fluid and reevaluated on a regular basis. If banks take a static approach, the solutions they implement could miss changing user preferences and, hence, produce only limited, short-term benefit. Worse yet, banks that adopt a wait-and-watch approach may never get started and be left completely behind.

Variability across mobile devices is perhaps the greatest challenge that mobile technology solutions face. Application features that work well on large screens may be impractical to implement on small screens. Also, certain hardware capabilities, such as near-field communications, may be accessible on some mobile devices, but not on others. As a result, web and mobile applications must be designed for and tested on different screen sizes, browsers, and operating systems, and then retested when operating systems and hardware are upgraded.

Transacting using mobile devices also introduces new security and operational concerns. So far, the malware protection and detection capabilities on mobile devices have significantly lagged behind what is available for desktop computers. It is important that this deficiency is addressed because as of 2016, 67 percent of consumers in the US who were not using mobile payments stated that concerns

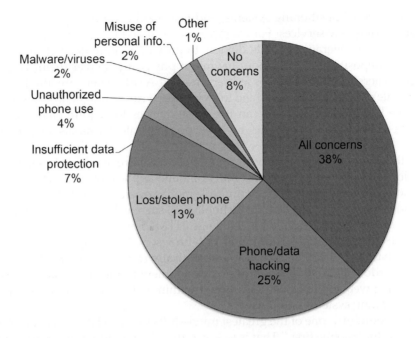

Figure 16-7 Consumers' security concerns related to mobile financial transactions

about security were a reason for not using that transaction method (Figure 16-7) [6]. Nevertheless, mobile banking has overtaken Internet banking in terms of customer usage in many countries. In turn, regulators have become more concerned about the potential risks of the services that banks provide on mobile platforms and how they can be mitigated.

It took banks many years to understand the many ways that fraud could be perpetrated after they began offering Internet banking services. A similar learning curve is likely with mobile banking services, particularly those that go beyond the existing services that Internet banking provides. Likewise, new operational complexities arise when different capabilities and functionalities are combined, such as when a mobile phone is used to perform point-of-sale credit card transactions. For instance, issues such as how credit card information is loaded into a phone, how it can be maintained and kept up to date, and what steps must be taken when a phone is lost or stolen all become new operational concerns. Furthermore, the responsibilities and legal liabilities of the various parties involved in facilitating and processing the transaction must also be clearly established and understood.

Moreover, the participants in the mobile banking ecosystem are, in many ways, misaligned. In many cases mobile phone manufacturers, operating system makers, telecommunication companies, and other intermediaries often put their own objectives and priorities ahead of those of consumers and other market participants. Case Study 9-1 highlights the complications that arise from a fragmented ecosystem in the context of mobile payments. Clearly, contactless credit and debit card payments using mobile phones are technologically feasible. Rather, it has been the lack of cooperation by market participants involved in the transactions that has held back the success of this mobile technology solution.

16.7.3 Mobile Banking Opportunities

For all their challenges and complications, mobile devices offer great potential for innovation. Their ability to integrate transactional and alert capabilities with other technologies, such as cameras, fingerprint scanners, global positioning systems, and near-field communication facilities, provides a ripe platform for offering new services. For example, as discussed in Chapter 7, financial institutions in the United States have leveraged mobile devices to provide remote deposit capture services that enable customers to deposit cheques without having to physically deliver them. This capability has helped reduce customers' need for services at branches and ATMs. There are also hardware add-ons that connect to mobile devices that enable them to swipe credit cards' magnetic strips and access cards' EMV chips. Mobile banking applications can use these devices to acquire credit card transactions, eliminating the need for small merchants to have point-of-sale terminals to process card-based transactions.

Historically, the wide variety of platforms and devices that are available has made it difficult for financial institutions to build web-based and native mobile applications. In many cases, technology solutions have had to be redesigned to run on multiple mobile operating systems and device types. The emergence and adoption of web application technologies, such as HTML5, Bootstrap, and Cordova, have gone a long way toward addressing this challenge. HTML5 provides capabilities for building rich, interactive interfaces for applications running in web browsers. Bootstrap provides a framework for designing browser-based applications that will automatically resize and adjust themselves according to the screen size. Cordova is a mobile application development framework that enables the front-end software from existing web applications to be reused within mobile applications and be deployed on multiple mobile operating systems and devices.

Perhaps most importantly, one of the greatest mind-shifts in financial services has been to develop technology solutions for "mobile first." That is to say, rather than building desktop solutions and then porting them to mobile devices as secondary activity, software applications should be designed from the start to work on mobile devices and then extended to better support desktop platforms. While this concept does not sound revolutionary in and of itself, it deviates significantly from decades of application design and development practices. But given the ever increasing usage of mobile devices and the innovation that is happening in that area, mobile first is a philosophy that financial institutions will need to adopt if they are going to claim their place in a mobile world.

16.8   SUMMARY

This chapter covered:

- the purpose and functions of channels, CRM, and BI;

- the opportunities and challenges that banks face with channels, CRM, and BI;

- how business processes underlie CRM's effectiveness;

- the concerns with silo-based channel implementations and architectural alternatives; and

- the challenges and complications involved with implementing mobile banking solutions.

The next chapter discusses cybersecurity in the context of financial institutions, and how controls and information technology can help address these concerns.

FURTHER READING

Books

Buttle, F., *Customer Relationship Management: Concepts and Technologies* (New York: Routledge, 2015).

Inmon, W. H., *Building the Data Warehouse* (Indiana: Wiley Publishing, 2005).

Knox, S., S. Maklan, A. Payne, J. Peppard, and L. Ryals, *Customer Relationship Management: Perspectives from the Marketplace* (Oxford: Butterworth-Heinemann, 2002).

Papers

Avery, J., Fournier, S., and Wittenbraker, J., "Unlock the Mysteries of Your Customer Relationships," *Harvard Business Review*, July–August 2014, https://hbr.org/2014/07/unlock-the-mysteries-of-your-customer-relationships.

Duran, R. E., L. Zhang, and T. Hayhurst, "Applying Soft Cluster Analysis Techniques to Customer Interaction Information," in *Marketing Intelligence Systems*, pp. 49–78 (Berlin: Springer-Verlag, 2010).

FDIC, "Brick-and-Mortar Banking Remains Prevalent in an Increasingly Virtual World," *FDIC Quarterly* 9, issue 1 (2015).

Maklan, S., S. Knox, and J. Peppard, "Why CRM Fails—And How to Fix It," *Sloan Management Review* (Summer 2011): 77–85.

Narayanan, L., "Data Warehousing and Analytics in Banking: Implementation," *Data Warehousing and Mining: Concepts, Methodologies, Tools, and Applications*, pp. 1825–1839 (Pennsylvania: IGI Global, 2008).

Peppard, J., "Customer Relationship Management (CRM) in Financial Services," *European Management Journal* 18 (2000): 312–327.

Pinedo, M., S. Seshadri, and J. G. Shanthikumar, "Call Centers in Financial Services: Strategies, Technologies, and Operations," in *Creating Value in Financial Services*, eds. E. L. Melnick, P. R. Nayyar, M. L. Pinedo, and S. Seshadri, pp. 357–388 (Massachusetts: Springer, 1999).

Rugimbana, R., "Generation Y: How Cultural Values Can Be Used to Predict Their Choice of Electronic Financial Services," *Journal of Financial Services Marketing* 11 (2007): 301–313.

Periodical

Journal of Financial Services Marketing

ENDNOTES

1. BSE Ltd., "Notices," http://www.bseindia.com/cirbrief/new_notice_detail.asp?noticeid={9FE8209F-9ADF-4A96-82C7-42F54751A90A}&noticeno=20120329-2&dt=3/29/2012&icount=2&totcount=6&flag=0.

2. Freed, D., "U.S. Banks Want to Cut Branches, but Customers Keep Coming," *Reuters*, August 22, 2016, http://www.reuters.com/article/us-usa-banks-branches-idUSKCN10X0D6.

3. Coltman, T., "Can Superior CRM Capabilities Improve Performance in Banking?" *Journal of Financial Services Marketing* 12 (2007): 102–114.

4. Kramer, A. E., "A Russian A.T.M. With an Ear for the Truth," *New York Times*, June 8, 2011, http://www.nytimes.com/2011/06/09/business/global/09atm.html?pagewanted=all.

5. Wixom, B. H. and H. J. Watson, "An Empirical Investigation of the Factors Affecting Data Warehousing Success," *MIS Quarterly* 25 (2001): 17–41.

6. Board of Governors of the Federal Reserve System, "Consumers and Mobile Financial Services 2016," March 2016.

— — —

7. Lohr, S., "In a New Web World, No Application Is an Island," *New York Times*, March 26, 2011, http://www.nytimes.com/2011/03/27/business/27unboxed.html.

8. Stellin, S., "Bank Will Allow Customers to Deposit Checks by iPhone," *New York Times*, August 10, 2009, http://www.nytimes.com/2009/08/10/technology/10check.html.

9. Pogue, D., "A Simple Swipe on a Phone, and You're Paid," *New York Times*, September 29, 2010, http://www.nytimes.com/2010/09/30/technology/personaltech/30pogue.html?pagewanted=all.

10. Ramsay, M. and P. Huntington, "Mildly Irritating: A WAP Usability Study," *Aslib Proceedings* 53 (2001): 141–258.

11. Kiili, K., "Evaluating WAP Usability: 'What Usability?'," Proceedings of the IEEE International Workshop on Wireless and Mobile Technologies in Education (WMTE'02) (2002): 169–170.

12. Dvorak, P. and S. Weinberg, "RIM, Carriers Fight over Digital Wallet," *Wall Street Journal*, March 18, 2011, http://online.wsj.com/article/SB10001424052748704360404576206412989185134.html.

13. Ho, V., "National Mobile Wallet Rolled Out," *Business Times*, August 4, 2012, http://www.businesstimes.com.sg/premium/top-stories/national-mobile-wallet-rolled-out.

14. Wisniewski, M., "Lessons from a Small Bank That Embraced Video Tellers," *American Banker*, July 24, 2014, http://www.americanbanker.com/issues/179_142/lessons-from-a-small-bank-that-embraced-video-tellers-1068985-1.html.

15. Browdie, B., "Why UMB Is Ramping Up Video Banking in Its Branches," *American Banker*, May 6, 2013, http://www.americanbanker.com/issues/178_87/why-umb-is-ramping-up-video-banking-in-its-branches-1058871-1.html.

16. Bhattarai, A., "Banks Turn to Video Tellers to Cut Costs," *Washington Post*, April 20, 2014, https://www.washingtonpost.com/business/capitalbusiness/banks-turn-to-video-tellers-to-cut-costs/2014/04/18/a7b28e7c-bb59-11e3-9a05-c739f29ccb08_story.html.

17. "The State of Social Media in Banking," American Bankers Association, 2017, http://www.aba.com/Products/Endorsed/Documents/ABASocialMedia_Report.pdf.

17 Cybersecurity

Liquid assets, such as cash and securities, are a prime target for theft. Because financial institutions hold large volumes of these assets, they must take extensive measures to protect and secure them. Both external and internal parties pose potential threats to financial institutions. External parties, such as bank robbers and computer hackers, may attack the IT systems of banks or their customers and inflict damage or steal money. Likewise, ill-intentioned customers may exploit failings in financial institutions' processes and IT systems to defraud them or perpetrate other crimes. Banks' employees may also take advantage of privileged access rights to circumvent controls and commit crimes against the institution or its customers. This last concern is, perhaps, the most critical since at least historically, the majority of thefts in banks involve insiders.

Over time, security mechanisms and control systems have been developed to address these threats. In ancient Egypt, locks were developed that could provide physical security for goods and valuables. In medieval times, records for financial transactions were made tamper-resistant by using split tally sticks. Tally sticks—pieces of wood with notches carved into them to represent amounts—were used to record debts and were then split down the middle lengthwise. Each party in the transaction would keep half of the tally stick so that when brought back together, the pieces of wood and notches cut into them would match, showing that the transaction record had not been altered. Double-entry bookkeeping became popular during the Renaissance period, and provided a systematic means of recording and verifying the accuracy of transaction information. Furthermore, functional **separation of duties** has been used as a means of preventing fraud, theft by insiders, and security breaches. Separation of duties can be found in many forms, including procedures that require "four eyes" (two pairs) and processes that are designed around "maker-checker" roles. For these controls to fail, both employees must either be corrupt or negligent.

The increasing use of information technology (IT) in financial services has had a far-reaching impact on security considerations, both positive and negative. IT has helped make it easier to monitor and track activities so that security-related exceptions can be detected quickly and acted upon when they occur. On the other hand, IT has exacerbated security concerns by increasing the number of entry points that must be guarded and removing the need for attackers to have physical access or close proximity to a bank's facilities. Additionally, IT has increased the overall complexity of the processes and systems that must be secured. Heightened complexity increases the likelihood of both design flaws and execution failures that can, in turn, lead to security weaknesses.

Over the past two decades cybersecurity has become a major concern for financial services and other industries (Case Study 17-1). Cyberattacks have become more frequent and increasingly clever in their design. Fraudsters, who seek monetary gain from compromising sensitive information or gaining access to online services, such as payment systems, are usually the perpetrators of cyberattacks. However, they may also come from foreign governments and terrorist organizations, whose motivations are oriented toward causing damage, as opposed to realizing financial gain. As cybercrime has increased, financial institutions' risk of financial loss from cybercrime and cost of cyberdefense have grown substantially. As of 2015, the cost to businesses from cyberattacks was estimated to be around $400 billion a year, and cybersecurity spending by financial institutions in the United States was expected to exceed $9 billion annually [1]. Of that, the top four banks in the United States spent around $1.5 billion on cybersecurity.

Within this book, security considerations for technology solutions have been touched upon in the context of architecture and payments in Chapters 3 and 9, respectively. Likewise, fraud is discussed in the context of operational risk in Chapter 19. In contrast, this chapter focuses on information security and cybersecurity as its central topic. First, it begins by reviewing some of the basic concepts that underlie information security. Second, common threats and attack vectors for cyberattacks are examined. Third, the importance of having a security framework and how it can be applied is presented. Fourth, considerations related to security operations are presented. Fifth, business opportunities and challenges related to information and cybersecurity are discussed. Sixth, information security considerations related to processes, architecture, and solutions are reviewed. Finally, the fallibility of security systems is considered. Note that the term *information security* pertains more to the protection of electronic data, whereas *cybersecurity* covers the protection of IT systems as well; however, the two terms will be used somewhat interchangeably within this chapter.

17.1 CONCEPTS

Authentication, authorization, confidentiality, nonrepudiation, and accountability are core security concepts. They are vital to both paper-based and electronic transactions, as well as manual and computerized processes. Table 17-1 provides a summary of these considerations and how they are implemented both manually and electronically.

It is important to understand that it is necessary for financial institutions to address all of these considerations to ensure security and prevent fraud. Front-end controls, such as authentication, must be complemented with back-end controls, such as monitoring and detection, so that limitations or failures

Case Study 17-1

The Never-ending Battle for Cybersecurity

While many things improve over time, financial institutions' Internet security does not seem to be one of those things. In 2011 and 2012, there was a spate of high-profile security breaches that affected financial firms, and in the United Kingdom, fraud hit a record high. After asset misappropriation, cybercrime was the second most common type of economic crime that financial services firms were facing. A large proportion of fraud cases involved misuse of the victims' private information, which in some cases also included taking over their accounts. Preventing criminals from accessing customers' personal and account information is a major concern across the financial services industry. Yet, there are regular reports of customer information being compromised by banks and related third parties. There have also been cases where the underlying mechanisms that support Internet security have been undermined.

In 2011, Citigroup disclosed that computer hackers had broken through the bank's network security and had stolen US$2.7 million from over 3,000 customer accounts. They also gained access to the names, accounts, and contact information of approximately 200,000 of its credit card customers. As a result, Citi had to replace the credit cards of more than 200,000 customers. While it is unlikely that the data loss would directly lead to fraudulent charges against all of these accounts, it did enable more effective social engineering attacks to be developed by hackers. Knowing the email address that customers use to receive email from the bank, along with other personal information, would help criminals pose as bank representatives. Using this false identity, they could then attempt to elicit additional personal information from customers that could be used to initiate fraudulent transactions. Later, in 2014, JPMorgan Chase's IT systems were hacked into, and customer name, address, telephone number and email address information of 76 million households was compromised. The breach affected nearly two-thirds of the households in the United States.

However, banks are not the only focus of attack for cybercriminals. In 2012, Visa and MasterCard warned their credit card holders that the systems of Global Payments, a third-party credit-card transaction processor, had been breached, and up to 1.5 million credit card numbers had potentially been stolen. Global Payments provided services to merchants, such as local retailers, collecting and forwarding credit and debit card purchase transaction information to Visa and MasterCard's payment networks.

Companies that help look after the Internet security infrastructure can also introduce vulnerabilities for cybercriminals to exploit. As a case in point, in 2011, hackers were able to break into the systems of an Internet security company, Comodo Group, which issued Secure Sockets Layer (SSL) certificates that guaranteed the authenticity of Internet websites to web browsers. Hackers were able to use Comodo's servers to create fake certificates for common websites, such as Google and Microsoft, enabling other parties to set up servers that could masquerade as those sites. The phony servers could fool web browsers into thinking that they were communicating with the actual companies' servers for secure transactions. While no financial institutions' certificates were affected, the case highlighted the vulnerabilities of the SSL certificate system that financial institutions depend on for online security.

A more significant crack in the security infrastructure that many financial institutions rely upon was created when the systems of authentication technology company RSA were breached by hackers. RSA provides hardware devices and software applications, also referred to as tokens, that generate one-time numeric passwords that many firms use to authenticate employees' access to internal systems. RSA tokens are also used to authenticate customers' access to Internet banking websites and to authorize online financial transactions. RSA, which had distributed close to 40 million tokens to more than 30,000 companies around the world, offered to replace its customers' tokens. However, substantial time and effort are required to manage and track the replacement of physical security tokens, making it a major undertaking for companies that have a large number of tokens deployed.

(Continued)

(Continued)

Beginning in 2013, criminals ramped up their efforts to use cyberattacks to steal money from banks' ATMs. Initially a bank in the Ukraine was targeted, and similar attacks hit banks in Taiwan and Thailand in 2016. In these cases, a cybercriminal gang remotely controlled the ATMs by hacking into bank IT systems and inserted payment cards with malware installed on them to make the ATMs repeatedly dispense cash. Human "mules" were used to collect the cash from the machines, often late at night, and deliver it to the criminal gang. The theft from the Thai bank amounted to a few hundred thousand dollars, whereas the Taiwanese bank suffered losses of $2.5 million.

In 2016, SWIFT, an international bank payment network, also became a channel for cybercrime. In a movie-like plot, cybercriminals stole $81 million from Bangladesh Bank, the country's central bank. The criminals hacked into the bank's network and then through surveillance were able to obtain the authentication credentials that the bank's employees used to access SWIFT. The perpetrators also were able to gain network access to the bank's SWIFT gateways, which enabled them to send fraudulent requests to the New York Federal Reserve Bank to transfer money to the cybercriminals' accounts. They attempted to steal $1 billion; however, the New York Fed rejected most of the transfer requests. Later it was determined that several other financial instructions, in different parts of the world, had also been the targets of similar cyberattacks, some of which had been successful.

Cyberattacks and data breaches are increasing as time goes on and will continue to result in significant losses for financial institutions and their customers. Likewise, security failures related to core technology infrastructure and third parties that banks depend on to provide their services, reduce consumers' confidence in the integrity of the overall financial system. Unfortunately, there are few signs that things will improve much going forward. When existing security vulnerabilities are fixed, new weaknesses are found and exploited by cybercriminals. Also, when new technologies are introduced and existing ones are updated, additional vulnerabilities are often introduced.

Sources: "Fraud Hits Record High in the UK," *Banking Technology,* March 9, 2012, http://www.bankingtech.com/bankingtech/article.do?articleid=20000221523; Steinert-Threlkeld, Tom, "Cyber Attacks Now 2nd Most Common Economic Crime," *Securities Technology Monitor,* March 27, 2012, http://www.securitiestechnologymonitor.com/news/cyber-attacks-economic-crime-big-30254-1.html; Richmond, Riva, "An Attack Sheds Light on Internet Security Holes," *New York Times,* April 6, 2011, http://www.nytimes.com/2011/04/07/technology/07hack.html; Schwartz, Nelson D. and Christopher Drew, "RSA Faces Angry Users After Breach," *New York Times,* June 7, 2011, http://www.nytimes.com/2011/06/08/business/08security.html?pagewanted=all; Palmer, Maija, "Breach Puts Pressure on Security Group RSA," *Financial Times,* June 7, 2011, http://www.ft.com/cms/s/2/2281463e-9132-11e0-9668-00144feab49a.html; Aspan, Maria and Narayanan Somasundaram, "Citi Says Hackers Access Bank Card Data," *Reuters,* June 10, 2011, http://www.reuters.com/article/2011/06/09/uk-citi-hacking-idUSLNE75800H20110609; Kapner, Suzanne and Justin Baer, "Hackers Took $2.7m in Citi Credit Cards Raid," *Financial Times,* June 25, 2011, http://www.ft.com/cms/s/0/fb87f304-9eb8-11e0-a4f1-00144feabdc0.html; Bullock, Nicole and Telis Demos, "MasterCard and Visa Warn of Data Breach," *Financial Times,* March 30, 2012, http://www.ft.com/cms/s/0/cf2c04a0-7a89-11e1-8ae6-00144feab49a.html; Braithwaite, Tom, "JPMorgan Cyber Attack Hits 76m Households," *Financial Times,* October 2, 2014, http://www.ft.com/intl/cms/s/0/961a31fa-4a7a-11e4-b8bc-00144feab7de.html#axzz3F5T1Pq9P; Sanger, David E. and Perlroth, Nicole, "Bank Hackers Steal Millions via Malware," *New York Times,* February 14, 2015, https://www.nytimes.com/2015/02/15/world/bank-hackers-steal-millions-via-malware.html; AFP, "Thai ATMs Hacked by Gang Linked to Taiwan Theft," *Channel News Asia,* August 24, 2016, http://www.channelnewsasia.com/news/asiapacific/thai-atms-hacked-by-gang/3070070.html; Burne, Katy, "Swift Finds Evidence of Second Malware Attack," *Wall Street Journal,* May 12, 2016, http://www.wsj.com/articles/swift-finds-evidence-of-second-malware-attack-1463102215.

Questions

1. For cases where it is not possible to prevent security breaches, what advance steps can financial institutions take to minimize the impact of incidents when they occur?
2. Why have authorities not cracked down on cybercriminals to eliminate or reduce the incidences of fraud?
3. Besides the direct costs of losses due to fraud, what are the indirect costs that financial institutions and their customers must bear?
4. What role should regulators play with respect to ensuring that online financial transactions are secure?

Table 17-1 Security concerns and management techniques

Security Concern	Description	Manual Techniques	Electronic Techniques
Authentication	Verifying the identity of customer and counterparties	Presentation of photo ID, passbook, security questions, signature	Username-password, PINs, digital certificates, PIN generation tokens
Authorization	Rights to perform specific functions or access information	Access lists, joint-signatory control rules, "permission to discuss"	Role-based permissions, access entitlement restrictions
Confidentiality	Restricting access to private or secret information	Need-to-know access controls, locked filing cabinets, opaque envelopes	Data encryption, data access restrictions
Non-repudiation	Ensuring customers or counterparties cannot refute transactions	Signatures and initialing, witnesses	Digital signatures, third-party verification
Accountability	Being able to determine what actions were taken by whom and at what time	Entry/exit log	Log files, database audit trails

in one area will be fortified by controls in other areas. The subsections that follow discuss each of these considerations. Later, Section 17.3.2 will discuss approaches for using technology to address them.

17.1.1 Authentication

Identity verification is critical for financial institutions, their customers, and other third parties involved in financial transactions. Financial firms must ensure that instructions they receive regarding customer accounts are genuine. Likewise, customers need to avoid divulging information that could enable others to falsely represent themselves as the customer. For example, customers who inadvertently use a fake automated teller machine (ATM) will likely end up revealing their card and PIN details to criminals. It behooves customers, therefore, to verify that the banking access points that they intend to use are authentic before using them.

The need for authentication has been around for centuries and is not specific to technology. Various approaches have been devised to manually authenticate individuals. Secret information such as passwords or less known details of the account holder is one means of authentication. Another is presentation of special credentials, such as a passport, driver's license, birth certificate, passbook, or special seal. Biometric methods such as signatures, fingerprints, and photo comparisons may also be used.

Unfortunately, all of these methods have their drawbacks. Secret information may be unintentionally leaked. Credentials may be copied or forged. Biometric methods, which are often imprecise, may be fooled by close resemblances. Hence, multiple authentication methods are often used in parallel to reduce the risk of fraud. Likewise, multiple authentication checks may occur at different stages of processes to help increase the chance of preventing illicit access.

17.1.2 Authorization

Once the identity of an individual is confirmed, it is necessary to determine what activities they are entitled to perform and what information they may access. For instance, retail account holders may authorize relatives to access information about their account. Employees will also have various levels of authorization, and access to information and transactional capabilities are often segregated between operational units. For instance, front-office employees should not be allowed to modify information maintained in the back office. Only very few trusted employees may be allowed to modify the authorization rules.

A number of mechanisms have been developed to manage authorization; access control lists and access matrices are two commonly used methods. Access control lists (ACLs) are descriptions of which users can perform what functions for a given entity. For example, the **general ledger (GL)** access control list might include three entries in its ACL as shown in Table 17-2. ACLs are flexible, but in complex cases, the current access state may be difficult to ascertain.

Alternatively, access matrices use the vertical axis to represent users and the horizontal axis to represent functions. Access matrices are simpler in design, but may become inefficient for managing large combinations of permissions. Table 17-3 shows how the GL permissions from the previous example would be managed using an access matrix. The principle of role-based access is generally applied for both ACLs and access matrices. Entitlements are defined for roles rather than individuals. Individuals are then associated with specific roles.

The complexity and effort associated with implementing and administering authorization controls should not be underestimated. First, each system must have inbuilt access restriction facilities, and the controls provided by various systems are likely to be different. Some may have coarse levels of control, whereas others may have finer-grained levels of restriction. Furthermore, designing, setting up, managing, maintaining, and reporting access rights are important but uninspiring tasks. A seemingly trivial mistake due to carelessness can introduce a major vulnerability. For example, forgetting to revoke permissions when an employee leaves the firm can provide criminals with an attack vector.

A common practice to help maintain data integrity is to designate a **system of record** for specific types of information. Downstream systems should receive their information from a system of record, not other sources of the same information, to ensure that the information they use is complete and correct. For example, the core banking system is often designated as the system of record for current and savings account transactions. Thus, to maintain data integrity, a bank's Internet banking channel should retrieve customer account balance and other transactional information from the core banking system, and not from its **data warehouse**. The access control implemented for other systems that

Table 17-2 An access control list

Entry	Role	Entitlement
1	Accounting Manager	Create Journal Entries
2	Accounting Manager	View Profit and Loss
3	Product Controller	View Profit and Loss
…	…	…

Table 17-3 An access matrix

Role	Create Journal Entries	Modify Journal Entries	View Profit and Loss
Accounting Manager	Yes	No	Yes
Product Controller	No	No	Yes

maintain the same information, such as data warehouses, may have fewer controls, allowing it to be modified locally, whereas the tighter access and change restrictions will be in place for systems of record. Generally, audit and data verification processes will also be used to help verify the integrity of the information stored in designated systems of record.

17.1.3 Confidentiality

Ensuring data privacy is a core aspect of information security. Although access control is one means of helping ensure confidentiality, it is also necessary to have other measures in place. Additional protection measures, such as encrypting information, are used to protect information, especially when it is transferred outside the bounds of a bank's secure network environment (Case Study 17-2). Likewise, encrypting information within a secure network environment provides another layer of protection from external actors who are able to break through the perimeter defenses of a bank's network, as well as threats from insiders who already have access to the internal network. This *defense in depth* approach is discussed further in section 17.8.1.

For many years, national governments have had systems in place for classifying and managing sensitive information, as leakage of certain information could clearly undermine a country's political or military standing. In contrast, most financial institutions' management of confidential information is not as rigorous. As concerns about privacy and confidentiality have grown, there is increased need for financial institutions to implement more comprehensive and proven models for managing sensitive information.

Central to managing privacy is determining what information is sensitive and the severity of loss should the information be divulged. In this regard, financial institutions must not only be concerned

---

Case Study 17-2

How Process Failures Can Compromise Customer Information

In 2008, Bank of New York Mellon admitted that it had lost a box of backup tapes in transit. This loss could potentially lead to the disclosure of personal information, including names, addresses, birth dates, and Social Security numbers, of up to 12.5 million of its customers. Besides generating negative publicity, this failing led the Connecticut state government to pursue legal action against the bank so as to make the bank compensate for its mistakes.

While the loss of the tapes was the trigger for this fiasco, the secondary, and perhaps more significant, cause was that the information on the tapes was not encrypted. Had the tapes been encrypted, the probability of the information being compromised would have been much lower. At the time of the incident, the need for encrypting backups was a well-understood industry best practice. Presumably, there was a failure in either the design or execution of the bank's processes.

This problem is in no way unique. Over the past decade, scores of banks, merchants, and other companies have reported customer data loss. In some cases, negligence was attributed as the factor, whereas in others, security breaches were blamed. Starting in 2002, most states in the United States began passing laws that required companies to notify consumers if their personal information is compromised. These laws have helped provide incentives for companies to ensure that their security practices are robust. Previously, it would have been easier to downplay the seriousness of such privacy breaches and allow substandard practices to persist.

Source: Stempel, Jonathan, "Bank of NY Mellon Data Breach Now Affects 12.5 Million," *Reuters*, August 8, 2008, http://www.reuters.com/ar ticle/2008/08/28/us-bankofnymellon-breach-idUSN2834717120080828.

about information that they maintain about themselves, but also information about customers, and sensitive information that is shared with partners. What is considered confidential information and how it should be treated has changed over time. Fifty years ago, it was of little concern that bank employees had access to customers' account numbers. Today, a common best practice is to limit most employees' access to only the last four digits.

17.1.4 Nonrepudiation

Repudiation is a concern related to contracts and transactions performed between the financial institution and its customers and with other financial firms. A transaction is repudiated when one party refutes the validity of their participation in the agreement. For instance, a common technique that supports nonrepudiation is the use of written signatures. However, written signatures can be forged or copied and, therefore, having the signature witnessed by a third party may also be required to reduce the chances of repudiation.

Transaction confirmation procedures are another way of reducing the chance of loss as a result of repudiation. In this case, the strategy is to make the counterparty responsible for validating any confirmations received prior to **settlement**. Subsequently, it will be difficult for either party to dispute the authenticity of the transaction. Alternatively, both parties might be required to lodge a copy of the transaction with one or more neutral third parties, who can then vouch for the legitimacy of the transaction.

Where the burden of proof lies for proving the authenticity of transactions will depend on the legal jurisdiction within which they are performed. Hence, it is critical that process and systems designers understand what is required to prove the authenticity of a transaction, in case of a legal claim. For example, Regulation E in the United States clearly places the responsibility of proving the authenticity of electronic transactions on banks. In the United Kingdom, historically, this responsibility was placed on customers, which seems contradictory since customers must use the banks' systems to perform transactions.

17.1.5 Accountability

Audit trails, a key means of enforcing accountability, are essential for supporting investigation of and forensics for cybersecurity events. They enable cybersecurity personnel to determine what happened, when it happened, and who was involved. This information is also crucial for validating the integrity of IT systems that have been involved in a cyberattack or may have been otherwise compromised. For example, an audit trail is used in software applications, such as accounting systems, to determine what changes were made to financial records. Similarly, operations executed as privileged user on a computer's operating system should be logged to be able to determine how those actions may have compromised the security of the system or used to carry out attacks on other systems. Ideally, audit trails should be implemented in a way so that they can only be added to and existing records cannot be changed, and in fact, some security standards require this mechanism to be implemented.

17.2   COMMON THREATS AND ATTACK VECTORS

In decades past, physical security was the primary security concern for banks. Cash notes, negotiable securities, and customer information were held and transported in physical form. In this context, criminals' main strategies were theft, robbery, and fraud. Today, digital assets have largely supplanted the physical ones. Theft, fraud, and extortion all can be perpetrated electronically now, without the need to have access to a bank's physical premises. Hence, the most common threats to financial institutions are logical security breaches—where cybercriminals are able to circumvent banks' access control restrictions and other protections for their IT systems—as opposed to physical security breaches. As with physical security, the greater the number of digital access points—e.g., websites, email severs, vendor connections, and externally accessible application programming interfaces—an institution has, the greater the attack surface there is for cybercriminals to try to exploit.

This section reviews some of the more common cybersecurity-related threats that financial institutions face and the typical attack vectors that cybercriminals use to compromise financial institutions' information security. While these are discussed independently, keep in mind that in many cases they are used in combination.

17.2.1 Malware Attacks

Malware, i.e., malicious software, can be broadly defined as software that is used to damage or gain access to computer systems. There are many types of malware that are used for different purposes. Some common types, which are often installed by computer viruses or worms, include:

- **Keyloggers and spyware**—that capture and exfiltrate details of users' keystrokes, mouse movements, and screen information.

- **Backdoors**—that provide a means for cybercriminals to access the computer remotely, typically to locate and exfiltrate data stored on and accessible to compromised devices and/ or serve as a launching pad for attacks on other computers.

- **Command and control/botnets**—that coerce compromised computers to participate in activities as directed by cybercriminals, e.g., being part of a distributed denial of service attack.

- **Password dumpers**—that locate and exfiltrate password-related information.

Besides the applications described above, malware may also disable controls and protective mechanisms on a computer and subvert the web applications that are accessed through infected web browsers. In some cases, the malware's purpose may be purely malicious, with the objective of deleting information and disabling systems.

Malware is delivered through multiple attack vectors including installation by users, clicking on email attachments, website "drive-by" attacks, remote installation, and installation by other malware. Users may inadvertently download and install "Trojan" malware by being tricked into thinking it is legitimate software. Email attachments may contain files, such as documents, that are designed to exploit vulnerabilities in the software that displays those files, allowing the malware to execute operating system-level commands on the affected system. Websites may intentionally or inadvertently be hosting malware that exploits vulnerabilities in web browsers when the websites are visited, allowing the malware to execute operating system-level commands on the affected system. Hackers that are able to access the operating system of a computer can then transfer and install malware on it. Likewise, some malware is designed to be a launching pad for downloading and installing other types of malware.

One type of malware that has gained popularity with cybercriminals in recent years is ransomware. After infecting a computer system, ransomware's *modus operandi* is to encrypt the system's data files and prevent user access on the system until a ransom amount is paid.* Typically, the ransom is paid via a digital currency such as bitcoin. In many cases, payment of the ransom may restore access, but there is no guarantee that access will be restored if the ransom demand is met. To date, ransomware has been one of the few means for cybercriminals to easily monetize malware, as it can be targeted at both individuals and businesses. The main defenses against ransomware are prevention of malware infections and maintaining up-to-date and well-protected backups.

---

* Unfortunately, digital currencies, such as bitcoin, were likely a catalyst and have been an enabler for ransomeware schemes. They provide a means for cybercriminals to collect ransom demands remotely, quickly, irrevocably, and with a high degree of anonymity.

17.2.2 Social Engineering Attacks

Social engineering attacks aim to mislead the victim into doing something that they would not normally do, thereby compromising their own security or someone else's security. In a nontechnical context, social engineering attacks are often aimed at contact centers, where a perpetrator will try to convince a contact center agent that he is a customer so that he or she can elicit nonpublic information about the customer or their account. Alternatively, the perpetrator may pose as a customer to try to take over the account by changing the contact information, such as the mailing address, email, and phone number, and then request a replacement debit or credit card be issued and sent to the new address.

Another common social engineering attack is for either a website, malware, or a phone call to mislead a user into thinking that his or her computer is infected with malware. The user is then told that he or she needs to download and install antimalware software from the Internet to fix the problem. In fact, the user's computer is not infected, and the software downloaded is actually malware.

Email **phishing**—where a message that directly includes or has a link to malicious content is sent with the objective of tricking the recipient into disclosing their private information or compromising their information security—has been a popular channel for social engineering attacks against companies and individuals.* In some cases, the aim has been to trick finance and payment staff into transferring money to the perpetrator. A cybercriminal will send an email on the pretext that a senior executive has requested that an electronic payment be made urgently and outside of the normal payment process. This approach has been successful in a number of cases. Alternatively, cybercriminals may send email that is made to look like it is coming from a legitimate external business, such as the customer's bank, prompting them to click on a website link. The website that is associated with the link is typically made to look like the business' website and will either try to trick users into logging in to the site, so as to capture their login credentials, or to have them divulge other confidential information, such as their identification and account numbers.

Most phishing attacks are targeted to have mass appeal. For example, a common phishing attack that has been used is to send users an email saying that they are about to exceed their email storage quota, and providing a link for them to "log in" to the system to increase their quota. In fact, the login page they are sent to is designed to capture their login credentials. On the other hand, *spear phishing* attacks are designed to appeal to a specific group or an individual that are high value targets. For example, an email advertising an information security conference might be sent to system administrators with a link to website providing fake information, which hosts malware designed to infect their workstations.

As illustrated by this last example, phishing is often used to trick the email recipients into infecting their computers with malware. Malware may be delivered as email attachments that, when opened, install and run themselves on the user's account. In some cases, just previewing the phishing email in an email application can compromise the receiver's system by exploiting vulnerabilities in software applications and/or the operating system. Alternatively, email may contain links to sites that host malware. In many cases the web address for the malware sites may be slightly misspelled names of legitimate sites, e.g., "wwwmybank.com" instead of "www.mybank.com", making it difficult for the email recipient to notice the difference. Likewise, the website that the phishing email links to may be a mockup copy of a legitimate website.

17.2.3 Hacking Attacks

Computer hacking may be done for financial gain, espionage, political reasons, or purely for malicious purposes. The cyberattack on the central bank of Bangladesh, discussed in Case Study 17-1, is an example of where cybercriminals hacked into the bank's systems for financial gain. Typically hackers will exploit vulnerabilities in external systems, such as web servers or network devices, to gain access to internal computer systems. More recently, hackers have been using spear phishing attacks to deliver

---

* While the discussion here focuses on email phishing, phishing attacks are also delivered through text messages on mobile phones as well.

malware that compromises internal systems. Once they are on the internal network, they will seek to compromise other systems to gain access to critical assets. Hackers often leverage malware, sometimes delivered through phishing campaigns, to create a backdoor entry point into an institution's network. The malware will create an outbound connection over a standard network protocol, such as HTTP or DNS, from the network to the cybercriminals' servers, generally via a *reverse shell*, creating a virtual tunnel that they can use to access the network.

Network firewalls, discussed in Chapter 5, limit what connections can come in from external networks. However, they generally allow outbound connections that use standard network protocols from the internal network to external networks. Hence, by using malware to create an outbound connection, cybercriminals are able to circumvent the firewall defenses. The primary strategy for addressing this threat is to closely monitor outbound network connections and look for anomalous behavior. For example, an Australian bank might detect an unexpected outbound connection to a server in Eastern Europe, and in response, isolate the internal computer that is making that connection from the network and scan it for malware and other signs of compromise.

17.2.4 Denial-of-service Attacks

Denial-of-service (DoS) attacks are designed to disable online services provided by banks and other institutions. Typically, they are achieved by flooding a system that is connected to the Internet with requests or other network traffic to overload the affected system and impede its availability to process legitimate requests. For example, a cybercriminal could send a large number of webpage requests in a short period of time to a web server so as to heavily load it and slow it down, possibly to the point that other requests to it are caused to time out. Alternatively, a DoS attack might make a large number of requests to specific pages on the web server that involves a complex database query, so that the database that the web application uses gets overloaded. Another DoS strategy would be to saturate a website's network connection to the Internet with network traffic so that few, if any, legitimate requests can be received. DoS attacks may also take aim at overloading an institution's domain network service (DNS).

It is difficult for any single computer to generate sufficient request traffic to overload banks' servers and networks. Likewise, when a single or a few computers participate in a DoS attack, banks can defend themselves by using their network firewalls to block the network traffic from the attacking computer or have their Internet service provider block the traffic. Cybercriminals typically use distributed denial-of-service (DDoS) attacks to get around these defenses. In the case of a DDoS attack, the attack emanates from many different computers on the Internet. This enables a greater volume of requests and/or network traffic to be generated and also makes it more difficult to block the network traffic from all of the different sources, which may number in the thousands or tens of thousands. The main defense in this case is for a bank to route all of its Internet traffic to its website through a firm that has specialized technology that can filter out the attack traffic and only route legitimate traffic back to the bank.

To effect DDoS attacks, cybercriminals typically instruct computers that have been infected with command and control malware to participate in the attack. As a group, these computers are referred to as a *botnet*. More recently, botnets have also included networked devices, such as video surveillance cameras, where cybercriminals were able to exploit software vulnerabilities in those devices to commandeer them. Historically, DDoS attacks were driven primarily by malicious intent, rather than financial gain. However, it is becoming more common for DDoS threats and demonstrations of capability to be made in conjunction with ransom demands.

17.2.5 Exploitable Vulnerabilities

Most of the threats and attack vectors discussed in this subsection rely on exploiting security vulnerabilities in software applications, web browsers, operating systems, and firmware that run on a variety of devices including workstations, servers, network routers, printers, mobile devices, and network appliances. As of the second quarter of 2016, web browsers were the most commonly exploited application (48%), followed by the Android mobile operating system (24%), Microsoft Office (14%), Java (7%), Adobe Flash Player (6%) and Adobe Reader (1%) [2]. Besides applications, vulnerabilities are commonly found in operating system components and communication protocols. For example, in 2014 the "shellshock" vulnerability was discovered in the Bash command shell, which was included in most Linux operating system distributions, and allowed attackers to remotely execute commands on those systems. Likewise, in 2017, the "Eternal Champion" vulnerability was exposed in the network protocol used to provide shared access to files in older versions of the Windows operating system. A cybercriminal could use the exploit to remotely execute commands on computers that were running a susceptible version of the operating system.

There are a number of ways that vulnerabilities may be identified. Typically security researchers will discover new vulnerabilities, and high risk ones will usually be disclosed by security industry news sources and security-related industry associations. Threat intelligence feeds also provide information about new vulnerabilities. Banks must analyze this information to determine if they are relevant to the IT systems and applications that are in use. External and internal vulnerability network scans, using specialized software that has up-to-date information about what vulnerabilities are potentially exploitable, can also be used to identify what vulnerabilities exist in a bank's IT environment. For software that is developed in-house, code reviews that are focused on information security best practices and software designed to scan web applications can be used to identify security weaknesses. For example, *cross-site scripting* is a common vulnerability that occurs in web applications that can easily be identified using scanning software and fixed before the applications are deployed.

The likelihood of exploitation is a key factor for determining the priority of vulnerabilities' mitigations. Vulnerabilities in externally facing systems have the greatest likelihood of exploitation because potentially anyone from anywhere in the world can try to exploit them over the Internet. Conversely, internal systems, which are protected from external threats by network firewalls, are less likely to be exploited. In general, the more protected a computer is on internal networks, e.g., if it is behind several network firewalls, the lower the risk that the vulnerability it has will be accessible and exploitable.

The potential impact of the vulnerability is another key factor that affects mitigation priority. For example, an operating system vulnerability that enables a hacker to gain privileged, i.e., system administrator, access would be considered to be of critical severity. Privileged access would enable a criminal to access all of the information on that computer system and possibly others, to install malware, and use the system as a springboard for attacking other computers on the network. In contrast, a vulnerability in a printer's software may only allow hackers to disable the printing services, which is clearly a much lower severity concern.

Vulnerabilities can be mitigated through several different means. In most cases, there are security-related software updates, i.e., patches, that can be applied to eliminate the risk of compromise. Regular patching, as discussed in Chapter 5, is the key defense against the exploitation of software vulnerabilities. Another mitigation approach is to disable or block the vulnerable component on a computer using a network firewall. This approach is practical when an application or service running on a computer that has the vulnerability is not actively used or required, or when there is no patch available to protect against the vulnerability. In some cases, the severity and likelihood of a vulnerability being exploited may be determined to be sufficiently low such that the effort to mitigate it is not worthwhile. Likewise, in some cases, the risk of exploitation may have to be accepted, with the primary mitigation being to closely monitor for signs of exploitation with rapid response to minimize the impact.

17.3   CYBERSECURITY FRAMEWORK

It is vital that financial institutions frame their activities using a cybersecurity framework. It provides a standard way for thinking about and communicating cybersecurity risk and mitigation approaches.

A cybersecurity framework provides a well-defined structure for assessing existing capabilities, identifying target states, and prioritizing actions that will improve an institution's security posture and reduce its cybersecurity risk. Two commonly used cybersecurity frameworks are ISO 27001 and the US National Institute of Standards and Technology (NIST) Cybersecurity Framework. The top-level activities of the NIST framework are shown in Figure 17-1 [3]. This section will review the NIST framework and discuss a few of its elements in more detail.

17.3.1 Identification

Cybersecurity requires identification of the potential risks to relevant assets—such as data, IT systems, and operational processes—so that they can be analyzed and so their mitigations can be prioritized. The starting point for identifying risks is being aware of all the things that are potentially at risk. Thus, asset management, i.e., creating and keeping up to date a register of all the assets that need to be protected, is essential. While this may sound elementary, in practice, asset management can be a major challenge. It requires the tracking of the current state of every networked device, the software that is installed and running on those devices, the information stored on those devices, and who has access to those devices. Likewise, this information must be kept up to date with every software patch, application upgrade, new application installation, and new user onboarding. In small companies, it is manageable to track this information by hand, but in more sizable operations, automated tools are required to maintain up-to-date information about IT assets and avoid excessive manual effort.

Once it is clear what assets need to be protected, a risk assessment and management plan can be developed. There are thousands of potential transaction and information risks; however, the resources to counter them are limited by available time and budgets. Hence, it is important to ensure that resources are applied most effectively. Security resources should be focused on the intersection between potential threats, known vulnerabilities, and vital resources, as shown in Figure 17-2. This subset of risks can then be evaluated, and resources allocated to minimize them based on their relative likelihood, potential damage, and cost to mitigate. Methodical and objective analysis is necessary to avoid flaws in human perception that can easily bias judgments and lead to suboptimal allocation of resources.

Wishful thinking, attention anomalies, social biases, and poor assessment of probabilities are all well-documented ways in which people's cognitive biases can unduly influence their perception of risk. For example, wishful thinking leads people to play the lottery, even though rationally it is a poor choice for allocating money given the expected return. Similarly, people are often more worried about the threats that have materialized most recently or have been publicized lately, even when it has a lower probability of occurring than many other threats. As a case in point, after reading news about an accident related to air travel, often people are more concerned about dying in a plane crash than in an automobile accident, even though the latter is much more likely to occur.

To help avoid these risk analysis biases and failings, formal risk assessment methodologies should be utilized. Standards such as AS/NZS 4360:2004 and its successor ISO 31000:2009 provide structured and objective methods for evaluating and treating risks, including those related to security. Risk assessment and management approaches typically follow a process similar to the one shown in Figure 17-3.

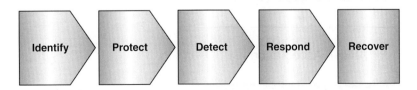

Figure 17-1 A cybersecurity framework

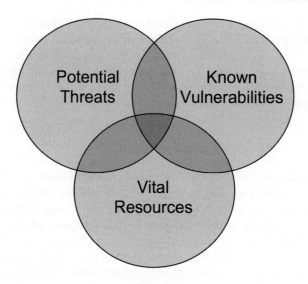

Figure 17-2 The critical focus areas for applying security resources

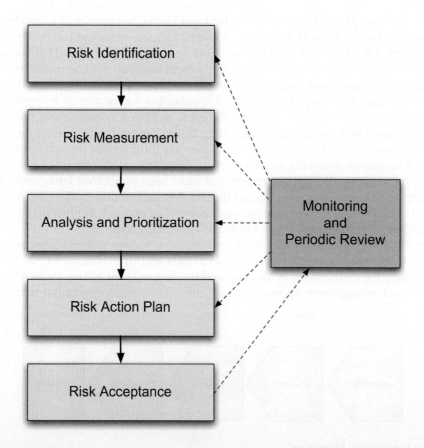

Figure 17-3 Risk assessment and management steps

Security risk analysis efforts will typically generate a list of potential risks and their overall severity rating, which is based on their likelihood and potential impact, as discussed in the context of security vulnerabilities in Section 17.2. The risks can then be categorized by their severity, as shown in Table 17-4. Mitigation steps can then be analyzed for the top risks that have been identified, and the cost of mitigation can be estimated. Based on these factors, a cost-benefit estimate can be produced, as shown in Table 17-5. Based on the risk severity assessment and cost-benefit analysis, informed decisions can be made about how best to allocate available budget and resources to address security concerns.

Typically, only the more severe risks that are identified will be carried forward for mitigation analysis, due to limited resources. Likewise, only some of those risks for which mitigation steps and costs are determined will actually be treated. Hence, a subset of the risks will need to be accepted; most likely, those risks that are less severe or are very costly to mitigate will fall in this category. There will also be some risks that cannot be treated; these fall into the category of residual risks.

The risk review process is not static; monitoring and regular reassessment is necessary. The likelihood or impact of risks that were acceptable at one point in time may change, requiring reevaluation and potential mitigation steps to be taken. New risks may arise due to organizational, environmental, and technological changes. Furthermore, the risks across the entire supply chain, including vendors, must be considered. For example, if a bank relies upon an external payment processor or cloud service provider, the risks associated with that vendor must also be considered as part of the bank's risk assessment.

17.3.2 Protection

Protective security measures aim to prevent security incidents by implementing safeguards for critical infrastructure and data. Where prevention is not possible, protective measures will be designed to limit the impact of security events. The processes and procedures related to information security

Table 17-4 Example of an assessment of potential risks

ID	Source	Consequences/Risk	Likelihood	Risk Rating
1	a. User passwords unchanged for over one year	IT security procedures are not being implemented as intended	4 LIKELY	16 VERY HIGH
	b. User accounts unnecessarily accessible on external web server	4 MAJOR		

Table 17-5 Example of a risk-mitigation evaluation

ID	Risk	Risk Treatment and Action Plan	Remediation Cost	Cost Effectiveness
1	IT security procedures are not being implemented as defined	a. Have division managers verify procedure and policy implementation details relevant to their business area on a quarterly basis and send report to group security b. Perform annual audits of (a) by group security	a. 20 labor days @ US$500/day = US$10,000 per annum b. 3 labor days @ US$500/day = US$1,500 per annum	HIGH Benefit/Cost

are the starting point for protection. Undocumented and/or inconsistent setup and management of computers, networks, and software is a common way in which vulnerabilities, which can be exploited by cybercriminals, are introduced to IT environments. Likewise, well-designed processes for reviewing and investigating security-related events are essential to ensure that potential threats that are detected are acted upon swiftly and effectively.

Access control, both physical and logical, is a fundamental mechanism for protecting information assets and IT systems. Physical access controls cover both computers and networks and are typically implemented by having these resources under lock and key. For instance, a bank's servers are typically only accessible physically in the bank's data center, which is a separate locked room, where only a small number of staff have the key to enter. Logical access controls include software-based mechanisms that provide capabilities that support authentication, authorization, and accountability. A software application that uses login credentials to control user access to information and services is an example of logical access control. Another example of how logical access control can be implemented is where networks are designed so that critical data assets are segregated on specific network segments that have very tight firewalls restrictions and limited user access.

There are a number of technologies that can be employed to help protect information and IT systems. Table 17-6 lists common technologies that are leveraged to support information security. Some, such as encryption algorithms, facilitate data security. Others, such as security information and event management systems, support detection and response. Chapter 5 discusses some of these

Table 17-6 Protective technologies for information security

Technology	Purpose	Description	Examples
Public key infrastructure	Authentication	Facilities to support the generation and management of public and private keys, and authentication of keys	Digital certificates, certificate authority, Pretty Good Privacy (PGP), GNU Privacy Guard (GPG)
Encryption algorithms	Data security/ confidentiality	Tools for converting plaintext information into cipher text and vice versa.	AES, Triple DES, RSA
Digital signatures	Nonrepudiation, authentication, data security	A means of generating and verifying a digital code that is used to demonstrate the authenticity of a block of information	Full domain hash, RSA-PSS, DSA
Intrusion prevention system (IPS)	Detection, protection	Monitors network traffic and alerts and/or blocks potentially malicious traffic	Next-generation firewalls (e.g., Palo Alto Networks, Cisco ASA, FireEye)
Intrusion detection system (IDS)	Detection	Monitors networks, systems, and/ or files for signs of unauthorized access	Security Onion, Snort, OSSEC, Tripwire
Security information and event management systems (SIEMS)	Detection	Aggregates and analyzes information from IPS, IDS, endpoint protection, and log files	OSSIM, Splunk, LogRhythm
Vulnerability scanners	Protection, validation	Scan for known vulnerabilities in networks, applications, websites, databases, and/or source code	Nessus, Fortify, Nikto2, Burp Suite

components in the context of technology infrastructure, and detailed information about some of these tools can be found in the Further Reading section at the end of this chapter.

Proper maintenance of hardware and software is a key means of preventing information security incidents. As mentioned throughout this chapter, patching of systems and keeping operating systems up to date are paramount for minimizing security vulnerabilities. Furthermore, the use of end-of-life components—i.e., those that are no longer supported by the vendor and, thus, are not provided with security patch updates—should be avoided at all costs. Of course, this is easier said than done, and Chapter 5 discusses some of the challenges with keeping software and hardware components current.

Moreover, the human element of security should not be overlooked when it comes to prevention. As discussed in Section 17.2.2, social engineering attacks are a common cyberthreat for banks and other institutions. Increasing awareness and ongoing education on concerns related to cybersecurity for both employees and customers can help address this weakness. For example, educating customers on how phishing scams work can help them be more cautious with regard to what appears to be email sent from their bank or another trusted entity. Likewise, simulated phishing exercises that send test phishing messages to employees to check their reaction, can be effective in sensitizing them to think twice before clicking on an attachment or link in an email.

In most cases, it is not practical to expect to avert all security threats. Thus, limiting the impact of security events and preventing significant damage are key objectives. For example, even with antivirus software in place, it is almost inevitable that a user's workstation will become infected with malware at some point in time. This is because antivirus software can defend against some, but not all forms of malware. Hence, swift detection and treatment of the infection serve as a secondary form of protection.

17.3.3 Detection

Prevention and management of security risks are vital, but use of detection mechanisms is also necessary to help minimize the damage in case of cybersecurity events. In many cases, detection can take place while security exceptions are in progress, that is, while the attack is ongoing. For example, real-time monitoring can help detect fraudulent credit card transactions. This monitoring usually relies on statistical analysis techniques to assess the likelihood that an in-process purchase is fraudulent and, accordingly, approve or decline the transaction. Intrusion prevention and detection systems are also usually relied upon for real-time detection.

Alternatively, in many cases, real-time monitoring and detection may not be possible, and post-transaction checks are performed. For instance, it may not be practical to verify the integrity of every transaction for high-volume, manual, paper-based transactions. Hence, periodic auditing is often used to monitor this type of activity. Statistical sampling is used to select a subset of the transactions for validation. Likewise, software system limitations may also limit the ability to monitor in real time. In such cases, end-of-day, weekly, or monthly reports may be generated to identify potential fraud and security breaches. However, timely detection is important, since, as shown in Figure 17-4, the estimated cost of security breaches in enterprises goes up substantially the longer it takes to discover them [4].

In the context of cyberattacks, operations staff will monitor for evidence of any various stages of incursion: entry, lateral movement, harvesting, and exfiltration. Entry will be typically indicated by the operation within the IT environment of malware that provides hackers with a platform to support the latter stages of activity. Lateral movement will be evidenced by the spread of the attack to multiple systems in the IT environment. Harvesting may be revealed by surreptitious activity involving data sources where information is being illicitly collected. Exfiltration will involve hackers extracting information out of the bank's environment.

Detection involves monitoring for unexpected events and anomalies (Case Study 17-3). Many false positives are often found and, thus, it is important to tune detection algorithms to minimize these cases. Otherwise, a substantial investment of time will be spent investigating cases that are not actually relevant. Investigating potential security events can be time consuming because it requires aggregating and comparing information from multiple sources—such as network monitors, antimalware software, and

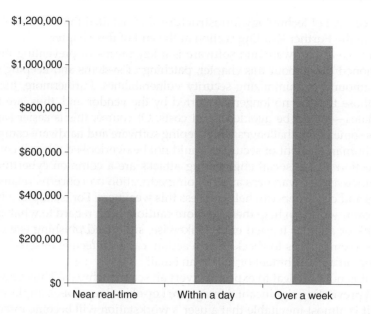

Figure 17-4 The estimated cost of recovering from a security breach versus how quickly it was discovered

system logs—to determine what actually happened. Security information and event management systems can greatly reduce the effort involved with these investigations by automating the data aggregation and providing analytical tools to help correlate and compare the information.

17.3.4 Response

Minor security events, such as malware infecting a user's workstation and the follow-up effort to clean up the workstation, may often be treated as business as usual if the risk and impact are negligible. Likewise, probes and attempted attacks on servers directly connected to the Internet are commonplace and are not usually considered to be of concern in and of themselves. On the other hand, where there is evidence of widespread infection, compromise of key data assets, evidence of data exfiltration, or other significant concerns, a cybersecurity incident may be declared and a formal response effort begun. One of the main goals of the response effort is to minimize the impact of the incident.

The response effort should begin long before any security incident occurs by going through an incident response planning exercise. As part of that exercise, an incident response plan will be developed and then followed when a security incident does occur. Part of this plan will identify which situations qualify as security "incidents" and, thus, require the plan be implemented. It may also provide guidelines for how incidents should be investigated and documented along with the roles and responsibilities of the individuals involved. The process for containing or eradicating threats should be outlined along with the steps for recovery if damage is incurred. The incident response plan should also include a communication strategy that is consistent with legal regulatory requirements and defines the information that should be communicated to specific parties and when it should be communicated. Relevant parties may include senior management and the board of directors, customers, law enforcement authorities, regulatory authorities, and the press. It is often the case that legal guidance will be used in conjunction with communication externally.

Given the myriad of situations that could lead to a security incident, incident response plans typically provide high-level guidance. That is to say, it is impractical to try to provide very specific guidance for each and every potential situation. Hence, situation-specific analysis and reaction will also be required during the actual response effort to address the specifics of the situation. For example, if the security incident was a distributed DoS attack, the high-level guidance within an incident

---

Case Study 17-3
The Importance of Having Effective Detection Capabilities

To prevent fraud by both insiders as well as external parties, it is important to have mechanisms to detect security breaches and control system irregularities. A fraud case that occurred in New Zealand highlights these considerations.

In this case, a bank manager created accounts for friends and relatives without their permission or knowledge, and then secured loans against each of the accounts. The addresses for the accounts were set up to be post office boxes that were kept by the perpetrator so that he could intercept any bank correspondence related to the accounts. Over NZ$400,000 was siphoned off over a 20-year period. The fraud was finally detected when the loan accounts became so large that the manager's interventions showed up in regional-level reports as exceptions.

One approach that has been mandated by some regulators to help prevent and detect such frauds is to institute mandatory "block leave" for certain categories of bank employees—ten consecutive working days of vacation without contact with any bank staff. The motivation behind this is that constant presence is required to contain the details of a fraud. This requirement will undoubtedly help detect and reduce the instances of some types of fraud. Even so, one can only assume that other types of fraud, which can survive a two-week absence, have found their way into practice.

There is no substitute for effective detection capabilities. While the fraud in this case may have been difficult to prevent entirely due to the managerial position of the perpetrator, it should have been detected much sooner. For example, the frequent shifting of money between accounts as the only source of revenue to pay off loan payments would be a clear indication that a Ponzi-like scheme was in progress. This type of analysis, however, requires that information from different paper-based sources and computer systems is aggregated and available for review.

Source: Isaac, Peter, "Inside Job," Chartered Accountant Journal (Institute of Chartered Accountants of New Zealand) (November 2009): 64.

---

response plan might be to email all customers to make them aware of a problem with the Internet banking website and suggest that they use voice or branch channels instead to access information and services. If a DDoS attack were to also affect other communication channels, that guidance will need to be adapted to fit the circumstances.

An incident response plan should also identify what information needs to be captured and documented to provide record of the incident and the response activities. Likewise, once the incident is over, a *post-mortem* review should be performed to identify lessons learned from the incident response and improvements that can be made going forward. This, in turn, will often lead to revision and enhancement of the incident response plan. The plan should also be reviewed and updated on a periodic basis to take into account changes in the industry and technology trends.

17.3.5 Recovery

Recovery involves planning for and implementing steps to restore services to normal operation that were compromised as a result of a cybersecurity incident. Recovery planning should consider how IT systems could be potentially impaired by a cyberattack and what steps would be required to restore those systems. For example, if malware deleted the data and software on a database server, the recovery plan would likely involve reinstalling the operating system and software applications on that server, restoring the data from backups, testing the integrity of the new server implementation, and reintroducing it back into service.

17.4 SECURITY OPERATIONS

IT operations and administration are critical for ensuring the integrity of an institution's cybersecurity. A robust information security architecture and protection tools will provide limited benefit if they are not managed effectively. Generally, security administration involves the following activities:

- controlling access to information and system functions;

- managing signature records and digital certificates;

- investigating incidents;

- identifying new potential cybersecurity-related threats and staying abreast of technology changes;

- ensuring that procedures and policies are enforced in all locations;

- updating and adapting security procedures and policies where necessary;

- performing security-related audits and reviews; and

- providing information security training.

As discussed in Chapter 5, a number of different components are used to monitor and manage information security. Antimalware software is installed and updated to provide endpoint protection on workstations and servers. Intrusion detection systems are used to monitor network traffic and identify anomalous behavior, such as the creation of unexpected connections to internal or external servers. Firewalls and intrusion prevention systems are used to block potentially harmful network traffic. Data loss prevention software is used to detect and stop any sensitive information, such as customer account information, from being inadvertently divulged using communication channels, such as email, or being intentionally exfiltrated using external media, such as a USB drive. Security information event monitors are used to aggregate security-related information from all of these and other systems, analyze the data, and trigger alerts on suspicious events. A bank's security operations staff must monitor and manage all of these components on a continuous basis. They must also assess the potential security implications of changes made to the hardware, software, and network environment. Adding a new component or upgrading an existing one could introduce new vulnerabilities. Likewise, configuration changes that are made to software applications and supporting infrastructure components, such as application servers, can also introduce security weaknesses.

Besides performing their operational roles, it is also beneficial for security administrators to participate in the design and implementation of systems. Design reviews can identify potential flaws that can lead to security vulnerabilities before deployment. Likewise, reviewing the test plan can ensure that potential attack vectors are covered as part of the user or operational acceptance testing. Further checks can be performed when a process or system is deployed to ensure that test modes or accounts that were enabled for testing are not carried over into the production environment.

Ultimately, those responsible for security and system administration, along with the most senior business managers, must have the highest level of integrity and trust. It is in the organization's best interest to make this group as small as possible and to monitor them closely. Finding staff who are well versed in information security is another major challenge for financial institutions and other organizations. The cybersecurity domain is both broad and deep, and it changes on a daily basis.

17.5 BUSINESS OPPORTUNITIES

With all the challenges and risks that are involved with cybersecurity, it may be hard to imagine business opportunities related to this area. In fact, the nature of financial institutions' trusted relationship with their customers and focus on security puts them in a unique position to offer special types of "secure" services. Likewise, they may be able to attract customers by marketing themselves as being safer than competitors. As discussed in Chapter 20, trust by customers is one of the advantages that banks maintain over their Fintech competitors.

An opportunity that financial institutions can take advantage of is their access to information about fraud patterns. It is common practice for banks to monitor credit card and other payment accounts for suspicious activity that might lead to fraud. The focus of these activities is usually to prevent fraud-related losses. However, these same techniques could also be applied as a service that is provided to merchants and corporate customers. For example, a bank could offer the option of sending businesses real-time alerts related to exceptional payments that are detected, that is, ones paid to new parties, for large amounts, or that correspond to suspicious patterns.

Banks are in a unique position for offering such services because they already have some of the necessary tools in place and also have access to a wide range of data to draw upon for reference. Whereas a customer only has access to its transaction history, its bank has access to all its customers' transaction histories. Once understood, a new fraud pattern that is observed on one customer's account can be monitored for on other customers' accounts.

17.6 BUSINESS CHALLENGES

Unfortunately, when it comes to cybersecurity and control systems, there are more challenges than opportunities. As previously mentioned, one key challenge is assessing the scale and scope of potential losses so as to determine what costs should be borne to prevent them. Likewise, because of the variety of threats and the diversity of operating environments, there is no standard recipe for implementing security that can be repeated with the assurance that it will be fully effective whenever and wherever it is used.

Shared security responsibility has become a major concern over the past several decades due to the rapid increase in interconnectivity and dependencies between banks, payment network providers, merchants, and customers. When financial firms improved their cybersecurity capabilities, criminals shifted their focus to target merchants and customers instead, so as to attack banks indirectly. Phishing scams targeted at end customers and breaches of merchants' systems can compromise the integrity of entry points used to access banks' systems, i.e., web browsers and point of sale systems. In response to these threats, financial firms have taken different approaches. In some situations, banks' have tried to shift the burden of liability onto other parties. In other cases, institutions have implemented additional security measures, such as second-factor authentication (2FA) and additional verification/confirmation checks.

The organizational evolution of financial firms has also created new security challenges. Distributed project teams and globally distributed operations have increased accessibility, thereby broadening the potential avenues of attack. Outsourcing practices have also made the security of financial institutions more dependent on their outsourcing partners' personnel and systems. With the increased use of technology-enabled mobile phones for digital communication, mobile devices have also become an attack vector. While much of the concern regarding security has focused on smart phones that are connected to the Internet, lower end mobile phones are susceptible to attack from short message service (SMS) messages.

In financial services, a good business idea can be undercut by potential security concerns, making it impractical to implement. Lateral thinking, experience, and good knowledge of history may serve high-level assessment of security risks better than detailed technical or business skills. The nature of most security breaches and frauds has not changed significantly over time; instead, they have found new instantiations. For instance, Ponzi schemes have been in existence for centuries and are well understood. Yet, they persist and continue to appear in new forms and flavors. Likewise, cyberattacks that disrupt the flow of secondary secondary services, such as information distribution, can also affect primary services, as highlighted by Case Study 17-4.

Case Study 17-4
Security Threats to Stock Exchanges

Security concerns related to Internet banking fraud tend to get the most press coverage; however, all types of financial institutions must be concerned about hacking attacks. For example, in 2011, an Internet-based attack brought down the Hong Kong Stock Exchange's (HKEx) website. While the attack did not affect the exchange's core matching or clearing and settlement systems, it did disrupt the delivery of market disclosure-related announcements by Hong Kong-listed companies, which were distributed via the HKEx's website. More importantly, the attack came prior to interim financial result announcements by the HKEx and several other companies. The disruption caused the exchange to suspend the share trading of seven companies, including one of its flagship listings, HSBC.

 Distributed denial of service (DDoS) attacks, such as the one suffered by the HKEx, are a common type of Internet hacking attack. They are difficult to defend against because they emanate from thousands of different computers that have been taken over by hackers. One approach to counter the attack is to decentralize the distribution of information so that there is not a single failure point that can be targeted. In the case of the HKEx, the company announcement information could be provided to several third-party news distribution services in parallel with its posting on the website. This strategy helps ensure that the information will be available to market participants even if the exchange's website was not accessible, eliminating the need to suspend trading.

Source: Cookson, Robert, "Hong Kong Exchange Hit by Hackers," *Financial Times*, August 10, 2011, http://www.ft.com/cms/s/0/f448a9b6-c33a-11e0-9109-00144feabdc0.html.

 Moreover, in many cases, business users, executives, and board members within financial institutions struggle to understand information security and cybersecurity risks, because of cyberthreats' often complex technical nature. As a result, management may become overly focused on the cybersecurity threat that has been publicized most recently by the media or by vendors, and not appreciate the relative importance compared with other security concerns. Hence, it is behooves financial institutions' senior management and boards to become educated on and briefed regularly about the specific cybersecurity risks that the institution faces and how the risks are being managed. Likewise, financial institutions' boards can benefit from having a technology expert who is knowledgeable in cybersecurity as a director or as an advisor to the board to help ensure that it provides adequate and well-directed oversight of cybersecurity.

17.7   PROCESS CONSIDERATIONS

The identification and modeling of security threats go hand in hand with the risk analysis process described in Section 17.3.1. Security threats must first be identified before they are prioritized, and prioritization will then determine the threats to be evaluated in depth. Contrary to standard business process analysis, which focuses on planned users and tasks, process analysis for security purposes must focus on the unexpected.

 When designing internal controls, a structured methodology should be used to ensure that security concerns throughout the entire end-to-end process, including related processes, are addressed. Security weaknesses may occur across functional or process boundaries. Hence, it is important to ensure that the methodology used addresses both intraprocess and cross-process security concerns. Two analysis approaches discussed in this section are misuse cases [5] and mal-activity diagrams [6]. These approaches provide graphical representation of security risks, which helps stakeholders visualize these concerns.

Misuse cases are based on the use case requirements specification methodology that was introduced in Chapter 4. Misuse cases provide extensions to use case diagrams and templates to capture the intended actions of "misusers"—those who intentionally or inadvertently bypass expected system or process usage. Misusers can be used to model the behavior of malicious users who seek to exploit security vulnerabilities. Figure 17-5 shows an example of a misuse case diagram. Misusers and their actions are represented in conjunction with normal usage actions, but are represented using an inverse color scheme, white on black.

Misuse cases can help identify threats and also analyze risks. They also provide a mechanism to support evaluation of security requirements at an early stage of the development process. Weaknesses of misuse cases are that they are not designed to represent extended sequences of actions or situations where there is no immediate actor. For example, a series of complex interactions, involving multiple external parties that are required to obtain and present falsified credentials, may not be readily described by misuse cases.

Mal-activity diagrams follow a strategy similar to misuse cases, but are based on unified modeling language (UML) activity diagrams rather than use cases. Mal-activity diagrams include extensions that represent malicious activities, actors, and decisions. As with misuse case diagrams, all of these extensions are shown using an inverse color scheme. This approach can also be used with diagrams based on business process modeling notation (BPMN), which was covered in Chapter 2. Whereas misuse cases are better oriented toward describing misuse of system functions, mal-activity diagrams are better suited for describing how malicious activities can be implemented across various roles and stages of a business process, crossing system boundaries. Mal-sequence diagrams provide yet another way for analyzing and explaining how malicious users can compromise communication message flows.

Besides finding weaknesses in existing system and business process definitions, it is also necessary to explicitly consider and specify security requirements. Too often, security is dealt with at a superficial level during the requirements and design process. As a result, major security concerns may be identified during testing or, worse, during or after deployment. The cost of reengineering the system to support security requirements after development has begun can be enormous. Hence, extensions to UML and BPMN have been proposed to help support the inclusion of nonfunctional, security-related requirements [7, 8].

An important reason for using tools, such as use cases and BPMN diagrams, to elucidate security requirements is to help communicate them to people who are not security experts. Due to the complex nature of vulnerabilities and attacks, security is very much a multidisciplinary effort. Many of those

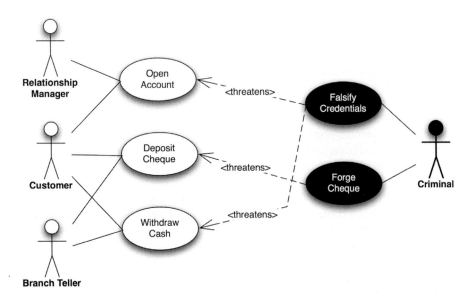

Figure 17-5 Example of a misuse case diagram

who should be involved with planning and evaluating security designs, such as software developers, system administrators, and operations staff, often do not have a security background. Using complex, formal, mathematics-based notations is, therefore, not practical; it may be more practical to adapt existing tools that those participants are familiar with to support end-to-end analysis.

17.8   ARCHITECTURE CONSIDERATIONS

This section examines two architecture considerations related to cybersecurity: layered security and managing security trade-offs.

17.8.1 Layered Security

It is critical that the architecture design is robust and resilient to one or more failures of security mechanisms. Layering is an architecture pattern that is commonly applied to achieve this goal, and in the context of information security, it is referred to as *defense in depth*. Multiple security layers ensure that no single point of failure will compromise security. Multiple different types of security barriers make attacks on solution security more difficult and less cost effective for perpetrators. A physical example of layered security is where a valuable item is locked in a combination lock safe that is kept in a room with ten-inch-thick concrete walls, a door that has a deadbolt key lock and electronic card magnetic lock, and a security guard posted outside. Extensive skills and effort will be required to break through the multiple security layers.

An example of layered security in the software development context is the multiple validation checks that can be performed to prevent SQL injection attacks, as discussed in Case 17-5. From an

---

Case Study 17-5

SQL Injection Attacks

In 2008, information relating to 130 million credit and debit card customers was stolen from multiple retailers' payment systems by hackers. The hackers used an SQL injection attack to extract information directly from the merchants' databases. The stolen information could potentially be used to facilitate fraudulent transactions that affect customers, merchants, and banks.

When executing an SQL injection attack, the hacker sends instructions directly to the database via an external interface, such as a data field that is entered on a website. If the application software that processes the input data does not validate that the input is "clean" in advance of passing it to the database, it is possible that commands embedded in the field input values may be executed by the database, potentially returning unauthorized information or modifying stored information.

SQL injection attacks and buffer overflow attacks have been well known and understood for decades. In the case of buffer overflow attacks, the design of modern programming languages has largely helped address this concern. For SQL injection attacks, performing validations at any of the various stages of the application processing can prevent the attack from being successful. Unfortunately, poor education, design, and testing practices have allowed and may continue to allow SQL injection attack vulnerabilities to persist indefinitely. As of 2017, SQL injection attacks were still the second most common means for hackers to breach the security of web applications.

Source: "US Man 'Stole 130m Card Numbers,'" *BBC News*, August 18, 2009, http://news.bbc.co.uk/2/hi/8206305.stm; "2017 Data Breach Investigations Report," *Verizon*, http://www.verizonenterprise.com/verizon-insights-lab/dbir/2017/.

architecture-design standpoint, the presentation layer could prevent punctuation symbols that are used in the syntax of injection commands being entered by users. The business layer might do syntactic checking to ensure that the inputs were well formed and did not contain SQL commands. The data layer should be designed to use stored procedures or compiled queries, instead of interpreting SQL commands. Even if one of the validation points failed or was removed, the others in place would prevent attacks from succeeding.

In the networking context, layered security can be implemented through the use of multiple firewalls to protect critical information assets. Perimeter firewalls could be used to protect outward facing web servers from unnecessary and unwanted network traffic coming from the Internet. Another set of firewalls could then be used to only allow network traffic from the bank's web servers to come further into the bank's network to communicate with application servers. Additional firewalls could be used to segregate corporate network traffic, such as that used for email and shared file access, from production business applications, such as Internet banking. Lastly, firewalls with very tight access restrictions could be used to protect the production system databases, only allowing traffic from the application servers and from a few select database administrators to reach the database servers. This example highlights that "flat" networks, where all components are able to communicate with one another, are not secure networks; network segmentation using firewalls helps contain security breaches and limit the damage they cause.

17.8.2 Security Trade-offs

An important architecture design trade-off related to security is that the more secure a system is, the less usable it becomes. There is a half-joke, half-truth that the most secure system is a locked room with no network and to which no one has access. The point is that such a system would be unusable and, hence, have little value, other than being secure. This extreme example is a good illustration of the trade-offs related to security.

Usually, for every benefit that security confers, there is a cost that is paid elsewhere. Adept security managers in banks understand this and work with technology designers and business users to find an appropriate balance. On the other hand, less effective security managers will focus more on defining what should and should not be done, ignoring the business impact and cost implications.

Another trade-off that must be considered is that the more complex a solution is, the greater the security risk it will present. Increasing the number of functions, interfaces, or process flow paths expands the scope for flaws that can be exploited. Complexity also makes business and system administration more difficult, which can lead to operational security failures. Complex solutions are also problematic to maintain by nature of difficulty in understanding their function or implementation. Misunderstandings of the solution design can also potentially undermine security. The effect of changes made may not be fully understood, resulting in modifications that unintentionally compromise security.

Decisions regarding trade-offs can be readily seen in different types of solution implementations. As discussed in Chapter 9, it is common for EMV chips to be embedded in credit cards. When making credit card purchases, the cardholder is required to enter a PIN, which is securely stored on the smart card, into a card reader to complete the transaction. This security design helps prevent stolen cards from being used because the thief would not know the PIN. This approach, while providing benefits, also has costs. Specifically, each card issued must have a smart card embedded in it and points of sale must have smart card readers with PIN keypads that customers are able to access when making a purchase.

Second factor authentication (2FA) is another example to consider. Whereas login-password authentication has a number of weaknesses associated with it, the security principle of 2FA helps improve security for online transactions. There are a number of design approaches for 2FA, such as security tokens, PINs sent to mobile phones via SMS*, and mobile phone PIN-generating applications.

---

* In 2016, the National Institute of Standards and Technology (NIST) began advising against the use of SMS messages for 2FA because they can be intercepted on the mobile telecommunications network or by malware that has infected a mobile device.

Each of these designs has implementation, administration, and maintenance costs. While improving security, 2FA is not foolproof. Man-in-the-middle attacks* can circumvent the security provided by PINs generated by simple, one-click tokens by reusing the PIN to authenticate additional transactions during the time window that the PIN is valid. In some cases, financial institutions may provide customers with more expensive PIN-generating tokens that have enhanced capabilities to improve security. Tokens with a numeric keyboard can generate unique PIN codes to verify transactions using a challenge-response model. For instance, when verifying an online transaction, a bank would present the customer with a numeric code that must be entered into the token, and the token would then provide a numeric response that is passed back to the bank for verification. Each challenge and response will be unique and cannot be replayed for subsequent transactions as part of a man-in-the-middle attack. Nevertheless, security based on challenge-response tokens is not foolproof and has also been undermined [9]. It is also more complicated and cumbersome for customers to use.

While some countries require the use of 2FA for financial transactions, others do not. Presumably, the cost-benefit trade-offs are judged differently in these cases. There is often signficant cost involved with deploying and managing security tokens. Likewise, there may be other mitigations against the financial risks, such as having rapid fraud detection and response capabilities.

17.9 SOLUTION CONSIDERATIONS

In the early days of computing, security architecture was relatively simple because the entire computing environment was hosted on the mainframe. Solutions could be designed largely based on the needs of operating systems' inbuilt security and audit facilities. Today, however, we live in a world of heterogeneous hardware systems, operating systems, and applications. These changes have required a number of security considerations to be addressed at the architecture level.

It is critical that information security and control requirements are clearly identified and understood at the outset of a project and incorporated into the architecture design. If this objective is not met, security concerns will most likely be uncovered during testing or deployment. Reworking designs after they have been implemented is a costly and time-consuming undertaking. Furthermore, the reworked design may end up being an overly complex, suboptimal hack of the existing design, rather than a robust design that could have been produced from the start, if security-related requirements had been fully considered.

There are a number of standard design practices that software applications should implement to mitigate cybersecurity risks. A few of the more common ones are listed in Table 17-7.

Table 17-7 Application design information security best practices

Best practice	Benefit
Store cryptograph hashes of passwords instead of the encrypted password value	Prevents passwords from being divulged if stored password data is compromised
Add a random value, referred to as "salt," to passwords before they are hashed	Makes it more difficult to apply a dictionary attack against hashed password values to determine the original passwords from the hashed values
Implement a timed lockout after multiple login attempt failures	Counters brute force attacks by stopping or slowing down the rate of repeated attempts

* In man-in-the-middle attacks, the fraudster intercepts communications and misrepresents itself to the customer as being the financial institution and to the institution as being the customer.

Best practice	Benefit
Validate and sanitize user inputs	Prevents injection attacks
Maintain log files of system activity	Supports cybersecurity event investigation and response
Enforce size limitations for data copied into memory buffers	Avoids memory buffer overflow attacks
Only transmit password credentials through encrypted communication sessions	Prevents network sniffers from capturing user login credentials
Require strong passwords	Hinders guessing of passwords and brute-force attacks by cybercriminals

Besides these, there are many other documented security standards that solution developers can benefit from. For instance, the Open Web Application Security Project (OWASP) provides guidance and tools for implementing secure web applications, including an analysis of the top ten critical web application security risks [10].

Security requirements are not static. Technology and business environments change continuously, making the maintenance of secure environments a significant challenge. Some of the major changes affect financial institutions' business and operational environments and, in turn, their security needs, which are summarized as follows:

- **White labeling**—helps by enabling other providers' systems and infrastructure to be leveraged, but provides exposure to additional security risks, both technical and operational, that are largely beyond the banks' control.

- **Outsourcing/offshoring**—can provide more flexible resourcing options and a lower cost base for resources, but exposes financial institutions to new personnel and system environment risks. The financial institution may become dependent on the security provided by the service provider.

- **New channels**—new ways of reaching customers become available on an ongoing basis. Social networking sites and mobile communications are two examples of relatively new channels that provide significant business opportunities. However, they are relatively immature with regard to cybersecurity.

- **Expansion into new geographies**—the relative level of security can vary widely from country to country. For example, bribing a security guard may be a relatively easy method of attack in some countries, whereas in others it may not be. If the rule of law is not strong, the disincentives provided by legal prosecution will be less effective. Also, in some countries, employee background checks may not be legal or practical to implement.

These complications highlight the need for well-defined and transparent processes, strategies, and technologies. Trying to achieve security by secrecy or obscurity is rarely effective. It is important that flaws can be identified and fixed rather than hoping that they do not exist and then finding that they have been exploited by cybercriminals or used for espionage purposes.

Moreover, it is necessary to keep reevaluating security risks and updating solutions on an ongoing basis. The latest fraud prevention and detection methods will be successful for some time, but as criminals adapt, new techniques will need to be implemented. Likewise, as technology changes and time passes, new vulnerabilities can appear. For instance, for many years the MD5 cryptographic hash function was used by applications to ensure password confidentiality. However, over time a number of security vulnerabilities were identified with the algorithm that made it no longer prudent to use for securing password information.

Information security should be managed in conjunction with other internal control functions, rather than being viewed solely as the purview of a dedicated function within the IT department. To ensure organizational-wide consideration, some organizations will appoint a chief information security officer, who is not part of the IT organization and reports to the COO, CEO, or the board of directors. Furthermore, solution designers must consider the threats that may be encountered in the broader usage context, rather than just focus on narrow areas with which they are more familiar.

17.10   FALLIBILITY OF SECURITY SYSTEMS

For financial institutions, security is by no means an issue that has been fully addressed or solved. Signature and identification forgery have been prevalent for centuries and continue to this day. A common reference to be aware of is "the illusion of security"; many security measures largely provide psychological comfort, but are not by any means flawless. Most security measures are designed to help prevent breaches, but they cannot completely eliminate them. Case Study 17-6 highlights that even some of the most secure IT systems have security flaws and weaknesses.

Case Study 17-6

The Difficulty of Securing Interfaces

A common strategy for compromising processes and systems is to attack their entry points, that is, their interfaces. The interfaces to modules running as software applications or embedded in hardware are commonly referred to as application program interfaces, or APIs. Designing APIs to be secure is a difficult challenge and often not achieved as intended. The greater the complexity of the interface, the more difficult it is to test and validate the security. Likewise, over time, changes to interfaces can introduce new weaknesses that undermine the system security.

Hardware security modules (HSMs) are an arcane but important part of security technology infrastructure used to secure financial transactions. As its name implies, an HSM is a hardware device that manages digital keys and facilitates security-related processes such as digital signing. These devices work in conjunction with other computer systems, but serve a specific and dedicated function. Unlike general-purpose computers, HSMs have restricted interfaces and are designed to be tamper resistant. HSMs are commonly used to protect PINs and the encryption keys that are used for electronic banking channels and ATM networks.

The core reasons for using HSMs is that they will be more secure than general-purpose hardware that runs software providing the same functions. In practice, though, the APIs provided by some HSMs had a number of flaws that made them vulnerable to different types of attacks. One nonobvious problem with the APIs was that functions that were secure individually could create vulnerabilities when used in combination. Another problem was that the conditions under which error messages returned for invalid transactions could also be used to derive PIN values stored in the HSM. Furthermore, certain API features made "brute force" cryptographic attacks practical, that is, being able to guess the right key in a reasonably short period of time.

Although the vulnerabilities were fixed using software updates to the HSMs after they had been identified, ongoing changes and additions to the APIs made security validation of these components a moving target. The problem was that there was an inherent trade-off between functional capabilities of an HSM and its integrity. The more features that were provided, the more API functions were required, and the greater the likelihood of vulnerabilities. Then again, an HSM with fewer features would be more secure, but would also be of limited use to customers.

This example highlights some of the practical challenges related to security. Multiple concerns can be observed with this relatively simple device that was designed to be secure. Imagine the difficulty in trying to ensure the security of solutions that are much more complex and where changes are more pervasive and frequent. What is more, when different components are used to put together solutions, it is common for each component to have its own API. Although only a handful of functions of these APIs may be used by a technology solution, they are all potential security vulnerabilities.

Source: Anderson, Ross J., *Security Engineering: A Guide to Building Dependable Distributed Systems,* 2nd ed. (New York: John Wiley & Sons, 2008).

In some ways, computers have made the perpetration of fraud easier. For instance, there have been scores of cases where sensitive customer information has been lost or compromised by banks. Hence, protection of customer data has become a major concern over the past decade. The problems involved with securing information are not surprising, given the fact that this information is spread across a number of systems, is easily duplicated, and is vulnerable to both external exploitation and internal weaknesses.

One of the challenges with data security is that it has evolved from a paper environment. Many of the security control processes have not been sufficiently adapted to address the new challenges that electronic storage and access present. One example of the challenges that new technology introduces can be seen with universal serial bus (USB) "thumb drives." They greatly simplify the ease with which information can be copied, taken off site, and then lost or compromised. A simple answer would be to ban them or disable the USB drives on computers. Unfortunately, enforcing bans is difficult, and disabling computer interface points may interfere with other necessary business functions.

Information security is often focused on the intricacies of encryption algorithms and user access control mechanisms for IT systems. However, physical controls and procedures continue to be as important as technical weaknesses; if hackers are able to physically access a computer, they will usually be able to compromise its security quite easily. Any weak link in the security chain can lead to a breach. Unfortunately, electronic systems and digital information do not eliminate all of the original problems; in fact, they tend to add more to the list. A common assumption of security and control systems designers and operators is that malefactors will adopt sophisticated and advanced hacking techniques. However, in practice, much simpler strategies are used, circumventing known patterns and taking advantage of simple but obscure weaknesses or by leveraging social engineering attacks. For example, why try to pick open a high security front-door lock when the third-story window has been left open?

Another major challenge with security is the paradox that security that is too onerous will defeat itself. Often, solution designers have good intentions but forget about the practical considerations of use. Systems that are difficult to use because of overly complex security mechanisms may not be used at all, or the security may be circumvented by users. Likewise, comprehensive control and security systems can themselves introduce excess complexity. This complexity, in turn, can lead to mistakes in configuration or modifications to the security environment, creating security vulnerabilities. Security policies that require passwords to be complicated and difficult to remember are one such example. If users are unable to easily remember their passwords, it is more likely that they will then write down the passwords somewhere, creating another type of security risk.

It is important for financial institutions to acknowledge their own strengths and limitations. It is usually best to go with well-understood and proven approaches to security. Trying to invent new security systems is usually a recipe for disaster. It is not practical from a cost standpoint for most firms to craft custom information security solutions, and often they are less secure than off-the-shelf options. Existing information security technologies may not be perfect, but at least their weaknesses are generally understood.

 Several different security-related standards covering areas such as security practices and evaluation have been defined, as mentioned in earlier parts of this chapter. Such standards are often useful as guidelines for identifying areas that need to be addressed and provide a structured analysis framework. However, these are not a panacea and, in many cases, can do more harm than good. One problem is that reliance on a recognized "standard" may lead to overconfidence, the expectation being that complying with the standard will be sufficient to identify and address all potential vulnerabilities. Another problem is that the effort directed toward achieving full and strict compliance with the standard might be better directed toward more practical defense measures. If too much focus is given to the means, the end goal can easily be neglected.

 Moreover, the expectation must be that vulnerabilities will persist and eventually be exploited. Human errors and technical failures cannot be eliminated. Likewise, it is not practical to perform exhaustive testing and, hence, flaws may be uncovered and used maliciously. Thus, the architecture considerations of resilience, robustness, and defense in depth are integral to security design. Although considering the response and recovery plans for security breach and fraud incidents is not necessarily pleasant, it is prudent to assess what actions should be taken, even in the worst-case scenarios. Such decisions are best thought through in advance, rather than in panic conditions.

 Information security is achieved through a combination of complex mathematics, planning, and effective management. The complex mathematics aspect is in the algorithms used to secure transactions and protect digital information. Planning prepares for the occurrence of security events and incidents, which are often inevitable. Good management helps ensure that cybersecurity-related processes, such as software patching and security event monitoring, are performed consistently and effectively. Furthermore, management requires making the necessary compromises and achieving the optimal balance that allow a financial institution's business to operate efficiently while managing cybersecurity risks.

17.11 SUMMARY

This chapter covered:

- information security concepts;
- cybersecurity threats and attack vectors;
- the purpose and components of a cybersecurity framework;
- the importance of security operations;
- business opportunities and challenges related to cybersecurity;
- information security-related considerations related to processes, architecture and solutions; and
- the limitations of security systems.

 The next chapter will review market risk management principles and the approaches used by financial institutions to measure and control their risk.

FURTHER READING

Books

Anderson, R. J., Security Engineering: *A Guide to Building Dependable Distributed Systems*, 2nd ed. (New York: John Wiley & Sons, 2008).

Ferguson, N. and B. Schneier, *Practical Cryptography* (Indiana: Wiley Publishing, 2003).

Schneier, B., *Secrets and Lies: Digital Security in a Networked World* (New York: John Wiley & Sons,2004).

Steven, B., *Thinking Security: Stopping Next Year's Hackers* (New Jersey: Pearson Education, 2015).

Tipton, H. F. and M. Krause, *Information Security Management Handbook*, 6th ed. (Massachusetts: CRC Press, 2007).

Vacca, J. (Editor), *Managing Information Security*, 2nd ed. (Massachusetts: Syngress, 2013).

Papers

Camillo, M., "Cybersecurity: Risks and Management of Risks for Global Banks and Financial Institutions," *Journal of Risk Management in Financial Institutions*, Vol. 10, 2 (2017): 196–200.

Cichonski, P., T. Millar, T. Grance, and K. Scarfone, "Computer Security Incident Handling Guide," National Institute of Standards and Technology, NIST Special Publication 800-61 Revision 2, August 2012.

European Central Bank, "Recommendations for the Security of Internet Payments," April 2012, http://www.ecb.europa.eu/pub/pdf/other/recommendationsforthesecurityofinternetpaymentsen.pdf.

Monetary Authority of Singapore, "Internet Banking and Technology Risk Management Guidelines," Version 3.0, June 2, 2008, http://www.mas.gov.sg/~/media/MAS/Regulations%20and%20Financial%20Stability/Regulations%20Guidance%20and%20Licensing/Commercial%20Banks/Regulations%20Guidance%20and%20Licensing/Guidelines/IBTRMV3.ashx.

Murdoch, S. J. and R. Anderson, "Verified by Visa and MasterCard SecureCode: or, How Not to Design Authentication," in *Financial Cryptography and Data Security*, Lecture Notes in Computer Science, vol. 6052, p. 336 (Berlin: IFCA/Springer-Verlag Berlin Heidelberg, 2010).

Murdoch, S. J., S. Drimer, R. Anderson, and M. Bond, "Chip and PIN Is Broken," *2010 IEEE Symposium on Security and Privacy* (2010): 433–446.

Ponemon Institute, "Managing Insider Risk through Training & Culture," May 2016, http://www.experian.com/assets/data-breach/white-papers/experian-2016-ponemon-insider-risk-report.pdf.

"Recommended Practice: Improving Industrial Control System Cybersecurity with Defense-in-Depth Strategies," US Department of Homeland Security, September 2016, https://ics-cert.us-cert.gov/sites/default/files/recommended_practices/NCCIC_ICS-CERT_Defense_in_Depth_2016_S508C.pdf.

Web

"Common Vulnerabilities and Exposures", http://cve.mitre.org/

"Cisco Security Reports," https://www.cisco.com/c/en/us/products/security/security-reports.html.

"FBI Internet Crime Complaint Center Annual Reports," https://www.ic3.gov/media/annualreports.aspx.

"Fraudscape," http://www.cifas.org.uk.

"Global Economic Crime Survey," http://www.pwc.com/crimesurvey.

"Kaspersky Lab Quarterly Malware Reports," https://securelist.com/all/?category=441.

"National Institute of Standards and Technology (NIST) Computer Security Resource Center Special Publications (800 Series)," http://csrc.nist.gov/publications/PubsSPs.html.

"National Vulnerability Database," https://nvd.nist.gov/.

"PwC The Global State of Information Security Survey," https://www.pwc.com/gx/en/issues/cyber-security/information-security-survey.html.

"SANS Critical Security Controls," https://www.sans.org/media/critical-security-controls/critical-controls-poster-2016.pdf.

"Schneier on Security," http://www.schneier.com.

"Security Engineering: A Guide to Building Dependable Distributed Systems, 1ˢᵗ Edition," http://www.cl.cam.ac.uk/~rja14/book.html.

"Top 25 Most Dangerous Software Errors," http://cwe.mitre.org/top25.

ENDNOTES

1. Morgan, S., "J.P. Morgan, Bank of America, Citibank And Wells Fargo Spending $1.5 Billion to Battle Cyber Crime," *Forbes*, December 13, 2015, http://www.forbes.com/sites/stevemorgan/2015/12/13/j-p-morgan-boa-citi-and-wells-spending-1-5-billion-to-battle-cyber-crime/#cd101d91112b.

2. Emm, D., R. Unuchek, M. Garnaeva, A. Ivanov, D. Makrushin, and F. Sinitsyn, "IT Threat Evolution in Q2 2016," Kaspersky Lab.

3. National Institute of Standards and Technology, "Framework for Improving Critical Infrastructure Cybersecurity," January 10, 2017, Draft Version 1.1.

4. Kaspersky Lab, "Report: Measuring the Financial Impact of IT Security on Businesses Executive Summary", 2016, https://usblog.kaspersky.com/security_risks_report_financial_impact.

5. Sindre, G. and A. Opdahl, "Eliciting Security Requirements with Misuse Cases," *Requirements Engineering* 10 (2005): 34–44.

6. Sindre, G., "Mal-activity Diagrams for Capturing Attacks on Business Processes," *Requirements Engineering: Foundation for Software Quality* (2007): 355–366.

7. Rodríguez A., E. Fernández-Medina, and M. Piattini, "Capturing Security Requirements in Business Processes through a UML 2.0 Activity Diagrams Profile," in *Lecture Notes in Computer Science*, vol. 4231, pp. 32–42 (Berlin: Springer-Verlag, 2006).

8. Rodríguez A., E. Fernández-Medina, and M. Piattini, "A BPMN Extension for the Modeling of Security Requirements in Business Processes," *IEICE—Transactions on Information and Systems* E90-D (2007): 745–752.

9. Kelly, Spencer, "Hackers Outwit Online Banking Identity Security Systems," *BBC News*, February 2, 2012, http://www.bbc.co.uk/news/technology-16812064.

10. Open Web Application Security Project, "OWASP Top 10 2013," https://www.owasp.org/images/f/f8/OWASP_Top_10_-_2013.pdf.

— — —

11. Anderson, R. J., *Security Engineering: A Guide to Building Dependable Distributed Systems*, 2nd ed. (New York: John Wiley & Sons, 2008).

12. Apostolou, N. and D. L. Crumbley, "The Tally Stick: The First Internal Control?" *Forensic Examiner*, Spring 2008, http://www.theforensicexaminer.com/archive/spring08/13/.

13. Nelms, J., "Managing Technology Risk in the Banking and Finance Sector," (presentation slides, 7th Annual Banking and Finance Technology Forum Asia 2011).

14. "War on Fraud Focusing on the Insider Front," *American Banker* 170 (2005), http://www.americanbanker.com/issues/170_62/-245063-1.html.

15. Naone, E., "'SMS of Death' Could Crash Many Mobile Phones," *Technology Review*, January 4, 2011, http://www.technologyreview.com/news/422272/sms-of-death-could-crash-many-mobile-phones.

16. "Eternal Champion Exploit Analysis," *Microsoft*, https://blogs.technet.microsoft.com/srd/2017/06/29/eternal-champion-exploit-analysis/.

17. Townsend, K., "NIST Denounces SMS 2FA—What are the Alternatives?" *Security Week*, August 17, 2016, http://www.securityweek.com/nist-denounces-sms-2fa-what-are-alternatives.

15. Nicole, C., "SMS of Death Could Crash Many Mobile Phones," *Technology Review*, January 4, 2011, http://www.technologyreview.com/news/422272/sms-of-death-could-crash-many-mobile-phones

16. "Eternal Champion Exploit Analysis," Microsoft, https://blogs.technet.microsoft.com/.../eternal-champion-exploit-analysis.

17. Townsend, K., "NIST Deprecates SMS 2FA. What are the Alternatives?" *Security Week*, August 17, 2016, http://www.securityweek.com/nist-deprecates-sms-2fa-what-are-alternatives.

18 Market Risk Management

Chapter Overview

Risk management is an integral part of financial services. Taking on too little risk can lead to underperformance relative to peers, and taking on too much risk can lead to catastrophic losses. In the short term, financial institutions may succeed by taking excessive risk so as to achieve high returns, but long-term success is often determined by avoiding certain risks and careful management of risk exposures. Advancements in the science of risk management as well as the development of financial instruments that offset specific risks have enabled financial institutions to manage their risks more effectively. However, there is still a wide gap between the understanding of risk management theory and its practical implications; major risk management failures have persisted over time.

As shown in Figure 18-1, over the past three decades there have been many cases of risk management failures that have adversely affected individual institutions and the financial services industry as a whole. In several cases, trading risk management failures occurred when "rogue traders" exposed their institutions to excessive risk through bets placed in financial markets. **Credit risk** management failures occurred when banks concentrated their lending business on market segments that ultimately proved to be unsound. Although one might expect that the amount of financial damage incurred would decrease over time with successive generations learning from previous incidents, to the contrary, losses have actually increased over time.

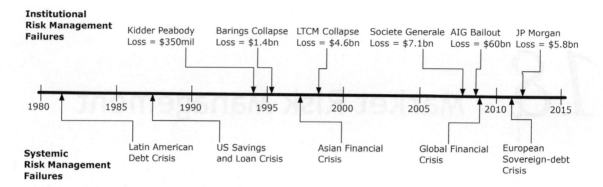

Figure 18-1 Risk management failure timeline[*]

As financial instruments have become more complex, it has become increasingly difficult for financial institutions to assess and monitor their risk exposure. For instance, a small, seemingly inconsequential, derivatives trading unit in London led to the insurance giant AIG's near collapse in 2007. Trading in derivatives instruments, in particular, has created a major source of risk even for banks with robust and well-respected risk management capabilities. As a case in point, JPMorgan Chase, which came out of the **Global Financial Crisis** relatively unscathed, was disfavored in 2012 by losses resulting from credit derivatives trading. When it first emerged publicly that there was a risk problem, it estimated its losses to be around US$2 billion, but within a few months, it had realized a loss of US$5.8 billion, and the bank's internal risk models predicted that the losses could potentially reach US$7.5 billion [1]. In many cases, derivatives positions can be viewed as "risk icebergs," where the visible risk represents only a small portion of the total potential downside.

IT systems are vital for determining risk exposures, but stale or incorrect data that is input into them can lead to inaccurate and invalid risk assessments. Banks have a long way to go to address this challenge. A 2016 benchmarking assessment of 19 large global banks found that over three quarters of them considered data quality and system automation as two of the top concerns related to their ability to execute and manage risk stress testing processes [2]. Accordingly, many banks' risk initiatives have been focused on data quality improvement, data reconciliation, and aggregation of data across disparate divisions and entities.

Risk management is as much an art as it is a science. That is, it depends as much on effective business management as it does on advanced quantitative techniques. For example, incentive structures, or bonuses, that reward employees individually for taking on risk can easily thwart other corporate-level risk management measures. In many cases, the parties who were responsible for or contributed to risk management failures were hailed and rewarded with large bonuses right up to the time the impact of imprudence was discovered. Besides poor incentive structures, deficient controls and lax enforcement of controls can also lead employees to perform improper transactions and to hide legitimate mistakes or bad business decisions (Case Study 18-1). Moreover, financial institutions' complexity can also diminish the effectiveness of risk management controls.

This chapter begins by reviewing the different types of common financial risks faced by financial institutions. **Market risk** concepts and measurement techniques are then discussed, followed by the opportunities and challenges that risk management presents. Business process, architecture, and solution concerns related to risk management are also examined. The focus of this chapter is on the risks that financial institutions can control, primarily in the context of market risk. Hence, the risk of widespread collapse of banks and financial markets, that is, systemic risk, is not considered.

---

[*] The loss amounts and crisis timings shown in Figure 18-1 are approximate—they spanned several years and had inexact beginning and end dates.

Case Study 18-1

Big Bets and Poor Risk Management Bring Down MF Global

In October 2011, multinational futures broker and bond dealer MF Global filed for bankruptcy after being unable to meet its creditors' payment demands. With $40 billion in liabilities, it was the second largest financial institution to fail, and one of the largest bankruptcies in US history. MF Global's demise came less than two years after Jon Corzine assumed office as its chief executive officer (CEO) and chairman, with the aim of transforming the firm from a third-tier commodities broker to a high-flying investment bank. Prior to leading MF Global, Corzine had been a bond trader and managing partner at Goldman Sachs, and had also been a US senator. MF Global's undoing was a result of the firm's highly leveraged trades in European sovereign debt.

MF Global's troubles began earlier in 2008 when a rogue trader's bets on wheat futures led to market losses of $141.5 million and a regulatory fine of $10 million for poor risk management. Leading up to 2011, the firm lost money on its traditional agency brokerage business, that is, facilitating market access for its customers, for three years, putting its longevity in doubt. It needed to generate profits quickly so that its investment-grade credit rating could be maintained, allowing it continued access to low-cost sources of funding. To achieve this goal, MF Global began to leverage its own capital to make bets by means of proprietary trading that exceeded $6 billion on the bonds of less secure eurozone governments. The bonds were trading at steep discounts and if all went well, the trades would provide large profits for little risk. What is more, accounting rules allowed MF Global to book the difference between the interest rates paid on the European bonds that it bought and the (lower) interest rate at which it borrowed to fund the bond as upfront profit. In 2011, it recorded profits of $122 million from these trades, keeping the firm alive. However, MF Global's high leverage ratio, over forty-to-one, made it highly sensitive to changes in European government bond prices.

In October 2011, the likelihood of European Union members defaulting on their sovereign debt increased, leading to a sharp drop in the value of their bonds. In turn, the Financial Industry Regulatory Authority ordered MF Global to increase its capital, its credit rating was downgraded, the firm reported a quarterly loss, and its stock value dropped more than 50%. This combination precipitated a **liquidity** crisis. The firm faced a sharp increase in collateral demands from customers, creditors, and exchanges. Because of MF Global's highly leveraged position, it had insufficient capital available to satisfy these demands.

A last-ditch attempt was made to save the firm by selling it to a competitor. However, the deal was scuttled when more than $700 million of MF Global's customer funds could not be accounted for. Later, this number would rise to $1.5 billion. The US Commodities Exchange Act, enacted during the Great Depression, required brokers to segregate customer's assets from the firm's assets. This law was passed to protect customers in cases where their broker failed. Five days before it became insolvent, MF Global began using customer funds to support its proprietary trading and avert bankruptcy. What is more, it did not notify regulators of the segregation breach as it was required to.

It was a surprise to many that this kind of failure could have occurred so soon after the Global Financial Crisis. Tighter regulations and oversight were intended to prevent excessive risk-taking by financial institutions, let alone loss of customer funds. Hubris may have been one factor that led to MF Global's fall. Allegedly, Corzine had personally championed the business strategy that amassed European sovereign bond positions, and he overruled the firm's chief risk officer's concerns over the excessive exposure to European sovereign debt. Also, in the year leading up to the bankruptcy, MF Global's board had approved increasing the limit for bond purchases from $4 billion to $8.5 billion. Rather ironically, a report by an independent consultancy issued in May of 2011 praised MF Global's risk management capabilities. Later, MF Global employees would testify in court that the organization had inadequate risk control frameworks and IT capabilities, and overall had primitive risk controls. When the firm shifted its focus from being a broker to prop trading, it did not upgrade its IT systems and back-office infrastructure to support the new business requirements. Leading up

(Continued)

(Continued)

to the bankruptcy, MF Global's IT systems and operations staff were overloaded by the frenzy of business activity, causing gaps and errors in the recording of transactions.

As with many financial calamities, there was an element of bad luck. If MF Global had been able to make it through its liquidity crisis, in the long term, its European bond positions may have turned out to be profitable after all. The failed **hedge fund** LTCM had faced a similar problem over a decade earlier. Hence, traders and risk managers should best keep in mind economist John Maynard Keynes's quip that the market can remain irrational longer than you can remain solvent.

Sources: "Broke Broker," *Economist*, November 5, 2011, http://www.economist.com/node/21536615; Burrough, Bryan, William D. Cohan, and Bethany McLean, "Jon Corzine's Riskiest Business," *Vanity Fair*, February 2012, http://www.vanityfair.com/business/2012/02/jon-corzine-201202; Gustin, Sam, "Did Jon Corzine Lie to Congress about Missing MF Global Funds?" *Time*, March 26, 2012, http://business.time.com/2012/03/26/did-jon-corzine-lie-to-congress-about-missing-mf-global-funds/; Scannell, Kara and Tom Braithwaite, "MF Global Won Praise for Risk Handling," *Financial Times*, March 27, 2012, http://www.ft.com/cms/s/0/8844c36c-7825-11e1-b237-00144feab49a.html; Parloff, R. "How MF Global's 'missing' $1.5 billion was lost—and found", Fortune, November 15, 2013, http://fortune.com/2013/11/15/how-mf-globals-missing-1-5-billion-was-lost-and-found; McLannahan, B., "PwC Suggests MF Global Was a Risk Culture Run Amok," *Financial Times*, March 14, 2017, https://www.ft.com/content/00de719a-086f-11e7-97d1-5e720a26771b?mhq5j=e3.

Questions

1. Which risk management principle(s) did MF Global's trading strategy violate?
2. When the default of European government bonds looked more likely, why did MF Global's CEO not take steps to reduce the firm's holdings of these instruments and, thus, save the firm from bankruptcy?
3. What would have been the likely outcome for MF Global's CEO if the European debt market had not dropped, as they did in October 2011?
4. What controls should have been in place to prevent the improper use of customer funds?

18.1   BUSINESS CONTEXT

Where rogue traders have been a concern, the failures have been primarily related to **operational risk** and failure of internal controls, discussed in Chapter 19. More recently, however, many of the problems that financial institutions have encountered have also involved market and credit risk management. As a case in point, record volatility encountered in equity, housing, and credit markets in 2008 and 2009 led to widespread concern among many different types of financial institutions.

18.1.1 Risk Considerations

A premise of the financial services industry is that profit and risk are inseparable. Larger profits are associated with larger risks, and lower risk will lead to smaller profits. Hence, risk cannot be completely eliminated without also eliminating profits. The challenge is to manage risk effectively so that the level of risk taken is not too great and is in line with expected profits. Risk management must also consider worst-case scenarios and ensure that their expected outcomes are also acceptable.

Given the uncertainty of future prices, both trading and investing have certain inherent elements of gambling. Psychologically, winning often makes people believe that they have skill and, therefore, leads them to increase the size of their wagers. Unfortunately, it is difficult to determine if it is skill or just luck that is producing strong returns. When luck is the primary factor determining profits, eventually the tide will change and losses will ensue.

Organizational structure underlies effective risk management. Front-office sales functions are rewarded for achieving sales targets, not minimizing risk. On the other hand, risk management functions in middle office are designed to serve as a counterbalance. Ideally, the middle office is rewarded for controlling risk and has the authority to counteract excessively risky actions that may be attempted by sales or management. To provide additional protection, regulators are responsible for ensuring that financial institutions' employees adequately protect their customers and the markets as a whole from undue risk.

18.1.2 Types of Risk

Financial institutions must constantly deal with different types of risks including the following five major risk categories.

Market risk is the risk associated with the value of institution-owned assets and positions in instruments such as equities, bonds, and currencies. The value may change with variations in market prices. Market prices will fluctuate due to changes in circumstances of a company or country to which the asset is related, or changes in other considerations that affect the valuation, such as interest rates.

For example, an increase in short-term interest rates will reduce the net present value calculations for equities and fixed-income instruments, which, in theory, should lower their prices in the market and, thus, their asset value. However, in practice, markets are not always rational. At times, speculation and market sentiment may have greater influence on prices than fundamental factors.

Market liquidity risk is the risk that a financial instrument may not have ready buyers or sellers, that is, is not liquid under either usual or unusual market conditions (Case Study 18-2). Low liquidity may mean that if the instrument must be traded, it will fetch an unfavorable price. For example, millions of ten-year US Treasury bond futures are traded daily. Hence, the **spread** between the price offered by buyers and sellers is small, and there is little risk that there will be no buyer or seller to take the other side of a trade. In contrast, options traded on stocks that have low trading volumes may have very few, if any, market participants offering to buy or sell. These options often have very wide bid-ask spreads, and may not have any counterparties willing to buy or sell during times of high volatility.

Credit risk is the risk that a counterparty to whom the institution provides a line of credit, or whose credit underlies debt instruments that are held, will default on its payment or delivery obligations. Credit may take the form of cash loans, securities lent, debt securities purchased, or obligations to fulfill a transaction at a future date. For example, when an institution enters into an interest rate swap agreement under certain future market conditions, the counterparty may "owe" the institution an amount in the future as a result of the swap, which translates to a counterparty credit risk.

Settlement risk is the risk, in cases where **gross settlement** (as discussed in Chapter 9) is used, that the institution makes its payment but does not receive payment from the counterparty. In the context of securities, such as stocks and bonds, there is also the risk that a counterparty will fail to deliver the security on the settlement date. This risk has largely been minimized, but not completely eliminated, through the use of net **settlement** and using **central counterparties (CCPs)**.

Case Study 18-2

The Dangers of Taking Corporate Liquidity for Granted

Corporate liquidity, which is different from market liquidity, relates to a company's ability to meet cash-flow demands through the maintenance of cash reserves and borrowing. Failure to maintain sufficient corporate liquidity can potentially lead to insolvency. For many years, corporate liquidity risk was a concern only for financially weak borrowers and holders of exotic instruments, such as emerging market debt. However, the Global Financial Crisis of 2008/09 made corporate liquidity a widespread concern when lending markets around the world effectively ceased to function for several months. Banks and corporations, both large and small, were affected.

(Continued)

(Continued)

The collapse of Bear Stearns and Lehman Brothers caused financial institutions to stop lending to one another, or only to lend at high interest rates. This caused major problems for financial institutions that had short-term funding needs. Many banks had to borrow from the Federal Reserve and/or raise equity, that is, issue more stock, to improve their overall liquidity position. Corporations were affected in a similar way when the short-term "commercial paper" lending market stopped functioning. In many cases, companies that relied upon rolling over short-term debt as part of their financing strategy had to shift to more expensive reserve lines of credit with their banks, if they had them or could get them.

The corporate liquidity crunch not only affected borrowers, but also those holding assets. Many corporate treasuries held commercial paper and other less liquid debt instruments to generate higher returns than savings deposits. Unfortunately, during the credit crunch many of these assets became illiquid—they either were not tradable or could only be sold at steep discounts. Also, some companies had strong balance sheets but were cash-poor, which led to day-to-day funding problems during the crisis.

Corporate liquidity risk, especially as severe as that which occurred during the credit crisis, is difficult to factor into risk models. It is primarily managed through **diversification** and by setting less aggressive targets for return on capital. By diversifying, corporations can avoid investing too much capital in instruments that may become illiquid. Likewise, being conservative ensures that more cash is on hand to deal with crises when they occur.

Sources: Johnston, Megan, "Corporate Liquidity Begins to Dry Up," *Financial Week*, March 24, 2008, http://www.financialweek.com/apps/pbcs.dll/article?AID=/20080324/REG/736472226; Webb, Andy, "Multinational Corporate Treasurers: Liquidity Decision-making at the Sharp End," *Finance Asia*, July 13, 2010, http://www.financeasia.com/News/219611,multinational-corporate-treasurers-liquidity-decision-making-at-the-sharp-end.aspx.

Operational risk is the risk that an institution may incur losses due to operational failures. Operational risk is a broad category and some examples of operational risk include failures of controls that lead to internal or external fraud, downtime of critical systems, and mistakes in the implementation of pricing or valuation models. Many of the case studies in this book are related to operational risks that have been observed in practice, and this topic is covered in its own right in Chapter 19.

Many books have been written about managing risk in financial institutions; it is a deep and complex subject. The next section will examine a few fundamental market risk management concepts to help provide the reader with context for understanding how technology supports the measurement and control of market risk.

18.2 MARKET RISK CONCEPTS

Fundamentally, risk management relies upon estimates of the expected value of an institution's holdings at some point in the future, based on uncertain knowledge about how prices of the assets and liabilities held will change. To develop estimates about potential risk, assumptions must be made about how prices will behave. Historic market price movements are typically used as a basis for estimating to what extent and in which direction prices will move in the future.

18.2.1 Return Distributions

When assessing risk, periodic returns of many financial instruments are modeled on the assumption of normal or lognormal distributions. Figure 18-2 shows the histograms for daily price changes of two asset classes, US stocks (S&P 500) and the euro currency, over a ten-year period. The bars show

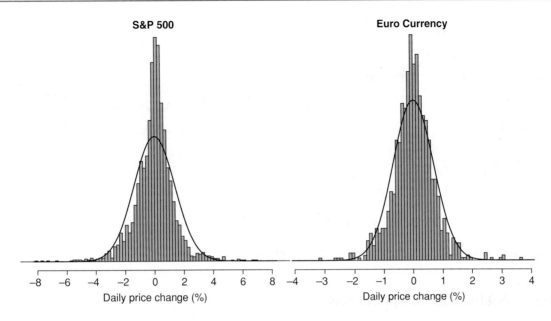

Figure 18-2 Histograms of price movements for two common asset classes

the actual price returns, and the solid lines show how a normal distribution would be fitted to the returns. It can be observed from the histograms that the actual price returns generally, but not perfectly, correspond to bell-shaped curves.

18.2.2 Correlation of Asset Prices

Another important concept of risk management is combining instruments that have different, and preferably negative, correlations. Figure 18-3 shows the inverse price movements of the S&P 500 and long-term US Treasury bonds over a two-year period. Hence, by holding both assets, it is possible to reduce the overall volatility, or risk, of the portfolio. Portfolio theory* is based on this principle and can be used to determine the optimal return on a set of assets with minimized risk.

To help illustrate this point, consider the example where a financial institution holds a portfolio that has some mix of the S&P 500 index and long-term US Treasury bonds. Assume that the expected return on the S&P 500 is 10% and the expected annualized volatility is 3%. Furthermore, assume that the return on the Treasury bonds is expected to be 5% with a volatility of 1% and that the price movements of the two assets are negatively correlated. According to **modern portfolio theory**, by combining the two assets it is possible to achieve a return that is between the return of the two assets at a risk level that is potentially lower than either asset. For example, by formulating a particular mix of the two assets, say 70% S&P 500 stocks and 30% Treasury bonds, it may be possible to achieve an 8.5% return at 2% volatility. Alternatively, with a different mix, say 30% S&P 500 stocks and 70% Treasury bonds, it may be possible to produce a 6% return with a volatility of only 0.5%.

Holding a mix of assets that are not closely correlated is referred to as diversification, and is the core principle of risk reduction. This concept can be simply summarized as: First, do not hold too much of any one type of asset, and second, make sure that the prices of different assets held do not follow one another too closely.

---

* For more background information, refer to Alexander, G. J., W. F. Sharpe, and J. V. Bailey, *Fundamentals of Investments*, 3rd ed. (New Jersey: Prentice Hall, 2000), Chapters 6 and 7.

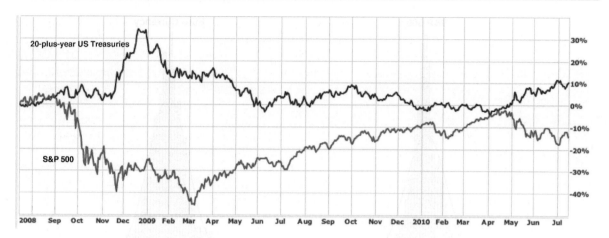

Figure 18-3 Comparison of price changes of S&P 500 and US Treasuries

18.2.3 Real-world Complications

The principles discussed above work well in theory, but using them effectively in practice can be complicated. For instance, many instruments' price distributions often will appear to be quite similar to normal or lognormal distributions. However, they may differ enough that using normal distributions to model their risk will result in underestimation of potential loses. As can be observed in Figure 18-2, the bars, which show observed variance, on the far left side of the S&P 500 distribution, are higher than the normal curve would estimate. In other words, if a normal distribution were used to model the risk of the likelihood of losses in excess of −4% of a portfolio of S&P 500 stocks, the actual loses would likely exceed the estimate.

This characteristic is referred to as kurtosis or "fat tail" risk, because the tail end of the distribution is larger than would be expected in a normal distribution. Hence, it is necessary to try to augment standard risk models to account for non-normal price return behavior [3]. Moreover, for some instruments, even fat-tailed normal distributions may not be relevant, and other types of distribution may need to be used.

Risk models' reliance on historical information is another concern. Expectations of asset price movements and available liquidity are based on previous years' data. Risk estimates may vary greatly depending on the time range of input data used to calculate volatility and cross-asset correlations. For example, the volatility of stocks and bonds issued by banks was relatively low in the five years leading up to the financial crisis of 2008. Hence, a risk model that was calculated using five-year historical data for a portfolio of bank stocks and bonds would produce a relatively low value in 2006. The same risk model calculations, however, would yield much significantly higher expected loss if calculated in 2010, because they would incorporate the stock and bond price volatility observed during the Global Financial Crisis.

Also, correlations for assets' price movements are not constant. Over time, there may be gradual or sharp shifts in their relationships to one another. In particular, during crises, it is not unusual for prices of different asset classes that normally have low correlation, such as equities and commodities, to move in tandem. Similarly, the prices of assets that normally move in tandem may deviate substantially. When this occurs, the effectiveness of risk management diversification and hedging strategies can be greatly reduced. For example, as shown in Figure 18-4, traditionally, the prices of US Treasury bonds and high-quality US corporate bonds moved fairly closely together, that is, they had a high positive correlation. However, during the financial crisis of 2008 and 2009, their prices exhibited almost the opposite behavior and showed a high negative correlation, causing complications for risk models that assumed that the positive correlation would persist under all conditions.

A further complication is that many instruments held in a portfolio may have been created only recently. For instance, new companies are listed on stock exchanges daily and complex derivatives are formulated on an ongoing basis. By their nature, new instruments will have little or no historical data available for use in risk analysis. Hence, estimating the future volatility of these instruments and how they will correlate with other instruments presents major challenges. Typically, "bootstrapping" techniques are used to model new instruments. Synthetic historical data may be created for the instrument based on the belief that it would have behaved in the past like other similar instruments. Alternatively, historical data may be synthesized based on the instruments' expected relationship with other principal components, such as interest rates. While bootstrapping helps risk managers accommodate new instruments, the technique is far from perfect for estimating their risk. Moreover, assumptions about trigger conditions, which have not been encountered previously, for payouts for certain types of financial instruments can also lead to risks of their own (Case Study 18-3).

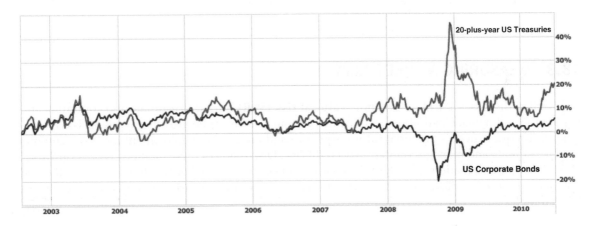

Figure 18-4 Comparison of price movements of Treasury and corporate bonds

Case Study 18-3
Mitigating the Risk of Sovereign Debt Default

Default by sovereign nations on their debt is a major concern for banks because they tend to hold large amounts of government debt. While this situation is generally considered to have low likelihood, the financial strain that Greece faced in 2010 was one of the rare examples of when banks faced significant risk of this type of financial loss. Within Europe, French banks had the greatest exposure to Greece. For instance, Société Générale's exposure to Greek government bonds amounted to a whopping $3.9 billion.

One approach that banks use to mitigate debt default risk is to use credit default swaps (CDS), an over-the-counter (OTC) derivative designed to pay out if default occurs. In theory, they can provide insurance against the situation that banks faced with Greece. As of 2012, there were over $3 billion worth of credit default swap contracts on Greek debt. However, in practice, it was less clear if CDS would really serve this purpose. When Greece restructured its debt, it did so as part of a "voluntary" arrangement, which brought into question whether it was a "true" default situation that should trigger the payment of related CDS contracts. The International Swaps and Derivatives Association, which is an industry group that is primarily governed by large banks, would make this decision. Ultimately it decided that the Greek restructuring did constitute an event that would trigger the CDS payouts, but for a long while the outcome remained in question.

(Continued)

(Continued)

Beyond CDS, other types of swap derivatives are also used to manage market risks. For example, equity swaps are used to hedge the risk of equity price movements, interest rate swaps protect against the adverse movement of interest rates, and commodity swaps mitigate the risk of losses due to changes in commodity prices. However, as shown in this case, these financial instruments are not without risks of their own. The nuances of the events they are meant to protect against are sometimes open to interpretation, which may in turn limit their effectiveness.

Sources: Daneshkhu, Scheherazade, "SocGen Has €3bn Greek Bond Exposure," *Financial Times*, May 5 2010, http://www.ft.com/cms/s/0/4b95c3e8-58a7-11df-a0c9-00144feab49a.html; Reuters, "Crédit Agricole Faces €3.8bn Greece Exposure," *Financial Times*, May 7, 2010, http://www.ft.com/cms/s/0/057d3d84-59b8-11df-ab25-00144feab49a.html; Morgenson, Gretchen, "Scare Tactics in Greece," *New York Times*, November 19, 2011, http://www.nytimes.com/2011/11/20/business/credit-default-swaps-as-a-scare-tactic-in-greece.html; Bases, Daniel, "ISDA Declares Greek Credit Event, CDS Payments Triggered," Reuters, March 9, 2012, http://www.reuters.com/article/us-greece-cds-isda-trigger-idUSBRE82817B20120309.

18.3   MEASURING MARKET RISK

This section discusses at a high level how **value at risk (VaR)** is used to estimate and communicate the market risk of financial institutions. VaR principles can also be applied to other types of risk. However, other techniques such as potential future exposure and credit value adjustment are more commonly used to estimate and manage counterparty credit risk. Discussion of these methods is outside the scope of this chapter and readers are referred to the references in the Further Reading section at the end of this chapter for more information. Considerations related to counterparty credit risk are also discussed in Chapter 8.

18.3.1 An Overview of Value at Risk

Based on the concepts outlined in the previous section, it is possible to estimate and measure market risk. Yet, a key question arises: How can risk be effectively communicated to relevant stakeholders? Where key stakeholders include management and regulators, their needs and risk comprehension skills vary considerably. Management, who may not have a strong quantitative or statistical background, need risk information to be communicated in a simple manner that belies the mathematical complexity. On the other hand, regulators with greater technical understanding are in a better position to understand more complicated and comprehensive risk measures. However, they must assess and compare risk across multiple financial institutions, so consistency of the risk measures reported by different institutions is important for them as well.

To address these requirements, VaR was developed in the 1980s to help simplify and standardize how financial institutions quantify risk. VaR is the expected loss expressed in monetary terms, for example, dollars, within a certain timeframe at a certain probability. For example, the daily VaR of a portfolio of assets with total value of $2 billion might be $60 million at a 95% confidence level. That is to say that on any given day, there is less than a 5% chance that the losses will exceed $60 million, or 3% of the portfolio value.

Fundamentally, a portfolio's VaR will be determined by the volatility of the portfolio and its overall size. Accordingly, more volatile portfolios, that is, those that hold instruments whose prices vary to a greater degree, will produce higher VaR. Figure 18-5 helps illustrate this concept by showing the histogram of ten-year historical daily returns in dollars for two hypothetical $1 billion portfolios: one consisting of US Treasury bonds and the other of S&P 500 stocks. As shown, only 5% of the daily losses for the bond portfolio exceed $2.7 million dollars, whereas 5% of the daily losses for the equity portfolio exceed $4.2 million dollars. The loss threshold for the equity portfolio is higher because the volatility, or expected variance of returns, of equities is greater than that of Treasury bonds.

VaR has been adopted as the primary tool by financial institutions and regulators to measure market risk (Case Study 18-4). The advantage of VaR is that it is simple. A single number that quantifies risk is beneficial to managers who have difficulty understanding the nuances of more complex measures. In this regard, VaR is similar to net present value, which enables managers to evaluate and compare expected returns of different investments without delving into the structure of the underlying cash flows and how the returns are generated. VaR's simplicity is also helpful to regulators—it provides a consistent means of evaluating and comparing risk between different institutions.

18.3.2 Value at Risk Calculation Methods

There are three primary techniques that are used to calculate VaR: the variance-covariance method, historical method, and Monte Carlo simulation method. Although the techniques vary significantly, in theory, they should all produce similar results. In practice, different financial institutions may choose different methods, depending on their comfort level with the approach, the ease with which it can be implemented, and the types of financial instruments that they hold.

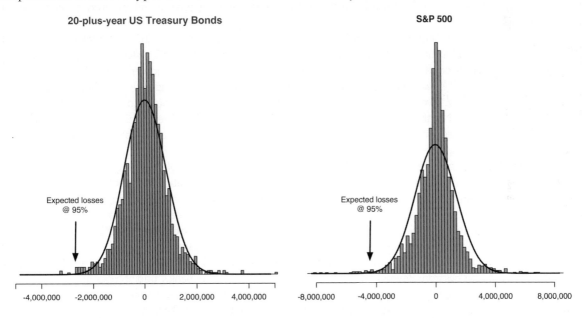

Figure 18-5 A comparison of VaR of portfolios based on two asset classes

Case Study 18-4
Evolution of the Basel Accords

The stability of financial institutions largely depends on the amount of leverage used, that is, the amount of debt versus equity on their balance sheet. Most financial institutions' business models rely on securing equity capital and borrowing money in the form of customer deposits or issuance of debt securities and then lending and investing amounts many times their equity capital amount. The greater the leverage used, the higher the

(Continued)

(Continued)

profits. However, high leverage can also lead to large losses. If a financial institution's losses exceed its equity capital, it will become insolvent.

To help prevent banks from becoming insolvent, regulators have set limits on the leverage that banks can use. In the early 1990s, leverage ratios were introduced in the United States, requiring that banks maintain a minimum amount of core capital that is a percentage of their assets. This measure was simple but inefficient. For example, the quality, that is, the risk of default, of the loans on the balance sheet was ignored. In 1998, the Basel Committee on Banking Supervision defined a similar model that included a simple weighting structure that required less capital to be allocated for certain categories of loans and investments and more for others. Both leverage ratios and the Basel approach did not take into account the risk benefits of diversification and inversely correlated hedging positions.

The second Basel Accord that was published in 2004 addressed some of these shortcomings. Basel II was designed to be an international standard for banking regulation that was focused on how much capital financial institutions should be required to maintain. Going beyond simple and weighted leverage ratios, Basel II was based on a more complex structure that allocates capital based on the different types of risks—market, credit, and operational—that financial institutions face. More advanced risk measurement techniques, such as VaR, were allowed as a means for determining the core capital required to offset risk exposures.

While the ideas behind Basel II were good in theory, they were much harder to implement. First, the costs for financial institutions to implement advanced risk management IT systems to support Basel II were substantial. Second, some regulators were concerned that it would lower capital requirements too much. Third, Basel II was defined as guidelines; different countries' implementation of those guidelines could vary substantially. Five years after Basel II was published, it had been put into practice primarily in Europe, and less so in North America and other parts of the world. Sadly, it seems that neither Basel II nor alternative risk management frameworks that were in place were robust enough to prevent the Global Financial Crisis.

Basel III was developed in the year 2010 and was meant to address many of the failings of Basel II. Among other changes, Basel III substantially increased banks' core tier-one capital ratios and reintroduced leverage ratios. The new rules are being phased in over a nine-year period that ends in 2019. From a process and IT perspective, Basel III's push to use CCPs for clearing of standardized OTC derivatives further increases the need for banks to integrate their systems to support **straight-through processing (STP)**. It also requires them to connect to CCPs and trade reporting services (discussed in Chapter 12).

From its outset, Basel III had inherent drawbacks, and as 2019 draws closer, the spectre of a Basel IV Accord is on the horizon. Beyond changing the capital treatment for bank's trading operations and the means of calculating capital ratios, it may also significantly affect how capital requirements are calculated for operational risk, including losses related to cybercrime and IT system failures. Banks may be required to use a more standardized calculation approach that is defined by global regulators. While Basel IV is still emerging as a concept, it is safe to say that it the Basel Accord will continue evolving well into the future.

Sources: D'Hulster, K., "The Leverage Ratio—A New Binding Limit on Banks," *Crisis Response Policy Briefs* (Washington, DC: The World Bank Group, December 2009), http://rru.worldbank.org/documents/CrisisResponse/Note11.pdf; "One Basel Leads to Another," *Economist*, May 18, 2006, http://www.economist.com/node/6908488; "A Battle over Basel II," *Economist*, November 2, 2006, http://www.economist.com/node/8109629; "The Banks Battle Back," *Economist*, May 27, 2010, http://www.economist.com/node/16231434; Masters, Brooke and Justin Baer, "Inconsistency Appears over Basel Compliance," *Financial Times*, November 21, 2010, http://www.ft.com/cms/s/0/df6ba944-f590-11df-99d6-00144feab49a.html; Brunsden, Jim, "Banks in Europe May Win EU Exemption from Basel Leverage Ratio," *Bloomberg*, November 17, 2010, http://www.bloomberg.com/news/2010-11-17/banks-in-europe-said-to-be-poised-to-escape-basel-rules-that-curtail-debt.html; Noonan, L., "Basel IV Spectre Looms for Battle-won Bankers," *Financial Times*, March 13, 2016, https://www.ft.com/content/a9d6eb94-ce5d-11e5-831d-09f7778e7377.

In the variance-covariance method, VaR is computed using matrix multiplication techniques. Matrices are constructed that describe:

- the standard deviations (that is, the volatility) of the instruments in the portfolio;

- the correlation between different instruments in the portfolio; and

- the weightings of the different instruments in the portfolio.

In essence, these matrices are multiplied together to yield the VaR in percentage terms, which can then be multiplied by the current value of the portfolio to determine the VaR in monetary terms. The variance-covariance method usually makes use of third-party vendor information that provides reference data related to instrument standard deviations and correlations. Keeping the reference information related to the standard deviation of and correlations between instruments up to date and ensuring that it is correct require substantial effort. Therefore, many financial institutions have chosen to outsource this function (see Case Study 18-7).

The historical method for calculating VaR requires risk managers to keep a record of the daily profit and loss of the portfolio over time and then measure which losses were in the top fifth percentile. For example, a financial institution's portfolio, based on data from the past five years, may show that 95% of the time, its daily losses on a portfolio of $2 billion were less than $40 million. This method is simple in theory, but becomes more complicated if either the weighting or composition of the instruments held in the portfolio is not stable over time.

The Monte Carlo simulation method uses computers to generate random values that simulate price movements of the underlying instruments in a portfolio and then determine the portfolio's return in a large number of hypothetical scenarios. This technique is computationally intensive. Hence, it only became practical to use as the performance of computer hardware increased and as distributed, grid, and cloud computing solutions became available. Whereas the variance-covariance and historical methods work well for portfolios that are composed of relatively simple financial instruments, the Monte Carlo simulation is better suited for portfolios that contain complex instruments. The risk characteristics of structured products and exotic options may be difficult to model accurately using variance-covariance techniques, and these products may not have sufficient past data to support historical VaR computation.

The availability of different VaR modeling techniques is both a curse and a blessing. On the one hand, it provides institutions with the flexibility to choose the most appropriate method. On the other hand, it raises doubts about which is the most appropriate method. Also, if each calculation method yields a significantly different result, it will be unclear which of them is really correct and can be trusted.

18.3.3 Limitations of Risk Measurement and Value at Risk

For all its benefits, VaR has a number of problems and limitations. As discussed in the previous section, VaR calculations assume that the future behavior of financial instruments will be similar to relatively recent past behavior. During a financial crisis, this is often not the case. To compensate for behavioral inconsistency, stress test parameters may be used as inputs to VaR models. For example, when using the variance-covariance method, correlation and volatility matrices that correspond to particular crisis periods may be used in along with the ones that match recent market conditions. But because no crash is quite like others in the past, the effectiveness of historical scenario stress testing is limited. Likewise, it is difficult to factor into VaR calculations the effects of abnormal market conditions, such as a liquidity crunch when the only buyers available are making offers at submarket prices.

VaR is also limited by its single number simplicity. Knowing that there may be a certain level of loss at a certain level of confidence does not provide insights regarding what extreme losses might occur. The extreme losses are by far the most worrisome. For example, two portfolios of $2 billion may have the same 99% VaR of $120 million. However, due to differences in the risk characteristics of the underlying holdings, one portfolio may have a 0.1% chance of losing $500 million, whereas the other portfolio may have a 0.1% chance of losing $1.5 billion. Hence, in some cases, the simplicity of VaR can lead to overconfidence, or underestimation of unlikely, but not impossible, losses.

Given VaR's sensitivity to the calculation method chosen and the input parameters used, the results may vary significantly based on the implementation. Hence, "back testing" is required to validate the VaR estimate. For example, consider a portfolio whose VaR percentage is calculated to be a loss of 2% at a 95% confidence level. A review of the previous year's daily valuation of the portfolio should observe no more than 11 days with losses of 2% or more. Similarly, going forward, if losses greater than 2% are observed on more than what would be statistically expected, the VaR estimate may be viewed as suspect and the VaR calculation method may need to be revised.

18.4   BUSINESS OPPORTUNITIES

While financial risk can be detrimental in some cases, it is also a necessary part of business and, thus, provides opportunities for financial institutions that excel in risk management. From the Global Financial Crisis of 2008, the financial institutions that had effectively managed their risk exposures came out stronger than before and were able to more aggressively pursue the business of their stricken rivals. For instance, many Asia-focused banks that had suffered severe losses during the Asian Financial Crisis in the late 1990s acted more conservatively in the following decade, which led them to come through the Global Financial Crisis relatively unscathed. On the other hand, some relatively conservative financial institutions in North America and Europe took on positions in financial derivatives that were beyond their risk-management depth and faced painful consequences as a result (Case Study 18-5).

Besides keeping their house in order, there are clear opportunities to help financial institutions' customers manage their risk. Because financial institutions are obliged to invest in risk management IT systems, they have a sunk cost that can be potentially turned into an asset if it can be leveraged to provide services to customers. Corporate customers can benefit from independent analysis of the potential risk involved with their holdings. Furthermore, helping corporate customers understand their risk could also encourage customers to purchase hedging instruments, such as FX forwards and interest rate swaps, thereby increasing transaction volumes for banks that offer risk advisory services. There are also opportunities for banks to provide capital protected financial products to their customers. Capital protected products typically provide upside that is linked to a particular index or asset class, with a downside of no interest payout under certain conditions. The deposit principle amount, however, will be returned irrespectively. Unfortunately, principle protected products were avoided in the wake of the Global Financial Crisis. Some products were touted as being capital protected but were constructed using corporate debt instruments, such as Lehman Brothers bonds, for which there was no guarantee of principal return, particularly when Lehman Brothers filed for bankruptcy in 2008. Constructing such products using highly rated government bonds would have been a more legitimate way of providing these types of products.

Moreover, new technologies can help banks improve the accuracy and timeliness of their risk calculations. For instance, JPMorgan used specialized hardware technology, field-programmable gate arrays (FPGA), to help reduce the time required to produce risk estimates from eight hours to just under four minutes [4]. Being able to perform near-real-time risk calculations enables financial institutions to respond more rapidly to market events that occur during the day, as opposed to having to wait for overnight reports to be generated. They can also test more risk scenarios, allowing additional concerns to be identified and mitigation steps to be planned in advance.

Case Study 18-5

Knowing Your Place in the Financial Risk Food Chain

While risk management may involve a great deal of complex mathematics, one of the most important principles is to stick to common sense guidelines. Financial institutions that do not have the human or technological capacity to accurately determine the valuations and manage the risks associated with complex financial derivatives should not be buying or selling them in the first place. The financial markets are not always fair, and ignorance is often punished.

As a case in point, Eastern Financial Florida Credit Union was a state chartered cooperative bank in the United States that was placed under conservatorship, an alternative to bankruptcy, in 2009. Credit unions are typically relatively small financial institutions that focus on real estate lending and are limited in the types of securities they can purchase. On the contrary, starting in 2007, Eastern Financial made bets on relatively obscure and complex collateralized debt obligations (CDOs) that led to losses of close to $150 million. These losses compounded the bank's problems of losses on property loans and led to its demise. Its assets were taken over by another credit union, and losses amounting to tens of millions of dollars were absorbed by the National Credit Union Share Insurance Fund.

Given its size and charter, it is highly unlikely that Eastern Financial was suited to invest in CDOs, which is confirmed by the timing of their investment. If they had a suitable risk management IT system, it should have shown that buying the CDOs would increase the credit union's exposure to credit defaults on property loans and would increase the bank's risk concentration, as opposed to providing diversification. This impact should have been visible by a sharp jump in Eastern Financial's VaR.

Moreover, some degree of management common sense might also have helped avoid disaster. That a relatively small, loan-oriented financial institution is going to be on the winning side of derivatives trading, a business that major investment banks pour hundreds of millions of dollars into to compete, seems difficult to imagine.

Source: Morgenson, Gretchen, "A Credit Union That Played with Fire," *New York Times*, May 15, 2010, http://www.nytimes.com/2010/05/16/business/16gret.html.

18.5 BUSINESS CHALLENGES

Risk management provides no shortage of challenges. Financial institutions are usually more focused on taking steps to not become casualties of risk management, rather than finding ways to turn risk management into a profit center. Risk management is like a chain that is only as strong as its weakest link. A bank may invest millions of dollars in an IT system that calculates VaR to great accuracy. However, if inaccurate information is fed into that system or information that comes out is misinterpreted or ignored, very little value will come out of that IT investment. Calculating a VaR amount is not the end solution.

Like security, any number of operational failures can lead to major risk management-related losses. When internal controls are loosely enforced, rogue traders will thrive. Poor validation built into IT systems may allow high-value erroneous trades to be entered and executed by mistake. Overly aggressive sales staff may mis-sell products to customers, leading to lawsuits and regulatory fines. Management may not understand or be concerned about the potential downsides of their actions, leading their firms to take on excessive risk. Risk management is a multifaceted problem of which mathematics and technology only solve a small part.

A well-designed risk management system requires a strong set of checks and balances. Those whose jobs are to take risks must be matched with those who are to control risks. Furthermore, the risk management function should be independent and not report to a sales-related function or business executive who has profit targets. In some cases, a financial institution's risk management function may report to the board of directors rather than to the CEO, who may have a strong sales or trading orientation.

Risk management considerations must also be incorporated into compensation structures across the institutions. Often for sales people and traders, their personal gains from taking risks outweigh their potential losses. For example, imprudent actions may either lead to receiving a million-dollar bonus or, in the worst case, having to find a new job at a different financial institution. Managers who stand to profit from a rogue trader's winnings may be more ready to turn a blind eye to unauthorized trades that initially appear to be profitable. In many cases, poorly designed incentive structures will lead people to maximize their own returns, to the detriment of their employer.

On the other hand, avoiding risk can lead to underperformance. Viable business opportunities may be passed up for competitors to take advantage of. As a case in point, consider that Bank A may refuse to lend to customers who it sees are likely to default. Alternatively, Bank B may choose to lend to the customers that Bank A avoided, but charge higher interest rates so as to make their business profitable. Over time, overly conservative institutions may survive, but lag behind their competitors who take on more risk, but not excessively (Case Study 18-6).

Risk management is often referred to as an art, rather than a science. Like medicine, too little or too much can kill you. The dosage should vary according to the patient's size, constitution, and pain threshold.

Case Study 18-6
Knowing When to Stop Dancing

In 2007, Citibank's chairman was quoted as saying "as long as the music is playing, you've got to get up and dance." This statement has been interpreted as relating to the challenges of managing a financial institution when performance is gauged relative to industry benchmarks. If the majority of a bank's peers are doing something profitable in the short term, though risky in the long term, it can be hazardous for management not to run with the pack. When managers choose to follow a more prudent path and begin underachieving relative to their peers, shareholders may doubt their abilities and consider replacement options. In other words, if everyone else is dancing, you had better too.

MP Bank was the only commercial bank in Iceland that did not fail as a result of investments that were made during Iceland's economic bubble period in the early 2000s. During the bubble, concerns that senior management had regarding overvaluation of investment opportunities in Iceland led the bank to shift its focus abroad and move the bulk of its assets into Icelandic government bonds. While it missed some of the upside of the boom, it remained profitable and after the bust, it ended up being the only independent commercial bank in Iceland. It is interesting to note that MP Bank is relatively small and privately held; its senior management holds a significant stake in the company. So, it would seem that it is easier to stop dancing when you get to help call the tune.

Sources: "The Gods Strike Back," *Economist*, February 13, 2010, http://www.economist.com/node/15474137; McClain, Dylan Loeb, "Caution Kept Icelandic Bank Clear of the Worst," *New York Times*, July 3, 2009, http://www.nytimes.com/2009/07/04/business/global/04spot.html.

18.6 PROCESS CONSIDERATIONS

Business process management (BPM) can help reduce financial firms' risk in a variety of ways. In some cases, there is an opportunity to transition risk management from being an art that is highly dependent on the capabilities of specific individuals to become more of a repeatable process that can evolve on its own and ensure continuity over time. BPM can also provide a means for tracking the business process so that important tasks related to risk management, such as reconciliation of positions, are not sidestepped or forgotten, creating operational risks in their own right.

Financial institutions' operational risk largely comes from processing exceptions. Losses do not usually occur when processes go as intended. System failures, missing or corrupted information, failed communications, skipped process steps, and fraudulent actions often cause exceptions (Figure 18-6). By tracking the ongoing state of transactions, monitoring their status, and detecting and taking rapid action when exceptions are detected, it is possible to minimize losses. BPM-related technology can help automate process flows, thus making exception detection and management more efficient.

Consider, for example, a trade that is booked to the wrong counterparty. Trade confirmation processes have been designed to detect such situations. Manual comparison of trade confirmations may be practical for low trade volumes; however, automation will be required for larger volumes. It is critical that any confirmation mismatches, that is, process exceptions, are identified and corrected promptly; otherwise, settlement deadlines may be missed, and cause interest and/or regulatory penalties to be incurred.

Process automation may have also helped avoid the collapse of Barings Bank, as reviewed in Case Study 19-1. Many exceptions occurred in many different processes leading to its collapse. If Barings had a more robust process implementation and monitoring system, it would have been easier to piece together much earlier that a fraud was underway. Audits are useful for uncovering process and accounting failures, but often only long after they have occurred. BPM is much more effective at detecting irregularities as they arise.

Figure 18-6 Paper-based transactions that require manual processing increase risk (© **DBS Bank. Reprinted with permission.**)

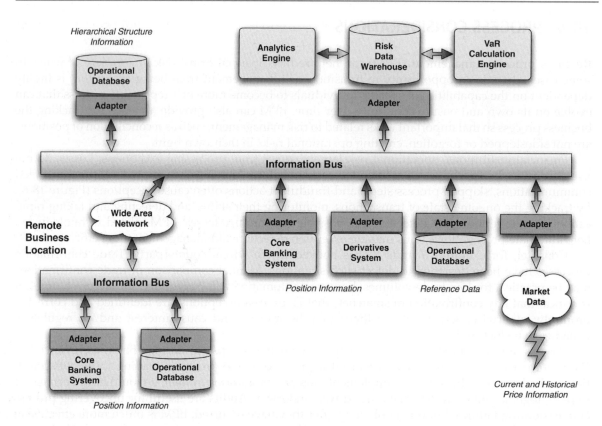

Figure 18-7 Risk management data aggregation architecture

18.7   ARCHITECTURE CONSIDERATIONS

As discussed in the introduction of this chapter, data quality of risk information and automation of risk processes are a current challenge for banks, but the concern has been ongoing for many years. In 2009, a review by bank supervisors found that many large banks had problems aggregating risk information [5]. Two-thirds of the banks surveyed were only able to partially aggregate their credit exposures in an automated and timely manner. During stress tests of US banks in the same year, some banks took days to calculate their exposure to counterparties' derivatives trades. In some cases, limitations involving **legacy system** integration were to blame. Hence, consolidating position information from disparate IT systems into a centralized risk management **data warehouse** is critical for generating timely and accurate risk estimates. Aggregated position information is necessary for financial institutions with multinational business operations to determine their overall exposures to specific countries (for example, exposure across all asset classes linked to Greece) and global exposure to multinational customers (for example, global exposure to Lehman Brothers). Furthermore, centralizing risk information in a data warehouse is essential for fulfilling Basel risk reporting requirements and other country-specific regulatory reporting demands.

Figure 18-7 shows the logical view of a data aggregation architecture for risk management. Adapters extract information on a real-time or periodic basis from the bank's transactional systems and databases. These systems may be in a single location, such as the bank's headquarters. For larger institutions, though, it is more likely that they will be distributed across multiple countries or regions. An information bus is used to distribute information that is necessary for risk calculations. Another

---

Case Study 18-7
Risk Data Solutions

To accurately calculate risk exposures, it is necessary that the data input into risk calculations is complete and consistent. Some input data, such as aggregated position data, is bank specific. However, other types of input data, such as price volatility correlations, historical price volatility, and default probabilities, are all information that many financial institutions require. Accordingly, a number of vendors provide technology-based risk solutions to address these common needs.

The Risk Metrics Group, a company established in 1998, was an offshoot of JPMorgan. Risk Metrics provided standard risk management methodologies and tools that can be used by a wide range of financial institutions. The company went on to provide risk management software, risk management data, and risk management software services. For example, Risk Metrics provided standard estimates of the volatilities and correlations required for variance-covariance VaR calculations. Many large investment managers, hedge funds, and central banks were its customers. MSCI acquired Risk Metrics in 2010 and provides Risk Metrics' data and services as part of its risk management product offerings.

Another company, FICO, previously known as the Fair Isaac Corporation, has chosen to focus on standardizing consumer credit risk data by providing credit-scoring solutions. FICO scores are commonly used in the United States to assess the likelihood that an individual will repay his or her debt obligations. Credit bureaus and banks often use these scores to help make decisions about granting credit to their customers. FICO provides a range of products and services related to credit scoring and decision analysis.

With regard to operational risk, a common problem that financial institutions face is collecting sufficient data about past operational risk events. To help address this issue, the Operational Riskdata eXchange Association (ORX) was formed as a nonprofit industry association. ORX provides a platform for the secure and anonymous exchange of operational risk loss data. Over 50 banks are members of ORX. They submit standardized operational risk information to ORX and can access the aggregate information stored in its global loss database, which includes information about tens of thousands of operational risk loss events.

Sources: MCSI website, http://www.msci.com; FICO website, http://www.fico.com; ORX Association website, http://www.orx.org.

---

adapter receives data from the information bus and stores it in the risk data warehouse.* The risk data warehouse will then serve the VaR calculation engine and other analytics engines, providing an aggregated and accurate source of information for computations. Often the multiple instances of the VaR calculation engine will be run in parallel using distributed, grid, or cloud computing platforms to increase performance and reduce processing time.

A wide range of information is required to support VaR calculations. Position information, that is, the quantities of different instruments, is required to determine the market exposure. A snapshot of current prices is required to evaluate the instruments and determine the current monetary value of the positions. Prices of some instruments may not be available, and their values will need to be estimated. Historical data is required for back testing and may also be used within the VaR computation. In some cases, correlation and volatility information may be sourced from third-party risk information vendors. Securities reference data, such as the cash-flow structure of securities and loans, is also required to perform risk sensitivity calculations. Furthermore, hierarchical information, that is, corporate legal entities' relations to one another, is necessary to calculate aggregated limit exposures.

---

* In cases where risk data is sourced primarily through files that are provided by source systems on a batch basis, an extract, transform, load (ETL) approach may be used in place of an information bus / adapter strategy.

To calculate VaR accurately, all position information must be consolidated and fed into a centralized VaR calculation engine. That is to say, producing separate VaR calculations, based on positions in different geographic locations, and then aggregating the individual VaR estimates will yield suboptimal results. VaR calculations take into account the correlation of positions to one another, that is, how one position's market movement may offset the effects of another position's movement. When all of the raw position information is available to the VaR calculation engine, every offsetting factor can be taken into account. However, when VaR is calculated locally in multiple locations, the benefits of offsetting positions across the locations cannot be taken into account. For example, consider the simplified case where a bank's New York business operation is long 100 Japanese Government Bond futures and its London operation is short the same amount. If New York and London calculate their VaR separately, they will each come up with VaR amounts that reflect the risk associated with their individual positions, and combining their VaR would result in a greater VaR amount that either of them would record individually. Alternatively, aggregating the New York and London positions before calculating VaR would cause the two positions to entirely offset one another for market risk calculation purposes and, thus, generate zero VaR.

Obtaining a complete and robust data model, which serves as the core of the risk data warehouse, is a major challenge underlying data aggregation. It is not easy to construct or source a data model that will cater for a wide range of instrument types and all their unique features. Likewise, the effort required to map system-specific information into the data warehouse's standardized form is another challenge. The adapters that connect to the source systems or, alternatively, an adapter linked to the data warehouse may perform the mapping function.

18.8   SOLUTION CONSIDERATIONS

Fortunately, over the past 20 years a variety of software solutions have been developed to help manage risk. Broad categories of solutions include VaR calculation engines, risk modeling toolkits, data services, and risk portals. Third-party VaR calculation engines are quite common and usually implement one or more of the techniques discussed in Section 18.3.2. Using proven, off-the-shelf risk calculation systems helps minimize the chance of software development mistakes that can potentially lead to incorrect risk estimations. Off-the-shelf software is usually more robust than homegrown implementations because it is more mature and has a larger user base. The more users a system has, the greater the chance that users will have already identified and reported to the vendor any relevant defects. Likewise, the older a system is, the more likely it is that known defects will have been fixed by the vendor.

Flexible modeling toolkits are also used for risk management. They can be used to help explore the risk characteristics of complex financial instruments and statistically model the effects of fat-tail distributions. These tools differ from VaR calculators in that they are usually very flexible, providing an interactive programming environment for manipulating and charting data. The open source R-Project (see the Further Reading section at the end of the chapter) is an example of a statistical modeling toolkit that can be used to help analyze financial risk.

As discussed in Case Study 18-7, a number of vendors provide standardized data that can be used for risk management calculations. Some services provide entire hosted risk portals that not only provide the risk data, but also host the VaR calculation engine and **market data**. With this type of solution, the only effort required of the user is to load the position information into the portal.

It is important to remember that while using prepackaged risk management solutions has many benefits, it also has its trade-offs. The features provided by the third-party risk products must be close enough to the user requirements to be viable solutions. In the worst case, some user requirements that are not met may have to be forgone. Alternatively, additional functionality may be built around the off-the-shelf system. Customizing an off-the-shelf risk solution is sometimes possible, but is often an expensive undertaking.

18.9 SUMMARY

This chapter covered:

- the common types of risks that financial institutions face;
- market risk concepts and value at risk;
- the need for data aggregation to support consolidated risk management; and
- process, architecture, and solution considerations related to risk management.

The next chapter reviews considerations related to operational and regulatory compliance risk. It also examines how the technology architectures and solutions that financial institutions implement are impacted by these types of risks.

FURTHER READING

Books

Bodie, Z., A. Kane, and A. Marcus, *Essentials of Investments* (New York: McGraw-Hill/Irwin, 2005).

Butler, C., *Mastering Value at Risk: A Step-by-Step Guide to Understanding and Applying VAR* (Essex: Financial Times/Prentice Hall, 1999).

Coleman, T. S., *A Practical Guide to Risk Management* (Virginia: Research Foundation of CFA Institute, 2011).

Hull, J. C., *Risk Management and Financial Institutions* (New Jersey: Wiley, 2012).

De Haan, L. and A. Ferreira, *Extreme Value Theory: An Introduction* (New York: Springer, 2006).

Jorion, P., *Value at Risk—The New Benchmark for Managing Financial Risk* (New York: McGraw-Hill, 2006).

Lewis, M., *The Big Short: Inside the Doomsday Machine* (New York: W. W. Norton & Company, 2010).

Papers and Articles

Bank for International Settlements, "Regulatory reform of over- the-counter derivatives: an assessment of incentives to clear centrally," October 2014, http://www.bis.org/publ/othp21.htm.

Canabarro, E. and D. Duffie, "Measuring and Marking Counterparty Risk," in *Asset/Liability Management of Financial Institutions*, ed. Leo M. Tilman, pp. 122–134 (London: Euromoney Books, 2003).

Ieraci, R., "RAROC: A Tool for Factoring Risk into Investment, Pricing, and Compensation," *The RMA Journal* (March 2009): 68–72.

Nocera, J., "Risk Mismanagement," *New York Times*, January 4, 2009, http://www.nytimes.com /2009/01/04/magazine/04risk-t.html?pagewanted=all.

"Special Report: Financial Risk," *Economist*, February 11, 2010, http://www.economist.com/ node/15474137.

Web

"Basel III: international regulatory framework for banks," http://www.bis.org/bcbs/basel3.htm.

"Basic Principles of Banking Supervision—Handbooks in Central Banking no. 7," http://www. bankofengland.co.uk/education/ccbs/handbooks/ccbshb07.htm.

International Convergence of Capital Measurement and Capital Standards, A Revised Framework (Basel II), Basel Committee on Banking Supervision, 2005, http://www.bis.org/publ/bcbs118.pdf.

"The R Project and RMetrics," http://www.r-project.org.

ENDNOTES

1. Greenberg, J. S., "New Fraud Inquiry as JPMorgan's Loss Mounts," *New York Times*, July 13, 2012, https://dealbook.nytimes.com/2012/07/13/jpmorgan-says-traders-obscured-losses-in-first-quarter/.

2. KPMG, "Stress Testing: A Bench Analysis of Systemically Important Financial Institutions," August 2016, https://assets.kpmg.com/content/dam/kpmg/xx/pdf/2016/11/stress-testing-a-benchmarking-analysis-of-systemically-important-financial-institutions.pdf.

3. Embrechts, P., S. I. Resnick, and G. Samorodnitsky, "Extreme Value Theory As a Risk Management Tool," *North American Actuarial Journal* 3 (1999): 30–41.

4. Nguyen, A., "JP Morgan Supercomputer Offers Risk Analysis in Near Real-time," *ComputerWorld UK*, July 11, 2011, http://www.computerworlduk.com/news/it-business/3290494/jp-morgan-supercomputer-offers-risk-analysis-in-near-real-time.

5. "Number–crunchers Crunched," *Economist*, February 13, 2010, http://www.economist.com/node/15474075.

19 Operational and Compliance Risk Management

Chapter Overview

19.1 OPERATIONAL RISK

19.2 COMPLIANCE RISK

19.3 SUMMARY

FURTHER READING

ENDNOTES

Historically, when it came to risk, banks focused most of their attention on credit and **market risk**. However, with the growth of banks' size and complexity over the past several decades, **operational risk** has advanced to become a core business concern. Likewise, the increase in the number and the complexity of financial products and expansion of the technology and communication channels that banks use have led to **compliance risk** becoming a major source of concern for financial institutions. Some of these risks, such as fraud, have been around for many years. Others, such as the risks related to technology outsourcing and compliance with rules related to digital communications, have emerged more recently.

Operational risk is defined by the Bank of International Settlements (BIS) in the Basel II accord as "the risk of loss resulting from inadequate or failed internal processes, people and systems or from external events."* This broad definition can cover a wide range of situations. Examples of faulty internal processes are those that, by design, lead to conflicts of interest, as highlighted in Case Study 19-2, and processes that are not executed as designed. Operational risk related to people could range from outright fraud to negligence due to inadequate training or management. Failures of IT systems can stem from surges in transaction volume, as described in Case Study 7-5, or software glitches, highlighted in Case Study 3-2. External events can include cyberattacks, such as denial of service attacks, as well as natural disasters, such as earthquakes and floods.

The BIS defines compliance risk as the losses or reputational damage that a financial institution may incur from failing to comply with laws, regulations, rules, and codes of conduct applicable to its activities. Examples of laws that banks must comply with include fair lending and debt collection practices. Regulations may cover liability for electronic fund transfers or the disclosures for home

---

* The BIS considers legal risk to be a subset of operational risk, but does not include reputational and strategic risk in its definition. Also, Basel III did not include any changes to regulations that were related to operational risk.

mortgages. Rules may be imposed by market bodies, such as stock exchanges and clearing houses, for instance, the National Automated Clearing House Association (NACHA), as discussed in Chapter 9. Furthermore, each financial institution may have its own code of conduct that addresses considerations like conflict of interest for employees and handling of customer complaints.

Operational and compliance risk go hand in hand, in that often failures that produce operational risk may also lead to compliance risk as well. Their impact can be significant, leading to financial losses, reputational damage, and in some cases institutional failure, as discussed with Barings Bank in Case Study 19-1. The scope of operational and compliance risks may be limited to a single institution, span multiple institutions, or even be systemic. In the case of Barings Bank, only the bank itself was involved with the process failures. Alternatively, the Libor interest rate fixing scandal involved multiple financial institutions [1]. In the case of the terror attacks in New York in 2001, the entire cheque clearing system in the United States was affected by the subsequent restrictions on air travel.

Like financial institutions, operational risk concerns apply directly to Fintech companies, but their exposure to compliance risk has been more limited. By their nature of not having a banking license, most Fintech companies have been able to avoid much of the regulatory scrutiny that financial institutions must endure. However, as the Fintech industry has grown and gained greater prominence, lawmakers and regulators have taken more notice and compliance is likely to become a greater concern going forward. As a case in point, historically in the US marketplace lenders (discussed in Chapter 8) have not been subject to fair lending rules. Even so, in 2017, the US congress began investigating whether the algorithms that they use were potentially discriminatory. These algorithms typically do not use prohibited factors, such as race and ethnicity; however, alternative inputs that they use may have close correlations to prohibited factors, leading to biased credit decisions.

Operational and compliance risk is largely managed through the design of processes and business practices, such as credit decisioning models and incentive schemes. Risks are identified and mitigating controls are put in place to address them. For example, a mistake in the manual entry of price information could create both operational and compliance risk. Designing a process so that a second person reviews the information that is entered before submission could be used as a mitigating control. Monitoring is also necessary to ensure that as things change, new risks are identified and mitigating controls work as intended. However, mitigations such as adding additional checks increase the cost

---

Case Study 19-1

Operational Risk Brings Down Barings Bank

Barings Bank had a long and prestigious history in the United Kingdom; however, as it entered the 1990s, the profitability of its core business, lending, was steadily being eroded. To help compensate for this change, Barings moved into proprietary trading (prop trading) in securities and derivatives markets, providing an important source of revenue for Barings' Asia operations. Besides executing trades on the futures exchanges on behalf of its customers, Barings also engaged in arbitrage trading on its own account. Arbitrage trading, which is buying and selling similar securities on different markets to take advantage of short-lived price differences, generates small but steady returns with relatively little risk.

The UK-based bank's troubles with its derivatives business began in 1993 when it appointed 25-year-old Nick Leeson as general manager of the new futures trading operation in Singapore. In his capacity as a trader, Leeson was authorized to make arbitrage trades, but was not authorized to take net long or short positions or hold positions overnight. In his capacity as general manager, he was in control of front-office trading as well as back-office accounting and settlement operations.

By 1994, the trading profits that Leeson reported represented around 8% of Barings Group's operating profits. Leeson stood to make hundreds of thousands of pounds in bonus for his trading activities in 1993 and

1994. The scale of his trading profits, however, did not correspond to what trading arbitrage strategies would be able to generate. In fact, Leeson made large unhedged trades on Japanese government bond futures, Japanese stock index futures, as well as options on Japanese stock index futures, and held them on Barings' account. These trades were unauthorized and were contrary to his trading remit, which did not allow holding long-term positions.

Unfortunately for Barings, Leeson's trades went sour and led to cumulative losses of hundreds of millions of pounds. As head of the back office, he was able to manipulate Barings' accounting systems to hide his trading losses. Furthermore, Barings' reconciliation processes, which compare trades recorded by different systems, were ineffective—they failed to uncover that Leeson's trades did not, as he claimed, correspond to customer orders. Nonetheless, Leeson continued to receive funding from Baring's headquarters in London even though the payments he received could not be matched with client positions.

The bank's headquarters was unaware that Leeson was booking his trades on its account, and thought that the increasingly large funds transfers that it made to its Singapore operation were necessary to cover the future exchanges' margin calls on its customers' positions. Partially because Barings Group lacked a centralized position monitoring system, it did not determine that the funds Leeson requested from the bank's headquarters on a regular basis were far in excess of what should have been required. In the end, the accumulated losses amounted to €800 million more than Barings Group's capital, leading it to file for bankruptcy.

Barings's failure was the result of weak systems and lax management. If the century-old internal control principle of separation of duties had been applied, Leeson would have never been given control of front- and back-office operations. This segregation would have prevented him from falsifying the accounting information. Likewise, better reconciliation processes could have flagged mismatches as fictitious trades. Centralized position keeping and risk monitoring systems should have also determined that the bank had an unjustifiably large exposure to positions in specific markets.

More critically, Barings' collapse was due to failures of management common sense. The Singapore trading operations requests for funding from Barings headquarters were continuous and increased over time to mind-boggling proportions. The business units' funding needs were inconsistent with the high profitability that Leeson purported. Even after Barings received warnings from the futures exchange about Leeson's trading activities months prior to its discovery of the fraud, the Barings Group continued to send over €400 million to fund his operation right up to the point of collapse. Had serious measures been taken earlier, the bank may have only faced considerable losses rather than a complete collapse.

While Barings Bank was one of many banks that has incurred significant losses due to derivatives and unauthorized trading, it was the first time that such losses were sufficiently large to cause a bank to become insolvent. Unfortunately, 15 years later, the problems that plagued Barings were still prevalent. As a case in point, in 2010, the Hong Kong trading unit of a global investment bank was fined close to half a million US dollars by regulators for "systems and controls failings." In this case, to hide losses, a senior manager illicitly changed the prices used to value exotic option positions in the bank's computer systems. Sounds familiar?

Questions

1. What types of technology solutions would have helped Barings' management identify that Leeson was engaging in unauthorized activity?
2. Were Barings' futures trading counterparties directly impacted by counterparty risk when Barings collapsed?
3. How is it that even with the corrective actions taken by regulators and banks after events like Barings, similar types of problems continue to occur in the future?
4. What factors might have led Leeson to engage in unauthorized trading activities?

Sources: Stonham, Paul, "Whatever Happened at Barings? Part One: The Lure of Derivatives and Collapse," *European Management Journal* 14, issue 2 (1996): 167–175; Stonham, Paul, "Whatever Happened at Barings? Part Two: Unauthorized Trading and the Failure of Controls," *European Management Journal* 14, issue 3 (1996): 269–278; Cookson, Robert, "HK Watchdog Slaps Fine on Merrill Units," *Financial Times*, May 31, 2010, http://www.ft.com/cms/s/0/6a550446-6cdf-11df-91c8-00144feab49a.html.

of processing and the complexity of processes, so they must be weighed against the likelihood and impact of the operational risks that they guard against.

Information technology (IT) can be a useful tool for implementing mitigating controls. For instance, automated checks can be implemented to verify that amounts that are entered are within an expected range. Technology also supports monitoring of operations and compliance. On the other hand, technology can also be a source of operational and compliance risk. IT systems can fail, and their complexity can lead to unintended compliance violations. Ironically, compliance and operational risk concerns are major contributors to the complexity of financial institutions' IT systems. This chapter highlights key considerations with regard to operational and compliance risks that relate to technology solutions.

19.1 OPERATIONAL RISK

The Basel II accord framework classifies operational risk losses into seven distinct event types:

- internal fraud;

- external fraud;

- employment practices and workplace safety;

- products and business practices;

- damage to physical assets;

- business disruption and system failures; and

- execution, delivery, and process management.

Given the focus of this book, only the subset of these categories that have a strong relation to technology, shown in Figure 19-1, are discussed in this chapter. The subsections that follow will review the types of operational risk, along with how those risks can be mitigated, and how operational risk is measured for capital allocation purposes.

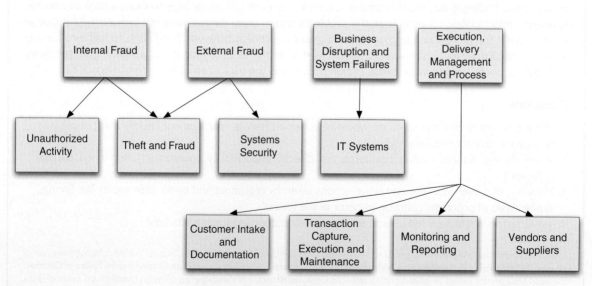

Figure 19-1 Technology-related categories of operational risk

19.1.1 Types and Sources of Operational Risk

Operational risk can be produced by internal and external sources. Internal sources of operational risk include people, processes, and technology, i.e., IT systems. External sources include people and natural disasters. Broad types of operational risk that are technology-related include unauthorized activity, theft and fraud, IT systems security, IT systems resilience, data management, and vendors.

19.1.1.1 Unauthorized activity

Case Study 19-1 highlights the risks of unauthorized activities, which initially occurred as unreported transactions and later included unauthorized transactions. The "rogue trader" problem, exemplified by Barings, is not uncommon. A number of similar cases have been publicly scrutinized over the years, and it is likely that many others have been handled internally without public review.

Intentional mismarking of positions is another common type of unauthorized activity, which is usually used to hide losses. Typically this occurs with financial instruments, such as complex over-the-counter (OTC) derivatives, that are not liquid and therefore do not have an easily discernable price and cannot be "marked to market." In these cases, they may be valued based on financial model-based pricing, "market to model," or using some other subjective valuation method. By manipulating the pricing model it may be possible to make positions appear more profitable than they would be if they had to be unwound. Additionally, unauthorized activity may involve entering into types of transactions that are not permitted for an individual or business unit.

Technology solutions can help implement mitigating controls for unauthorized and unreported transactions, chiefly through automation of reporting, monitoring, and reconciliation. In particular, exception-based reporting and monitoring can help identify inconsistencies and inaccuracies that result from unauthorized activities. Often, just knowing that reporting and monitoring mechanisms are in place can provide strong disincentive for employees to engage in unauthorized activity.

19.1.1.2 Theft and fraud

Theft and fraud are a major source of operational risk for financial institutions. For as long as there have been banks, there have been bank robbers. Internal theft and fraud are a key concern because insiders, by nature of their roles, are able to bypass a number of physical and logical controls that provide protection against theft and fraud. For instance, a branch manager who has access to the bank vault and knows the combination clearly is able to bypass these controls. Not surprisingly, insiders are responsible for the majority of fraud; it is estimated that around 75% of fraud is perpetrated or facilitated by insiders [2]. Furthermore, as shown in Figure 19-2, while the main driver of fraud is personal gain and greed, other factors are involved as well.

There are many types of fraud, many of which do not directly involve technology, as highlighted by Case Study 19-2. If anything, the lack of technology, that is, relying on copies of paper documents as supporting evidence for financial transactions, can contribute fraud. Likewise, customer's personal and financial information that has been leaked through data breaches or is exposed through social media enables external fraud via account takeovers and identity theft, which have grown as concerns in recent years. Account takeovers are perpetrated by fraudsters who have enough information about a customer to impersonate him or her. Typically, the fraudster uses this deception to change the address on the customer's account to be the fraudster's address, report a debit or credit card as lost or stolen, and then have a replacement card sent to the new address. In the case of identity theft, fraudsters will apply for loans or credit accounts using an individual's personally identifiable information.

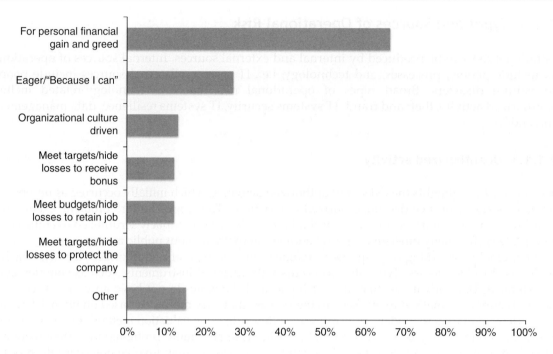

Figure 19-2 Motivations for fraud

Case Study 19-2

Forgery Still a Common Means for Fraud

One consideration that was not discussed in Case Study 19-1 was the fact that Leeson's fraud was enabled by forging documents that were provided to auditors to help hide his malefaction. Surprisingly, forgery is still a common means of committing internal fraud. Two examples follow to illustrate how the practice is accomplished on different scales and in different countries.

In Singapore, a former bank executive was jailed for his participation in a fraudulent loan scam. In this case the bank executive colluded with two housing agents to use forged proof-of-income documents to provide mortgage loans to people whose incomes did not qualify them. The banker was set to gain by receiving an agent referral fee from the bank for the transactions totaling several thousand dollars and also over fifteen thousand dollars from the housing agents. As a result of the fraud, the bank lost over a hundred thousand dollars because the borrowers were unable fully to repay the loans. The three perpetrators were sentenced to five years in jail.

In the United States, the collapse of a futures broker, Peregrine Financial Group, resulted from embezzlement of $215 million by the head of the firm. The fraud was perpetrated for over a decade and was sustained by submitting forged bank statements to auditors and regulators. The failure of Peregrine compounded concerns about the security of customer deposits following MF Global's downfall two years earlier (discussed in Case Study 18-1). The head of Peregrine was sentenced to 50 years in jail.

Implementation of controls and use of technology to monitor activities are helpful in preventing and minimizing fraud. However, unfortunately simple paper-based techniques such as forgery, in some cases, are still able to bypass those protections.

Sources: "3 Jailed for 5 Years Each for OCBC Housing Loan Scam," *AsiaOne*, Dec 15, 2011, http://news.asiaone.com/print/News/AsiaOne%2BNews/Singapore/Story/A1Story20111215-316374.html; Munshi, Neil, "Wasendorf Jailed for 50 Years for Fraud," *Financial Times*, January 31, 2013, http://www.ft.com/intl/cms/s/0/cdf6ce16-6bd4-11e2-a17d-00144feab49a.html#axzz2JaMHBbBq.

More recently, technology-based attacks, discussed in Chapter 17, have become an increasingly common avenue for fraud. A few examples are:

- hackers break into merchant's point-of-sales systems to capture card account information and then sell that information to be used to create cloned cards that are used for fraudulent purchases;

- fraudsters send email impersonating a company's senior executive instructing someone in finance to make a payment to the fraudster's bank account;

- hackers are able to install **ransomware** on a company's workstations that encrypts data files and demands payment to unlock the files;

- hackers gain access to payment gateway systems, e.g., ACH or SWIFT, and initiate transfers using those systems.

While historically, fraud risk has been largely an internal concern, technology has made it easier for fraudsters to go after financial institutions remotely, and often from foreign nations. A cartoon depicting a bank robber holding up a bank teller, and the teller responding that it was easier to do it online, is quite fitting for modern times.

Technology is used to implement many of the controls that are used to prevent fraud. Controls, such as two-stage approval, transaction amount limits, and transaction frequency limits, are often built into software solutions. Technology also helps to monitor for and detect exceptions and anomalies that can be the symptoms of fraudulent activity. Business process modeling, discussed in Chapter 2, is also helpful to identify points where fraud could occur and to identify mitigating controls that can be applied to prevent fraud.

19.1.1.3 IT systems security

Two main concerns related to IT systems security in the context of operational risk are damage done by hacking and the theft of information. Damage done by hacking is typically through **denial of service attacks** and malware that is designed to erase information or render IT systems unusable. Both types of activities are typically performed by external actors and are done maliciously for political or ideological reasons, as opposed to for financial gain. As mentioned in Section 19.1.1.2, hacking may also be targeted at fraud or theft of money. Such theft may be achieved by initiating falsified payment instructions or by accessing IT systems that have direct access to cash such as automated teller machines (ATMs). As a case in point, in 2016, cybercriminals from Europe and Russia used malware to hack into a Taiwanese bank's ATMs, enabling them to illicitly withdraw $2.5 million from the ATMs [3].

Theft of information can occur in many different ways and involves different types of data. Historically, the primary concern has been cybercriminals stealing customer contact and account information from financial institutions. Confidential merger and acquisition information has also been a target of information theft, since it can be used for insider trading. More recently, the threat of insiders, who have legitimate access to internal IT systems, stealing sensitive information has become a growing concern. The damage done to the US government by Edward Snowden highlights the potential risk that this threat poses.

A variety of technologies and operational practices are used to mitigate IT systems security risk. These topics are discussed in depth in Chapter 17.

19.1.1.4 IT systems resilience

Failure of IT systems can lead to financial and reputational damage as well as regulatory sanctions and, thus, systems resilience is a major focus for banks. Failures and disruptions can occur at many different levels including hardware, software, networks and telecommunications, and power. Failures may be limited to individual software applications or systems, or may affect entire sites or geographic areas. The causes of failures include bugs in software, equipment failure, operational mistakes, flooding, fires, terrorism, and even from cosmic rays hitting and affecting computer processing components. None of these can be entirely prevented. Natural and man-made disasters are a major concern because of their widespread impact and unpredictability. The 2001 terrorist attacks on the World Trade Center in New York, the 2005 flooding of New Orleans caused by Hurricane Katrina, and the 2011 Fukushima earthquake and nuclear disaster in Japan are just a few examples of the calamities that lead to major IT systems failures or inaccessibility.

Systems and communications redundancy is the primary means of mitigating the risk of systems failures. Mission-critical systems will usually have backup systems in the same or a different location. Data centers will have a geographically separate backup data center that can be used for disaster recovery. Redundant communication lines will be used between critical locations, usually routed through different telecommunication providers. Offsite, offline data backups will be used to protect against inadvertent or intentional damage to online data stores. Paradoxically, adding components to provide redundancy to reduce operational risk increases the complexity of the overall system architecture, which increases operational risk.

Redundancy of skills and knowledge across operational staff is also required. While some failovers to backup systems may be automated, it is common for larger-scale recovery activities to require manual intervention. Thus, it is important that IT operations staff that have the requisite skills and experience are available to support failover and disaster recovery activities. It follows that operational risk can increase significantly in cases of mass attrition or layoffs of IT operations staff, because the remaining employees and new hires may not be sufficiently versed in the IT systems or business environment. Furthermore, the risk of unintentional mistakes as well as outright sabotage by IT operations staff are other operational risks that must be considered, as highlighted by Case Study 19-3.

Case Study 19-3

Rogue System Administrators Are a Major Source of Operational Risk

By nature of their security privileges and extended access, IT system administrators are a large source of operational risk. By incorrectly typing a command or pushing the wrong button, they have the potential to render systems inoperable and permanently delete information. Most of the time, operational loss incidents caused by system administrators are purely accidental; however, the risk of intentional damage is also a real concern. Cases where system administrators go rogue are particularly dangerous because they know best how to cause the most damage in the IT environment. In 2013, Citibank faced this situation in its US operations.

After being reprimanded by his manager and believing that he was going to be fired, a system administrator deleted the configuration files on nine core network routers. This caused network traffic to be routed through backup routers leading to network congestion that disrupted phone and network service at 110 branches across the country. Ultimately, the system administrator pleaded guilty to intentional damage to a computer and was sentenced to 21 months in jail and ordered to pay a $77,000 fine.

It is common practice when terminating staff that have enhanced security privileges, to immediately cut off their access to systems and walk them out of the building. While this procedure may seem harsh and callous, especially for longstanding employees, it mitigates the operational risk that may ensue from having a disgruntled employee with the potential to do material damage to the IT systems or information. As shown by Citibank's misfortune, similar precautions may also need to be taken leading up to termination as well.

Sources: Nichols, Shaun, "Ex-Citibank IT Bloke Wiped Bank's Core Routers, Will Now Spend 21 Months in the Clink," *The Register*, 27 July 2016, http://www.theregister.co.uk/2016/07/27/citibank_network_wipe_man_jailed/.

Having good architecture documentation is important for supporting the analysis of potential failure points across the many IT components that banks rely upon. IT system resilience is discussed in more depth in Chapters 5 and 7.

19.1.1.5 Information management

A large contributor to operational risk is the mismanagement of information. Often it is related to human error, such as an amount entered with an extra zero at the end or clicking the buy button instead of the sell button for an order. Data may also not be maintained properly, such as having a customer address updated in the core banking system but not in the credit card account system. Reference data, such as SWIFT bank identifier codes (BIC), may not be up to date, leading to failed payments. Overnight update files can fail to be transferred properly, leading to stale data potentially being used the next morning. The requirements specification for an interest payment calculation may be unclear, leading to its implementation in a software application being incorrect. Copies of customer identification documents used for account opening may be lost or misplaced, leading to audit issues. These are just a few of the many examples of how things related to information management can go wrong and produce operational risk and potential losses.

There are many different mitigating controls that are used to try to minimize the damage that these types of problems cause. Electronic forms can use a confirmation screen to help the user verify that the information is correct before the transaction is completed. Master data management systems can be used to centralize the management and distribution of static and reference data, such as customer addresses and BIC codes. Redundant file transfers can be implemented along with automated monitoring to alert if any transfer failure has occurred. Multiple people can be assigned to review requirements specifications to help identify and address any ambiguities. Documents can be scanned and stored electronically, helping to prevent loss. Many of these mitigating controls are implemented through technology solutions. Hence, when designing solutions it is important to think about the types of operational risk that could arise related to data management, and design and build in safeguards to help avoid that risk.

19.1.1.6 Vendor and supplier risk

Financial institutions have many dependencies on vendors and suppliers, which can lead to operational risk. For example, smaller banks may rely on payment processors to host their core banking and payment systems. The possibility that the service provider might have an outage is operational risk for the bank. Likewise, all financial institutions are dependent on power and telecommunications utilities. If power or data links are disrupted, the institution could face losses related to operational risk as a result. Where certain business functions such as call data center management or call center services are outsourced, there is risk that the incorrect performance of those services by the outsourcing vendor will lead to problems such as compliance failures. As financial services IT systems move more toward decentralized hosting, i.e., cloud-based services, and as application programming interfaces (API) are used to leverage third-party components and services, these operational risk related to vendor and supplier services will grow. Because of the significant risks associated with vendor and supplier risk, many regulatory jurisdictions require financial institutions to have vendor management programs, which is discussed in Section 19.2.

For suppliers, risk mitigation is usually achieved by having multiple, independent suppliers, where possible, or have backup capabilities that can be implemented internally. For example, while it is usually impractical to use an alternate payment processor as backup, if the core processor has an outage, it might be possible to have tellers or contact center agents reference the previous day's closing balances and manually record transactions on paper, and then enter them into the core banking application later when the core processor's system is available. Typically, multiple telecommunication providers are used to limit the impact of service disruptions. Having multiple power suppliers is usually not an option, but uninterruptable power supplies (UPS) and backup generators can be used to limit the impact of power failures.

To mitigate the risks associated with outsourced service providers, it is critical to have a well-defined and well-designed service level agreement in place and monitor performance. If monitoring were to show that outsourced management of data center facility was not meeting service levels, the service provider could be penalized as a means of providing it with an incentive to improve. That said, sometimes using incentives can be counterproductive, as discussed in Case Study 19-4. Alternatively, the service provider could be terminated and replaced with a better one. Likewise, call monitoring of outsourced contact center services can identify potential compliance violations. Remediation then could be achieved through additional training or replacement of contact center staff.

Case Study 19-4

Phantom Account Openings Wipe Billions off of Wells Fargo's Valuation

Incentive schemes have long been a source of operational risk for financial institutions. Front-office staff who are incentivized by sales targets have been known to cut corners or falsify records to seemingly meet their goals to achieve greater compensation or simply retain their jobs. US-based Wells Fargo Bank, which for many years had a sales-driven culture that focused on cross-selling financial products, faced dire consequences when this risk eventuated in 2016.

Over the course of several years, Wells Fargo branch staff opened up to two million "phantom" credit card and deposit accounts without the knowledge or permission of the customers whose names the accounts were associated with. Aggressive sales targets were the primary motivation for this behavior. Branch staff that achieved their targets could receive quarterly bonuses of between $500 and $2,000 and district managers' sales-target bonuses ran from $10,000 to $20,000. Those who failed to meet their targets faced potential criticism and/or termination. In response to the phantom account scandal, Wells Fargo dropped product-focused sales goals from its branches starting in 2017.

The fallout from this scandal was massive. The bank fired over 5,000 employees for misconduct. The bank suffered major reputational damage from the news coverage that ensued and paid a $185 million fine. The bank's CEO was grilled by congressional committees and subsequently resigned. Furthermore, the bank's stock market valuation was reduced by over $8 billion, causing it to lose its place as the world's most valuable bank.

This case provides a good example of how incentive structures that are implemented without sufficient controls and monitoring can lead to significant losses stemming from operational risk. It is unusual that the problem persisted for so long and was so widespread. Moreover, given that the vast majority of the phantom accounts were not profitable, it is surprising that management information reporting did not raise questions about the value and effectiveness of the overall sales strategy.

Sources: Glazer, Emily, "How Wells Fargo's High-Pressure Sales Culture Spiraled Out of Control," *Wall Street Journal*, September 16, 2016, http://www.wsj.com/articles/how-wells-fargos-high-pressure-sales-culture-spiraled-out-of-control-1474053044; Glazer, Emily, "Wells Fargo CEO John Stumpf Steps Down," *Wall Street Journal*, October 12, 2016, http://www.wsj.com/articles/wells-fargo-ceo-stumpf-to-retire-1476306019; Gray, Alistair, "Wells Fargo Loses Status As World's Most Valuable Bank," *Financial Times*, September 13, 2016, https://www.ft.com/content/cfda2e06-79ba-11e6-97ae-647294649b28.

19.1.2 Operational Risk Measurement and Capital Allocation

Basel II provides several options that banks can use to measure and determine how much capital must be set aside to provide a sufficient buffer for losses that may stem from operational risk:

- **Basic Indicator Approach**—is based on the average annual gross income of the financial institution over the past three years and is a fixed percentage of that average, e.g., 15%. This method does not take into account actual operational risks that were realized by the financial institution in previous years.

- **Standardized Approach**—similar to the Basic Indicator Approach, but uses the average gross income of individual lines of business and uses different fixed percentages depending on the line of business, e.g., 12% for retail banking, 15% for commercial banking, and 18% for trading and sales. This method does not take into account actual operational risks that were realized by the financial institution in previous years.

- **Advanced Measurement Approach**—relies upon a risk measurement framework based upon statistical models that the financial institution develops internally that complies with standards specified by Basel II. The framework includes factors such as the institutions' historical losses due to operational risk, industry operational risk loss information, and planning that estimates future potential losses based on specific operational risk scenarios.

The three methods provide a spectrum from very simple to very complex. The Basic Indicator Approach and Standardized Approach use gross income as a means of estimating the size of business operations and assume that the operational risk they incur are linearly proportionate to their size. While simple and straightforward, it uses a one-size-fits-all approach that may penalize banks that effectively manage their operational risk more effectively and, thus, suffer lower related losses. On the other hand, the Advanced Measurement Approach requires much more effort to implement, but can potentially provide a more accurate estimation of operational risk and lead to lower capital charges. This method has been criticized for being overly complex and overly reliant on statistical models. Note that as of 2016, Basel Committee on Banking Supervision was moving toward abandoning the Basic Indicator and Advanced Measurement Approach and have the Standardized Approach applied to all institutions.

19.2 COMPLIANCE RISK

This section briefly reviews the concepts behind compliance risk, and the types of regulatory guidance that financial institutions must comply with. It discusses compliance primarily in the context of the United States, which has one of the most complex and extensive regulatory regimes. First, regulatory and compliance concepts are reviewed. Then, technology solution considerations related to regulatory compliance are explored in the areas of payments and trade reporting. Chapter 20 further discusses how new technology is being developed to help financial institutions tackle regulatory challenges.

The following subsections will outline key concepts related to banking compliance, specifically regulatory objectives, discuss regulatory bodies, and survey the types of laws and regulatory guidance.

19.2.1 Regulatory Objectives

No single entity has been responsible for designing the regulatory system in the United States. Rather, it has evolved from the late 1700s to its current form with changes often made along the way in reaction to financial crises and political agendas. The result is a patchwork of laws, regulations, and supervisory bodies with which financial institutions must comply. While the regulatory goals have shifted, and sometimes reversed, over time, there are a few broad objectives that regulators in the United States and other countries aim to meet; namely, those goals that focus on protecting depositors and consumers, maintaining financial stability, and ensuring that the financial system is efficient.

The protection of depositor funds is at the heart of banking regulation. Throughout history there have been many bank failures, and most customers are not in a position to evaluate the health and safety of the banks with which they deposit their money. Likewise, as part of their everyday business operations, banks must take risks, such as the potential that a borrower may not repay a loan or a trader will enter into unauthorized trading activity. Thus, regulation focuses largely on defining appropriate limits on the risks that banks can take and ensuring that banks consider relevant risks and address them accordingly.

Beyond ensuring the solvency of individual financial institutions, regulators aim to ensure that the overall financial services ecosystem is stable as well. In particular, a stable and efficient payment system underpins the banking services and the financial markets. Regulators, on behalf of the public that they serve, will also seek to ensure that banking and other financial services are provided at competitive prices and with high quality. Regulators may achieve these objectives by allowing new entrants into the market to increase competition, as well as by penalizing uncompetitive behavior by incumbent institutions. Moreover, regulators are responsible for protecting consumers from being sold products that may be unsuitable for them and from unfair practices, providing a counterbalance to banks' profit-making objectives.

19.2.1.1 Regulatory bodies

Federal authorities are the predominant regulators for banks and other financial institutions in the United States. There are several different government agencies that provide oversight, including the Federal Reserve (Fed), Office of the Comptroller of the Currency (OCC), and Federal Deposit Insurance Corporation (FDIC). The Fed is responsible for promoting the safety and soundness of financial institutions in the United States and ensuring that they are compliant with applicable regulations and laws. It primarily regulates and supervises bank and financial holding companies with federal charters and banks with state charters that are part of the Federal Reserve System. The OCC is part of the US Department of the Treasury and is responsible for providing federal charters and regulating US-based banks and branches of foreign banks. The FDIC is an independent government agency that insures deposits as well as supervises and examines financial institutions to ensure their safety and soundness. It is the main supervisor for state-chartered banks that are not part of the Federal Reserve System. The determination of which agencies will supervise domestic banks is determined by whether the bank operates under a federal or state charter and which authority granted the bank's charter.

Additionally, the Consumer Financial Protection Bureau (CFPB) is an independent government agency that was formed in 2011 in the wake of the Global Financial Crisis and was designed to centralize responsibility for protecting consumers and enforcing federal consumer protection laws related to financial services. Its scope of supervision includes banking-related financial institutions with assets exceeding $10 billion as well as payday lenders, mortgage originators and servicers, consumer reporting agencies, consumer debt collection agencies, international money transfer agents, and entities that provide automobile financing. The CFPB accepts consumer complaints related to financial products and services and engages with the the applicable financial institutions to get responses and may take additional enforcement action where necessary. The CFPB provides a public database of consumer complaints. A snapshot of the over 15,000 consumer complaints that the CFPB collected over six months in 2016 is shown in Figure 19-3.

Besides being supervised by federal regulators, state regulators will also oversee state-chartered banks. US banks that operate in foreign countries will be supervised by regulators in those jurisdictions as well. If a bank holding company has insurance as a subsidiary, it will also be supervised by state

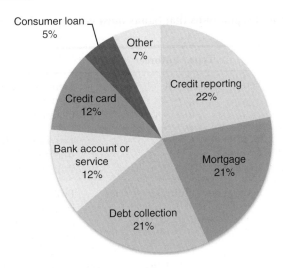

Figure 19-3 Consumer complaints about financial institutions

insurance regulators. Likewise, if a bank holding company has a broker-dealer subsidiary, it will also be governed by the Securities and Exchange Commission.

Depending on the type of financial services that a bank provides, industry bodies may also regulate and supervise banks' activities. For instance, credit and debit card issuers are bound by the rules of the card associations, such as Visa and MasterCard. Bank holding companies that own broker-dealer subsidiaries are supervised by the Financial Industry Regulatory Authority (FINRA), which is a nongovernment, not-for-profit organization.

19.2.2 Types of Laws of Regulatory Guidance

To help readers appreciate the range of compliance requirements that financial institutions in the United States have to deal with, Table 19-1 shows a survey of laws and regulatory guidance that

Table 19-1 Examples of laws and regulations that banks must comply with

Name	Type / Enforcer	Coverage (Highlights)
Americans with Disabilities Act (ADA)	Federal law/Department of Justice	Requires that websites and mobile applications are compliant with the Web Content Accessibility Guidelines (WCAG) 2.0 standard.
Bank Secrecy Act (BSA)	Federal law/OCC	Requires that banks assist US government agencies in preventing and detecting money laundering. Banks must keep records of certain types of transactions, file reports on them, and report specious activity.
CAN-SPAM Act	Federal law/Federal Trade Commission	Defines rules for content and methods of sending advertising or promotional emails.

(continued)

Table 19-1 Examples of laws and regulations that banks must comply with (*Continued*)

Name	Type / Enforcer	Coverage (Highlights)
Credit Card Accountability Responsibility and Disclosure (CARD) Act	Federal law/CFPB	Defines additional rules regarding how credit card issuers can market cards, charge fees, and handle payments.
Electronic Signatures in Global and National Commerce Act (ESIGN)	Federal law	Provides guidelines for use of electronic documents and electronic signatures in interstate and foreign commerce.
Equal Credit Opportunity Act (ECOA)	Federal law/multiple agencies	Prohibits banks from taking into account customers' race, color, religion, national origin, sex, marital status, age, and source of income when deciding to provide credit or when setting the terms of credit.
Fair Credit Reporting Act (FCRA)	Federal law/CFPB	Provides guidance on how banks collect, distribute, and use consumer credit information in conjunction with credit bureaus.
Fair Debt Collection Practices Act (FDCPA)	Federal law/CFPB	Provides guidelines for how banks interact with customers when collecting debt, explicitly prohibiting various types of conduct that are considered abusive and deceptive.
Gramm-Leach-Bliley Act (GLBA)	Federal law/Federal Trade Commission	Requires banks to disclose what information is collected about customers, how the information is used, with whom it is shared, and also to develop plans for safeguarding that information.
Massachusetts Debt Collection Regulations, 940 CMR 7.00	State law/Massachusetts Attorney General	Provides guidelines for how banks interact with customers who are residents of Massachusetts when collecting debt, with specific provisions, such as limiting collection calls to a customer's home to twice per week.
Payment Card Industry Data Security Standard (PCI DSS)	Proprietary standard/card associations (e.g., Visa)	Defines information security controls to be implemented to help reduce credit card fraud.
Servicemembers Civil Relief Act (SCRA)	Federal law	Postpones or suspends outstanding credit card debt and mortgage payments for bank customers who have active military service obligations.
Telephone Consumer Protection Act (TCPA)	Federal law	Prohibits the use of automated dialers to call customer mobile phones without having received the customer's prior express consent.
Unfair, Deceptive, or Abusive Acts and Practices (UDAAP)	Federal law/CFPB and Federal Trade Commission	Prohibits banks from misleading and/or taking advantage of consumers.

may be applicable to banks and also affect how technology solutions are implemented. Note that this is only a partial set, listed in alphabetical order, and does not by any means define the entire set of guidance that banks, and other financial institutions, must abide by.

The United States provides an extreme example of regulatory complexity both in terms of the number of regulatory bodies involved and the types of regulatory guidance that must be complied with. Other countries—such as Singapore, where the Monetary Authority of Singapore is the single government agency that licenses and regulates a wide range of financial institutions—are much simpler in both regards. Moreover, within any given regime the scope and scale of regulation can also change over time, as highlighted in Case Study 19-5.

Case Study 19-5
The Banking Regulatory Pendulum

Regulating banks and financial markets is a difficult task. To start with, regulators must accommodate competing political ideologies and government agendas. Free-market proponents push to reduce regulation, whereas those with less faith in the markets advocate for increased government intervention. What is more, new financial products and changing market practices generally require regulators to operate in a reactive mode. Consequently, regulation is often focused on the excesses and problems of the recent past. When the markets have been stable, less oversight becomes the norm. Then, when problems ensue, increased supervision takes hold again. This phenomenon can be clearly seen in the United States, a major contributor to the development of capital markets.

Following an investment bubble and the subsequent stock market crash in 1929, the US Congress enacted the Glass-Steagall Act in 1933. One of the key provisions of the legislation was to separate commercial banking and investment banking. Commercial banks were barred from underwriting and dealing securities, and investment banks were prohibited from taking deposits. The Glass-Steagall Act helped to restore public confidence in the US banking system following the failure of thousands of banks at the start of the Great Depression.

As banks and markets remained stable over the course of several decades, the Depression-era banking restrictions were gradually relaxed. The climax was in 1999, when commercial banks were once again allowed to underwrite securities and investment banks were allowed to take deposits. This shift enabled commercial and investment banks to merge, forming larger financial institutions that would be more competitive in globalized financial markets. These changes set the scene for the blazing, but brief, era of universal banking.

Critics claimed that repealing the Glass-Steagall Act led to the creation of financial institutions that were considered too large to be allowed to fail. They also claimed that these combined entities contributed to the proliferation of "toxic" derivatives that undermined the financial system. At least in theory, the failure of standalone investment banks such as Bear Stearns and Lehman Brothers, which did not take retail deposits, could be tolerated by the financial system. However, allowing the failure of large amalgamated financial institutions was not an option.

Following the public bailouts of private-sector financial firms that were required during the Global Financial Crisis, the pendulum very quickly began to swing back toward more stringent regulation. The Dodd-Frank Act passed by Congress in 2010 required banks in the United States to spin off significant portions of their proprietary trading (prop trading), derivatives, and private equity businesses. Although the Dodd-Frank Act is not as stringent as the Glass-Steagall Act, it has had considerable impact on the financial services industry, particularly the largest institutions.

In the 1990s and 2000s, much of the emphasis was on integrating organizational structures, processes, and IT systems that multiplied due to bank mergers and acquisitions. On the other hand, the separation of business activities mandated by the Dodd-Frank Act potentially created very different types of challenges for financial institutions. It is usually easier to consolidate IT systems than to break them apart to support

(continued)

(continued)

the division of business units. Business systems have dependencies on core components, such as centralized databases, that complicate disaggregation efforts. Likewise, replicating core business systems so that they can be used by the divested entities is also problematic. Concerns related to intellectual property, software licensing, and support capability must be addressed.

Legislation such as the Dodd-Frank Act takes years to be fully defined and implemented. Even at 2,319 pages, the Dodd-Frank Bill has ambiguities that require clarification through new regulations. It will take many years, therefore, before the impact is fully realized. Likewise, even before legislation is fully implemented, political conditions can change again, shifting the pendulum's direction, again undoing earlier reforms.

Sources: Sanati, Cyrus, "10 Years Later, Looking at Repeal of Glass-Steagall," *New York Times*, November 12, 2009, http://dealbook. nytimes.com/2009/11/12/10-years-later-looking-at-repeal-of-glass-steagall; Van Duyn, Aline and Francesco Guerrera, "Dodd-Frank Bill Is No Glass-Steagall," *Financial Times*, June 27, 2010, http://www.ft.com/cms/s/0/e355c680-8212-11df-938f-00144feabdc0.html.

19.2.2.1 Vendor management

Bank's reliance on third-party service providers to execute business processes and implement IT systems effectively makes the third parties an extension of the bank. Accordingly, from a regulatory perspective, third parties need to be factored into banks' risk planning and must be effectively managed to ensure that the risks that they bring are well understood and controlled as best as possible. Vendor-related risks are especially of concern when a third party has access to customer information and/or is handling customer transactions.

Often regulators will provide specific guidance on vendor management and outsourcing of technology services, for instance, the Monetary Authority of Singapore's *Guidelines on Outsourcing*. Typically they address risk assessment and management, service provider selection, contract considerations, ongoing monitoring as well as related concerns such as business continuity planning, information security, and safeguarding of sensitive information. In some cases, regulatory guidance on outsourcing has been updated to include provisions related to the use of cloud-based services, such as data commingling, multi-tenancy, and processing location variability considerations. Banks typically put vendor management programs in place to address these requirements.

Vendor management programs define the responsibilities of the board and management of the bank with regard to third-party vendors. Broadly, vendor management programs specify the roles, responsibilities, procedures, and reporting mechanisms for overseeing and managing the vendor relationship. Much of the focus is on identifying and assessing the risks associated with the use of a vendor and how controls can be implemented to address those risks. Vendor management programs also prescribe how vendor risks will be monitored and what reporting mechanisms will be used to inform management and the board about vendor risks.

One of the challenges that banks face when they rely on third parties is that they have limited visibility into their vendors' technology operations and infrastructure. This limitation makes it difficult to assess risks related to third-parties' business continuity capabilities and information security. As a result, it is common for technology service providers to have independent auditors assess these areas and issue audit reports that can be shared with the vendor's customers. The SSAE 16 SOC1 audit report is commonly used to provide third-party service provider's customers with an independent assessment of the vendor's control environment with respect to availability and system security.

19.2.3 Technology Solution Considerations

This section looks more specifically at how regulatory compliance affects technology solutions. Two business areas are discussed: payments and trade reporting.

19.2.3.1 Payments

In the United States, payments have a wide range of laws and regulatory guidance that must be complied with. Processing of cheques are governed by the Uniform Commercial Code (UCC) as well as other laws, such as the Expedited Funds Availability Act (EFAA), which is also known as Regulation CC. Credit card payments fall under laws such as the CARD act as well as industry compliance requirements, such as the PCI DSS. Automated clearing house (ACH) payments fall under the NACHA operating rules and the UCC, as well as laws such as Regulation E and the Code of Federal Regulations. Moreover, all payments must comply with the Bank Secrecy Act, which is aimed at stopping money laundering and fraud.

Over the past two decades, money-laundering practices have been put in the spotlight by governments to help stifle drug trafficking and terrorist activities. As a result, banks have had to comply with a plethora of anti-money laundering (AML) rules. One of the complicating factors with AML compliance is that its rules span across different business units, many business processes, and multiple IT systems. Hence, it is difficult to come up with a universal AML solution. Rather, AML compliance rules checks must be woven into a number of existing business processes that involve account opening, payments, and the transfer of assets, for example, securities.

Money laundering generally involves three key activities: placing illicit proceeds into the financial system, obscuring the source of proceeds by "laundering" them through a number of financial transactions, and using subsequent asset purchases to make them appear legitimate. For instance, according to US officials, part of a money-laundering scheme uncovered in 2011 involved combining profits from the sale of drugs in Europe with legitimate profits from the sale of used cars in Africa, and then routing the mixed proceeds to a Lebanese bank via money-exchange houses. Ultimately, some of the funds were routed to a militant group in Lebanon [4].

To get an idea of the scope and scale of AML compliance requirements, all financial institutions with operations in the United States are required to institute AML compliance and customer identification programs, record and report suspicious transactions, and block or reject financial transactions involving people, entities, and countries who are on the US government's Specially Designated Nationals and Blocked Persons lists. As part of the account opening process, banks must obtain and verify customer identity information, maintain records of that information, and check if the customer is on the lists of known terrorist organizations.

Furthermore, if the account is a private banking account, the bank must check whether the customer or beneficial owners of the account are "senior foreign political figures," determine the account's purpose, verify the source of funds for deposits into the account, and report suspicious activities, such as transactions that involve certain senior foreign political figures. With respect to payments, international transactions involving $10,000 or more, whether in a single transaction or multiple over the course of a single day, must be reported to the US Treasury, and detailed records must be maintained of fund transfers, for example, wire transfers, of $3,000 or more.

While failing to comply with AML requirements can lead to severe penalties, there are also major costs and drawbacks of implementing these checks. For one thing, the processes for acquiring new customers can become much more complex and onerous as a result of AML regulations. For example, if a multinational company wants to open an account with its bank in a new country, it may have to produce several forms of proof-of-identity materials so that the bank can comply with local AML requirements even though the bank already has copies of the same information that was provided when the customer opened previous accounts. Likewise, AML can hinder new banking business models, such as digital-only retail banking, where there is no direct face-to-face contact through which customers can be verified in person against their photo identification.

From a technology solutions perspective, the impact of BSA/AML compliance requirements is multifold. First of all, software requirements specifications must address the applicable laws and regulations and should be reviewed by legal and compliance staff to ensure that they are compliant. The effort and time required to meet compliance requirements are significant, is highlighted in

Case Study 7-2. In many cases, Fintech companies are not burdened by many of these requirements which provides them with a significant advantage over banks, in terms of the cost and speed at which solutions can be delivered and deployed.

Not all regulatory requirements will be able to be incorporated into software solutions and, thus, will need to be addressed by the broader business processes that they support. Additionally, it is not just sufficient for banks to be compliant; they must also be able to demonstrate that they are compliant. This involves extensive reporting as well as undergoing audits and regulatory examinations, which add significant overhead to banks' technology and operations. Moreover, the complexity that results from effectively implementing so many rules and checks, both automated and manual, to comply with the labyrinthine set of laws and regulations, creates operational risk. Conversely, cutting corners and insufficient implementations can lead to significant penalties (Case Study 19-6).

Case Study 19-6

Anti-money Laundering Oversights Create Problems for Major Banks

Ineffective implementation of anti-money laundering rules has plagued banks for many years. For instance, Citigroup had regulatory challenges related to AML requirements in its private banking division. One of the more conspicuous cases involved Citi's compliance with "know your customer" (KYC) rules. In 2005, a US Senate report stated that deposed Chilean dictator Augusto Pinochet and his family had maintained accounts with Citibank for 23 years. Unlike some other banks, it was not suggested that Citibank was actively trying to help hide funds; rather, sloppy application of control processes was cited.

Another major multinational bank, HSBC, had major AML problems in the US that led to a five-year investigation which culminated in 2012 with HSBC agreeing to pay more than $1.2 billion in fines to the Department of Justice and an additional $665m to regulators. Authorities claimed that Mexican and Colombian drug cartels had laundered over $800 million worth of proceeds from drug trafficking through HSBC's US operations. The bank also was said to have helped countries such as Iran and Libya avoid sanctions and send over $600 million to accounts in the United States. Furthermore, as part of the settlement with regulators, HSBC agreed to spend $700 million to implement a global KYC program to better vet its customers.

Also in 2012, Standard Chartered Bank agreed to pay $660 million in AML-related penalties to the US Department of Justice, the Department of the Treasury, the Federal Reserve Board, the Manhattan District Attorney's Office, and the New York Department of Financial Services. Standard Chartered was accused of processing US dollar payments on behalf of Iranian and Sudanese customers. Authorities claimed that the bank provided clients with advice on how to avoid scrutiny by US regulators and removed information from payments that would have shown that they originated from countries sanctioned by the United States.

These examples highlight the potential costs that poor AML practices can lead to. The larger the organization is, the greater its complexity will be, making it more difficult to manage operational and compliance risks. Fintech companies are not impervious to AML compliance concerns either. For example, in 2015, the US Financial Crimes Enforcement Network (FinCEN) fined Ripple Labs, a digital currency company, $700,000 for violating the Bank Secrecy Act (BSA) and acting as an unregistered money services business.

Sources: "Pinochet's Web of Bank Accounts Exposed," *The Guardian*, March 16, 2005, http://www.guardian.co.uk/business/2005/mar/16/chile.pinochet; Jenkins, Patrick and Tom Braithwaite, "HSBC to Spend $700m Vetting Clients," *Financial Times*, December 11, 2012, http://www.ft.com/intl/cms/s/0/4f6bd806-43b7-11e2-844c-00144feabdc0.html#axzz2EhX95zKl; Browdie, Brian, "Standard Chartered to Pay $327M to Settle Money-laundering Probes," *American Banker*, December 10, 2012, http://www.americanbanker.com/issues/177_236/standard-chartered-to-pay-327-million-to-settle-money-laundering-probes-1055050-1.html; "FinCEN Fines Ripple Labs Inc. in First Civil Enforcement," Financial Crimes Enforcement Network, http://www.fincen.gov/news_room/nr/pdf/20150505.pdf..

19.2.3.2 Trade reporting

While this chapter has primarily focused on regulation and compliance risk in the context of retail banking, this subsection will draw on an example that affects capital market participants, such as investment banks, and nonbanking entities, such as asset managers. Over the past decade, one of the major areas of regulatory change in the OTC derivatives market, discussed in Chapter 12, has been in the area of trade reporting. During the Global Financial Crisis of 2008, counterparty risk, and to some extent market risk, related to OTC derivatives undermined the global banking system, almost bringing it to systemic failure. One of the critical problems during that period was for banks and regulators to understand where risk was concentrated. Due to the bilateral nature of OTC derivatives agreements, there was no central clearing facility that kept track of how many and what types of OTC derivatives contracts were held between market participants.

Subsequently, to address this concern, regulators across the globe introduced trade-reporting requirements for OTC derivatives. The United States led the charge by ordering market participants to report the details of derivatives trades to trade repositories. Europe followed with similar requirements a few years later. In Asia, Japan was the first country to require trade reporting, and was followed by Singapore, Australia, and Hong Kong. MiFID II regulation, discussed in Chapter 13, also includes a complex set of trade reporting requirements that affect both buy-side and sell-side firms globally. While the specific requirements varied by jurisdiction, the general principle applied was that existing exchanges and clearing houses would serve as trade repositories,* collecting information about OTC derivatives trades from market participants and providing it to the regulator. However, each jurisdiction had different requirements as to how trades were to be reported, at what point in time the requirement would apply to different types of derivatives, and when different types of market participants would need to comply with trade reporting.

One key difference between jurisdictions requirements was the time delay allowed in reporting trades. The United States was most stringent, requiring near real-time, T + 15 minutes reporting. Europe and Australia allowed next day, T + 1, reporting and Japan, Singapore, and Hong Kong elected to allow T + 2 reporting. From a technology and operations standpoint, the trade reporting timing makes a big difference in the cost and complexity of the solution required to support trade reporting. Requiring near real-time reporting usually necessitates the use of messaging middleware, as opposed to using batch file transfer to communicate the trade information on an end-of-day basis. Likewise, a 15-minute window provides very little time to fix problems when things go wrong. Hence, ongoing monitoring and management of the information flows are critical to solutions that are implemented to address US reporting.

Larger market participants, such as banks, had the additional solution challenge of aggregating and homogenizing trade reporting data from different systems. For example, whereas interest rate swap trade information might come from one system in an industry standard format, commodity swap trade information could come from another system in a proprietary format. Hence, substantial integration and data transformation could be involved to consolidate trade data from multiple sources and convert it into the format required by the trade repository. Likewise, multinational entities may need to report to different trade repositories in different jurisdictions, further complicating their solution architecture.

Overall, trade reporting has increased the overhead and compliance risk for OTC derivatives trading. Besides banks, other financial institutions, including brokers, pension funds, and asset managers, have also had to meet trade-reporting obligations. While, in some jurisdictions, financial institutions with small derivatives operations are able to perform the process manually, those with large derivatives businesses have had to purchase an off-the-shelf product or invest in building an in-house solution to address their needs.

---

* Note that trade reporting is new line of business within these firms and uses different technology than their order matching and clearing platforms.

19.3 SUMMARY

This chapter covered:

- technology-related types and sources of operational risk;
- how operational risk can be measured;
- vendor management and risk assessment;
- regulatory compliance risk concepts; and
- technology solutions considerations related to compliance.

The next and closing chapter looks at the process of and trends around technology innovation within financial services.

FURTHER READING

Books

Leeson, N., *Rogue Trader*, London: Sphere, 2016.

Spong, K., *Banking Regulation*, Division of Supervision and Risk Management, Federal Reserve Bank of Kansas City, 2000.

Periodicals

ABA Bank Compliance

Papers

Courchange, M. and Skanderson, D., "Fair Lending in the Brave New World of Big Data," *ABA Bank Compliance*, May-June 2017.

Rawlings, P., A. Georgosouli, and C. Russo, "Regulation of Financial Services: Aims and Methods," April 2014; http://www.ccls.qmul.ac.uk/docs/research/138683.pdf.

"Operational Risk Capital: Nowhere to Hide," PWC, November 2014, http://www.pwc.com/us/en/financial-services/regulatory-services/publications/operational-risk-capital.html.

Xu, Y., Pinedo, M., and Xue, M., "Operational Risk in Financial Services: A Review and New Research Opportunities," *Production & Operations Management*, March 2017, vol. 26 issue 3, pp. 426-445.

Web

Standardised Measurement Approach for Operational Risk, http://www.bis.org/bcbs/publ/d355.htm.

Guidelines on Outsourcing – Monetary Authority of Singapore, http://www.mas.gov.sg/Regulations-and-Financial-Stability/Regulatory-and-Supervisory-Framework/Risk-Management/Operational-Risk.aspx.

US Bank Code of Ethics and Business Conduct, https://www.usbank.com/hr/docs/policies/coeHandbook.pdf.

ENDNOTES

1. Murphy, M., B. Masters, and C. Binham, "Probe Reveals Scale of Libor Abuse," *Financial Times*, February 9, 2012, http://www.ft.com/cms/s/0/5ae1f598-5264-11e1-a155-00144feabdc0.html.

2. Basel Committee on Banking Supervision, "International Convergence of Capital Measurement and Capital Standards," June 2006.

3. Basel Committee on Banking Supervision, "QIS 2: Operational Risk Loss Data," May 4, 2001.

4. Becker, J.,"Beirut Bank Seenasa Hub of Hezbollah's Financing," *NewYorkTimes*, December 13, 2011, http://www.nytimes.com/2011/12/14/world/middleeast/beirut-bank-seen-as-a-hub-of-hezbollahs-financing.html?pagewanted=all.

— — —

5. KPMG, "Global Profiles of the Fraudster: Technology Enables and Weak Controls Fuel the Fraud," May 2016.

6. McMillan, R., "Hackers Program Bank ATMs to Spew Cash," *Wall Street Journal*, November 20, 2016, http://www.wsj.com/articles/hackers-program-bank-atms-to-spew-cash-1479683814.

7. US Securities and Exchange Commission,"Anti-Money Laundering (AML) SourceTool for Broker-Dealers," January 14, 2010, http://www.sec.gov/about/offices/ocie/amlsourcetool.htm.

8. Office of the Comptroller of the Currency, Washington DC, "Money Laundering: A Banker's Guide to Avoiding Problems," December 2002, http://www.occ.gov/topics/bank-operations/financial-crime/money-laundering/money-laundering-2002.pdf.

9. KPMG, "Revised Operational Risk Capital Framework," March 2016.

10. Spong, K., *Banking Regulation*, Division of Supervision and Risk Management Federal Reserve Bank of Kansas City, 2000.

11. The Federal Reserve, *The Federal Reserve System: Purposes and Functions*, October 2016.

12. Gaffen, D., "CFTC Fines Barclays $560,000 for Inaccurate Swaps Position Reports," Reuters, July 6, 2016, http://www.reuters.com/article/us-cftc-barclays-fine-idUSKCN0ZM26V.

13. Catena Technologies, "Trade Reporting: Fifty Shades of Grey," 2014.

14. Clozel, L., "Is Your AI Racist? A Lawmaker Wants to Know," *American Banker*, June 30, 2017, https://www.americanbanker.com/news/is-your-ai-racist-a-lawmaker-wants-to-know.

20 Innovation

Chapter Overview

20.1 **BANK INNOVATION**

20.2 **FINTECH INNOVATION**

20.3 **DISTRIBUTED LEDGER TECHNOLOGY**

20.4 **SMART CONTRACTS**

20.5 **INNOVATION OPPORTUNITIES**

20.6 **SUMMARY**

CONCLUSION

FURTHER READING

ENDNOTES

The past decade has been a challenging time for banks and other financial institutions. Ultra-low interest rates have squeezed profits. Regulatory requirements and restrictions have significantly increased. Customer preferences and demographics have shifted. New financial technology (Fintech) competitors have emerged, levering technology in new ways and threatening longstanding business models. Now more than ever, banks need to innovate to maintain their position and, more importantly, to continue growing.

Like other industries, financial institutions are under pressure to provide a wider range of products and services with higher quality at lower costs. For many years, competition in the financial services marketplace was driven by innovative financial institutions, such as digital-only banks and discount brokers, that pioneered new business models that removed inefficiencies from basic services, such as retail banking, retail brokerage, and foreign exchange trading. Over time, competitive pressure moved up-market to include other business areas such as payments, lending, and derivatives trading. Competition in these areas came not only from financial institutions, but also from Fintech companies, many of them startups.

Fintech companies have capitalized on opportunities to use technology in ways that banks have been slow to take advantage of or feared to tread, often due to potential cannibalization of their existing lines of business. In many cases, Fintech competitors have been able to better leverage customer information and offer new and improved products and services to customers. They have also taken advantage of changing expectations and preferences of the Millennial generation. This mobile-oriented and technology-astute part of the market has been more willing to use financial services that were not provided by mainstream institutions.

Banks have struggled to keep up with the pace of change in the technology world. While not so long ago, banks would routinely take 18 months to roll out a new technology solution to customers, today, in many business areas that approach is impractical. During that time, the underlying technology could change substantially, making the solution less relevant by the time it reaches customers. Likewise, if a delivery cycle is too long, Fintech startups could bring competing solutions to market much earlier and capture significant market share. Accordingly, banks have had to rethink how they deliver technology solutions and reimagine how their core businesses can be improved by making better use of technology (Case Study 20-1).

In recent years, many banks have defined new goals related to innovation. After seeing how technology-savvy competitors quickly upended other industries—for example, Amazon displacing brick-and-mortar bookstores and Uber engulfing a large part of taxicabs' business—financial institutions have had little choice but to adapt their strategy to remain relevant. Banks have had to invest in new technologies to stay ahead of the curve, or at least remain with the curve, understanding that not all of those investments will yield major benefits. In a fast-moving environment, it is not possible to determine in advance which innovations will ultimately be winners and losers. However, not all banks have become first movers. Many have chosen to be "fast followers" that invest in and adopt new technologies shortly after their credibility and effectiveness has been established.

Earlier chapters have examined, in the context of specific lines of business, how financial institutions and Fintech companies are using technology to provide new products and services and establish new business models. Chapter 6 reviewed how Fintech competition and new regulations are changing how investment advisory services are provided to customers. Chapter 8 examined how marketplace lenders are encroaching on banks' core lending business. Chapter 9 looked at how a variety of market participants were taking different approaches to make inroads into mobile payments.

Case Study 20-1

Changes at Bank of New York Mellon Help Drive Innovation

Bank of New York (BNY) Mellon is over 230 years old and is the one of the ten largest banks in the United States. Part of its strategy for providing competitive services was to function more like a technology company and less like a bank. To support this strategy, three initiatives were pursued: setting up innovation centers, shifting the bank's mentality to become more like that in the Silicon Valley, and encouraging an entrepreneurial way of thinking.

BNY Mellon set up six innovation centers, three in the United States and three overseas. Within the United States, one center was set up in New Jersey to help maintain close alignment and communicate with the bank's corporate headquarters. Another was set up in Silicon Valley to access the Fintech culture and emerging technology practices. The third was set up in Pittsburg, collocated with the bank's technology and operations group that was based there. Overseas, BNY Mellon set up two innovation centers in India, in Chennai and Pune. The last center was set up in London to collaborate on industry problems and solutions with European customers.

Part of shifting the bank toward having more of a Silicon Valley mindset was to move away from a highly structured, project-oriented delivery model, and move toward techniques like continuous delivery and continuous integration[*]. Using these approaches, products could be delivered to market more quickly,

---

[*] Continuous integration is discussed in Chapter 4.

so that customer feedback could be obtained quickly and products could, in a short period of time, be adapted to better address their needs. Another part of the mind-shift was to increase the reuse of software components and actively consider whether it would be more beneficial to use third-party components rather than build components in-house.

To help instill an entrepreneurial mindset, BNY Mellon identified all the IT services that it provided and assigned an internal "owner" to each service. The owner was responsible for understanding the clients who use the service, the costs and risks associated with providing the service, and for developing a strategy to improve the service offering. By focusing service owners and their groups more narrowly on these considerations, BNY Mellon aimed to apply an operating model that was more similar to the ones used by Fintech companies.

With over 12,000 employees, BNY Mellon's information technology (IT) division accounted for a quarter of the bank's overall headcount. Accordingly, to remain competitive, it was critical for BNY Mellon to find ways to help them to become more nimble and adapt to a fast-changing business environment. As shown by this example, in many cases innovation is less about the technology itself and more about people and the approaches they take.

Questions

1. Why would banks want to set up separate innovation centers rather than have just have a research and development function within the main IT organization?
2. How could BNY Mellon help ensure that service owners embrace and follow through with their responsibility to make the service successful?
3. What challenges might a financial institution encounter when trying to take advantage of continuous delivery?
4. What other approaches could banks use to help spur technology innovation within the organization?

Source: Streeter, Bill, "More Tech Than Bank," *Banking Exchange*, July 2015.

This chapter examines financial institutions' and Fintech companies' strengths and weaknesses and how they approach the process of innovation. Innovation opportunities related to distributed ledgers, i.e., blockchain, will also be reviewed in depth. Then, several other technologies that have disruptive potential within the financial services industry, including artificial intelligence and application programming interfaces, are discussed. Finally, a short conclusion to this book is provided.

20.1 BANK INNOVATION

By definition, innovation relates to change, changing something that exists and is already in place. It is also about introducing something new, such as new ideas, methods, or products. Achieving both of these objectives together is often difficult. Things that are established may not change easily and new things can be difficult to move forward.

In financial services, like most industries, innovation is a core principle of competitive strategy. These days, there is an expectation that any bank of considerable size will have a technology innovation function, and large banks will likely have that function located in multiple locations around the world. While much of the focus of banks' management is on operational effectiveness—i.e., efficient utilization of resources and execution of processes—a survey of over 200 CEOs from around the world found that only a quarter of them thought that operational effectiveness was more important than innovation [1].

This is not surprising because growth is a primary goal for most banks, and technology innovation provides the means for providing new products and services that enable growth.

A financial institution's innovation program should have a clear purpose that is aligned with overall technology strategy. For example, if the program's purpose is to facilitate technology transfer, the design of the innovation program will be very different than if the main goal is to achieve cultural transformation. Likewise, it is important to define the area(s) on which innovation is to be focused, e.g., whether the focus is on technology innovation, product innovation, service innovation, process innovation, or business model innovation. Innovation programs should also be well structured and formalized so that the participants in it understand their role and what they are intended to contribute to or get out of it.

To support technology innovation, many larger financial institutions have set up dedicated innovation centers, as discussed in Case Study 20-2. Often a key goal for these centers is to facilitate transfer of new technology into the financial institution. In this capacity, they help serve as a bridge between internal needs and opportunities and new technology and services that are being developed externally, in some cases by Fintech companies. It might seem counterintuitive that banks would want to work with potential Fintech competitors; however, as shown in Figure 20-1, collaboration was identified as a top competitive strategy in a 2016 survey of global banking executives [2]. Having separate innovation centers provides insulation from the day-to-day operational concerns, so that business and technology managers take time out to learn about and focus on new technology. Innovation centers also provide a vehicle for educating staff about new technology and helping to drive collaboration. Furthermore, setting up innovation centers demonstrates to an institution's shareholders that it is taking innovation seriously and is committed to bringing in new technology and ideas.

With regard to technology transfer, to a large extent, innovation functions act as matchmakers. They marry internal needs and goals with external capabilities. The starting point for achieving this is to be in touch with and understand both sides of this equation. The innovation function must maintain an ongoing dialog with internal stakeholders to understand their current challenges and opportunities. It must also engage with external technology providers to identify and narrow down amongst the thousands of potential offerings, which technologies are actually suitable for use within the institution; internal constraints must be taken into consideration. For instance, if the external company providing the technology is not sufficiently established or funded, a bank's vendor management procedures may determine that the company is too risky to depend upon. Alternatively, the potential technology provider may utilize a cloud platform that does not meet a bank's security requirements.

Financial institutions face a number of barriers when pursuing innovation goals. One major challenge is being able to take new technology or ideas and translate them into business solutions

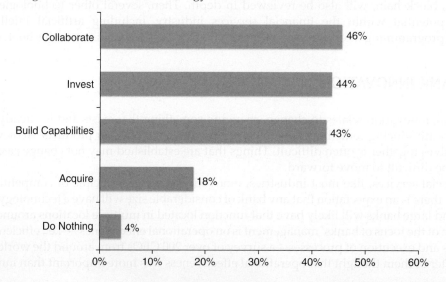

Figure 20-1 Banks' strategies for competing with Fintechs

quickly and on a sufficiently large enough scale to produce meaningful benefit. Finding, attracting and retaining people with the aptitude for and orientation toward innovation can also prove to be difficult for banks. The freethinking, break-the-rules attitude that is frequently associated with innovators is in many ways at odds with the structured and controlled environments that characterize banks. Another challenge that banks encounter is being able to break away from the standard operating models and performance assessment approaches that they use for their other business activities; these are often poorly suited for managing and measuring the value of innovation functions.

Quantifying the success of innovation measures and functions is complicated, yet it is essential for determining whether they are effective and are worth the often considerable investment to set up and maintain. In the case of technology transfer, an assessment objective could be rather simply defined as the level of adoption of new external technology. However, a more meaningful measure might be to assess the business benefit that was realized through the adoption of that technology. In some cases, the business benefit might be measured quantitatively, i.e., in terms of additional products

---

Case Study 20-2

Banking on Innovation Centers

Over the past decade, banks have formally embraced the idea of having innovation functions within their organizations, often in the form of separate innovation centers or "labs." Skeptics have suggested this approach is impractical because innovation is something that needs to be ingrained across the entire organization, as opposed to segregated within a single functional area and small number of individuals. However, many banks around the world including Citibank, Wells Fargo, BNY Mellon, Deutsche Bank, Bank of Tokyo-Mitsubishi UFJ, Standard Chartered, and the Development Bank of Singapore (DBS) have moved forward with the strategy of having separate innovation functions.

Some of the common themes that these banks are pursuing include the exploration and use of technology related to artificial intelligence (AI), big data, cloud computing, distributed ledger, and information security. Likewise, most banks' innovation functions are tasked with strengthening relationships with established and startup Fintech companies and becoming more deeply embedded in the innovation ecosystem, to help drive the adoption of new technology throughout the bank. There is also a focus on rapid prototyping and experimentation with new technologies.

Banks have different views on how best to approach innovation. For example, Citibank's Singapore-based innovation lab is focused on collaborating with institutional customers to develop technology solutions. Wells Fargo set up an accelerator where it invests up to $500,000 in startup companies with technology that is relevant to the bank and helps them understand what is necessary to integrate their solutions into the bank's IT environment. BNY Mellon provides an innovation boot camp program for its staff, in conjunction with Carnegie Mellon University. Deutsche Bank's goal is to identify and evaluate 500 Fintech companies per year and, for a select group of them, leverage their technology within the bank and foster their further growth and development. Bank of Tokyo-Mitsubishi UFJ's holding company, MUFG, has used "hackathons" to engage with Fintech startups. Standard Chartered and DBS partnered together with Singapore's Infocomm Development Authority to develop proof-of-concept technology solutions.

Clearly, there are many different strategies that banks are using to promote innovation. The wide range of approaches being used is not surprising though, given banks' diversity of cultures, competencies, and customers.

Sources: Citibank, "Citi Launches Innovation Lab in Singapore," http://www.citigroup.com/citi/citiforcities/home_articles/n_singapore.htm; http://accelerator.wellsfargo.com; Broughton, Kristin, "BNY Mellon Opens Silicon Valley Innovation Center," *American Banker*, November 17, 2014, http://www.americanbanker.com/news/bank-technology/bny-mellon-opens-silicon-valley-innovation-center-1071275-1.html; Atkins, Thomas and Andreas Kröner, "Deutsche Bank to Launch Three Tech Startup Labs in 2015," *Reuters*, June 2, 2015, http://www.reuters.com/article/us-deutschebank-tech-idUSKBN0OI28Y20150602; MFUG, "MUFG—Embracing Innovation for Change," http://www.bk.mufg.jp/global/newsroom/featuredarticle/2016_01.html; Standard Chartered, "We've Opened the eXellerator—the Bank's New Innovation Lab," March 23, 2016, https://www.sc.com/en/news-and-media/news/asia/2016-03-23-singapore-opens-the-eXellerator.html.

or services sold. In other cases, benefit could be measured qualitatively, i.e., in terms of customer satisfaction. Alternatively, the time required to deliver externally sourced, innovative technology to market could also be important to banks for assessment purposes. It is unclear even where to start when trying to measure a goal such as cultural transformation. Hence, it can be difficult to define and apply meaningful and consistent measurement standards.

20.2 FINTECH INNOVATION

That Fintech companies have been able to outpace banks at innovation should come as no surprise, given that Fintechs have a different operating model and are unencumbered by many of the constraints that banks are bound by. Likewise, typically banks have a formalized approach toward innovation that starts with objectives, which determine strategy, which is translated into an operating model. In contrast, Fintech startups might only have a technology vision and a few eager technologists. Solution developers at financial institutions may be weighed down by regulatory and audit requirements, ongoing operational issues, corporate technology standards, and directives to increase efficiency and productivity. In contrast, developers at Fintech startups have the luxury of focusing more on the underlying business problems and finding the best technology to create solutions. For the most part, Fintechs do not try to govern or measure innovation, other than by demonstrating the success of their technology solutions.

In contrast to banks, which must innovate to maintain their relevance, Fintechs must innovate to become relevant. This leads to a different mindset that helps drive innovation. For instance, in many cases, banks would not demonstrate solutions that are far from being production-ready to customers. In contrast, at startups the idea of waiting to provide a demonstration until a solution was almost ready for production would seem like a substantial waste of time and money; it would be too late to incorporate feedback from the demonstration at such a late stage of the development cycle. Customer expectations drive these attitudes to some extent. While consumers may be willing to put up with a buggy application that provides cutting-edge features from a Fintech startup, they tend to have higher expectations from an application that their main street bank provides.

Another factor that weighs in favor for Fintechs when it comes to innovation is their age and their size. With respect to age, the number of years the company has been operating and the age of its employees are both relevant. While new companies may struggle to get off the ground, they are also not weighed down by legacy systems and distracted by ongoing software maintenance and customer support. Likewise, unlike senior managers at a bank, who are typically in their 50s and 60s, the senior managers in a Fintech startup are commonly in their 20s and 30s. Hence, Fintech firms tend to be better oriented toward the needs and preferences of the Millennial generation, which is often the target audience for innovative solutions. With regard to size, Fintech startups' small size presents limitations, such as lack of resources; however, it also provides benefits that support innovation. Being small means that decisions regarding strategic direction need not be filtered up through layers of management or approved by cross-organizational committees. Rather, they can be agreed upon by a few people in a room and then quickly implemented.

In many ways, financial institutions and Fintech companies are complementary. Banks need to incorporate innovation in their products and services, but are challenged to innovate from within. At the same time, Fintech companies are well positioned to innovate, but need someone to use and fund the technology solutions they create. Hence, the idea of banks' internal innovation functions focusing on transferring technology from Fintech startups into the institution makes perfect sense (Case Study 20-2). However, where this model has broken down in recent years is where Fintech companies have been able to sidestep banks and deliver financial service solutions directly to consumers, becoming competitors to banks in the process.

Historically, with a few exceptions such as Paypal, the threat that Fintech companies have posed to banks has been relatively small. Regulatory restrictions limited the scope of activities that Fintechs could directly engage in. More recently, this competitive threat has become greater as regulators have shifted their stance to be more supportive of nonbank innovation in the offering of financial services. For example, in the United States toward the end of 2016, the Office of the Comptroller of Currency (OCC), which issues banking licenses, began exploring the issuance of special-purpose national bank charters for Fintech companies. It is likely to be a double-edged sword, enabling Fintechs to provide financial services more easily by no longer having to comply with many different state-level laws and regulations, but also increasing regulatory compliance that is required. In other countries, regulators have begun testing new approaches that provide more regulatory flexibility but still maintain an adequate level of oversight. For instance, the Monetary Authority of Singapore has created a regulatory sandbox that relaxes of some legal and regulatory requirements which allows Fintech companies and financial institutions to experiment with new offerings within a "well-defined space and duration".

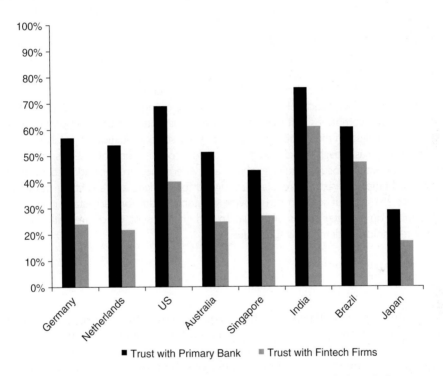

Figure 20-2 Consumers' trust of their primary banks versus their trust of Fintech firms

---

Case Study 20-3

An Innovative Solution for Finding Innovative Technology

It takes significant effort for banks to identify new technology that can be potentially adopted and utilized. Typically, a funnel approach is used to filter potential matches; for every hundred companies that are researched and engaged at a preliminary level, something like ten will be evaluated in depth, and one will be chosen to move forward with. It is crucial that the front end of this process works effectively, so that viable candidates are not overlooked and omitted from consideration. Yet, finding and selecting the right Fintech companies from the tens of thousands that exist around the world is a major challenge.

(Continued)

(Continued)

Part of the challenge is for banks to clearly define their requirements in terms of what they are looking for in external technology providers. That is to say, banks need to clearly specify what types of solutions and vendors will actually be feasible to integrate into the banks' technology and business infrastructure. Another part of the challenge is tracking the interactions of team members within an innovation group with external companies. Managing that information is paramount for being able to identify potential matches for new technology requirements. For example, consider a bank based in Europe that has an innovation center based in Silicon Valley, where a staff member meets with a startup focused on cybersecurity. A year later, a cybersecurity-related business requirement is identified at headquarters. If the information from the meeting with the cybersecurity startup is not well documented and easily locatable, the startup may not be considered to fulfill the bank's need. While technology can support this need, a high level of discipline from bank staff to record their interactions is also required.

Price Waterhouse Cooper (PWC) saw this problem as an opportunity and developed a technology solution called De Novo that, combined with its innovation strategy consulting services, helps banks address this problem. The solution integrates data from over 40,000 proprietary and public sources and combines it with information gathered by PWC's consultants. It helps banks identify how innovation will potentially affect different business areas and what technologies are driving those changes. Furthermore, De Novo helps banks identify potential Fintech companies that may match their requirements in any part of the world. Banks can also leverage PWC's analysis of the company to support early-stage evaluation of suitability.

While it might seem as though banks would want to do all of this work themselves, they are constrained by the number of innovation-focused staff they have, and where they are located. Also, most banks do not have their own technology infrastructure that is designed for tracking and searching through this type of information. Hence, this type of solution can provide greater breadth for early-stage investigation, enabling banks to focus more on the later stages of evaluation and engagement, which are critical for ensuring that adoption of the technologies identified is successful.

Source: http://www.strategyand.pwc.com/denovo.

The impact of this change will be interesting to observe over the coming years and will be largely determined by details of how it is implemented. It could easily increase Fintech growth, but reduce the speed at which they are able to change and innovate. Also, increased regulation may help increase the level of trust that consumers have in Fintech offerings, helping to solidify their place in the market as legitimate competition to established financial institutions. As shown in Figure 20-2, which is based on a survey of 16,000 customers in 32 countries, there is a wide variation in the level of trust that consumers place in their bank versus Fintech firms. In Germany, the Netherlands, and the United States, the difference in trust of banks over Fintechs is greater than 25%. Hence, in some markets, significantly increasing customers' level of trust in Fintech companies could have a major impact on the market. Also, keep in mind that in developing markets, fraud risks related to Fintech firms' financial products are quite real concerns for consumers. As a case in point, a criminal trial began in China in 2016 related to an alleged fraud by an online peer-to-peer lending platform that involved over US$8 billion in investor funds [3].

20.3 DISTRIBUTED LEDGER TECHNOLOGY

Blockchain is a classic example of innovation in financial services. It has provided financial institutions of all types and sizes as well as Fintech companies with a clear area to focus on for innovation. Much of interest in blockchain has been focused on using it to create new solutions. At the same time, much of the activity has been driven by the fear of not understanding the technology and the opportunities and threats that it presents. Financial institutions have been concerned that technology advances such as blockchain could be the next Uber-like event for the financial services industry. That is, a new disruptive technology could quickly upend the existing business model of banks without them being aware early enough to take defensive action. This section discusses basic concepts, applications, challenges, and prospects related to distributed ledger technology. Digital currencies that make use of digital ledger technology are covered in Chapter 7.

20.3.1 Concepts

20.3.1.1 Overview

To begin with, it is important to clarify the meaning of the terms *distributed ledger* and *blockchain*. The term *ledger* is taken from the field of accounting where it refers to a permanent record of financial transactions. Typically for payments and other financial transactions, participants rely upon a clearing house or central counterparty that maintains a *centralized ledger* that keeps track of ownership and transaction flows between participants. A *distributed ledger* serves the same purpose, but is not managed and maintained by a central authority. Instead, it is maintained by multiple parties that perform the recordkeeping and updating activities on copies of the ledger in parallel. The term *blockchain* originated from the seminal paper that launched the Bitcoin digital currency, describing the digital ledger implementation that it used. Today, the term *blockchain* is generally used to describe the data structure and management process of a distributed ledger based on the general principles of the one used for Bitcoin.

Thought of another way, distributed ledgers are a type of database that exists in multiple locations and is shared amongst its users and possibly other entities. In many applications, they enable users to demonstrate ownership of virtual assets. For instance, Bitcoin's blockchain contains the transaction history of every Bitcoin in circulation and can determine which Bitcoin addresses were the owners of any coin at any given point in time. Bitcoin's blockchain uses a data structure and management process that provide a permanent record that is immutable, transparent, and secure. Generally, cryptography is used to secure the information stored in the blockchain and authenticate the parties involved in the transactions it records. In essence, it is a chain of validated transaction records, which are grouped together into blocks, that grows with each new set of transactions that is added to it. Moreover, there is no single blockchain implementation. The blockchain data structure and management process have been adapted and customized for many different purposes.

20.3.1.2 Structure and mechanics

With regard to the structure and mechanics of blockchain, there are three key components:

- a network protocol that supports communication between participants;

- a network of computers that store and manage transaction data; and

- a process for managing records that is based on achieving consensus between participants.

A key feature of blockchain is that its data, in part or in its entirety, is maintained on many different computers, "nodes", within the network. Nodes coordinate with one another to maintain the consistency of the distributed ledger. *Permissionless* blockchain implementations, such as the one used by Bitcoin, allow free and open access to the distributed ledger. Since the ledger is publically available, anyone can retrieve the entire blockchain transaction record history from nodes on the network.

Input String	Hash Value
"Credit $10.00 to acct 12345678 from acct 87654321"	4D4B4E362E1E1C491A2742ADB5A8EBF5
"Credit $10.01 to acct 12345678 from acct 87654321"	E8E394F751072093606966C1DB670F4D

Figure 20-3 A comparison of the hash values for two different strings

This feature provides transparence and resilience. If the network of participants is sufficiently large, the unavailability of any single node or small group of nodes will not affect the ability to process transactions. In contrast, often when central authorities manage ledgers, their records are not publicly accessible. If the central authority is unavailable, transactions cannot take place. On the other hand, *permissioned* blockchain implementations limit who can participate in the network and do not usually make the transaction information publically available.

When a blockchain transaction is processed, the initiator of the transaction will first distribute the transaction request to nodes on the network that validate the transaction's digital signature and review previous transactions that have been recorded by the blockchain to verify that the address transferring the funds actually owns them. The transaction will then be grouped with other verified transactions into a "block" that is proposed as an update to the distributed ledger. Miner nodes will perform computationally intensive verification of the block and, when they reach a consensus that the transaction information is valid, the transaction is approved for inclusion in the ledger. The block is then distributed to all the nodes in the network for inclusion in their copy of the ledger. The nodes that contribute the computing resources to validate transactions are rewarded with a small amount of its underlying digital currency, either as part of the protocol or by users voluntarily paying "transaction fees" to miners to encourage them to incorporate the users' transactions into the blockchain.

The consensus mechanism helps prevent fraudulent activity by a small number of bad actors entering false information into the blockchain. The process for achieving consensus between network participants varies between blockchain implementations. One consensus mechanism, which is used by the Bitcoin blockchain, is referred to as a proof-of-work scheme. Proof-of-work requires miners to solve computationally difficult problems to "win" the block and gain the reward. The problem used for proof-of-work must be hard to solve but easy to validate. Alternatively, proof-of-stake schemes may also be used. In this case, network participants need only prove how much of the digital currency they own. The participants' proportion of overall ownership, i.e., their stake, is used to weigh their vote in determining consensus. Proof-of-stake schemes avoid the hardware and energy costs associated with mining in proof-of-work schemes and ensure that the entities responsible for validating transactions have a vested interest in the integrity of the blockchain.

Blockchain also uses a cryptographic hash function to provide security. The hash function takes as input all of the transactions in the block as well as the block's meta-data and generates a string that serves as a digital signature that is recorded alongside the transaction records in the blockchain. When nodes verify information stored in the blockchain, they rerun the hash function on the record information to verify that the same digital signature is generated. If the record information has been modified, the hash function will generate a different digital signature. Figure 20-3 shows an example of how even a very minor change to the hash input value will generate a completely different hash value. The hashing algorithm used for this example was MD5*.

20.3.1.3 Special Characteristics

To identify and evaluate use cases and applications that are suitable for distributed ledgers, it is useful to consider some of the unique characteristics of that technology. Perhaps the most distinctive and

---

* The MD5 hashing algorithm was used in this example for convenience. Readers should note that it is no longer considered to be secure and, therefore, should not be used in solution implementations.

important characteristic of blockchain is its decentralized nature. There is no "owner" of the blockchain and there is no single point of failure. The peer-to-peer design of the system enables new participants to join the network at anytime and in any location, without any formal application or approval process. This decentralized architecture also helps provide scalability. While having a decentralized structure has many advantages, it also comes with downsides. For instance, some network participants may not agree with design changes that are made to the blockchain implementation and opt to continue using an older version. Such schisms can lead to divergent blockchains that are used in parallel, and potentially compete and conflict with one another.

Another key characteristic of blockchains is trust. The transaction history in the blockchain is transparent and openly auditable. Furthermore, in contrast to the implementation of most other ledger systems where users' trust is in the central authorities that are responsible for maintaining the account ledger, the trust of the users of blockchain is in the design of the system. For example, people who deposit their money in banks in the United Kingdom place their trust in their local bank and the Bank of England to faithfully maintain records of their holdings. In contrast, owners of Bitcoin do not trust individual miners or other participants in the Bitcoin network per se. Rather, they trust the mechanisms designed into Bitcoin's blockchain implementation that ensure that the participants involved in processing transactions perform their duties and that the fidelity of the account records are maintained. The security provided by blockchain's use of cryptography is another aspect that instills trust in its users. While the behavior of software algorithms is more predictable than the behavior of people, there is the risk that potential defects in the design or implementation of computer code used for the blockchain could compromise trust in the overall function that it provides.

The immutability of blockchain is an important characteristic in that it ensures that verified transactions are final and irrevocable. In most cases, transactions recorded in ledgers that are maintained by central authorities may be undone or reversed at the discretion of that entity. For example, stock exchanges have been known to reverse trade executions in cases of exceptional market conditions. Alternatively, banks can reverse charges to a customer's credit card account that they believe are fraudulent. In the case of transactions recorded on a blockchain, particularly those that are public and fully decentralized, undoing transactions is not an option[*]. While irrevocability provides a strong level of assurance to blockchain users, it also limits the ability to correct mistakes, recover funds in the case of theft, and comply with interventions by legal authorities.

The fully automated nature of blockchain implementations is another characteristic that is unique and is attractive to its users. Avoiding manual processing eliminates the potential of human error in transaction processing and eliminates discretionary decisions regarding how transactions will be handled. As discussed in Case Study 18-3, decisions made by individuals or organizations can potentially undercut the validity of transactions. Automation also enables fast transaction processing. Moreover, blockchains' potential to automate the execution of agreements that are formally specified, by means of implementing smart contracts, may be where their greatest value lies.

20.3.1.4 Smart Contracts

Smart contracts are an offshoot of blockchain technology. While the idea behind smart contracts has been around for over a decade, the Bitcoin blockchain was the first practical implementation of one. However, the blockchain that Bitcoin uses was not designed to support the execution of smart contracts. In contrast, other blockchain implementations, such as Ethereum, which is discussed in Chapter 7, provide open and flexible smart contract capabilities that can be applied for a broader range of uses.

In essence, smart contracts are computer programs that can execute the terms of an agreement, which is specified in a programming-like language, between users of the blockchain network. Typically, network participants who are not directly involved with the transaction hold the value to be transferred

---

[*] The closest option to undoing transactions on a blockchain is to create a hard fork, as discussed in Case Study 7-6, whereby a new instance of the blockchain is created and must be adopted by users.

in escrow and control the delivery of the whole or parts of that amount based on verifying that conditions specified within the smart contract are met. For example, a smart contract could be used to implement a coupon-based debt security, similar to a bond. The smart contract would specify the amount of the coupons and when they should be paid, as well as when principal should be returned. Once parties involved in the transaction are committed to it, the blockchain would automatically facilitate the initial fund transfer, the subsequent coupon payments, and return of principal at the end of the term.[*]

Smart contracts provide a number of benefits compared with traditional paper-based contracts. Since no manual processing is involved, the execution cost will be lower, the speed of transactions will be faster, and the risk of human errors occurring will be minimized. The execution risk is also reduced because it is a trusted set of network participants who carry out the terms of the agreement and performance is not dependent on the parties who formed the agreement. That said, it is critical that the specification of smart contracts be precise and fully match the intent of the parties involved. With traditional agreements, the parties involved can address flaws with the way an agreement was drafted by subsequently agreeing to a particular interpretation or by following through with the spirit of the agreement. On the other hand, smart contracts generally do not provide this type of flexibility.

20.3.2 Applications

While there are many potential applications for blockchain technology, it is best suited to those that take advantage of its unique characteristics, which were discussed in Section 20.3.1.3. In particular, processes that involve multiple writers of information to a shared repository are a natural fit for using blockchain. Situations where blockchain can eliminate the need for one or more intermediaries in a transaction process also provide a compelling reason to use it. Likewise, where participants in the process are distributed geographically, especially across international borders, blockchain can provide benefits. Typically the advantages provided by using blockchain are related to speeding up transaction processing times, lowering costs, and improving resilience. Nevertheless, before basing a solution on blockchain technology, it is prudent for technology architects to consider whether using other time-proven technologies could provide the same or possibly greater benefits.

Besides determining the underlying rationale for using blockchain technology, it is important to consider the context of problem and business process that must be supported. For instance, using blockchain may increase the complexity of the overall process leading to increased operational risk. If the use of blockchain introduces new potential security vulnerabilities, they must also be factored into the overall value that the solution provides. Furthermore, when collaboration between stakeholders—such as end users, innovators, established institutions, lawmakers, and regulatorsis required, the likelihood and timeliness of their cooperation must be considered. These are critical factors in the overall success of blockchain-based solutions. Nontechnical considerations can easily derail blockchain solutions when the replacement of infrastructure, significant changes to existing processes, or alterations to legal or regulatory frameworks are required. It is important to note that blockchain-based digital currencies have been able to thrive because they addressed a need that was able to sidestep many of these complicating factors.

Table 20-1 lists some of the many proof-of-concept projects and commercially oriented initiatives that are focused on creating blockchain-based technology solutions. In some cases, multiple institutions have been involved, but only one or two are listed for brevity. Of note, many of the institutions that are experimenting with blockchain are trusted intermediaries, which run the risk of potentially being displaced by that technology. The last example in the table was included to highlight that blockchain has potential applications outside of financial services as well.

---

[*] Counterparty credit risk is ignored in this simplified example; it is assumed that the funds would be available when required for transfer.

Table 20-1 Digital ledger solution development initiatives

Business Application	Institution(s)	Description
Cross-border payments	Santander Bank	Uses a mobile application to perform next-day international money transfers that are processed using blockchain.
Trade finance	Standard Chartered, DBS	Tracks the processing status of trade invoices using the Ripple distributed ledger.
Interbank and cross-border payments	Visa	Uses blockchain for international bank-to-bank transfers and smart contracts to support regulatory and compliance requirements.
Property title registry	Swedish government	Records the real estate transactions on blockchain enabling involved parties—e.g., the government, banks, brokers, buyers, and sellers—to track their state of progress.
Digital sovereign currency	Bank of Canada	Developing a digital version of the Canadian dollar using blockchain.
Interbank and cross-border payments	Monetary Authority of Singapore (MAS)	Banks deposit cash as collateral with the MAS in exchange for blockchain-based digital currency that is issued by the MAS. Banks can then pay one another directly using digital currency without sending payment instructions via the MAS.
Cheque payments	Bank of Tokyo-Mitsubishi UFJ	Uses blockchain technology to issue, transfer, and collect electronic checks.
Trade finance	HSBC, Bank of America Merrill Lynch	Uses blockchain to model a letter of credit transaction.
Syndicated loans	R3	Uses blockchain to process syndicated loan information, eliminating the need for each bank to maintain its own lending platform.
Repurchase (repo) market transactions	Depository Trust & Clearing Corp.	Uses blockchain to manage mortgage-backed repurchase transactions in real time, with support for netting and offsets.
Settlement of securities	Deutsche Bundesbank, Deutsche Börse	Uses blockchain to implement payments and securities transfers and support settlement of securities transactions.
Trade finance	Barclays	Executed a letter of credit transaction using blockchain.
Food supply chain tracking	Walmart	Uses blockchain record and track details about each party in the food-handling supply chain and transactions between them.

One of the most evident applications for blockchain technology is the clearing and settlement of payments. Bitcoin and other digital currencies have clearly demonstrated the applicability of blockchain in this area. By eliminating traditional intermediaries—such as SWIFT, correspondent banks, and national automated clearing house (ACH) operators—in the international remittance processing chain, Bitcoin has enabled transactions to be processed faster, more reliably, and at lower cost. While consumers have been the main users of digital currencies, banks can also benefit from using blockchain to more efficiently process interbank payments.

Another application for blockchain that has garnered significant attention is trade finance. In this context, blockchain technology can support the secure sharing of transaction-processing information between multiple parties in near-real time. Accelerating this communication process can greatly reduce the time required for payment settlement and speed up the delivery of goods. Blockchain technology can also be used to increase the transparency of asset ownership and the placement of liens on collateral that is used in trade finance transactions. Better availability of this information can help reduce the risk of fraud, as discussed in Section 10.1.1. What is more, using smart contracts to automate the fulfillment of trade finance transactions, which is a very manual process today, could greatly reduce the processing costs and operational risk.

It is unclear which of these applications will actually lead to meaningful solutions, as opposed to just being research and development exercises. For all the work being done with blockchain, as of 2017, there were many proof of concepts using distributed ledgers, but little in the way of mainstream commercial applications.

20.3.3 Challenges

Many of the use cases that blockchain is being employed to experiment with sound compelling. For instance, reducing the time and cost to perform payment and trade finance transactions would produce significant benefits for the parties involved. However, the question is whether blockchain is really required to solve these problems or whether the same objective could be achieved using traditional technologies. For instance, as discussed in Chapter 9, many countries are already migrating their payment infrastructure to support near-real-time transactions without using blockchain technology. Likewise, as discussed in Chapter 10, banks have struggled for years with digitizing trade finance documentation. While blockchain appears well suited to improve the efficency of trade finance processes, it is difficult to imagine that just by using this technology, it will be possible to sidestep the inertia that has plagued the shipping industry and limited the effectiveness of other technology solutions. Furthermore, blockchain use cases often require participants to use standard data formats and communication mechanisms for transferring information electronically. Yet history has shown that achieving that goal is, in many cases, very difficult.

One of the key changes that are necessary to raise the maturity and digital ledger technology is the availability and widespread use of open standards that solution developers and users can rally around. As seen with the case of mobile payments, discussed in Chapter 9, competition between the ecosystem participants could easily derail progress toward bringing innovative technology into the mainstream. Even where financial institutions have teamed up to push blockchain technology forward, as in the case of the R3 CEV consortium, some major banks eventually left it and stopped funding initiatives through that body. To date, there have been many different blockchain infrastructure initiatives going in different directions. It is unclear how participants' strategies can be drawn together so that the negative effects of market fragmentation are minimized. Even Bitcoin has been subject to technology-related schisms, which in 2017 led to a fork in its blockchain and the creation of another version of the digital currency, Bitcoin Cash.

Privacy and security concerns could also hold back the use and acceptance of distributed ledger technology. The transparency that publicly accessible blockchains provide can work against them in terms of providing privacy for their users. Security flaws in the design or implementation of a blockchain may only be uncovered after it is in use, compromising the solutions that have been built upon it. Likewise, components built on top of blockchain may have security vulnerabilities that bring the integrity of the overall technology solution into question. As discussed in Chapter 7, the cyberthefts of Bitcoin and Ether digital currencies show how limited understanding of the security risks of new technology can materialize into financial losses and cast doubt on the underlying technology[*].

---

[*] Besides the cybertheft of ether digital currency that occurred in 2016, in 2017, around $30 million dollars worth of ether was stolen through the exploitation of a vulnerability in a digital wallet implementation.

Furthermore, regulatory and legal uncertainty may hinder the growth of solutions that are based on blockchain. So far, regulators have encouraged blockchain initiatives within the industry; however, it is unclear how they will treat solutions that make it past the proof-of-concept stage and are put forward for customers to use. Given the inherent and unknown risks with this new technology, it would not be surprising if regulators set a high bar for banks to show that they have adequately identified, evaluated, and mitigated the potential risks related to solutions using distributed ledger technology. Additionally, related legal considerations, such as whether blockchain records can be used for financial audit purposes or for transaction confirmation purposes, need to be established. For instance, uncertainty over how smart contracts will be treated in a court of law, which became a very real concern with the hacking of the DAO (discussed in Case Study 7-6), could present barriers to widespread use and adoption of this technology.

20.3.4 Prospects

A survey of 200 international banks in 2016 showed that 15% of the respondents planned to launch products based on blockchain in 2017, and 65% expected to do so by 2019 [4]. Another survey of over 300 senior executives who were knowledgeable with regard to blockchain found that more than a quarter of the respondents reported that their companies had already spent over $5 million on blockchain technology and that a quarter also expected to spend more than $5 million on this technology in 2017 [5]. Additionally, during 2016 there has been a surge of patent applications on technology related to blockchain.

With all the focus on and resources applied to blockchain technology by financial institutions and Fintech firms around the world, one would hope that some significant applications will eventually result. Clearly, distributed ledger technology powered the rise of digital currencies; however, banks had little, if anything, to do with the course of that innovation. Perhaps the biggest question is whether banks or Fintech firms will be able to find another compelling application that provides new or improved services that is dependent on the use of distributed ledger technology. Interbank payments is one application area that has gained some traction. To support new use cases, some banks and Fintech companies are creating their own proprietary blockchain infrastructure that provide improved features. For example, JP Morgan's Quorum platform is based on Ethereum, but provides additional privacy, performance, scalability, and governance capabilities. Likewise, Ripple's blockchain implementation increases the speed at which transactions are completed.

Blockchain technology may find specific niches that it can be applied successfully within, which are less affected by its current limitations and shortcomings. Digital currencies provide a good example of such a niche. Users have not been put off by their potential risks, and regulators have, to a large extent, have not tried to directly govern them. Likewise, land and title registries appear to be a natural fit for the structure and purpose of blockchain technology. Beyond providing distributed ledger capabilities, blockchain may spawn other innovations as it evolves. For example, smart contracts show promise for enabling the complete automation of business transactions between organizations where there is no inherent trust relationship, and, hence, may be where the greatest potential lies.

20.4 TECHNOLOGY INNOVATION OPPORTUNITIES

Beyond digital ledgers, there are many other areas where financial institutions can innovate. First, this section reviews three technology areas, open application programming interfaces (APIs), artificial intelligence (AI), and predictive analytics, which banks are in the process of adopting. Then it discusses other technologies that may have significant impact in the future: digital identity management, quantum computing, and augmented reality. Other innovation areas—such as big data, cybersecurity, analytics, cloud computing, and mobile devices—are discussed in other chapters.

20.4.1 Open APIS

In recent years, it has become increasingly important for financial institutions to provide APIs that can be accessed externally by third parties and provide access to customer data and transactional capabilities. There are several factors that are driving the shift to provide open APIs. One factor has been the opportunity to address new business needs. For example, banks that have provided open APIs for processing payment card transactions have been able to better serve business' websites and mobile applications that accept card payments from their customers. Another factor is the pressure that regulators have applied to financial instructions to provide greater access to their customers' information and support an "open banking" environment. For instance, European Union member states will begin implementing the Second Payment Services Directive (PSD2) in 2018 which requires banks to allow third parties, which have customers' authorization, to access their account information without a contractual agreement in place with the banks. The regulators' view is that customers are the owners of the information that financial institutions hold about them, and if they provide consent, should be able to allow third parties access that information. Also, an important factor for providing open APIs is to provide a channel for collaboration with Fintech companies, which can use the APIs to create innovative services and experiences for customers.

Financial institutions that already have channel-services architectures in place, as discussed in Chapter 3, are well positioned for providing APIs that are externally accessible. Most of the work that they will need to perform to provide these services is to rewrap existing APIs that are already used internally. In that process, the API wrappers will need to conform to whatever standard is used to present APIs externally. Access through open APIs will need to be limited only to the functions and data that are designated for external use. It will be necessary to determine how best, from a security standpoint, to allow external access to the open APIs. Such considerations include deciding whether the open APIs should be accessed via existing servers or new ones, determining what additional "holes" in the network firewalls will need to be opened to allow external access, setting up additional monitoring for the new API services, and analyzing what potential attack vectors may be introduced. In some cases, new vulnerabilities may be created, but not by the APIs themselves. Rather, vulnerabilities may arise from the use of new communication platforms that are put in place to support external network access to API functions.

Financial institutions that do not have channel-services architectures in place will find it much more difficult to provide open APIs. If the APIs do not already exist internally, the work to create them will likely be an enormous challenge. The effort involved in designing, building, and testing APIs is considerable. If the APIs are not being used internally, there is a good chance that they have a potentially large number of defects that will be discovered when they are used externally. In turn, customer satisfaction could suffer if too many defects are encountered.

Besides reviewing how open APIs can be supported by banks' internal technology infrastructure, strategies for providing external access to APIs must also be considered. One strategy is for banks to develop their own API developer portals. In this case, the bank designs the APIs and hosts the API connectivity services. This approach provides banks with the greatest level of control but also requires substantial implementation and maintenance effort. Another strategy is for banks to partner with third-party service providers or data aggregators and provide access to customer information through their API portals. This strategy reduces the time and effort required to provide open APIs, but also limits banks' influence over how the APIs will be presented and accessed. Alternatively, in cases where a bank outsources the operation and maintenance of its core IT systems to a third-party processor, the processor may provide hosted API services on behalf of the bank.

While there are potential advantages that come from providing open APIs, there are also downsides. One downside is the added cost of testing and maintaining another communication channel. Any time underlying systems are upgraded and enhanced, the externally accessible APIs that are dependent on them will need to be tested and may need to be modified. Likewise, once services or data have been made available externally, they can be difficult to withdraw later. A future decision to drop support for some or all of a bank's open APIs may invite a public backlash from customers and partners who use applications that employ those APIs. Furthermore, if the open APIs prove to be wildly popular, there is the risk that the high usage volume could cause systems to become overloaded and provide poor performance, once again leading to potential backlash.

Open APIs can also introduce business risks. Banks are already struggling to avoid being disintermediated by Fintech companies. By providing access to proprietary information to potential competitors, banks risk accelerating this process and devaluing one of their key assets and competitive advantages—customer trust. By opening these doors, banks run the risk their relationships with customers may become further removed, and their ability to directly reach and make a positive impression on customers will be diminished. Moreover, allowing third parties to access customer information will only increase the likelihood that it will be leaked at some point through a data breach at one of the third parties that is accessing it.

20.4.2 Artificial Intelligence

For several decades, AI has been touted as the next big thing for financial services, but at least thus far, banks have not realized major benefit from this technology. However, the increased availability of supercomputing power, ongoing research, and renewed interest of Fintech and other companies in AI may lead to greater fruition in the coming years. In particular, machine learning—the ability for computers to learn on their own from exposure to information and without being programmed for a specific purpose—holds promise. This technology automatically creates analytical models based on the historical data to predict future outcomes. Machine-learning algorithms can adapt to changing conditions by continuously processing new information. They can also process a large number of input variables—much greater than a human analyst could manage—and determine how much they relate to specific outcomes. In a 2016 letter to shareholders, JP Morgan's chief operating officer identified machine learning as one of the key innovation areas that the bank was focusing on. Specifically, the bank was looking to machine learning to support cybersecurity, trading strategies, communication channel, and automated service response activities. Banks can use machine-learning strategies to deconstruct business process activities, model those activities, and then replicate and automate routine tasks (Case Study 20-4). While this approach is not suitable for all banking activities, it holds promise for certain areas, such as basic customer-service interactions. Chatbots, which provide automated service responses as part of web chat sessions, already use AI to automatically answer straightforward customer questions. The challenge for AI is to be able to address more complex queries and consistently

---

Case Study 20-4

Financial Institutions' API Developer Portals Make Their Debut

During 2016 and 2017, a number of banks launched API Portals for software developers. Spanish bank BBVA launched eight open APIs after spending a year working with businesses and developers to test its API services. BBVA's APIs support integration with merchants' checkout processes so that customers have the option to finance their purchases with loans from the bank. BBVA also provides anonymous aggregated customer information through its APIs as a commercial offering to other businesses. To use the production APIs and access live customer data, developers must go through a vetting process with the bank in a test environment. Citi, Capital One, and Standard Chartered also launched API developer portals. The services that they provide through APIs include marketing offers, rewards, account information access, transaction authorization, fund transfers, account acquisition, and business transaction banking.

Visa was another financial institution that has provided API-based developer platforms. As of 2017, it offered approximately 60 APIs that catered to the needs of banks, merchants, and Fintech companies. Furthermore, Visa's APIs support payments made by Internet-enabled household devices and cars. In some cases, they have been designed to support business-specific requirements, such as the distribution of funds to drivers by ride-sharing services.

Also, in the US, NACHA-The Electronic Payments Association set up an API Standardization Industry Group to help proactively manage the proliferation of bank-specific APIs. Its overarching goal is to provide guidance for the financial services industry on governance and standards that will help support the adoption, consistency, and security of APIs. During its inaugural meeting in May of 2017, it identified common API use-case categories, such as data sharing and payment access. It also identified key concerns, including how standardization can be enforced, whether interoperability is likely to be achieved through API standardization, what security requirements should be in place for APIs, and how standardization will affect competition.

Sources: Castellanos, S., "Visa Prepares for the Future of Payments With API Push," *Wall Street Journal*, June 20, 2017, https://blogs.wsj.com/cio/2017/06/20/visa-prepares-for-the-future-of-payments-with-api-push/; Mondres, T., "How Banks Are Using APIs to Balance Security and Openness," *ABA Banking Journal*, May 10, 2017, http://bankingjournal.aba.com/2017/05/how-banks-are-using-apis-to-balance-security-and-openness/?utm_campaign=Fintech%202017051280utm_medium=email&utm_source=Eloqua; Peyton, A., "Standard Chartered Launches Open Banking API Developer Portal," *Banking Technology*, February 10, 2017, http://www.bankingtech.com/727781/standard-chartered-launches-open-banking-api-developer-portal/; "BBVA Launches Open API Marketplace," *Finextra*, May 24, 2017; https://www.finextra.com/newsarticle/30614/bbva-launches-open-api-marketplace; API Standardization Industry Group, "Inaugural Meeting Summary Report," NACHA-The Electronic Payments Association, May 2017, https://www.nacha.org/system/files/resources/API-Standardization-Industry-Group-Inaugural-Meeting-Summary-Report-May-2017.pdf.

come up with the right answers. AI may also be combined with other emerging technologies such as speech analytics, as discussed in Chapter 16, to help increase the rate of response of contact center agents to customer queries.

Marketplace lenders have used machine-learning models to make credit decisions, as a supplement or an alternative to traditional credit-scoring approaches. Machine learning can identify complex relationships between data available from a wide variety of sources and resultant consumer behavior. The large number of potential variable combinations makes it impractical to use traditional, human-driven analysis approaches. Machine learning also enables credit decision criteria and scoring models to be dynamic and adapt to changing market conditions. Nevertheless, using machine learning to make credit decisions can run afoul of fair lending regulations. For instance, biased credit-approval decisions may occur in cases where a machine-learning algorithm uses variables that are correlated with ethnicity, even though ethnicity itself is not a direct input. Accordingly, in some cases, being able to understand how AI makes a decision can be as important as the decision itself.

There are a number of different machine-learning algorithms that can be used. Many of them, such as deep-learning algorithms, are computationally intensive. In turn, vendors have created cloud-based platforms that are specifically designed to support the execution of machine learning algorithms. Some machine-learning algorithms have also been designed to run on graphics processing unit (GPU) chip sets, to take advantage of their large-scale parallel-processing architecture and reduce the time required for computation.

There are many potential applications for artificial intelligence in financial services. AI is well suited for analyzing volumes of data to find patterns and anomalies, the nature of which vary and change over time. This information can be useful for identifying fraud, abusive trading practices, and cyberattacks. AI can also automate the analysis of complex documents, greatly reducing processing costs. As a case in point, JP Morgan has leveraged machine learning to extract 150 key data elements from 12,000 commercial credit agreements. A task that would take the bank's staff as many as 360,000 hours to perform, AI technology was able to complete within seconds [6]. Eliminating inconsistencies in the interpretation of document information, from one person to the next, and eliminating manual data-entry errors can avoid processing mistakes. This is particularly important in business areas that are document-intensive, such as trade finance and regulatory compliance.

Over the past several decades, many functions that were performed by people—such as processing of equity and foreign exchange orders, handling paper cheque deposits, and executing trading strategies—have already been automated. It is a foregone conclusion that over time, AI will automate many more business activities. In many cases, AI can perform tasks more efficiently, quickly, and cost effectively. Yet, overshadowing AI's use are claims that automating cognitive tasks will cut employment in the financial-services industry. There is a long history of similar concerns, going as far back as the 19th century when machines began automating manual tasks that factory workers performed. Generally, automation of both manual and cognitive tasks has focused on routine, repetitive tasks. As a result, jobs have shifted to non-routine tasks and those that require greater judgment and more dynamic skills. Rather than destroying jobs, to a large extent, automation has redefined them.

20.4.3 Predictive Analytics

AI can also be used to implement predictive analytics, which is an important area where financial institutions can innovate. While the ideas and technologies that underlie predictive analytics are not new, outside of areas such as fraud detection and marketing, this capability has not been broadly adopted for other purposes. There has been a lot of hype around using big data for predictive analytics; yet, in many cases, financial institutions can benefit from applying predictive analytics to relatively small datasets that can be aggregated and processed more quickly and easily than big data.

Predictive analytics uses past data to create models that can forecast outcomes based on new data. A wide range of techniques can be used to implement predictive analytics. Regression methods are one of the main types of techniques that are used, with linear and logistic regression being two of the most common. Machine-learning techniques are also commonly used, including neural networks and cluster analysis. Off-the-shelf software can be used to perform predictive analysis, including commercially available and open-source packages, the latter of which are often accessed using the python or R programming languages.

With regards to applications for predictive analytics, it is commonly used for fraud detection and identification of cross-selling opportunities. However, operations and risk management are two other areas within financial services where it could also provide significant benefits. In the context of operations, improving the ability to predict demand and utilization could help managers allocate resources more efficiently. That is to say, inaccurate estimates of demand can lead to allocating too few resources, which can negatively affect service levels, or allocating too many resources and unnecessarily driving up expenses. This is particularly relevant to the allocation of staff in contact centers and branches. In terms of reducing risk, predictive analytics can help make debt collection strategies to be more effective and orient them to more closely match specific customer characteristics and circumstances. Predictive analytics can also help manage risk related to cybersecurity threats by predicting when and how cyberattacks may occur.

There are several reasons why the predictive analytics is not pervasively used across banks' different business areas. Lack of data availability and poor data quality are common hindrances. In particular, where real-time information is necessary, an information-bus architecture (discussed in Chapter 2) may be required. Also, managers may lack knowledge about predictive analytics and fail to understand how it can be applied in business and operational contexts. Unfortunately, analytics solution vendors will sometimes promote their systems as almost magical solutions that can, by themselves, transform business. In reality however, it is critical that the people who use those tools understand the business context in which they will be used, their capabilities, and potential applications. Rather than making major investments in software platforms, greater value can be often achieved by performing experiments and implementing small-scale projects that serve as learning opportunities.

20.4.4 Digital Identity Management

Digital identity management—the identification of users and control over their access to online resources—is a prime area for innovation. Traditional authentication mechanisms, such as using username and password credentials, have a number of concerns. Most critically, they can become compromised through security breaches and malware attacks. Also, as the volume of online services has grown, the number of online credentials that users must keep track of has increased to a state where many people are unable to manage them securely. For example, it is not uncommon for people to use the same username and password across multiple accounts. Furthermore, security breaches, such as the Equifax breach in 2017, have compromised personally identifiable information (PII) for hundreds of millions of people. As a result, it is unclear how effective PPI information will continue to be for identity-verification purposes.

There are several opportunities to improve and streamline digital identity management. Leveraging biometric information is at the forefront. Already, fingerprints, voiceprints, eye images, and facial recognition have been used to authenticate users for specific applications. The wide-scale use of mobile phones and their ability to capture biometric information is a key advancement that can facilitate the use of this approach on a broader scale. Individuals can also be identified by their location and movement patterns, which can be tracked by global positioning system (GPS) and accelerometer technologies within mobile phones. While each of these identification mechanisms has security weaknesses individually, in combination they have the potential to identify users more securely and with less effort than other existing mechanisms.

Moreover, centralizing the management of digital identity information could greatly improve the users' experience with authenticating to online services. It could eliminate the need for different online services, i.e., Internet-banking websites, to implement their own solutions. National governments are well positioned to act as centralized authorities for digital identity management. However, for the most part, they have not embraced the opportunity. Alternatively, blockchain technology could be used to support decentralized identity managment services. Although digital identity management solutions are still emerging in their own right, they are likely to have major impact on financial institutions in the future.

20.4.5 Quantum Computing

While quantum computing—using the quantum properties of atoms to perform computational operations—is still in its infancy, the development of this technology could have profound implications for the financial services industry. This technology can decrease the computational time required for some algorithms tremendously. In particular, it makes it practical to use algorithms that can compromise traditional public-key encryption methods and thus, potentially rendering them unsecure. Given that so much of financial services technology is underpinned by secure communication that is achieved through encryption, it is difficult to imagine the consequences that would ensue if and when quantum computing technology advances further and becomes more widely available. Already, the National Institute of Standards and Technology (NIST) in the United States has begun working with researchers to develop new encryption algorithms that provide stronger defenses against quantum computing capabilities.

20.4.6 Augmented Reality

New hardware technology also holds promise for innovation in financial services. While, from a banking perspective, next-generation watches that provide connectivity to mobile devices turned out to be a damp squib, advances in other areas hold promise. New hardware technology that supports virtual and augmented reality has the potential to provide a new and unique customer communication channel that could enable services that do not exist today. Virtual reality headsets could provide a better way of communicating complex information within banks and also to customers. Likewise, augmented reality applications, particularly when combined with mobile devices, provide an opportunity for financial institutions and Fintech companies to develop creative solutions that have widespread appeal to customers. The global popularity of the Pokémon Go application provided just

---

Case Study 20-5

Regtech Enters the Spotlight

One of the most recent branches to emerge within Fintech is Regtech, companies that develop innovative solutions to help financial institutions better address regulatory needs. One key area of focus has been on driving down the compliance costs, which, along with costs related to risk and governance, are estimated to represent 15–20% of the banks' ongoing operational costs. To put things in perspective, in 2013, JPMorgan added 4,000 compliance staff and spent $1 billion implementing additional controls. The same year, HSBC planned to add 3,000 compliance staff and its headcount in this area totaled over 7,000 employees. Another Regtech area of focus is analytics. The goal of applying analytics is to better organize and sift through the masses of information that financial institutions maintain. By generating higher-quality reports more quickly, banks can identify risks and address potential compliance issues more effectively.

Regtech companies bring a technology-oriented view to compliance operations, which traditionally have been dominated by manual processes. In many cases, the approach banks' compliance functions have taken when faced with new regulatory challenges has been to add headcount. The agility and speed that characterize Fintech companies are important assets for driving change, especially in a conservative and deeply embedded part of banks' business. Regulators have been a proponent of Regtech and have emphasized the need for financial institutions to innovate and to use technology to fulfill regulatory and compliance requirements more effectively. In particular, the Financial Conduct Authority (FCA) in the United Kingdom has encouraged banks there to leverage systems and tools when implementing and monitoring controls.

One interesting development in the Regtech space was the planned purchase of a consulting firm focused on regulation and compliance that has over 600 employees by IBM. The goal of the purchase is to provide IBM's AI supercomputer, Watson, with the background knowledge and training it needs to understand the regulatory compliance domain. While it is unlikely that computers will ever be able to fully replace compliance staff, it does hold the promise of automating some routine and mundane work, so as to reduce the number of staff that is required.

Sources: Noonan, Laura, "Banks Face Pushback over Surging Compliance and Regulatory Costs," *Financial Times*, May 28, 2015, https://next.ft.com/content/e1323e18-0478-11e5-95ad-00144feabdc0; Memmingerm, Matthias, Mike Baxter, and Edmund Lin, "You've Heard of Fintech, Get Ready for 'Regtech'," *American Banker*, September 7, 2016, http://www.americanbanker.com/bankthink/youve-heard-of-fintech-get-ready-for-regtech-1091148-1.html; Ernst & Young, "Innovating with RegTech," 2016; Crosman, Penny, "IBM Buying Promontory Clinches It: Regtech Is Real," *American Banker*, September 29, 2016, http://www.americanbanker.com/news/bank-technology/ibm-buying-promontory-clinches-it-regtech-is-real-1091692-1.html.

a taste of what was possible with augmented reality using mobile devices. As this technology becomes more mainstream and is directly supported by mobile devices and their operating systems, more innovative applications will emerge. The challenge, and opportunity, will be in identifying how this technology can be made relevant to financial services customers.

20.5 SUMMARY

This chapter covered:

- how financial institutions and Fintech companies are approaching the process of innovation;
- innovation opportunities related to blockchain technology; and;
- various technologies that have the potential to disrupt the financial services industry.

This is the final chapter; however, additional information related to the topics covered in this book can be found at the author's website: www.financialservicestechbook.com.

20.6 CONCLUSION

As discussed throughout this book, the importance of "digital bankers" is growing, and their numbers will continue to increase in the coming years. As a case in point, at Goldman Sachs, the IT staff account for close to a third of the bank's employees. It is hard to predict just how pervasive the role played by technologists in the financial services industry will be another ten years from now, but it is clear that the growth trend is likely to continue. There is little doubt that as time progresses, the line between business and technology will become more difficult to define. To be effective, bankers will need to have technical proficiency and, conversely, IT staff will be required to understand business practices and operations. To remain relevant in a world that is being redefined by technological advancements such as blockchain and AI, workers must be ready to acquire new knowledge and find ways to improve existing processes using technology. Financial institutions can help themselves too by developing digital banking skills in their employees and improving their understanding of innovative technologies. Moreover, both executives and frontline staff need this knowledge to effectively compete and collaborate with Fintech companies.

It has been the aim of this book to provide the reader with background knowledge that will be helpful for improving the financial services industry. Understanding the fundamental concepts, process structures, and designs of financial services solutions will provide a solid base for making informed decisions and beneficial changes. Likewise, the case studies presented have provided perspectives on previous industry successes and failures.

However, there is no substitute for experience. Every situation has its own unique challenges; hence, it is impossible to create repeatable recipes for success. Only through practice and reflection can we begin to understand specific business contexts and which courses of action will be most effective to change them. It is often said that we learn more from our setbacks than from our advances. Therefore, although we may strive to avoid setbacks, when they do occur, we should be prepared to learn from those experiences.

Processes and technology are merely tools and cannot make improvements by changing or applying themselves; only people can make these tools effective. There is an opportunity for the older generation of financial services workers, who understand how processes and systems currently work and how they have evolved over time, to collaborate with the upcoming generation, who can better imagine how they can work more effectively in the future. By bringing together people, processes, and technology, we can all help improve the financial services industry.

FURTHER READING

Books

Antonopoulos, A., *Mastering Bitcoin: Programming the Open Blockchain* (California: O'Reilly Media, 2017).

Chollet, F., *Deep Learning with Python* (New York: Manning Publications, 2017).

Kumar, A., *Learning Predictive Analytics with Python* (California: O'Reilly Media, 2016).

Monetary Authority of Singapore, *MAS-ABS API Conference EBook*, 2016.

Muller, A. C., *Introduction to Machine Learning with Python* (California: O'Reilly Media, 2016).

Papers and Articles

Basel Committee on Banking Supervision, "Sound Practices: Implications of Fintech Developments for Banks and Bank Supervisors," August 2017, http://www.bis.org/bcbs/publ/d415.pdf.

Chakraborty, C. and Joseph, A., "Machine Learning at Central Banks," Bank of England, September 2017, http://www.bankofengland.co.uk/research/Documents/workingpapers/2017/swp674.pdf.

EBA_May2016_eAPWG_Applying_cryptotechnologies_to_Trade_Finance.pdf.

EBA Working Group on Electronic Alternative Payments, "Applying Cryptotechnologies to Trade Finance," Euro Banking Association, May 2016, https://www.abe-eba.eu/downloads/knowledge-and-research/

Office of the Comptroller of the Currency,"Exploring Special Purpose National Bank Charters for Fintech Companies," December 2016.

"Special Report on Artificial Intelligence," *Economist*, June 25, 2016, https://www.economist.com/news/special-report/21700761-after-many-false-starts-artificial-intelligence-has-taken-will-it-cause-mass.

UK Government Office for Science, "Distributed Ledger Technology: Beyond Block Chain," January 2016, https://www.gov.uk/government/uploads/system/uploads/attachment_data/file/492972/gs-16-1-distributed-ledger-technology.pdf.

Web

"ABA Banking Journal Special Report: Fintech and New Frontiers in Bank Innovation," http://bankingjournal.aba.com/2016/10/fintech-and-new-frontiers-in-bank-innovation/.

ABA Fintech, http://aba.com/fintech.

ENDNOTES

1. PWC, "Unleashing the Power of Innovation," 2013.

2. Capgemini, "World Retail Banking Report 2016."

3. Miller, M. "China's $8.6 billion P2P fraud trial starts: Xinhua," *Reuters*, December 15, 2016, http://www.reuters.com/article/us-china-fraud-ezubao/chinas-8-6-billion-p2p-fraud-trial-starts-xinhua-idUSKBN1450I2.

4. Schaus, P., "Blockchain Projects Will Pay Off—10 Years from Now," *American Banker*, December 2, 2016, http://www.americanbanker.com/bankthink/blockchain-projects-will-pay-off-226128-10-years-from-now-1092670-1.html.

5. Deloitte, "Deloitte Survey: Blockchain Reaches Beyond Financial Services with Some Industries Moving Faster," *PR Newswire*, December 13, 2016, http://www.prnewswire.com/news-releases/deloitte-survey-blockchain-reaches-beyond-financial-services-with-some-industries-moving-faster-300376792.html.

6. Zames, M. "2016 Letter to Shareholders: Redefining the Financial Services Industry," JP Morgan, https://www.jpmorganchase.com/corporate/annual-report/2016/ar-ceo-letter-matt-zames.htm.

— — —

7. Irrera, A. and Gertrude Chavez-Dreyfuss, G. "Bitcoin splits, but clone off to slow start," *Reuters*, August 2, 2017, http://www.reuters.com/article/us-bitcoin-split-idUSKBN1AH5F1.

8. Graham, L., "$32 Million Worth of Digital Currency Ether Stolen by Hackers," *CNBC*, July 20, 2017, https://www.cnbc.com/2017/07/20/32-million-worth-of-digital-currency-ether-stolen-by-hackers.html.

9. Horlacher, C., "Centralized Blockchain Projects are Doomed to Failure," *American Banker*, January 31, 2017, January 31 2017, https://www.americanbanker.com/opinion/centralized-blockchain-projects-are-doomed-to-failure.

10. World Economic Forum, "The Future of Financial Infrastructure," August 2016, http://www3.weforum.org/docs/WEF_The_future_of_financial_infrastructure.pdf.

11. Miller, M., "China's $8.6 Billion P2P Fraud Trial Starts: Xinhua," *Reuters*, December 15, 2016, http://www.reuters.com/article/us-china-fraud-ezubao/chinas-8-6-billion-p2p-fraud-trial-starts-xinhua-idUSKBN1450I2.

12. American Bankers Association, "Understanding APIs".

13. Courchange, M. and Skanderson, D., "Fair Lending in the Brave New World of Big Data," *ABA Bank Compliance*, May-June 2017.

14. "Automation and Anxiety," *Economist*, June 25, 2016, https://www.economist.com/news/special-report/21700758-will-smarter-machines-cause-mass-unemployment-automation-and-anxiety.

15. "Answering the Machinery Question," *Economist*, PWC, "Breakthrough Innovation and Growth," September 2013.

16. "FinTech Regulatory Sandbox," http://www.mas.gov.sg/Singapore-Financial-Centre/Smart-Financial-Centre/FinTech-Regulatory-Sandbox.aspx.   https://www.jpmorgan.com/global/Quorumhttps://ripple.com/.

17. Chavez-Dreyfuss, G., "Sweden Tests Blockchain Technology for Land Registry," *Reuters*, June 16, 2016, http://www.reuters.com/article/us-sweden-blockchain-idUSKCN0Z22KV.

18. Nash, K. S., "Wal-Mart Readies Blockchain Pilot for Tracking US Produce, China Pork," *Wall Street Journal*, December 16, 2016, http://blogs.wsj.com/cio/2016/12/16/wal-mart-readies-blockchain-pilot-for-tracking-u-s-produce-china-pork/.

19. Chanjaroen, C. and D. Boey, "StanChart, DBS's Trade Finance Distributed Ledger: How It Works," *Bloomberg*, May 22, 2016, https://www.bloomberg.com/news/articles/2016-05-22/stanchart-dbs-s-trade-finance-distributed-ledger-how-it-works.

20. Dunkley, E., "Santander Pilots Blockchain Payments App," *Financial Times*, May 26, 2016, http://www.ft.com/cms/s/0/2df2f65c-234f-11e6-9d4d-c11776a5124d.html.

21. Arnold, M., "Visa Eyes New Link in Blockchain Payments," *Financial Times*, September 1, 2016, http://www.ft.com/cms/s/0/483e315e-6fa6-11e6-a0c9-1365ce54b926.html.

22. Stafford, P., "Canada Experiments with Digital Dollar on Blockchain," *Financial Times*, June 16, 2016, https://www.ft.com/content/1117c780-3397-11e6-bda0-04585c31b153.

23. Monetary Authority of Singapore, "Singapore's FinTech Journey—Where We Are, What Is Next," November 16, 2016, http://www.mas.gov.sg/News-and-Publications/Speeches-and-Monetary-Policy-Statements/Speeches/2016/Singapore-FinTech-Journey.aspx.

24. MUFG, "Hitachi and BTMU Start Proof of Concept Testing for Utilizing Blockchain Technology for Check Digitalization in Singapore," August 22, 2016, http://www.bk.mufg.jp/global/newsroom/news2016/pdf/newse0822.pdf.

25. Barreto, E., "Banks and Tech Firms Apply Blockchain to Trade Finance," *Reuters*, August 10, 2016, http://www.reuters.com/article/us-asia-trade-blockchain-idUSKCN10L17D.

26. Macheel, T., "Banks Test Blockchain for Syndicated Loans with Symbiont, R3," *American Banker*, September 27, 2016, http://www.americanbanker.com/news/bank-technology/banks-test-blockchain-for-syndicated-loans-with-symbiont-r3-1091625-1.html.

27. Macheel, T., "DTCC, Digital Asset Holdings Build Blockchain for Repurchase market," *American Banker*, March 29, 2016, http://www.americanbanker.com/news/bank-technology/dtcc-digital-asset-holdings-build-blockchain-for-repurchase-market-1080142-1.html.

28. Deutsche Bundesbank, "Joint Deutsche Bundesbank and Deutsche Börse Blockchain Prototype," November 28, 2016, https://www.bundesbank.de/Redaktion/EN/Pressemitteilungen/BBK/2016/2016_11_28_blockchain_prototype.html.

29. Kelly, J., "Barclays Says Conducts First Blockchain-based Trade-finance Deal," *Reuters*, September 7, 2016, http://www.reuters.com/article/us-banks-barclays-blockchain-idUSKCN11D23B.

30. Chirgwin, R., "NIST Readies 'Post-quantum' Crypto Competition," *The Register*, May 4, 2016, http://www.theregister.co.uk/2016/05/04/nist_readies_postquantum_crypto_competition.

31. Guerrera, F., "How the Financial Sector Sees Technology As Its Saviour," *Financial Times*, February 21, 2011, http://www.ft.com/cms/s/0/a8ff2548-3de3-11e0-99ac-00144feabdc0.html.

32. Nash, K. S. and S. Norton, "Morgan Stanley Plans to Drop Out of R3 Blockchain Group," November 22, 2016, http://blogs.wsj.com/cio/2016/11/22/morgan-stanley-plans-to-drop-out-of-r3-blockchain-group/.

33. "The great chain of being sure about things", *Economist*, Oct 31, 2015, http://www.economist.com/news/briefing/21677228-technology-behind-bitcoin-lets-people-who-do-not-know-or-trust-each-other-build-dependable

GLOSSARY

account takeover Where a criminal is able to gain access to a customer's financial account, typically for the purpose of making fraudulent transactions. (88, 531)

active-active configuration A configuration where two or more active services are run in parallel, sharing the processing load and providing resilience to one another in case of failure. (79, 189)

active-passive configuration A configuration where only one service is actively processing and one or more other services will be on standby, waiting to take over in case the primary service fails. Also referred to as primary/secondary fault tolerant configuration. (79, 189)

agency broker A financial market intermediary who acts as an agent for its clients, performing transactions on its customers' behalf and without serving as a counterparty in the transaction. (301, 413)

algorithmic order execution The use of well-defined and repeatable methods to execute orders in the market, typically by dividing an order into parts and executing them over a period of time. (435)

algorithmic trading A somewhat ambiguous term that often refers to the execution of algorithmic trading strategies, but sometimes may also be used to refer to algorithmic order execution. (356, 418, 435)

algorithmic trading strategy A trading strategy that uses a predefined set of rules, in the form of an algorithm, to determine the timing, price, and quantity of orders placed in the market, usually implemented using an electronic platform. (357, 435)

allocation matching utility (AMU) A clearing house that aggregates, matches, and reconciles trade settlement allocation instructions provided by an institutional customer and trade details supplied by its broker. (401)

alpha The excess return of a trading strategy or portfolio over a specified benchmark; it is negative if the strategy underperforms the benchmark. (365)

anti-money laundering (AML) A term used to refer to the prevention of hiding and distribution of funds obtained from illicit activities. Also referred to indirectly as know your customer (KYC for short) verification. (211, 263)

automated clearing house (ACH) An electronic network or system that is used to clear financial transactions for banks and other financial institutions.(178, 194, 232, 245, 249, 543, 561)

back-to-back transaction A second and opposite transaction performed by a financial intermediary with another financial firm that offsets the position and exposure created by the initial transaction. (310, 326)

basis point An increment of 1/100th of 1%. (303)

best execution A broker's obligation to route customer orders to the execution venue that is "best" for the customer as defined by a predetermined set of rules. This is in contrast to cases where a broker routes orders to an execution venue because it provides monetary incentives to the broker for providing order flow or an execution venue in which the broker has a beneficial interest. (356)

beta The volatility, or risk, of a trading strategy or portfolio that is directly attributable to the market. (365)

bid price The price at which a market participant is willing to buy a security. (359, 385, 417)

big data An excessively large volume of information, some of which may be unstructured. (128, 443, 444, 567)

bill of exchange An unconditional order drawn by the payee instructing the payer to pay the payee, or the bearer of the bill, a sum of money immediately or at a specified future date. Also referred to as trade bill, term bill, and sight bill. (282)

blockchain See distributed ledger.

blocking and allocation A situation in which an institutional customer instructs its broker to split a trade's settlement across multiple settlement accounts. (401)

book entry system The recording of changes in ownership through computerized accounting entries. (364, 401)

broker-dealer A financial market intermediary that fills orders on behalf of its customers, but also trades in the market on its own account. (319, 392, 421)

business continuity plan (BCP)   A documented plan that considers potential business or operational failure points and conditions, identifies steps, and defines procedures for alleviating critical failures. Also referred to as disaster recovery plan. (189)

business process management (BPM)   A set of tools and techniques that help companies systematically control and improve their business processes. (12, 32, 170, 229, 295, 462, 521)

business process management system (BPMS)   An IT system that orchestrates process activities performed by both people and IT systems and that integrates the content of both information contained in documents and data stored in IT systems. Also referred to as business process management suite. (12, 33, 34, 171, 235, 296, 415, 442)

card associations   Organizations, such as MasterCard and Visa, which provide the underlying payment network infrastructure and sets the rules governing payment card transactions. (253, 254, 256, 539)

cash equities   The trading of stocks, that is, equity securities, in contrast to the trading of futures or option contracts on stock indices. (392)

cashier's cheque   A cheque that is secured by a bank's account rather than a customer's account. Also referred to as banker's draft, bank cheque, and certified cheque. (245)

central counterparty (CCP)   An entity that intermediates between counterparties so that the settlement risk is borne by the central counterparty, rather than the individual parties. (245, 331, 361)

central limit order book   A mechanism that matches customer orders limit and market based on a predefined set of rules that typically are prioritized by the orders' price specification and time of arrival. (388)

central securities depository (CSD)   An entity that maintains an official record of share ownership and facilitates the transfer of securities between counterparties by recording the changes as computerized accounting book entries. (364, 401)

clearing   The process of communicating and reconciling security transfer and payment instructions prior to settlement. (245, 331, 361, 392, 415)

clearing house   A centralized facility that coordinates the communication of instructions related to the payment of funds or delivery of securities between market participants. (245, 346, 364, 396, 412)

clearing member   A financial institution that acts as a financial intermediary between counterparties, taking on the counterparties' settlement obligation with a central counterparty. (246, 304, 360, 398)

cold standby configuration   A software solution that is installed on servers but not actively run; however, it can be started up, with some delay, in case of a major systems failure. (189)

commercial banking   Banking services provided to businesses and corporations. Also referred to as wholesale banking, and corporate and institutional banking. (73, 435, 444)

committed line of credit   A lending agreement whereby the bank is legally obliged to lend the funds up to the credit limit specified in the lending agreement to the customer as long as the covenants of the lending agreement are not breached. (210)

complex event processing (CEP)   A method of analyzing real-time information streams so that when patterns are matched, corresponding actions are triggered. (59, 373, 430, 453)

compliance risk   The losses or reputational damage that a financial institution may incur from failing to comply with laws, regulations, rules, and codes of conduct applicable to its activities. (527)

consolidated tape   An electronic system that continuously reports the price and volume data for trades executed across multiple execution venues, including stock exchanges, electronic communications networks, and trades internalized by brokers. (391)

core banking system (also core banking platform)   The primary IT system used to store and maintain account information related to one or more lines of business, such as deposits and lending, trade finance, or treasury. (176)

correspondent bank   A bank that performs transactions or collects documents on behalf of another bank, which may not have direct access to a domestic market that the correspondent bank operates in. (252)

credit risk   The risk that a counterparty to whom the institution provides a line of credit, or whose credit underlies debt instruments that are held, will default on its obligations. (152, 223, 246, 278, 302, 332, 397, 505)

crossing engine   A trading system component that maintains an internal limit order book and matches customer orders against it. Also referred to as matching engine. (422)

custodian   A financial institution that provides safekeeping and transfer of securities, such as stocks and bonds, particularly where a customer is not in a position to take possession or ownership of the securities itself. (364)

customer information file (CIF)   Historically, the key reference data contained in a file related to a customer, including their name, address, national tax identification number, and phone numbers. In practice, the information is no longer maintained in a file but, rather, in a database that is accessed through a service; yet the acronym CIF remains. (86)

cyberattack An information technology-related attack designed to damage computer systems, disable computer networks, or exfiltrate confidential information. (19, 20, 256, 472, 474, 478, 480, 487, 489, 527)

cycle time The total time, i.e. duration, taken to complete a business process. (52)

dark pool A trade execution venue where information related to open orders is not exposed publicly in advance of execution. (361, 382, 421)

data warehouse A central database that consolidates bankwide information and makes it available to multiple business functions and systems; it is often used for marketing and management information purposes. (458, 476, 522)

delivery versus payment (DvP) The process whereby the transfer of securities and payment for them happens simultaneously between counterparties. (247, 401)

denial-of-service (DoS) attack An attack is designed to disable or limit the availability of online services. (481)

depth of market The volume of buy or sell orders available at different prices for a security in an exchange's order book. (385, 428)

depth-of-market information Market data that includes detailed information about the orders available for matching in a limit order book, not just the best bid and best offer. Also referred to as level 2 market data. (395, 428)

digital currency A store of value that only exists in digital form and facilitates electronic payments. Also sometimes referred to as a virtual currency or a cryptocurrency. (193, 195, 196, 197, 198, 200, 479, 557, 558)

digital wallet A software application that enables users to access account balances, access transaction history information, perform transactions, and in some cases store cryptographic keys. (195, 196)

direct market access (DMA) A service whereby customer orders are sent electronically to the broker, who then routes the order to the relevant exchange with minimal involvement and delay. (357, 418)

disaster recovery site (DR Site) A remote location that has key software components installed and the necessary external connectivity so that it can be used to continue business operations in cases where a financial institution's primary business operations have been compromised. (79, 189)

discretionary trading A trading strategy that relies on the trader's ongoing judgment, rather than following a systematized plan. (371)

distributed ledger A database that is shared and replicated across multiple parties and has no centralized storage or administration. (193)

distributed system A set of software components that are installed and run on separate servers and communicate with one another over the network. (10)

diversification The strategy of holding multiple investments that do not have identical performance characteristics to help reduce the volatility of a portfolio. (5, 152, 306, 367, 417, 510)

dual currency investments (DCIs) Structured investment products that provide a higher yield on local currency deposits, but depending on exchange rate fluctuations may return the deposit in another currency that at current exchange rates may be less than the original deposit amount. (12, 178, 310, 338)

EMV chip Computer chips that are embedded in payment cards to support authentication using the EMV standard for credit and debit card transactions. (255, 257, 468, 495)

enterprise application integration (EAI) The practice of integrating IT systems using consistent tools and techniques across the enterprise, rather than choosing how to integrate systems on a case-by-case basis. (11, 48)

enterprise content management (ECM) The provision of a common means of storing, managing, and accessing the content of documents, email, and websites across business divisions and geographies. (53)

enterprise data management (EDM) Providing a centralized means of storing, validating, managing, and distributing reference data that is used across all key IT systems. Also referred to as master data management (MDM for short). (86, 106, 167)

enterprise service bus (ESB) An "information bus" model used to implement service-oriented architecture, whereby applications integrate with one another using a standardized set of services. Each application provides its own set of services that other systems can utilize. Also referred to as information bus. (11, 73)

execution management system (EMS) A component in a trading system architecture for managing the execution of orders electronically, and with no manual intervention, often by using algorithms to execute orders over an extended period of time. (418)

factoring Purchasing a company's invoices or accounts receivable at a discount, thus providing the company with faster access to those funds. This service is provided by a factor. (285)

federated Autonomy that is provided to functional groups or regions, rather than being managed centrally. (176)

foreign exchange spot (FX spot) The standard foreign exchange settlement period, which for most currencies is two days after the trade date. (302, 310, 424)

forward points   Basis points that are added to the spot rate to determine the forward rate. In some cases, the forward points may be negative. (303)

forward rate   The foreign exchange rate that is quoted for exchange of currencies with a settlement date falling on a date different from the spot date. (167, 303, 333)

front running   When a broker or other financial intermediary uses knowledge about a customer's order that it is handling to trade in the market, to obtain a profit, before the customer's order is executed. (360, 389)

general ledger (GL)   The IT system that maintains the firm's central accounting repository. (181, 345, 476)

Global Financial Crisis   The financial crisis that began in 2007 and that led to the failure of several large banks and required government bailouts for many other financial institutions. (1, 177, 182, 288, 329, 416, 506)

gross settlement   Settlement of transactions on an individual basis. (246, 336, 509)

haircut   The discount in percentage terms that is applied when valuing an asset for collateral or margining purposes that takes into account the risk that the asset's market value may fall or that the asset may become illiquid. (212)

hardware clustering   An approach that uses hardware level failover to achieve software application resilience typically by restarting applications on a second server when a fault occurs on the primary server. (189)

hedge fund   A pooled investment vehicle similar to a mutual fund, but that is leveraged, has few restrictions on the investment strategies it uses, and which typically requires significant initial upfront investment amounts and, thus, is not available to retail customers. (301, 358, 412, 508)

high availability (HA)   A characteristic of IT systems that are resilient and typically have some level of redundancy to ensure continuous uptime under normal, i.e. noncatastrophic, conditions. (141, 433, 450)

high-touch order management system   A system that supports manual order execution and requires people to be involved in the execution process. (418)

horizontal scaling   Maintaining the performance of a software application by adding more servers as transaction volumes or the number of users increases. (79, 321, 348, 405)

host virtualization   Where multiple virtual machines are run together on the same hardware, sharing its resources. (126)

hot standby configuration   A resilience model where passive service is run in parallel with active service and receives the same input information, but does not follow through the actions that the active service performs unless the passive service takes over because of an active service failure. (189, 321)

injection attack   A type of cyberattack that is injects source code into a form input field so that the code is inadvertently executed by a software application or database. (494)

insurance company   A company that offers compensation for potential losses in the future in exchange for premium payments from the party that it insures. (172, 358)

interbank foreign exchange (interbank FX)   Foreign exchange transactions that occur between banks, as opposed to between banks and their customers. (301, 308)

interchange fees   Fees that are typically imposed by a bank that issues a payment card on the merchant's bank, and thus indirectly upon the merchant, for each card transaction processed. (254)

investment banking   Banking activities related to issuance of equity and debt securities for customers, and trading of those securities in secondary markets. (32, 149, 341, 413, 444)

key performance indicator (KPI)   The metrics by which business or operational units are formally evaluated, for example, average transaction processing time. (20)

know your customer (KYC)   The due diligence processes that financial institutions perform to verify the identity of their customers and ensure compliance with antimoney laundering regulations. (211)

latency   The delay or time incurred between when a transaction is sent for processing and when it is received back after completion. (114, 319, 347, 404, 411)

Lean   A process improvement approach that focuses on optimizing existing processes by identifying and eliminating process steps that do not directly contribute toward business value, thus reducing waste from the processes. (33, 37)

legacy system   An IT system that is depended upon for ongoing business, but which is dated and would ideally be replaced by a more modern system. (9, 104, 219, 522)

letter of credit (L/C)   A document issued by a seller's bank that guarantees, if the specified conditions are met, that the seller will receive payment for the goods sold, even if the buyer fails to meet its payment obligations. Also referred to as documentary credits. (44, 276)

limit order   An order to buy or sell a security or derivative at a specific price, or better. (383, 417)

liquidity   In the context of trading, the level of demand for an instrument in the market as measured by the number of buyers and sellers and the quantities that they are willing to trade. Also referred to as market depth. (164, 176, 177, 281, 300, 338, 356, 382, 423, 446, 507)

lit pool   A trade execution venue that makes information publicly available about outstanding orders to buy and sell. Also referred to as lit execution venue. (361)

mainframe computer   A high-powered, centralized computer system that is typically used for large volume batch processing and hosting of large-scale user applications, such as core banking systems. Also referred to as a host. (9)

malware   Malicious software that is used to damage or gain access to computer systems. (141, 466, 479–481, 487, 533, 568)

margin   The difference between the rate that a bank offers to customers and the rate at which it must pay for lending of funds or foreign exchange, that is, its profit margin on the transaction. Alternatively, a "margin account" is a securities trading account where a customer can buy and sell securities using money that is lent to it by the broker and that is secured by the customer using "margin collateral," usually the customer's cash or securities which are held by or assigned to the broker. (5, 153, 180, 305, 361, 398, 416)

market access gateway   A trading architecture component that connects and communicate orders to an execution venue, such as an exchange. Also referred to as line handler. (419)

market data   Information related to current market prices, trades, and trading volume that is distributed directly by exchanges and other financial institutions, or by vendors who serve as data aggregators and specialist information providers. (10, 160, 346, 371, 381, 411, 435, 524)

market depth   *see depth of market.*

market liquidity risk   The risk that a financial instrument may not have ready buyers or sellers, that is, is not liquid under either usual or unusual market conditions. (509)

market maker   A market participant that offers to buy or sell on an ongoing basis, thus providing market liquidity. (7, 362, 382, 417, 435)

market order   An order that is executed immediately at the best available trading price when it is received by an execution venue. (78, 385, 417)

market risk   The risk associated with fluctuations in value of assets and positions in instruments such as equities, bonds, currencies, and derivatives held by financial institutions. (218, 506, 527)

marketplace lending   The facilitation of loans between investors and individuals or businesses that seek capital, also referred to as peer-to-peer lending. (164, 208, 216, 217)

mean reversion   The expectation is that the price of a financial instrument will temporarily fluctuate around its true market value, and profits can be made from trading on the temporary fluctuations. (370)

messaging middleware   A software platform that facilitates message-level communication between applications, eliminating the need for low-level network communication programming. (73, 425)

Millennials   The generation of people born between 1980 and 1994. (8)

mobile wallet   A software application on a mobile device that enables users to transfer money or make payments electronically. In some cases it may store and make use of payment card information. (14, 16, 243, 244)

modern portfolio theory   An approach for maximizing the return of a portfolio and minimizing its volatility by optimizing the assets held and their relative percentage of holdings. (511)

multifactor authentication   An mechanism where multiple factors are used authenticate users. Factors may include: what a user knows, such as a password; what a user has, such as a passcode-generating digital token; or what a user is, such as a biometric identifier, i.e. a fingerprint. (255, 258)

mutual funds   An investment vehicle that allows investors to pool their funds to take advantage of economies of scale and gain access to professional managers. (154, 358, 401)

netting   The reduction of settlement obligations between parties by taking into account a series of payments or trades and calculating the overall positions that result when they are combined. (176, 182, 220, 247, 248, 249, 397, 401)

nostro account   An accounting term that refers to an account held by a bank at another financial institution. (276)

notional amount   For financial instruments, such as derivatives, the face value of the underlying asset or related instrument that the instrument is based on. The notional amount is not exchanged between counterparties. Also referred to as notional principal (for interest rate swaps) or notional value. (218, 303, 329, 399)

offer price   The price at which a market participant is willing to sell a security. Also referred to as ask price. (331, 362, 381, 417)

online dealing system   An IT system that provides electronic foreign exchange dealing services, such as price quotation, order capture, and position keeping, to the a bank's corporate customers. Also referred to as a single dealer platform. (308)

operational data store (ODS)   A database that consolidates and maintains current information used by multiple systems for transactional purposes. In contrast, a data warehouse usually has day-, week-, or month-old snapshot data and is intended for marketing and reporting purposes, not for supporting business transactions. (73, 457)

operational risk   The risk that an institution may incur losses due to operational failures, such as failure of controls that lead to internal or external fraud, downtime of critical systems, and mistakes in the implementation of pricing or valuation models. (16, 42, 224, 247, 349, 373, 508, 527)

opportunistic algorithm   A trade execution algorithm that targets to execute as much of the order as possible at times when there is ample liquidity available at or near the current market price. Also referred to as liquidity-seeking algorithm. (426)

order book   The central data structure used in an order matching facility, such as an exchange, to track market participants' outstanding orders to buy and sell at different price levels and at various quantities. (384, 385, 387, 388, 391, 395, 404, 406, 417, 420, 428, 435)

order flow internalization (internalization)   When a bank or broker matches customer orders internally with other customers' orders or proprietary positions before routing them to external execution venues. (421)

order management system (OMS)   A trading system component that supports manual order-capture, position monitoring, accounting, reporting, and compliance functions. (346, 375, 418)

order spoofing   The practice of rapidly placing orders without the intent of actually filling them, then canceling them before they can be executed as trades. (374)

out-of-sample data   Historical market data that is intentionally not used to tune a trading strategy. This data can then be used to more robustly test the strategy's hypothetical performance. (372)

over-the-counter product (OTC product)   A financial product that is traded bilaterally between a broker- dealer and a customer, rather than on a centralized exchange. Typically, an OTC product is customized to meet specific customer needs. (303, 332)

partial fill   When only part of an order is matched and executed. (385)

patching   The application of software updates to operating systems, drivers, or applications. (121, 126, 127, 139, 140, 141, 482, 487, 500)

payment versus payment (PvP)   A mechanism that ensures that the settlement of foreign currencies occurs simultaneously, thus avoiding settlement risk. (247)

pension funds   Investment funds set up by large corporations or public entities to collect, invest, and distribute pensions to employees. (160, 358)

phishing   Where a message that directly includes or has a link to malicious content is sent with the objective of tricking the recipient into disclosing their private information or compromising their information security. (480, 487, 491)

point-of-sale terminal   An electronic device used by retailers to process payment card transactions. (158, 468)

POS terminal   see point-of-sale terminal.

presettlement credit limit   The maximum allowable exposure to the risk that future settlement obligations will not be met by a counterparty. (218)

price slippage   When the market price moves adversely prior to or while an order is being filled. Also referred to as slippage. (359)

prime brokerage services   Bundled service packages offered by brokers that are designed to support smaller fund managers. Common services provided include securities lending, centralized clearing, global custody, provision of trading and order management systems, and leasing of office space. (411)

process reengineering   A process improvement technique that aims to totally redesign business processes so as to eliminate inherent inefficiencies. (58)

proprietary trading (prop trading)   Trades executed by a financial market intermediary for its own profit rather than by generating commission fees for processing customer trades. (362, 412, 416)

ransomware   A type of malware that locks access to an affected system and renders files on the system unusable until a ransom payment is made. (141, 479, 533)

real-time gross settlement (RTGS)   When payment or securities transactions are settled individually and processed without any settlement lag. (249)

reference data   Underlying information used by IT systems that are relatively static and nontransactional in nature, for example, settlement calendar/holiday information and securities master data. Also referred to as static data. (86, 377)

relationship banking   Banking services that rely on a close connection between the bank and the customer so that the bank can make use of qualitative information that it has or can obtain about their customers to offer services and make credit decisions. (227)

relationship manager (RM)   A financial institution's representative, typically in a branch or call center, that deals directly with customer requests. (155, 223, 308, 415, 441)

remittance   A sum of money that is sent between companies or individuals. This term commonly used in banking contexts to describe outbound customer payments. (97, 158, 464)

remote deposit capture   Technology that enables cheque images to be scanned remotely by customers, transmitted electronically to their bank, and then cleared and deposited directly to the customer's bank account. The bank does not need receive or directly access the physical cheque. (14, 178)

request for quote (RFQ) In the context of trading, when a market user requests a tradable price from a market maker to buy or sell a specific amount of a security, derivative, or currency. Also referred to as request for quotation. (308, 424)

reset date In context of an interest rate swap, the date that the benchmark interest rate will be referenced and used to calculate the amount due for the floating rate portion of the swap settlement. Also referred to as fixing date. (336)

retail banking Banking services provided to individual consumers. Also referred to as consumer banking. (58, 152, , 183, 210, 259, 271, 306, 338, 444, 452, 537, 545, 549)

rules engine An architecture component designed for managing and executing business rules. (53, 434)

schedule-driven algorithm An order execution algorithm that is designed to execute portions of an order at predefined or calculated time increments. (425)

scripless Securities that have no physical form, and are maintained by a book entry system. (364, 401)

securitization The process of transforming illiquid assets, such as debt payment receivables, into securities so that they can be sold to investors. (294)

separation of duties An internal control principle that prevents any one individual or group from controlling a process from start to finish, typically implemented by separating key process functions such as creation and verification of transactions. (23, 47, 317, 472)

service-level agreement (SLA) The acceptable ranges for providing services, often described in terms of the average and maximum allowable processing time and throughput or in terms of absolute cutoff times by which processing must be completed. (23, 52, 235, 267)

service-oriented architecture (SOA) A software design approach whereby applications are implemented as components that provide interoperable service interfaces so as to simplify integration and development of composite applications. (53, 71)

settlement The process of transferring funds and securities to fulfill payment and trade execution obligations. (31, 86, 158, 217, 245, 282, 301, 331, 336, 361, 478, 509)

settlement agent A financial institution that is a clearing member of a payment system that clears and settles transactions on that system on behalf of its customers. (246, 401)

settlement credit limit The total difference between gross outbound and inbound payments allowed with a given counterparty during the settlement cycle, usually between one and a few days. (218)

settlement lag The delay between the acceptance of a payment instruction and its final settlement. (246)

settlement risk When gross settlement is used, the risk that one institution makes payments to its counterparty but does not receive the corresponding payment or delivery of securities. (364, 397, 509)

silos Business functions or IT systems that are connected together within their own organizational context, but are segregated from functions and/or systems in other business areas. (457)

single view of the customer The ability to integrate customer data from multiple backend systems so that users can see all the current customer information at the same time in one application or desktop environment. (86, 457)

Six Sigma A process improvement methodology that aims to reduce variance in process output by identifying and eliminating defects. (44)

spread The difference in the bid and offer prices of a financial instrument. (308, 362, 384, 417, 509)

stateful process orchestration A form of business process execution whereby the process activities are long-lived and require a persistent state to be maintained. (38)

stateless process orchestration A form of business process execution whereby the process activities are short-lived and require little, if any, persistent state to be maintained. (38)

storage virtualization Where many different storage devices are made to appear as a single storage service. (125)

straight-through processing (STP) The processing of a transaction entirely electronically from start to finish. (12, 31, 86, 109, 226, 261, 301, 340, 464, 516)

syndicated lending Where multiple lenders join together to make a loan to a single borrower. (54)

system of record An IT system that is designated as the master source for a particular set of information. (82, 403, 476)

technical debt The result of choosing a suboptimal technical design or implementation that is easiest to deliver in the short term, but creates more work in the long term in terms of maintenance. (16, 83)

telegraphic transfers (TTs) An international electronic funds transfer. Also referred to as wire transfer. (258, 282)

thick client A software application that requires its user interface to be installed or downloaded and then to be run locally on the user's workstation. (72)

thin client A software application that has its user interface run within a web browser locally on the user's workstation without requiring additional software to be installed. (10)

throughput   The volume of transactions that can be processed in a given period of time. (23, 52, 84, 114, 321, 347, 404, 419, 455)

trade blotter   A paper-based or electronic presentation of order and execution details, such as buy or sell, trade date and time, execution price, and quantity, for a given period of time. (376)

trade reporting facility (TRF)   A facility that enables financial market participants to publicly report off-exchange trade executions, thereby contributing to a consolidated tape. (391)

transactional banking   Banking services that focus on selling high volumes of standardized products, relying on quantitative assessment measures that can be assessed quickly and with minimal effort. (227)

two-factor authentication   see multifactor authentication.

uncommitted line of credit   A credit facility where the lender has the option to cancel or suspend the credit line without cause. (210)

universal banking   Providing a comprehensive set of banking products and services, including deposit taking and lending, derivatives trading, securities trading and underwriting, fund management, and insurance. (5, 164)

use case   A description of interactions between actors and a software system that that achieve a specific goal, typically used to specify software system requirements. (102)

user story   A description of a software feature from an end-user perspective, typically used to specify software system requirements. (102)

usury laws   Laws that limit the interest rate that may be levied by lenders on customers. (207)

value at risk (VaR)   The expected loss of a portfolio expressed in monetary terms within a certain timeframe at a certain probability. (399, 514)

vertical scaling   Maintaining the performance of a software application by increasing the capacity of existing servers as transaction volumes or the number of users increases. (79, 348)

video teller   Automated teller-like machines that are equipped with video and audio, cash deposit and withdrawal, cheque deposit, and signature pad capabilities. They connect to bank staff at other locations, usually contact centers, and can accommodate many of the same activities as a branch teller. (449)

virtual machine (VM)   An instance of operating system software that shares a physical server's resources –i.e. microprocessors, memory, disk, network connectivity, and hardware peripherals– usually with other operating system instances that are running on the same hardware. (79, 126, 127, 131)

voice dealing   The process of requesting price quotations, placing orders, and executing transactions using person-to-person telephone-based communications. Also referred to as voice-based trading, voice trading, and voice execution. (307, 331)

volume participation algorithm   An order execution algorithm that aims to execute a proportion of the order that corresponds to a percentage of the volume of the instrument traded in the market during a specific time period. (425)

vostro account   An accounting term that refers to an account held by the bank for another financial institution. (276)

wallet share   In the context of banking, a bank's proportion of a customer's aggregate business across all of the banks that he or she uses. (183, 455)

warm standby configuration   A resilience model where passive service does not begin running until the active service fails. (189)

waterfall methodology   A software development methodology where each phase of development follows the other sequentially to produce the end deliverable. (98)

white labeling   When a financial institution provides IT systems or services to another institution's customers on behalf of that institution without the end users being aware of the arrangement. (106, 288, 326, 497)

INDEX

Note: Page numbers followed by "n" refer to footnotes.

economies of scale, 5, 16, 48, 58, 84, 91, 107, 112, 126, 176, 181, 209, 253, 263, 288, 295, 311, 326, 359, 368, 376, 401

EDI, *see* electronic data interchange

EDM, *see* enterprise data management

electronic commerce network, 301, 423

electronic data interchange, 166, 176, 181, 464

emerging markets, 3, 112, 162, 163, 215, 224, 261, 281, 406, 444, 509

EMS, *see* execution management systems

EMV, 254, 255–258, 255n, 468, 495

enterprise

application integration technology, 11, 12, 48, 53

content management, 53

data management, 11, 19, 86, 106, 167

service bus, 11, 73, 86

enterprise application integration technology, 11, 12, 48, 53

enterprise content management, 53

enterprise data management, 11, 19, 86, 106, 167

enterprise service bus, 11, 73, 86

equities, 15, 16, 154, 159, 161, 177, 212, 221, 229, 299, 301, 320, 337, 338, 339, 340, 346, 355, 356, 358–368, 370, 374, 377, 379, 392, 394, 396, 400, 402, 412, 413, 415, 418, 422, 425, 429, 433, 435, 451, 508, 509, 510, 512, 514–516, 541, 567

ESB, *see* enterprise service bus

ESP, *see* event stream processing

ETFs, *see* exchange traded funds

Ethereum, 198, 199, 201, 559, 563

Europe, 8, 19, 49, 50, 78, 97, 107, 112, 150, 162, 172, 178, 185, 191, 207, 256, 259, 263, 275, 299, 330, 331, 340, 356, 361, 362, 363, 365, 395, 422, 466, 481, 513, 516, 518, 533, 543, 545, 556

event stream processing, 434

exchange traded funds, 340, 367, 369

execution management systems, 418, 420, 422, 427, 431, 434

execution venue, 301, 356, 357, 360–364, 382, 389, 391, 392, 394, 395–397, 402–404, 414, 418–425, 427, 430, 436

F

factoring, 285, 287

FAST protocol, *see* FIX adapted for streaming protocol

Faster Payments Service, 245, 263, 269, 270

FATCA, *see* Foreign Account Tax Compliance Act

fee revenue, 13, 101, 194, 212

field-programmable gate arrays, 518

financial information exchange, 66, 391, 392, 412–413, 418, 422, 425, 431–435

Financial products Mark-up Language, 349

Financial Services Authority, 164, 190

Fintech, 5, 13, 15, 16, 25, 91, 98, 99, 111, 143, 150, 151, 157, 161, 164, 183, 184, 187, 200, 208, 210, 216,

217, 242, 259, 269, 288, 289, 300, 311, 312, 368, 491, 528, 544, 549–556, 563–566, 569, 570

FIX, *see* financial information exchange

FIX adapted for streaming protocol, 413, 433–434

Foreign Account Tax Compliance Act, 19

foreign exchange

forwards, 158, 302–305, 312–316, 343, 397, 399, 518

spot, 157, 302, 303, 310, 424

foreign exchange forwards, 158, 302–305, 312–316, 343, 397, 399, 518

foreign exchange spot, 157, 302, 303, 310, 425

forward

foreign exchange swaps, 247, 302, 304, 312–316

FX swaps, *see* forward foreign exchange swaps

points, 303, 304

forward foreign exchange swaps, 247, 302, 304, 312–316

FPGA, *see* field-programmable gate arrays

FpML, *see* Financial products Mark-up Language

FPS, *see* Faster Payments Service

fraud, 18, 22, 31, 47n, 50, 59, 81, 155, 179, 185, 187, 191, 195, 197, 213, 217, 223, 224, 234, 242, 252, 253, 256, 259, 263, 264, 270, 278, 288, 290, 317, 376, 436, 444, 467, 472, 473, 475, 478, 487, 489, 491, 492, 496, 497, 499, 500, 510, 521, 527, 529, 530, 531–533, 540, 543, 556, 562, 566, 567

front running, 360, 389

FSA, *see* Financial Services Authority

fund

hedge, 18, 154, 160, 209, 301, 340, 358, 359, 362, 368, 375, 412, 416, 425, 508, 523

management, 5, 400

pension, 160, 209, 358, 359, 545

FX forwards, *see* foreign exchange forwards

FX spot, *see* foreign exchange spot

G

Glass-Steagall Act, 541

Global Financial Crisis, 1, 8, 164, 177, 182, 193, 288, 329, 330, 340, 341, 342, 417, 506, 507, 509, 512, 516, 518, 538, 541, 545

H

hardware

clustering, 189

security module, 498–499

hardware security module, 498–499

hedging, 152, 158, 159, 160, 180, 200, 303–306, 333–334, 337–339, 356, 367, 415, 512, 516, 518

HFT, *see* high frequency trading

high frequency trading, 325, 356, 362, 371, 373, 375, 403, 406, 411

high-net-worth individuals, 155

HSM, *see* hardware security module